OOIS'98

T0211686

Springer

London
Berlin
Heidelberg
New York
Barcelona
Budapest
Hong Kong
Milan
Paris
Santa Clara
Singapore
Tokyo

Also Available:

OOIS'94
1994 International Conference on Object Oriented Information Systems
19-21 December 1994, London

Edited by D. Patel, Y. Sun and S. Patel

OOIS'95
1995 International Conference on Object Oriented Information Systems
18-20 December 1995, Dublin

Edited by John Murphy and Brian Stone

OOIS'96
1996 International Conference on Object Oriented Information Systems
16-18 December 1996, London

Edited by D. Patel, Y. Sun and S. Patel

OOIS'97
1997 International Conference on Object Oriented Information Systems
10-12 November 1997, Brisbane

Edited by Maria E. Orlowska and Roberto Zicari

OOIS'98

**1998 International Conference on
Object Oriented Information Systems
9-11 September 1998, Paris**

Proceedings

Edited by
Colette Rolland and Georges Grosz
University of Paris - IUT, Paris, France

CENTRE NATIONAL
DE LA RECHERCHE
SCIENTIFIQUE

DE PARIS
UNIVERSITE PARIS 1
PANTHEON-SORBONNE

U - PANTHÉON - SORBONNE -
NIVERSITÉ PARIS 1

Springer

Colette Rolland and George Grosz

Centre de Recherche en Informatique, Université Paris I - La Sorbonne, Paris, FRANCE

ISBN-13:978-1-85233-046-0   e-ISBN-13:978-1-4471-0895-5
DOI: 10.1007/978-1-4471-0895-5

Springer-Verlag London Berlin Heidelberg

British Library Cataloguing in Publication Data
A catalogue record for this book is available from the British Library

Typesetting: Camera ready by editors

34/3830-543210 Printed on acid-free paper

Preface

The Sorbonne University is very proud to host this year the OOIS Conference on Object Oriented Information Systems. There is a growing awareness of the importance of object oriented techniques, methods and tools to support information systems engineering. The term information systems implies that the computer based systems are designed to provide adequate and timely information to human users in organizations. The term engineering implies the application of a rigorous set of problem solving approaches analogous to those found in traditional engineering disciplines. The intent of this conference is to present a selected number of those approaches which favor an object oriented view of systems engineering. OOIS '98 is the fifth edition of a series of conferences. Starting in 1994 in London, this series evolved from a British audience to a truly European one. The goal is to build a world wide acknowledged forum dedicated to object oriented information systems engineering. This conference is organized with the aim to bring together researchers and practitioners in Information Systems, Databases and Software Engineering who have interests in object oriented information systems. The objective is to advance understanding about how the object technology can empower information systems in organizations, on techniques for designing effective and efficient information systems and methods and development tools for information systems engineering. The conference aims also at discussing the lessons learned from large scale projects using objects. The call for OOIS was given international audience. The program committee was chosen from very well reputed researchers in the international information systems, databases and software design. Twenty six papers have been selected for presentation and discussion during the conference. The spectrum of the contributions in the present proceedings extends from issues regarding the modeling and design of information systems in an object oriented manner, to various novel views for some specific aspects of information systems development such as modeling and querying spatial and temporal aspects of object oriented applications, reuse, evolution and new topics such as model and method engineering. The editors express the hope that these papers will contribute to improvements in both the understanding and practice of object technologies in information systems. The OOIS '98 conference would not have been possible without the efforts of the authors, the program committee members and the additional referees. They deserve our deepest thanks.

Colette Rolland

Programme Chair
Professor Colette Rolland, CRI, University of Paris, France

Organizing Chair
George Grosz, CRI, University of Paris 1, France

Programme Committee

S. Lautemann (Germany)
J. Bezivin, LRSG (France)
F. Lochovsky (China)
S. Brinkkemper (The Netherlands)
P. Loucopoulos (United Kingdom)
J. Brunet (France)
R. Meersman (Belgium)
X. Castellani (France)
M. Orlowska (Australia)
C. Cauvet (France)
D. Patel (United Kingdom)
C. Chrisment (France)
B. Pernici (Italy)
W. Emmerich (United Kingdom)
N. Prakash (India)
A. Flory (France)
D. Rieu (France)
M. Franckson (France)

M. Saeki (Japan)
C. Ghezzi (Italy)
F. Saltor (Spain)
P. Gray (United Kingdom)
M. Schneider (France)
J. Grimson (Ireland)
C. Souveyet (France)
H. Habrias (France)
J. Stage (Denmark)
B. Henderson-Sellers (Australia)
K. Subieta (Poland)
M. Jarke (Germany)
Y. Sun (United Kingdom)
K. Jeffery (United Kingdom)
Y. Vassiliou (Greece)
L. Kalinichenko (Russia)
H. Zullighoven (Germany)
R. King (USA)

Organizing Commitee

Camille Ben Achour (France)
Rebecca Deneckere (France)
Saefd Assar (France)
Setthachai Jungjariyanonn (France)
Joel Brunet (France)
Vincent Motte (France)
Adolphe Benjamen (France)
Farida Semmak (France)

Alphabetical List of OOIS'98 Contributors

Y. Arapha, Imperial College of Science, Technology and Medicine, Department of Electrical and Electronic Engineering, Exhibition Road, London, SW7 2BT, UK

F. Barbier, IRIN, University of Nantes, 2 rue de la Houssiniere, BP 92208, 44322 Nantes cedex 3, France

P.J. Barclay, Department of Computer Studies, Napier University, Edinburgh, Scotland

L. Bellatreche, Department of Computer Science, Hong Kong University of Science and Technology, Clear Water Bay, Kowloon, Hong Kong

W. Benn, Department of Computer Science, Technical University of Chemnitz-Zwickau, 09107 Chemnitz, Germany

H. Briand, IRIN, Rue de la Houssiniere, BP 92208, 44322 Nantes cedex 3, France

J. Brunet, C.R.I., Universite Paris 1, 90 rue de Tolbiac, 75013 Paris, France

X. Castellani, CEDRIC IIE (CNAM) Research Laboratory, 18 allee Jean Rostand, 91025 Evry cedex, France

M. Chabre-Peccoud, Laboratoire Logiciels Systemes Reseaux - IMAG, BP 72, 38402 Saint Martin d'Heres cedex, France

E. Chang, La Trobe University, Department of Computer Science and Computer Engineering, Bundora, Victoria 3083, Australia

P. Charlton, Imperial College of Science, Technology and Medicine, Department of Electrical and Electronic Engineering, Exhibition Road, London, SW7 2BT, UK

Y. Chen, IPSI Institute, GMD GmbH, Dolovostr. 15, 64293 Darmstadt, Germany

T.Y. Cheung, 3/F., University Administration Building Department of Computer Science, The Chinese University of Hong Kong, Shatin, NT, Hong Kong

K. S. Cheung, 3/F., University Administration Building Department of Computer Science, The Chinese University of Hong Kong, Shatin, NT, Hong Kong

I. Choudhury, South Bank University, School of Computing, Information Systems and Maths, 103 Borough Road, London SEI OAA, UK

K.O. Chow, 3/F., University Administration Building Department of Computer Science, The Chinese University of Hong Kong, Shatin, NT, Hong Kong

S. Clarke, School of Computer Applications, Dublin City University, Dublin 9, Ireland

C. Delobel, INRIA, LRI-Universite de Paris-Sud, France

P. Delorme, Department of Computer Science, Trinity College, Dublin

R. Deneckere, C.R.I., Universite Paris l, 90 rue de Tolbiac, 75013 Paris, France

T. S. Dillon, La Trobe University, Department of Computer Science and Computer Engineering, Bundora, Victoria 3083, Australia

Y. Ehou, Department of Computer Science, Worcester Polytechnic Institute, 100 Institute Road, Worcester, MA, 01609 2280, USA

A. Finkelstein, Department of Computer Science, University College London, Gower Street, London, WC1E 6BT, UK

R.B. France, Department of Computer Science & Engineering, Florida Atlantic University, Boca Raton FL 33431 0991, USA

J. C. Freire Junior, UNESP, Faculdade de Engenharia, CP 205, 15 500 000 Guaratinguet, Brazil

A. Front, Laboratoire Logiciels Systemes Reseaux - IMAG, BP 72, 38402 Saint Martin d'Heres cedex, France

J.-P. Giraudin, Laboratoire Logiciels Systemes Reseaux - IMAG, BP 72, 38402 Saint Martin d'Heres cedex, France

W. Goebl, CFC Informations Systeme, Baeckerstrasse 1/2/7, 1010 Vienna, Austria

J. Grimson, Department of Computer Science, Trinity College, Dublin, Ireland

N. Hamamouche, CEDRIC IIE (CNAM) Research Laboratory, 18 allee Jean Rostand, 91025 Evry cedex, France

M.L. Hines, Software Architecture Department, Computer Science Telecommunications, University of Missouri-Kansas City, 5100 Rockhill Road, Kansas City, MO 64110, USA

K. Hung, Department of Computer Science, The University of Sheffield, Regent Court, 211 Portobello Street, Sheffield, SI 4DP, UK

M. Jouve, Laboratoire CEDRIC-IIE (CNAM), 18 allee Jean Rostand, 91025 Evry, France

K. Karlapalem, Department of Computer Science, University of Science and Technology, Clear Water Bay, Kowloon, Hong Kong

J.B. Kennedy, Dept. of Computer Studies, Napier University, Edinburgh, Scotland

B.B. Kristensen, The Maersk Mc-Kinney Moller Institute for Production Technology, Odense University, DK 5230 Odense, Denmark

H. Kuno, R&D Instrument Support Sol. Div., Hewlett-Packard Company, Santa Clara CA 95052 8059, USA

R. Laleau, Laboratoire CEDRIC-IIE (CNAM), 18 allee Jean Rostand, 91025 Evry, France

N.W. Lammari, Laboratoire CEDRIC-IIE (CNAM), 18 allec Jean Rostand, 91025 Evry, France

M.M. Larrondo-Petrie, Department of Computer Science & Engineering, Florida Atlantic University, Boca Raton FL 33431 0991, USA

A. Le Grand, Centre Universitaire d'Informatique, Universite de Geneve, Rue General Dufour 24, CH1211 Geneve 4

A.J. Lee, Department of EECS, University of Michigan, Ann Arbor MI 48109 2122, USA

H. Lehmann, Department of Management Science and Information Systems, University of Auckland, Private Bag 92019, Auckland, New Zealand

Q. Li, Department of Computing, Hong Kong Polytechnic University, Hung Hom, Kowloon, Hong Kong

M. Magnan, LGI2P EMA-EERIE, Parc Scientifique Georges BESSE, 30000 Neemes, France

R, McGuigan, Department of Computer Science, Trinity College, Dublin, Ireland

J. Murphy, School of Computer Applications, Dublin City University, Dublin 9, Ireland

J. Odell, James Odell Associates, 1315 Hutchins Avenue, Ann Arbor, MI 48103, USA

C. Oussalah, LGI2P EMA-EERIE, Parc Scientifique Georges BESSE, 30000 Neemes, France

S. Patel, School of Computing, Information Systems and Mathematics, South Bank University, 103 Borough Road, London SEI OAA, UK

D. Patel, School of Computing, Information Svstems and Mathematics, South Bank University, 103 Borough Road, London SEI OAA, UK

N.W. Paton, Department of Computer Science, University of Manchester, 0xford Road, Manchester M13 9PL, UK

Y.-G. Ra, Department of EECS, University of Michigan, Ann Arbor MI 48109 2122, USA

W. Rahayu, La Trobe University, Department of Computer Science and Computer Engineering, Bundora, Victoria 3083, Australia

S. Rideau, GC2i, 5 et 7 rue des Piliers de la Chauviniere, 44800 Saint-Herbain, France

M. Roantree, School of Computer Applications, Dublin City University, Dublin 9, Ireland

T. Rose, CAD Consultants Ltd., 797 London Road, Thornton Heath, Surrey, CR7 6XA, UK

E.A. Rundensteiner, Department of Computer Science, Worcester Polytechnic Institute, 100 Institute Road, Worcester, MA 01609 2280, USA

M. Saksena, Department of Computer Science & Engineering, Florida Atlantic University, Boca Raton FL 33431 0991, USA

P.R.F. Sampaio, Department of Computer Science, University of Manchester, Oxford Road, Manchester, M13 9PL, UK

T. Simons, Department of Compter Science, University of Sheffield, Regent Court, 211 Portobello Street, Sheffield SI 4DP, UK

A.J.H. Simons, Department of Computer Science, The University of Sheffield, Regent Court, 211 Portobello Street, Sheffield, S1 4DP, UK

M. Snoeck, Universite Libre de Bruxelles, Brussels, Belgium

C. Souveyet, C.R.I., Universite Paris l, 90 rue de Tolbiac, 75013 Paris, France

G. Spanoudakis, Department of Computer Science, City University, Northampton Square, London, ECIV OHB, UK

D. Tamzalit, LGI2P EMA-EERIE, Parc Scientifique Georges BESSE, 30000 Neemes, France

F. Velez, Ardent Software Inc, France

T. Vianna de Arafjo, ISEG, Technical University of Lisbon, UECE - Research Unit on Sciences of Complexity, 1200 Lisboa, Portugal

Y.Wang, Centre for Software Engineering, IVF, Argongatan 30, S-431 53 Gothenburg, Sweden

Y. Zhou, Department of Computer Science, Worcester Polytechnic Institute, 100 Institute Road, Worcester, MA 01609 2280, USA

Additional Reviewers

OOIS98
Centre de recherche en informatique
University of Paris 1 - Sorbonne
90, rue de Tolbiac
75013 PARIS
FRANCE
Phone: 33 1 40 77 46 34 / 46 04
Fax: 33 1 40 77 19 54

email: oois98@univ-paris1.fr
http://panoramix.univ-paris1.fr/CRINFO/OOIS98

Contents

INVITED TALKS

MODELLING ISSUES 1

QUERIES AND VIEWS

REUSE

METHOD ISSUES 1

DESIGN ISSUES 1

MODELLING ISSUES 2

EVOLUTION AND INTEROPERABILITY

METHOD ISSUES 2

DESIGN ISSUES 2

PANEL: OO TRENDS AND PERSPECTIVES

INVITED TALKS

Object Databases: Connectivity with Relational Systems and ODMG Standard (Summary)

C. Delobel

LRI-University of Paris-Sud, INRIA

F. Velez

Ardent Software, Inc.

June 15, 1998

Object databases have been introduced since 1987. The first version of ODMG standard appeared in 1991, and the new release 2.0 is from 1997. During ten year period, object database technology has received considerable attention and improvements. Today products are mature and proved their efficiency in many real applications (telecommunication, energy distribution, spatial data management, Web, etc.) where gigabytes of data are manipulated. The goal of this paper is to present two key subjects: (i) why the ODMG standard is crucial, and (ii) how to implement an open architecture to connect object and relational databases.

The first subject is related with the ODMG standard. The ODMG Object Model is the core of the standard. The ODMG standard has evolved from the Release 1.2 (1993) to Release 2.0 (1997). The ODMG standard is composed of three parts: the Object Model (OM) with the Object Definition Language (ODL), the Object Query Language (OQL) and the bindings for the Object Model onto each programming languages such as C++, Smalltalk and Java which turn these languages into true Object Manipulation Language (OML) for persistent objects.

Recently a paper written by Alagic has raised a number of problems. Many problems come from the fact that the Object Model should serve as a common basis for different paradigms underlying the typing system of each programming languages like C++, Smalltalk or Java. The criticisms can be classified into different categories :

- The type expressions associated with the OM are not enough well defined and may be too rigid.

- In some cases dynamic type checking is required in spite of applying only static type checking. When the type safety is verified by the type checker, it is not always guaranteed at run time. These two elements are not independant. When defining a type system for an OM, one should

3

have in mind the features that he wants and what solutions are feasible an efficient.

- Persistence definition is not orthogonal to types.

As Alagic's paper suggests, the use of more modern type systems: "self" types, parametrized types, higher order typing, "meet" and "join" operators on types would be perfectly reasonable to consider to define an OML with built-in persistence associated to the ODMG data model. But we are not in this situation. All the benefits of this typing technology won't match with C++, Smalltalk and Java as DMLs for this object model. Why would one try to introduce a data model with safe types and high order types and then map it to languages that don't have these concepts? One should clearly understand that the only manipulation language in the ODMG model is the one provided by the programming language. Given these constraints, we gave ourselves to define the standard, namely add persistence to non-persistent languages, and we got a result which makes sense.

The second subject deals with the connection between the relational and the object world. Todays large entreprise information is distributed over multiple database management systems, and relational technology is the dominant technology for data storage. On the other hand, the object paradigm has clearly gained acceptance among developers as the best way to develop applications: they are faster to built and much easier to maintain and extend. Solving the connections between ODMG technology and relational storage and access becomes crucial, as this would provide a portable way of developing object-based database applications on existing relational data. The paper will present the necessary technology to solve the following basic *connections cases*:

- Object developers who use an object-oriented language want to store their data in a transparent way into a relational database system.

- Object developers who use an object-oriented language want to define applications over an existing relational database.

- Finally, the last case is *migration* where the relational database and its application are completely moved in a new object environment.

In the first case, we are facing the problem of how to introduce persistency concepts into an object programming language. Data move back and reverse from the object environment to the relational database and only the relational database keeps persistent data. In this environment, the object developers define their schema as composed of classes and the object data model associated with the language is mapped onto a fixed relational schema which guarantees data conversion. This situation is called an *import* functionality. When data is created or updated within the object environment, the mapping is defined in a such way that data is modified into the relational database.

This second case is different from the first one and it is both an extension and a reverse case. We assume the existence of a relational database, therefore the source relational schema has to be mapped onto class definitions. These class definitions have to be consistent with the preexisting relational schema and the mapping has to be always invertible for updating data. We call that an *export* functionality.

In the last case, once the migration is finished users and applications have to cope with only the object database. Since existing relational databases are often huge, the efficient migration of bulk data into object databases is a problem frequently encountered in practice. This occurs when applications are moved from relational to object systems, but more often, in applications relying on external data that has to be refreshed regularly. Indeed, one finds more and more object replications of data that are used by satellite Java or C++ persistent applications. The migration problem turns out to be extremely complicated. It is not rare to find migration programs requiring hours and even days to be processed. Furthermore, efficiency is not the only aspect of the problem. As we will see, flexibility in terms of database physical organization and decomposition of the migration process is at least as important for efficency or security purposes.

In all of these cases, communication between an object application and a new or existing relational database is done by invoking SQL-statements and receiving tuples. This access can exploit software like ODBC (Open Database Connectivity) which provides access to a variety of relational systems across different platforms. However, when developing his application, the programmer faces three main problems: (i) he has to define a mapping between objet concepts and the relational ones, (ii) he has to translate OQL queries into SQL ones, (iii) he has to write code for converting tuples into object structures according to the defined mapping.

Of course, there are industrial connectivity products which makes the life of developers easier. However, they are far to be satisfactory. For instanmce, no optimization techniques are provided. On other hand, the scientific community has mainly focused on modeling issues and has provided sound solutions to the problem of automatically generating object schemas from relational ones. These works left out the manipulation of data (read, write, update). They do not integrate the schema translation problems within the scope of the execution environment.

In summary, what is missing is an environment which supports the three cases: export, import and migration where the definition of schema mappings and query translation from SQL to OQL and vice-versa are the central elements. Therefore, the user can friendly modify the schema mapping without rebuilting completely the application code. In the presentation, we will propose an open architecture based on a mapping language where the three issues: import, export and migration are considered. Prototypes and products developed around the O_2 systems will illustrate the presentation.

Standardization for OO A&D?

J. J. Odell
James Odell Associates
1315 Hutchins Avenue
Ann Arbor, MI 48103 USA
Tel: +1 734 994-0844
email: jodell@compuserve.com

What if there were a standard set of core concepts for OO analysis and design (OO A&D)? What if there were a prescribed set of diagrams for communicating these concepts? Imagine how much simpler our OO A&D world would be—not to mention the world of OO-CASE vendors. We could all speak a common OO A&D language, rather than some dialect based on a particular methodologist or OO-CASE vendor. I'm not sure such an event would ever meet everyone's satisfaction. Furthermore, I'm not sure that one fixed set of diagrams can (or should) express everything we need to say. But, a way to express most of our A&D knowledge is within sight. With the OMG's Object Analysis and Design Taskforce (OA&DTF) a standard could soon exist for:
- o a common meta-model for maintaining our OO A&D knowledge,
- o a technique for exchanging this knowledge, and
- o a suggested notation for expressing our OO A&D knowledge.

A LITTLE HISTORY

Grady Booch was the first to organize an OO A&D standardization effort. In the spring of 1993, he asked a handful of major methodologists if they wished to create an OO A&D standard. (Jim Rumbaugh, Ivar Jacobson, Stephen Mellor, Peter Coad, and I were included.) However, assembling these people for even one day proved too daunting as we could only agree on a short breakfast meeting at OOPSLA '93 in Washington, DC. Since the idea of standardization was considered undesirable by the majority at the meeting, the standards movement floundered—but not for long. In

October 1995, Rational Corporation succeeded in hiring Jim Rumbaugh. With the combined force of Booch and Rumbaugh, Rational decided to produce its own standard approach, then called the Unified Method. Its rollout occurred at OOPSLA '95 in Austin accompanied by singing (Jim) and merriment (Grady). When Ivar Jacobson joined Rational about a year later, the resulting unified approach became stronger and broader.

The downside of this was that Rational positioned its unified approach as *the* new world standard. Supporters of any other approach were expected to lay down and die, because Rational considered itself king. As you can imagine, this attitude did not go down well with those of us who differed from Rational. Around the world, there was a hue and cry by newly formed Anti-Booch Coalitions (ABC). Among those of us who initially banded together were Peter Coad, Larry Constantine, Don Firesmith, Ian Graham, Brian Henderson-Sellers, Ivar Jacobson (before he joined Rational), Bertrand Meyer, Meilir Page-Jones, and Rebecca Wirfs-Brock. This new alliance, initially known as COMMA and Omega, is now known as the OPEN (Object-Oriented Process, Environment, and Notation) Alliance.

The OPEN Alliance gradually lost several members to apathy, disagreement, and other reasons. (Peter Coad, Ivar Jacobson, Bertrand Meyer, Meilir Page-Jones, and I were among those who left.) One important reason for leaving the OPEN Alliance was that Rational had changed its apparent stance and had begun actively inviting other points of view. Rational's approach—now called the UML (Unified Modeling Language)—became a unification of more than Booch, Rumbaugh, and Jacobson. However, this invitation did not mean that Rational was accepting *all* approaches. Rational made it clear that it was only opening the door to those approaches that made sense to Rational. While this tactic did not please everybody, it ushered in a more cooperative atmosphere.

ENTER THE OA&D TASKFORCE

By 1995, OO A&D unification and standardization were certainly in the wind and on June 29, 1995, a new special interest group was formed within the OMG. This special interest group is now known as the Object Analysis and Design Taskforce (OA&DTF) and I am its co-chair. After an initial period of data gathering and discussion in 1995, the OA&DTF submitted its first Request for Proposal (RFP) in June 1996. As of November 1997, the proposal entitled *Unified Modeling Langauge* was accepted by the OMG. A copy of the proposal is available from www.omg.org/members/doclist-97.html (documents ad/97-08-02 through ad/97-08-11). Or, if you are not a member of the OMG, the proposal can also be downloaded from www.rational.com/uml.

MODELLING ISSUES 1

A Characterization of Aggregation

Monika Saksena, Robert B. France, María M. Larrondo-Petrie

Department of Computer Science & Engineering
Florida Atlantic University
Boca Raton, FL-33431-0991, USA
{msaksena,robert,maria}@cse.fau.edu

Abstract. Most popular object-oriented modeling techniques (OOMTs) provide good support for the creation of structured conceptual models of system behavior and structure. A serious drawback of these techniques is that the concepts and notations used are loosely defined. This can lead to the creation of ambiguous models, and to disagreements over the proper use and interpretation of modeling constructs. An important modeling construct that is often loosely defined is aggregation. In this paper we present a characterization of aggregation that can help developers identify appropriate applications of the concept.

1 Introduction

There are several reasons for the popularity of graphical object-oriented (OO) modeling techniques (OOMTs) such as OMT [9] and Fusion [2]. They provide modeling concepts and constructs that allow developers to create conceptual models that closely reflect the real-world concerns that are pertinent to the system under development. These models can help developers gain insights into the essential behavior of systems.

A major drawback of popular OOMTs is that the notations and concepts they use are loosely defined. A result of this is that the models they produce can be ambiguous, and their interpretation often relies heavily on human intuition aided by the use of suggestive names and knowledge of the problem domain. Another serious consequence of poorly defined modeling concepts is that developers can waste considerable time resolving disagreements over usage and interpretation of the modeling constructs. For example, it is often not clear to developers when aggregation is to be preferred over general associations.

It is sometimes argued that loose interpretations are to be favoured because they allow the modeling concepts to be tailored to particular usages. This is indeed a strength if developers make clear the precise interpretation they used in creating their models. If this interpretation is not communicated to the reader of the model then the door is open for misinterpretation.

In this paper, we provide a characterization of *aggregation*, a modeling concept that is often the topic of heated discussions. In developing the characterization we examined published works on aggregation and analysed our OO modeling experiences. The characterization presented in this paper is the result of a careful analysis and distillation of these works and experiences, and is the first step towards formulating a formal semantics for aggregate structures. The ultimate goal of our research on aggregation is to provide a formal characterization that allows one to distinguish aggregation from the more general notion of association. The characterization presented in this paper is not presented in formal terms because it relects our initial understanding of properties pertinent to aggregate structures. As our understanding of aggregation properties deepens, a more formal characterization will evolve.

The characteristics we discuss are grouped into two classes: *primary* and *secondary* characteristics. Primary characteristics are properties that are essential to aggregation. They are invariant in the sense that they hold for all aggregate structures. Secondary characteristics are non-essential in the sense that they are not true for all aggregate structures. The secondary characteristics we discuss in this paper can also be found in other OO modeling constructs, however, in aggregation their manifestations can have special connotations.

In Section 2 we list the works that influenced our characterization. Section 3 presents the characteristics that we consider to be essential (the primary characteristics) and Section 4 presents some of the major secondary characteristics. We conclude in Section 5 with an outline of our planned work in this area.

2 Background and Related Works

In the OO community there is much debate on the usefulness of distinguishing aggregation as a special form of association. From the programming perspective the distinction between the two concepts is probably not useful because they can both be implemented in the same manner: as references to other objects (e.g., pointers to associated objects). We feel that a distinction can usefully be made at the conceptual modeling level. Modeling an association as an aggregation imparts additional information about the association. Unfortunately, this additional information is seldom clearly defined in published works on OO modeling techniques. This has led to confusion over the appropriate use of the aggregate construct, and has caused modelers to avoid using the construct.

The notion of aggregation has been explored by many authors in the software engineering, knowledge representation, conceptual modeling, and database communities. Winston *et al.* [11] characterize different kinds of aggregations from a knowledge representation perspective. In 1994, Odell mapped the work of Winston *et al.* to the OO modeling perspective [8]. Civello studied properties of whole-part associations in a case study [1], and Moreira and Clark present a rigorous treatment of aggregation [7]. Kilov and Ross [6] give a rigorous treatment of aggregation in terms of invariant properties.

This paper attempts to unify and extend the above works on aggregation. The Unified Modeling Language (UML)[4, 5], a recently approved Object Management Group OO notation standard, is used to represent the aggregation concepts discussed in this paper.

Our characterization of aggregation is expressed in terms of primary (essential) and secondary (non-essential) characteristics. Fig. 1 shows the organization of the characteristics discussed in this paper.

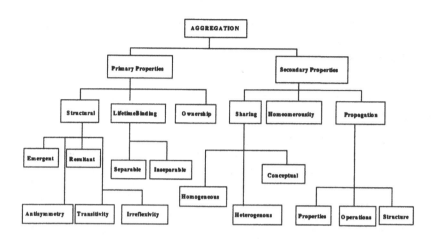

Fig. 1. Properties of Aggregation

3 Primary Characteristics of Aggregation

The primary characteristics are grouped under three views:

- **Structural:** This view focuses on the static structure of aggregates.
- **Lifetime Binding:** This view focuses on lifetime relationships between parts and their whole.
- **Ownership:** This view focuses on the behavioral relationship between the parts and their whole.

In the following subsections we elaborate on the characteristics in each of these views.

3.1 Structural Characteristics

Structural characteristics constrain the static aspects of aggregate structures. The transitivity, antisymmetry, and irreflexive characteristics are widely known and we simply state them below.
Transitivity

If object A is part of object B and object B is part of object C, then object A is part of object C.

Antisymmetry

If object A is part of object B then object B cannot be part of object A.

Irreflexivity

Object A cannot be a part of itself either directly or indirectly. This means that the irreflexive property must hold for the transitive closure of the aggregate structure.

The Resultant Property and the Emergent Property characteristics determine the types of properties (e.g., attributes) that an aggregate must have.

Resultant Property

A resultant property of an aggregate structure is one that is dependent on a subset of the properties of the aggregate's parts. It is dependent in the sense that a change in the properties in the subset results in a change to the resultant property. Every aggregate must have at least one resultant property [6].

For example, in Fig. 2, *numberofsamples* is a property that is derived from the *Sample* parts.

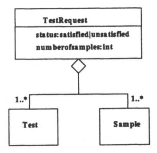

Fig. 2. Resultant and Emergent Properties

Emergent Property

An emergent property is one that is independent of the properties of the component instances. Every aggregate structure must have at least one emergent property [6].

An example of an emergent property is the unique identifier associated with an aggregate instance. This property distinguishes an aggregate from its parts and justifies its existence. Emergent properties are independent of component properties, thus changing the properties of parts, or adding and deleting parts will not change the identity of an aggregate. An example of a non-identity emergent property is the *status* attribute of *TestRequest*.

It is important to note that resultant attributes of an aggregate class should not be modeled as attributes of the class if the relationships between it and its parts are modeled as associations rather than aggregations (see Fig. 3). The presence of resultant properties is a good indication that an association should be modeled as an aggregation.

Fig. 3. Alternative modeling as an association

3.2 Lifetime Binding Characteristics

Lifetime binding refers to the relationship between the lifetimes of the whole and the parts. In the Unified Modeling Language (UML) [5] the strong form of aggregation is defined with coincident lifetime binding between the part and the whole. The weaker form of aggregation relaxes this rule to allow sharing of parts across wholes. Civello [1] puts forward the idea that parts and wholes can outlive each other. In the Rumbaugh *et al.* [10] characterization of aggregation, the lifetime of the part is "contained" within the lifetime of the whole (i.e., parts do not outlive the whole). Cook and Daniels [3] concur with this notion of containment.

In our characterization of aggregation, we use the weakest form of lifetime binding that seemed consistent with the notion of aggregation:

Lifetime Binding

> *In an aggregate structure, the lifetime of the part must overlap the lifetime of the whole.*

All the possible relationships between lifetimes of parts and wholes allowed by our characterization are given in Fig. 4. Case 4 corresponds to the UML notion of coincident lifetimes. Cases 1-4 correspond to Rumbaugh's notion of contained lifetimes. Civello's notion of the part outliving the whole corresponds to Cases 6 and 7.

Cases 1 to 4 are scenarios of lifetime bindings where the lifetime of the part is described as "contained" within the lifetime of the whole. In these cases the parts cannot be separated from their wholes and must always be associated with a whole. This group of lifetime dependencies is referred to as *inseparable parts*. Cases 5 to 8 allow parts to exist without associated wholes. This group of dependencies is referred to as *separable parts*. In Cases 5 to 7 the death of a part is independent of the death of the whole. In Case 8, a part can exist on its own, but if it is associated with a whole, it dies when the whole dies.

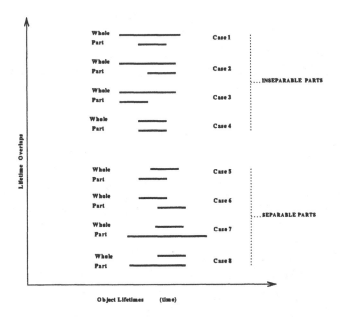

Fig. 4. Lifetime Bindings between the part and the whole

3.3 Ownership Characteristic

Ownership pertains to the control the whole has over the behavior of its parts. According to Odell, it is a term that describes the destiny of the whole viz a viz its parts [8]. We consider the following notion of ownership as essential to aggregation:

Ownership

> *An object owns its part in the sense that it controls the behavior of its parts, that is, the whole controls how and when the services of its parts are used. This requires that an aggregate class have methods that call the methods of the parts.*

Note that the above notion of ownership does not preclude other objects from interacting directly with the part. Ownership means that manipulation of the whole can involve manipulation of the parts. This notion of ownership facilitates the propagation of operations from the whole to its parts (see next section). A part may be owned by one or more wholes at a particular time, and its owners may change over the part's lifetime.

4 Secondary Characteristics

As stated earlier, secondary properties are non-essential properties of aggregation. Combinations of secondary characteristics yield different flavors of aggregation. The following classes of secondary characteristics are discussed in this section: parts sharing, homeomerousity (sameness of part and whole), and propagation of features.

4.1   Sharing of parts

Sharing of parts occurs when a part is associated with more than one whole at a particular time. Shared parts are necessarily separable.

The notion of sharing may seem alien to aggregation. Often, aggregation is based on the idea of "object containment", wherein parts are inseparable from their whole and can only be part of a single whole. In our characterization containment is not an essential characteristic of aggregation. Three types of parts sharing can be identified:

- *Homogeneous Sharing*: An instance of a part class can be shared among different instances of the same aggregate class. For example, in Fig. 5 an instance of *Person* can belong to two different instances of *ResearchGroup*.
- *Heterogeneous Sharing*: An instance of a class can be shared by wholes that are instances of different classes. For example, in Fig. 6 an instance of *Person* can be simultaneously shared by an instance of *Family* and by an instance of *ResearchGroup*.
- *Conceptual Sharing*: The concept represented by a class is shared. Conceptual sharing does not imply sharing of instances. Fig. 7 illustrates an *Engine* which is a class in two different aggregate classes: *Car* and *Plane*. However, an instance of *Engine* for a *Plane* cannot be used as a part of an instance of *Car*. The concept of the *Engine* is being shared, not instances of *Engine*.

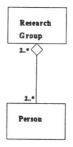

Fig. 5. Homogeneous sharing

Sharing implies that if the membership of the part in one aggregate is nullified then the part can continue to exist. *Constrained Sharing* occurs when a part exists only if it is a part of an aggregate structure (i.e., at any point in time when the structure is not being manipulated by an operation, the part must be associated with a whole).

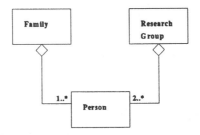

Fig. 6. Heterogeneous sharing

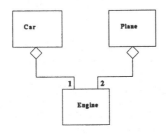

Fig. 7. Conceptual sharing

4.2 Homeomerousity

Parts in an aggregate structure are said to be homeomerous when they have properties in common with their whole or with other parts in the structure. For example, a homeomerous part class can be a specialization of its whole class. Such parts are often used to form recursive aggregate structures.

4.3 Property Propagation

Properties of the whole (attributes, operations, references) can propagate to its parts. Such propagation is a powerful and concise way of specifying an entire continuum of behavior.

For an example of behavior propagation, consider a triangle modeled as an aggregate with edges as parts. Moving the triangle requires the movement of the edges. The move operation of the whole is propagated to its parts.

For an example of attribute propagation consider the *Car* composed of an *Engine*, *Body* and *Chassis*. The color of the body is the color of the car, that is, the color of the car propagates to the body.

5 Conclusions

In this paper we propose a method independent characterization of aggregation. The characterization is expressed in terms of primary and secondary characteristics. This work is part of an ongoing effort to formalize OO modeling concepts. The objective is to create modeling notations that can be used to build precise and rigorously analyzable models. We are currently developing extensions of the UML that reflect the characteristics of aggregation outlined in this paper.

References

1. F. Civello. Roles for composite objects in object-oriented analysis and design. *OOPSLA*, pages 376–393, 1993.
2. Derek Coleman, Patrick Arnold, Stephanie Bodoff, Chris Dollin, Helena Gilchrist, Fiona Hayes, and Paul Jeremaes. *Object-Oriented Development: The Fusion Method*. Prentice Hall, Englewood Cliffs, NJ, Object-Oriented Series edition, 1994.
3. S. Cook and J. Daniels. *Designing Object Systems Object Oriented Modelling with Syntropy*. Prentice Hall, Englewood Cliffs, NJ, 1994.
4. The UML Group. *Unified Modeling Language, Notation Guide, Ver 1.1*, August 1997.
5. The UML Group. *Unified Modeling Language, Semantic Guide, Ver 1.0*, January 1997.
6. H. Kilov and J. Ross. *Information Modeling An Object-Oriented Approach*. PTR Prentice Hall, Englewood Cilffs, New Jersey, 1994.
7. A. M. D. Moreira and R. G. Clark. Complex Objects: Aggregates. Technical Report TR-CSM-123, Department of Computing Science and Mathematics, University of Stirling, FK9 4LA, Scotland, August 1994.
8. J. Odell. Six Different Kinds of Composition. *Journal of Object Oriented Programming*, 6(8):10–15, January 1994.
9. J. Rumbaugh, M. Blaha, W. Premerlani, F. Eddy, and W. Lorensen. *Object-Oriented Modeling and Design*. Prentice Hall, 1991.
10. J. Rumbaugh, M. Blaha, W. Premerlani, F. Eddy, and W. Lorensen. *Object Oriented Modeling and Design*. Prentice Hall, Englewood Cliffs, New Jersey, 1991.
11. M. E. Winston, R. Chaffin, and D. Herrman. A Taxonomy of Part-Whole Relations. *Cognitive Science*, 11:417–444, 1987.

Object-Oriented Hierarchies and Their Resulting Complex Systems

Tanya Vianna de Araújo

ISEG - Technical University of Lisbon
UECE - Research Unit on Complexity in Economics

Abstract

Information Systems can be considered complex in a great many ways. This paper focus on the hierarchical structures used in Object-Oriented Modelling and MetaModelling. Models are described as emerging structures within aggregation and generalization hierarchies, and acquiring the characteristics of a complex system is imputed to the role of (free) associations whose semantics is exogenous to those hierarchies.

1 Introduction

While Computer Aided Software Engineering tools deal with the most mechanical features of such an engineering process, advanced CASE and MetaCASE Environments try to move away from a pure technological perspective. New paradigm proposals are being considered and the Object-Oriented paradigm appeared as a new way of modelling Information Systems. Underlying every modelling effort there is an attempt to deal with complexity.

Epistemological approaches have been suggested as the most promising way for reasoning about complex systems (see, for instance, [1] and [2]). They raise many new fundamental questions on the form of our knowledge, and, in so doing, address the need for *Meta-Scientific* reassessments. In the Information Systems Development (ISD) field, an increasingly attention on Meta-Modelling concerns can be observed. Ontologies for Object, Process and Structural Modelling have been adopted in academia and industrial research ([3], [4], [5]). There is a clear trend in applying *second order* models and an increasingly popular use of the term *meta* so as to designate issues that go beyond the regular modelling concerns.

The adoption of Object-Oriented concepts in meta-modelling has appeared as a straightforward contribution for describing modelling techniques. By means of applying the uniform notion of Object, together with concepts like aggregation and inheritance, it has been possible to model methods structure and behaviour at various levels of abstraction and detail.

We envision that, contributions coming from the Science of Complexity can be of great help in Object-Oriented modelling and meta-modelling. Hierarchical constructions are ubiquitous in Science. In Object-Oriented Analysis, aggregation and generalization hierarchies play a central role. But describing knowledge from a pure analytical approach can lead us to "reductionistic" views. Whenever the complexity perspective is adopted, the concept of emergence allows reductionism to be counterbalanced, and new structures to be described as resulting of the interaction of multiples hierarchies ([1], [6],[7]).

This paper focus on the hierarchical structures applied in Object-Oriented modelling and meta-modelling. In so doing, models and metamodels are described as intermediate structures emerging from both aggregation (or systemic) (*partOf*) and generalization (*kindOf*) hierarchies.

The concept of association is an extremely important one in the context of every modelling process. Metamodelling approaches ([8], [9], [10], [11], [12], [13]) vary in the way associations are described and therefore applied in conceptual modelling. Some Object-Oriented approaches do not treat associations on an equal foot with objects and classes, preserving encapsulation has been the main reason to proceed this way.

Encapsulation is, however, a concern of the Design and Implementation phases. Discussing on the role that associations play in modelling and metamodelling, we address the description of associations whose semantics is exogenous to both *partOf* and *kindOf* relationships. It is shown how, considering the (free) associations in the description of a model, brings to models and metamodels the characteristic of a complex system.

This paper is organised in five sections. In the next section we focus on the use of the aggregation and generalization hierarchies in analysis. In the third section, models and metamodels are defined by means of combining aggregation and generalizing frameworks. In the forth section we apply the concepts of Emergence and Non-Linearity in order to describe models from the complexity perspective. The paper ends with the appropriate conclusions and outline of the future work.

2 Conceptual Modelling

Modelling concerns can be found in every branch of Science and deal with the interpretation (and representation) of a given reality. A model can be defined as *an attempt to gain reductive understanding of a system through a simplified representation of it* ([2]).

The gain of reductive understanding results from an *abstraction process*. Producing a simplified representation of a given reality is a *conscious choice* leaded by the need for abstracting from less important aspects of such reality so as to better understand the relevant ones. Thus, we can say that a model results from the interpretation of a given reality, which is seen through a chosen Concept Structure on a particular *Level of Abstraction*.

Although the expression Level of Abstraction is often applied in conceptual modelling it is not always explicitly stated *what* one is supposed *to abstract from*. The most usual meaning concerns the abstraction levels that are supported in CASE environments. The scope of abstraction in a CASE environment may range from Analysis concerns (a high-level of abstraction) to programming or machine-oriented concerns ([14]). The following scheme shows the scope of Abstraction seen from the CASE perspective.

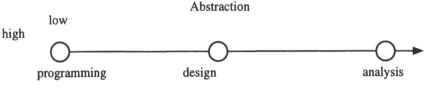

Figure 1: CASE Abstraction Levels

As shown in figure 1, the aspects which are considered to be relevant from such a CASE perspective are those allowing to identify a model as a result of one of the classical IS Development phases.

Modelling issues are also closely related to CASE concerns. Meanwhile, the expression Level of Abstraction as it is applied in the Conceptual Modelling field has a different meaning: it is targeted at identifying modelling levels where each level represents the intention (the scheme) of the lower (extension) one. This perspective is based on the *generalization* principle and the resulting structure is a *hierarchy of types*. Whenever this perspective is adopted, each component of a given level is related to at least one component of the higher level by means of a *KindOf* (or *IS-A*) relationship.

The following scheme (figure 2) shows Abstraction Levels seen from the Conceptual Modelling perspective.

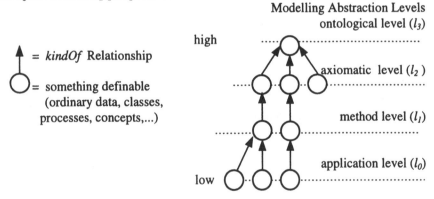

Figure 2: Conceptual Modelling Abstraction Levels

The aspects which are considered to be relevant from such a modelling perspective are those allowing to identify any abstraction (ex: data, classes, processes, concepts) as something definable, i.e., something whose definition is known and thus can be represented in a hierarchical generalizing framework.

The ontological level (l_3) is the one comprising human-readable text, which is targeted at providing definitions of existing concepts. Within ontological definitions the names of concepts are associated with human-readable text describing what the names are meant to denote ([4],([5],[15]). The axiomatic level (l_2) comprises the primitive notions or concepts existing in the metamodelling approach(es). The method level (l_1) consists of ordinary modelling concepts, like those of entity, process and class. Finally, the application level (l_0) comprises the relevant abstractions of a given Universe of Discourse (UoD).

2.1 Defining Abstractions : the Hierarchy of Types

Although Conceptual Modelling and IS Analysis are equivalent expressions we advocate that the former has a twofold nature. Conceptual Modelling is carried out through a combination of both analysis and synthesis. While analysis is mostly concerned with the definition of abstractions, synthesis is carried out by means of describing associations so as to related them.

An abstraction is considered something existing on its own, and thus, having a large degree of autonomy. In conceptual modelling, the definition of abstractions is performed by means of mapping each abstraction being defined in a hierarchy of types. The abstractions being defined must fit in with a certain level of the hierarchy of types.

Figure 3 :Defining Abstractions

As presented in figure 3, the definition of an abstraction A_i at the Modelling abstraction level l_i can be represented by the binary relation $kindOf (l_i, A_i, l_{i+1}, A_{i+1})$, where A_i is an abstraction at the abstraction level l_i. The vertical arrow which links the two nodes comprised in the above scheme (figure 3) provides a graphical representation of this binary relation.

In Object-Oriented modelling ([16], [17] and [18]), defining abstractions is performed through classification and inheritance. The concept of Class is applied to describe a set of objects sharing structure and behaviour, where each object is said to be an instance of a class and contains an implicit reference to it. Essentially, the objects in a class share a common semantic purpose.

Semantic purposes are further exploited through the concept of inheritance. Inheritance describes the relationship between a class and one or more refined versions of it. Applying this concept is also based on the *generalization* principle, where the classes being related fit in with the same level of the hierarchy of types earlier presented.

In the work herein presented we avoided describing inheritance occurring inside each modelling level, because, applying this concept would introduce difficulties (especially in graphical representations) in differentiating internal level (inheritance) from external level (*kindOf* or *generalization* relationships). The differentiation of these two forms of applying the *generalization* principle is strongly recommended.

In order to illustrate our approach, we shall consider at least two distinct modelling techniques: data flow diagramming (DFD) and entity relationship modelling (ERM). Defining the abstractions found in the context of these techniques will be provided by means of applying the concept of Object, as it is defined in the GOPRR ([8], [12] and [19]) metamodelling approach*.

The corresponding binary relations.

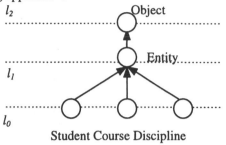

kindOf (l_1.Entity, l_2.Object)

kindOf (l_0.Course, l_1.Entity)
kindOf (l_0.Discipline, l_1.Entity)
kindOf (l_0.Student, l_1.Entity)

Figure 4 : example ERM - GOPRR

Within the context of the ERM, defining abstractions at the method level, provides the definition of an entity as an GOPRR object. Whenever the UoD concerns academic issues, performing the definition of abstractions at the application level provides the definition of three entities, named Student, Course and Discipline, as shown in figure 4.

The next scheme presents the DFD example applying the GOPRR concept of Object. In the data flow diagram context, performing the definition of abstractions at the method level provides the concepts named Process, External and Store to be defined as GOPRR objects. Whenever the UoD concerns issues of an Automatic Teller Machine (ATM) system, defining abstractions at the application level provides the definition of two processes (Withdraw and Deposit), an external entity (Customer) and a data store (Account), as figure 5 shows.

The corresponding binary relations.

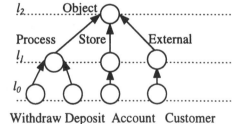

kindOf (l_1.Process, l_2.Object)
kindOf (l_1.External, l_2.Object)
kindOf (l_1.Store, l_2.Object)

kindOf (l_0.Withdraw, l_1.Process)
kindOf (l_0.Deposit, l_1.Process)
kindOf (l_0.Customer, l_1.External)

kindOf (l_0.Account, l_1.Store)

Figure 5 : example DFD - GOPRR

Defining abstractions through a hierarchy of types is an analytical feature. When an abstraction is defined the observer (IS engineer or software analyst) performs a decomposition task: the abstraction being defined is made free from other possible (previous) concepts and acquires its own identity with respect to the present context.

---

* Representing the GOPRR notions of Property and Role was avoided for simplification reasons, and since, it would not contribute to a better understanding of this work. Discussions on our work on GOPRR metamodelling can be found in ([20], [21], [22], and [23]).

This seems to be the very nature of any interpretation process, to free the object under interpretation from previous conceptualizations, which may be suggested by its name or its role in other contexts.

As it happens in chemical decomposition processes, the role of analysis is to free the various components from the characteristics of the whole, in so doing it is possible to identify each component and to learn what the compound is made up of. Being free of other characteristics, they are allowed to be combined in order to capture the semantics of the underlying UoD. It is accomplished through synthesis.

2.2 Describing "Free" Associations

Synthesis is carried out by means of associating abstractions previously defined. In associating abstractions the observer performs a composition task : an association establishes a link between a pair of components (abstractions) creating a compound element. Representing the result of this feature implies the inclusion of horizontal links (or single level links) in the Modelling hierarchy of types, as figure 6 shows.

association $(l_i.A_{ix}, l_i.A_{iy})$

Figure 6: Describing Associations

As presented in figure 6, an association S_i at the Modelling abstraction level l_i can be represented by the binary relation *association* $(l_i.A_{ix}, l_i.A_{iy})$, where A_{ix} and A_{iy} are abstractions at the Modelling abstraction level l_i . The horizontal link, which associates the two nodes comprised at the same abstraction level (figure 6) provides a graphical representation of this binary relation.

Figure 7 presents a graphical description of how DFD abstractions are associated at the method and application levels. The following binary relations provide the corresponding textual description.

flow1 $(l_1.\text{Process}, l_1.\text{Process})$
flow2 $(l_1.\text{Process}, l_1.\text{Store})$
flow3 $(l_1.\text{Process}, l_1.\text{External})$

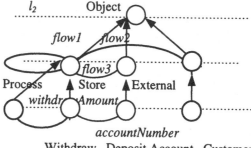

Figure 7: Representing DFD Associations

accountNumber $(l_0.\text{Deposit}, l_0.\text{Account})$
withdrawAmount $(l_0.\text{Withdraw}, l_0.\text{Deposit})$

26

The method level (l_1) comprises the representation of three associations named *flow1*, *flow2* and *flow3*. They are, accordingly to DFD rules, targeted at relating processes to processes, processes to stores, and processes to external entities, respectively[*].

At the application level (l_0), an arc represents the association named *withdrawAmount* (between Withdraw and Deposit), while another arc represent the association named *accountNumber* (between Deposit and Account). These arcs are simplified representations of data flows. Their names are targeted at describing the semantics of each association.

Figure 8 shows another example of describing associations at the method and application levels of the hierarchy of types. At the application level, there is an association named *enrol* which relates the entities Student and Course. At the method level we have another association being represented, it is named *relationship* and is targeted at relating entities within the ERM context.

These associations are described by the following binary relations.

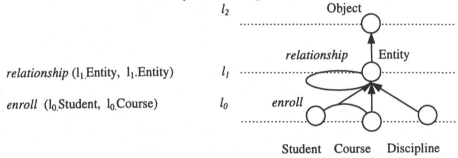

relationship (l_1.Entity, l_1.Entity)

enroll (l_0.Student, l_0.Course)

Figure 8: Representing ERM Associations

In applying an ontology-based approach [3], the axiomatic level comprises the representation of two associations named *inComing* and *outGoing* (links). These associations are targeted at relating nodes. At the method level there is a single association named *link*, which is targeted at relating the abstractions named Method and Class. At the application level, the method M may be related to the class Q through the association named *methodOf*, as figure 9 shows.

The following relations provide the corresponding textual representation of sNet abstractions and associations.

kindOf (l_0.Q, l_1.Class)   *kindOf* (l_0.M, l_1.Method)
methodOf (l_0.M, l_0.Q)   *link* (l_1.Method , l_1.Class)

---

[*] The associations named *flow1*, *flow2* and *flow3* were described instead of the GOPRR *FromFromProcess* and *FlowFromNonProcess*. In so doing, we avoided the use of the concept of inheritance because, applying this concept would introduce difficulties (especially in graphical representations) in differentiating internal level (inheritance) from external level (*kindOf* relationships). The differentiation of these two forms of applying the *generalization* principle is strongly recommended.

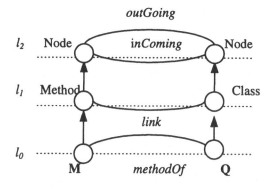

kindOf (l₁.Class,   l₂.Node)   *kindOf* (l₁.Method, l₂.Node)
inComing (l₂.Node,l₂.Node)   *outGoing* (l₂.Node, l₂.Node)

Figure 9: Representing sNet for OSMOSIS

From the previous examples we observe that each association has a name (that provides its identification) and the purpose of relating abstractions which are at the same abstraction level of the Modelling hierarchy of types.

The concept of association is an extremely important one in the context of every interpretation process. Metamodelling approaches vary in the way associations are described and therefore applied in conceptual modelling. These approaches, through different ways, aim at capturing the semantics of associations in order to provide within CASE and MetaCASE Environments the required modelling support.

A sounding attempt to capture the semantics of a specific kind of association is accomplished with the notion of *aggregation* (or modularity). This notion allows a group of abstractions and related associations to be described as being clustered in a context or universe.

In the Object-Oriented context, aggregation or assembly structures are largely used in describing associations with richer semantics. Aggregation is a firmly coupled form of association with relevant properties like being transitive and asymmetric. In the next section we address the contributions of this particular kind of association to the description of conceptual models.

2.3 Aggregating Abstractions : the *PartOf* Hierarchy

IS conceptual models can be described as resulting from clustering related abstractions in modules. So does the whole Information System at each of its developing phases. In so doing, we are applying the *whole-part* principle and the resulting structure is a *Part-Of Hierarchy*. When applying the *whole-part* principle we are adopting a *systemic approach*.

Whole-Part Abstraction Levels

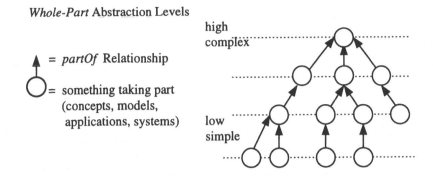

= *partOf* Relationship

= something taking part
(concepts, models,
applications, systems)

Figure 10: Abstraction Levels from the *Whole-Part* (Complexity) perspective

As shown in figure 10, within this framework each element of a given level is related to at least one element existing at the higher level by means of a *Part-Of* relationship.

The following figure shows the abstractions named Student, Course and Discipline being described as taking part in a model named Students, which, together with a model named Enrollment, participates in the application named Academic.

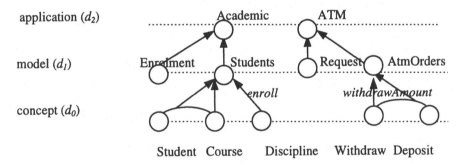

Figure 11: The *partOf* hierarchy relating models, concepts and applications

As also shown in figure 11, the abstractions named Withdraw and Deposit are described as taking part in a model named ATMOrders, which, together with a model named Request, participates in the application named ATM. Textually representing the relationships between the two lower levels is provided by means of the following specification:

$$partOf\ (d_0.\text{Student}, \quad d_1.\text{Students})$$
$$partOf\ (d_0.\text{Course}, \quad d_1.\text{Students})$$
$$partOf\ (d_0.\text{Discipline}, \quad d_1.\text{Students})$$

and

$$partOf\ (d_0.\text{Withdraw}, \quad d_1.\text{AtmOrders})$$
$$partOf\ (d_0.\text{Deposit}, \quad d_1.\text{AtmOrders})$$

From the *partOf* relations above presented we are able to describe the models named Student and ATMOrders throughout the shorter specifications, which are shown bellow. These specifications comprise the definitions of the model elements (those to which the *partOf* relation holds) and the description of the associations which are targeted at relating them.

d_1.Students = {d_0.Student, d_0.Course, d_0.Discipline, *enroll* (Student, Course)}

d_1.AtmOrders = {d_0.Withdraw, d_0.Deposit, *withdrawAmount* (Withdraw, Deposit)}

Although *partOf* relationships are well suited for describing a model through a list of its elements and related associations, this kind of description does not provide the proper identification of the model being described. Entities, processes, models and systems have their own identity and, although systemic approaches are targeted at presenting a system by means of the description of its parts, the preservation of some degree of autonomy is required, in order that they can be distinguished from other things.

A conceptual model is identified by its name and *type*. The type of a model concerns the aspects of the reality it is able to capture (ER models, for example, are targeted at capturing structural aspects while State Transition Diagrams are targeted at capturing the dynamic ones).

The proper identification of a model may be provided by means of simultaneously applying the *whole-part* principle and the *generalization* one. The interaction between these two main hierarchical constructions allows a conceptual model to acquire its own identity as well as to keep the necessary references within a systemic approach.

3 Defining Models through the Interaction of Hierarchies

Embracing the model type within every model representation is fundamental whenever conceptual modelling is addressed from either a corporative (enterprise widely) or an evolutionary (time extensive) approach.

Including the necessary references to each element type may be accomplished by means of adding an extension to the names of the elements comprised in the *partOf* hierarchy. The extensions are targeted at bringing information on the element type to *partOf* descriptions. Throughout extent-naming, systemic descriptions convey the necessary references, which allow the identification of each comprised element accordingly to the previously presented hierarchy of types.

The following scheme shows a graphical representation of a *partOf* hierarchy where extent-naming was adopted. Accordingly to this scheme, the models named respectively Student and ATMOrders are instances of the ERM and DFD types. The extent-names show that, at the concept level, the elements named Student, Course and Discipline are entities, while the elements named Withdraw and Deposit are processes, and Account is a data store.

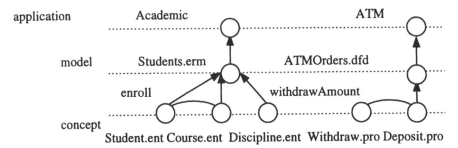

Figure 12: The *partOf* hierarchy with extent-names

Textually representing the relationships between the two lower levels is provided by means of the following specification:

partOf (d_0.Student.ent, d_1.Students.erm)
partOf (d_0.Course.ent, d_1.Students.erm)
partOf (d_0.Discipline.ent, d_1.Students.erm)

in short:

d_1.Students.erm = { d_0.Student.ent, d_0.Course.ent, d_0.Discipline.ent, *enroll* (l_0.Student,

l_0.Course)}

and   *partOf* (d_0.Withdraw.pro, d_1.AtmOrders.dfd)
           partOf (d_0.Deposit.pro, d_1.AtmOrders.dfd)

in short:

d_1.AtmOrders = { d_0.Withdraw.pro, d_0.Deposit.pro, *withdrawAmount* (Withdraw,

Deposit)}

An equivalent representation is provided by means of overloading the hierarchy of types framework with frames clustering the representation of the intention (scheme) and the extension of the abstractions which take part in a conceptual model.

The following scheme shows the combination of hierarchy of types and complex hierarchy concerns being presented at the same diagrammatical context.

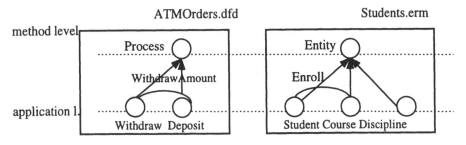

Figure 13: The *kindOf* hierarchy with frames

When this representation is adopted to describe ordinary models, each frame encompasses the hierarchy of types method level and application level. The earlier described ERM and DFD models are represented by means of the corresponding frames.

Some metamodelling techniques adopt a similar description in order to combine in the same diagrammatical context the representation of these two fundamental aspects of a model: its type and its modular, systemic or complex concern.

In the GOPRR context it is achieved by means of relating a model type to object types (modelling concepts). This relation is represented through the GOPRR *Inclusion Relationship* ([19]). A simplified representation of GOPRR *Inclusion Relationship* is presented in figure 14. At the method level of the hierarchy of types, the *Inclusion Relationship* describes that a DFD comprises processes, stores and external (entities). The same relationship describes an ERM as comprising entities.

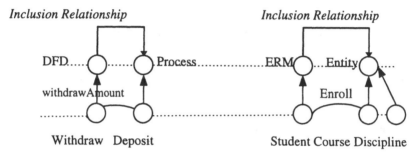

Figure 14 : The *kindOf* hierarchy with GOPRR *Inclusion Relationship*

In applying an ontology-based approach (as sNet in OSMOSIS platform [3]) , the notion of modularity is added to metamodelling by means of framing semantic universes, which are related through a *meta* relationship.

The *partOf* hierarchies also play a central role within the context of the concept-based approaches. As presented in reference ([24]), the building of a System of Concepts applies the *Containing* (*partOf*) relationships in associating primitive and derived concepts.

The approaches herein discussed offer powerful metamodelling techniques by means of providing model descriptions where the model type and its modular aspect can be identified. Consequences are that the modelling concepts and the resulting models can be described in a uniform way. However, and although uniformity is an important issue, this concern should not prevent us to adopt a more ambitious approach. In the next section, describing (and prescribing) conceptual models is carried out through the concept of emergence.

4 Conceptual Models as Emerging Complex Systems

As presented in reference ([14]) the descriptive representations of a system are targeted at describing states of things as they are here and now or have been in the past. Conversely, prescriptive representations are targeted at prescribing states of things that are intended to take place in the future. As an example, comparing IS

Development methodologies can be accomplished through a pure descriptive metamodelling approach; while, enabling customization of methodologies in MetaCASE tools requires the adoption of a prescriptive metamodelling approach.

Prescriptive approaches are well suited for representing complex systems. They help to counterbalance the reduced views of the system that are provided through the application of systemic analysis. Prescribing states of things that are intended to take place in the future is accomplished by means of considering new organization forms and their resulting (emerging) structures.

4.1 Emerging Models

The concept of emergence concerns spontaneous organizations, i.e., organizations that provide new structures to come out. In the Science of Complexity, emergence and hierarchical structures are concepts closely related. When emergence takes place (within a hierarchical framework), the new structures coming out are intermediate structures, due to the fact that, they do not fit in with a specific level of the hierarchy of types.

Conceptual modelling and metamodelling can be described as intermediate structures, since, they do not fit in with a single level of the Modelling hierarchy of types. Their definition (and representation) encompasses abstractions at the intention (scheme) and the extension levels.

The following textual representations allow the bi-level nature of a conceptual model to be further verified. In these specifications, each model element is represented by the corresponding binary relation which is targeted at defining it. These relations are bi-level relations as the following specification shows.

The models named Student and ATMOrders can be described as follows.

Students.erm = { *enroll* (l_0Student, l_0Course),

$\qquad$ *kindOf* (l_0Student, l_1Entity), *kindOf* (l_0Course, l_1Entity),

$\qquad$ *kindOf* (l_0Discipline, l_1Entity) }

ATMOrders.dfd ={ *withdrawAmount* (l_0Withdraw, l_0Deposit),

$\qquad$ *kindOf* (l_0Withdraw, l_1Process), *kindOf* (l_0Deposit, l_1Process) }

and the meta-model named DFD.soprr (the soprr extension stands for Simplified OPRR) can be described as:

DFD.soprr = { *flow1*(l_1Process,l_1Process),

$\qquad$ *flow2*(l_1Process,l_1Store), *flow3*(l_1Process,l_1External),

$\qquad$ *kindOf* (l_1Process, l_2Object), *kindOf* (l_1Store,l_2Object),

$\qquad$ *kindOf* (l_1External,l_2Object) }

The corresponding graphical representations allow the bi-level nature of models and metamodels to be further verified.

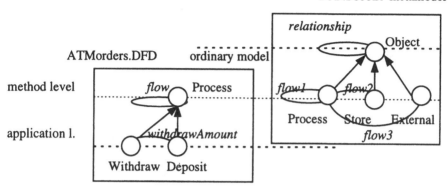

Figure 15: Intermediate Structures

In the Science of Complexity, the emerging structures are said to be new, in the sense that, their properties can not be deduced from other properties of the system. As we see it, in conceptual modelling and metamodelling, the new properties are the associations at the application and method levels of the hierarchy of types. They are new with respect to the generalizing and systemic arrangements that govern the corresponding hierarchies. The role of these associations, is addressed through the focus on the characteristics of a non-linear system.

4.2 Conceptual Models as Non-Linear Systems

Linearity is almost always a synonym of simplicity. Within the context of a linear system the whole is precisely equal to the sum of its parts, being each system component free to act regardless of what is happening elsewhere in the system ([25]).

We argue that, IS conceptual models behave like complex systems, since non-linearity characterizes the derivation of their descriptions at the various levels of the *partOf* hierarchy.

In the previous examples, models and metamodels were described as consisting of abstractions, as well as, associations targeted at relating abstractions. When a framed description is used, the horizontal links that represent associations are also comprised within the frame, as figures 12 and 15 show.

As an example, the model named ATMOrders has been described as:

ATMOrders.dfd $=\{kindOf\,(l_0\text{Withdraw},l_1\text{Process}), kindOf\,(l_0\text{Deposit},l_1\text{Process}),$

$withdrawAmount\,(l_0\text{Withdraw},l_0\text{Deposit})\}$

or shortly : $d_1.\text{ATMOrders.dfd}=\{d_0\text{Withdraw.pro}, d_0\text{Deposit.pro},$

$withdrawAmount\,(l_0\text{Withdraw},l_0\text{Deposit})\}$

Considering it a linear system, its description should be provided by the aggregation (sum) of the descriptions of its elements. In section 3, it was noticed that the elements of a given conceptual model are those to which the *partOf* relation holds.

Aggregating the descriptions of each element of the model named ATMOrders provides the following specification:

$$\{d_0.\text{Withdraw. pro}, d_0.\text{Deposit.pro}\}$$

If the meta-model example is considered the same property holds. The meta-model named DFD.soprr is described as:

DFD.soprr $=\{kindOf\,(l_1\text{Process},l_2\text{Object}),\ kindOf\,(l_1\text{Store},l_2\text{Object}),$
$\qquad kindOf\,(l_1\text{External},l_2\text{Object}),$

$\qquad flow1(l_1\text{Process},l_1\text{Process}),\ flow2(l_1\text{Process},l_1\text{Store}),$

$\qquad flow3(l_1\text{Process},l_1\text{External})\}$

or shortly: $\qquad d_1.\text{DFD.soprr} =\{d_0.\text{Process.obj}, d_0.\text{Store.obj}, d_0.\text{External.obj},$

$\qquad\qquad flow1(l_1\text{Process},l_1\text{Process}),\ flow2(l_1\text{Process},l_1\text{Store}),$

$\qquad\qquad flow3(l_1\text{Process},l_1\text{External})\}$

while, aggregating the description of the DFD.soprr elements provides:

$$\{d_0.\text{Process.obj}, d_0.\text{Store.obj}, d_0.\text{External.obj}\}$$

We may conclude that, regarding the description of a conceptual model, linearity is accomplished whenever free associations are not considered. The description of abstractions is therefore uniformly propagated and analytical simplicity is achieved. The need to consider the results of synthesis, which are provided by the description of associations, brings to models and metamodels the characteristic of a complex system.

Non-linearity is thus introduced by the need to consider the (free) associations in the description of a model.

From the previous examples we observe that in the description of conceptual models and metamodels, complexity comes from the need to simultaneously apply two hierarchical structures - *partOf* and *kindOf* hierarchies - plus a particular kind of relationship whose semantic is exogenous to any of these two hierarchies: the single level associations, herein designated free associations.

4.3 Object-Orientation and the Complexity Perspective

The conceptual nature of our work should not prevent us to approach the complexity perspective in modelling from a more pragmatic view. There is yet not enough evidence on how describing modelling features from the complexity perspective can improve Object-Oriented Analysis of IS.

Systemic analysis has been always motivated by the need for dealing with complexity and modelling is certainly its fundamental tool. Describing a system as being comprised of elements, which are in turn made of simpler units, produces a simplified representation of a given reality. But systemic analysis is also said to contribute to reductionism by means of producing parcelled and loosely connected descriptions of the whole.

Within the context of a complex system, the associations existing among the system elements are considered to be much more important then the elements themselves. Creating suitable conditions for investigating on the semantics of these associations seems to be the better way to counterbalance reduced views. To this end Object-Orientation brought uniformity.

Within Object Oriented approaches it is claimed that the very notion of object conveys the synthesis of several common notions as those of record, message, process and module [18]. The uniformity purposes underlying this claim are particularly welcome. Moreover when the concept of object supports the integration of both structural and behavioural aspects of the reality.

Describing the elements of a system through a uniform notion helps to concentrate on the associations which are targeted at relating them. When conceptual modelling is approached from the complexity perspective, models are described as being shaped by a collection of associations. Perceiving models and metamodels as non-linear and intermediate structures (that do not fit in with a specific level of the hierarchy of types) helps to counterbalance the reductionism inherent to analytical views.

Some other relevant issues have been approached from the complexity perspective, like supporting incompleteness in conceptual modelling. This issue relies on differentiating completeness from consistency within the context of CASE and MetaCASE tools. As a conceptual model is not developed at once, it should be possible to recognize relevant stages of a model while it evolves along with the analysis phase. In so doing, intermediate structures (intermediate in time) should be acknowledge as resulting of specific modelling stages (see reference [26]).

If the scope of conceptual modelling is intended to go out the analysis phase, this issue leads to *supporting adaptive design and feedback learning*. It has been strongly addressed within some proposals (see references [24] and [27]). These proposals, moving away from a pure technological perspective, apply the metaphor of Evolution to the whole IS Development process.

5 Conclusions and Future Work

Hierarchical constructions play a central role in conceptual modelling. The herein discussed hierarchy of types and complex hierarchy settle the basis for modelling efforts of analysis and synthesis to be jointly described. The interaction of these two fundamental constructions provides support for describing modelling elements from both a *generalization* and a systemic approach. In so doing, models and metamodels are shown to be intermediate structures, emerging from the interaction of elements comprised at two consecutive levels of abstraction of the modelling hierarchy of types.

The *partOf* and *kindOf* relationships are special types of associations, which are governed by the *whole-part* and *generalization* principles, respectively. But when caring out IS conceptual modelling and metamodelling, we are also required to represent associations whose semantics is exogenous to any of these principles. It was demonstrated that, considering the (free) associations in the description of models and metamodels, brings to models and metamodels the characteristic of a complex system.

As we see it, it results from the role that associations play in knowledge representation, in every branch of Science. Associations may be considered the primal form of (understanding) scientific knowledge [1], and dealing with knowledge representation there is much to learn about relational concepts.

Metamodelling has proved to be of great help in investigating on ontological solutions. Present and future work is concerned to the development of a Meta-Modelling Ontology and its application in the definition of Object-Oriented concepts.

References

1. Jackson A. The Second Metamorphosis of Science: a Second View. In: the Santa Fe Institute Working Papers, 1996
2. Voorhees B. Reasoning about Complex Systems: Towards an Epistemology for the Science of Complexity. In: the Proceedings of the International Conference on Complex Systems, Nashua, 1997
3. Bézivin J. OSMOSIS: an Ontology-Based MetaCASE . In: the Proceedings of the sixth CAiSE International Workshop on the Next Generation of CASE Tools, Jyvaskyla, 1995
4. Gruber T. Ontolingua: a mechanism to support portable ontologies. Knowledge Systems Laboratory Technical Report, Standford University, 1992
5. Gruber T. Towards Principles for the Design of Ontologies Used for Knowledge Sharing. Knowledge Systems Laboratory Technical Report, Standford University, 1993
6. Baas N. Emergence, Hierarchies and Hyperstructures. Artificial Life III, Addison-Wesley, 1994
7. Zhuge H. et al. Abstraction and Analogy in cognitive Space: A Software Process Model. Information and Software Technology, n.39, 1997
8. Smolander K. OPRR - A Model for Modelling Systems Development Methods. In: the Proceedings of the second Workshop on the Next Generation of CASE Tools, Trondheim,1990.
9. Brimkkemper S. Formalization of Information Systems Modelling. PhD thesis, Thesis Publishers, Nijmegen, Holland, 1990
10. Domingues E. et al. A Conceptual Approach to Meta-Modelling. In: the Proceedings of the 9th International Conference CAiSE*97, Barcelona, 1997
11. Heym M., Osterle H. A Semantic Data Model for Methodology Engineering. In: the Proceedings of the fifth International Workshop on Computer-Aided Software Engineering, Montreal, 1992
12. Marttiin P., Lyytinen K., Rossi M., Tahvanainen V-P., Tolvanen J-P. Modelling Requirements for Future CASE: issues and implementation considerations. In: the Proceedings of the third European Workshop on Next Generation of CASE Tools - NGCT*92 , Manchester, 1992
13. Wijers G. Modelling Support in Information Systems Development. PhD thesis, Thesis Publishers, Amsterdam, 1991
14. Lyytinen K., Smolander K., Tahvanainen V-P. Modelling CASE Environments in Systems Development. In: the Proceedings of the first Nordic Conference on Advanced Systems Engineering, 1989

15. Sowa J.(Eds) Principles of Semantic Networks : Explorations in the Representation of Knowledge. Morgan Kaufmann Publishers, USA, 1991
16. Booch G. Object Oriented Design with Applications, The Benjamin Cummings Publishing Company, USA, 1991
17. Rumbaugh J. et al.: Object-Oriented Modelling and Design, Prentice-Hall, USA, 1991
18. Sernadas A. et al. Object-Oriented Logic - An Informal Introduction, INESC, Lisbon, 1990
19. Smolander K., Lyytinen K., Tahvanainen V., Marttiin P. MetaEdit - A flexible Graphical Environment for Methodology Modelling. In: the Proceedings of the third International Conference on Advanced Information Systems Engineering CAiSE91, 1991
20. Araújo T. Modelling Methodological Support for the Information Systems Development Process. PhD thesis, Technical University of Lisbon, 1995
21. Araújo T., Carapuça R. Issues for a Future CASE. In: the Proceedings of the third CAiSE European Workshop on the Next Generation of CASE Tools, Manchester, 1992
22. Araújo T., Rossi M. Process Models for CASE Shell Environments. In: the Proceedings of the forth CAiSE International Workshop on the Next Generation of CASE Tools, Paris, 1993
23. Araújo T., Carapuça R. Overloading Class Structure Diagram to Represent Objects Behaviour. In: the proceedings of the ERCIM EDRG Workshop 4, Crete, 1993.
24. Dolado J., Moreno A. Assessing Software Organizations from a Complex Systems Perspective. In: the Proceedings of the International Conference on Complex Systems, Nashua, 1997
25. Waldrop M. Complexity - the Emerging Science at the Edge of Order and Chaos. Penguin Books, England, 1992
26. Araújo T., Carapuça R. : Process Management Support for CASE Environments. In: the Proceedings of the sixth CAiSE International Workshop on the Next Generation of CASE Tools, Jyvaskyla, 1995
27. King S. Tool Support for Systems Emergence: a multimedia CASE Tool. Information and Software Technology, n.39, 1997

Multiple Viewpoints of IS-A Inheritance Hierarchies through Normalization and Denormalization Mechanisms

Nadira Lammari, Régine Laleau, Mireille Jouve
Laboratoire CEDRIC-IIE (CNAM)
18 allée Jean Rostand 91025 Evry - France
Email: {lammari, laleau, jouve}@iie.cnam.fr

Abstract

This paper presents a two-steps process for reorganizing IS-A hierarchies in conceptual schemas of object-oriented databases. First, a normalized schema is derived, containing all the possible IS-A inheritances, according to applicability constraints. Then, the process executes groupings, defined by the designer, by deleting the relevant inheritance links and replacing them by applicability constraints in order to preserve the initial schema semantics.

1 Introduction

The object model provides a natural and close view of the real world since it does supply a variety of semantic concepts and doesn't enforce constraints on their use. This is specially true for inheritances. So, different schemas may be obtained depending on the designer aims. On one hand, to deal properly with reusability, the designer must have a clear and complete view of all possible inheritances. On the other hand, an Object-Oriented (OO) schema should be application significant for both designers and users. To be understandable the schema may be less detailed, some sub-classes being regrouped in one class. Several optimization criteria have been proposed in the literature (e.g.: [1], [2], [3]), to decide either to decompose a class or to merge classes.

In order to satisfy these two aims, we need a reorganization mechanism responsible for the execution of the grouping of several classes into one, which will replace the suppressed inheritance links by some information semantically equivalent so that the process will be reversible. Indeed, an optimized schema must be prone to modifications to be adapted, for example, to a new operational environment, to some volumetric changes in applications or to the introduction of new classes.

To have a clear and complete view of all inheritances, the inheritances concealed in a schema must be exhibited. There are two ways for an inheritance to be concealed. The first one is to have, in different classes, common structures and behaviour which are not actually shared. This approach is used by the inheritance derivation mechanisms known as factorization. In the second approach, inheritances are concealed through optional attributes that is attributes which are not applicable to all the instances of their class. This is a well known mechanism used to translate an OO schema in a relational one.

The factorization mechanisms ([4], [5], [6], [7]) regroup classes by comparing class characteristics from a syntactic (same name) and/or semantic (same type or signature) point of view. Therefore they ignore possible inclusion relations between instance sets. Thus the derived inheritances are indifferently IS-A or implementation inheritances, the choice can be done by the designer. Only [8] proposes a mechanism to derive IS-A inheritances but only from a structural point of view. Furthermore, none of them take into account optional attributes so they can derive equivalencies of classes that are semantically different, what we have demonstrated in [9].

We have chosen the second approach and this paper presents a process for reorganizing inheritances in an object-oriented schema which includes both a normalization and a denormalization mechanisms. The normalization process derives all the possible IS-A inheritances concealed in a schema through optional attributes. The main idea is to find among the instances of a class, subsets sharing the same behaviour, that is instances which have values for the same attributes and which are used by the same methods. According to the inclusion links between those subsets, an IS-A inheritance hierarchy is associated with the initial class. This normalization process needs some semantic information about the class characteristics (attributes and methods). This information is captured by constraints between characteristics which we call applicability constraints.

The denormalization mechanism is processing a normalized schema. It aims to carry out groupings of classes defined by the designer according to some optimization criteria, for example the minimum number of instances in a class or the depth of an inheritance hierarchy. To carry out groupings while preserving the schema semantics, applicability constraints between characteristics are added automatically. These added constraints can thereafter be expressed as integrity constraints in a target DBMS.

No specific object-oriented model is assumed for reorganizing OO schemas. We are dealing with object concepts that exist in most OO methods. We consider that classes regroup objects defined with the same attributes and methods. The type of a class is defined by the tuple constructor applied to its attributes. An attribute is defined by its name and its type that can be atomic or complex by using the tuple or the set constructor. It can also be optional or mandatory. Associations can link objects of different classes. An association is represented by an attribute whose value is an object reference. We call characteristic of a class either an attribute or a method of this class.

Classes are organized according to IS-A inheritance hierarchies. IS-A hierarchy has a set inclusion semantics, that is the set of objects of a class is included in the set of objects of all its superclasses. It is based on the subtyping relation between classes [10], [11], [12]. We allow simple or multiple inheritance. However we consider that there is no inheritance conflict, that is the IS-A inheritance hierarchies are correct according to [13], [14].

The graphical notations we use in the examples of the paper are those of the Unified Modeling Language (UML) [15].

In this space-limited paper, the presentation of the reorganization process is intentionally informal and rather intuitive. However, the reader who is interested by a formal description of the process can find it in [9].

The remainder of this paper is organized as follows. The example to which we refer all through the paper is presented in Section 2. Applicability constraints are defined in Section 3. Section 4 describes the whole process of schema reorganization. Finally, Section 5 concludes the paper.

2 Example

This section is presenting a simple example of a complete execution of the schema reorganization process. The schema is about a travel agency application managing touristic information: the description of the places to visit in a town (see Figure 1).

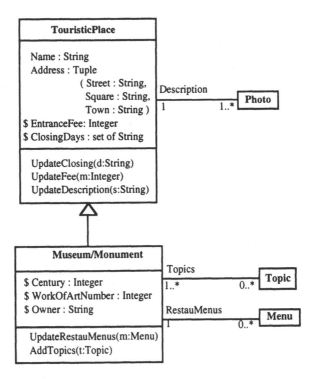

Caption : UML has no particular symbol to specify an optional attribute, we use $

Figure 1. Example of a schema to be reorganized

We assume that the schema designer supplies also some constraints, that we call applicability constraints, such as the following :

a) The attributes EntranceFee and ClosingDays are applicable only to a subset of the instances of the class TouristicPlace, but they are applicable to all instances of Museum/Monument.

b) All the specific attributes of the class Museum/Monument are only applicable to some of its instances.

c) Century and Topics never have values together in one instance of Museum/Monument.

d) The method UpdateDescription can be applied to all the instances of TouristicPlace which is not the case of UpdateFee. We say that UpdateDescription is applicable to all the instances of its class.

e) EntranceFee and UpdateFee are applicable to the same instances of TouristicPlace.

The first step of the reorganization process is to get a normalized inheritance schema according to the supplied applicability constraints. The result of this normalization is the schema of Figure 2 where attributes and associations are applicable to all the instances of their classes and where methods are associated with classes which they really handle. Of course, the name of the various new classes are given, a posteriori, by the designer and not by the process.

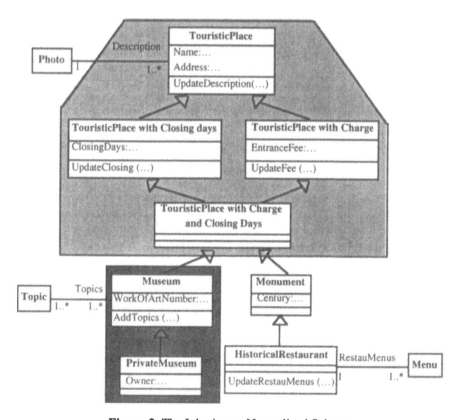

Figure 2. The Inheritance Normalized Schema

Then the designer may decide to group together the classes of each dark rectangle in Figure 2, according to its own criteria - note that the aim of the process is not to evaluate or judge the pertinence of the grouping criteria used by the designer. The denormalization mechanism will process these groupings, which yields the schema of Figure 3. The suppressed inheritance links are replaced by applicability constraints such as:
- The attribute Owner is only applicable to a subset of the instances of the class Museum.

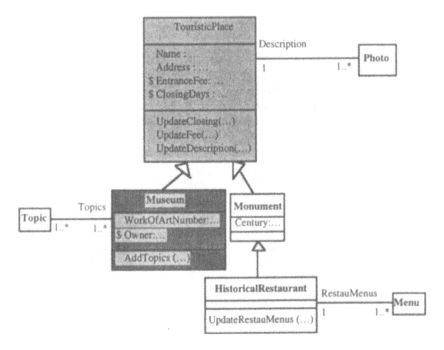

Figure 3. The Reorganized Schema

3 Applicability Constraints Definition

As in the other approaches of normalization, for exhibiting IS-A inheritances concealed in a class, we need to take into account constraints between the characteristics of this class. They are of the same family as the null value constraints studied in the relational context ([16], [17], [18], [19]) or used to translate a conceptual schema into a relational schema [20], [21]. In this paper we present a generalization of these constraints to the characteristics of a class. Since it is difficult to give a meaning to null values for a method, we call our constraints applicability constraints. Their definition is found on the applicability domain concept which is first presented.

3.1 Applicability Domain of a Characteristic

3.1.1 Applicability Domain of an Attribute

According to Codd [22], an attribute may have a null value in an instance for two reasons, either because the value is temporarily unknown but applicable, or because the value will never be known since this attribute is inapplicable for this instance. To distinguish between those two situations, Codd gives a value *A-mark* to an attribute if its value is *absent but applicable*, and an *I-mark* if the value is *absent and inapplicable*. So, we can associate with each attribute of a class, an applicability domain which is the set of the instances where this attribute is applicable. When the applicability domain of an attribute is equal to all the instances of the class, then the attribute is called mandatory: it will never contain an *I-mark*, but it can temporarily contain an *A-mark*. On the contrary, it is called optional.

This definition is meant for attributes with a simple type: boolean, string or object reference. It can easily be extended to deal with complex types using constructors such as tuple, set or list. If an attribute is constructed with the tuple or the set constructor for example, it is applicable to an instance if it has at least one value for this instance (a value for one component of the tuple or one value in the set). Since the constructors can be recursively used to build complex types, the applicability domain of a complex attribute is defined as the *distributed union* of the applicability domains of the attributes which compose it.

3.1.2 Applicability Domain of a Method

A method has also an applicability domain. It is the set of all the instances which can be selected, updated, deleted or created by this method. For example the method UpdateDescription is applicable to all the instances of TouristicPlace since the description of all the instances may be changed. So the applicability domain of UpdateDescription is equal to all the possible instances of TouristicPlace. On the contrary the applicability domain of UpdateFee is restricted to the instances of TouristicPlace representing places which are not free of charge while some instances of TouristicPlace are free of charge.

3.2 Applicability Constraints

Our goal is to group in a single class all the characteristics which have the same applicability domain. But the applicability domain cannot be defined in extension especially at the conceptual design level. On the other hand it is possible to compare applicability domains. The applicability constraints are capturing these comparisons.

3.2.1 Applicability Constraints between Characteristics

• An exclusive applicability constraint between two characteristics x and y of a class, denoted by x ↮ y, captures the fact that in each instance where x is applicable then y is not applicable and vice versa. In other words, the applicability domains of x and y have no intersection. In our example (Section 2), Constraint "c" is of this type: Century ↮ Topics.

• A mutual applicability constraint between two characteristics x and y of a class, denoted by x↔y, captures the fact that in each instance where x is applicable, then y is also applicable and vice versa. In other words the applicability domains of x and y are equal. In our example, Constraint "e" is of this type: EntranceFee ↔ UpdateFee.

• A conditioned applicability constraint between two characteristics x and y of a class, denoted by x↦ y, captures the fact that in each instance where x is applicable, then y is also applicable but the reverse is not always true. We also say that x requires y . In other words the applicability domain of x is included in the applicability domain of y. In the example of Section 2, Constraint "d" is of this type: UpdateFee ↦ UpdateDescription.

To summarize :

Let : - C(A, M) be a class, A the set of its attributes, M the set of its methods
  - x and y two characteristics of A ∪ M
  - D_x and D_y the applicability domains of x and y
Then we say that:
  - x ↮ y if and only if $D_x \cap D_y = \varnothing$
  - x↔y if and only if $D_x = D_y$
  - x↦ y if and only if $D_x \subseteq D_y$

3.2.2 Remarks

1) Applicability constraints are used, as we will see in the next section, to reorganize the classes of a schema. But, during this process, we don't want to modify the structure of the attributes of the initial classes. Therefore we only use the constraints between attributes which are not component of other attributes. Hereafter, we call those attributes "first level attributes".

2) Some properties of these three types of applicability constraints and of their interactions may be stated as inference rules and axioms. Axioms are used to define validation rules. Inference rules lead to the minimal cover and closure of the set of each type of constraints. Those properties are described in [9]. The completeness and soundness of the inference rules systems are also described.

3) Applicability constraints can also be defined between set of characteristics. The formal definition of this generalization can be found in [23].

3.3 Applicability Constraints and Inheritance Hierarchy

An applicability constraint is an intra-class constraint. It may concern either an abstract class or a class with instances. All the possible instances of the class must satisfy it whether they are instances of the class or of one of its subclasses. Let us consider Figure 4. It describes the applicability constraints of each classes of Figure 1.

TouristicPlace
Applicability Constraints
EntranceFee $\mapsto$ Name
ClosingDays $\mapsto$ Name
Name $\leftrightarrow$ Description
Name $\leftrightarrow$ Address
ClosingDays $\leftrightarrow$ UpdateClosing
EntranceFee $\leftrightarrow$ UpdateFee
Description $\leftrightarrow$ UpdateDescription

Museum/Monument
Applicability Constraints
EntranceFee $\leftrightarrow$ ClosingDays
Name $\leftrightarrow$ EntranceFee
Century $\nleftrightarrow$ Topics
RestauMenus $\mapsto$ Century
UpdateRestauMenus $\leftrightarrow$ RestauMenus
UpdateTopics $\leftrightarrow$ Topics
Owner $\mapsto$ Topics
Workof ArtNumber $\leftrightarrow$ Topics

Figure 4. Applicability Constraints of the Figure 1 classes

All the constraints specified in the class TouristicPlace are also satisfied in the class Museum/Monument by definition of the IS-A inheritance. For the Museum/Monument class, these constraints are inherited. Museum/Monument has also specific constraints such as Century $\nleftrightarrow$ Topics.
We distinguish, in a class, between the inherited constraints and the specific ones.

3.3.1 Inherited Applicability Constraint

An inherited applicability constraint is a constraint defined in a subclass and involving only characteristics inherited from the same superclass. There exists two types of inherited applicability constraint:

• constraints inherited as is. Examples are Name $\leftrightarrow$ Description and Name $\leftrightarrow$ Address in Figure 4. All the constraints defined in the class TouristicPlace are inherited in Museum/Monument, so they are not mentioned in the description of Museum/Monument.
A constraint B inherited from a constraint A, is of the same type (for example mutual). Moreover, if A involves an attribute x, B involves an attribute y corresponding to x by a subtyping relation [10]. We say that B is a subtype of A.

• constraints added in subclasses and that allow to distinguish the behaviour between a superclass and its subclasses. In the example such a constraint is EntranceFee $\leftrightarrow$ ClosingDays in Museum/Monument. This constraint is added to specify that the museums and historical monuments are both closed certain days and not free of charge which is not the case of all the touristic places.

3.3.2 *Specific Applicability Constraint*

There are three types of specific applicability constraints:

• constraints involving only specific characteristics; they may lead to a reorganization of the class whether this class inherits or not from other classes.

• constraints involving inherited and specific characteristics; they are used after the normalization of the initial class to determine some inheritance links between subclasses of the initial class and new subclasses of the resulting inheritance hierarchy.

• constraints between characteristics inherited from different superclasses; they are only specified in multiple inheritances. For a given inheritance, they can be considered as constraints of the previous type. They have the same purpose.

Some properties of the specific applicability constraints can be demonstrated such as: every specific characteristic of a class B requires in B every characteristic inherited by B from A if these characteristics are applicable to all the instances of A. These properties are demonstrated in [9]. They are used to define validation rules in order to control the consistency of the applicability constraints supplied by the designer. They are also used to generate a minimum set of applicability constraints during the denormalization process.

4 Schema Reorganization

From any schema with applicability constraints, the reorganization process builds a new schema that satisfies criteria chosen by the designer. The process is defined so as to preserve the initial schema semantics in the final schema. The process encompasses two main steps (Figure 5):

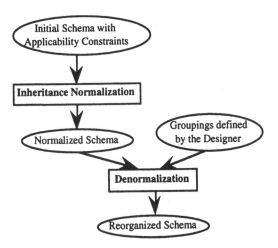

Figure 5. Principle of the reorganization process

The first step is a normalization one. It computes a normalized schema by deriving from an initial schema all the possible IS-A inheritances, according to the applicability constraints supplied by the designer.

A class is normalized if it satisfies the two following properties :

• (i) all its attributes are mandatory, that is applicable to all its instances (classes with no more *I-mark* but possibly *A-marks*);

• (ii) its methods manipulate (that is update, delete, select or create) at least one instance of the class.

The second step consists in restructuring the normalized schema : it is a denormalization process. Indeed, the schema can contain a huge number of classes and become hard to manage and to understand. To avoid this, the designer can merge some classes, belonging to the same inheritance hierarchy, according to criteria he has chosen. Their definition is not the purpose of this paper, other works have already dealt with (e.g.: [1], [2], [6]). Then the denormalization mechanism performs the chosen groupings and replaces the undone inheritances by applicability constraints in order to preserve the initial semantics.

4.1 Normalization Mechanism

First of all, the consistency of the initial schema constraints is verified according to the validation rules mentioned in Sections 3.2.2 and 3.3. The inconsistent constraints are indicated to the designer, sometimes with possible solutions. Then the schema is split into partitions, each one corresponding to a single inheritance hierarchy. Lastly - part described below - the process computes the normalized hierarchy associated to each partition. The set of all these hierarchies forms the normalized schema.

In fact, the previous conditions (i) and (ii) express that a normalized class C belonging to the normalized inheritance hierarchy associated to a partition P must be compatible with the applicability constraints defined between its characteristics, more precisely :

(i) let S be the set of the first level attributes of C (Remark 1, § 3.2.2), called structure of C, S must satisfy the three following rules :

• *Homogeneity rule* : Any attribute of P linked to an attribute of S by a mutual applicability constraint is in S,

• *Unpartionnability rule* : There is no exclusive applicability constraint between attributes of S,

• *Convexity rule* : Any attribute required by a group of attributes of S is in S (to comply with the conditioned applicability constraints).

Then S is called the normalized structure of C.

(ii) a method m linked to C must satisfy :

• let $X_{m,\mapsto} = \{x \in P / m \mapsto x\}$ the set of attributes of P that m requires,

$\quad X_{m,\nleftrightarrow} = \{x \in P / m \nleftrightarrow x\}$ the set of attributes of P linked to m by an exclusive constraint

then $X_{m,\mapsto} \subseteq S$ and $X_{m,\nleftrightarrow} \cap S = \varnothing$

Indeed, and roughly speaking, these properties express that the applicability domain of m is included in that of S and that there is no attribute of P in S such that its applicability domain and that of m are disjoined.

The normalization process is based on the definition of the normalized inclusion graph of a class or of a partition. This is a connected graph whose nodes are the different normalized structures derived from the class or the different classes of the partition. Let S_1 and S_2 be two normalized structures, an edge from S_1 to S_2 expresses the inclusion of S_2 in S_1 (recall that a structure is a set of attributes).

Hereafter we give the high-level algorithm for the normalization process:

Algorithm:

Input : a partition P
Output : H(P) : the normalized inheritance hierarchy of P
Notations :   G(C) : the normalized inclusion graph of a class C,
                  G(P) : the normalized inclusion graph of P

Begin

>   for each Class C in P do
>   **compute** G(C) by considering the applicability constraints (specific and inherited) between attributes and rule (i)
>   endfor
>
>   G(P) = **merge** all G(C) and **delete** the redundant nodes

// redundant nodes are nodes represented by the same set of attributes. It can happen when subclasses in the initial inheritance graph are distinguished from their superclasses only by methods or when all their specific attributes are optional.

>   for each Method m in P do
>   **link** m to the relevant structures of G(P) by considering the constraints between attributes and methods and rule (ii).
>   endfor
>
>   **deduce** H(P) from G(P)

// straightforward process except when a method is not linked to a complete branch of the graph. In this case, new classes, probably abstract, are added.

End

For lack of space, the full text of the algorithm is not included. The procedure that computes each G(C) can be found in [24], the ones that link a method to its structures and deduce H(P) can be found in [23]. Finally the one that computes G(P) is described in [25].

By applying this algorithm on the schema of Figure 1 completed by the applicability constraints of Figure 4, we obtain the normalized schema of Figure 2.

4.2 Denormalization

The groupings proposed by the designer must be valid, that is, they must respect the inclusions of instance sets described by the inheritance links. We have proved that a grouping G of classes is valid if every external ancestor of a class of G is also an ancestor of every class of G.
There exists only two types of valid groupings (Figure 6).

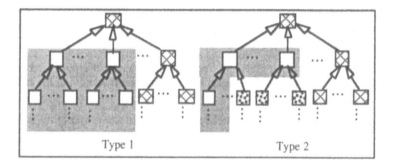

Figure 6. An example for each of the two valid grouping types

The first one represents all the valid groupings defined by a set of classes whose all the descendants are part of the grouping. The second one represents all the other cases.

To obtain the final denormalized schema, each grouping G is replaced by a class C_G. C_G must be semantically equivalent to G and therefore describes all the entity sets contained in G and all the inclusion or exclusion relations linking these entity sets. These relations are expressed in G through inheritance links, they will be translated in C_G by applicability constraints.

To compute C_G and specially its applicability constraints, we consider the denormalization process as the *reverse* of the normalization process. That is, if the normalization process is performed again on C_G, the same classes as those contained in the grouping are deduced. Thus, C_G characteristics must be the union of the characteristic sets of each class of G, C_G must contain the applicability constraints between attributes that have allowed to obtain the normalized structures of G and the applicability constraints between attributes and methods that have allowed to link methods to the different classes of G. Note that the applicability constraints between attributes can be translated by integrity constraints in a database implementation, which is not possible for applicability constraints between attributes and methods. However, they must be kept because they can be used in a possible schema evolution.

Therefore, to deduce the applicability constraints between attributes, the four following rules have been used :

• *Coexistence rule* : any two attributes, specific to a same class of G, coexist in C_G, that is they are linked by a mutual applicability constraint.

• *Generalization/specialization rule* : If in G class B inherits from class A, then in C_G every specific attribute of B requires every attribute of A.

• *Specializations exclusion rule* : if in G two classes A and B don't share any subclass then in C_G the applicability of every specific attribute of A excludes the applicability of every specific attribute of B.

• *Multiple inheritance rule* : if in G class D is the only direct subclass of classes A and B then in C_G every couple composed of an attribute of A and an attribute of B requires every attribute of D.

Obviously, the set of all the applicability constraints generated by the denormalization process can be reduced to a minimal set by applying the inference rules (§ 3.2.2).

Integrating C_G in the initial schema depends on the grouping type (Figure 7).

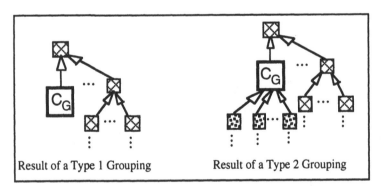

| Result of a Type 1 Grouping | Result of a Type 2 Grouping |

Figure 7. Integration of C_G according to the grouping type

In case of a Type 2 grouping, the C_G characteristics that don't belong to its new subclasses must be hidden. Therefore we add constraints in the subclasses in order to express that the inherited characteristics are inapplicable to all the instances of these subclasses.

For instance, suppose that in the example of Figure 2, we have chosen the grouping (Museum, PrivateMuseum, Monument), instead of the grouping (Museum, PrivateMuseum). It is a Type 2 grouping. We obtain a new class Monument2, corresponding to the grouping, and HistoricRestaurant inherits from this class. Since, in the normalized schema, HistoricRestaurant inherits only from Monument, characteristics of Museum must be hidden in the HistoricRestaurant class of the denormalized schema. Thus the following applicability constraints are added in this class: AddTopics ↭ Topics; WorkofArtNumber ↭ Topics; Owner ↦ Century.

5 Conclusion

In this paper, we proposed a two-steps process for reorganizing IS-A inheritance hierarchies. The normalization mechanism allows to obtain a maximal splitting of classes by derivation of IS-A inheritances. It defines a normal form for the classes of the schema. The denormalization mechanism allows, according to criteria supplied by the designer, groupings of classes belonging to the same inheritance hierarchies. It is applied to a normalized schema. The process can be used at the end of the conceptual design stage[1]. However, it can also be used at the logical stage depending on the retained denormalization criteria.

Furthermore, to obtain a complete view of all inheritances, a factorization mechanism, as described in the Introduction Section, should be added to our normalization process. However, only IS-A inheritances must be considered because they are the only application significant at this level of design.

We have shown in [9] that a factorization mechanism combined with the proposed normalization process contributes to an accurate schemes integration. In the other hand, the proposed denormalization mechanism provides to the designer the possibility to develop multiple viewpoints that correspond to different application specialists.

A logical extension to our work is to use our process during a schema evolution. However new problems will arise due to the fact that in this case the database already exists, and then classes are populated. Thus, if class structures change, then we have to consider problems of object migration.

The normalization mechanism is also an interesting tool in the perspective of evolving from a traditional design, where data and operations are independent, to an object-oriented design where data and operations are encapsulated. More precisely, we intend to use the procedure of the normalization algorithm that links methods to the structures of the normalized inclusion graph.

We are also studying how to extract applicability constraints (specially those defined between attributes and methods) from formal specifications like B or VDM. We expect this will appreciably reduce the task of the designer and avoid mistakes while constraints are collected.

---

[1] It is commonly accepted that the database design process consists in three levels : conceptual design, logical design and physical design, also called implementation level [26].

References

1. Chidamber S. R. and Kemerer C. F., *A Metrics Suite for Object-Oriented Design*. IEEE Transactions on Software Engineering 1994; vol.20; 6: 476-493.

2. Eick C. F., *A Methodology for the Design and Transformation of Conceptual Schema*. Proceedings of VLDB'91 (International Conference on Very Large Data Bases), Barcelona, Spain, september 1991, pp 25-34.

3. Thieme C. and Siebes A., *An approach to Schema Integration based on Transformations and Behaviour*. Research report CS-R9403, january 94.

4. Godin R. and Mili H., *Building and Maintaining Analysis-Level Class Hierarchies Using Galois Lattices*. OOPSLA'93 (International Conference on Object-Oriented Programming Languages and Applications). ACM SIGPLAN notices 1993; vol.28; 10:394-410.

5. Lieberherr L., Bergstein P. and Silva-Lepe I., *From Objects to Classes: Algorithms for Optimal Object-oriented Design*. Software Engineering 1991; vol.6; 4:205-228.

6. Thieme C. and Siebes A., *Schema Integration in Object-Oriented Databases*. CAISE'93. Lecture Notes in Computer Science n°685, Springer-Verlag, Paris, France, June 1993, pp 54-70.

7. Yahia A., Lakhal L. and Cicchetti R., *Building Inheritance Graphs In Object Database Design*. DEXA'96. Lecture Notes in Computer Science n°1134, Springer-Verlag, Zurich, Switzerland, September 1996, pp 11-28.

8. Andonnof E., Sallaberry C. and Zurfluh G., *Interactive design of object oriented databases*. CAISE'92 (International Conference on Advanced Information System Engineering), Lecture Notes in Computer Science n°593, Springer-Verlag, Manchester, UK, may 1992.

9. Lammari N., *Réorganisation des hiérarchies d'héritages dans un schéma conceptuel objet*. PHD Thesis, Conservatoire National des Arts et Métiers, Paris, France, october 1996.

10. Cardelli L., *A Semantics of Multiple Inheritance*. Readings in Object-Oriented Database Systems, S.B. Zdonik and D. Maier (Eds), 1990.

11. Delobel C, Lecluse C., Richard P., *Bases de donnees : des systemes relationnels aux systemes a objets*, Intereditions, France, 1991.

12. Taivalsaari A., *On the Notion of Inheritance*. ACM Computing Surveys 1996, Vol. 28, 3: 438-479.

13. Formica A., Missikoff M., *Correctness of ISA Hierarchies in Object-Oriented Database Schemas*. EDBT94, Lecture Notes in Computer Science n°779, Springer-Verlag, Cambridge, UK, March 1994, pp 231-244.

14. Formica A., Groger H.D., Missikoff M., *Object-Oriented Database Schema Analysis and inheritance processing : A Graph_Theoric Approach*, Data and Knowledge Engineering 1997; 24:157-181.

15. Booch G., Rumbaugh J., Jacobson I., *Unified Modeling Language version 1.0*, Rational Software Corporation, Santa Clara, USA, January 1997.

16. Goldstein B., *Formal Properties of Constraints on Null Values in Relational Databases*. Technical Report 80-013-REV, Computer Science Department, University of New York, USA, november 1980 and July 1981 .

17. Atzeni P. and Morfuni M., *Functional dependencies and existence constraints in databases relations with null values*. Technical report n°R77, Information System Analysis Institute, University of Roma, Italy, december 1983.

18. Atzeni P. and Morfuni M., *Functional Dependencies and Constraints on Null Values in Databases*. Technical report n°R111, Information System Analysis Institute,University of Roma, Italy, 1985.

19. Kornatzky Y. and Shoval P., *Conceptual Design of Object-oriented Database Schemas using the Binary-relationship Model*. Data and Knowledge Engineering 1995; vol.14; 3:265-288.

20. Halpin T., *A Fact-oriented Approach to Schema Transformation*. Proceedings of MFDBS'91, Lecture Notes in Computer Science n°495, Springer-Verlag, Rostock, 1991, pp 342-356.

21. Blaha M., Premerlani W. and Shen H., *Converting OO Models into RDBMS Schema*. IEEE software 1994; 28-39.

22. Codd E. F. *The Relational Model for Database Management. Version 2.*Addison-Wesley Publishing Company, Inc., 1990.

23. Lammari N., Laleau R., Jouve M. and Castellani X., *Deriving Normalized Is_A Hierarchies by Using Applicability Constraints*. CAISE'96. Lecture Notes in Computer Science, Springer-Verlag, Heraklion, Greece, 20-24 may 1996, pp 562-580.

24. Lammari N., Jouve M., Laleau R. and Castellani X., *An algorithm for IS_A Hierarchy Derivation*. Proc. OOIS'94 (International Conference on Object-Oriented Information systems), Springer-Verlag editor, London, december 1994, pp 469-479.

25. Lammari N., Laleau R., Jouve M., *Schema Transformation Mechanisms for Reorganizing IS_A Inheritance Hierarchies*, Research Report, CEDRIC-CNAM Laboratory, Paris, March 1998.

26. Navathe S. B., *Evolution of Data Modeling for Databases*. Communication of the ACM 1992; vol.35; 9:112-123.

QUERIES AND VIEWS

Deductive Queries in ODMG Databases: the DOQL Approach

Pedro R. F. Sampaio and Norman W. Paton
Department of Computer Science
University of Manchester
Oxford Road, Manchester, M13 9PL, UK
(sampaiop,norm)@cs.man.ac.uk

Abstract

The Deductive Object Query Language (DOQL) is a rule-based query language designed to provide recursion, aggregates, grouping and virtual collections in the context of an ODMG compliant object database system. This paper provides a description of the constructs supported by DOQL and the algebraic operational semantics induced by DOQL's query translation approach to implementation. The translation consists of a logical rewriting step used to normalise DOQL expressions into molecular forms, and a mapping step that transforms the canonical molecular form into algebraic expressions. The paper thus not only describes a deductive language for use with ODMG databases, but indicates how this language can be implemented using conventional query processing techniques.

1   Introduction

The ODMG standard is an important step forward due to the provision of a reference architecture for object databases. This architecture encompasses an object model and type system, a set of imperative language bindings and the OQL declarative query language. Perhaps the cornerstone contribution of the ODMG specification is the definition of a standard object model that can be accessed and manipulated by different languages, catering for portability and supporting different paradigms of interaction with object databases (currently, imperative by way of language bindings and functional, by way of OQL).

Besides the programming API supported by the DML of the ODMG imperative language bindings (viz. C++, Java and Smalltalk) and the OQL query language that supports interactive and embedded declarative access modes in a functional style, new modes of interaction with ODMG compliant databases are being investigated in the fields of visual query languages [7, 13] and computationally complete query language extensions [17].

In this paper we report on the use of the deductive paradigm for querying ODMG databases through DOQL. DOQL is a rule-based database query language that provides a deductive interface to an ODMG compliant object database. DOQL is designed to integrate object-oriented and deductive language constructs, and to support recursion, aggregates, grouping and virtual collections (views).

This paper presents the main features of DOQL, and the algebraic operational semantics of DOQL. The remainder of this paper is structured as follows. An overview of the features supported in DOQL is presented in section 2, followed by a description of the query translation approach defining the operational semantics of DOQL in section 3. Related work is presented in section 4, and the paper concludes in section 5 with a summary of the work and a discussion of future directions.

```
extern const char _boss[] = "boss";
extern const char _subordinates[] = "subordinates";
extern const char _workers[] = "workers";
extern const char _works_for[] = "works_for";

class Skill : public d_Object {
    d_String s_name;
    d_String rating;
};

class Person : public d_Object {
    d_String name;
    d_String surname;
    d_Ref<Person> father;
    d_Ref<Person> mother;
    d_UShort age;
    d_Set<d_Ref<Person>> dependents;
    d_Set<d_Ref<Skill>> skills;
};

class Employee : public Person {
    d_Rel_Set<Employee,_boss> subordinates;
    d_Rel_Ref<Employee,_subordinates> boss;
    d_Rel_Ref<Department,_workers> works_for;
};

class Department : public d_Object {
    d_String name;
    d_Rel_Set <Employee,_works_for> workers;
};
```

Figure 1: Database schema in C++ ODL.

Figure 1 describes the application schema used throughout the paper, specified in C++ ODL [14, 4]. The database conforming to the application schema supports the extents *persons*, *employees* and *departments*. It is assumed that readers have some familiarity with the ODMG standard, and with deductive database technologies, as described in [4] and [5], respectively.

2   An Overview of DOQL

DOQL is designed to exploit language integration [1, 15], where a deductive language is integrated with an imperative programming language in the context of an object model or type system. In this strategy, the resulting system supports a range of standard object-oriented mechanisms for structuring both data and programs, while allowing different and complementary programming paradigms to be used for different tasks, or for different parts of the same task. The idea of integrating deductive and imperative language constructs for different parts of a task was pioneered in the Glue-Nail deductive relational database [9], and is now adapted for ODMG compliant object-oriented databases. The success of this strategy depends on the seamlessness of the integration of the deductive language and the imperative language, which is achieved by adopting ODMG types as the type system underlying the integration.

The architecture adopted for DOQL is illustrated in figure 2. The DOQL compiler and evaluator is a class library that stores and accesses rules from the ODMG database – the rule base is itself represented as database objects. The class library is linked with application programs and the interactive DOQL interface. The interactive interface is itself a form of application program. The system is designed with the goal of serving as a complementary and non-invasive query layer that can be used by application designers without the need to change existing data or programs.

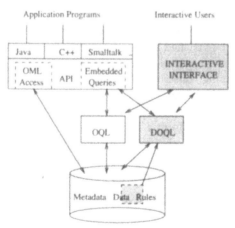

Figure 2: Architecture diagram showing location of DOQL compiler/evaluator.

2.1 DOQL Methods and Rules

Rules are used to define virtual collections and deductive methods over ODMG databases. A rule is a clause of the form: $H \leftarrow L_1, L_2, L_3, \ldots L_n$, where H is the *Head* of the rule and the body is a sequence of literals denoting a formula. The syntactic form of the head depends on whether the rule is a *regular clause* or a *method clause*.

2.1.1 Regular Clauses

Regular clauses are rules that specify a virtual collection (intensional database predicate) over the stored database. Virtual collections can be used to define new types that can model associations, aggregations and specializations involving stored objects. In regular clauses, the head of the rule is of the form:

$$< rulename > (arg_1, ..., arg_n)$$

where each arg_i is a variable, an atomic constant, a compound constant, or a grouping expression applied to a term. Rules can be recursive, can range over collections, can traverse ODMG relationships (collection valued relationships using the operator $\Rightarrow$, and single valued using $\rightarrow$), and combine positional (access to arguments of rule heads) and named approaches (access to properties and operations of objects) to attribute denotation. The following rule defines a virtual collection formed by the names of same aged siblings of a person object.

```
sameAgeSiblings(N1,N2)  :- persons[dependents=>P1,dependents=>P2],
                           P1 != P2, P1.age = P2.age,
                           P1.name = N1, P2.name = N2.
```

Grouping is the process of grouping elements into a collection by defining properties that must be satisfied by the elements. Grouping is restricted to rules that contain a single clause and to a single argument position in the head of the clause. The grouping construct is expressed using the symbols { Var_Name } for set groupings, < Var_Name > to group elements as bags and [Var_Name | $a_i : o_i, \ldots a_n : o_n$] to group as lists, sorting the list according to the attributes $a_i, \ldots, a_n$, each attribute defining a letter (a=ascending, d=descending) for the ordering field o_i that defines the order of the elements of the list according to that attribute. The following example shows the grouping of the relatives of a person as a list sorted in ascending order of the age attribute.

```
ancestor(X,Y)  :- persons(X), X.father->Y.
ancestor(X,Y)  :- persons(X), X.mother->Y.
ancestor(X,Y)  :- ancestor(X,Z), ancestor(Z,Y).

relatives_of(X,[Y|age:a])  :- ancestor(X,Y).
```

2.1.2 Method Clauses

Method clauses are rules that specify deductive methods attached to classes. Method clauses extend the interface of the recipient object type and can be used to define derived properties associated with classes. In method clauses, the head of the rule is of the form:

$$< recipient >::< method-name > (arg_1, ..., arg_n)$$

where *recipient* is a variable, and arg_i are as for regular clauses. For example, the following method rule reinterprets ancestor as a deductive method on person. In the deductive method definition, the typing information for variables is obtained from the class to which the deductive method is attached, instead of explicitly stating the extent over which the variable ranges, as was done in the example describing regular clauses.

```
P::ancestor(R)  :- P.father->R.
P::ancestor(R)  :- P.mother->R.
P::ancestor(R)  :- P::ancestor(Z), Z::ancestor(R).
```

Deductive methods can be overriden along the sub-typing hierarchy, specializing the behaviour of a rule. The approach to overriding and late binding follows that of ROCK & ROLL [10]. In essence, methods can be overridden, and the definition that is used is the most specialised one defined for the object fulfilling the role of the message recipient.

2.2   Rule Management

Rules can be created either transiently, or in rule bases that are stored persistently in the ODMG compliant database. Rule bases are created using the create_rulebase operation, which takes as parameter the name of the rulebase to be created. The inverse of create_rulebase is delete_rulebase. These commands can be run from the operating system command line, from the interactive DOQL system, or from executing programs.

Once a rulebase has been created, rules can be added to it using the extend rulebase command, which can also be run from the operating system command line, from the interactive DOQL system, or from executing programs. For example, figure 3 extends the rulebase employment with both regular and method rules.

The above environment for creating and storing rules has a role analogous to that of ODL for describing ODMG databases. We do not propose an extension to ODL, as implementation of such an extension requires access to the source of the underlying database.

2.3   Queries and Rule Invocation

Queries are evaluated over the current state of the database and rule base, with different query formats depending on the nature of the query. Rules can only be invoked directly from within DOQL queries and rules. The different formats are:

```
extend rulebase employment
{
  // Extend EMPLOYEE with an operation related_subordinate that associates
  // the EMPLOYEE with subordinates who are related to them.
  extend interface EMPLOYEE
  {
      Emp::related_subordinate(R)  :-
           Emp::relative(R), Emp::subordinate(R).

      Emp::subordinate(S)  :- Emp[subordinates=>S].
      Emp::subordinate(S)  :- Emp[subordinates=>Int],
                              Int::subordinate(S).

      Emp::relative(R)  :- Emp::ancestor(Z), R::ancestor(Z), Emp != R.
  }

  // A dodgy manager is one who is the boss of a relative.

  dodgy_manager(M)  :- employees(M), exists(S: M::related_subordinate(S)).
}
```

Figure 3: Extending a rule base.

- Single element queries (SELECT ANY): this form of query returns a single element from the set of elements that results from the evaluation of the goal. The choice of the element to be returned is non-deterministic.

- Set of elements queries (SELECT): this form of query returns all elements that satisfy the goal.

- Boolean queries (VERIFY): this form of query has a boolean type as result. The result is the value yielded by the boolean formula given as a parameter.

The query formats can be summarized according to the following general expressions:

```
SELECT [ANY] Result_Specifier
    FROM     DOQL Query
    [WITH    Rule_Statements]
    [USING   Rulebase]

VERIFY Boolean_Formula
    [WITH    Rule_Statements]
    [USING   Rulebase]
```

The Result_Specifier is a comma separated list of arguments that are the same as the arguments allowed in a rule head, and Rulebase is a comma separated list of persistent rulebase names. For example, the following query associates each employee with a set of their related subordinates, using rules from the employment rulebase.

```
SELECT E,{S}
FROM    E::related_subordinate(S)
USING   employment
```

The verification format requires that the operand of the verify returns a boolean value:

```
VERIFY  exists(E:employees(E), E.age < 18)
USING   employment
```

The WITH clause is used to allow the specification of rules that exist solely for the purpose of answering the query (i.e. that are not to be stored in the persistent rule base). For example, the following query retrieves the names of the employees who have more than 5 related subordinates:

```
SELECT Name
FROM    employees(E)[name=Name], num_related_subordinates(E,Num), Num > 5
WITH    num_related_subordinates(E,count({S})) :- E::related_subordinate(S).
```

The above query forms can be used either in the interactive DOQL interface or in embedded DOQL.

2.4 Embedded DOQL

DOQL programs can be embedded in host programming languages in a manner similar to that used for OQL [4]. DOQL statements are embedded as parameters of calls to the API function d_doql_execute (d_DOQL_Query Q, Type_Res Result)[1]. The function receives two parameters. The first parameter is a query container object formed by the query form described in section 2.3 along with any input arguments to the query. The second parameter is the program variable that will receive the result of the query.

```
d_Ref <Person> adam = ...;
d_Set <d_Ref<Person>> *ancestors = new Set(Person);
d_DOQL_Query
    q1("SELECT Y
        FROM ancestor($1,Y)
        WITH
        ancestor(X,Y) :- persons(X), X.father->Y.
        ancestor(X,Y) :- persons(X), X.mother->Y.
        ancestor(X,Y) :- ancestor(X,Z),
                         ancestor(Z,Y)."
    );
q1 << adam;
d_doql_execute(q1, ancestors);
```

Figure 4: Example embedded DOQL code fragment

---

[1]A general syntax is used to show concepts. The specific syntax varies for each language binding (e.g. for C++, template<class T> void d_doql_execute(d_DOQL_Query &query, T &result)).

Figure 4 is a code fragment that shows the embedded form of DOQL for C++. First some variables are declared for the input parameter to the query (adam) and the result (ancestors). Then the query object q1 is created with the query as the parameter of the constructor function. It is then indicated that adam is the (first and only) parameter of q1 – this parameter is referred to within the text of the query as $1. Finally, the query is executed by d_doql_execute, and the results are placed in ancestors.

2.5 Stratification, Safety and Restrictions

DOQL adopts conventional restrictions on rule construction to guarantee that queries have finite and deterministic results. In particular: each variable appearing in a rule head must also appear in a positive literal in the rule body; each variable occurring as an argument of a built-in predicate or a user-defined ODMG operation must also occur in an ordinary predicate in the same rule body or must be bound by an equality (or a sequence of equalities) to a variable of such an ordinary predicate or to a constant; all rules are stratified; a rule head can have at most one grouping expression; the type of each argument of an overridden DOQL method must be the same as the type of the corresponding argument in the overriding method; all rules are statically type checked, using a type inference system.

3 DOQL Translation

The translation of DOQL to the object algebra is done following a two-step approach:

1. *Rewriting:* in this step, method clauses are rewritten as regular clauses and a normalisation process transforms a rule into a canonical form (DO-QLc) where some types of nested queries are unnested and DOQL statements are rewritten as molecular expressions.

2. *Mapping:* in this step, DOQLc molecules are translated into an object algebra, capable of dealing with multiple collection types, grouping and aggregation.

The translation approach is highlighted in figure 5, which also shows the overall steps involved in the processing of a DOQL query. The operational semantic underpinned by the algebraic translation approach is useful in the sense that it provides a road to optimization and evaluation based on traditional algebraic query processing techniques.

3.1 Rewriting

In deductive object-oriented databases (DOODs), objects, classes and class members (structure and behaviour) play a central role in the organisation of

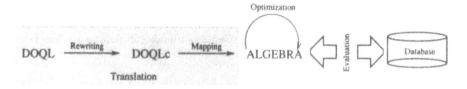

Figure 5: Translation Approach in DOQL Query Processing

information, contrasting with deductive relational databases where tuples, relations and attributes define the main abstractions.

Query processing technology for deductive databases is mainly targeted to the relational data model, which leaves to DOOD languages the options of conceiving new query processing techniques or rewriting the queries in a form that adapts the existing technology. The first approach is still an open research problem, while the latter approach has been employed in several systems and is also adopted by DOQL.

The rewriting process in DOQL is based on bundling the information directly related to collections in terms of molecules. Molecules are used to group formulas regarding properties and operations with the objects that belong to the collection. The molecular form can exploit classical query evaluation methods which are centered on the evaluation of variables and predicates. The following example shows a DOQL rule containing two molecules on the right hand side of the rule:

```
p_Kids(N1,N2) :- persons[name=N1,dependents=>Z],
                 Z[age < 2, name=N2].
```

Although it is possible to encode certain deductive object-oriented database languages in terms of Datalog as a preliminary step of rule evaluation, this process can generate complex recursive patterns and drastically increase the number of predicates [18]. In DOQL, instead of completely breaking the object information structure as is done in the process of translating DOOD languages to Datalog, the notion of collection expressions organized in terms of DOQL molecules is kept during the query evaluation process, with method clauses transformed into regular clauses in order to simplify the translation. This latter transformation doesn't change the recursive patterns within the program.

Method clauses in DOQL have the form $< recipient >::< method\text{-}name > (arg_1, \ldots, arg_n)$, where $recipient$ and arg_i are variables. Method clauses are transformed into regular clauses using the following rewrite rule:

$$< recipient >::< method - name > (arg_1, \ldots, arg_n)$$
$$\longmapsto$$
$$method - name(recipient, arg_1, \ldots, arg_n)$$

The rewriting process also applies the normalisation operations *Associate* ($\otimes$), *Compose* ($\propto$), and *PullOut*($\odot$) introduced in [18] to obtain a canonical form for DOQL. The symbol ($\rightsquigarrow$) is used to denote a formula operator in DOQL (i.e. $\rightarrow$ or $\Rightarrow$).

The *Associate* operator binds the collection membership information between objects and collections:

$$p(X), X[l_1 \rightsquigarrow p_1, \ldots, l_n \rightsquigarrow p_n]$$
$$\overset{\odot}{\longmapsto}$$
$$p(X)[l_1 \rightsquigarrow p_1, \ldots, l_n \rightsquigarrow p_n]$$

The following example illustrates the application of the *Associate* rewrite to a DOQL expression:

```
persons(X), X[name = N, skills =>S[s_name = 'cycling', rating = R]]
```

$$\overset{\odot}{\longmapsto}$$

```
persons(X)[name = N, skills =>S[s_name = 'cycling', rating = R]]
```

The *Compose* operator bundles all formulas regarding properties and operations of an object into the same molecule:

$$p[l_1 \rightsquigarrow p_1], \ldots, p[l_n \rightsquigarrow p_n] \overset{\otimes}{\longmapsto} p[l_1 \rightsquigarrow p_1, \ldots, l_n \rightsquigarrow p_n]$$

The following example illustrates the application of the *Compose* rewrite to a DOQL expression:

```
persons(X)[name = N], X.skills => S[s_name = 'cycling', rating = R]
```

$$\overset{\otimes}{\longmapsto}$$

```
persons(X)[name = N, skills =>S[s_name = 'cycling', rating = R]]
```

In case of a formula describing relational properties such as equalities, inequalties, greater than, etc., between more than one object (variables of two different molecules appearing in the left and right hand sides of the relational operator), the *Compose* is not applied, as in the formula:

```
persons(X)[age < 21], departments(Y), X.surname = Y.name.
```

In the previous DOQL expression, the formula X.surname = Y.name relates to two objects appearing in different molecules. The *Compose* rewrite is not applied in this case. This is explained by the fact that in the mapping stage, formulas involving relational properties between objects of different molecules will appear as predicates of joins between the scans of the two extents corresponding to the molecules, while formulas that involve an object of a single molecule will be translated as filters of scan operations over a single extent. In the latter case, the *Compose* helps to bundle the predicate inside the molecule, simplifying the translation in terms of algebra.

The *PullOut* operation flattens a DOQL rule containing a nested collection expression.

$$p[l_1 \rightsquigarrow p_1, \ldots, l_i \rightsquigarrow p_i[l \Rightarrow v], \ldots, l_n \rightsquigarrow p_n]$$
$$\xmapsto{\propto}$$
$$p[l_1 \rightsquigarrow p_1, \ldots, l_i \rightsquigarrow p_i, \ldots, l_n \rightsquigarrow p_n], p_i[l \Rightarrow v]$$

The following example illustrates the application of the *PullOut* rewrite to a DOQL expression:

```
persons(X)[name = N, skills =>S[s_name = 'cycling', rating = R]]
```

$$\xmapsto{\propto}$$

```
persons(X)[name = N, skills => S], S[s_name = 'cycling', rating = R]
```

A *canonical* DOQL program is a DOQL program that has been normalised by the rewriting process.

3.2 Mapping

The rationale behind the use of an algebraic approach to DOOD query processing stems from the following points:

- A significant part of many DOOD queries involves nesting and path expressions which are mainly covered by research on algebraic approaches to OO query optimization.

- Logical rewriting techniques developed for deductive databases can be applied in the rewriting step and orthogonally complemented by the algebraic optimization stage.

- Where DBMS source code is available, the integrated architecture could benefit from an existing optmizer/evaluator implementation for OQL.

The object algebra underlying the DOQL translation approach is based on the algebras presented in [2, 8, 11]. The bulk operators of the algebra reflect the extent oriented nature of access to ODMG databases and also have a straightforward representation in terms of the algebraic interfaces supported by query optimization tools. The following bulk operators are supported:

join(A,B,*pred,outer*)   the join operation joins two collections *A*, *B* using the predicate *pred*. The value of *outer* can be *false*, *left* or *right*, indicating if the join is a standard join or an outer join. The operation returns sets of tuples.

select(A,*a,pred*)   the select operation returns the elements *a* of collection *A* such that *pred* holds.

apply(A, *a*, f(*a*))   the apply operation applies the function *f* to the elements *a* of collection *A*.

unnest(*E,path*, *v*, *pred*, *outer*)   the unnest operation unnests the nested collection *E* by retrieving the *path* component into variable *v*. If *outer* is *false*, elements of the input which have a NULL path or that do not satisfy *pred* are not kept in the output.

nest(*E,group_var*, *v*, *pred*)   the nest operation creates a nested collection from *E*, by grouping each element in *E* according to the value of the variable appearing in *group_var*. The groups formed relative to each value of *group_var* are accessible through *v*. The variable in *group_var* must have been previously defined in *E*.

fixpoint(Δ)   the fixpoint operator computes the fixpoint of a set Δ of algebraic expressions.

union(*C1,C2*)   the union operator merges the elements of two union compatible collections *C1* and *C2*.

The overall mapping process works by a left to right translation of the body of a DOQL canonical rule where each rule literal is mapped into a corresponding algebraic expression. The algebraic equivalent of a literal can be used as a parameter in algebraic expressions resulting from the translation of other DOQL literals. The last literal translated is the head of a rule.

Pre-processing steps to the mapping of a rule involve changing constants and replicated variables (with the generation of equalities) on the left-hand side of a rule, and also the generation of equality conditions due to the presence of replicated variables on the right-hand side of the rule. This process transforms the notion of repeated occurrences of the same variable (common in deductive languages) in terms of predicates that can serve as parameters to algebraic operations.

As a first example of the translation process, the following DOQL rule involves a join, retrieving the employees with a surname that coincides with the name of a department.

```
odd_surname(X) :- employees[surname=X], departments[name=X].
```

After the mapping step, the following algebraic expression represents the translation of the rule:

```
apply
(join (select(employees,v1,and(eq(project(v1,surname),x1))),
       select(departments,v2,and(eq(project(v2,name),x2))),
       and(eq(x1,x2)),
       false
      ),
 a,
 tuple(bind(!X,project(a,surname))
)
```

In the next example, consider the DOQL rule that groups the female dependents under 18 of the employees with surname "Smith":

```
empDeps(X,<D>) :- employees(X)[surname='Smith'],
                  X.dependents=>D,
                  D.age < 18, D.sex = 'Female'.
```

After the normalisation step, the equivalent canonical form is as follows:

```
empDeps(X,<D>) :- employees(X)[surname='Smith', dependents=>D],
                  D[age < 18, sex = 'Female'].
```

After the mapping step, the following algebraic expression represents the translation of the rule:

```
apply
(nest
 (unnest
  (select(employees,x,and(eq(project(x,surname),'Smith')))),
   project(x,dependents),
   d,
   and(lt(project(d,age),18),eq(project(d,sex),'Female')),
   true),
  x,
  v,
  and()
),
e,
tuple(bind(!X,x),bind(!D,v)),
)
```

The following example involves the translation of a recursive predicate that computes all direct and indirect supervisors of an employee.

```
super(X,Y) :- employees(X)[boss->Y].
super(X,Y) :- employees(X)[boss->K], super(K,Y).
```

After the mapping step, the following set of algebraic expressions represents the translation of the rule:

```
apply
(fixpoint
 (union(
        apply (select(employees,x,and(refchase(boss,y)))),
               e,
               tuple(bind(X1,x),bind(Y1,y))),
        apply (join
               (select(employees,x,and(refchase(boss,k)))),
                select(super,v1,and(project(v1,@1),project(v1,@2)))),
                and(eq(k,@1)),
                false),
              E,
              tuple(bind(X1,x),bind(Y1,y)))
        )
 ),
 E,
 tuple(bind(!X,X1),bind(!Y,Y1))
)
```

Negation: prior to the translation of a set of rules in a DOQL program, it is necessary to order the set of rules that form the program to reflect the stratification conditions. This affects the order of translation such that rules containing atoms in higher strata levels are translated after rules with atoms in lower strata levels.

Solutions for negated atoms are defined when all unbound goal arguments of the atom are of type object, meaning that their domain is finite. In such a case, the result for the negated atom can be obtained by subtracting the result of the non-negated atom from the cross-product of the unbound arguments' domains.

Algorithm 1 Translation of Canonical Rule Body

Require: Canonical Rule Body (CRB): $L_1, \ldots, L_n$

$Result \leftarrow \emptyset$

for all Molecular Literals $L_i \in CRB$ **do**

  if L_i is a collection molecule **then**

    if NotGivenVarInMolecule(L_i) **then**

      CreateVar(L_i)

      $\{L_i$ has the form ext_name(Var_i)$[exp_1, \ldots, exp_k, colexp_1, \ldots, colexp_j]\}$

    end if

    $A_i \leftarrow$ select(ext_name,Var_i,$pred\_i = and(exp_1, \ldots, exp_k)$)

    for all nested collection expressions $colexp_j \in L_i$, of the form $path_j \Rightarrow var_j$ **do**

      $B_k \leftarrow$ unnest(A_i,project(Var_i,$path_j$),Var_j,$pred_j$)

      $\{pred_j$ is formed by the conjunction of the expressions appearing in the molecule Var_j [...]$\}$

    end for

  else if L_i is an object molecule **then**

    for all nested collection expressions $colexp_j \in L_i$, of the form $path_j \Rightarrow var_j$ **do**

      $B_x^y \leftarrow$ unnest(B_k,project(Var_i,$path_j$),Var_j,$pred_j$)

      $\{pred_j$ is formed by the conjunction of the expressions appearing in the molecule Var_j [...]$\}$

    end for

  end if

  $Result \leftarrow$ generate joins between all B_x^y, and all B_x not appearing as a parameter of a B_x^y

end for

for all Non Molecular Literals $L_i \in CRB$ **do**

  Place the formulas defined by the literals as parameters of the join predicates between the algebraic expressions resulting from the translation of the two molecules involved in the literal

end for

The general steps of the algorithm that maps the body of a canonical DOQL rule into a nested relational algebra expression are described in algorithm 1.

If there are no grouping constructs, the rule head is translated into an *apply* operator, otherwise, the rule head is translated into a *nest* operator followed by an *apply*.

In the mapping process, the following operators supporting path expressions and built-in predicates are used:

project($a,path$)   the project operator retrieves the *path* component of the element a. The *path* component can be a position (n) of a field of the element belonging to a virtual collection (positional approach akin to Datalog) or the name of a property defined for an element belonging to a stored collection (named approach to attribute denotation).

eq(a,b)   the value equality operator returns true if the values a and b are equal.

lt(a,b)   the less than operator returns true if the value a is less than b.

Other operators regarding object equality, relational built-in predicates, aggregations, and arithmetic predicates are also supported in the underlying target implementation algebra, defining the fully-fledged algebraic interface to the database engine.

4   Related Work

This section outlines a range of features that can be used to compare the query components of proposals that integrate declarative query languages and imperative OO programming languages in the context of OODBs.

Bidirectionality of calls: relates to the flexibility of the integration approach. In unidirectional systems, one of the languages can call the other, but not vice-versa.

Restructuring: relates to the operations available in the declarative language that can be used to reorganize the queried data elements to yield more desirable output formats.

Type system: relates to the underlying type system used across the integrated languages.

Query power: relates to the query classes supported by the query language (FOLQ = first-order queries, FIXP = fixpoint queries, HOQ = higher-order queries).

Table 1 shows a comparison between the query facilities supported by DOQL and the query components of Chimera [6], Coral++ [16], OQL [4], OQLC++ [3], Noodle [12] and ROCK & ROLL [1].

Some important aspects of our design are:

Language	Criteria			
	Bidirection of Calls	Restruct. Operators	Type System	Query Power
Chimera	no	unnest	Chimera object model	FOLQ, FIXP
Coral++	no	set group., unnest	C++	FOLQ, FIXP
DOQL	yes	(set,bag,list) group., unnest	ODMG object model	FOLQ, FIXP
Noodle	yes	(set,bag) group., unnest	Sword object model	FOLQ, FIXP, HOQ
OQL	yes	(set,bag,list) group., unnest	ODMG object model	FOLQ
OQLC++	yes	unnest	C++	FOLQ
ROCK & ROLL	yes	unnest	Semantic object model	FOLQ, FIXP

Table 1: Query languages for object databases

- language integration is done using a standard object-model as the underlying data model of the deductive system.

- the approach to integration complies with the call level interface defined by the ODMG standard, reusing existing compiler technology for other ODMG compliant languages and providing portable deduction within the imperative languages without the need for changes in syntax or to the underlying DBMS.

- bidirectionality of calls between the integrated languages.

- powerful aggregate and grouping operators that can be used for restructuring data in applications that require summaries, classifications and data dredging.

- updating and control features are confined within the imperative language

Language integration proposals can also be compared based on the seamlessness of the language integration (see [1]) or based on the object-oriented and deductive capabilities supported (see [15]). Using the criteria of [1], DOQL can be seen to support evaluation strategy compatibility, (reasonable) type system uniformity and bidirectionality, but to lack type checker capability and syntactic consistency. The lack of type checker capability means that embedded DOQL programs can cause type errors at runtime – obtaining compile time type checking of embedded DOQL would require changes to be made to the host language compiler. The lack of syntactic consistency is unavoidable, as DOQL can be embedded in any of a range of host languages, and thus cannot hope to have a syntax that is consistent with all of them.

5 Summary

DOQL is a deductive query language designed to complement existing query language facilities for ODMG databases that is being implemented on top of the Poet SDK 5.0 C++ ODMG binding [14].

In this paper, the translation approach adopted in the query processing of DOQL has been presented. The paper addresses the rewriting and mapping steps that translate DOQL rules involving conjunctive queries, recursion, negation and grouping into algebraic expressions that are evaluated against the underlying object base. The query transformation technique used in the rewriting step together with the functionality supported in the algebraic operators enable the early application of constraints such as inequalities and equalities, limiting the amount of data generated in the query processing flow.

The choice of a combined approach (logical + algebraic) to the translation of DOQL allows the exploitation of deductive optimization techniques and object-oriented optimization techniques, as well as laying the foundation for the use of query optimization tools like [11] to optimize the algebraic expressions.

Acknowledgements: The first author is sponsored by Conselho Nacional de Desenvolvimento Científico e Tecnológico - CNPq (Brazil) – Grant 200372/96-3.

References

[1] M. L. Barja, N. W. Paton, A. A. Fernandes, M. Howard Williams, and Andrew Dinn. An effective deductive object-oriented database through language integration. In *Proc. of the 20th VLDB Conference*, pages 463–474, 1994.

[2] C. Beeri and T. Milo. Functional and predicative programming in oodb's. In *Proc. of the ACM Principles of Database Systems Conference (PODS 92)*, pages 176–190, 1992.

[3] J. Blakeley. OQLC++: Extending C++ with an object query capability. In Won Kim, editor, *Modern Database Systems*, chapter 4, pages 69–88. Addison-Wesley, 1995.

[4] R. Cattel and Douglas Barry, editors. *The Object Database Standard: ODMG 2.0*. Morgan Kaufman, 1997.

[5] S. Ceri, G. Gottlob, and L. Tanca. *Logic Programming and Databases*. Springer-Verlag, 1990.

[6] S. Ceri and R. Manthey. Consolidated specification of chimera (cm and cl). Technical Report IDEA.DE.2P.006.1, IDEA - ESPRIT project 6333, 1993.

[7] M. Chavda and P. Wood. Towards an odmg-compliant visual object query language. In *Proc. of the VLDB Conference*, pages 456–465, 1997.

[8] S. Cluet and C. Delobel. A general framework for the optimization of object-oriented queries. In *Proc. of the ACM SIGMOD Intl. Conference on Management of Data*, pages 383–392, 1992.

[9] M. A. Derr and S. Morishita. Design and implementation of the glue-nail database system. In *Proc. of the ACM SIGMOD Intl. Conference on Management of Data*, pages 147–156, 1993.

[10] A. Dinn, N. W. Paton, M. Howard Williams, A. A. Fernandes, and M. L. Barja. The implementation of a deductive query language over an OODB. In *Proc. 4th Int. Conference on Deductive and Object-Oriented Databases*, pages 143–160, 1995.

[11] Leonidas Fegaras. An experimental optimizer for OQL. Technical Report TR-CSE-97-007, CSE, University of Texas at Arlington, 1997.

[12] I. S. Mumick and K. A. Ross. Noodle: A language for declarative querying in an object-oriented database. In *Proc. of the Third Intl. Conference on Deductive and Object-Oriented Databases*, volume 760 of *LNCS*, pages 360–378. Springer-Verlag, 1993.

[13] N. Murray, N. Paton, and C. Goble. Kaleidoquery: A visual query language for object databases. In *Proc. of the Working Conference on Advanced Visual Interfaces - AVI*, 1998.

[14] Poet Software. *Poet V5.0 ODMG Programmer's Guide*, 1997.

[15] Pedro R. F. Sampaio and Norman W. Paton. Deductive object-oriented database systems: A survey. In *Proceedings of the 3rd International Workshop on Rules in Database Systems*, volume 1312 of *LNCS*, pages 1–19. Springer-Verlag, 1997.

[16] D. Srivastava, R. Ramakrishnan, P. Seshadri, and S. Sudarshan. Coral++: Adding object-orientation to a logic database language. In *Proc. of the 19th VLDB Conference, Dublin, Ireland*, pages 158–170, 1993.

[17] K. Subieta. Object-oriented standards: can ODMG OQL be extended to a programming language. In *Proc. of the International Symposium on Cooperative Database Systems for Advanced Applications*, pages 546–555, Kyoto, Japan, 1996.

[18] Z. Xie and J. Han. Normalization and compilation of deductive and object-oriented database programs for efficient query evaluation. In *Proc. of the 4th Intl. Conference on Deductive and Object-Oriented Databases (DOOD' 95)*, pages 485–502, 1995.

Incremental Maintenance of Materialized Path Query Views*

Elke A. Rundensteiner

Department of Computer Science, Worcester Polytechnic Institute
Worcester, MA 01609-2280, USA
rundenst@cs.wpi.edu

Harumi A. Kuno

R&D Instrument Support Sol. Div., Hewlett-Packard Company
Santa Clara, CA 95052-8059, USA
harumi.kuno@hp.com

Yijing Zhou

Department of Computer Science, Worcester Polytechnic Institute
Worcester, MA 01609-2280, USA
yjzhou@cs.wpi.edu

Abstract

In this paper we address the problem of incrementally maintaining object-oriented database (OODB) views formed using path queries. We demonstrate that traditional indices organizations, designed for query support, are not well suited for this task. As a solution, we introduce a new *Satisfiability Indicating Multi-Index (SMX)* organization, which maintains partial information indicating whether or not a given endpoint satisfies the query predicate rather than what the exact value of the endpoint is. We have implemented SMX as well as competing index structures in the MultiView OODB system over Gemstone, and conducted experiments on this system. The results of our evaluations indicate that the SMX dramatically improves upon the performance of traditional indices.

Keywords: Incremental view maintenance, path queries, data warehousing, view materialization, and object-oriented databases.

1 Introduction

Recent advances in information technology have issued a new set of challenges to the database community. There is a growing need for strategies that provide the means

*This work was supported in part by the NSF RIA grant #IRI-9309076, NSF NYI grant #IRI 94-57609, and the University of Michigan Faculty Award Program, IBM Partnership Program, Intel, and AT&T. Harumi A. Kuno is also grateful for support from the NASA Graduate Student Researchers Program.

to cache and use query results, for mechanisms that support customized interfaces to shared data, and for the integration of such mechanisms with the powerful constructs of the object-oriented programming model. For example, the need for improved access to diverse data sources has spurred a recent interest in supporting queries across multiple information sources in a transparent fashion (e.g., *data warehouses* and *digital libraries* [20, 1]). Materialized database views are a recognized means of achieving such interoperability among applications, allowing applications to benefit from the powerful flexibility of view technology while minimizing the performance penalties traditionally associated with views. However, the fact that updates must be propagated to affected materialized views limits the variety of queries that can be used to define materialized views.

We have previously discussed the problem of view materialization in the context of object-oriented databases (OODBs) and proposed algorithms that exploit object-oriented characteristics in order to provide the incremental maintenance of materialized virtual classes created using the standard view query operators [10, 13, 14, 15]. In this paper we address the problem of the incremental maintenance of materialized virtual classes formed using selection queries on aggregation paths (or short, *path query views*). To the best of our knowledge, only two other research groups have addressed this topic. Kemper et al.'s work on *function materialization* addresses the problem of precomputing function results [6, 7]. Konomi et al. discuss a solution to supporting a type of join class that is formed along the aggregation graph [8].

Traditional indexing techniques are not well suited for this task of maintenance. The indexing needs of the path query view problem are unique in that because the contents of the materialized view are cached and can be queried directly, the primary use for a supplemental index is for the propagation of updates rather than for query processing. Because traditional index organizations are tailored for use during general query processing (i.e., primarily for data retrieval), they are not optimized to evaluate path instantiations with regard to a static predetermined predicate condition such as would be associated with a path query view. Furthermore, traditional index organizations do not distinguish between single-valued and multi-valued attributes, and thus do not account for the fact that multi-valued attributes enable a single object at the head of a path to be associated with multiple instantiations of the path, any number of which could satisfy the specific path query predicate. This means that if an updated path involves a multi-valued attribute then the aggregation hierarchy of the object at the head of the path must be completely re-calculated in order to determine whether or not that object participates in an alternative instantiation that fulfills the view query predicate despite the update.

As a solution, we introduce a new *Satisfiability Indicating Multi-Index (SMX)* organization that is specifically tailored to handle the issues of path query view maintenance [12]. SMX maintains partial information indicating whether or not a given endpoint satisfies the query predicate rather than the exact values of endpoints. This strategy offers a number of benefits. (1) Instead of traversing all instantiations in which an object participates to their endpoints, with the SMX organization at most two path positions forward must be examined in order to determine whether or not the endpoint of an instantiation fulfills a given path query predicate. (2) The SMX index structure only needs to be updated when the validity of an object's instantiation (in terms of the query predicate) changes. (3) Instead of having to fully traverse all instantiations of an object to identify whether or not it participates in any alternative instantiations (due to multi-valued attributes) that affect its membership in a path query view, with the SMX organization we only need to check at most one forward reference.

We have implemented SMX and competing index structures in our object-oriented view system *MultiView* , which is built on top of the commercial Gemstone OODB [9, 17, 13, 10]. In this paper, we now report upon experimental studies we have conducted evaluating the performance of SMX and other traditional index structures both in terms of materialized view generation and continued maintenance under updates. Our results indicate that the SMX dramatically improves upon the performance of traditional index structures.

In Section 2, we review the *MultiView* object model. Section 3 presents three issues with the maintenance of path query views, including a discussion of the limitations of utilizing traditional index organizations to address these problems. We describe SMX in Section 4. Sections 5 and 6 present our experimental setup and performance results. We discuss related work in Section 7, and present conclusions in Section 8.

2 The *MultiView* Model and System

In this section, we briefly review the basic object model principles of the *MultiView* system. More details are given in [16] and [10]. Let O be an infinite set of **object instances**, or short, **objects**. Each object $O_i \in O$ consists of state (**instance variables** or **attributes**), behavior (**methods** to which the object can respond), and a **unique object identifier**. The domain of an instance variable can be **constrained** to objects or sets of objects of a specific class. If an instance variable is constrained to sets of objects, then we say that the instance variable is **multi-valued**. Because our model is object-oriented and assumes full encapsulation, access to the state of an object is only through **accessing methods**. Together, the **methods** and **instance variables** of an object are referred to as its **properties.**

Objects that share a common structure and behavior are grouped into **classes**. We use the term **type** to indicate the set of applicable property functions shared by all members of the class. Let C be the set of all classes in a database. A **class** $C_i \in C$ has a unique class name, a **type**, and a set membership denoted by **extent**(C_i).

We use both class type and class extent to determine subsumption relationships. For two classes C_i and $C_j \in C$, C_i is a **subtype** of C_j, denoted $C_i \preceq C_j$ if and only if (iff) (**properties**$(C_i) \supseteq$ **properties**(C_j)). All properties defined for a supertype are **inherited** by its subtypes. Similarly, C_i is a **subset** of C_j, denoted $C_i \subseteq C_j$, iff $(\forall o \in O)((o \in C_i) \Rightarrow (o \in C_j))$. C_i is a **subclass** of C_j, denoted C_i *is-a* C_j, iff $(C_i \subseteq C_j)$ and $(C_i \preceq C_j)$. C_i is a **direct subclass** of C_j if $\nexists C_k \in C$ s.t. $k \neq i \neq j$, C_i *is-a* of C_k, and C_k *is-a* of C_j.

An **object schema** is a rooted directed acyclic graph $G = (V, E)$, where the finite set of vertices V corresponds to classes $C_i \in C$ and the finite set of directed edges E corresponds to a binary relation on $V \times V$ representing all direct *is-a* relationships. Each directed edge $e \in E$ from V_i to V_j represents the relationship C_i *is-a* C_j. Two classes $C_i, C_j \in C$ share a common property iff they inherit it from the same superclass. The designated root node, *Object*, has a global extent equal to the set containing all instances and an empty type description.

An **aggregation path** P_i is defined as $C_{i,1}.A_{i,2}.A_{i,3} \ldots A_{i,n}$ where $C_{i,1}$ is the path's source class, $A_{i,2}$ is an instance variable of $C_{i,1}$, and $\forall A_{i,k}, 1 < k \leq n, A_{i,k}$ is an instance variable of the class to which instance variable $A_{i,k-1}$'s values are constrained. We use the term **instantiation** of path P_i to refer to a sequence of objects $O_1, O_2, \ldots, O_n$ s.t. O_1 belongs to class $C_{i,1}$, O_2 belongs to class $C_{i,2}$, etc., and $\forall k$ s.t. $1 < k \leq n$, the value of O_{k-1}'s $A_{i,k}$ instance variable refers to O_k. We identify an **instantiation** of subpath $P_i(j, k), j \leq k$ of path P_i as a sequence of objects $O_j, O_{j+1}, \ldots, O_k$ s.t. O_j belongs to class $C_{i,j}$, O_{j+1} belongs to class $C_{i,j+1}$, etc., and $\forall l$ s.t. $j < l \leq k, O_{l-1}$'s $A_{i,l}$ instance variable refers to O_l. Given an instantiation of a path $P_i = C_{i,1}.A_{i,2}.A_{i,3} \ldots A_{i,n}$, we call the object in the 1st position (e.g., the object from class $C_{i,1}$) the **head** and the object in the nth position (e.g., the object from class $C_{i,n}$) the **endpoint** of the instantiated path. An object $O_j, 1 \leq j \leq n$, can participate in multiple **instantiations** of a path P_i.

Virtual classes are defined by the application of a query operator to one or two classes that restructures the source classes' type and/or extent membership. *MultiView* provides a virtual-class-forming algebra that includes the following operators: difference, hide, intersect, join, refine, select, and union [16, 13]. These queries determine the methods, instance variables, and extent of the virtual classes. The join operator can be *object-generating*; all other operators are *object-preserving*.

Let Q be the set of all possible queries. We constrain a **query** $Q_i \in Q$ used to define a virtual class to correspond to a single algebra operation, and refer to the query $Q_i \in Q$ that defines a virtual class, $VC_i \in VC$, as **query**(VC_i). We identify three types of predicates used in virtual-class defining queries. **Class membership predicates** (intrinsic to hide, union, intersect, refine, and difference queries) are predicate terms that depend upon the classes to which an object belongs [1]. **Value predicates**, used by select and join queries, are predicate terms constraining instances based on the values of their local instance variables. In addition, our select operator supports the formation of virtual classes using **path queries** (queries that refer to a value along an object's aggregation path). A **path query**, which consists of a path and a value predicate upon the endpoint of that path, takes the form $PQ_i = C_{i,1}.[\Theta]A_{i,2}.[\Theta]A_{i,3} \ldots [\Theta]A_{i,n}\theta value$, where if attribute $A_{i,j}$ is a multi-valued attribute then the quantifier $\Theta \in \{\exists, \forall\}$ indicates whether the multi-valued attribute should be handled in an existential or universal manner, and the comparison operator θ is defined for $C_{i,n}$ [2].

---

[1] Set operations are typical of queries using class membership predicates, because they function by using the presence of objects in source classes rather than by checking value-based predicates.

[2] Typically, $\theta \in \{=, <, \neq, \leq, >, \geq\}$.

Given an instantiation of a subpath $P_i(j,n)$ $O_j, O_{j+1}, \ldots, O_n$ s.t. O_j belongs to class $C_{i,j}$, O_{j+1} belongs to class $C_{i,j+1}$, etc., and $\forall l$ s.t. $j < l \leq k, O_{l-1}$'s $A_{i,l}$ instance variable refers to O_l and $A_{i,j+1}$ is a single-valued attribute, if O_n satisfies the predicate $O_n \theta value$ then we say that the subpath instantiation is a **satisfying subpath instantiation**, or short, that it is **satisfying**. If $A_{i,j+1}$ is a multi-valued attribute and $\Theta = \forall$, then we say that the subpath instantiation is **satisfying** if and only if all the objects that serve as object $O_{i,j}$'s values for attribute $A_{i,j+1}$ participate in **satisfying subpath instantiations** of subpath $P_i(j+1, n)$. The extent of a virtual class that is defined by a path query PQ_i contains all objects $O_1 \in C_{i,1}$ that satisfy PQ_i. In the current paper we assume that virtual classes are materialized, and refer to a single virtual class that is defined using a path query as a **path query view** (PQV).

3 Path Query View Maintenance

3.1 Example Schema

Figure 1 shows an initial aggregation schema composed of four classes. *Person* has an attribute, age, which is constrained to the *Number* class. *Person* also has a multi-valued instance variable—cars, which associates each person with the set of cars they own. *Car* has one instance variable, maker, which is constrained to the class *Company*. *Company* has two instance variables: stockPrice, which is constrained to the *Number* class; and owner, which is constrained to the *Person* class.

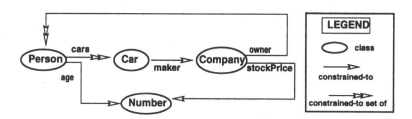

Figure 1: The example schema.

Figure 2 shows instances of the base classes and the aggregation relationships between them. For example, the *person1* object is an instance of the *Person* class, *car1* is an instance of the *Car* class, and *company1* is an instance of the *Company* class. The *person1* object has both *car1* and *car2* as values for her cars attribute.

Suppose that we were to define a virtual class *PathSelect1* for the schema in Figure 1 using the (existential) path query select from Person where [:person | person.∃cars.maker.stockPrice < 40]. Those instances of the *Person* class whose cars instance variable includes an instance of *Car* that has a maker value whose stockPrice instance variable has a value less than 40 qualify to belong to the *PathSelect1* class. As shown in Figure 3, the initial extent membership of the *PathSelect1* class contains the *person1* and *person2* objects. Figure 4 depicts

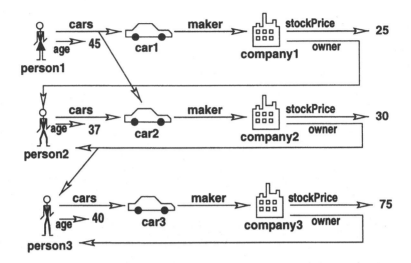

Figure 2: Initial base instances and aggregation relationships for Figure 1.

the index structures created for our example schema under the traditional multi-index (MX), path index (PX), and nested index (NX) organizations.

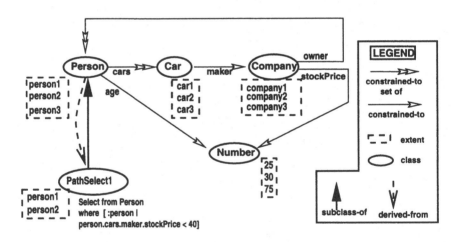

Figure 3: The *PathSelect1* is derived from the base schema using a path query.

3.2 Path Query View Maintenance Issues

We now outline issues that must be addressed when maintaining the extents of materialized path query views.

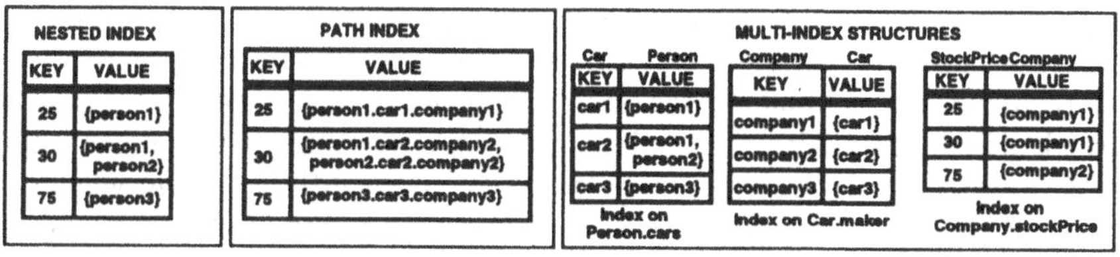

NESTED INDEX		PATH INDEX		MULTI-INDEX STRUCTURES							

KEY	VALUE
25	{person1}
30	{person1, person2}
75	{person3}

KEY	VALUE
25	{person1.car1.company1}
30	{person1.car2.company2, person2.car2.company2}
75	{person3.car3.company3}

Car Person
KEY	VALUE
car1	{person1}
car2	{person1, person2}
car3	{person3}

Index on Person.cars

Company Car
KEY	VALUE
company1	{car1}
company2	{car2}
company3	{car3}

Index on Car.maker

StockPrice Company
KEY	VALUE
25	{company1}
30	{company1}
75	{company2}

Index on Company.stockPrice

Figure 4: Traditional index organizations for the path person.cars.maker.stockPrice.

Determining instantiation validity. First we must determine whether or not the original and new endpoints of the path instantiations in which the updated object participates fulfill the path query. The traditional index organizations shown in Figure 4 facilitate the identification of head objects of instantiations, but not their endpoints. For all three index structures, we must thus traverse each of the updated object's path instantiations to their original and new endpoints in order to determine if the update affects whether or not that instantiation satisfies the path query predicate.

For example, if the *car2* object from Figure 2 were to change the value of its maker instance variable to refer to *company3* instead of *company2*, then (with the PX, NX, and MX organizations) we would have to traverse both the *company2* and the *company3* objects' instantiations of the *PathSelect1(2,4)* subpath and determine that while the original endpoint of *car2*'s path instantiation was '30' (which does fulfill *PathSelect1*'s query predicate), the new endpoint is '75' (which does not fulfill *PathSelect1*'s query predicate).

Finding head objects. If the original and new endpoints of a given path instantiation differ in that one satisfies the query predicate but the other does not, then we must identify the head object of the path instantiation. The membership of this head object in path query views based on the path instantiation is potentially affected by the update.

Given a path $P_i = C_{i,1}.A_{i,2}.A_{i,3} \ldots A_{i,n}$ and a modified object O_j of class $C_{i,j}$, we use the PX and NX organizations by first finding the endpoint objects of instantiations involving the updated object by traversing the object's instantiations of the $P_i(j,n)$ subpath (as already done in step 1), then looking these endpoints up in the index structure. With the PX organization, we can then scan the paths retrieved from the PX, determine which involve O_j, and thus identify the head objects of the instantiations in which O_j participates. However, because the NX structure does not include any path information, if multiple heads are associated with a given endpoint then we must traverse these heads' instantiations of the $P_i(1,j)$ subpath forward in order to identify which instantiations (and thus head objects) involve object O_j. We can use the reverse references provided by the MX organization to avoid such forward traversals and instead identify the head objects of O_j's instantiations of the $P_i(i,j)$ subpath by performing lookups in the $j-1$ indices of the $C_{i,1}$ through $C_{i,j+1}$ classes.

For example, if the *car2* object from Figure 2 were to change the value of its maker instance variable to refer to *company3* instead of *company2*, then with the PX and NX organizations we would first traverse the *company2* object's instantiation of the $P_i(3,5)$ subpath and find that the original endpoint is *30*. We would then look up *30* as a key in the index. Because multiple values are associated with that key, under the PX organization we would examine each path to identify the one in which the *car2* object participates and thus determine that both the *person1* and *person2* objects are potentially affected by this update. However, with the NX organization, we must traverse all the instantiations of each object associated with the key of '30' in order to determine which objects' aggregation hierarchies involve the *car2* object. With the MX organization, we traverse backwards through all multi-index structures (e.g., we could look up the *car2* object in the *Person.cars* index and identify that both the *person1* and *person2* objects are potentially-affected head objects).

Identifying alternative instantiations. The presence of even one multi-valued attribute in the path of the query greatly increases the cost of evaluating the effects of updates using any traditional index structure. If an update changes whether or not an instantiation fulfills a path query's predicate and the path includes at least one multi-valued attribute, then we must determine if each involved head object participates in any alternative instantiations that cause the head object membership in the path query view to remain the same despite the update. With the PX, NX, and MX organizations, this means that in addition to the cost of identifying each head object, we must also traverse all of that head object's path instantiations completely forward in order to determine if it participates in any alternative *satisfying instantiations*.

For example, if the *car2* object were to update its maker instance variable to remove the reference to *company3* instead of *company2*, then although we could use traditional index structures to identify that the *person1* object is potentially affected by the update, we would have to traverse all of the path instantiations of the *person1* class, in particular *person1.car1.company1.25*, in order to determine that *person1* still satisfies *PathSelect1*'s query predicate and thus should not be removed from the extent of the *PathSelect1* class.

4 SMX Solution

4.1 The SMX Structure

From the above discussion, we can identify three characteristics of the path query view problem. First, we use the supplemental index structures at the time of *updates* instead of queries. Second, because our focus is on updates rather than queries, we do not need to know exact endpoints of updated instantiated subpaths—we really need only to know whether or not these endpoints satisfy the path query view predicate. Finally, we need to be able to determine whether or not, due to multi-valued attributes, head objects participate in alternative path instantiations that affect the impact of the update on a head object's membership in the path query view.

Our *Satisfiability-Indicating Multi-Index* (SMX) exploits these characteristics to maintain path query views in an efficient and incremental fashion. The fundamental principle of the SMX solution is that we do not need to know the exact endpoint of path instantiations—we only need to know whether or not that endpoint satisfies the query's predicate. SMX therefore extends each multi-index (MX) entry with a *satisfiability indicator* (or $SatInd$ for short) that indicates whether the key value object participates in any instantiations that fulfills the query predicate. Because the satisfiability of a path instantiation is determined by its endpoint object, we can consider satisfiability to be a transitive property in that if we know for all objects $O_j \in$ class $C_{i,j}$ whether or not O_j leads to endpoints that satisfy the path query predicate, then we also know for any object $O_{j-1} \in C_{i,j-1}$ that refers to O_j as the value for its $A_{i,j}$ attribute whether or not O_{j-1} leads to endpoints that satisfy the path query predicate.

We can initialize the SMX index recursively. First, for each endpoint object O_n of class $C_{i,n}$ that serves as a value for the $A_{i,n}$ attribute of at least one object O_{n-1} of class $C_{i,n-1}$ (i.e., the last component of the path), we store $SatInd(O_n)$, which indicates whether or not O_n satisfies the path query predicate, i.e., $O_n \theta value$ evaluates to true. Next, for each object O_j of class $C_{i,j}$ that serves as a value for the $A_{i,j}$ attribute of at least one object O_{j-1} of class $C_{i,j-1}$ (i.e., the $C_{i,j-1}.C_{i,j}$ component of the path), we store $SatInd(O_j)$, which indicates either (1) (if the predicate expression's quantifier for the $C_{i,j-1}.C_{i,j}$ component is *existential*) whether or not $\exists O_{j+1}$ s.t. O_j's $A_{i,j+1}$ attribute value is set to O_{j+1} and $SatInd(O_{j+1})$ is true; or (2) (if the component's quantifier is *universal*) whether or not $\forall O_{j+1}$ s.t. O_j's $A_{i,j+1}$ attribute value contains O_{j+1}, $SatInd(O_{j+1})$ is true.

When an update takes place, we can use the SMX index to look up whether or not an object O_j leads to an endpoint that satisfies the path query predicate (i.e., $SatInd(O_j)$). If a value of true is associated with O_j in the index, then O_j leads to an endpoint that satisfies the path query predicate; otherwise (if a value of false is associated with O_j's record) it does not. If O_j does not already have an index record associated with it because no object previously referred to it, then we must look up the O_{j+1} objects referred to by O_j as values for attribute $A_{i,j+1}$ in the $C_{i,j}.A_{i,j+1}$ index. Because of the entries corresponding to the $O_j.O_{j+1}$ relationship, we are guaranteed to find these objects in the index, and thus no other traversal is needed.

If the *satisfiability indicator* value of an updated object $O_j \in C_{i,j}$ does not change as the result of an update, then the *satisfiability indicator* value of any object $O_{j-1} \in C_{i,j-1}$ that refers to members of class $C_{i,j}$ as the value for its $A_{i,j}$ attribute will not change as a result of the update. For example, Figure 5 shows the *satisfiability indicators* for the objects from Figure 2. The initial path instantiations of the *person1* and *person2* objects fulfill the predicate person.cars.maker.owners.stockPrice < 40 (introduced in Section 3). Now suppose that the *car2* object were updated as shown in Figure 5, changing the value of its maker instance variable to refer to *company1* instead of *company2*. We can compare the satisfiability indicators associated with the *company2* and *company1* objects, thus determining that because both lead to satisfying endpoints, the update will not affect the satisfiability of *car2*'s path instantiations and nothing needs to be done. Figure 6 shows the SMX index structures that correspond to the objects and classes shown in Figure 5.

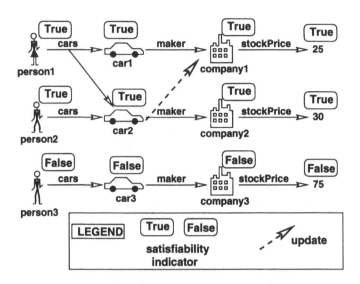

Figure 5: *Satisfiability Indicators* allow us to maintain path satisfiability information incrementally.

4.2   Incremental Processing Strategy

We can maintain the SMX structures efficiently under all three update operations (create, delete, and modify). Suppose that there exists a virtual class PQV_i defined by the query $PQ_i = C_{i,1}.A_{i,2}.A_{i,3} \ldots A_{i,n} \theta value$, and that some object O_j belonging to class $C_{i,j}$, $1 \leq j \leq n$ is updated. The *satisfiability indicators* can be maintained in an incremental fashion; when object O_j is updated, we can use the index to determine the old and new values for $SatInd(O_j)$. If $SatInd(O_j)$ changes as a result of the update, then we must iteratively traverse backwards through the multi-index components of SMX to update the *satisfiability indicators* of O_j and the objects that directly or indirectly refer to O_j in their path instantiations until either (1) we reach an object at the head of the path, in which case this object's membership in PQV_i could potentially have to change, or else (2) we find an element whose $SatInd$ is already set to the correct value.

Note that if $C_{j-1}.A_j$ is a multi-valued attribute, then potentially we might have to check all other values for the updated attribute in order to determine whether not the modified attribute value fulfills the quantifier. For example, if the quantifier were *existential* ($\Theta = \exists$), $SatInd(O_{new})$ were false, and $SatInd(O_{old})$ true, then we would have to check to make sure that no other value for $O_{j-1}.A_{i,j}$ has a positive $SatInd$ before we could determine that $SatInd(O_{j-1})$ should be reset to false. Similarly, if the query predicate were *universal* ($\Theta = \forall$) and $SatInd(O_{new})$ were true and $SatInd(O_{old})$ were false, then all other values of the multi-valued attribute must be checked in order to confirm that their *satisfaction indicators* are positive before we could determine that $SatInd(O_{j-1})$ should be reset to true.

SATISFACTION-INDICATING MULTI-INDEX STRUCTURES

Car KEY	Person VALUE
car1	{True, {person1}}
car2	{True, {person1, person2}}
car3	{False, {person3}}

Index on Person.cars

Company KEY	Car VALUE
company1	{True, {car1}}
company2	{True, {car2}}
company3	{False, {car3}}

Index on Car.maker

stockPrice KEY	Company VALUE
25	{True, {company1}}
30	{True, {company2}}
75	{False, {company3}}

Index on Company.stockPrice

Figure 6: *Satisfaction-Indicating Multi-Index* (SMX) organization.

5 Experimental Setup

System Implementation. As described in [19], in order to evaluate the relative performance of the index structures in a real system implementation, we implemented the four index structures in the *MultiView* system using *GemStone* . *MultiView* provides a hierarchical registration service that supports the registration of virtual classes with other classes that they are dependent upon (derived from) and the notification of the former upon modifications performed on the latter [9, 17, 13, 10]. We now extend the system to register all classes along the path query PQ_j with their respective PQV_j view. Our platform is a Sun4m running SunOS 4.1.3 with 32 megabytes of memory.

Test Data. While benchmarks for OODB performance evaluations exist (e.g., the OO7 benchmark [3]), none is designed to evaluate the performance of view systems [11]. Thus, for the purpose of evaluating materialized path query views, we designed a benchmark schema consisting of up to 12 classes named A, B, C, ... L, and M with A at the head and M at the end of the path, each containing one attribute constrained to the set of instances of the next class in the path. Each class includes an instance variable constrained to instances of the next class in the path. For example, class B has an attribute ccc, which is constrained to instances of class C. A path query can thus be expressed: *aaa.bbb.ccc. . .*

Our key parameters include:

- Size of Object (ObjSize)

- Number of Objects per Class (NumObjPerClass)

- Multi-Valued Attribute (ForkWidth): The number of objects referred to by a multi-valued attribute.

- Path Length (PathLen)

- Update position (UpPos): The position of the updated object in the path.

- Fork position (ForkPos): The position(s) of the multi-valued link(s) in the path.

6 Performance Studies

Although we conducted an extensive set of experiments [19], due to space constraints we present only a small subset of these at this time.

6.1 Experiment 1: Materialized v.s. Non-Materialized Views

Our first set of experiments evaluated the cost and benefit of path query view materialization by comparing the cost of performing a variable number (k) of updates and one query (returning the extent of the view). The results indicate that (using the SMX strategy to maintain the materialized view) given a path of length 7, view selectivity around 15%, 1000 forks of width 3 evenly distributed among 7000 objects, object size of 18 bytes, the cost of performing a single query on a non-materialized view is counter-balanced by the cost of propagating approximately 750 updates to a materialized view. This large update/query ratio indicates that materialization of path query views would benefit most applications.

6.2 Experiment 2: Changing the Length of the Path

In order to compare the performance of the SMX indexing strategy to other indexing strategies in the maintainance of materialized path query views, we measured the time needed to maintain a path query view in the face of updates while varying the path length from 3 to 11. We measured both the time for initializing the index and the time for a single update (averaged over 1000 updates). We consider only paths with single-valued attributes, which, as the next experiment demonstrates, is the worst case for SMX.

Figure 7 compares the cost of initializing the index structures. Given a path of length 5, SMX (and MX) takes four times longer than either NX or PX to initialize; given a path of length 11, the (S)MX index is 5.5 times more expensive.

Figure 8 compares the average cost of propagating an update using all four index structures. SMX is the fastest because it doesn't need to traverse forward to identify the exact value of either the original or new end point. MX, NX, and PX all must traverse forward to both new and original end points in order to determine whether or not the update affects the view. In addition, if multiple head objects are associated with the original endpoint, then NX must traverse forward from the head points to the update point in order to identify which were affected by the update. MX is the slowest, because it must also traverse backwards in order to identify affected head points. Note that while in Figure 8 PX performs as well as SMX, this is only true

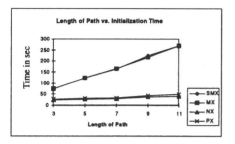

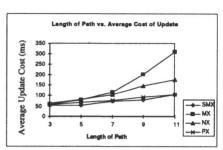

Figure 7: Time to initialize index structures (varying path length). NumObjPerClass=1000, ObjSize=18, No Fork, No multi-references, Update at the middle of path, Selectivity=20%

Figure 8: Update cost (varying path length). NumObjPerClass=1000, ObjSize=18, No Fork, No multi-references, Update at the middle of path, Selectivity=20%

when no multi-valued attribute is present. SMX significantly outperforms PX when multi-valued attributes are introduced (as demonstrated in the next set of experiments).

6.3 Experiment 3: Forks and Multi-Valued References

According to the analytic model [9], multi-valued attributes (forks) and multi-references (converge) greatly increase the cost of maintaining the path query view in the face of updates. We validated that hypothesis by fixing the size of the database (to its default) and the length of the path (to 7), while varying the forking factor of the fifth path element's attribute. That is, given path aaa.bbb.ccc.ddd.eee.fff.ggg.hhh, we vary the fork width at 'eee' from 1 to 6. All other attributes are single-valued.

Figures 9 and 10 show the average time needed to perform updates before (at link 'ddd') and after (at link 'fff') the multi-valued attribute, respectively. The cost of maintaining the view using either the NX and PX increase quickly, because the affected head-points must be identified in order to maintain the index strucutres regardless of whether or not the view content is affected. As shown in Figure 10, SMX consistently outperforms MX by about 50 percent, because the MX strategy must traverse forward to both endpoints in order to determine whether or not the view is affected (whereas the SMX strategy can exploit the *SatInd* boolean for this purpose).

6.4 Experiment 4: Changing the Position of the Update

The position where the update takes place potentially impacts the performance of different index structures. For this experiment, we varied the position of the update from the front to the end of the path (i.e., over positions bbb, ccc, ddd, eee, fff, ggg). We used a long path (PathLen=11) and default settings for all other values. We used no multi-valued attributes or multi-references.

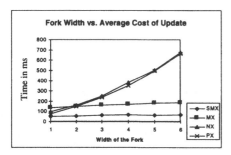

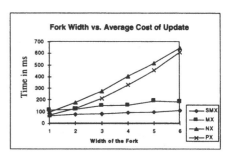

Figure 9: Average cost for one update before the fork (varying width of fork). NumObjPerClass=1000, ObjSize=18, PathLen=7, Fork position = eee, Selectivity=20%, Update position=ddd.

Figure 10: Average time cost for one update after the fork (varying width of fork). NumObjPerClass=1000, ObjSize=18, PathLen=7, Fork Position = eee, Selectivity=20%, Update position=fff.

As shown in Figure 11, both PX and SMX perform very well in the absence of multi-valued attributes. According to the analytic model [9], the closer the updated object is to the head of the path, the higher the costs of traversing forward from it to its endpoints become. This will affect the traditional indices but not SMX. And the closer the updated object is to the end of the path, the lower the costs of traversing forward from the update site to its endpoints becomes. This benefits the traditional indices and would not lead to any advantage for SMX, because SMX never traverses forward. However, when the updated object is closer to the end of the path, then it becomes more expensive to use the multi-index structures to identify the heads of its instantiations. This increases the cost of evaluating updates with SMX and MX. In the case of MX, these two conflicting factors will compete, and the average cost of going one step forward v.s. one step backwards will be a determining factor.

6.5 Experiment 5: Varying the Number of Objects per Class

In this test, we vary the number of objects per class from 100 to 1300 while fixing the length of the path query to seven. The total number of objects in the database thus varies from 100*7 = 700 to 1300*7 = 9100 objects. There is a fork of width three in the middle of the path. Figure 12 shows the average cost of update at "ddd". All four lines go up as the number of objects increases. This is because as the total number of objects increases, the cost of looking up an individual object increases. Also all the index structures become larger, which makes the access more expensive.

6.6 Experiment 6: Evenly Distributed Fork Scenario

In this experiment, we evenly distribute 1000 forks of width 3 among all the 7000 objects in the database. On the average, about 17% of the objects of each class were

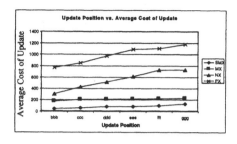

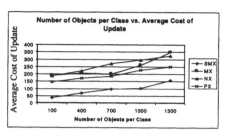

Figure 11: Average cost for update (varying position of update). NumObjPerClass=1000, ObjSize=18, PathLen=11, No Fork, Selectivity=20%.

Figure 12: Average cost for update (varying the number of objects per class). SizeofObject=18, Selectivity=20%, PathLen=7, Fork width=3, Fork at eee, Update at ddd.

multi-valued. The update position was varied while other parameters are fixed to their defaults. Due to space constraints, we omit graphs showing the results of this set of experiments. We found that SMX performs two to ten times faster on average per update. PX and NX become much slower because of the fork. Their trends of higher cost at the end of the path were magnified. On the contrary, SMX and MX become faster since the path length is shorter.

6.7 Discussion

Overall, the *multi-valued* attributes are a chief determining factor. For any fork width greater than 1, SMX performs 2-10 times faster than others. When no multi-valued or multiply-referenced attributes are involved, the performance of SMX is equivalent to PX. Because PX is faster to initialize than SMX, in this scenario it out-performs SMX.

Since SMX takes a longer time to initialize but helps us to update the view faster, the construction of SMX structure is only beneficial if there are *numerous updates*. We found that when there are multi-valued attributes, the cost difference between initializing SMX and traditional indices can typically be balanced by the benefit of using SMX for about (0.01 * Total Number of Objects in Database) updates. When there are no multi-valued attributes, it takes 2 to 3 times more updates to balance the cost difference of initialization.

To find the head points when updating the view, SMX needs to traverse backward. When updates take place at a position close to the end of the path, SMX will need to traverse a longer distance backward. However, even in the worst case for SMX (no multi-valued attributes), on average, SMX was the fastest together with PX.

7 Related Work

Project-Select-Join Views. Although traditional relational databases (RDBs) don't have complex attributes of the object-oriented variety, foreign keys allow tuples to include references to other tuples. Multiple tables can be "joined" using foreign keys to form a relational equivalent to the OO aggregation hierarchy. The relational equivalent of a path query is a select-project-join (SPJ) query. However, path query views, as defined in this paper, are less powerful than the more general SPJ views – and our solution is tuned to take advantage of this fact. A common expense of relational SPJ is the cost of finding a join match in a relational table after following a reference, which our SMX solution allows us to avoid such traversals.

A number of researchers have investigated the problem of maintaining materialized SPJ views in RDBs. Gupta and Blakeley [5] infer knowledge about the state of underlying base relations using local information (such as the view definition, the update, and varying amounts of base relation replicas). They identify classes of materialized views according to the amount of information needed to maintain them in the face of updates and demonstrate necessary and sufficient conditions for determining the amount of information needed to update a materialized SPJ view. Segev and Zhao propose a join pattern indexing technique for materialized rule-derived data that allows the identification of join completion without reading base relations [18]. Join patterns more resemble a PX than an MX, and thus need to be maintained in the face of all updates (unlike the SMX satisfaction indicators).

OODB View Materialization. The only previous work on materialized path query views for OODBs that we are aware of is that of Konomi et al. [8], who use superkey classes to maintain consistency for a particular type of join class formed along an existing path in the aggregation graph. Superkey classes facilitate the incremental update and elimination of duplicates for materialized views produced by relational expressions that include projections. Instead of using external index structures, the authors provide a procedure that transforms class schemas to add new classes that will allow it to satisfy the super-key condition and thus permit incremental updates of the join class. They do not address the more general problem of path query views, which is the focus of this paper, nor do they provide any cost models or performance analyses.

Function Materialization. The work of Kemper et al. on *function materialization* is closely related to OODB view materialization [6, 7]. The goal of function materialization is the precomputation and maintenance of function results. Similar to the SMX *satisfaction indicator* solution, Kemper et al. associate a "validity" value with each object that can serve as an argument to a function. However, our *satisfaction indicators* indicate whether or not the object can be used to reach endpoints that satisfy the path view predicate and allows us to avoid evaluating updates that don't affect view membership. The "validity" value, on the other hand, indicates whether or not the object has been updated and thereby invalidated the stored result. The goal of keeping "validity" values is to facilitate *lazy rematerialization* of the function result.

Indexing Techniques. We utilized the work by Bertino et al. regarding the performance of basic operations with traditional index organizations [2, 4].

8   Conclusions

To the best of our knowledge, ours is the first work to address the specific needs of the path query view problem for OODBs and to present a solution that is tailored to these needs. We introduce a new *Satisfiability Indicating Multi-Index (SMX)* organization, which maintains partial information indicating whether or not the endpoints reachable from an object satisfies the query predicate. We identify a number of tasks required to maintain materialized path query views that involve multiple forward traversals with traditional indices. SMX can be used to eliminate these forward traversals. We also discuss experimental studies we have conducted on a working system implementation in *MultiView* . Our results indicate that the SMX dramatically improves upon the performance of traditional index structures for path query view maintenance.

References

[1] E. Baralis and S. Ceria nd S. Paraboschi. Conservative timestamp revisited for materialized view maintenance in a data warehouse. *Proceedings of the SIG-MOD Workshop on Materialized Views: Techniques and Applications*, pages 1–9, 1996.

[2] E. Bertino and P. Foscoli. Index organizations for object-oriented database systems. *IEEE Transactions on Knowledge and Data Engineering*, 7(2):193–209, April 1995.

[3] M. J. Carey, D. J. DeWitt, and J. F. Naughton. The OO7 Benchmark. *SIGMOD*, pages 12–21, 1993.

[4] S. Choenni, E. Bertino, H. M. Blanken, and T. Chang. On the selection of optimal index configurations in OO databases. In *IEEE Int. Conf. on Data Engineering*, pages 526–537, 1994.

[5] A. Gupta and J.A. Blakeley. Using partial information to update materialized views. *Information Systems*, 20(8):641–662, 1995.

[6] A. Kemper, C. Kilger, and G. Moerkotte. Function materialization in object bases. *SIGMOD*, pages 258–267, 1991.

[7] A. Kemper, C. Kilger, and G. Moerkotte. Function materialization in object bases: Design, realization, and evaluation. *IEEE Transactions on Knowledge and Data Engineering*, pages 587–608, 1994.

[8] S. Konomi, T. Furukawa, and Y. Kambayashi. Super-key classes for updating materialized derived classes in object bases. In *Int. Conference on Deductive and Object-Oriented Databases*, pages 310–326, July 1993.

[9] H. A. Kuno. *View Materialization Issues in Object-Oriented Databases*. PhD thesis, University of Michigan, Ann Arbor, June 1996.

[10] H. A. Kuno and E. A. Rundensteiner. Materialized object-oriented views in *MultiView*. In *ACM Research Issues in Data Engineering Workshop*, pages 78–85, March 1995.

[11] H. A. Kuno and E. A. Rundensteiner. New Benchmark Issues for Object-Oriented View Systems. In *OOPSLA Workshop on Object-Oriented Database Benchmarking*, October 1995.

[12] H. A. Kuno and E. A. Rundensteiner. The satisfiability-indicating multi-index organization for maintaining materialized path query oodb views. Technical Report CSE-TR-302-96, University of Michigan, Ann Arbor, 1996.

[13] H. A. Kuno and E. A. Rundensteiner. The *MultiView* OODB View System: Design and Implementation. In Harold Ossher and William Harrison, editors, *Theory and Practice of Object Systems (TAPOS), Special Issue on Subjectivity in Object-Oriented Systems*. John Wiley New York, 1996.

[14] H. A. Kuno and E. A. Rundensteiner. Using Object-Oriented Principles to Optimize Update Propagation to Materialized Views. In *IEEE Int. Conf. on Data Engineering*, pages 310–317, 1996.

[15] H. A. Kuno and E. A. Rundensteiner. Incremental maintenance of materialized object-oriented views in *multiview*: Strategies and performance evaluation. *To appear in IEEE TKDE*, 1998.

[16] E. A. Rundensteiner. *MultiView*: Methodology for Supporting Multiple Views in Object-Oriented Databases". In *18th VLDB Conference*, pages 187–198, 1992.

[17] E. A. Rundensteiner, H. A. Kuno, Y.-G. Ra, V. Crestana-Taube, M. C. Jones, and P. J. Marron. Demonstration paper: The MultiView Project: Object-Oriented View Technology and Applications. *SIGMOD*, page 555, 1996.

[18] A. Segev and J. L. Zhao. Efficient maintenance of rule-derived data through join pattern indexing. In *Int. Conference on Information and Knowledge Management*, pages 194–205, December 1993.

[19] Y. J. Zhou. Experimental evaluation of materializing path query views in multiview. In *Master's Thesis, WPI*, February 1998.

[20] Y. Zhuge, H. Garcia-Molina, J. Hammer, and J. Widom. View maintenance in a warehousing environment. In *SIGMOD*, 1995.

A Multidatabase Layer for the ODMG Object Model

Mark Roantree

School of Computer Applications, Dublin City University. Ireland.
mark.roantree@compapp.dcu.ie

Jessie B. Kennedy   Peter J. Barclay

Dept. of Computer Studies, Napier University, Scotland.
jessie,pete@dcs.napier.ac.uk

Abstract

The lack of a common object model has been addressed to some extent by the specification of the ODMG Object Model standard. However, the problem still exists for designers of object-oriented multidatabase systems. In this research we propose to use the ODMG object model in a multidatabase environment by specifying an additional layer to manage the further requirements of these applications. This paper describes our definition of a view mechanism and a series of integration operators required for restructuring schemas based on the ODMG-93 standard.

Keywords: Multidatabases, Interoperable Systems, Views, ODMG.

1   Introduction

The ODMG Object Model (ODMG OM) has been proposed as a standard for object-oriented databases in an attempt to provide a uniform model for object-oriented database design [5, 6]. The model's attraction as a standard has seen it employed in a multidatabase environment [7] although it is not necessarily suited to this type of application [16]. If the ODMG OM is to be used in multidatabase environments, a multidatabase layer is required to facilitate additional requirements such as the definition of export and federated schemas [20]. Our research has focused on extending the functionality of the object model through the definition of a Multidatabase Object Definition Language (MODL), based on ODMG's ODL, and a Multidatabase Object Query Language (MOQL), based on ODMG's OQL. This paper describes our work on view support for MOQL to define export and federated schemas.

The paper is structured as follows: the remainder of §1 provides an overview of multidatabase systems; §2 introduces MODL and MOQL and describes our basic view mechanism; §3 describes the MOQL operators we adopt to create federated schemas; §4 illustrates a healthcare example; finally §5 provides some conclusions.

1.1 Background and Motivation

The term *multidatabase* or *federated database* system is used to denote a collection of autonomous heterogenous software systems. They first emerged in [9], and in [20] they proposed a five-layer schema architecture for federated databases which is now the widely accepted standard for these systems. A detailed classification of federated and multidatabase systems can be found in [4]. A more specialised form of multidatabase systems has emerged in the form of object-oriented multidatabase systems [2], where these systems used an object model to represent the global schema.

In the five layer architecture described in [20], the lowest level is occupied by the *local schema* of each participating system which can be any data model. At the next level upwards, we have the *component schema* level. There is one component schema for each local schema in the federation, and each represents the local schema transformed to the common model of the multidatabase system. It may not be desirable to convert the entire local schema to canonical model format and some component schemas may comprise a subset of local schemas. The issues involved in data model transformation are described in [3, 15] among others. The next layer up in the hierarchy is used to provide security. A number of *export schemas* are derived from each component schema in the same manner as views are derived in traditional database systems. Export schemas from separate databases are used to form the next layer, which is the federated schema layer (see *figure 1*). The component, export and federated schemas are all in the multidatabase common model format. At the top level external schemas are derived from federated schemas using the preferred data model of the user. The component and export layers contain views from single schemas, while the federated and external layers contain views across multiple data sources.

Our motivation is to define a view mechanism which can retrieve data from both single and multiple data sources. It is intended that the research is both theoretical and practical in nature as it will be applied to applications in an existing healthcare environment. To this extent, we employ a simple architecture (*figure 1*) which uses CORBA [14, 13] to provide distribution for all schemas from component layers upwards. Component schemas will contain the complex functionality required to interface with local schemas.

Research has shown that object-oriented data models are the most suitable candidate for canonical models [19] owing to their expressive qualities and degree of semantic relativity. By employing the ODMG OM we make use of these characteristics and benefit from using an emerging standard. Our proposed architecture illustrated in *figure 1* demonstrates how we intend to use the ODMG OM to model a multidatabase architecture and our multidatabase extensions ensure that we remain as close as possible to the existing standard. At present we are concentrating on read-only views as existing requirements are to view a more complete patient record in a single view. However, by employing the view architecture described in §2 which attaches oids to derived attributes we will be in a position to offer a limited write facility in the future.

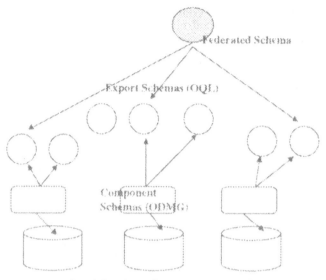

Figure 1: *A Multidatabase Architecture using the ODMG Object Model.*

1.2 Applying the ODMG Model

Although we use ODL to define our schemas, they exist as attribute-function pairs rather than attribute-value pairs. To use ODL in the traditional sense involves creating base schemas rather than virtual schemas and attributes contain physical data as opposed to mapping details. We assume that by specifying an ODL schema, a collection of get() and set() functions are derived for each attribute. We overload these functions with retrieval and (in later work) update operations which communicate with the local schema. This approach has the effect of adding encapsulation at the ODL schema level and provides a means of employing complex functionality to retrieve values from local data sources. A simple example of how this might work could see the following ODL definition for a component schema:

```
interface Patient
( extent Patients
  keys id)
{
    attribute id string;
    attribute lastname string;
    attribute firstname string;
}
```

However, each attribute is a function which returns a string with the exception of one attribute (id for example) which is used to bind each component schema object to an object (or tuple or record) in the local data store. If the component schema is mapped to a relational database then the lastname attribute might look like:

```
lastname()
{
select LastName from Node.Tablename.Name
where Node.Tablename.id = id
}
```

An OQL query which retrieves lastname remains unchanged. Note that this only provides an example of how mapping between component and local schemas might be constructed. A multidatabase system still requires a fully functional Query Service which can use these direct mappings to construct sub-queries and handle inter-schema dependencies.

The layer above the Component Schema Layer is the Export Schema Layer which contains a number of views (export schemas) for each component schema. At present, no formal mechanism exists for view definition in the ODMG OM. Our first task was to provide a view definition mechanism. A discussion on creating views is provided in §2. Export schemas exist as views, defined using MOQL, a superset of OQL. The fourth layer is called the Federated Schema Layer and contains the multiviews (federated schemas) which are constructed from a number of export schemas. They are also defined using MOQL. In simple terms, they are views created on top of existing views.

2 The Object Model and Query Language

We use the core ODMG model for defining schemas by creating types using the Object Definition Language (ODL). In this respect we are fully compliant with the ODMG-93 standard when operating in a centralised database environment. To provide multidatabase functionality, we provide an enhanced Object Query Language which we have called MOQL, as it was designed to handle only the multidatabase components of the system architecture. The view mechanism is included in this layer to retain compliance with the core model. Note that the Unified Modelling Language [8] is used for all object schema illustrations.

2.1 Multidatabase OQL

On one hand, we have provided additional modelling capabilities for ODMG's Object Query Language (OQL) to cater for the advanced needs of multidatabase systems. However, we have found it necessary to restrict the usage of OQL [18] to provide closure for and allow the definition of views for multidatabase modelling. Note that we have included closure and views only in the multidatabase layer to retain compatibility for centralised OODBs with the core ODMG object model.

The core ODMG-93 model provides a mechanism for constructing a type hierarchy and creating instances of user-defined types. We have included a class hierarchy to facilitate collections and views, and treat them as virtual types. This leads to two separate hierarchies: a type hierarchy defined using MODL; and a class hierarchy based on the type hierarchy, but defined using MOQL. This is similar to earlier research [21] where a distinction was drawn between a type hierarchy and a class hierarchy.

2.2 Mapping Virtual Attributes to Base Attributes

In this section we discuss how MOQL can be used to provide a view mechanism similar to that of the relational model. OQL as it stands has no problem creating a query or view on a base type. Using the named query definition feature a query can be created and stored persistently and also serve as a view. The difficulty arises when trying to reuse the view for subsequent view definitions [18]. Since export schemas are views in a multidatabase architecture and federated schemas will be defined using export schemas, it is a necessary to reuse views.

We have adopted an object preserving design for our view mechanism which implies that new oids are not generated for derived objects. Generating new oids leads to well-documented problems [10, 11] which we will discuss briefly in §4.

ODMG defines a type instance as

$$T = \{oid, v\}$$

where oid is a unique identifier and v is a set of attributes $\{a_1, ... a_n\}$ where attributes may be either simple or aggregate types, or simple or complex functions. If we relate an object-oriented type to a relation definition, where an identifier is a primary key, then we could use the object's oid and the theory of functional dependencies to state:

$$oid \longrightarrow \{a_1, a_2, a_3, ..., a_n\}$$

In other words, the oid is acting as a superkey for the set of attributes which describe the type and the superkey functionally determines the attribute set. Using functional dependency axioms [1] the following also holds:

$$oid \longrightarrow \{a_1\}, oid \longrightarrow \{a_2\}, oid \longrightarrow \{a_3\}, ..., oid \longrightarrow \{a_n\}.$$

Thus, an object's identity defines each individual attribute in the object's type. In fact, this represents the minimal set of dependencies in canonical form. Thus, we could also represent a type as

$$T = \{array(oid), v\}$$

where the cardinality of v represents the number of elements in the array of ids. Functional dependencies have been applied to object-oriented databases in the past [22] where the dependencies could navigate through relationships; however, attributes rather than oids were used as the left-hand side of dependencies.

This representation is used in the multidatabase layer to extend the ODMG model although one is easily derived from the other. An ODL type can be transformed to an MODL type by applying the function MODLtype() which converts {oid,v} to {array(oid), v}, by creating an array of oids where the array size equals the number of attributes[1]. Each element of the array is populated with the same oid value. To convert between MODL base types and ODL base types, a function ODLtype() is used to reduce the arrays of oids to a singleton set containing the first element in the array (any element will suffice as they are all equal).

In practical terms, it is not necessary to store an array of equal identifiers for a base object as it would require a major storage overhead. However, MOQL classes will be restructured many times to form derived classes (see §4) and so each derived attribute requires its own individual mapping to its base attribute. Note that we do not provide a mapping to each attribute of a nested type. We rely upon ODMG access paths to retrieve these attributes.

An object can be a member of only one type extent although it may belong to more than one class. For example, a base type may appear in many forms eg a Patient may have a rare bloodtype, may be seeing more than one consultant, and may be resident outside the county. The ODMG model facilitates the creation of groups of objects by defining collections and storing these groups in the type hierarchy. However, they are not dynamic and it may not be practical to design a type hierarchy which takes all of these factors into account when classifying schema types. A view mechanism allows us to group or classify Patient objects using predicates and provides a dynamic picture of each collection at a given time. To facilitate the definition of views we have created a class hierarchy which is separate from the type hierarchy. We use the expanded representation of $T = \{array(oid), v\}$ to model a class to ensure that we can map all derived attributes to their base values.

2.3 On View Semantics

When an object is selected in a view definition, the object and all of its superclasses will be retrieved as part of the view. If no attributes are retrieved that belong to its superclasses, then these will exist as virtual classes only. Thus, by selecting the cd4count attribute in the HIV_Schema database (*figure 2*), the HIV_Patient, Patient, Person and Object classes are retrieved.

The CreateView operator is used to define and store a view, and is composed of a view name and a query specification. For most queries, the query definition part is identical to the OQL syntax used in the standard model's query language. The exceptions are when queries return either values or sets: we permit only the retrieval of sets of objects [18].

---

[1]For the purpose of this discussion, an attribute may have single or multiple values, or can be a system- or user-defined function.

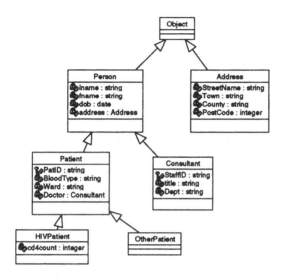

Figure 2: *The HIV_Schema database from the HIV clinic*

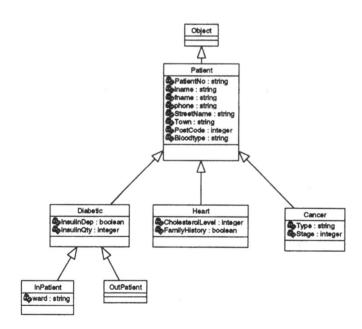

Figure 3: *The PAS_Schema taken from the Patient Administration System.*

2.3.1 Basic Select, Project and Join Views

Using the HIV_Schema database in *figure 2* a selection query to return all HIV
patients who are seeing Doctor Ryan could be defined as:

```
CreateView Ryans_Patients as
select P from Patient P
  where P.Consultant.lname = 'Ryan'
```

This view contains Patient objects, their generalisations, and relationships
for the Patient and any of its generalisations. In this example the view contains
the Object, Person, Address, Patient and Consultant objects. A selection on
the same type might be interested in patients with a bloodtype of 'O' for the
same doctor.

```
CreateView Ryans_Patients_Type0 as
select P from Patient P
where P.Consultant.lname = 'Ryan' AND P.bloodtype = 'O'
```

This view will be structurally identical to the previous but will contain
a projection of its dataset. It is considered unusual to require a join on two
objects from the same schema but it can be accommodated using the integration
operators; in §3 we describe different join operators where objects from different
schemas are combined.

2.3.2 Nested Attributes

A view may contain a base attribute which is a relationship, or may contain a
base type which exists as an attribute in the view. In the first case, it is treated
as a single attribute, and its base type is used to navigate to each attribute
in the nested type. For example, in either of the previous view definitions it
is possible to access the StreetName of each Patient indirectly through their
Address attribute.

In the second example, we require a list of patients and a list of nearby
addresses of consultants. The following query will provide a set of patient
names and a list of addresses for each patient.

```
CreateView Potential_Callout as
select P.FirstName, P.LastName, C.Consultant.Address
  from Patient P, Consultant C
  where P.Address.PostCode = C.Address.PostCode
```

The result is a view which contains a set of Address objects (which resembles
a two-dimensional array of attribute oids) which can be used to navigate to
individual attributes. Suppose two consultants have the same address and this
is stored once physically in the database and we wish to check that two address
objects are the same (the same object as opposed to the same value). Since no
new oids are generated it is necessary to examine the set of attribute oids to
determine if it is the same object.

2.3.3 Views As Attributes

In this section we examine the implication of reusing a view by including it as an attribute in a subsequent view. Assume we wish to reuse the view containing Dr. Ryan's patients in a requirement to list all patients with bloodtype 'O' and match each of these with patients of Doctor Ryan who live in the same area.

```
CreateView AddressList as
select P.FirstName, P.LastName, R.Ryans_Patients
from Patient P, RyanPatients R
where
 Patients.Address.PostCode = Ryans_Patients.Address.PostCode
```

Once again the view will contain a a list of objects containing a oids which map to base attributes and which can be used to retrieve (and provide possible future updates to) the physical values.

3 Schema Integration Operators

In multidatabase systems it is often necessary to restructure schemas prior to integration. For example, two export schemas from two separate component schemas might come from similar environments (eg. General Practitioner (GP) Systems) but may have been designed differently. To integrate schemas requires the restructuring of one or more of them. This requires a set of operators designed for manipulation of object-oriented schemas. The ODMG OM has no need to cater for such operations and these are therefore part of the multidatabase layer.

Most of the operators described below exist elsewhere already [12], but we believe that this particular collection is unique so we will describe them briefly. A large amount of restructuring takes place when the local data model is transformed to a canonical representation. However, restructuring also takes place at the export schema level, as part of the schema integration process. This is necessary as the global DBA uses export schemas from various sources (which are not aware of each other and may be dissimilar) to form the federated schema. In our architecture, this take place on virtual types (views) as the physical objects themselves will never be restructured. The integration operators facilitate the construction of a federated schema. Each federated schema has its own class hierarchy. They share initial class hierarchies constructed from component schema views (as export schemas) but will require their own specialised restructuring layers to generate them. Thus, we begin with a base set of virtual classes (export schemas) and through a series of integration operations (view definitions) compose a federated schema.

3.1 Single Class Operators

The first set of operators are used to restructure a single object-oriented schema. There are a total of six single schema operators: aggregate, separate, subclass, superclass, flatten, and addattr.

The aggregate operator forms a new class from an existing set of attributes inside an existing type or class. The attributes will be replaced with a relationship to the new class.[2] Assume we wish to create a new class from the StreetName, Town, and PostCode atributes from the Patient class in the PAS schema in figure 3. The format for aggregate is :

```
Address = aggregate(StreetName, Town, PostCode) FROM (Patient)
```

The result of this operation is shown in figure 7 where the aggregation is taken from the Person class. The separate operator performs the reverse of the aggregate operator by replacing a relationship with the attributes which make up the related class. Thus, the inverse of the last operation would be:

```
separate(address)
```

All classes which contain a reference to Address will acquire its attributes directly.

There are three operators which deal with inheritance. The subclass operator creates a new subclass C_2 from an existing class C_1 and removes n attributes ($n \geq 0$) from the class C_1 and places them in the C_2, which inherits the remaining attributes from C_1. Assume we wish to create two types of patients: out patients and hospitalised patients from the Patient class in the HIV_Schema database in *figure 2*. We could begin by creating a subclass InP which takes the attribute ward from Patient, and then create a second subclass which initially contains no new attributes. These may be added later using addattr. The format for the operation is :

```
InP = subclass (ward) FROM Patient OutP = subclass FROM Patient
```

The superclass operator creates a new superclass C_0 and places n attributes ($n \geq 0$) from the existing class C_1 inside C_0. This has the effect of creating a generalisation of an existing class. Using the Patient class in figure 3, a new class Person could be created which contains non-medical attributes, and Patient would become a subclass, inheriting the attributes from Person. For example, to create a generalisation Person containing just lastname and firstname

```
Person = superclass(lastname, firstname) FROM Patients
```

The flatten operator has the effect of removing a subclass from the hierarchy and placing its attributes in one of its superclasses. This has the effect of making the schema more relational in structure. For example, we can undo the effects of the previous superclass operation with :

```
flatten Patient INTO Person
```

The addattr operator adds a new attribute to a class while we can delete attributes by defining a projection view.

```
addattr (Bloodtype, string) INTO Patients
```

---

[2]This relationship exists as multiple relationships to individual atrributes when implemented.

3.2 Multiple Class Operators

There are a total of 8 binary operators: join, ojoin, subjoin, osubjoin, superjoin, osuperjoin, nulljoin, and union

Before joining two classes C_1 and C_2 it is necessary to determine what they have in common. There are four possibilities listed below with the operator names in parenthesis:

- C_1 is a subclass of C_2 (subjoin);

- C_1 is equal to C_2 (join);

- C_1 overlaps with C_2 (join or superjoin);

- they have nothing in common (nulljoin).

The basic join operator which joins two classes C_1 and C_2, removes C_2 from the hierarchy but places its attributes inside C_1. For example, we may have a Doctor object from one database, and a Surgeon object from a separate database. In some cases, this will be the same person. The following example demonstrates the join of two such objects where the joining attribute a may be a staff number which is consistent across the hospital.

$$C_1 = \{a,b,c,d,e,f\}$$
$$C_2 = \{a,b,c,g,h\}$$
$$C_3 = \text{join } C_1, \ C_2 \text{ ON a}$$
$$C_3 = \{a,b,c,d,e,f,g,h\}$$

After C_1 and C_2 have been joined on a the result is one single class (C_3) with two added attributes. There are a number of well-documented problems with this type of integration operator. For example, what if $C_1.a = C_2.a$, but $C_1.b \neq C_2.b$? There are a number of possible strategies, based on a predefined ruleset which are outside the scope of this discussion.

The subjoin operator is used to join C_1 and C_2 where C_1 is a subset of C_2. The result places C_2 as a subclass of C_1 in the class hierarchy and removes some attributes from C_2 as they are now inherited from C_1. For example, we may have a Patient object from one database and a Diabetic object from another database. Since Patient is a more general class we can subjoin the specialisation class Diabetic to Patient which results in specialisation attributes remaining in Diabetic and the common attributes residing in the Patient class.

$$C_1 = \{a,b,c\}$$
$$C_2 = \{a,b,c,d,e,f\}$$
$$C_2 = \text{subjoin } C_1, \ C_2 \text{ ON a}$$
$$C_1 = \{a,b,c\}$$
$$C_2 = \{d,e,f\} : \ C_1 \text{ (inherits from } C_1)$$

The superjoin operator has the same semantics as meet in [12]. Two classes C_1 and C_2 are joined through a new superclass C_0 which contains the common attributes from each class. For example, one database exports diabetic patients, and the other database exports HIV patients. We wish to join both databases to provide a larger patient record for those patients who are in both databases.

$$C_1 = \{a,b,c,d,e,f\}$$
$$C_2 = \{a,b,x,y,z\}$$
$$C_0 = \text{superjoin } C_1, \; C_2 \text{ ON a}$$
$$C_0 = \{a,b\}$$
$$C_1 = \{c,d,e,f\} \; : \; C_0 \text{ (inherits from } C_0)$$
$$C_2 = \{x,y,z\} \; : \; C_0 \text{ (inherits from } C_0)$$

The ojoin, osubjoin and osuperjoin operators are outerjoin equivalents of join, subjoin and superjoin respectively. Note that common attributes used in any of the join operations cannot be updated when we examine these issues in the future as our view mechanism maps to a single physical source and these attributes will contain a 1-to-many mapping between derived and base attributes.

The nulljoin operator is used to join two classes C_1 and C_2 which have nothing in common. Although it may be rarely used, it is included for completeness. The result is a new class C_0 with is a superclass of both C_1 and C_2.

$$C_1 = \{a,b,c\}$$
$$C_2 = \{x,y,z\}$$
$$C_0 = \text{nulljoin } C_1, \; C_2$$
$$C_0 = \{\}$$
$$C_1 = \{a,b,c\} \; : \; C_0 \text{ (inherits from } C_0)$$
$$C_2 = \{x,y,z\} \; : \; C_0 \text{ (inherits from } C_0)$$

An example of a nulljoin could be where two different laboratory tests are being run in two separate databases. Neither test has any attributes in common (the test name is the name of the class) but hospital consultants require a printout of all test entries for both test types. We can create a generalisation using nulljoin to provide a abstraction for both tests.

The union operator combines two datasets of indentical structure and is used, for example, to combine two different datasets.

4 A Sample Healthcare Application

In figures 2 and 3 two sample component schemas were illustrated: HIV_Schema from the HIV clinic and PAS_Schema from a Patient Administration Schema dealing with diabetic, heart and cancer patients. Both schemas have been converted to the canonical data model (ODMG) and are modelled using UML notation. An export schema has been defined for each component schema (figures 2 and 3) using MOQL for a department studying patients who are HIV

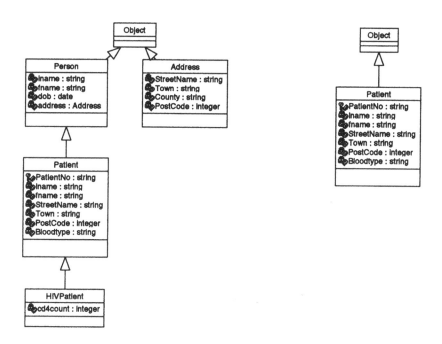

Figure 4: *The HIV Export Schema defined as node1.HIV_Exp1 and the PAS Export Schema defined as node2.PAS_Exp1*

positive, diabetic, and have bloodtype 'O'. It is not necessary to state the location of attributes as it is implied that they are from the subclass (HIV_Patient) in the select statement or in one of its superclasses. Note that this research concentrates on the restructuring and merging operations which take place above the component schema. We must assume that many name differences have been resolved during transformation from local to component schemas.

4.1 Constructing the Federated Schema

To generate a federated schema from the export schemas defined in *figure 4* it is necessary to restructure the PAS_Exp1 view to enable it to resemble the HIV_Exp1 view. There are three steps involved which are illustrated in figures 5, 6 and 7. We begin by creating a supertype for Patient which is called Person.

```
Step 1
    CreateView node2.TempView1 as
    (Person = superclass (lname,fname,StreetName,Town,PostCode)
    FROM Patient)
    FROM node2.PAS_Exp1
```

At an implementation level, this is a straightforward mapping of attributes in the current view (containing classes Object, Person, Patient) to attributes

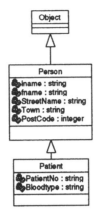

Figure 5: *PAS View after step 1*

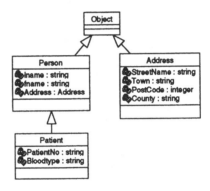

Figure 6: *PAS View after step 2*

in the original view (containing classes Object, Patient). We then create a new class called *Address* from *Patient*.

    Step 2
      CreateView node2.TempView2 as
      (address = aggregate(StreetName,Town,PostCode) FROM Patient,
      addattr (County, string) into Address)
      FROM node2.TempView1

Our current design maps new attributes to NULL values as no attribute exists in the physical database to hold a newly derived attribute, and we are presently concerned with read-only views. We now add some attributes to the existing classes.

    Step 3
      CreateView node2.TempView4 AS

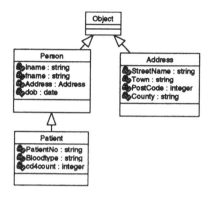

Figure 7: *PAS View after step 3*

```
(addattr (dob, date) into Person
addattr (cd4count, integer) into Person)
FROM node2.TempView3
```
Before joining the schemas it is necessary to restructure the *HIV_Exp1* schema slightly. Since we are only dealing with one type of patient (an HIV patient) in the *HIV_Exp1* export schema, we can *flatten* the *HIVPatient* subclass into its superclass.

Step 4
```
CreateView node1.TempView1
(flatten HIVPatient INTO Patient)
from node1.HIV_Patient
```
This has the effect of placing the *cd4count* into the *Patient* class and removing the *HIVPatient* from the hierarchy. Finally, we can use the *join* operator to construct the federated schema. This has the effect of creating a federated view which contains only those patients which occur in both databases. If we wished to include all patients from both databases, then we would use the *ojoin* operator.

Step 5
```
CreateView Diabetic_HIV_Patients AS
(join node1.TempView1, node2.TempView3 on PatID)
```

4.2   Federated Queries

Using the federated schema constructed in §4.1, we can generate a list of patients and their addresses living in Dublin with a cd4count of '15'. The following OQL query is passed to the *Diabetic_HIV_Patients* by the global user:
```
select lname, fname, address
from Diabetic_HIV_Patients
where address.county = 'Dublin' AND cd4count = '15'
```

The query is broken down until it can be passed to a single node. Thus, the above query becomes :

```
select lname, fname, address
from node1.TempView1
where address.county = 'Dublin' AND cd4count = '15'
select lname, fname, address
from node2.TempView3
where address.county = 'Dublin' AND cd4count = '15'
```

The second subquery is dropped as it has no *cd4count* attribute and thus, cannot return a result. The first subquery must be restructured and passed to the *PAS_Schema* component schema using the reverse set of operations used to construct the federated schema. In this example, we have only one more step to reverse (step 4 in §4.1) which flattened the *HIVPatient* specialisation into *Patient*. The subquery can then be passed to the component schema which queries the local schema and passes the results back to the federated schema. A post-processing query is then required (the set of restructuring operators used to construct the federated schema) to restructure the result set for the federated schema. The federated schema query (itself a view) is populated with objects containing attribute mappings to objects in various component schemas (in this case, a single component schema).

4.3 Component to Local Schema Mappings

To explain how we map to physical data it is necessary to understand the structure of the component schema. It is necessary for the component schema to contain one object for every object in the local database (or for every object the local database is willing to share). We assume that an ODL compiler generates a list of get() and set() functions for each attribute in the schema. These methods are overloaded with the functionality required to read and write the physical attributes in local schemas (described briefly in §2 and in some detail in [17]). It is intended that the component schema contain only one physical attribute i.e. the identifier of the mapped object in the local schema. This may be an oid for an object-oriented database, a tuple identifer for a relational database, or a primary key. With an ODMG database, an oid is automatically generated for each object added to the component schema. These oids are used by views to map to the base objects in component schemas, and from there, it is possible to query physical data values.

Each of the attributes in the PAS Export Schema defined in figure 3 will have an oid attached to it. As the object presented to the user is restructured (see figures 5, 6 and 7), attributes must exist as (name, oid mapping) pairs but no new oids are created for newly derived classes. Programmers may wish to materialise some views and make use of their oids to pass object identifiers to some application process. This has the effect of creating a snapshot of the database. This is one mechanism for overcoming limitations of an object preserving semantics.

5 Conclusions and Future Research

In this paper we described a design for a multidatabase layer which lies above the ODMG object model. One of our objectives is to retain compliance with the ODMG standard. We achieve this when our ODMG database is used in a centralised environment. This compliance is only compromised for operations which are distributed in nature but we still retain a close compatibility. We described a viewing mechanism which uses ODMG oids to map between derived and base attributes, and can be used to define export and federated schemas in a multidatabase environment. We also included a collection of integration operators which operate on export schemas (views or virtual classes) to form federated schemas. The examples provided in §4 demonstrate how the distributed architecture is expected to work in a target healthcare environment. At present we support read-only operations but we feel that our object preserving semantics will allow some write capability in future revisions.

Our current research is focused on finalising the multidatabase version of ODL (MODL) and on examining ways to integrate behaviour in the view mechanism. We feel that our architecture is practical in nature and are planning a prototype implementation which will be employed at St. James' Hospital in Dublin as part of the research effort at Dublin City University. We are also concentrating on porting our current specification to work with the recently published ODMG 2.0 standard [6] which now uses a combination of classes and interfaces to define ODMG types.

References

[1] Armstrong W. Dependency Structures of Database Relationships. *Proceedings of IFIP Congress*, 1974.

[2] Bukhres O. and Elmagarmid A. (eds). *Object-Oriented Multidatabase Systems*. Prentice Hall, 1996.

[3] Batini C., Lenzerini M. and Navathe S. A Comparative Analysis of Methodologies for Database Schema Integration. *ACM Computing Surveys*, vol. 18, no. 4, December 1986.

[4] Bright M., Hurson A. and Pakzad S. A Taxonomy and Current Issues in Multidatabase Systems. *IEEE Computer*, December 1991.

[5] Cattell R. (editor). *The Object Database Standard: ODMG-93*. Morgan Kaufmann, 1996.

[6] Catell R. and Barry D.(eds). *The Object Database Standard: ODMG 2.0*. Morgan Kaufmann, 1997.

[7] Conrad S., Hasselbring W., Heuer A., Saake G.. Engineering Federated Database Systems. *Proceedings of the CAISE 97 Workshop*, Preprint 6/1997, University of Magdeburg, 1997.

[8] Eriksson H. and Penker M. *The UML Toolkit*, Wiley, 1998.

[9] Heimbigner D. and McLeod D. A Federated Architecture for Information Management. *ACM Transactions on Office Information Systems*, Vol. 3, No. 3, 1985.

[10] Kim W. and Kelley W. On View Support in Object-Oriented Database Systems in *Modern Database Systems: The Object Model, Interoperability, and Beyond*, Won Kim (ed), Addison-Wesley, 1995.

[11] Lausen G. and Vossen G. *Models and Languages of Object Oriented Databases*. Addison Wesley, 1997.

[12] Motro A. Superviews: Visual Integration of Multiple Databases. *IEEE Transactions on Software Engineering*, vol. se-13. no. 7, 1987.

[13] Mowbray T. and Zahavi R. *The Essential CORBA: System Integration Using Distributed Objects*. Wiley, 1996.

[14] Orfali R., Harkey D. and Edwards J. *The Essential Distributed Objects Survival Guide*. Wiley, 1996.

[15] Pitoura E., Bukhres O. and Elmagarmid A. Object Orientation in Multidatabase Systems. *ACM Computing Surveys*, Vol. 27, No. 2, June 1995.

[16] Roantree M. Evaluating the ODMG Object Model for Usage in a Multidatabase Environment. *Technical Report No. CA-2597*, Dublin City University, 1997.

[17] Roantree M., Hickey P., Crilly A., Cardiff J., Murphy J. Metadata Modelling for Healthcare Applications in a Federated Database System. *Intl. Workshop on Trends in Distributed Systems*, LNCS No. 1161, 1996.

[18] Roantree M., Kennedy J. and Barclay P. Providing Views and Closure for the ODMG Object Model. *Submitted for publication*, 1998.

[19] Saltor F., Castellanos M. and Garcia-Solaco M. Suitability of Data Models as Canonical Models for Federated Databases. *SIGMOD Record* vol. 20, no. 4, 1991.

[20] Sheth A. and Larson J. Federated Database Systems for Managing Distributed, Heterogeneous, and Autonomous Databases. *ACM Computing Surveys*, vol. 22, no. 3, September 1990.

[21] Scholl M., Schek M and Tresch M. Object Algebra and Views for Multi-Objectbases. *Proceedings of Workshop on Distributed Object Management*, 1992.

[22] Weddell G. A Theory of Functional Dependencies for Object-Oriented Data Models. *Proceedings of 1st DOOD*, North Holland, 1989.

REUSE

The re-use of Multimedia Objects by Software Agents in the Kimsac system

Ray Mc Guigan, Patrice Delorme, Professor Jane Grimson,
Department of Computer Science, Trinity College Dublin
Patricia Charlton, Yasmin Arapha, Professor E. Mamdani
Department of Electrical and Electronic Engineering
Imperial College of Science, Technology and Medicine, London

Abstract:
The Kimsac system is an agent mediated multimedia system running on a touch-screen kiosk and providing real-time information on jobs vacancies, training and income support to Irish citizens. The distributed system accesses legacy databases. Multimedia objects are described (using an asset description tool which associates a script with each asset) and this description is used by the agent infrastructure for the rendering of screen assets through a Presentation System. Content Handlers, written in Java, allow for the reuse of the multimedia objects by enabling the display of atomic or composite objects.

Introduction

The Kimsac system (ACTS AC030) is an agent-mediated multimedia system, which provides public service information to citizens through a touchscreen kiosk. It is a distributed system with 12 PC-based kiosks running from a central server in a major public trial in Government offices and libraries in the Republic of Ireland during the first half of 1998.

In Kimsac the user is interacting with a number of agents through the metaphor of a Personal Services Assistant. Interactions by the user (pressing a button, selecting a service or entering a magnetic card) are passed to a relevant agent which carries out any processing required and returns a number of objects to the Presentation System for display. The Presentation system then uses abstractions known as Content Handlers to present these objects on the screen. The Content Handlers instantiate objects on the screen and some of these objects will be interactive - allowing the user to make further choices.

In order to make efficient use of multimedia objects, and allow the agents to make selections, there is an object ontology, a domain database and asset descriptions which allow the agent make decisions on what object to use. Objects are decomposed to their simplest definition and then given attributes, combined with other objects as necessary. In other words there is one object "button". It may have various attributes such as colour, placement etc. In some circumstances it will be combined with other objects to make a navigation bar or some other composite object. Thus in terms of assets it is only necessary to have one "button object" on the system and its attributes can be supplied when it is necessary to render it. To more fully explain the interaction between objects, asset model and agents we will describe each in more detail.

1.0 Asset Model

Multimedia content is viewed in terms of service-provisioned descriptions that provide visual meaning for the presentation system as well as augmented attributes instantiated when used within a particular application domain. The contextual semantic, visualisation entities, as well as the relation-ships among objects are what explicitly model the assets. The assets are abstracted encapsulations of this information providing a means by which the asset manager can interpret the underlying semantics of the object being used and the by presentation system to understand the mechanisms and services required for rendering the multimedia objects.

The underlying conceptual model of these assets is that they are object abstractions that provide content-based data which translates into knowledge about the multimedia objects. Assets are conceptually characterised as objects in the sense that are encapsulated, inherit parent characteristics, are visible, have a defined location and contain functional methods. The asset abstractions are described as meta-data templates that encapsulate semantic annotations of the Media Content, Domain (service provided), Tasks and Actions as defined earlier.

1.1 Meta Data Template

The meta-data template is defined by a meta-data language. The syntax of which is expressed in BNF (terms, expressions etc.), that determine the grammar that defines the meta-data structure. The structure is the ontological level between the meta-data template and the meta-data language and is necessary if the language definitions need to be changed (this is common in computationally reflective systems). This is the level at which asset descriptions and service descriptions have a common model. The actual structure for an asset template takes the following set of terms: header, content (composite or atomic), domain, script and task. Each term is specialised by a set of phrases, which are applicable within a service model. The syntax has to be refined using delimiters.

The multimedia data model defined here, addresses the aspects related to data presentation, manipulation and content-based retrieval. It provides a set of requirements based on which the asset manager can function. The asset model is to contain many asset descriptions which will allow the selection of assets for potentially any purpose. The purpose of this model is to dynamically generate objects for the Presentation System to render or for use with other applications that require objects of similar characteristics. The importance of the flexibility of the model is to not only to facilitate asset reuse with one application but moreover to allow other applications to also reuse these dynamically generated assets, thus supporting an open service architecture.

The base Asset model consists of:

- Multimedia Description, providing an annotated view of the raw data;
- Visual Description, aiding a presentation service in describing the temporal and spatial relationships among different assets;
- Content Semantics, giving a semantic view of the stored multimedia objects; in addition to
- Service Description, instantiated according to a application domain.

The asset model identifies two types of assets: atomic assets and composite assets. An Atomic asset is the smallest and (in principle) indivisible object that can comprise part of one or more aggregate assets. A composite asset is an aggregate of atomic assets or other composite assets that collectively form a more complex abstraction of the content. These assets are expressed in the form of meta-data descriptions that encompass abstract information about the multimedia objects into a compact representation.

Most multimedia environments are likely to require a rich variety of devices to support presentation services for handling the various types of media, by so, creating a large degree of heterogeneity. The Kimsac asset model augments the data model with system specific information required to reference the content as well as to present the data. As such, Asset descriptors are defined on two levels: descriptors that are directly derived from the data content in terms of its underlying contextual emphasises, and descriptors that are not directly determined from the content but are related to the ontology, or the physical characteristics (which include geometric specifications such as position and orientation).

The latter are included so that they may be decomposed into retrieval entities, which when combined with content-based retrieval entities provide for successive layers of retrieval detail. These descriptions are modifiers of the media types and as such do not fundamentally affect the nature of the content. The set of meaningful properties defined greatly depends on the media type itself, and according to our experimental results within the Kimsac system, the properties identified have proven to be sufficient enough to form an infrastructure for a general Asset Model while remaining specific enough to fulfill presentation service requirements.

1.2 Descriptor Properties of Assets

Assets used in the Kimsac systems are basically defined in terms of entities that make up a screen display, providing some type of multimedia service. The Atomic Asset content defined in our system are buttons, images, sound, video, fields, text, as well as several others. Among the various Assets defined, the Button asset is the most widely used, mainly because it is the most appropriate means of user interaction with kiosk-based touch screen interfaces. We shall, therefore, use it as an example to illustrate the descriptor properties defined for this kind of Asset.

The following illustration box shows the physical properties used to describe a Button atomic asset. The content_handler_details define content-based properties related to a Button as a visualised object, whereas, the layout_details determine the non content-based properties related to layout, geometry and orientation. Properties describing the Domain, Task and Action information, discussed earlier, give the asset a semantic outlook of its intended functionality and purpose. These are instantiated in association with the particular application domain in which an Asset will be used. The Assets are, thus, independent of the application domain and can be reused regardless of the application they are used in.

```
atomic([id,bbatom,
       layout_details(workarea, [preferredLocation, [80,234],

       alignment,south,layout,horizontal,
                                 padding,0,expand,both,color,gray
                  ]),
       content_handler_details('ButtonCH', [setUpImage,string,
                                 'drbutup.GIF',setDnImage,string,
                                 'drbutdn.GIF',setOffImage,string

                                 'drbutoff.GIF',setActiveSound,st
                  ring,
                                 'snd1.au',setInactiveSound,strin
                  g,
                                 'sndmain.wav',setEnabled,string,
                                 true,setLabel,string,'Financial
                  Details',
                                 setFontName,string,helvetica,set
                  FontSize,
                                 integer,36,setFontStyle,string,p
                  lain,
                                 setFontColor,string,magenta,
                                 setTextAreaSize,integer,[300,220
                  ]]),
       domain_properties(['SWS']),
```

Figure 1; Physical properties used to describe a Button atomic asset

The illustration box (Figure 2 below) demonstrates the use of the above atomic description to build a composite asset that could contain one or more atomic asset descriptions. The composite description format follows a similar structure to that of an atomic description. Again, physical and content-based details are defined, here, describing the composite entity as a whole.

Embedded atomics would inherit the layout-details defined on this level unless overridden by layout-details at lower levels based on a set of priority rules. Such composite asset can either be described at the development phase by manual user entry or can be dynamically generated at runtime as a result of an agent request for an asset that satisfies given criteria of required functionality and visual effects.

For simplicity, the following description is an extract of a more complex description, but it does demonstrate the general components of the description structure. Any additions to the above would follow the same format.

```
composite([id,wserv,
        layout_details(workarea,[preferredLocation,[80,234],
              alignment,south,layout,horizontal,padding,
              0,expand,both,color,gray]),
atomic([id,bbatom,
        layout_details(workarea,[preferredLocation,[80,234],

alignment,south,layout,horizontal,padding,
                    0,expand,both,color,gray]),
        content_handler_details('ButtonCH',[setUpImage,string,
                            'drbutup.GIF',setDnImage,string,
                            'drbutdn.GIF',setOffImage,string,
                    'drbutoff.GIF',setActiveSound,string,
                    'snd1.au',setInactiveSound,string,
                    'sndmain.wav',setEnabled,string,
                    true,setLabel,string,'Financial Details',
                    setFontName,string,helvetica,setFontSize,
                            integer,36,setFontStyle,string,plain,
                    setFontColor,string,magenta,
                    setTextAreaSize,integer,[300,220]]),
                        domain_properties(['SWS']),
                        script([[dotask,
                        buildProfile_FinanceDetails,
                         meta(bindables(RP trans:bp
                        buildProfile_FinanceDetails)}]]),
        task([buildProfile_FinanceDetails]]])
atomic([id,bbatom,
            layout_details([]),

        content_handler_details('ButtonCH',[setUpImage,'drbutup.GIF',
                    setOffImage,string,'drbutoff.GIF',setActiveSound,
                    string 'snd1.au',setInactiveSound,string,
                    'sndmain.wav',setEnabled,string,true,setLabel,
                    string,'Income Support', ...]
            domain_properties(['SWS']),
            script([[dotask,income_support,script]]),
            task([income_support])]),
    .
    .
    .
    domain_properties(['SWS']),
    script([[dotask,domain,script]]),
    task([domain])]])
```

Figure 2; Building a composite asset that could contain one or more atomic asset descriptions

1.3 Asset Description syntax

We have developed a syntax and a structure for describing Assets. The description language-base includes a terminology and a set of basic atomic properties that are defined as contextual implications giving the described objects their functional semantics. The language adopted is of limited expressiveness but does promote the simplicity of use as its most important feature.

This syntax is modelled in terms of the following entities.

Object type   specifying the multimedia type,

Content-based properties   describing the object content which will contribute to its functional semantics,

Non-content-based properties, including conceptual and physical properties, where:

Conceptual properties include:

domain   denoting a subset of the ontology

tasks   denoting actions or functional roles

scripts   tasks are associated with scripts that are used to represent a sequence of instructions

Physical properties, such as layout and location, denote attributes that aid in the physical representation of objects when passed to the Presentation System.

The structure uses a set of constructors for building the Atomic Asset descriptions. Defining combined instances of these, build up the composite description where each component is a variant of the atomic building blocks providing information layering for more complex assets. The content definition structure is defined in the form (see section 3 for the conceptual details of the asset description):

Header

        asset-identifier

        asset-type (atomic, composite)

Body

        content-handler-Properties

        layout-properties

        domain-properties

        tasks

        script

The Kimsac system attempts to identify all domain objects and classify relationships between various subsets based on their physical properties and relevant actions. These actions are taken as indicators of semantic associations between subsets of assets. Asynchronous instantiations of which are initiated at run-time by user interaction or agent back-calls. When used within the presentation system these actions will notify the agent world for appropriate reaction.

2.0 Agents and Multimedia Objects; Ontological View

The understanding of content for Agents is based on a logical view. For example an agent providing a service, such as access to database information, does not need to know the presentation format of that database information. This permits flexibility in both the presentation of information and service delivery. The content provided is understood by a service agent at an abstract level, either via a task or domain object level. The semantics of the content at an abstract level is encapsulated as an asset description. Understanding this asset description, from a distributed perspective, is termed as a base-ontological level. This simply means an interface to the multimedia objects.

However, the service agent does not understand multimedia content but reasons about content at a task and domain level and can apply an "action" to this multimedia content and hence specialise its interaction. The selection of multimedia objects and management of the objects is at an asset description level. A relationship between the components that make an asset description are statically supported by an asset tool where the first level of asset development is done.

The retrieval of the assets for agents is via the component called the asset manager, which permits changes to the asset description though adding bindings into the asset description. At one level this binding is just data that has a particular format. However, once the asset description is converted from a semantic structure to a visual multimedia display the result of an interaction is determined by these bindings. This design separation of agents from multimedia objects means that the multimedia objects can change without effecting the agents and the service agents can change without effecting the multimedia presentation as domain data is dynamically initialised at run time.

2.1 Asset Description Models

The asset description permits the sharing of four models across a distributed system to allow open service provision (see also figure 3):

- Media content: defines properties, types and values to be understood by the presentation system, which will render the media content interpreting the property values to specialise the content.
- (Service) Domain view: defines intended use of the content, that is, which service is this intended for. This is used as one level of integration between the service agents and the asset manager and another level between the content description and the presentation system.
- Task model: this is used by the agents and can be used by the presentation end to support navigation.
- Action model: supports the understanding what should happen when the media object is interacted with. This action model is supported by a scripting language. Certain actions are dynamic and are replaceable. This allows the agents to specialise the type of actions that should be executed when the user interacts with a media object. Some actions are static and are directly related to visual changes, which will occur. The actions specialised by an agent usually specify the type of return information about the current event that the agent is interested in.

The asset description shows how the ontology of the four main models can be shared to enable an open service architecture. Of course there are other ontologies required as well, but these ontologies do not affect multimedia content integration but are necessary for distributed service provision. For example, the asset manager has a knowledge base which contains a set of asset descriptions.

These asset descriptions in the Kimsac architecture co-ordinate the four models. The asset manager only reasons about three of these models, the task model (used for selecting the asset description), the domain model and the action model. The action model represents the relationship between the task and the domain. When the asset manager is operating with other agents this script is supplied dynamically by other agents. Part of the asset manager's task is to bind in new actions for an agent. Also, the asset manager binds new values for domain properties.

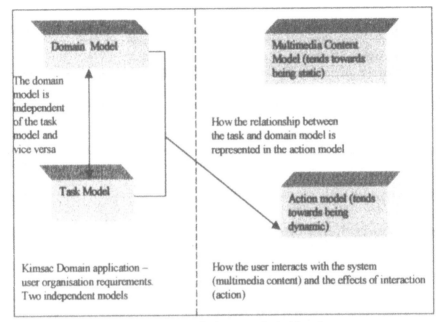

Figure 3: Asset Description Supporting the Base-ontological Level

The ontological level means the intended interpretation and can be considered as a set of constraints. These constraints provide the mechanism for understanding the intended meaning of the knowledge representation as applied to the conceptual level. For the asset manager the ontological level *is* the asset description. The asset description is understood as a template, which enables the asset manager to impose an intended meaning of the content. In the main the asset manager ignores the multimedia content, as the asset manager is concerned with the logical understanding of the information and not the visual representation. By logical we mean the semantic abstraction without having to understand an image file etc. An asset description is selected via a task request. The asset manager has a syntax model of the asset description template. This syntax model of the asset description model allows the asset manager to reason about the descriptions finding where new bindings are necessary.

When knowledge representation formalism is constrained in such a way that its intended models are made explicit, it can be classified as belonging to the ontological framework. For this to apply to the asset description, a deeper understanding of the different models is required. The asset description is the base meta-level of the ontological level. However, the intention of the asset description is to be understood by both the asset manager and the presentation system (of course there is a certain level of understanding by the agents). These two components have two views of the asset description. The syntax of the asset description is part of the ontological level as this enables the asset manager and the presentation system to understand the description in a way that is relative to the context of the user's interaction. This context originates from the user's interaction and is interpreted by the agents reasoning about the user's context based on the type of tasks the user has initiated.

Figure 3 also shows the content not directly used/linked to the other shared models. In reality it is associated with the domain. The domain contains the information requirements while the multimedia content is the visualisation. However, there is no dynamic task directly associated with the multimedia content and the dynamic action (bound at run time) is only associated via the task domain relationship (static actions can be associated either before or during system run time). This means that if new content is developed and associated with the same domain properties and tasks, the content can be selected with out making any changes to the Kimsac service architecture. This is only one of the levels where this architecture provides an open service mechanism.

3.0 Content Handlers

In order to keep the presentation system open and to insulate the interface designers, agents, and databases from any specific code, the asset description is rendered by Content Handlers (CHs) which are developed independently from the rest of the system. They are the "lego bricks" on which the application relies to display information. A content handler is a piece of self contained code which renders a specific media. It sits on the presentation end, and is instantiated by the Presentation System (PS) which passes to it the asset descriptions.

The CHs extend a very small common interface, well known by the PS, that suffices for the PS to forward what ever asset description it receives from the back end. The PS role is to deal with screen layout and to offer communication mechanisms between the content handlers and the back end. The content handlers take in charge the loading of media files, their rendering and give a consistent feedback of the user interaction with itself. Because of this architecture Content handlers and asset description are tightly coupled. A number of simple content handlers have been created: image, text, button, video, HTML and audio.

3.1 Composite Content Handlers

From a theoretical point of view those CHs should be able to handle any type of user interaction. However to limit the complexity of the asset description, to achieve better reuse of specific configuration of content handlers and for reasons of efficiency a second set of content handler has been developed : Counter, Header, Navigation bar, Numerical Keyboard, Generic Choice Mechanism. This second set of content handlers is application specific and implements some special effects not achievable using the basic CHs. For instance the Navigation bar is intended to remain on the screen all the time and might render some specific animation so that it's interface mechanism is better understood by the user.

3.2 Specialisation

A content handler is a piece of UI expert code ready for specification. It doesn't contain any reference to any media file it has to render before they are instantiated. After creation and before initialisation, their properties are set by the PS using a set of specific setter methods. Those methods are unknown by the PS and given by the asset description. Once the initialization is done the Content handler is ready to display its data. From this point onward the content handler is rendered and the user can start to interact with its interface.

3.3 Events

When the user interacts with the CH, the event is filtered by the CH, and relayed to the back end by sending a predefined message. For instance, in the case of a button it would send "button-pushed" which is then caught at the back end. As always the PS only forwards the message to who ever it belongs.

3.3.1 Updates and communications

In order to refresh information displayed by a content handler, a second mechanism has been put in place. Content handlers can subscribe to a specified field in the Domain Object Database (DODB) owned by the PS. When the information changes in the subscribed field, the content handler is warned and the new value is passed on. The information (image, audio, text, value) can then be updated on the screen as soon as it changes in the system. This Domain Object Database can be used as well to send messages in the other direction. For instance the Numerical Keyboard updates the field in the DODB each time the users presses a key so that when there is a requirement for the user to enter a number it can be aware of the user input by subscribing to the same field in the DODB. This DODB mechanism is very important in the openness of the content handlers because it handles all the communication transparently. The content handler doesn't need to know about its task partners nor the partners need to know about the specificity of one content handler.

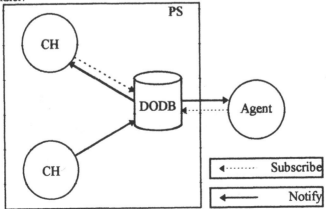

Figure 4; Composite content handler.

The PS knows how to deal with two types of content handlers. Atomic and composite. Composite CHs are containers of content handlers. They are used only for layout purposes and can handle various ways of laying down atomic or composite content handlers. Typically a screen is defined as composites of composites of atomics. This way the designer has a control on how the atomics are going to be laid.

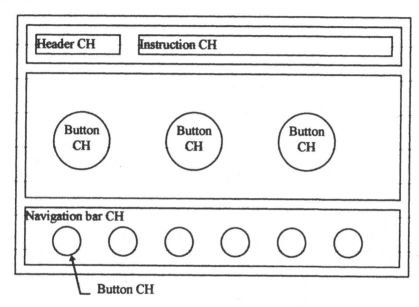

Figure 5; Making up a composite from atomic content handlers

A composite doesn't do anything else than dealing with layout. It can how ever be extended to create customised content handler. For instance the navigation bar extends a composite. That easier the development when other content handlers can be reused and unable the implementation of global behaviours i.e. "Navigation bar button #3 pressed" rather than "button #445 pressed". Another example would be a calculator CH extending composite so that the calculator doesn't care much about the layout.

4.0 Using the Asset Tool in Interface Design

The flexibility which the Asset Tool allows in describing a core set of main assets which can then be slightly altered within the asset description and reused was ideal for the generic model of Kimsac.

The typical Kimsac client was identified early in the design process as someone with little or no previous interaction with the type of multimedia kiosk that was being proposed. Therefore, it was viewed as vital that the Graphical User Interface was one that they would become quickly familiar with. The primary goal in designing the interface was to keep it is as consistent and generic as possible, to create an environment where the user could quickly and confidently achieve his goals.

The following diagram shows the description of the screen

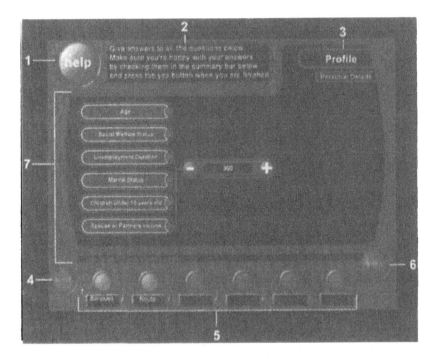

Figure 6; The Kimsac User Interface showing instantiated objects

1. This is where KIM, the helper or guide, is positioned. She introduces each new screen with a short video explaining what the user should do. When the video stops playing, she turns into a help button, as seen above.

2. This is the instruction text which KIM speaks at the introduction of each screen.

3. This is the header or title of the screen.

4. This is the exit button allowing the user to quit.

5. This is the navigation bar, showing the user where they have come from and allowing them track back to a previous screen if they need to.

6. This is the Yes button, allowing the user confirm certain actions that he makes in the work area.

7. This is the main part of the screen, the workarea, where the user does most of their interaction. All the other parts described above are consistent throughout the entire system and were easily described by making minor modifications to the Atomic Assets within the Asset Tool. Within the work area, there is more complexity with 5 templates being used. The one shown above is the generic choice mechanism which the client uses to give answers to a set of values.

The work area above is described in the following way in the Asset Tool:

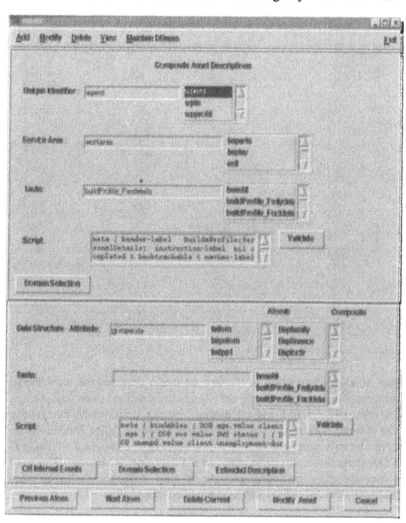

Figure 7, Using the asset tool to describe objects

This is the component screen outlining the main attributes associated with this asset – identifier, service area, task, etc. The data structure is displayed in the lower half of the screen, allowing the asset designer review what collection of atomics or composites aerve to make up the full asset. From a multimedia design point of view, the next screen is the more interesting. This is what we see when we check the extended description of any particular object.

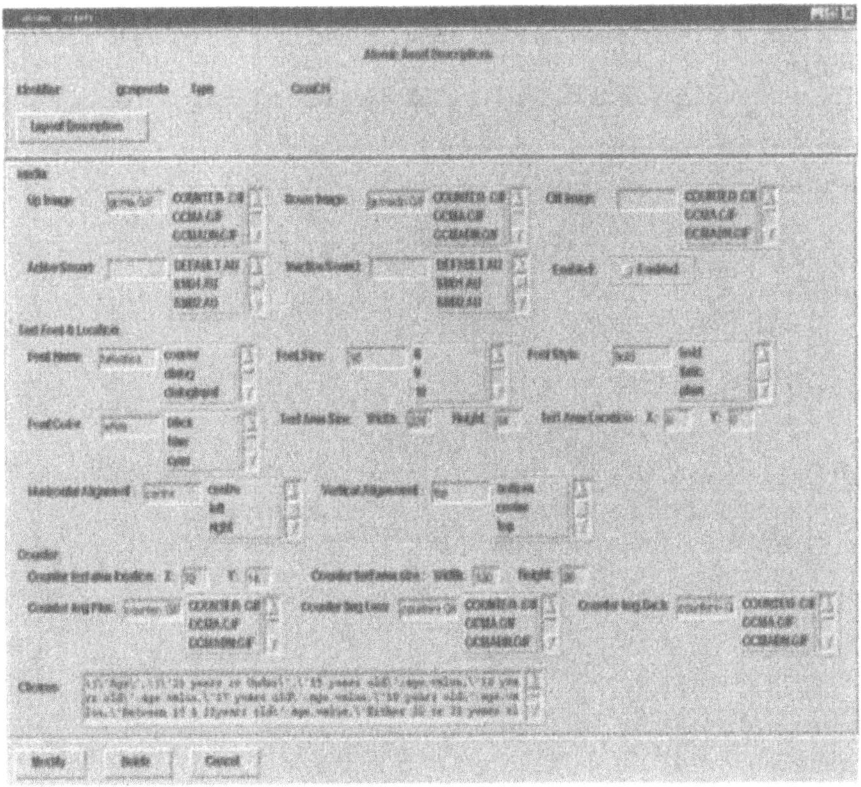

Figure 8, Extended Object Description

This gives an exact description of the various media elements that combine to make up the asset. This, of course really only needs to be defined once. The buttons and sounds, font sizes for text and positioning remains static, given the generic nature of the system. Given that this describes the Generic Choice Mechanism as seen in the Kimsac screengrab, the data structure which can be seen in the "Choices" field is the only thing that needs to be modified if a new asset is required. This is an advantage over the more traditional method of asset description whereby each button would have to saved individually, and modified individually.

5.0 Conclusion

The Kimsac system makes use of re-usable multimedia objects through use of an Asset Model, a Domain Database and an Object Ontology displaying these objects using Content Handlers. By doing so the extension or maintenance of the system is greatly simplified. The complexity of object storage is greatly reduced and the work of interface design is abstracted from the mechanics of object rendering.

The Kimsac consortium consists of seven partner organisations in five countries and receives funding from the European Commission under the ACTS Programme.

References

[1] P. Charlton, E. Mamdani, O. Olsson, J. Pitt, F. Somers, A. Waern, "An Open Agent Architecture Supporting Multimedia Services on Public Information Kiosks," *Proc. 2nd Int. Conf Practical Application of Intelligent Agents and Multi-Agent Technology (PAAM '97)*, pp 445-465, 1997.

[2] P. Charlton, E. Mamdani, O. Olsson, J. Pitt, F. Somers, A. Waern, "Using an Asset Model for integration of Agents and Multimedia to Provide an Open Service Architecture, Multimedia Applications, Services and Techniques," *Lecture Notes in Computer Science, (ECMAST '97)*, pp 635-650, 1997.

[3] P. Maes, "Agents that Reduce Work and Information Overload". Communications of the ACM, Vol. 37 No. 7. 1994.

[4] SJ Poslad, P. Charlton, & E. Mamdani " Agent based support for open multimedia services on PDAs. " *IEE Microprocessors and Microsystems: special issue on PDAs*. 21, 1997 (to appear).

[5] R. Walker, P. Foster, S. Banthorpe, "Content production and delivery for interactive multimedia services – a new approach," *BT Technol J*, vol. 15, no. 2, pp 74-82, 1997.

[6] S. Hedberg "Agents for Sale: First Wave of Intelligent Agents go Commercial",IEE Expert, Intelligent Systems & Their Applications, Vol(11), Number (6). Pages 16-23, 1996.

[7] J. M. Bradshaw, S. Dutfield, P. Benoit, and J. Woolley " KaoS: Toward An Industrial-Strength Open Agent Architecture", *Software Agents*, (Ed) J. M. Bradshaw. Pages 375-418, Chapter 17. 1997.

[8] R. Neches, R. Fikes, T. Finin, et al "Enabling Technology for Knowledge Sharing", AI Magazine 12(3): pages 36-56, 1991.

[9] T. Finn, J. Weber, G. Wiederhold, M. Gensereth, DRAFT Specification of the KQML Agent-Communication Language. *Report from the DARPA knowledge sharing initiative*. 1993.

[10] P. Hayes "The Second Naïve Physics Manifesto" In J.R. Hobbs & R. C. Moore, Eds. Formal Theories of the Commonsense World, pp. 1-36. Norwood, NJ: Ablex. 1985.

[11] N. Guarino "Formal Ontology, Conceptual Analysis and Knowledge Representation", *International Journal Of Human-Computer Studies*, Number 5/6, Page 625-640, 1995.

[12] M. Genesereth and R. Fikes, "Knowledge Interchange Format, Version 3.0" Reference manual, Technical Report, Computer Science Department, Stanford University. 1992.

[13] M. Wooldrige, & N. Jennings. 1994, "Agent Theories, Architectures, and Languages: A Survey.

Design Patterns as Litmus Paper to Test the Strength of Object-Oriented Methods

Anthony J H Simons[1], Monique Snoeck[2] and Kitty S Y Hung[1]

[1] Department of Computer Science, University of Sheffield,
Sheffield, United Kingdom
[2] Département d'Informatique, Université Libre de Bruxelles,
Brussels, Belgium

Abstract

This paper shows how Design Patterns may be used to reveal properties of object-oriented development methods. The responsibility-driven and event-driven design methods are contrasted in the way they transform and layer systems. Each method elevates a different modularising principle: contract minimisation and existence dependency. Different design patterns, such as *Mediator, Chain of Responsibility, Template Method, Command* and *Composite* emerge for each method, illustrating the particular bias and the different design decisions each makes.

Keywords: Object-oriented design, system layering, subsystem identification, design patterns, responsibility-driven design (RDD), event-driven design (EDD), minimisation of contracts, existence dependency

1 Introduction

The vast majority of object-oriented analysis and design methods are in agreement that the identification of subsystems is an important task. Subsystems are the building blocks that allow a system to be decoupled for various reasons, such as (i) to run on different processors; (ii) to be developed by different teams; (iii) to compile as a separate module; (iv) to facilitate substitution and extension; or (v) simply because the subsystem is itself an important domain abstraction. However, not many object-oriented methods offer any kind of *systematic process*, in the form of *axiomatised steps*, for developing subsystems that are optimally partitioned according to some design criteria. Indeed, some methods, such as Booch [3], p229, emphasise the continual need for creativity and intuition, believing that it is impossible to codify the design process. Other methods, such as OMT [20] choose to split systems up according to subjective criteria, such as *layers* (code substrates, virtual machines) and *partitions* (intuitively-determined subsystem modules). Instead, it would be better if subsystems were selected according to measurable internal criteria, such as the degree of inter-module coupling [18], which corresponds to the number of inter-object references needed for message sending in the object-oriented model. A good system design method should minimise inter-object coupling across subsystem boundaries and thereby also foster *subsystem reuse* in new contexts.

More recently, *Design Patterns* have emerged as the "distilled products" of high-quality object-oriented designs [10]. Each pattern is a solution to a small-scale design problem, created according to the single principle: "Encapsulate the part that changes". Patterns as diverse as *Abstract Factory* (creational), *Composite* (structural) and *Command* (behavioural) all rely directly on this principle, by reorganising designs around polymorphic plug-in points, which may subsequently be filled by specialised concrete components. The application of Design Patterns is normally a *system design* activity, in the sense we are seeking above. But, Design Patterns are again applied *intuitively* to particular problem/solution spaces [10] by expert developers who recognise these situations. In the rest of this paper, we use Design Patterns in a quite different way, as the "litmus paper" to judge the quality or strength of particular object-oriented development methods.

Because we were interested in comparing the kinds of *systematic guidance* provided by object-oriented design methods to non-expert developers, we needed to select methods which were obviously directive in their modelling approach. We considered that Booch [3] and OOSE [15] rely over-much on expert developer intuition in the identification of object concepts and subsystems. OMT [20], Coad-Yourdon [6, 7] and Shlaer-Mellor [22] all have a data-driven foundation that is amenable to systematic entity-relationship modelling (ERM), which elevates *data dependency* as its system modularisation principle. The deliverable of ERM is a set of normalised data files (equiv. 3NF) which says nothing about the procedural structure of the system interrogating the data. We did eventually find two methods which satisfied our criteria for providing proper direction for object-oriented design. Section 2 reformulates the *Responsibility-Driven* Design method [28, 29, 27] from a systematic viewpoint, especially the much-neglected system design stage, which elevates *contract minimisation* as its modularising principle. Section 3 presents an original *Event-Driven* approach adapted from the work of the second author and her colleagues [24, 25], which elevates *existence dependency* as its guiding principle for modular decomposition. Both approaches are evaluated for their potential to identify properly-layered subsystems with loose external coupling. In our assessment of these two contrasting methods, we use Design Patterns in an unusual way: as indicators of the design decisions taken by the methods. We allow the *systematic application of the methods themselves* to generate the Patterns which they naturally tend to promote. We regard the emergence of Design Patterns as evidence of the quality of the methods, and the generation of different Design Patterns as an indication of the particular bias of each method. This connection has not been made before.

2 Responsibility-Driven Design: Contract Minimisation

Responsibility-Driven Design (RDD) regards objects as behavioural abstractions, characterised at a coarse scale by the "responsibilities" that they bear, which translate 1:M at a finer scale into the services they provide [28]. Data attributes are assigned later, on a need-to-know basis [4]. The design method [29] operates in two phases: the first generative phase produces new object abstractions using the CRC-card modelling technique [2]; and the second transformational phase identifies tightly-coupled regions and layers the system using a coupling metric called "minimisation of contracts". RDD is especially good for decentralising control, distributing system behaviour throughout a society of objects [27].

Most second-hand treatments of RDD [4, 3, 13] mistakenly focus only on the informal aspects of the first phase; and then sometimes misunderstand its purpose. It is true that RDD and CRC-card modelling are helpful to promote more active (*viz* behavioural) object concepts, such as *manager* or *controller* abstractions [3]. However, the generative phase of RDD is best applied *ab initio*, not after the prior construction of object models. It is important to keep entity boundaries plastic while responsibilities are being elicited and redistributed - prior object modelling tends to fix these boundaries too early. RDD is compatible with other behaviour-centred approaches [11, 21, 12] which use scripts/scenarios/use-cases [15] to explore system requirements before assigning behaviours to objects. However, very few authors have picked up on the systematic layering offered by the second transformational phase of RDD, which we believe has been unfairly neglected.

2.1 The Rules of RDD

We are chiefly interested in RDD for its power to transform system designs, especially the much-neglected and often misunderstood second phase. However, for completeness' sake, the whole RDD process has been codified in the following 10 rules (an arbitrary number, but sufficient for our purposes), shown in table 1. The rules are an original semiformal characterisation of published informal descriptions of the RDD method [29, 4, 27]. We have made certain aspects of the RDD process more explicit (rules 1, 3), introduced a halting-condition (rule 4) and a novel decision function (rules 5, 6) for determining *how* an entity should be split when it is judged too large (by rule 1). A novel coupling weighting (rule 8), which we have found useful in the *Discovery* method [23] helps to show the degree of functional dependency expressed in a static client-server coupling. Rules 1-3 govern the initial conceptualisation of domain entities. Rules 4-6 generate more esoteric entities to decentralise computation; and determine their final granularity by the size constraint and single-purpose requirement. Rules 7-10 govern the systematic restructuring of the system, generating design-level entities needed to reduce system coupling ("minimise contracts", in [29]).

RDD rule 1: Identify entities on the basis that they fulfil a small (2-7) cohesive set of responsibilities, each a coarse-grained statement of (part of) the purpose of the entity; concepts which bear no responsibility are either simple attributes, or vacuous.

RDD rule 2: Consider how each entity fulfils its responsibilities, establishing collaborations with subcontractor entities, to which it delegates some parts of its responsibilities.

RDD rule 3: Add data attributes, on a need-to-know basis, to those entities bearing a primary responsibility for managing the data; convert passive concepts into attributes.

RDD rule 4: Continue subcontracting until the coarse-grained statements of responsibility reach the fine granularity of single services (methods).

RDD rule 5: If an entity acquires too many responsibilities, and these are cohesive, restate the responsibilities more generally and delegate the detail to new (invented) subcontractors.

RDD rule 6: If an entity acquires too many responsibilities, and these are not cohesive, partition the entity into two or more peer entities according to grouped responsibilities.

RDD rule 7: For each entity, group its services into contracts, one contract per set of services invoked by a distinct set of clients; index the contracts.

RDD rule 8: Draw a collaboration graph, linking clients via directed arcs to contracts indexed in each server entity; log the per-service weighted strength of each collaboration.

RDD rule 9: Aggregate tightly-coupled subsystems inside new mediator entities; uncouple the components and have their contracts migrate outwards to the aggregate entity.

RDD rule 10: Generalise groups of entities that offer, or that invoke the same, or similar contracts; merge communication paths to and from the general entity; add dynamic binding.

Table 1: Ten Rules of Responsibility-Driven Design

The terms used in RDD are sometimes misunderstood, in particular: *responsibility, collaboration* and *contract*.

- A *responsibility* is not necessarily the same thing as a service, but may be (rules 1 and 4); it is a statement of purpose, not the name of a method; keeping this coarser-grained view affects the operation of rules 5-6.

- A *collaboration* is best thought of as a connection, or coupling, between a client and a server [29], rather than the messages sent between them [19]; the coupling view is needed for rule 9 to operate correctly.

- The transformational stage depends crucially on identifying *contracts*, sets of services in a class interface *that are used by common sets of clients* [29]. Meyer's use of the term "contract" is different [16], standing for the reciprocal agreement between a client and a server governing correct invocation and exception-handling *in a single method.*

Henderson-Sellers and Edwards distinguish Meyer's "method contracts" from Wirfs-Brock's "class contracts", understood to be the set of method contracts used by each client [13]. Each client-server collaboration would then be governed by a single contract. RDD is slightly more subtle than this, grouping services into contracts according to *each distinct set of clients* which invoke them. This means that a given client-server collaboration may eventually be governed by one or more contracts, depending on whether the server has other clients which invoke intersecting groups of services. This distinction affects the operation of rule 10 above. In summary, RDD is a *responsibility-driven* approach, which optimises the communication pattern among entities, by transferring the responsibility for handling message requests around the system. The cleverness in RDD lies in its ability to merge communication paths, so reducing the degree of static inter-entity coupling required. This is consonant with Parnas' dictum on modularity [18].

2.2 Transformations in RDD

A version of the well-known ATM banking machine example is presented to illustrate the operation of the RDD process. Nouns from the original problem description, such as *Teller, Money, CheckingAccount* are selected as candidate object abstractions ("entities", hereafter). Sets of responsibilities are constructed for each of these entities, for example, according to the grammar:

P ::= R I R "and" R I R "or" R I (R)

where R is the set of atomic natural language statements and P are non-atomic statements of responsibility constructed from these. The initial entities are filtered and retained only if they can be conceived as bearing some kind of responsibility (rule 1), so concepts like *Money* do not survive, except as the *balance* attribute of a *CheckingAccount* entity (rule 3). Collaborators are elicited (rule 2) where these server-entities are obviously involved in the fulfilling of client responsibilities; this information is entered on CRC cards. Figure 1 shows the initial collaboration pattern between these first-cut domain entities.

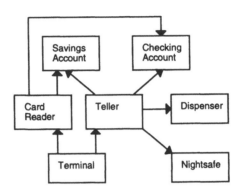

Figure 1: Pre-transformed RDD collaborations

Clearly, there is a degree of arbitrary interpretation in the early selection of object abstractions; nonetheless all entities selected must have the required behavioural properties. The elicitation rules (1-3) are perhaps less automatic than the later rules, but this is inevitable and not a fault. We have deliberately chosen the most obvious domain-influenced initial model, which fails to differentiate the activities of the *Teller* and fails to generalise on types of *Account*, although the RDD method would equally accept a more perceptive initial conceptualisation. The strength of RDD lies in its ability to reorganise the initial model according to modularising principles, forcing the invention of new abstractions.

In figure 2, the design process is more advanced, but not yet complete. An early and obvious generalisation on common responsibilities in the interfaces of *SavingsAccount* and *CheckingAccount* has generated the abstract *Account* parent class (rule 10). When all the responsibilities of the existing entities are listed, the two most overburdened entities are *Teller* and *CardReader*, both of which have over 7 responsibilities (rule 1), so these need to be split.

The *CardReader* must read, validate, encode and transmit account and PIN numbers, search for accounts and authorise connections to them. The choice of applying rule 5 over rule 6 to split *CardReader* is determined by the fact that its responsibilities are judged cohesive, since they all involve the same collaborators and attributes. According to rule 5, a new entity, *Verifier*, is spun off as a delegate of *CardReader* with the responsibility to handle and validate PINs. In retrospect, this is a good design decision, since *CardReader* has no need to retain the PIN number (rule 3) once it has read the card and PIN number [4]. Notice how this is an instance of the *Chain of Responsibility* pattern [10], p223, in which the responsibility to *verify PIN number* is passed onto a delegate object. RDD will tend to generate a *Chain of Responsibility* pattern every time rule 5 is invoked.

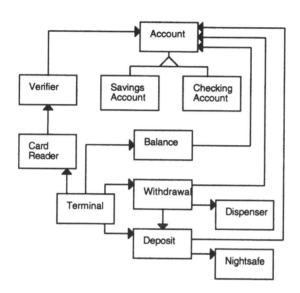

Figure 2: Partially-elaborated RDD collaborations

In contrast with this, the *Teller* entity must be partitioned into peers, because its many responsibilities are not cohesive (rule 6), even when restated. This is judged by observing how *deposit money* requires collaborating with the *NightSafe* and *Account*, whereas *withdraw money* requires collaborating with the *Dispenser* and *Account* and lastly, *inspect balance* only requires collaborating with the *Account*. So, three peer "manager entities" (rule 6) are devised to handle each distinct type of *Teller*-transaction. Note that the rule requires invention of new entities; and it is up to the developer to provide significant names, based on the partitioning of responsibilities. The elaborational rules 4-6 of RDD tend to generate manager entities to handle different system functions, by virtue of the constraint (rule 1) on the number of responsibilities assigned to each entity. We shall see later how this leads inevitably to instances of the *Command* behavioural pattern [10].

By drawing the collaboration graph (rule 8) after the proper determination of contracts (rule 7), we see in a more visual way how individual clients are coupled with their servers. At this time, areas of strong and weak coupling may be identified. In our example, one of the kinds of withdrawal to be supported is really a transfer of funds, which leads to the undesired cross-coupling highlighted in figure 3 (a): *Withdrawal* is the only manager-entity with a cross-linkage to one of its peers. This is strong evidence that rule 9 should be applied to remove the cross-coupling. This rule mandates the introduction of a new entity to aggregate over the subsystem and manage the communication between the parts. Calling this new entity the *Transfer* manager, we encapsulate *Withdrawal* and *Deposit*, as shown in figure 3 (b). *Withdrawal* no longer needs a direct reference to *Deposit*. Notice how this is an instance of the *Mediator* pattern [10], p273: the *Transfer* entity coordinates the sequence of interactions between the *Deposit* and *Withdrawal* managers, such that these do not need to refer to each other; the anomalous *transfer money* contract is moved from *Withdrawal* to this new entity. RDD rule 9 always generates *Mediator* patterns, where other object-oriented methods might be content to let the cross-coupling remain.

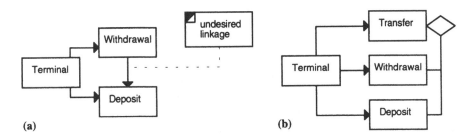

(a)   (b)

Figure 3: Aggregating over a closed subsystem

The last group of transformations involves considering how the contracts of *Account* are invoked by clients. Once *Account* responsibilities have been refined down to the level of individual services (by rule 4), these may be grouped into named and indexed contracts according to the distinct sets of clients which invoke them. According to rule 7, *Account* eventually offers five contracts, many of which only contain one service each: (1) *inspect balance* is used by *Balance*, *Deposit* and *Withdrawal*; (2) *make deposit* is used by *Deposit*; (3) *make withdrawal* is used by *Withdrawal* (grouping together the services *request withdrawal* and *withdraw amount*); (4) *commit changes* is used by *Deposit* and *Withdrawal*; and finally (5) *connect to account* is used by *Verifier*, (grouping together the services *valid a/c?*, *valid PIN?* and *a/c frozen?*).

Figure 4 (a) is a fragment of the system, showing how *Deposit* and *Withdrawal* invoke the *Account* contract (4) in common, but otherwise invoke apparently separate contracts (2) and (3) each. This is nonetheless suggestive, according to rule 10, that some generalisation of *Withdrawal* and *Deposit* should handle all communication with *Account*. Calling this new abstract entity a *Transaction* manager, the responsibility for invoking *Account* contracts migrates upwards to *Transaction*. In figure 4 (b), contract (4) *commit changes* is now invoked directly by *Transaction* (instead of separately by *Account* and *Withdrawal*). Contracts (2) *make deposit* and (3) *make withdrawal* are judged sufficiently similar, from the perspective of *performing a transaction*, that an abstract method *transact(int)* may be provided in *Transaction,* which is subsequently redefined and dynamically bound in the descendants *Deposit* and *Withdrawal* to perform the appropriate deposit or withdrawal action. The effect of this transformation is to merge the communication paths leading from different manager-entities to *Account.* First, the duplicate paths to contract (4) are merged, then the paths to contracts (2) and (3) are merged (on the basis of polymorphism).

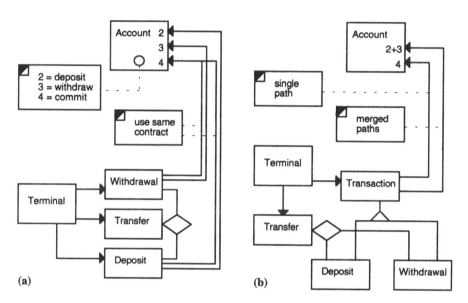

Figure 4: Generalising on commonly-invoked contracts

From figure 4 (b), it is clear that the revised contracts (2+3) and (4) are now only used by the client *Transaction,* so these may also be merged (by rule 7), making it possible to combine the *transact(int)* and *commit()* methods. Notice how these transformations lead systematically to an instance of the *Template Method* pattern [10], p325, in the form of *Transaction's handleRequest(Account&)* method. This method is the template for all single transactions on an *Account.* First, it invokes a virtual *transact(int)* method stub, followed by a concrete *commit()* method, on an *Account* instance. *Transaction's* descendants will provide appropriate concrete implementations for *transact(int);* c.f. [10], p327.

The continuing process of generalisation (rules 10, 7) eventually predicts an abstract superclass for *Balance, Transfer* and *Transaction,* which all communicate with *Account.* Since this entity will be the root of all managers handling banking requests, we reintroduce *Teller* as the abstract superclass in the final design in figure 5, having a single contract (1+2+3+4) with *Account.* We emphasise that it is the similarity in the way different manager-entities communicate with *Account,* judged according to contracts, which motivates the introduction of the *Teller* entity; the fact that this corresponds to an existing concept in the analysis domain is serendipitous. Notice how *Teller* is an instance of the *Command* pattern [10], p233: *Teller* encapsulates different kinds of abstract banking requests, which are fielded by its more concrete subclasses. This could be represented by a polymorphic *handleRequest(Account&)* method. Further merging of *Teller* and *Verifier* is prevented by their too-different external interfaces.

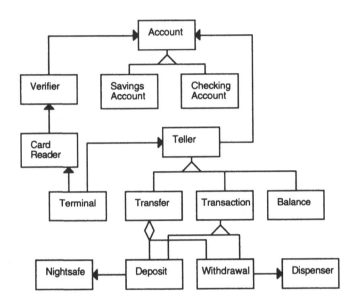

Figure 5: Fully-transformed RDD collaboration graph

2.3 Subsystems and Coupling in RDD

The kinds of subsystems identified by RDD are equivalent to well-factored modules with minimal inter-module procedure calls. We emphasise that it is the systematic application of rules 7-10 which layers systems properly; and this is the aspect of RDD which is most often neglected. The per-service weighting measure (rule 7) lets the designer see how many services each collaboration is carrying, in highly-coupled systems. It provides a rationale for placing subsystem boundaries: you aggregate over the most tightly-coupled parts of the system (with high per-service counts) and break the system at weakly-coupled points (with low per-service counts). RDD subsystems are eventually much better motivated than Coad-Yourdon *subjects* [6].

RDD supports the bottom-up discovery of *Mediator* patterns, where each *Mediator* is a properly-layered subsystem. The aggregate subsystem *Transfer* obviates the need for its component *Transaction* managers to be coupled directly to each other. Instead, it initiates the communcation between them, handling the transfer of requests and money in a controlled sequence, possibly recording state information in the process (rule 3). For example, the withdrawal request may be refused, in which case the deposit cannot go ahead. This is ideally handled internally by the *Transfer* manager.

Most methods encourage clustering of classes with similar external interfaces (we showed this with the grouping of *SavingsAccount* and *CheckingAccount* under *Account*), in other words, their similar behaviour is grouped according to *how they act as servers*. RDD is unique in its ability to cluster classes systematically according to *how they invoke their clients*. We emphasise how clever this is - it is the only approach which can optimise the opposite (usually invisible, encapsulated) end of the collaboration relationship. Through the partitioning of class services into contracts (rule 7) and the construction of fine-grained collaboration graphs (rule 8) RDD supports the bottom-up discovery of *Template Method* and *Command* patterns. In particular, it is the *per-client-set* identification of contracts which allows the designer to see similarities in the global pattern of invocation. Coarser-grained definitions of a collaboration graph [13, 19] do not show patterns of invocation; but only patterns of coupling. This will permit the aggregation activity (rule 9) to proceed, but not the generalisation activity (rule 10).

3 Event-Driven Design: Existence Dependency

The second object-oriented design method we consider is an original one, based on a process algebra [25, 8] and a conceptual modelling approach [24]. We call it *Event-driven design* (EDD) because it takes the viewpoint that all computation is made up of events, on which objects must synchronise in order to participate. The notion of event participation is deliberately abstract, avoiding early assignment of responsibility to objects for carrying out actions. A motivating example is where a *Copy* of a library book is taken out on loan by a *Borrower*: which object is responsible for performing this action? The event-driven approach says that neither is, instead both participate in a *borrowing event*. This viewpoint is similar to the view of communication defined in CSP [14]; whereas traditional message-passing is more like CCS [17].

Entities are identified initially as simple data abstractions and are inserted into an object-event table (OET). Every entity should have one or more associated creation and deletion events bounding the lifetime of its existence (see figure 6 for examples); these are logged in the table. Further events, which trigger the main system operations, are also logged against all those entities which participate in each event. An existence dependency graph (EDG) is constructed, in parallel with the OET (see also figure 6). This is different from an entity-relationship diagram in that every link is an existence- or lifetime-dependency relationship, between a master and one or more dependent entities. For example, a library may acquire a new *Title* and several *Copies* of that book. The existence of the *Copies* is directly dependent on that of the *Title*; without the *Title* first being created, no *Copies* can exist; and if the *Title* is ever withdrawn, then all *Copies* must necessarily cease to exist. The EDG starts as a set of nodes, only some of which may initially depend on each other and so be connected. Eventually, the EDG becomes an acyclic graph (transitive, antisymmetric, non-reflexive) as further nodes and connections are added.

The system elaboration phase extends the OET and EDG by considering groups of entities which must synchronise to participate in events. If they are not already linked by dependency in the EDG, then some new entity must be invented to represent the time-bounded association between the participating entities. This is added to the EDG and appropriate creation and deletion events are logged in the OET for the new entity. An example is the *borrow* and *return* events, in which a *Copy* of a book and a *Borrower* participate. Since *Copy* and *Borrower* are so far unrelated in the EDG, a new associative entity, named *Loan*, is introduced. The *borrow* event marks the creation of the *Loan* entity, which is deleted when a corresponding *return* event signals the return of the book to the library. The *Loan* encapsulates the keys (pointers, IDs) of its participants.

In the system consolidation phase, polymorphic families of methods are devised corresponding to one method per system event handled in each entity. The flow of control is initiated from the dependent associative entity to the participating master entities, each of which must have a version of the method to react to the event. The polymorphic *borrow* method constructs a *Loan*, dispatching the same *borrow*-message to the participants, where it (variously) decrements a *Borrower's* book allowance and marks a *Copy* as unavailable to other library users.

3.1 The Rules of EDD

Once more, we are interested in the potential of EDD as a systematic design process. In table 2, we have distilled 10 rules (coincidentally, the same number as for RDD) from the principal sources [8, 24, 25], by ignoring the more subjective aspects of the design processes described there. Rules 1-4 govern the identification of entities and events; rules 5-8 govern the elaboration phase which layers the system according to the principle of existence dependency; and rules 9-10 govern the consolidation phase which converts events into chains of methods. There is a pleasing simplicity about the EDG, since all relationships have the same semantics and are already normalised (in ERM terms) when they are constructed. Also, the mutual influence of the OET and EDG allows the two principles of *event participation* and *existence dependency* to drive the invention of associative entity-abstractions.

EDD rule 1: Entities are data or association concepts, existing for a period of time, bounded by one or more creation and deletion events and involved in possibly many other events.

EDD rule 2: Primary data entities group atomic, non-overlapping sets of attributes, which they are responsible for maintaining.

EDD rule 3: Associative (dependent) entities group the keys of the master entities on which they depend; and may manage further relationship attributes.

EDD rule 4: Events are defined as atomic, non-decomposable actions which (C)reate, (I)nvolve or (D)elete entities; an atomic event must impact on a finite, known number of entities.

EDD rule 5: An object-event table arranges entities (x-axis) against events (y-axis); C, I, D are entered at appropriate intersections; every entity should have at least one C and D; every event should have at least one C, or I, or D.

EDD rule 6: An existence dependency graph connects 1:1 and M:1 simultaneous dependents to their master(s); the lifetime of each dependent is strictly contained within that of its masters.

EDD rule 7: A new associative entity is created for each distinct set of entities participating in 2 or more common events; the C, I, D events for this new dependent entity must correspond respectively to: [C or I], I, [D or I] events for its masters.

EDD rule 8: Continue the process until all nodes in the EDG are connected; and all joint participations in events in the OET have been encapsulated in dependent associative entities, or all but one, since two events are needed to bound the lifetime of a dependent entity.

EDD rule 9: All events become methods invoked on the dependent entities, delegating to the participating master entities; dependents handle the intersection of their masters' events.

EDD rule 10: Branches in method-trees are renamed according to the rôles played by each participating entity; similar rôles are clustered; degenerate methods are eliminated.

Table 2: Ten Rules of Event-Driven Design

3.2 Transformations in EDD

Most of the system layering activity is performed during the elaboration phase (rules 5-8), in which new entities are devised according to the principle of *existence dependency*. Less structural re-design is required, since the event-participation model deliberately leaves the initial message pattern plastic; however, transformations are made to the OET. Figures 6 and 7 illustrate the lending library system before and after a *Reservation* entity has been added.

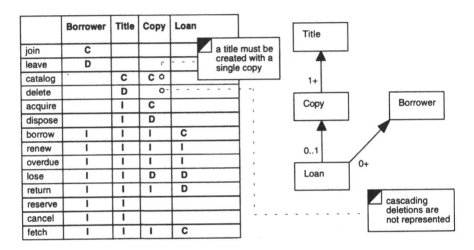

	Borrower	Title	Copy	Loan
join	C			
leave	D		┌	
catalog	·	C	C ○	
delete		D	○	
acquire		I	C	
dispose		I	D	
borrow	I	I	I	C
renew	I	I	I	I
overdue	I	I	I	I
lose	I	I	D	D
return	I	I	I	D
reserve	I	I		
cancel	I	I		
fetch	I	I	I	C

a title must be created with a single copy

Title

1+

Copy

Borrower

0..1

0+

Loan

cascading deletions are not represented

Figure 6: OET and EDG after addition of Loan

In figure 6, *Loan* is the latest associative entity introduced, according to rule 7, to manage the common events {*borrow, renew, overdue* and *return*}, in which the unique set of entities {*Copy, Borrower*} participate. *Loan* has also been attached as the latest child in the EDG, and made dependent on *Copy* and *Borrower*. The multiplicity figures state how many *Loans* may exist for each *Copy* or *Borrower*. Note how, in accordance with rule 7, the OET contains I-events for *all* the the master entities, viz. {*Borrower, Copy, Title*}, impacted by *Loan* C-, I- or D-events, such as *renew*. This allows *renew*'s consequences to propagate to all the master entities (*eg* the *Borrower* may have certain privileges restored by renewing an overdue book; the *Copy* may have its time-to-inspection reduced); but it is difficult to imagine what impact *renew* might have on *Title* - it is possible for an event to have a null effect; we show how this is handled below.

In figure 6, the existence of at least two events {*reserve, cancel*} which involve two participants {*Title, Borrower*} not already covered by the existing *Loan* association motivates the separate creation of the *Reservation* associative entity (by rule 7). This is shown added to the OET and EDG in figure 7. Note how there are no longer any I-entries in the OET which are not covered by some existing association, indicating that the elaboration phase is now complete. Every time a new entity is introduced, existing events are examined for their impact on this entity (rule 1). For example, the *fetch* event is identified as a (D)elete-event for a *Reservation* and a simultaneous (C)reate-event for a *Loan*. This is the only event to involve both a *Loan* and a *Reservation*. No new associative entity need be created (according to rule 8), since a pair of time-separated events is always necessary to (C)reate and (D)elete each new associative entity introduced. Furthermore, there are no unconnected entities in the EDG (rule 8).

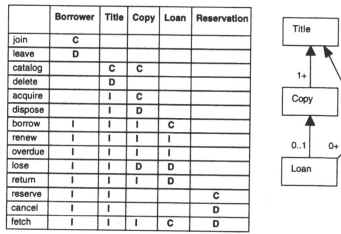
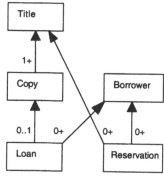

	Borrower	Title	Copy	Loan	Reservation
join	C				
leave	D				
catalog		C	C		
delete		D			
acquire		I	C		
dispose		I	D		
borrow	I	I	I	C	
renew	I	I	I	I	
overdue	I	I	I	I	
lose	I	I	D	D	
return	I	I	I	D	
reserve	I	I			C
cancel	I	I			D
fetch	I	I	I	C	D

Figure 7: OET and EDG after addition of Reservation

Rule 9 is applied to convert *all* event-participations into methods (one method per entity-event). A large number of methods are generated. Every associative entity automatically becomes the root of a call-graph for each event it manages. For example, the *renew* event is translated into: *Loan::renew()* - update the due date of the loan, which dispatches to: *Copy::renew()* - reduce the time to inspection; and also to *Borrower::renew()* - restore borrowing privileges. *Copy::renew()* dispatches to *Title::renew()*, which eventually is a null operation, a degenerate method. Notice the similarities between the method interfaces of each associative entity and the participating entities it manages: every dependent entity manages the intersection of its masters' events. Just like a *Composite* pattern [10], p163, associations encapsulate part-whole hierarchies which respond to the same sets of messages. Just like the *Chain of Responsibility* pattern [10], p223, the events are handed on to the next component in the hierarchy, until components are reached which perform significant parts of the computation. EDD will always generate these two patterns in abundance. Finally, rule 10 is applied to eliminate degenerate methods, such as *Title::renew()*. Groups of methods may be renamed, to increase their mnemonic salience, for example: *transact* may convert into *buy()* and *sell()* for objects playing these complementary rôles.

3.3 Subsystems and Coupling in EDD

Dependent entities in EDD have some of the characteristics of ERM's linker entities (they represent associations and store foreign keys) but also have characteristics of RDD's *Mediator* patterns (they are devised in response to a need to communicate events to their participants). However, data aggregations may be handled differently in EDD than in other object modelling approaches [22, 20, 5, 19, 9]. Aggregations representing *existence dependencies* are modelled the same way: *eg* the *Lines* of an order are dependent on the *Order*. However, new associative entities must always be devised to relate an assembly to its *non-existence-dependent* parts, such as the components of a PC. Here, an associative entity manages the collaboration between the whole and each part, which is presumed to have a separate existence (it may be exchanged, substituted into other PCs). This tends to promote a distributed pattern of control: the logic of the PC is handled by a society of existence-dependent controllers governing the throughput between the PC and each of its hardware components. EDD optimises the *construction order* of a system. It is easy to draw *entity life history* diagrams (ELHs) [1] for each entity and derive the life-history of the system from this. The logic handling other events during the life of an entity is either pure selection (all events equally likely), or some sequencing of events is required.

EDD layers the composition structure similarly to RDD; but it suggests a quite different generalisation structure. Consider that *Borrower* and *Copy* satisfy the interface of *Loan* (because they respond to all *Loan*'s events, and also to other events). It is tempting, but wrong, to think of *Loan* as a generalisation of *Borrower* and *Copy*, since *Loan* implements the common events differently from either class. Instead, all three classes should inherit from an abstract class which defines the *Loan* interface (but not the implementation). This abstract class is an instance of the *Composite* pattern base class [10], p163, whose concrete descendants respond to each message and then delegate these messages to their own components. EDD inevitably produces large numbers of composite patterns, because of the emphasis on shared participation in events. More important master entities will participate in more than one *Composite* pattern, suggesting the use of multiple inheritance from several abstract base classes. Where one or other master entity is chiefly accountable in handling an event, this is also an instance of *Chain of Responsibility* [10], p223, which allows events to be dispatched to one starting point, then forwarded down the line to some object which eventually executes the major part of the response.

4 Conclusions

This paper has examined two different approaches to object-oriented design, each of which elevates a different modularising principle: *contract minimisation* and *existence dependency.* Different *Design Patterns* emerged during the application of the methods, showing how they take different design decisions when structuring a system. We showed above how these *Design Patterns* emerged naturally and are in fact an inevitable part of the layering and transformational rules of each method. We characterised each method in a semiformal way, so that the reader could see more easily the link between the "rules" of the methods and the particular *Design Patterns* generated.

4.1 Emergent Patterns and Coupling Characteristics

The kinds of subsystems and layering suggested by each approach are different. EDD promotes unidirectional data coupling in its modelling, so is unable to handle inverse effects, such as a cascading deletion (see note in Figure 6), which is formally forbidden. An *Observer* pattern [10], p293, could be used to register master entities with their dependents, although this would significantly worsen the coupling characteristics. RDD is most successful in eliminating mutual and closed-loop couplings because of the perspective offered by the collaboration graph. In the same circumstances, where EDD requires an *Observer* pattern, RDD will generate a *Mediator* pattern. RDD is unique in its generalisation strategy, because it merges communication paths at both the source and destination ends. RDD and EDD contrast strongly in the way they generalise - whereas RDD will generate *Command* and *Template Method* patterns, EDD will generate *Composite* and *Chain of Responsibility* patterns. It is no accident that RDD generates all *behavioural* patterns (*Mediator, Command, Template Method, Chain of Responsibility*), since its focus is on responsibilities and behaviour. EDD, on the other hand, is dominated by the *structural* pattern, *Composite*, determined by the EDG structure. The event-participation model leads directly from this to the emergent *Chain of Responsibility* pattern.

Both approaches reduce the number of subsystems which interact directly. In some cases, they will suggest the same structures, but for different reasons. A *Purchaser*, *Vendor* and *Product* will end up encapsulated in a *Sale* using both approaches. In RDD, *Sale* will be invented at a later stage to aggregate over the closed ring of collaborations involved in transferring money, goods and ownership; whereas in EDD, *Sale* will necessarily exist from the beginning, by virtue of the existence dependency rules, but only for the duration of the agreement to purchase until the final transaction is complete.

4.2 Pattern Metrics for System Design

There is far more to object-oriented system design than elaborating analysis models to the point where they can be implemented. This is not truly appreciated by seamless approaches [6, 7, 26, 13, 19]. System partitioning has only been treated informally in many other presentations [20, 15, 3, 13]. Initially, we had set out to identify, codify and then compare two design approaches which offered some leverage in the system design stage. When we applied our semi-formal rules to example designs, we found again and again that recognisable Design Patterns emerged. In particular, we gave examples of instances of *Mediator, Command, Chain of Responsibility, Template Method* and *Composite* that were generated automatically. These five patterns all have the property that they reduce cross-coupling in system design. The *Façade* pattern [10], p185, also exhibits this property, but whereas the other five may be derived from the internal coupling characteristics of systems, *Façade* is always imposed externally, in situations where components are being bundled for convenience. Some patterns, such as *Adapter* [10], p139 and *Bridge* [10], p151, are neutral with respect to cross-coupling: they introduce an extra layer of composition to reduce the number of specialised variants of a class. Other patterns, such as *Proxy* [10], p207, *Flyweight* [10], p195 and especially *Observer* [10], p293, actually increase cross-coupling and mutual dependency. This reinforces our confidence in the five emergent patterns as indicators of high-quality system designs. We note that Design Patterns have not been used in this manner before - as litmus paper for testing the strengths, weaknesses and preferences of design methods.

References

1. Ashworth, C. and Goodland, M., *SSADM: A Practical Approach*, McGraw-Hill, 1990.

2. Beck, K. and Cunningham, W., "A laboratory for teaching object-oriented thinking", *Proc. 4th ACM Conf. Object-Oriented Prog. Sys., Lang. and Appl.*, pub. *Sigplan Notices, 25(10)*, 1989, 1-6.

3. Booch, G., *Object-Oriented Analysis and Design with Applications, 2nd edn.* Benjamin-Cummings, 1994.

4. Budd, T., *Introduction to Object-Oriented Programming* Addison-Wesley, Reading MA, 1991.

5. Coleman, D., Arnold, P., Bodoff, S., et al., *Object-Oriented Development: The Fusion Method,* Prentice Hall, 1994.

6. Coad, P. and Yourdon, E., *Object-Oriented Analysis*, Yourdon Press, 1991.

7. Coad, P. and Yourdon, E., *Object-Oriented Design*, Yourdon Press, 1991.

8. Dedene, G. and Snoeck, M., "Formal deadlock elimination in an object-oriented conceptual schema", *Data and Knowledge Engineering, 15,* 1995, 1-30.

9. Firesmith, D., Henderson-Sellers, B. and Graham, I., *OPEN Modelling Language (OML) Reference Manual*, SIGS Books, 1997.

10. Gamma, E., Helm, R., Johnson, R. and Vlissídes, J., *Design Patterns: Elements of Reusable Object-Oriented Software*, Addison-Wesley, 1995.

11. Gibson, E. A., "Objects born and bred", *BYTE magazine, 15(10),* 1990, 255-264.

12. Graham, I. M., *Migrating to Object Technology,* Addison-Wesley, 1995.

13. Henderson-Sellers, B. and Edwards, J., *Book Two of Object-Oriented Knowledge: The Working Object,* Prentice Hall, 1996.

14. Hoare, C. A. R., *Communicating Sequential Processes,* Prentice-Hall, 1985.

15. Jacobson, I., Christerson, M., Jonsson P. and Övergaard, G., *Object-Oriented Software Engineering: a Use-Case Driven Approach,* Addison-Wesley, 1992.

16. Meyer, B., *Object-Oriented Software Construction, 2nd. edn. rev. and enl.,* *Prentice-Hall,* 1997.

17. Milner, R., "A calculus of communicating systems", *Lecture Notes in Computer Science,* Springer, 1980.

18. Parnas, D., "On the criteria to be used in decomposing systems into modules", *Comm. ACM, 15(12),* 1972, 1053-1058; reprinted in: *Classics in Software Engineering,* ed. E Yourdon, Yourdon Press, 1979.

19. Rational, *UML 1.1 Reference Manual,* Rational Software Corp., September, 1997; also available through: *http://www.rational.com/uml/* .

20. Rumbaugh, J., Blaha, M., Premerlani, W., Eddy, F. and Lorensen, W., *Object-Oriented Modeling and Design,* Prentice-Hall, 1991.

21. Rubin, K. and Goldberg, A. "Object-behaviour analysis", *Comm. ACM, 35(9)* 1992.

22. Shlaer, S. and Mellor, S., *Object-Oriented Analysis: Modelling the World in Data,* Yourdon Press, 1988.

23. Simons, A. J. H., "Object Discovery: a process for developing medium-sized object-oriented applications", *Tutorial 14, European Conf. Object-Oriented Prog.,* Brussels (1998); see also: *http://www.dcs.shef.ac.uk/~ajhs/discovery.*

24. Snoeck, M. and Dedene, G., "Generalisation/specialisation and rôle in object-oriented conceptual modelling", *Data and Knowledge Engineering, 19(2),* 1996.

25. Snoeck, M., "On a process algebra approach to the construction and analysis of MERODE-based conceptual models", *PhD thesis, Katholieke Universität Leuven* 1995.

26. Waldén, K. and Nerson, J.-M., *Seamless Object-Oriented Architecture,* Prentice-Hall, 1995

27. Wirfs-Brock, R., "Responsibility-Driven Design" *Tutorial Notes, ACM Conf. Object-Oriented Prog. Sys., Lang. and Appl.,* 1996.

28. Wirfs-Brock, R. and Wiener, L., "Responsibility-driven design: a responsibility-driven approach", *Proc. 4th ACM Conf. Object-Oriented Prog. Sys., Lang. and Appl.,* pub. *Sigplan Notices, 25(10),* 1989, 71-76.

29. Wirfs-Brock, R., Wilkerson, B. and Wiener, L., *Designing Object-Oriented Software,* Prentice Hall, 1990.

Reuse by Appropriation of Software Elements in Information Systems

Stéphane Rideau*, Franck Barbier**, Henri Briand**
*GC2i, 44800 Saint-Herblain - France
**IRIN, BP 92208, 44322 Nantes Cedex 3, France

Abstract

If reuse seems to be the magic wand in software industry, non-reuse is certainly the most encountered situation. Human factors of non-reuse have especially to be taken into account while providing models and associated tools to consider and manage software as data. The mixing of numerous, old and new software parts, especially the most recent ones based on object technology, leads to deal with large original information systems including these parts. The management of such information systems raises in particular the problem of standardizing the way reuse daily happens. The idea of appropriation presented in this paper is based on an object wrapping of information systems where software elements are just grains. Such an approach allows a smooth integration of new object-oriented software pieces (classes, patterns...) into a DBMS based on a Web architecture. For that, one turns attention in this paper to the definition of a generic model, named MARST, on which we designed the framework RENET, a generic implementation for a reuse support tool. In this framework, access, request and handling of software parts occur while offering a unified presentation of software data. All reusable assets are in particular managed in a standard way, because those coming from legacy systems are presented as object-wrapped software parts.

1 Introduction

Reuse is often presented, considered and studied according to its technical aspects. As far as object technology is concerned, a main trend is to encourage generic, parameterized and abstract features of software pieces: classes, components [1], design patterns [2, 3, 4], frameworks [5], conceptual patterns [6]... Although these reuse research directions seem promising, they seldom deal with the associated process in which reuse aspects such as documentation activities, human factors, appropriation decisions of software parts or their rejects, large-scale management of these parts in dedicated information systems and so on, are described. In this respect, this paper presents some practical lessons from the implementation of a CASE tool to help a developer, in its daily work, to really become a reuser. This CASE tool has been built during a migration towards object-oriented development, and basically includes a DBMS where data is software. It is based on an object-oriented metamodel representing common reuse concepts, namely software asset, document, software medium (file), reuse metrics (statistics) and reuse scenarios. Such a metamodel, the kernel of the tool presented in this paper, allows to standardize the way users deal with reusable elements. As a result, presentation of software assets takes place in a uniform object-oriented context, even if some of these parts come from legacy systems. In conventional corporate organizations, software applications and libraries are voluminous information systems. In fact, software items are the information pieces of a reuse support tool: data in databases. This metaphor is that of Isakowitz and Kauffman in [7] and is used to justify the need of reuse-dedicated tools. Furthermore, these authors distinguish:

• classification from search, that is to say manufacturing versus consumption of software elements. In this paper, one outlines that among these two basic activities, human factors are keys of failures/sucesses in an overall reuse strategy. In this connection, this paper focuses on the design by reuse activity, and more precisely on reuse consumers. For them an empirical, intuitive and informal approach tends to facilitate the appropriation of reusable object-oriented elements. In order to achieve it, one must provide reuse-based tools with a suitable functionality set, as for instance, online testing, online downloading, available documentation concerning existing micro-architectures or illustrate a given reuse which occurred in the past and so on.

• managerial aspects from technical aspects of reuse. In this paper, the implementation of a reuse support tool using a Web architecture is detailed. Owing to dissemination of software elements and coexistence of heterogeneous types of software pieces (UML packages, Java/C++ classes, binary libraries, entity/relationship diagrams...), administration of reusable data is a critical task.

Thus, after this introduction, the second section of this paper exposes conventional approaches to deal with a reuse strategy in an industrial context. Then, in the third section, we define a generic model called MARST (Model of A Reuse Support Tool). This described model, using UML [8], supports the idea of reuse guided by appropriation, to bypass human obstacles in a reuse strategy. The fourth section presents the RENET framework (REuse with the NET), which is both developed from MARST model and built upon a Web technical architecture. This architecture provides a uniform presentation to deal with the software data heterogeneity. This framework can be used as a computable base in a reuse support tool development. The fifth part taking place in the industrial context of GC2i, presents a RENET adaptation that exploits legacy components [9], and the perspectives which emanate from this research.

2 Appropriation of Software Elements

The idea of appropriation implies that to succeed in reuse adoption one must develop a feeling of confidence between the reuser and the software element. Two dimensions can be distinguished.

2.1 Technical Features

Several methods to facilitate appropriation of software parts have been proposed in the literature. Meyer in [1] essentially advocates assertions as code members. Because a client component knows the contract ensured by a reusable component, reuse is then facilitated. More theoretical approaches [10] outline the problem of observability and controllability of components. They insist "on the expressiveness of the mathematics used in a specification (of a given reusable software component)". Generally speaking, many approaches rely on the understanding of the component which are not dependent of the implementation. This is well illustrated in CORBA specification where the main concept of interface provides modularity thus reusability [11]. For the software parts which are larger and more sophisticated than components, namely frameworks, Johnson in [5] introduces patterns to be used as framework documentation supports, since they "are an informal technique aimed primarily at describing how to use a framework". Often twined with framework, we can mention the buzzing concept of business object. In [12], Casanave claims that business objects are understandable reusable structures, since they match a business concept. Another trend is to capitalize a shareable knowledge base upon software development through the description of repetitive micro-architectures called patterns. For the analysis patterns developed in [6], Fowler illustrates how a pattern can be adapted depending on the desired abstraction. In one of the most popular work in pattern area, Gamma et al. provide a detailed <problem, solution, context> description to support reuse [2]. A matching operation between respectively a problem and the problem section of the design pattern, and a context and the design pattern one, leads to select the good design pattern.

Despite the existence of these contributions that support reuse at each step of software development, studies of large scale implications of object-oriented reuse [13, 14, 15, 16] demonstrate that non-technical aspects are often keys for success or failure. Contrasting with Meyer's opinion, the Not Invented Here syndrome is invoked in these four extracts to explain the failure in adopting a reuse strategy in an industrial context. In this respect, our work presents a manner to wrap the software assets in such a way that it facilitates the appropriation stage to bypass human obstacles in a reuse strategy adoption. More often, "successful reuse generally requires the presence of certain key non-technical prerequisites like political, organizational, economic, and psychological factors" [17].

2.2 Non-Technical Features

Succeeding in the reuse adoption also needs organizational changes. A first commonplace appearing both from literature and as a return of experience, is that an organization should change to assign reuse mission to an independent specific team, the activity of which is asynchronous, and clearly disjointed from the software production activity [15, 18, 13, 16]. "The component factory's ability to efficiently answer requests from the project organization is critical for the successful application of the reuse technology" [19]. The cost of reuse for an organization is a second commonplace of the literature [20, 13, 21, 22]. So, to minimize this investment, legacy software assets must be wrapped and not re-invented. "Please say no to reverse engineering, reengineering or forward engineering and use wrapper or object shell instead" [17]. Furthermore, according to Rada and Moore, the reusable software assets need to be relevant for the organization business domain. This idea is developed by Rine when he says that "a product-line management approach [...] is higher predictors of decreased effort and increased quality". Hence, information system models and business models must become closer and closer. This close resemblance between them allows the information system to evolve directly with the business [23].

A set of tools is needed to support all of these non-technical constraints. "The technology and method upon reuse include lack of tools to carry out reuse procedures" [15]. Tools are needed to materialize the reuse team activity, in order to justify the reuse investment for the organization management, to adapt the legacy system and to present software data in the business area.

3 A Generic Model to Design a Reuse Support Tool

So, different tools are needed, but they share the same goal: helping and supporting an organization in the adoption of a reuse strategy. These tools are also sharing the presented element types: data in an information system for reuse are the software assets. These assets should be illustrated in such a way that it makes their reuse easier in developing the feeling of appropriation for the reuser. We can define a common model that describes the obstacles and offers a solution. Before this generic design, let us have a look at a typology of software data we need to deal with.

3.1 Extendible Typology of Software Assets.

This section can not be viewed as an exhaustive list of software assets. We can identify five main categories:

• *Legacy components*. The banking business is made of 500 functional procedures. Each of them are split up into n operating ranges, which are in turn divided in m logic treatment units that are implemented through a set of functions in a run-time binary library.

• *OOAD elements*. These data are produced during the analysis and design steps: this can be diverse diagrams (like sequence diagram, use-case diagram, class diagram,...), static elements (package, classes,...), and so on. In fact, these elements and their organization are described by the method metamodel.

• *Knowledge upon software engineering*. These knowledge is mainly capitalized with patterns. Generally speaking, patterns are represented through a triplet structure <problem, solution, context>. [4].

• *Coding elements*. These data are representing the code like C, function or library, C++/Java class, Java package or interface and so on. Their organization depends on used language.

• *Distributed binary components.* These elements are linked with the used middleware. Today, we both work on DCOM model and CORBA architecture. The hierarchy of components at this level also depends on the middleware type, since for instance, you can use inheritance and composition with CORBA while DCOM only admits composition.

You can notice that except for legacy software assets, the four other types of software assets encompass all software development stages.

3.2 Synthesis: Three Main Causes of Non-Reuse

The general issue is to avoid human reuse obstacles. It is also known as the "Not Invented Here", a syndrome which is encountered when a developer would rather re-design than reuse. For example, developers easily find a list of persuasive ideas to avoid reuse of components and to encourage themselves to reinvent software pieces [24]. We study first, some non technical reuse reticence to identify the benefits expected from a tool. Let us suppose that we already have a component set. In fact, Client/Server systems have been designed since 1991 in the banking development area. Thus, since 1991 we are developing structures namely DLL (Dynamic Link Library) which are our components. Three main obstacles are arising now, blocking a wide acceptance of a design by reuse policy.

• First of all, a good component for a precise request is not quickly found or not found at all.

• Secondly, the software data are not fully understood and are not presented in the component hierarchy. So the reuser may misunderstand it, and the reuse phase may become a nightmare for him.

• Finally, it is difficult to reuse when you know that you are able to make it yourself. It is made more important by the fact that, generally speaking, the required work is under-estimated by developers.

When a potential reuser cannot quickly find the adequate component, when he doesn't understand it, and when is not able to evaluate software element efficiency or capability, as a genius developer, he may make it himself. Let us have a look at the definition of reusability appearing in [19] but coming from Prieto-Diaz: "a software component is reusable if the effort required to reuse it is remarkably smaller than the effort required to implement a component with the same functions". Reuse activity comes with an important contradiction because by definition, reusable means more abstract which means more difficult to understand; thus more difficult to reuse. Hence, the greatest goal of a reuse support tool is to reduce the effort of reuse by making the component much more understandable.

3.3 Requirements of a Reuse Support Tool

3.3.1 To reduce reuse effort, three axes are investigated.

First, we need to facilitate integration of components into applications by giving a better understanding to the reuser. Then, we must show the components in their component repository to illustrate their relationships with each other. Finally, a reuse support tool must allow whenever it is possible, online use of components. The general idea of these three propositions is to facilitate the appropriation of the components by the reuser.

• *Presenting a component with its documentation.* A key aspect relating to the observability of computations offered by a given component is the specification of its interface, which establishes how other components can interact with it. But, as this contract is defined, we must also facilitate the future reuse. Hence a software asset must expose a precise and well documented interface. Furthermore, the building block also needs to provide its administrative history like its author, its versions and so on [24]. Moreover, to promote its reuse, a component must "wear" its statistics, like for example the number of times it has been already used. This documentation can also provide a past reuse example that explains the way this software asset has already been integrated. By exposing such a documentation, the component may give more confidence to the user. Finally, if they're available, the quality properties (time complexity of services, memory cost, internal function call graph...) may favor any appropriation.

• *Showing the component in components hierarchy.* When potentially reusable components are memorized with all required information such as model or history, their organization issue arises [24]. Depending on the software data type, their hierarchy can be thought in technical terms or in business terms. Presenting software elements in their organization enforces the definition of a metamodel for each asset types (legacy components, OOAD elements, coding elements, binary components).

Another difficulty arises from component hierarchy and dependencies. It clearly appears that if a software element is useful, it is already reused by other assets. Our work is focused "on (specific) software domain whose components are not stand-alone, that are designed to be plug-compatible and interoperable with other components (...)" [25]. Hence, in a specific domain, components depend on each others. Showing the component in its repository and in its organization is crucial because the reuser may know dependencies among components in order to have a good control of it.

• *Online use of components.* The purpose here is to evaluate the advantages when the reuser is able to test the component online in the tool environment. As we said before, one obstacle of reuse is the ability of the potential reuser in re-doing a component himself. As mentioned in [24], a developer uses all sorts of personal and persuasive arguments like "reinventing is fun", "why buying when you can build", "if somebody else built it, could you really trust it", etc., in order to avoid to reuse. A good way to persuade the reuser that he should better reuse instead of rewriting is to show him the component capabilities. Hence, he can evaluate component strength, efficiency, capability, and complexity. For elements like OOAD assets, a reuse support tool should offer a downloading capability.

However, one can notice that our approach is quite distinct from techniques, like for instance in [10], where components are highly abstract considering their mathematical description. Nevertheless, despite these differences, understandability remains a key idea for reuse

3.3.2 Object-Oriented Static Structure:

The key concept is clearly the software asset concept (you can read component). An asset, is at least illustrated by a document, it can be tested through a sample program or it can be used or imported in a computable format, a file. Assets are organized recursively in a hierarchy and assets at the same level can also be related by a usage relation. A document can serve as a support reading for many assets.

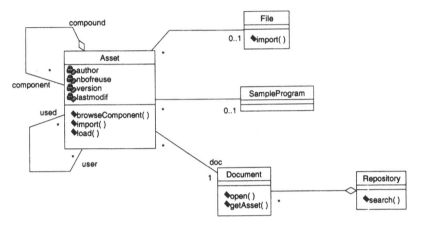

Figure 1: MARST structure through a class diagram.

• Asset: software assets are related with each others in two different manners: through a compound/component hierarchy or through a usage relationship. This structure is so generic that it can be applied whatever the level of abstraction is (see paragraph 3.1). Depending on it, this generic structure can be specified more precisely using the metamodel of the level. For instance, if we try to reuse UML analysis class diagram, the relationship between a package asset and classe asset can be better specified using the metamodel. This structure between assets must be represented in the tool to provide component browsing capabilities.

• Document: Each asset must be attached with a document that illustrates it. A document can be the reading support for many assets

• Repository: All documents are recorded in a repository. The main goal of this repository is to provide full text retrieval and search by key-words capabilities.

• File: A file (computable format) is attached to each asset. So, the reuser is able to reuse code. He can also test online a component or import class diagrams...

• Sample Program: To illustrate the capability of a software asset, it is associated with a executable demonstration program whenever it is possible.

3.3.3 Dynamic study through the description of a reuse scenario.

The collaboration of the whole is studied through a reuse sequence diagram. Let us describe a typical reuse activity. First of all, the reuser, can qualify his need with keywords. Based on them, he can request the repository to obtain documents that are matching keywords. Then, the reuser can consult a document to choose a software asset. He can evaluate dependencies between assets by browsing their organization. Finally, the reuser can import the software data as a computable structure (a file) and can exploit it to answer his need. In a sequence diagram, this collaboration can be designed like in figure 2.

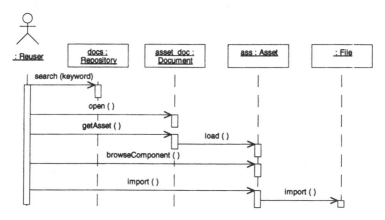

Figure 2: An architecture-independent sequence diagram of a reuse activity.

This sequence diagram can be extended. Indeed, the reuser can filter his request in specifying an asset type. He can also test online the component through a sample program, and so on...

3.4 Applicability and Consequences

As a generic model, MARST defines a common design kernel that must be adapted for concrete software assets.

3.4.1 Applicability

Use this model whenever you need to develop the appropriation feeling for a reuser. The documentation part makes the asset much more understandable, the browsing capability make the asset much more manageable and finally the online functionalities give more confidence to the reuser, since he can test the software asset online. All these three qualities are essential to develop the feeling of appropriation and to avoid human obstacles in a reuse strategy.

3.4.2 Consequences

Each reusable asset must be added in the repository with at least two characteristics: its documentation and its computable format (a file). Hence, for this architecture, adding an asset that can be reusable imposes its adaptation. At this stage many questions arise. What is a good grain for a component? Is it possible to select the asset type? Finally, we can claim that the efficiency of a tool built on this generic model also comes from the quality of the information recorded. It must be the responsibility of the reuse support team to adjust these parameters to provide efficient tools.

4   RENET, a Framework to Support Reuse Using a Web Architecture

Upon the MARST generic model, we define a framework that generates a computable reuse support tool. Figure 3 presents the coarse grain architecture of a reuse support tool.

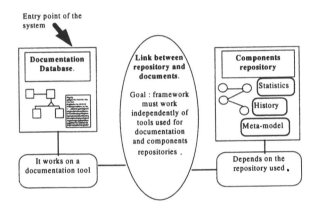

Figure 3: Coarse grain architecture of the RENET framework.

So, the main goal of this architecture is to link a component with its associated documentation. The documentation database gives a good entry point in the system by which the reuser will be able to search a software asset requesting the documentation set in a free language.

4.1   Basic Technical Properties

Some key aspects of a reuse support tool are its availability, its accessibility and the quality of components presentation. A tool must be designed to guarantee three axes to increase the potential reuse of all the components, like these specified in MARST.

• Component presentation. The documentation depends on software element type. For the legacy system we use documents (i.e. specifications) which already exist. For new components, we think that a pattern card presentation could be a convenient way to clearly document reusable software data [2]. The user must be able to evaluate and understand the component as easily as possible. Therefore, we add to the component presentation some qualitative and quantitative information like the number of reuse, test cases, the author or an example of an anterior reuse, etc.

• Availability. To help the developer in its daily work, a tool must always be available and must be in accordance to the existing component set. So the tool may load its data from a centralized database which is up to date. We can notice that this tool also helps to adopt a new working organization in which a specific team is explicitly responsible for guarantee a reuse policy. We think that this team needs reuse support tools to help its acceptance and its integration in the organization and to promote the components they maintain.

• Activities of the reuse support tool. After having studied technical and functional requirements, we can design an activity diagram of a reuse support tool. First of all, let us describe the different functions the user needs in a reuse support tool. The reuser, identified as the main actor, can begin to use a tool in two ways. First of all, if he knows the component he needs, he can access it directly through the component hierarchy. If he only knows his requirements, he can search with keywords a component which may be adapted to his requirements. Once the component is identified, the potential reuser will be able to browse the component hierarchy, to read and to study the online documentation and even to test online, or to import the building block. Using UML notation, these activities can be modeled in a use case diagram (see figure 4).

So reusing activity is separated in five use cases. "Component browsing" and "Component searching" are the two entry points of the system. These two alternatives will appear on the first screen of the application.

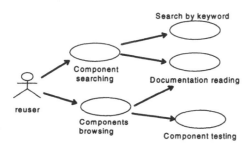

Figure 4: Use case diagram.

4.2 Technical Choices for the Development

The technical target of the framework is based on two tools: the first one is responsible of the documentation issue and the second one deals with components repository. Let us describe what the "documentation database" and "repository" mean in this RENET framework area. A documentation tool serves to collect documents, but it also serves to retrieve pertinent information from this document set. Generally speaking, these tools are exploited in two steps. The first one called indexing process prepares a keyword table from a full text document set. The second one uses the first one and consists in answering to many requests from the user who wants to consult document on a particular subject. The repository tool is responsible for assets organized in a hierarchy. This repository also exposes the metamodel of assets to leave the reuser choose his needed type of component. These two tools are independent and can be used together through and by the reuse support software.

Any documentation functionality, like document retrieval by keywords, is under the responsibility of the documentation tool. It allows a good autonomy of changing the tool whenever a better one is needed. In the same idea, the component repository depends on software asset types. Like documentation support tool, the component repository tool can be changed or can be mixed with another one. So we must define a set of uniform interfaces called APIs (Application Program Interface), independently of underlying used tools. In respect with these constraints, one solution is to develop this tool around a Web server; available on the local network.

The Web server architecture offers a lot of advantages for such a tool. First, a lot of HTTP servers are twined with documentation tool. Therefore, the dialog is facilitated between them because the APIs of the documentation tool are adapted to the Web server. Moreover, HTML language is naturally adapted to represent component hierarchy: "Hypertext applies well to domains where relationships among domain elements are important" [7]. Indeed, we can notice that the same word "browse" is used as well as for a Web area as for a component repository. Finally, Web architecture is widely accepted by our developers.

4.3 Static Design of RENET

Such technical choices have consequences on the design target. The Web server architecture and the documentation database together rely on the same technique which is namely a file organization. A component may also be visualized in the run of a binary file (executable) or via a documentation file. To reach an asset, whatever its type is, we need to declare in a HTML file a referential link to its documentation support file and to its location. Finally, we can also notice that searching requests work on a documentation database. A file serves as a support both for a document and for a software element. The resulting class diagram is presented in figure 5.

This diagram puts the stress on some key-ideas. It shows that this design is adapted to a technical target, mainly the technical target of the software. It also serves as a transition between MARST and its implementation to illustrate how analysis concepts will be implemented in the chosen technical target is. In that sense, "[RENET] framework can be viewed as a more concrete form of [PARST] pattern" [5].

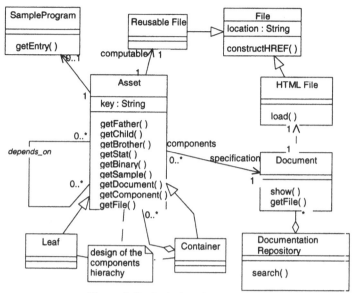

Figure 5: Static design class diagram.

4.4 RENET Dynamic Design

Operations in precedent class diagram were obtained after having designed many sequence diagrams. One sequence diagram is presented in figure 6 as an example. The sequence diagram presented is first described in a free language, then specified in a sequence diagram.

Let us describe the scenario entitled *"component retrieval using the documentation database"* (we use a searching/indexing engine on the documentation database). First, let us imagine that the reuser knows his requirements and is looking for a software asset that is conform to his requirements. In that case, the reuser defines his need by keywords and submits it to the documentation database tool. The request result presents a list of documents to the user. The user chooses one document and asks the system to display it. An HTML page is dynamically composed to present both textual documents and all referential links which show the place of the asset in the repository (child, parent, brother). Thanks to the Web architecture, our tool enables the user to browse the assets hierarchy with hyper-link capability. Moreover, the system illustrates the component by its statistics of reuse and its quantitative history (author, date, version, etc.). Once he has chosen the asset, the reuser can import the computable file linked with it (see figure 6).

We need to develop other sequence diagrams for "documentation reading", "online test of a component" , "components hierarchy browsing". Once critical sequence diagrams are made, we add the discovered operations to the static class

160

diagram. The complete class diagram with all added operations is presented in figure 5.

We can notice that as HTML language is adapted to visualize component browsing activity, sequence diagram is a good representation for a Web server design. Indeed, figure 6 shows that dynamic aspects in HTTP server can be classified in two categories: when a request is submitted to the server, the server first loads the HTML answer page, then it prepares future links that the user will be able to invoke. For example, when you want to visualize a component documentation, the resulting HTML page must show the requested document and the hyper-links that illustrate component place in the repository. Furthermore, we can notice that sequence diagram of figure 6 extends that of figure 2 in adding architecture-dependent details. In figure 6, we focus on the "showing component step" and we describe more precisely how the dynamic making of HTML page prepares future request of the reuser such as "browse components hierarchy" or "online test of component ".

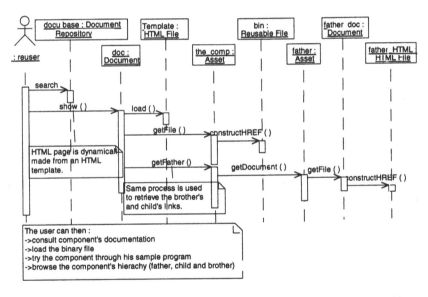

Figure 6: An example of a sequence diagram strongly depending of the chosen architecture.

4.5 Implementation

Once the design step is achieved, we develop the framework that will provide a skeleton to implement the reuse support tools. RENET relies on two other existing software systems. One of them manages documentation database and the other one deals with the component repository. Our framework may be independent of these software and needs to interact with them by standard APIs (see table 1).

Documentation Tool	Components repository
search	getSister
index	getFather
show	getChild
getLocation	getLocation

Table 1: Standards APIs for documentation tool and component repository software.

The RENET framework uses a relational database in which we maintain the referential links between software components and documents, relationships between assets and import files and statistics of reuse and component history. Based on this architecture, the Web server dynamically builds HTML pages interacting with the database, the components repository and the documentation database.

So, each operation that must be implemented, is coded in a scripting language in HTML pages. We use the Microsoft ASP for Active Server Page that are like CGI programs. When an ASP request is invoked on HTTP server, the server interprets the scripting code and the result, an HTML page, is sent back to the client. This technique is efficient in a full Microsoft environment. Indeed, we works with Microsoft index server as a documentation tool, with Microsoft INTERNET information server as a Web server, and with Microsoft SQL server as a database.

The technical architecture in figure 7 represents the five main processes used in the RENET framework. The client computer where a Web browser is running, is the interface between system and reuser. Therefore, the global established dialog goes through this Web RENET.

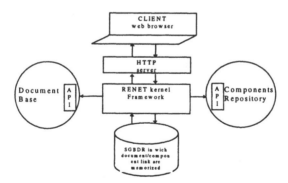

Figure 7: Technical architecture of RENET.

4.6 Customizing RENET

Building a reuse support tool from RENET can be divided in four stages.

1. *Providing a document database that must be indexed. This stage gives the entry point of the search by keywords activity.*

2. Describing and recording in a database the assets, their link with their documentation and their link with their online import file and sample program.

3. Describing and recording the metamodel of the assets type to enable the reuser to filter his requests depending on type.

4. Implementing standard APIs of a repository (see Table 1), in specific embedded APIs of the current repository into component.

5 Actual Work: a Tool to Present Legacy Components

The predominance of software components coming from legacy systems leads to concentrate our works on them. Each component is documented and takes place in the banking business scheme as follows:

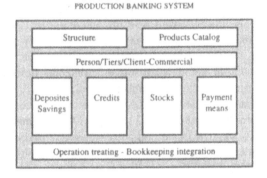

Figure 8: GC2i information system organization.

Presented in its environment the component becomes much more understandable and the appropriation phase is made easier.

5.1.1 Using RENET to present the legacy components.

Hence, the reuser has all the necessary information to understand each component but there is a lack of tool around reuse to structure this information. So, we have built a support tool upon the RENET. The smallest component is the DLL and the all is organized around a functional decomposition of the banking business.

See figure 9 to notice the resulted HTML page of a legacy software asset. This screen hard copy represents the vision that the reuser has from a component. The main menu of the Web server takes place on the left side. The right side is divided into two parts. At the top, the reuser can see the component name and he can browse the component hierarchy (see the hyper links "father", "son" and "sister"). He can also download the component. Finally, in the middle of the screen we present documentation relative to the components. Thus, the reuser owns a complete view of the components. So, he can understand them better in reading design choices in the document or evaluate their dependencies with each other in visualizing its place in the repository. After all, we may think that this reuse support tool achieves its main goal in facilitating the appropriation step in a design by reuse process.

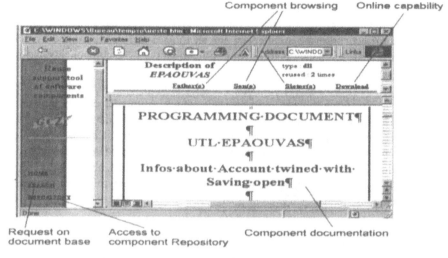

Figure 9: Component presentation sample.

5.1.2   Utility and arising issues.

This tool is the answer to different needs. First of all, adopting a reuse strategy means having useful components for reuse. Economically, rebuilding a banking software platform is impossible. Thus, this tool can constitute a first step in the reuse strategy adoption in wrapping current applications to design a component repository. The second advantage of this tool occurs in maintenance phase. Indeed it offers an online documentation tool for maintenance workers. The third advantage is to provide a structured base to identify and to build reusable business components from existing ones. In such a way, we avoid both the "a priori" building which leads to too generic structures and the "a posteriori" manner which gives too specialized objects [18].

6   Conclusion and Future Work

Today, another issue arises from a bad definition of the components. Indeed, in each component, graphical information, business logic and database requests are mixed. Moreover, components suffer from a lack of explanation on the design and technical choices. Each component is described through its functional utility but design choices remain at a coding level, so that the reuser can not acquire a satisfactory knowledge of each of them. So, in future developments, we will adopt two strategic choices. First, we will tend to clearly separate the three levels: presentation, business logic and access to database like in [26]. All technical and business aspects like persistence, concurrency, confidentiality, security and so on will be in charge of a middleware tool (for example a CORBA compliant broker). The second axis of the development is to enforce design step in order to explain each choice made during the making of the component. Developing with an OOAD method seems to be a convenient way to really specify a software. In such a development environment, the reuse support tools will become more and more important. In fact, once the architecture for all tools is defined through MARST and RENET, their efficiency is to be seen in the quality of the components and in their presentation.

As we noticed it throughout our paper, "the technology and method deficiencies include a lack of tools to carry out reuse procedures. A number of new tools are needed" [15]. Thus, to promote reuse, these tools must serve to the "reuse team" in guiding development process to this new and promising way of development. In that case, the main goal of reuse team consists in making the phase of component appropriation easier for the assemblers who reuse building blocks to design software. In our opinion, object oriented technology can lead to reuse but we must define a real reuse plan to achieve our goal.

Références

1. B. Meyer, Reusable Software, the basic of object-oriented libraries, Prenctice Hall object-oriented series 1994.

2. E. Gamma, R. Helm, R. Johnson, J. Vlissides, Design Patterns, Elements of Reusable Object-Oriented Software, Addison-Wesley, 1995.

3. W. Pree, Design Patterns for Object-Oriented, Addison Wesley 1994.

4. D. Riehle, H. Zullighoven, Understanding and Using Patterns in Software Development, Theory and Practice of Object Systems, Vol. 2, n°1, 1996

5. R. Johnson, Frameworks = (Components + Patterns), Communications of the ACM, Vol 40, No 10, pp39-42, October 1997

6. M. Fowler, Analysis Patterns, Reusable Object-Oriented Models, Addison Wesley, 1997

7. T. Isakowist and R. J. Kauffman, Supporting Search for Reusable Software Objects, IEEE Transactions on Software Engineering, Vol 22, No 6, June 1996.

8. Rational et al., UML Summary, Semantics and Notation Guide, http://www.rational.com/uml, September 1997.

9. S. Rideau, F. Barbier and H. Briand, Identifying Reuse Obstacles : A Tool Favoring Software Component Appropriation, proceedings of « Reverse Engineering of Information Systems », INSA de Lyon, France, April 1-2, 1998.

10. B. W. Weide, S. H. Edwards, W. D. Heym, T. J. Long and W. F. Odgen, Characterizing Observability and Controllability of Software Components, proceedings of the 4th International Conference on Software Reuse (ICSR4) p.62-71, IEEE Computer Society Press, 19

11. T. J. Mowbray and R. Zahavi. The Essential of CORBA. System Integration Using Distributed Objects. J. Wiley. 1995.

12. C. Casanave, Business-Object Architectures and Standards, http://www.omg.org, 1997.
13. C. M. Pancake, The Promise and the Cost of Object Technology: a Five Year Forecast, Communications of the ACM. Vol. 38, n°10, October 1995
14. R. Fichman and C. Kemerer, Object Technology and Reuse: Lessons from Early Adopters, IEEE Computer, pp 44-59, October 1997.
15. I. Jacobson, M. L. Griss and P. Jonsson, Software Reuse: Architecture, Process and Organization for Business Success, Addison Wesley, 1997.
16. D. Rine, Supporting Reuse with Object Technology, IEEE Computer, pp 43-45, October 1997.
17. D. Schmidt and M. Fayad, Lessons Learned, Building Reusable OO Frameworks for Distributed Software. Communications of the ACM, Vol 40, No 10, pp 85-87, October 1997.
18. B. Meyer, Object Success, In the object oriented series of Prenctice Hall, 1995.
19. G. Caldiera an V.R. Basili, Identifying and Qualifying Reusable Software Components, IEEE Computer, February 1991.
20. R. Wirfs-Brock, R. Johnson, Current Research in Object-Oriented Design, Communications of the ACM. Vol. 33, n°9, September 1990.
21. Poulin S., Measuring Software Reuse. Addison Wesley 1997.
22. R. Rada and J. Moore. Standardizing Reuse. Communications of the ACM, Vol. 40, n°3, March 1997.
23. I. Jacobson, The Object Advantage, Business Process Reengineering with Object Technology, Addison Wesley, 1994.
24. P. A. V. Hall. Overview of Reverse Engineering and Reuse Research, Information and Software Technology, Butterworth-Heinemann, Vol. 34, n°4, April 1992.
25. D. Batory and B. J. Geraci, Validating Component Compositions in Software System Generators, proceedings of the 4th International Conference on Software Reuse (ICSR4) p.72-81, IEEE Computer Society Press, 1996.
26. O. Sims, Business Objects, Delivering Cooperative Objects for Client-Server, McGraw-Hill, 1994.

Improving Productivity in Building Data-Oriented Information Systems - Why Object Frameworks Are Not Enough

Wolfgang Goebl
CFC Informationssysteme
Vienna, Austria

Abstract

In recent years the development of object frameworks has become state of the practice for building object-oriented information systems. We show that the pure framework approach fails to take advantage of the vast reuse potential of patterns occurring in our domain. We describe our generative approach for building data-oriented information systems and compare it to the pure object framework approach.

1   Introduction

Although many ideas for a more efficient software reuse in order to improve productivity have been presented since 1968 [1], the productivity of building computer programs is still dissatisfying. This situation is mentioned in many papers as the 'software crisis'. Typical symptoms of the crisis are (i) software is delivered late, (ii) software quality is low, (iii) too much of software engineers capabilities are spent on maintenance [2]. State of the art techniques like object frameworks do improve the productivity of building data-oriented information systems but are still not enough to close the gap between the demands placed on the software industry and what the state of the practice can deliver [3]. It seems as if the capability of the software engineering technology is always one step behind the demands of the software users.

The ideas to improve software reuse, to find a way out of the software crisis presented   in the last 3 decades can be divided roughly into composition technologies and generation technologies [4]. A few years ago the paths of research on composition-based reuse and on generative reuse were quite separate. Researchers on program synthesis tried to combine artificial intelligence with software engineering to generate complete computer programs automatically. Today it is believed that most attempts at program synthesis have either failed or enjoyed only limited success. Certainly, none of them has found its way into common software engineering practice [5].

Looking at the common software engineering practice of building data-oriented information systems, we find that reuse strategies today are mainly based on composition techniques. Usually the part of reuse strategy is reduced to the search for a suitable class-library or framework. Even further it might be observed that most research still concentrates on components [2]. Generative techniques are used only for very small portions of the code (e.g. generative CASE-Tools). Even though the reuse potential benefit of generative techniques has been mentioned in many papers for more than a decade (e.g. [6], [7], [8], [9], [10]), the use of code generators seems to be a somewhat forgotten technology. But it is just the domain of data-oriented information systems where most of the processing consists of associative data access, that shows lots of reusable patterns and has great potential for the use of generators. The object framework approach fails to take advantage of these patterns, and therefore the increase in productivity in our domain is insufficient.

To underline the insufficiency of frameworks in data-oriented information systems and the importance to reuse the vast amount of patterns, we present our approach which is a combination of object frameworks (composition technique) and domain-specific code generators (generation technique). Instead of implementing the framework code and the application code by hand, we just implement the framework code and the generator code manually. The application programmer builds a model of the application and starts the generators which produce most of the application code and the relational database table- and index structure out of this model by applying the reusable patterns.

The remainder of this paper is organized as follows: In section 2 we describe the characteristics of our domain to show the potential it offers for the use of generators. Section 3 gives a brief overview of the concept of object frameworks and discusses why it is not satisfying for applications in our domain. Section 4 presents our approach, discusses its benefits and compares it to the object framework approach. Finally we will present related work, our conclusions and a brief survey of our future research.

2 The Domain of Data-Oriented Information Systems

2.1 Brief Description of the Domain

The data-oriented information systems (DOIS) we build are used to administrate structured information. Most of the processing consists of associative data access. Usually the information is stored on one or more server(s). Data is entered by the clients using a graphical user interface. This data is then sent to the server(s) which store(s) it in a relational database. Clients which want to edit already stored information send a request to the server which provides the requested data. We use relational databases for storing the information on the server(s). Examples for such systems are: customer administration systems, product administration systems, etc. Workflow-Management systems on the other hand, are outside the borders of DOISs because they provide lots of calculations and processing. The description of such systems sounds quite trivial. It is "just" data entering, storing and providing, there are no complex logics or calculations as in other domains (e.g. real time systems). The complexity of building such systems arises from topics that can be grouped into 2 major categories:

2.1.1 Technical Issues

Examples for technical issues that have to be solved are: distributed transaction management, data replication between the servers, asynchronous communication of the data, performance issues, etc. Technical issues have to be addressed in the implementation not for just one concrete information system, but for all systems with "the same architecture".

2.1.2 Complex Structure of the Data

A medium object-oriented information system like we build, may have 500-1000 business object (BO) classes. Each of the BO classes has to be stored in the database, sent over the network, edited in a user-interface, etc. The BO model is usually custom-made for a concrete information system.

2.2 Patterns inside the Implementation

The following example illustrates the vast amount of patterns which can be found inside the implementation of DOISs. Consider a simple DOIS for processing the first name, surname and hobbies of a person. Figure 1 shows the BO model for this information system consisting of two BOs, namely Person and Hobby.

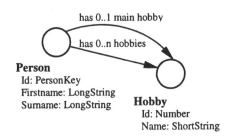

Figure 1: Business object model of an example information system

If we take a closer look at the structure of the code which has to be implemented to build a DOIS for displaying these 2 BO classes (Figure 2 shows the code in pseudo syntax), we find lots of repetitive patterns which can be grouped into two classes as described below:

2.2.1 Redundant Implicity of the BO-Model

One portion of knowledge from the BO model is spread redundantly and orthogonally across the application code.

The design decisions are scattered throughout the code, resulting in "tangled" code that is excessively difficult to develop and maintain [11]. The design decisions which attributes of which type a BO class has, effect for example the table structure of the relational database, the implementation of the request for the data of the BO class, the SQL queries to retrieve the data of the BO class, the implementation of the response to send the BO class' data back to the client and the GUI layout to display and edit the attributes. For the example in Figure 2: the

---

0. **Server:** Execute a SQL statement to create the tables of the relational database to store the attributes of the person, the hobby and the many-relationship between the two:
   CREATE TABLE **PERSON** (ID NUMBER, **FIRSTNAME CHAR(40)**,
                                   SURNAME CHAR(40), MAINHOBBY NUMBER)
   CREATE TABLE **HOBBY** (ID NUMBER, **NAME CHAR(12)**)
   CREATE TABLE **PERSONHOBBIES** (**PERSONID** NUMBER, **HOBBYID** NUMBER)

1. **Client:** Request the **FIRSTNAME**, the **SURNAME,** the **MAINHOBBY** and the other **HOBBIES** of a person with ID = *someID*

2. **Server:** Execute SQL statements to query the according tables of the relational database:
   SELECT **FIRSTNAME, SURNAME, MAINHOBBY** FROM **PERSON**
        WHERE ID = *someID*
   SELECT B.**NAME** FROM **PERSONHOBBIES** A, **HOBBY** B
        WHERE A.**HOBBYID** = B.**ID** AND A.**PERSONID** = *someID*

3. **Server:** Send the **FIRSTNAME**, the **SURNAME**, the **MAINHOBBY** and the other **HOBBIES** back to the client

4. **Client:** Read the **FIRSTNAME**, the **SURNAME** the **MAINHOBBY** and the other **HOBBIES** from the network

5. **Client:** Display the **FIRSTNAME**, the **SURNAME** and all the **HOBBIES** in some kind of GUI. Highlight the **MAINHOBBY**. The size of the text field for the **FIRSTNAME** and the **SURNAME** must be to display 40 characters, the width of the list of **HOBBIES** must be 12 characters

---

Figure 2: Tasks for displaying the information in the user-interface (pseudo-code). The BO-model from Figure 1 effects lots of places in the application code (written in **bold**).

knowledge that a person has a first name effects six places in the application code. The BO model is implicitly and redundantly hidden inside the application code.

2.2.2   *Similarities in the Implementation of the BOs*

Lots of similarities in the implementation of the BO classes of an information system can be found [12], or in other words: it is often "quite the same task" to

- create a database table for the BO class X or to create a database table for the BO class Y
- communicate the attributes of the BO class X or to communicate the attributes of the BO class Y
- query the relational database for the attributes of BO class X or to query it for the attributes of BO class Y
- display the attributes of BO class X in the GUI or to display the attributes of BO class Y in the GUI

In our example it is e.g. "quite the same task" to create a table for the BO class Person and to create a table for the BO class Hobby (Figure 2, Step 0.)

3   Object Frameworks

The idea of object frameworks captured significant attention recently [3]. A framework is a skeleton program defining a reusable software architecture in terms of collaboration contracts between abstract classes and a set of variation points

[13]. The framework classes abstract all structures which are common to the applications in the domain. The application code uses these framework classes and subclasses them for a new application. The classes of the application code are implemented "on top" of the framework classes. Framework reusability leverages the domain knowledge and prior effort of experienced developers in order to avoid recreating and revalidating common solutions to recurring application requirements and software design challenges [14]. Frameworks apply a great amount of uniformity to the applications built using them, and this uniformity reduces the cost of maintenance [15]. For the domain of DOIS frameworks are an excellent way to handle the technical issues as mentioned in section 2.1.1.

Usually an application doesn't only consist of application code in one programming language. It is e.g. common that the database stored procedures of the application are implemented in a language the database vendor provides. For the purpose of our work we name code of this kind "Other Code". Figure 3 shows the concept of the framework approach.

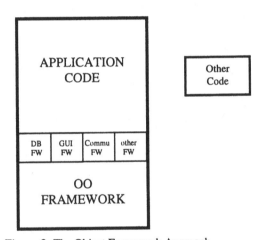

Figure 3: The Object Framework Approach

3.1.1 Problems of Object Frameworks In Our Domain

What does it mean to implement our simple DOIS from Figure 1 using the framework approach? To achieve a well-structured design („separation of concerns") the framework usually consists of a number of separated sub-frameworks (typically database framework, user interface framework, communication framework, etc.). The classes of the application code implementing e.g. the user interface are implemented on top of the GUI framework while the classes implementing the communication between client and server are implemented on top of the communication framework. The problem is that the design decisions (like the BO model in Figure 1) cross-cut the structure of this sub-frameworks. More concrete: it is e.g. necessary to implement Figure 2, Task 5.: "Display the **FIRSTNAME**, the **SURNAME** and all the **HOBBIES** in some kind of GUI" on top of the GUI framework and to implement Figure 2, Task 3.: "Send the value of the **FIRSTNAME**, the **SURNAME**, the **MAINHOBBY** and all the other **HOBBIES** back to the client" on top of the communication framework. The design decisions are still scattered throughout the application. Things get even worse if the design decisions are scattered throughout "Other Code" also. The implementation of database stored procedures is for example highly dependent on the BO-model of the application. Developers have to manually keep the BO-model, the application code and "Other Code" consistent.

Another major problem with object frameworks is mentioned in [14]: Application requirements change frequently. Therefore, the requirements of frameworks often change as well. As frameworks evolve, the applications that use them must evolve as well. For our domain this means that a change in one of the subframeworks makes it necessary to change the implementation of all 500-1000 BOs respectively - a really tedious, error-prone activity.

Object frameworks are very suitable for dealing with the technical issues which have to be solved just once for DOISs with a "similar architecture" (mentioned in section 2.1.1) but fail to offer a good concept to manage the complex structure of the data (see section 2.1.2) usually occurring in our domain – they fail to take advantage of the vast reuse potential of patterns as mentioned in section 2.2.

4   The Object-Framework + Generator Approach

Our approach (introduced first by [16]) shown in Figure 4 extends the pure object-framework approach by the massive use of generators. The important difference to the pure framework approach presented in the previous section is, that we generate

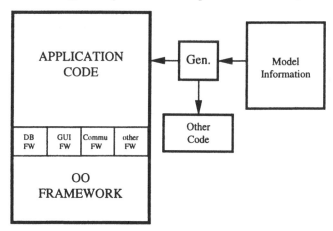

Figure 4: The Object-Framework + Generator Approach

most of the application code, instead of implementing it by hand. The application programmer builds a model of the application (writes down the model information) and starts the generators which produce the application code and "Other code" by applying the patterns as described in Section 2.2.

The structure of the application code is very different from the structure of the framework code. The *application code* built on top of the framework subclasses the framework classes for a concrete application. This code is highly dependent on the BO model and shows patterns like mentioned in section 2.2. The application code is a highly redundant moloch which is very hard to develop and maintain. As the BO-model of one DOIS is usually very different from the BO-model of another, this code itself has a very small reuse factor. What should be reused are the patterns like mentioned in section 2.2. Generators are an excellent technique to make the complex structure of the data (implicitly hidden inside the application code) manageable. The *framework code* implements common solutions for the technical issues of our domain mentioned in Section 2.1. Implementing this code requires human intelligence and it doesn't show any patterns like the application code. The framework code has a large reuse factor when implementing several DOISs with a similar architecture.

4.1   Model Information

Model information can be seen as the knowledge which is necessary to generate the code of an application on top of the framework. The more semantically-rich the model information the greater the amount of application code which can be generated. We've implemented an object-oriented meta-model on which the programmer can program the model information for a concrete application. The base of our meta-model are the meta-model constructs from the "classic" BO model (e.g. BO classes, one-, many-relationships between BO classes). For our example DOIS the BO model is shown in Figure 1. As this is usually not enough knowledge to generate a sufficient amount of code for an application, our meta-model extends the "classic" BO model. The model information is provided to the generators by Smalltalk definition-classes (Figure 5 shows a part of the model information for our example DOIS).

Our meta-model is designed to hold the following model information:

```
Person class>>definition
^self
    keyAttribute: 'Id' to: Key mandatory: true;
    oneAttribute: 'firstName' to: LongString mandatory: true;
    oneAttribute: 'surname' to: LongString mandatory: true;
    manyReference: 'hobbies' to: Hobby;
    oneOf: 'hobbies' reference: 'mainHobby';

Hobby class>>definition
^self
    keyAttribute: 'Id' to: Key mandatory: true;
    oneAttribute: 'name' to: ShortString
        mandatory: true

LongString class>>databaseType
    ^'Char(40)'

ShortString class>>databaseType
    ^'Char(12)'

Key class>>databaseType
    ^'Number'
```

Figure 5: A part of the model information (Smalltalk syntax) for our example DOIS from Figure 1.

4.1.1   "Classic" BO Model

Each BO has a class method >>definition like in Figure 5 which defines its attributes and relationships to other BO classes.

4.1.2   Extension of the Business-Object Model

New relationship classes. The classical object meta-model defines only a small number of classes of relationships between BOs (e.g. one-, many relationships). Our meta-model introduces a number of new classes of relationships. In our example, Person defines a one-of-"hobbies"-reference "mainHobby". This new kind of relationship has important semantic differences to a simple one-reference: the one-of-"hobbies"-reference always refers to one of the hobbies. We will see later that this semantic difference has important consequences on the generated GUI and database schema.
Information if an attribute is mandatory or not. This effects e.g. if a column in a database table is allowed to be NULL or not ('NOT NULL' clause in the CREATE TABLE statement) and if a client is allowed to leave a GUI dialog without filling in a certain edit-field.
Class of an attribute. In Figure 5 the classes 'Key' and 'Longstring' represent simple datatypes. 'PhoneNumber' represents a BO class.
Subsets of the business-object model which are processed in one user interaction (not shown in Figure 5). Typically a client wants to display or edit a certain subset of the business-object model. In our example the client might want to display the lastname and the main hobby of a certain person in a GUI. This kind of model information effects e.g. the generated code which sends the data across the network.

4.1.3   Other Model Information

Technical information about the used Relational Database Management System. For the generation of the database tables and SQL-statements on these tables it is important to have the knowledge of the available data-types and naming conventions of the Relational Database Management System inside the model information. In Figure 5 for example, the class 'Longstring' knows its database type, Char(40).

Generally the meta-model should be designed that it is:
Well structured (from the application developer's view). It should be easy for the application developer to understand the semantics of the meta-model and to build the model of the DOIS.
Well structured (from the generator's view). It should be easy for the generators to process the model information.
Non-redundant. This makes the model maintainable. A late change (e.g. a BO class needs another attribute) effects just one place in the model information.
Easy to extend. Getting more and more domain knowledge (identifying more and more commonalties of applications within the domain) it is possible to improve the percentage of generated code vs. manually implemented code by extending the meta-model and generators accordingly.

4.2 Generators

A generator projects a subset of the model information onto a segment of application code or "Other Code". Each generator applies a pattern on it's part of the model information to generate it's product. These patterns are identified during the design of the framework. All of our generators are implemented in Smalltalk and most of them generate Smalltalk classes or methods. Usually the generated classes are subclasses of framework classes and the methods are generated for a generated class or a framework class. Therefore the generators are strongly coupled with the design of the framework – designing a framework class which is relevant for a generator identifying the according pattern and designing the generator is the same task.

Currently we generate nearly the complete server application code and approx. 50% of the client application code - Figure 6 shows what we generate out of the model information.

1) The *GUI generator* just produces the basic contents of our dialogs. For the example dialog in Figure 6 which just displays the attributes of a person and its hobbies, the rules implemented in the generator are:

- For each attribute (first name, surname) create a text field of the width of its class (Longstring → 40 characters)
- For each many-reference (hobbies) create a listbox of the width of its class (ShortString → 12 characters)
- For each one-of-reference (mainhobby) highlight the according row in the list of its many-reference (hobbies)

The final GUI layout is done manually.

2) For each subset of the BO model which are processed in one user interaction, the *communication generator* produces a method that writes the data of this subset on the network and one that reads it from the network. In our example the only subset is the complete BO model (first name, surname, mainHobby of Person, name of Hobbies).

3) The *relational database schema generator* generates the complete database schema for our applications (tables, indices, referential integrity constraints). The (simplified) rules for generating the tables are:

- For each BO class: create a table with the appropriate name (PERSON, HOBBY) and a column with the appropriate name and data-type for each one-attribute of the BO class (PERSON: FIRSTNAME, SURNAME, MAINHOBBY; HOBBY: NAME).
  For each one-relationship to another BO class create a column with the data-type for ID (MAINHOBBY)
- For each many-relationship to another BO class create a table (PERSONHOBBIES) for resolving the many-relationship using two columns with data-type for ID.

The appropriate table- and column names are calculated out of the names of the BO classes and their attributes.

In reality the rules and the necessary model information for creating tables are more complex (for database performance reasons the table structure is also dependent from the expected number of rows in a table, from the kind of queries etc.).

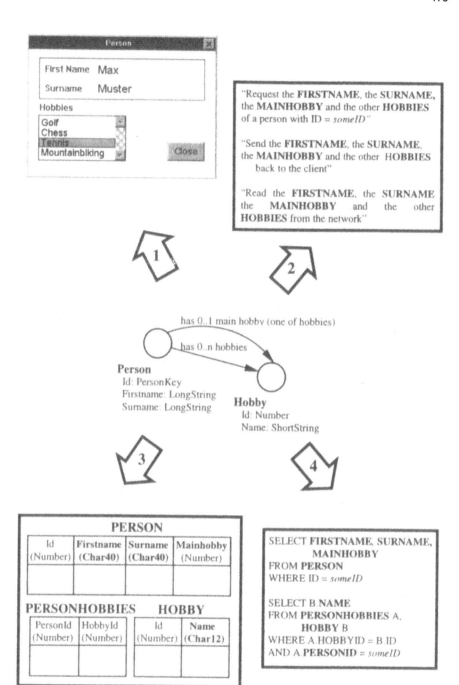

Figure 6: Overview of our generators

A number of rules produce all necessary indices and referential integrity constraints. For our example, the relational database schema generator generates a referential integrity constraint which makes sure that the column MAINHOBBY refers to a valid HOBBY.

4) The *SQL generator* produces nearly all SQL-statements for inserting, updating, deleting, and selecting data of all BO-classes and their relationships. The SQL-statements can be generated as stored procedures in an external file. Our experience shows, that the great majority of the SQL-statements for applications in our domain are "simple" and can easily be generated. Only the SQL-statements for performing searches tend to be more complex. Currently we write the more complex SQL-statements by hand.

Our domain offers great potential for the massive use of generators. The low-complexity, data-intensive structure of the information systems we build promotes the identification of the patterns, the design of the according model information and the implementation of the generators. However there are structures inside the application code where it doesn't make sense to reuse them as patterns because (i) these structures just appear once and are therefore no pattern, (ii) the pattern is very hard to identify or to implement in a generator.

The reason for the big difference of the percentage between the client and the server code which can be generated results from a big difference in the complexity of their tasks. All a server for a concrete application does is waiting for requests, doing the according database queries and sending the responses back to the client. A server for a concrete application X and a server for a concrete application Y do very much the same job. This makes it easy to identify the necessary model information and the patterns to be applied by the generators. Usually the clients of a concrete application provide much greater variety. There are GUI layouts, logics inside the GUI, etc. which aren't common for a domain but needed just by one concrete application. This fact prevents the use of generators, it is more productive to implement these parts of the client by hand.

[8] defines criteria for the use of program synthesis to have in mind when deciding whether to use generators for a certain part of the application code or not:
- „How complex is the program synthesis process?"
- „How much effort will it take to identify and represent the necessary domain knowledge?"
- „How much of the programming task can be automated using the program synthesis system? "

We only use generators where it makes sense from a productivity point of view considering the above mentioned criteria.

4.3 The Development Process

Developers implementing systems in the same domain get more and more domain knowledge overtime. Getting more domain knowledge means that a greater number of common characteristics of applications can potentially be identified. These common characteristics could be abstracted inside the framework code (as done using the pure object framework approach) or identified as an additional pattern which means to implement an additional generator and possibly to extend the meta-model. It is possible to improve the percentage of generated code vs. manually implemented code incrementally when getting more domain knowledge.

Our framework, meta-model and generators have been improved incrementally driven by the needs of concrete applications we are implementing. Finding a new abstraction for a common structure of a domain, building the according framework component and/or generator and the eventually necessary extension of the meta-model is done within the same design task.

4.4 Benefits of Our Approach Compared to the Pure Framework Approach

4.4.1 Very small amount of application code has to be implemented by hand

All the "standard work" is done by the generators. Only the tasks which require human intelligence have to be done by the application programmer.

4.4.2 Model-centered view of the application

The application programmer can concentrate on the real important thing – the model behind the concrete application he is building. It is much easier to lose the eye on the model behind a concrete application if implementing the application code by hand.

4.4.3 Maintainability

The generators keep the moloch of application code manageable. The model of the application is explicit and non redundant inside the model information. If a requirement changes late in the development cycle, a small change of the BO model effects just one place in the model information – the application programmer just has to do the according change of the model information and start the generators.

If a part of the framework changes, it is not necessary to change the relevant part of the implementation of all the BO classes as well. Instead we identify the changed pattern, re-implement the relevant generators which then project the new pattern to produce the change in the implementation of all the BO classes.

Although we have no experience with porting our applications to another OO language like C++, we believe that it is much more easy to port the framework and the generators than to port the framework and the implementation of all the hundreds of BO classes.

The large maintainability improvement compared to the pure object framework approach comes from the fact, that it is much less work to build or change a generator than to implement or change the code of hundreds of BO's. The generators can simply be implemented with much less code than the redundant application code.

4.4.4 Meta-model keeps model information clear, well structured and extendible

The information used to specify the concrete application on top of the framework is based on a meta-model which keeps it clear and well structured. The real productivity improvement can only be reached if the meta-model is extendible like in our approach. Simply speaking: the more model information is available the more application code can be generated. To reach a sufficient amount of generated application code the meta-model must be custom-made for a domain rather than off-the-shelf like in the generative CASE-tools. The extendibility of the meta-model enables the incremental improvement of the amount of generated code when getting more domain knowledge.

4.4.5   Generation of "Other Code"

Usually an application doesn't only consist of code in just one language. It is e.g. common, that the database stored procedures of the application are implemented in a language the database vendor provides. The implementation of these stored procedures is highly dependent on the BO-model of the application. The model information is the central starting point for the generation. Any code can be generated from the model information, not just application code in a certain target language. The generation of the relational database tables for an application from its model information helps keeping the BO-model and the according relation database tables consistent. No one has to take care that the BO-model and the database structure are consistent. [7] mentions that generators are very useful to facilitate the integration of several "tools" (in this context "tool" means: database management system, documentation system, programming languages, etc.) to build an application.

It seems possible that we will generate code segments in other target languages (e.g. HTML....) in the future.

5   Related Work

The goal of Gregor Kiczales' new programming paradigm called Aspect-Oriented Programming [11] is to enable programmers to express each of the different issues they want to program in an appropriately natural form. These issues are called "Aspects". Instead of manually implementing the code with all these issues "tangled" inside, the programmer expresses each of the aspects in an appropriately natural form. Tangled code is excessively difficult to develop and maintain. The reason why these issues have been hard to capture is that they cross-cut the system's basic functionality. [11] gives the following examples for aspects in a digital library application: failure handling, synchronization constraints, communication strategy. A special form of compiler (generator) called an Aspect Weaver automatically combines these separate aspect descriptions and generates an executable form.

We see aspect-oriented programming very closely related to our work. Our approach and aspect oriented programming have the same intention: to prevent the necessity of implementing non-maintainable code with design decisions tangled into. While aspect-oriented programming is a very general concept with some concrete example applications implemented using it, our approach has been used to implement a real application in the very narrow domain of data-oriented information systems.

6 Conclusion and Further Research

It was shown that the pure object-framework approach does not achieve a sufficient amount of productivity gain in the domain of data-oriented information systems. It fails to take advantage of the vast reuse potential of patterns which occur in our domain. The problem is that the design decisions (like the BO model) cross-cut the structure of subframeworks. In our opinion it is the generative reuse of patterns which has a great unleashed potential to improve the productivity in building applications in our domain. We believe that the use of semantically rich object models are a strong argument for reconsidering the application of domain specific automatic programming.

[8] argues that a domain should be analyzed focusing on the suitable combination of reuse techniques. A reuse strategy must be driven by the needs of an application program instead of adopting the software development strategy around a reuse program. The needs of application programs in our domain are bestimmt by the two groups of complexity namely the complex structure of the data and technical issues. Separating this two groups leads to a hybrid approach to software reuse. The method of choice for managing the complex structure of the data are domain specific generators while object frameworks are a good concept to abstract the common solutions of our domain (e.g. the technical issues described in section 2.1.1).

A prevalent software engineer's opinion is mentioned in [12]: "In the object-oriented world no code generation is needed, we use inheritance instead. The standard behavior in a system is just implemented once in a superclass (which is part of the object-framework) from which all BO classes inherit. The BO classes implement just customizing parameters". We showed that this opinion is not true for our domain. The generative technique has a number of benefits compared to a parameterized approach (generation of "Other Code", concentration on the model of the application).

Currently we edit the model information directly in the according definition classes using the Smalltalk class browser. It is planned to implement a graphical editor which makes the model information of a concrete application more visible and editable. We are incrementally improving our model information adding more and more relevant knowledge to the model information. Our current estimate is that we will be able to generate the complete server- and approx. 80% of the client application code in the near future. Currently our generators are written in Smalltalk, a multiple purpose language. Generators are difficult to build [6] and the implementation of the generators itself shows patterns which could be abstracted by something like a „generator framework". We believe that building a framework of abstractions for implementing generators will decrease time and difficulty to implement one.

References

1. McIlroy M.D. Mass-Produced Software Components. In Buxton J.M., Naur P. and Randell B. (ed) Software Engineering Concepts and Techniques. 1968 NATO Conference on Software Engineering. Petrocelli/Charter, Belgium, 1976, pp. 88-98

2. Dusink L., Katwijk J. v. Reuse Dimensions. Proc. of the Symposion on Software Reusability 1995. ACM Software Engineering Notes 1995; Special Issue August:137-149

3. Mili H., Mili F., Mili A. Reusing Software: Issues and Research Directions. IEEE Transactions on Software Engineering 1995; 6:528-562

4. Biggerstaff T., Richter C. Reusability Framework, Assessment and Directions. IEEE Software 1987; 3:41-49

5. Willis C., Paddon D. A Software Engineering Paradigm for Program Synthesis. Software Engineering Journal 1994; 9:213-220

6. Cleaveland J. Building Application Generators. IEEE Software 1988; 7:25-33

7. Bernstein D.B., Farrow R. Automatic maintenance of routine programming tasks based on a declarative description. Proc. of the 12th International Conference on Software Engineering 1990, IEEE CS Press, 1990, pp.310-315

8. Bhansali S. A Hybrid Approach to Software Reuse. Proc. of the Symposion on Software Reusability 1995, Proc. of the Symposion on Software Reusability 1995. ACM Software Engineering Notes 1995; Special Issue August:215-218

9. Jarzabek S. From reuse library experiences to application generation architectures. Proc. of the Symposion on Software Reusability 1995. ACM Software Engineering Notes 1995; Special Issue August:114-122

10. Kieburtz et. al. A Software Engineering Experiment in Software Component Generation. Proc. of the 18th International Conference on Software Engineering 1996, IEEE CS Press, 1996, pp. 542-552

11. Kiczales G. Aspect Oriented Programming. 8th Annual Workshop on Institutionalizing Software Reuse, WISR8, March 23-26 1997

12. Rösch M. Generierungstechnik für die Implementierung von Business-Objekten. OBJECTspektrum 1996; 6: 28-29

13. Codenie W., De Hondt K., Steyaert P., Vercammen A. From Custom Applications to Domain-Specific Frameworks. Communications of the ACM 1997; 10: 71-77

14. Fayad M.E., Schmidt D.C. Object-Oriented Application Frameworks. Communications of the ACM 1997; 10: 32-38

15. Johnson R.E. Frameworks = (Components + Patterns). Communications of the ACM 1997; 10: 39-42

16. Pieber B., Goebl W. A Genererative Approach for Building Data-Oriented Information Systems. To appear in: Proc. of the 22nd Computer Software and Application Conference 1998, IEEE CS Press, 1998

METHOD ISSUES 1

"The Truth Is Out There?": A Survey of Business Objects

[1] Kitty Hung, [2] Tony Simons, [3] Tony Rose

[1 & 2] Department of Computer Science, The University of Sheffield
Regent Court, 211 Portobello Street, Sheffield, S1 4DP, U.K.
[3] CAD Consultants Ltd.
797 London Road, Thornton Heath, Surrey, CR7 6XA, U.K.
Email : [1] k.hung@dcs.shef.ac.uk
[2] a.simons@dcs.shef.ac.uk
[3] tony.rose@btrinc.com

ABSTRACT

Since the term "Business Objects"(BOs) was first coined, little tangible evidence has emerged to support the claim that BOs have any beneficial impact on information systems (IS) development. A survey was therefore conducted into attitudes to, and adoption of, BOs across a wide spectrum of IS disciplines. Results of the survey revealed that the concept of BOs was not stable and the adoption of BOs was still understrength.

KEY WORDS : *Business Objects, information system development, survey, definition, adoption, standardisation*

1.   INTRODUCTION

The concept of "Business Objects" (BOs) first arose during the deliberations of the Object Management Group (OMG)'s Business Objects Management Special Interest Group (BOMSIG) which later changed its name to Business Objects Domain Task Force (BODTF) [16].   Over the last five years since BOs were first targeted for investigation, there has been an increasingly widely held belief that the goal of **'delivering software'** in line with **'delivering business solutions'** could be addressed by adopting BOs for information system (IS) development.   Academic researchers and industrial developers have now started focusing their attention on a more business-driven approach to software development.

1.1 Expectation

The goal of the BODTF is to bridge the gap between software system models and business enterprise models. The strategy adopted is to raise the level of abstraction at which information systems are described, through the medium of BOs. The expectation is that BOs somehow provide a common framework within which business professionals and software developers may communicate [8]. A "Business Object Model" is then a representation of the client's business, in terms of the operational procedures followed. The anticipated consequence is that the analysis of business systems will proceed more effectively, since the client and developer will use the same representational framework. A longer-term goal is to establish standardised "Business Object" templates that are applicable across individual business domains, and eventually across different types of industry [1] [2].

1.2 Definitions

The OMG define a BO as: *"A representation of a thing active in the business domain including at least its business attributes, behaviour, relationships and constraints. A Business Object may represent, for example, a person, place, event, business process, or concept. Typical examples of Business Objects are: employee, product, invoice and payment. The representation may be in a natural language, a modelling language, or a programming language"* [20]. This definition emphasises the importance of a one-to-one correspondence between natural business concepts and object-oriented modelling concepts. BOs have also been advocated by prominent practitioners of object technology. According to [24], *"Business Objects encapsulate traditional lower-level objects that implement a business process (i.e. they are a collection of lower-level objects that behave as single, reusable units)."* [18] [19] support this view by saying that : *"... current use of objects is primarily restricted to a small-town, technology oriented perspective. Reuse of low level components such as 'windows', 'widgets', 'queries' and 'sets' is possible, but these are clearly not the elements that users and enterprises expect. To make object technology work for large industrial IS environments, we need greater business orientation and the ability to genuinely involve users..."*

The above remarks tend to support the idea that a Business Object is a coarser-grained higher level object abstraction, which corresponds directly to some natural business concept, in contrast with finer-grained lower level software system components. Not every practitioner focuses on this perspective. For example, according to [7], *"A Business Object is an entity that has a significant life history - perhaps an entity that experiences state changes other than insert and delete...".* This puts the emphasis on the complexity of interactions. [13] [14] identifies a Business Object with the coherent block of data presented to a user as a result of a query: *"A Business Object is the data structure gathered by an event or enquiry from several objects for display at the user interface - the response - a kind of database view. It is a representation layer thing - often a block of data displayed on a screen that users see as one coherent thing".* Some authors have used the term BO almost synonymously with "domain" object, meaning an object concept that maps onto a primary noun in the domain of discourse. In this last sense, a BO corresponds simply to what Smalltalk [17] would call a Model object in the MVC paradigm - an object, which manages the primary data of the application concerned.

While these later definitions are not incompatible with the earlier focus on business accents, the above-mentioned various definitions are indicative that some confusion may still exist in the community at large regarding the meaning of the term "Business Objects".

1.3 Motivation and Related Work

Although much has been claimed about the impact of BOs on IS development and many research papers [23] [4], industrial reports [11] [3] [12] [25] [5] [22] [15] [6] and even software products have advocated BOs, there appears to be little tangible evidence to demonstrate whether BOs influence the development of business applications in any positive way. Where BOs have been developed and adopted by information technology (IT) professionals, business management still remains to be convinced whether they are appropriate, cost-effective, or whether they provide any assurances on system quality or increase the success-rate of completed projects. This raises the question: *"Can BOs deliver on their promises?"* A major survey was therefore conducted through the Object-Oriented Programming Systems Languages and Applications (OOPSLA'97) Conference in October 1997 in Atlanta, USA. 1,500 survey forms were distributed to the conference attendees with 201 forms returned to the authors of this paper. The feedback of only 13% seems quite low and one might question the significance of 'representation' amongst the conference delegates. Reason for that is quite understandable, the survey was not part of the OOPSLA's formal technical programmes, it was neither a compulsory exercise nor there was any monetary reward. Delegates participated in the survey in their own accord and out of their own favour.

The purpose of this survey was to investigate how IT professionals worldwide view BOs in their organisations. The investigation attempted to establish an understanding of the appreciation and deployment of BOs in terms their perceived maturity, the role they play in current system development and their likely future prospects. The results suggest that although the general notion of BOs is familiar to most of the respondents from the survey, the exact nature of a Business Object remains rather ill-defined. For this reason, few organisations have adopted a development strategy based upon BOs. There is a growing concern about the hype surrounding BOs, a suspicion that this may be a case of "*The Emperor's New Clothes*" [21], that is, BOs may simply turn out to be ordinary objects dressed up in new packaging.

Rather than debate these issues in the abstract, this paper seeks to assess the attitude within the community towards BOs and to determine their current usefulness and future prospects. The findings from this survey are revealing. They provide many useful pointers for advocates of BOs, showing what direction this trend must take if the drive to higher business abstractions is really to take off. As far as the authors are aware, this is the first ever survey of attitudes to, and deployment of, Business Objects.

2.   SURVEY METHOD

The survey was conducted in the OOPSLA'97 conference. The choice of the venue was based on the fact that OOPSLA is the world's largest OO conference attracting 2-3,000 delegates each year since the firs one was held in 1986. Delegates are ranging from industrial developers to academic researchers, from technical developers to business end users, from students to corporate executives - all with a common interest in OO. The variety of delegate portfolio has made it easier for the authors to target OO professionals from different sectors.

The survey method in this paper is based on the survey technique adopted by the Gartner Group Company Inc (http://www.gartner.com). The Gartner Group is a well known research company specialising in information technology (IT). The company regularly publishes its survey reports in leading computer journals and periodicals. In August 1995, Gartner Group published a survey report in BYTE Magazine. The survey was called "OO Methodologies Adoption Study" where the company conducted a survey to 260 selected IT professionals. Developers, senior corporate managers, IT managers, system analysts, programmers, researchers made up the bulk of the survey pool.

The survey framework used by the Gartner Group was firstly to identify the target survey group through their sources. The sources carry the information on their occupations, the size of their organisation they work for which is measured by number of employees and sales turnover. Having formed an understanding of their background, appropriate candidates are then selected and invited to participate in the survey. The questionnaire structure starts with knowledge and understanding about the subject matter, history of adoption , views and experiences on using the product / tool / methodology, comments on future prospects. The response to questions is mainly expressed as a percentage of the respondents. However, over and above the numerical representation, the extra comments from the surveyed candidates have also brought a significant impact to the findings of the survey.

The survey presented in this paper has followed the questionnaire structure from Gartner Group. However, there is a slight difference in the selection of candidates. Due to the limited resources, the authors were unable to identify prospective candidates on an individual basis. The OOPSLA Conference has provided an attractive alternative for it being the world's biggest OO conference and an ideal rendezvous for OO professionals.

Although no survey can represent the whole spectrum across the board, at least it voices the opinions from a fair proportion of people within the community.

3. SURVEY FINDINGS

A total of 1,500 questionnaires were distributed throughout the OOPSLA conference. By the end of the conference, 201 delegates returned the survey form to the authors of this paper. Of the 201 respondents, more than half had provided their name, occupation and email address for follow-up contact and further survey which authors plan to conduct during the next OOPSLA conference in October 1998.

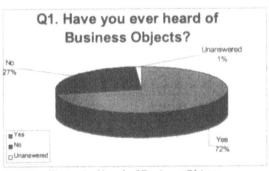

Figure 1 : Heard of Business Objects

Although the response to the first question: "Have you ever heard of Business Objects?" is quite encouraging with 72% answering yes and only 27% answering no, some people still do not understand what BOs really mean. Extra comments from respondents were: *"What is a Business Object? Until we have a good answer to that, we won't be using them. We know of commercial availability but if we don't know what a Business Objects is, how can we tell if there are any?" "If you mean a particular tool called Business Objects, then ignore this form because I've never heard of it. If you mean analysis objects that correspond to real world objects, this counts."*

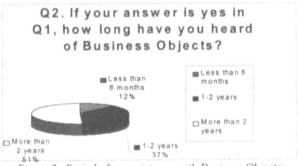

Figure 2 : Period of acquaintance with Business Objects

In question 2, when asked: "If your answer is yes in question 1, how long have your heard of Business Objects?" Half of the respondents (51%) said they have heard about Business Objects for more than 2 years, 37% said between one and two years and only 12% said less than 6 months. This figure is quite alarming. It can be seen that the number of new BO adopters is falling. However, one might argue that the 51% is the accumulation of years of adoption and it is quite natural that the growth rate is progressive year by year. Even so, the growth rate seems to be slower than average growth rate.

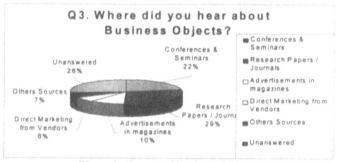

Figure 3 : Source of Business Objects

Question 3 asked the respondents : "Where did you hear about Business Objects?" 29% was from research papers/journals, 22% from conferences & seminars, 10% from advertisements in magazines, 6% from Direct Marketing, 7% from other source. 28% of the respondents did not answer this question. This indicates most of the sources of information for BOs are from conferences and journals where topics still under research are mostly discussed while advertisement and direct marketing media usually promote commercial products and tools. Such phenomenon has indicated that BOs are more academic driven with more of a concept under research rather than a 'commercial-product-off-the-shelf'.

Figure 4 : Started using Business Objects

Question 4 asked: "Have you started using Business Objects in your organisation?" 39% answered yes and 36% answered no. Although the numbers are very close to each other, 25% of the respondents did not answer this question. Overall, only one-third of the respondents said they had started using BOs.

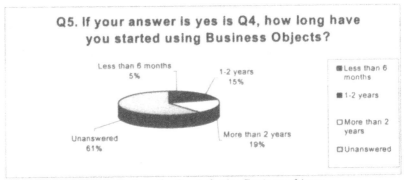

Figure 5 : Length of period using Business objects

In question 5, when asked: "If your answer is yes in question 4, how long have you been using Business Objects?" 19% answered more than 2 years, 15% answered 1 - 2 years and 5% answered less than 6 months. 61% of the respondents did not answer this question. Looking at the period of usage, nearly half of the organisations have been using Business Objects for more than 2 years. However, as stated above, the number of new adopters is actually declining with 5% less than 6 months compared with 10% more than 2 years. This has posed a potential threat to the future development of Business Object,

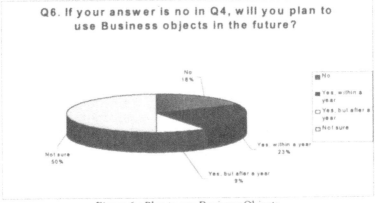

Figure 6 : Plan to use Business Objects

Question 6 asked: "If your answer is no is question 4, will you plan to use Business Objects in the future?" 23% answered yes and within a year, 9% answered yes but after a year, 18% answered no and 50% said not sure. The result is quite disappointing with less than one-third of the respondents have a definite plan to start using Business Objects. The 50% of the respondents who were not sure have reflected the lack of confidence about the concept and maturity of the technology.

Q7. If you are currently using Business Objects, are you using any CASE tools to support?

Figure 7 : CASE tools to support Business Objects

Question 7 asked: "If you are currently using Business Objects, are you using any CASE tools to support them?" 53% answered yes. Some of the respondents expressed that their reliance on CASE tool support has become inevitable due to the complexity of Business Objects. This also means that organisations have to spend more on purchase, consultancy and staff training for CASE tools. Such investment has discouraged some organisations from adopting Business Objects, as they are not sure how long it will be before they can see the return on their investment.

Q8. If you are already using Business Objects, did you:

Figure 8 : How to develop Business Objects

Question 8 asked: "If you are already using Business Objects, did you buy the Business Objects off-the-shelf? Or did you develop the Business Objects in-house? Or both?". 75% developed Business Objects in-house with only 3% buying the Business Objects off-the-shelf. 22% responded both. Some respondents expressed the difficulty in locating the commercial packaged Business Objects suitable for their needs as there are too few options. Even when available, they find that the price is too high.

For these reasons, they considered that the "do-it-yourself" one is more economical and appropriate to their requirements. This has created a situation that in every organisation, people just get together and create their own Business Objects for their organisation. Then different organisations have different ways of developing Business Objects, which are highly unlikely to integrate with another organisation's Business Objects. This situation has not only discouraged reuse but also has made the interpretation of BOs very inconsistent amongst business organisations across the domain [9]. Currently there is still a lack of industrial standards for Business Objects.

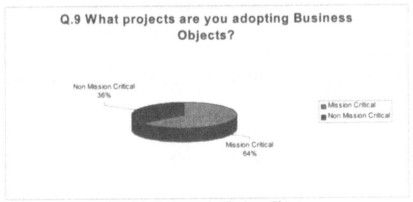

Figure 9 : Projects using Business Objects

Question 9 asked: "In what projects are you adopting Business Objects?" 64% said they already use Business Objects in their mission critical projects and only 36% use in non-mission critical projects. The result is quite enlightening . At least nearly two-third of the respondents feel that BOs can handle important projects.

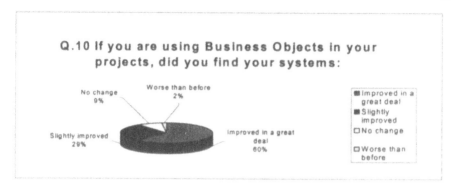

Question 10 asked: "If you are using Business Objects in your projects, did you find that the impact on your systems was: "No change?" "Or slightly improved?" "Or improved by a great deal?" "Or worse than before?" 60% said Business Objects have improved in systems by a great deal while only 2% overall said the systems are worse than before. So overall, the comments from people are satisfactory.

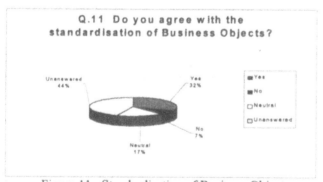

Figure 11 : Standardisation of Business Objects

Question 11 asked: "Do you agree with the standardisation of Business Objects?" 32% said yes, 7% said no and 7% said neutral. However, 44% of the respondents did not answer this question. It appears that many of them are not sure what the benefits will bring from standardisation.

The ultimate goal of OMG's BODTF is to standardise the Business Objects as a uniformity measurement towards both the quantitative and qualitative values. To achieve this goal, the BODTF must win more people's appreciation and support on standardisation.

Figure 12 : Reasons for adopting Business Objects

Question 12 asked: "What reasons make you adopt Business Objects?" 19% said BOs enhance reuse, 13% said IT developers will understand the business better, 16% believed that Business Objects will improve software quality, 15% reckoned that systems will be easier to maintain and 11% thought that it will be cost saving. Other reasons include: *"increase direct participation of domain experts"*, *"greater capability"*, *"reduce development time"*, *"better design"*, *"convenient place to put information for display"*, *"currently developing corporate engineering application architecture for future, mental hygiene"*, *"we sell them"*, *"business analysts will understand software better"*, *"support enterprise-scale architectures"*, *"closer to real world model"*, *"Commercial-Off-The-Shelf (COTS) vendor products have Business Objects and Sales Objects"*, *"faster development"*, *"shorten learning curve"*, *"better interface"*.

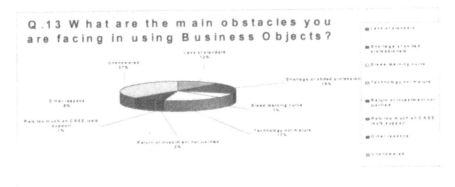

Figure 13 : Obstacles when using Business Objects

Question 13 asked: "What are the main obstacles you are facing in using Business Objects?" Not surprisingly, 18% of the respondents found that there are shortages of skilled professionals who know how to use or develop Business Objects. 17% respondents found that the technology not mature. 12% said there is a lack of standard to follow. 7% said learning curve is steep. 2% said the return of investment not justified. 1% said relying too much on CASE tools to support BOs constitutes a problem. 37% of the respondents did not answer this question.

The above result is interesting because it is co-incidental to the question 7 where 53% of the respondents use CASE tools to support their development of Business Objects. Out of this figure, there was only 1% of the respondents saying that relying too much on CASE tools to support. This indicates that there is a big potential in the CASE tools market to support Business Objects.

Other reasons include: *"performance impact uncertainties"*, *"lack of funding"*, *"implementation to diverse systems"*, *"building and deploying quickly"*, *"management don't understand"*, *"management ignorance"*, *"what are Business Objects? any description?"*, *"need to educate organisations"*, *"lack of understanding of business domain"*, *"unfamiliar"*, *"applicability to engineering applications unknown"*, *"management lack of understanding in reading the written materials from software engineers"*, *"management ignorance"*, *"very hard to get business domain aware developers"*, *"management buy off"*, *"understanding real business needs / requirements"*, *"process methodology support vs. vendor COTS"*, *"problems we have is that the Business Objects is not the natural way we do business and consequently IS is routine the business comments into a computer section"*, *"initially - steep learning curve after learning it is shorter"*, *"skill level of the developers is varied"*.

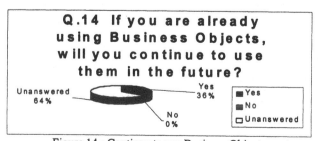

Figure 14 : Continue to use Business Objects

Question 14 asked: "If you are already using Business Objects, will you continue to use them in the future?" 36% said yes but the 64% of the respondents did not answer this question. This has reflected that most people are still in the "Trial-and-Test" stage. They did not have long term investment plans or strategies for the future adoption of Business Objects. Only one-third of the respondents felt any degree of certainty.

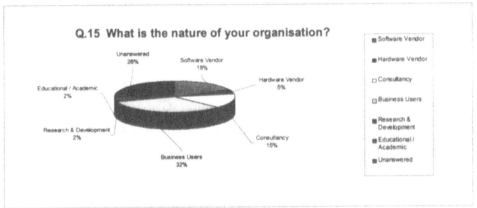

Figure 15 : Nature of organisation

Question 15 asked: "What is the nature of your organisation?" 18% are software vendors, 5% are hardware vendors, 15% are in consultancy, 32% are business users, 2% are in research and development, 2% are from educational / academic sectors, 28% did not answer this question.

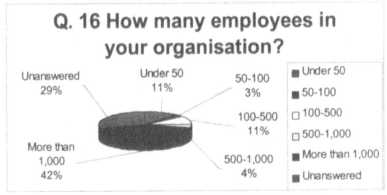

Figure 16 : Number of Employees

Question 16 asked: "How many employees are there in your organisation?" 42% came from large organisations with more than 1,000 employees, 4% came from medium-to-large firms, 11% came from medium firms with 100-500 employees, 3% are small-to-medium firms with 50-100 employees, 11% came from small firms with less than 50 employees. 29% of the respondents did not answer this question.

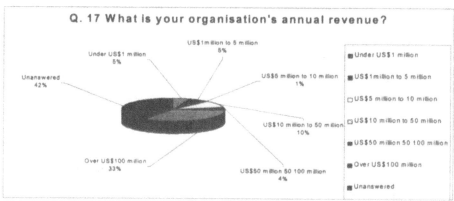

Figure 17: Annual Revenue

Question 17 asked: "What is your organisation's annual revenue?" 33% of the respondents said over US$100 million, 4% said between US$50 million and US$100 million, 10% said between US$10 million and US$50 million, 1% said between US$5 million and US$10 million, 5% said between US$1 million and US$5 million and 5% said under US$1 million. 42% of the respondents did not answer this question due to commercial confidentiality.

In view of questions 16 and 17, the majority of respondents work for large organisations employing more than 1,000 people with more than US$100 million annual revenue. We are confident that this survey reflects the viewpoint of several major industrial players where they play a relatively influential role in the advancement of software technology.

4.   SURVEY EVALUATION

The above survey has given both positive and negative views on BOs. In general, respondents are not sceptical about the principle of BOs and most of them appreciate the benefits brought by BOs, for example, they believe strongly that BOs can form a bridge to communicate between IT developers and business users. They also believe that software systems produced out of BOs will reflect better than the real business concerns of their user community, something contributing to the quality of the system [10].

Nevertheless, most respondents found the definition of BOs very vague. Many respondents explained that the reason why they still have not adopted such technology is largely attributable to the lack of knowledge of what BOs really are and how to use them.

In summary, respondents generally view that BOs have the value and usefulness to become a promising technology. The immaturity of the technology itself, shortage of skilled professionals and lack of industrial standards have hindered the potential of BOs development.

5. CONCLUSION AND FURTHER RESEARCH WORK

In view of the above findings and evaluation, one important question remains: *"What should we do about it?"* It seems that effort could be invested most productively in the definition of standardised Business Objects. This would ensure their adoption in a range of organisations and help with the integration and reuse aspects. More training would have to be provided, to help developers profit from this resource. However, without an agreeable standard, it would be very hard to benchmark the Business Objects. In conclusion, there are four major elements missing in the Business Objects: (1) Consistency; (2) Completeness; (3) Modularization; and (4) Adaptation.

The current survey focussed on the respondents' acquaintance with, and attitudes towards, Business Objects. The next stage will be to follow up many of the issues raised here. The authors anticipate conducting a follow-up survey at the next OOPSLA, which will give an interesting perspective on how attitudes have changed over one year.

6. ACKNOWLEDGEMENT

The Object Management Group's Business Objects Domain Task Force (OMGBODTF)'s chairman Mr. Cory Casanave and the Conference of Object-Oriented Programming Systems Languages and Applications (OOPSLA) Business Objects Workshop's chairman Dr. Jeff Sutherland play a great role in the development of Business Objects technology and have given us great inspiration and tremendous support during the tenure of this survey. Our heartfelt thanks to Ms. Mary Loomis, Chair of the OOPSLA'97 conference, Ms. Carol Mann, Conference Registrar and Professor Ken Bauer, Captain of Student Volunteers for their assistance throughout the conference.

7. REFERENCES

1. [Casanave 95]   CASANAVE, C.   "Business Objects Architectures And Standards" in the Proceedings of *Object-Oriented Programming, Systems, Languages & Applications (OOPSLA)'95 Conference Business Objects Design And Implementation Workshop*, Austin, Texas, USA, October 1995 (Eds. Sutherland et al) (Springer-Verlag, London) pp 7-28. ISBN 3-540-76096-2.
2. [Casanave 97]   CASANAVE, C.   "Standardised Business Objects" in the *Conference of Building & Using Financial Business Objects*, London, UK, 22-23 October 1997 (http://www.omg.org).
3. [Data Access et al 97] DATA ACCESS TECHNOLOGIES, SEMATECH, INC., PRISM TECHNOLOGIES, IONA TECHNOLOGIES LTD.   *"Business Object Facilities Submission"* in the Object Management Group's Request For Proposal-4. Source: http://www.omg.org.
4. [Digre 96]   DIGRE, T. "Business Objects Facility Presentation in the *OOPSLA'96 Conference Business Objects Design and Implementation II Workshop*, 5-10 October 1996, San Jose, California. Source : http://www.tiac.net/users/jsuth/
5. [EDS 97]   ELECTRONIC DATA SYSTEMS CORP. *"Business Object Facilities Submission"* in the Object Management Group's Request For Proposal-4.   Source: http://www.omg.org.
6. [Genesis/Visigenic 97] GENESIS   DEVELOPMENT   CORP   &   VISIGENIC SOFTWARE INC. *"Business Object Facility Submission"* in the Object Management Group's Request for Proposal-4. Source: http://www.omg.org.
7. [Graham 94] GRAHAM I, *Migration to Object Technology, 1994*, Addison-Wesley, N.Y,. ISBN 0-201-59389-0.
8. [Hung et al 97 (a)]   HUNG, K., SUN, Y., ROSE, A. "A Dynamic Business Objects Architecture For An Insurance Industry" in the *Proceedings of Object-Oriented Information Systems (OOIS)'97 Conference*, Brisbane, Queensland, Australia, 10-12 November 1997 (Eds. Orlowska et al) (Springer-Verlag, London) pp 145-156. ISBN 3-540-76170-5.
9. [Hung et al 97 (b)]   HUNG, K., PATEL, D.   "Modelling Domain Specific Application Frameworks with a Dynamic Business Object Architecture; An Approach and Implementation" in the *Object-Oriented Programming Systems Languages*

Applications (OOPSLA'97) Conference Business Object Workshop, Atlanta, USA, 5-9 October 1997. Source: http://jeffsutherland.org/oopsla97/oo97final.html.

10. [Hung et al 98]   HUNG, K, SIMONS, A & ROSE, A. "Can You Have It All?: Managing the time and budget against quality issue in a Dynamic Business Objects architecture Development" in the *Proceedings of the British Computer Society Software Quality Management (BCSSQM'98) conference,* 23-25 March 1998, Amsterdam, the Netherlands. Springer, London, 1998.

11. [IBM 97]   IBM CORP. *"Common Business Objects Submission"* in the Object Management Group's Request For Proposal-4. Source: http://www.omg.org.

12. [IBM/Oracle 97]   IBM CORP & ORACLE CORP. *"Business Object Facilities Submission"* in the Object Management Group's Request For Proposal-4. Source: http://www.omg.org.

13. [Jacobson et al 94]   JACOBSON I et al, *The Object Advantages: Business Process Reengineering With Object Technology,* 1994 (Addison-Wesley, New York), ISBN 0-201-42289-1

14. [Jacobson 96]JACOBSON I, "Use Case Engineering Tutorial" in *the Object-Oriented Programming, Systems, Languages & Applications (OOPSLA)'96 Conference, San Jose, California, USA,* October 1996.

15. [NIIIP 97]   NIIIP CONSORTIUM. *"Common Business Objects Submission"* in the Object Management Group's Request for Proposal-4. Source: http://www.omg.org.

16. [OMG 95]   *OMG, Object Management Group - Object Management Architecture Guide,* 1995 (John Wiley & Sons, Inc., New York). ISBN 0-471-14193-3.

17. [Par90]   ParcPlace Systems, Mountain View, CA. *ObjectWorks\Smalltalk Release 4 Users Guide,* 1990. Source: http://www.parcplace.com

18. [Ramackers et al 95]   RAMACKERS G and CLEGG, D. "Object Business Modelling Request & Approach" in the Proceedings of *Object-Oriented Programming, Systems, Languages & Applications (OOPSLA)'95 Conference,* Austin, Texas, USA, Oct 1995 (Eds. Sutherland et al) (Springer-Verlag, London) pp 77-86. ISBN 3-540-76096-2.

19. [Ramackers et al 96] RAMACKERS, G & CLEGG, D. "Business Process Re-engineering with Extended use Cases and Business Objects" in the *Object World '96 UK Conference,* June 1996, London.

20. [Shelton et al 96]   SHELTON, R et al. "OMG Business Application Architecture White Paper" in the *OMG Business Object Domain Task Force.* Source: http://www.omg.org.

21. [Spottiwood 96]   SPOTIWOOD, C. "The Emperor's New Clothes" in the *OOPSLA'96 Conference Business Objects Design & Implementation Workshop II",* 5-9 October 1996, San Jose, CA, USA (Source: (http://www.tiac.net/users/jsuth/).

22. [SSA 97]   SSA INC. *"Business Object Facility Submission"* in the Object Management Group's Request For Proposal-4. Source: http://www.omg.org.

23. [Sutherland 95 (a)]   SUTHERLAND, J et al. *OOPSLA'95 Business Object Design and Implementation Proceedings,* 1996, Springer, London, ISBN 3-540-76096-2.

24. [Sutherland 95 (b)]   SUTHERLAND J, "The Object Technology Architecture: Business Objects For Corporate Information Systems" in *the 1995 Symposium for VMARK Users,* Albuquerque, USA, 1995 (http://www.tiac.net/users/jsuth/).

25. [TRC 97]   TECHNICAL RESOURCE CONNECTION INC. *"Common Business Objects Submission"* in the Object Management Group's Request For Proposal-4. Source: http://www.omg.org.

Patterns for Extending an OO Model with Temporal Features

Rébecca Deneckère, Carine Souveyet

Université Paris 1 Panthéon-Sorbonne, Centre de recherche en informatique
90 rue de Tolbiac 75013 PARIS, France, tel : + 33 (0) 1 40 77 46 34, fax : + 33 (0) 1 40 77 19 54,
email : {denecker, souveyet}@univ-paris1.fr

Abstract

We identify a set of generic patterns which can be used to introduce temporal features in existing OO models. Patterns are generic in the sense that they are applicable to any OO model having the basic features of class, attribute, domain and class association. The paper shows the application of these patterns to the O* model.

keywords : method engineering, patterns and frameworks, object-oriented method, temporal database.

1. Introduction

Several method engineering approaches [1] have been developed for adapting existing methods to the project at hand [2][3][4][5]. Assembling components from various methods for constructing a method « on the fly » [4] is the approach we are exploring in the CREWS Esprit project[1]. This assembly process relies on two types of components : those that can be used directly and those that have to be generated from generic patterns. In this paper, we focus only on the second type of components called « generic patterns ».

The concept of pattern has been widely used in the software development community during the last 20 years in particular by those practising Object-Oriented (OO) approaches. It has been more recently introduced in the Method Engineering community. All these efforts aim to reuse the best practices of a method in another one. Therefore, this concept is usually used in the context of reuse.

In the OO community, the focus has been put on patterns useful during the design of software and independent of any particular domain [6][7][8][9][10][11][12][13] In the Method Engineering community, generic patterns aim at proposing a means for constructing situation specific methods. Such patterns encapsulate knowledge

---

[1] Basic Research Action CREWS (ESPRIT N°21.903). CREWS stands for Cooperative Requirements Engineering With scenarios.

about processes that can be reused and applied in different settings. They allow to guide method engineers in the construction of methods.

Much of the contemporary work on patterns has been inspired by the work of C. Alexander on the use of patterns within the domain of architecture [14]. In [15] a pattern is described as *"a problem which occurs over an over again in our environment and then describes the core of the solution to that problem, in such a way that you can use this solution a million times over, without ever doing the same twice"*. Here, the emphasis is put on the fact that a pattern describes a recurrent problem and is defined with its associate core solution.

The paper aims at proposing a set of generic patterns which can be used to introduce temporal features in existing OO models having the basic features of class, attribute, domain and class association. These patterns have been developed and used in the TOOBIS esprit project[2] for defining the TOOBIS method [16] which has been used to develop two real temporal applications, of general scope : one in the management of treatment protocols for health applications and the other one in the management and distribution implementation of Fresh Milk products.

The paper is organised as follows. The « pattern » notion is discussed in section 2. An overview of specific requirements of temporal database applications is given in Section 3. Then, section 4 presents the set of generic patterns extending any OO model with temporal features and their appliance to the O* model [17][18]. Finally, we conclude in Section 5.

2. The notion of a pattern

The key idea concerning patterns is the fact that a pattern relates a *problem* to its *solution*. Therefore, a set of desirable properties for a pattern must include the *problem* for which the pattern proposes a reusable knowledge, the *solution* describing this knowledge and its *context* of use. A context refers to a recurring set of situations in which the pattern applies.

The solution proposed by a pattern is a process chunk to apply on a particular product. Therefore, the *body* of a pattern encapsulated the process description as well as the definition of the product under modification. The *guideline* part (see figure 1) represents the process description whereas the *product* part (see figure 1) corresponds to the product definition. The body contains the guidelines to be followed when the pattern is applied. The body can have either a formal or an informal expression. Formal bodies are expressed using the NATURE process modelling formalism [19], [20]. Detailed examples of such descriptions can be found in [3], [5]. Informal bodies are expressed in natural language.

---

[2] TOOBIS (ESPRIT N° 20671) stands for Temporal Object Oriented dataBases & Information Systems. This project aims to define a temporal OO DBMS on the DBMS O2 with a specific conceptual method.

The application of the guidelines embedded in the body leads in our case to update the OO model of the method to be extended. Therefore, the product part represents the set of concepts of a OO model to extend. The aim of our generic patterns is to extend this set of concepts in order to handle specific temporal features at the modelling level.

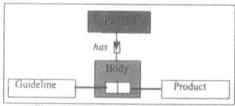

Figure 1 : The Body part of a pattern.

The *interface* of a pattern explains in which situation and for which intention the pattern is applicable. Therefore, it is a triplet <situation, intention, target> associated to a body. The interface is the visible part of the pattern.

The *situation* is a part of the OO model to be extended. The *intention* refers to the extension. The interface <situation = (*OO model.M*) intention = *Extend OO model.M by defining a calendar class description* > is an example. The result of the application will be the OO model including the calendar class. The body explains how to proceed to fulfil the intention in that particular situation.

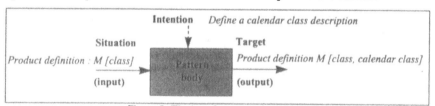

Figure 2: The interface part of a pattern

Figure 3 shows the structure of a pattern as counting of three aspects: the reusability, applicability and the reusable knowledge. The reusability aspects are managed by the *descriptor* part whereas the applicability aspects are handled by the interface part. The reusable knowledge is described in the body. The *descriptor* part of a pattern identifies the context in which it will be useful to reuse it. A descriptor is a couple <situation intention>. The pattern supporting the intention « Define a calendar class description », is described by the following situation : (application requirements : « *Need for time referential* » ; current model situation : « *The model doesn't include specific concept for describing user defined time referential* »).

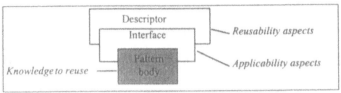

Figure 3: The pattern-structure

The pattern notion explained in this section is used to define solutions to the problems identified in the following section.

3. Temporal database applications domain

The importance of time in the database area has been realised since 1975. Applications require to deal with past, present and future data. Conventional databases are designed to store and retrieve current data. During update operations, data are erased and replaced by their new values. This means that past data are no longer available in the database and only current data are kept. This justifies the addition of mechanisms dedicated to model, retrieve, store and modify time dependent data. This has led to the introduction of SQL/T (temporal extension of SQL) in SQL3. This new generation of temporal DBMS integrates time into the data model in order to facilitate the management of temporal aspects at the application layer. Such DBMS have simplified the storage and the retrieval of temporal data. But, they don't solve design problems such as the definition of the data schema, specification of the activities of the application, verification of the consistency of the temporal database and provide no guideline to administer a database. The introduction of temporal features into OO models is still under investigation [21].

We have identified the six following temporal requirements which are required for designing temporal database applications, of general scope :

Time referential problem

The concept usually used to measure time is the one of a calendar. It is a metric system to apply on the time line. Most of the basic OO models use the time of the system clock which is the *Gregorian* calendar. But in the reality, an organisation needs to manage different calendars or different granularities at the same time for synchronising different kinds of activity. For instance, an hospital organises the salary management with the *Gregorian* Calendar whereas observation of patients is managed with a specific *Observation* Calendar (a turn is every 6 hours) for instance. Meanwhile the accounting activities of this hospital follow a specific *accounting* calendar (a year begins in September). Because applications may need specific calendar (one or several) and may need also to manage time at different level (week, second, hour etc.), OO models should provide specific concepts for modelling the use of different calendars and granularities.

Temporal domains problem

In classical OO models, the only way for an attribute to have a time domain is to select one of the following types : Date, Time and Timezone. However, these collection of types may not be sufficient for applications. For instance, a period of time (which is often modelled with two Date attributes *begin* and *end*) or a quantity of time called interval (which is designed as a numeric type) are abstractions useful to use with their associated operators. For instance, when you want to add 20 days to a period of time or when you want to add 10 months to an interval etc..

Besides absolute time, there is a need for managing relative time in applications of general scope. For example, the attribute *starting_date* of a task may be expressed relatively (20 days after) to the end of a previous one which is not yet finished.

In addition to the time referential problem (explained above), OO models should provide rich temporal domains allowing to manipulate absolute and relative time but also help in the management of periods of time and quantities of time.

Object time stamping problem

The application engineer may want to time stamp data with different time semantics. For instance, the attribute *order-date* represents the ordering date of the client : the true date of the reality, whereas the attribute *last-modification* represents the time when the order is registered is known in the database. The former is called valid time and the latter is called transaction time. Time stamping with valid and/or transaction time of data is often used and managed by at the application. However, OO models should provide specific concepts for supporting the time semantic definition and its management during the database operations such as insertion, update and deletion.

External event time stamping problem

Happening of external stimuli recognised by the application needs to be situated in the time line according to their valid time. It is required for organisations which are led to perform sensitive activities in advance or with a certain delay. For example, *"increase the salary of an employee"* induces different treatments according to its valid date. If the treatment is done in advance, the salary change must be taken into account only when its valid date becomes the current date whereas a delayed salary change requires a corrective payment. Therefore, OO models should provide specific concepts to differentiate these three different happenings of the same external stimuli.

Object historisation problem

Histories are sometimes required by applications. For instance, some may need to look at the evolution of the *salary* of an employee, and it is impossible if the application only keeps one state for this attribute. In addition, *Replay* function is more and more required for tracking decisional process of an organisation.

Therefore, the information system should provide for each state of an object when it is/was true but also when it is/was exploitable.

From this point of view, OO models should provide specific concepts to manage the object historisation with valid or/and transaction time.

Time constraint problem

The application engineer may want to constrain the evolution of the data present in the database. Most of the OO models contain constraints on the objects. However, if the application engineer wants to handle time, the problem will be to constrain data evolution. For instance, the application may need to constrain the attribute *Salary* in order to *forbid more than three increasing of its amount in one year*. Therefore, OO models must include concepts helping the application engineer to define his constraints which are related to time or not.

From each of these temporal problems, we have defined a generic solution that we have embedded in a pattern. Each of these patterns guides a method engineer in the adaptation process of his OO model for managing the temporal features associated to the pattern. The following section describes the six generic patterns dedicated to temporal features.

4. The temporal patterns

This section presents six patterns dealing with the temporal features introduced in the previous section. Each pattern is presented as follows : the objective of the pattern, a table containing the pattern descriptor (situation and intention) and the pattern interface (the intention), a textual explanation of the body and an example of the use of the pattern. The examples take as the baseline the O* model.

4.1 Time referential pattern

- Objective

The pattern aims at generating the description of calendars.

Descriptor : Situation		Descriptor : Intention	Interface : Intention
Application requirements	Current model situation		
Need for time referential	The model doesn't include specific concept for describing user defined time referential	Extend OO model by defining a calendar class description	Define a calendar class description

Figure 4: time referential pattern

- Explanation

The result of the pattern enactment is one calendar class description. The body of the pattern guides the generation of the calendar class description using a calendar template. As shown in Figure 4 the calendar class description has three parts :

name, property and operation. The property comprises the origin of the calendar which is an instant and an ordered list of granules of different granularity constructed out of a basic granule. The operation part corresponds to the set of operations to perform conversion between granules of different granularities and also to perform conversion from this calendar to the *Gregorian* one.

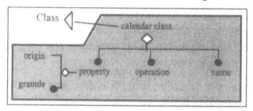

Figure 5: meta-model obtained following the application of the time referential pattern

This pattern provides a calendar class which can be instantiated several times to get several calendars. In addition, the pattern provides also a default calendar which is the *Gregorian* calendar (instance of the Calendar class, defined in Figure 6). If the OO model doesn't take this necessity into account, the pattern will adapt it for this use. For instance, an enterprise may use the *Gregorian* calendar in all its departments and *working-days* as the calendar in the staff department. As a result, it is necessary to define two calendars in the application (and also the mapping functions that will make the conversion between the two calendars).

```
Calendar class Gregorian
origin "01/01/0001:00:00:00"  basic unit = chronon
granules
second : {1 basic unit, basic unit=1second}
minute :  {irregular}
hour :  {60 minutes, minute=1/60hour}
day :  {24 hours, hour=1/24day}
month :  {irregular}
year :  {12 months, mois=1/12 year}
operations
instant<Gregorian, *> operator+ (instant<Gregorian, *>, interval<Gregorian, *>)
instant<Gregorian, *> operator+ (interval<Gregorian, *>, instant<Gregorian, *>)
interval<Gregorian, *> operator- (instant<Gregorian, *>, instant<Gregorian, *>)
EndCalendarClass
```

Figure 6: Definition of the Gregorian calendar

The minute and the month are irregular granules because their time quantity is not fixed. The minute represent usually 60 seconds (except when we add an intermediate second). On the same way, the number of days in a month is not fixed (28,29,30 or 31).

- O* example

The O* model matches the descriptor situation of the calendar class pattern. Indeed the model has the concept of calendar class in order to attach temporal events to it.

At the object level, the calendar class has only one instance : the clock of the Gregorian calendar (which is not explicitly defined).

Assume now that the application to be developed requires a specific calendar called « observation » calendar. Then, the pattern can be instantiated to generate « observation» calendar as shown in Figure 7. However, as this calendar requires a precise definition of the Gregorian calendar to which it refers, the pattern suggests in its body to formally define the Gregorian calendar too and guides the generation of the Gregorian calendar according to the template. The result is shown in Figure 6.

This extension proposes to describe, in an extensive way, the calendars used in the application by the way of a name, an origin (instant), a basic unit (granule), an ordered list of granules with their finer and coarser conversions, an operation of translation from an instant to a period, an operation of conversion between granules of the same calendar. If there is more than one calendar in the application, two conversion operations, one to the Predefined calendar and the other one coming from it (these two operations allow the conversions between calendars) are added to their definition.

```
Calendar class ObservationCalendar
origin ="1/01/01/0000" basic unit = hour of Gregorian  calendar
granules
turn : { 6 basic unit, basic unit = 6 turns}
day : { 4 turns, turn=1/4 day}
month : { irregular}
year : {12 months, month=1/12 year}
operations
instant<ObservationCalendar, *> operator + (instant<ObservationCalendar, *>,
interval<ObservationCalendar, *>)
interval<ObservationCalendar, *> operator + (instant<ObservationCalendar, *>,
instant<ObservationCalendar, *>)
instant<ObservationCalendar, *> operator - (instant<ObservationCalendar, *>,
instant<ObservationCalendar, *>)
instant <Gregorian, *> conversion (<instant<ObservationCalendar>)
instant <ObservationCalendar ,*> conversion (<instant<Gregorian>)
EndClass
```

Figure 7: Definition of the O* Observation calendar

4.2 Temporal domain pattern

- Objective:

The pattern aims at supporting the generation of various temporal domains. It offers a menu of temporal domains from which the method engineer can select the ones of interest for the model extension he is performing. These temporal types will be used in turn by the application engineers to associate domains to temporal attributes.

Descriptor : Situation		Descriptor : Intention	Interface : Intention
Application requirements	**Current model situation**		
Need of a time representing data	The model has no specific concept for describing a time representing data	Extend OO model by defining a set of temporal domains	Define a set of temporal domains

Figure 8: Temporal domain pattern

- Explanation:

The result of the pattern application will be the definition of a new set of domain : the *temporal domains*. There are three possible different temporal domains: instant, period and interval. On the same way, the domain can be absolute or relative. These types are expressed with one granularity of one calendar.

In the classical OO methods, the only way for an attribute to have a time domain is to use the Date, Time or Timezone types. For instance, the attributes *birthday* of a person or *end-of-project* of a project will be absolute dates, even if they could be more refined. So, these types may not be sufficient for the application and it may be necessary to create new temporal domains that will be used to represent time into database (to define the value set of the temporal attributes). Moreover, if the analyst wants to represent data that are relative to other ones, the pattern proposes to extend the Instant and Period domain types in two directions: one for relative time and the other for absolute time, as it is shown on Figure 9.

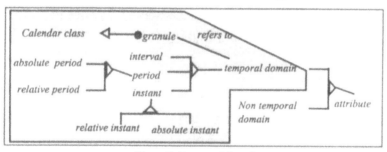

Figure 9: Temporal domains

An instant represents an isolated point on the time line (for instance *1996-12-12*). The generic temporal domain *INSTANT<calendar, granule>* replace the classical type DATE found in the classical DBMS. The domain *INSTANT-A<calendar, granule>* is used to specify an absolute instant. The domain *INSTANT-R<calendar, granule>* is used to specify a relative instant.

An interval is an unanchored quantity of time (for instance, *3months* is an interval). The generic temporal domain *INTERVAL<calendar, granule>* replace the classical type DATETIME found in the classical DBMS.

A period represents the quantity of time between two instants. The temporal domain *PERIOD<calendar, granule>* replace the type TIME found in the DBMS. The domain *PERIOD-A<calendar, granule>* is used to specify an absolute period.

The relative time is introduced in the period concept by the new temporal domain *PERIOD-R<calendar, granule>*

- O* example:

O* hasn't developed the concept of representing the time, only the usual DATE type is used. If the application needs a data representation for any of the three types of time, the application engineer will extend the O* model with a new set of domains called « *temporal domain* », as it is explained in Figure 9.

Figure 10 illustrates the use of the temporal domain types. The attribute *Project-beginning* is an absolute instant whereas the attribute *Project-ending* is a relative instant. The attribute *end-of-project* can be an absolute instant *(01/07/98)* or a relative one *(01/01/98+6months)*.

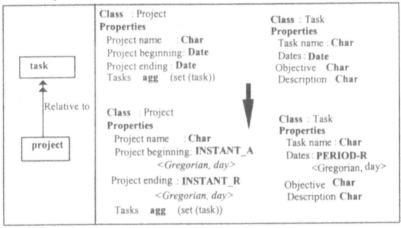

Figure 10 : Example of relative temporal attributes in O* and in the temporal extension

4.3 Object time stamping pattern

- Objective:

In the basic OO methods, the only way to represent the time is the type DATE. However, there are different kinds of time. According to the necessity of recording the « true » time of the reality, or/and the time of the database transaction, it can be useful to define different ways of stamping an object with the *valid time* or/and the *transaction time* as it is explained in [22].

Descriptor : Situation		Descriptor : Intention	Interface : Intention
Application requirements	Current model situation		
Need of a time stamped data	The model has no specific concept for describing time stamp	Extend OO model by defining a set of time stamped class	Define a set of time stamped class

Figure 11: Object time stamping pattern

- Explanation:

The result of the pattern enactment is the definition of a hierarchy of « *time stamped classes* ». There are three different kinds of time stamp : one with valid time stamping, one with transaction time and one with the *both (bi-temporal)*. As it is shown in Figure 12, each of this time stamps is represented by a class.

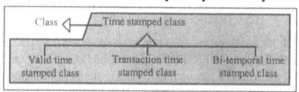

Figure 12: meta model following the application of the object time stamping pattern

The valid time of a fact is the time when it is true in the modelled reality. For instance, *James.B.* has been employed by *Expert Company* from *1995-02-01*. This definition allows to represent either the instant or the period when the fact is valid.

The transaction time of a database fact is the time when the fact is current in the database and may be retrieved. For instance, the employment of *James.B.* by the *Expert company* is available in the database from *1995-01-10 14:56:50*.

- O* example :

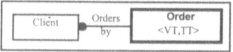

Figure 13: Example of a time stamped class

As we can see in the Figure 13, the *Order* class is a time stamped class. The application engineer needs to know when the order has been made by the client (time in the reality) but also when it has been inputted in the database (in order to have the possibility to manage the possible delays between them). As a result, the *Order* class is time stamped by the Valid time and the Transaction time (it is a bi-temporal time stamped class).

4.4 External stimuli time stamping pattern

- Objective:

The pattern aims at defining a classification of the external stimuli and generates in the OO model the sub-typing of the time stamp attribute which is appropriate to the model extension.

Descriptor : Situation		Descriptor : Intention	Interface : Intention
Application requirements	**Current model situation**		
Need of time stamped external stimuli	The model has no specific concept for describing time stamped external stimuli	Extend OO model by defining a set of time-subtypes of the external stimuli concept	Define a set of time-subtypes of the external stimuli concept

Figure 14: External stimuli time stamping pattern

- Explanation

External stimuli may need to be time-stamped. According to the use of distinguishing if the stimulus have a time nature in the past, in the present or in the future, the application engineer will need a way to differentiate them. The pattern offers a set of different types of external stimuli from which the engineer can select the ones of interest. There are three types of external stimuli time stamping: in time, a priori, a posteriori, as it is shown in Figure 15.

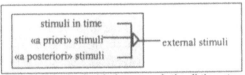

Figure 15: meta model obtained with the external stimuli time stamping pattern

An external stimulus materialises the emission of a message from the environment to the application. This last one answers to this message by performing a specific treatment. The valid time of an external stimuli is the valid time associated to the message. Three cases have to be considered : (a) a message received in advance, (b) a message received with delay and (c) a message received in time.

To receive a message by anticipation : Sometimes, the analyst wants to allow to trigger treatment in advance. However, in order to avoid problems relative to the management of post-actions (to maintain the coherence of the database through time), even if the acquisition of the message is done in advance, the treatment associated to the stimulus is executed in time. An « a priori » stimulus has a valid time in the future.

To receive a message with delay: On the same way, the analyst may want to correct the modelled real world stored in the database (it is limited to exceptional cases). An « a posteriori » stimulus has a valid time in the past. For instance, the correction of the customer's account related to a registered cheque in a bank is an example of « a posteriori » stimulus. The treatment associated to this stimulus has to correct the situation by erasing the treatment made with the « wrong » account and apply the treatment with the « right » one.

To receive a message when it happens : If the external stimulus is neither an anticipating nor a delayed one, it is a stimulus that affects the database exactly when it happens (they are the more common ones). A stimulus in time is a stimulus whose valid time is the present time.

- O* example :

The external event is the O* concept corresponding to the external stimulus. Examples of O* external events are shown in the Figure 16. *Salary update in advance* is an example of an a priori event, *delayed salary update* is an a posteriori event and *salary update* is an event in time.

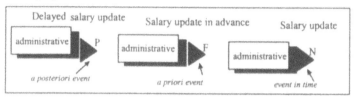

Figure 16: Examples of external stimuli

4.5 Object historisation pattern

- Objective:

The pattern identifies nine types of object historisation, and guides the method engineer in the selection of the types appropriated to the model extension he/she is working on. The output of the pattern is the sub-typing of the class concept reflecting the choice made by the method engineer.

Descriptor : Situation		Descriptor :	Interface :
Application requirements	Current model situation	Intention	Intention
Need of an historisation of the data evolution	The model has no specific concept for describing the historisation of data evolution	Extend OO model by defining a temporal and a non-temporal sub-typing of the class concept	Define a temporal and a non temporal sub-typing of the class concept

Figure 17: Class historisation pattern

- Explanation

The analyst may want to historise the data in order to have a trace of its evolution. As shown in Figure 18, the pattern will adapt the OO model in order to allow the application engineer to describe a new type of class : a temporal class that will keep the evolution of this attribute. There is two types of temporal class following the historisation desired : on the last state or on the history of the class. Two time dimensions taken into account are the real world time and the database time.

In order to maintain the consistency of the database, temporal objects need to be linked to non temporal objects. They are called **snapshot classes**. In the OO paradigm, there is at least one property that never changes : the identity of the object. As a result, an temporal class is a temporal variation of a snapshot class. Moreover, a snapshot class can have more than one temporal variation. The link between an historical class and its snapshot class is called a « temporal variation ». For instance, an employee can be characterised by some permanent properties and

214

some properties that evolve in the course of time and from which we need to keep track their change.

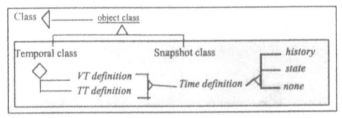

Figure 18: meta-model obtained following the application of the class historisation pattern

A snapshot class is a class which does not require time management. The properties of such classes are not related to time. For instance, The *Employee class* is a snapshot class because the evolution of its properties (that is to say : name, forename, address and phone number) is not relevant.

A temporal class is a class with time management (for instance, the *salary* of an employee is a temporal class because its evolution has to be kept in the database). The temporal class permits to integrate the valid or/and the transaction times management into the class definition. It is used to group properties that evolve at the same time and that are linked to the same temporal dimension.

The state of a class is composed of a set of values (a value for each property) at a given point of time. A state is associated to a time stamp (valid and/or transaction times). A state is called valid when it is associated to the valid time whereas it is named database state when it is related to the transaction time. And finally, a bi-temporal state of a class integrates its valid and its transaction times.

The notion of history permits to keep all states of a class in order to have its evolution over time. The valid history of a class reflects its evolution from the real world point of view (valid time management). The database history of a class represents its evolution according to the database viewpoint (transaction time management). And finally, a bi-temporal history of a class combines the real world and database viewpoints.

The temporal class concept permits to choose the time dimension to manage and, for each time dimension, two possibilities are offered : last state or history. The possible combinations offers by the temporal class concept are summarised in Figure 19.

		transaction time		
		none	state	history
valid time	none	no time management	last database state	database history
	state	last state with its valid time	last bi-temporal state	database history and its last valid state
	history	valid history	valid history and its last database state	bi-temporal history

Figure 19: time management defined in a temporal class

- O* example:

O* doesn't handle the data historisation. If the application engineer wants to historise a data, it become necessary to adapt the OO model in order to have the concept of *temporal class*, as it is shown in the Figure 18.

Figure 20 illustrates an example of a temporal class. The application wants to keep the evolution of the *family status* attribute. As a result, the application engineer has to transform it into a temporal class.

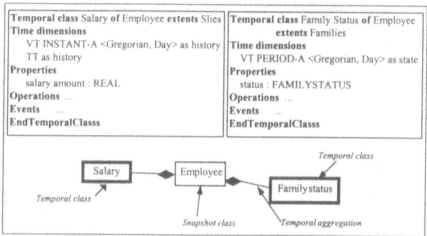

Figure 20: Example of temporal classes and their equivalent in O*

4.6 Time constraint pattern

- Objective:

The pattern uses the classification of constraints defined by Gehani [23] on active databases into intra-object and inter-object constraints, and the distinction between intra-time and inter-time constraints. This leads to four types of constraints for historical object bases which are explained to the method engineer in order he/she can select the appropriated ones for the model extension. The output of the pattern execution is an extended constraint type definition that takes the selected types into account.

Descriptor : Situation		Descriptor : Intention	Interface : Intention
Application requirements	Current model situation		
Need to constrain the evolution of data	The model has no specific concept for constraining the evolution of data	Extend OO model by defining the constraint classification hierarchy	Define the constraint classification hierarchy

Figure 21: Time constraint pattern

- Explanation

To use temporal time stamp on the data of the application involve a possibility to constrain their evolution. Most of the OO models don't handle this possibility. If the application engineer has chosen to historize data, it is necessary to constrain their evolution in order to keep the consistency of the database. For instance, one of the constraint that the engineer can't take into account (into an application designed with an OO model without the data time stamping) is « *the employee salary can't increase more than three times in one year* ». This constraint can't be designed in the static neither than in the dynamic of the application. The salary has to be designed as a time stamped data in order to have the possibility to constrain its evolution over the time.

The result of the pattern enactment is the definition of a new framework for classifying constraints. It permits to classify the constraints following two points of view : the time one and the object one, as it is shown in Figure 22.

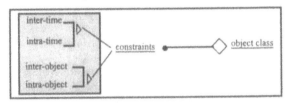

Figure 22: meta-model obtained following the time constrain pattern application

In the active OO DBMS such as [23], constraints are classified in two groups : intra-object and inter-object constraints. This distinction allows us to determine when they have to be verified.

⇒ An intra-object constraint is defined locally to an object and can be checked at the end of each method execution (for instance, the *weight of a patient* can not exceed *200 kilos*).

⇒ An inter-object constraint uses several objects, thus it has to be checked at the end of the database transaction (for instance, the *effort declared by an employee for a week must be equal to the sum of efforts per project declared by this employee for this week*).

The second classification comes from the temporal database field [24]. They group the constraints in two main categories : intra-time and inter-time constraints.

⇒ An intra-time constraint is only dependent of an instant t (each instant t should verify the constraint). Three semantics of constraints are derived from the time dimensions to consider : intra-VT, intra-TT and intra-Bi constraints. For instances, for *each week* declared in the *Weekly effort*, an *assignment* of this *employee* for this *project* must exist is an intra-VT constraint, the *name of a company* must be unique in each database state is an intra-TT constraint and the valid time of a *weight* value cannot be superior to its transaction time is an intra-Bi constraint.

⇒ An inter-time constraint is defined by using information available or valid at different instants. Each instant t should verify the constraint. Three semantics of constraints are derived from the time dimensions to consider : inter-VT, inter-TT and inter-Bi constraints. For instances, the valid time stamp must be unique in the temporal class with history<VT> is an inter-VT constraint, the name of a person cannot change more than three times is an inter-TT constraint and the weight of a patient for a specific valid time cannot be corrected more than three times is an inter-Bi constraint.

- O* example :

For instance, « *the salary of an employee can't change more than three times in one year* » is a constraint intra-object (only on the employee object) and inter-time (history of this object).

On the contrary, « *an employee can be affected only to a project belonging to the same department* » is an inter-object (employee and project) and intra-time (only one instant) constraint.

5. Conclusion

We have presented a set of generic patterns aiming at extending OO models with temporal features. They are called "generic" because they can be applied on any OO model.

These patterns lead to adapt an existing OO model to the specific requirements of the application to develop.

For this paper, we have selected six temporal features identified from temporal database applications, of general scope, explored in the TOOBIS project. These six patterns have been used and exemplified through the adaptation of the O* model, as we have done for defining the TOOBIS method.

The approach we have followed permits to reuse the know-how we have gained during this project, at the method engineering level, as well as at the temporal applications level.

We are currently working in three directions :

- extending the capability of the patterns for adapting, not only the concept definition, but to consider also the concept representation as well as the process definition associated to a OO model,

- extending the set of temporal patterns for handling more temporal aspects which are not specific to applications of general scope,

- evaluating and validating the temporal adaptation process with the UML method.

References

1. Proc. of the Conference on Methods Engineering, IFIP WG 8.1, eds. Chapman & hall, Atlanta, 1996.

2. Harmsen F., Brinkkemper S., Oei H. Situational Method Engineering for Information System Project Approaches. In : Proc. of the conference on Methods and associated Tools for Information Systems Life Cycle, eds. A.A. Verrijn-Stuart and T.W. Olle, pub. North Holland, IFIP WG 8.1, 1994.

3. Rolland C., Plihon V. Using generic chunks to generate process model fragments. Proc. of the 2nd Conference on Requirements Engineering, ICRE'96. Colorado Springs, 1996 .

4. Plihon V., Ralyte J., Benjamen A., et al. A Reuse-Oriented Approach for the Construction of Scenario based Methods. In ICSP'98. Chicago, 1998.

5. Rolland C., Plihon V., Ralyté J. Specifying the reuse context of scenario method chunks. In : Proc. of the conference CAiSE'98, Pise, 1998.

6. Coad, P. Object-Oriented Patterns. In : Communications of the ACM, Vol. 35, No. 9, 152-159. 1992

7. Beck, K. Smalltalk. Best Practice Patterns. Volume 1: Coding, Prentice Hall, Englewood Cliffs, NJ. 1997

8. Buschmann, F., Meunier, R., Rohnert, et al. Pattern-Oriented Software Architecture - A System of Patterns, John Wiley. 1996

9. Coplien, J.O. and Schmidt, D.O. (ed.) Pattern Languages of Program Design. Addison-Wesley, Reading, MA. 1995

10. Gamma E., Helm R., Johnson R., et al. Design Patterns: Elements of Reusable Object-Oriented Software. Addison-Wesley, MA. 1994

11. Vlissides, J.M., Coplien, J.O. and Kerth, N.L. (ed.) Pattern Languages of Program Design 2, Addison-Wesley. 1996.

12. Hay, D. Data Model Patterns: Conventions of Thought. Dorset House, NY. 1996

13. Fowler, M. Analysis Patterns: Reusable Object Models. Addison-Wesley. 1997

14. Alexander C. The Timeless Way of Building. Oxford University Press, NY. 1979

15. Alexander C., Ishikawa S., Silverstein M., et al. A Pattern Language. Oxford University Press, New York. 1977

16. Deliverables of the TOOBIS esprit project are available to http://www.di.uoa.gr/~toobis/Deliverables.html

17. Brunet J.. Analyse Conceptuelle orientée-objet. PhD Thesis, University of Paris 6, Paris. 1993.

18. Lee S. P. Formalisation et aide outillée à la modelisation conceptuelle. PhD Thesis, University of Paris 1, Paris. 1994.

19. Rolland C., Grosz G. A General Framework for Describing the Requirements Engineering Process. In : Proc. of the IEEE Conference on Systems Man and Cybernetics. CSMC94, San Antonio, Texas. 1994.

20. Plihon V., Rolland C. Modelling Ways-of-Working. In : Proc. of the 7th Int. Conference on «Advanced Information Systems Engineering», (CAISE). Springer Verlag (Pub.). 1995.

21. Theodoulidis B., Svinterikou M.. Temporal Unified Modelling Language (TUML). Technical Report CH-97-11. In : Chorochronos TMR Research Project (n° ERBFMRXCT960056). 1997.

22. Snodgrass, I. Ahn. A taxonomy of time in databases. In : Proc. of ACM SIGMOD Conference. 1985.

23. Gehani N., Jagadish H.V. Ode as an active database : constraints and triggers. In : Proc. of the 17th VLDB, Barcelona, Spain, pp. 327-336. 1991.

24. Böhlen M. H. Valid time integrity constraint. Report TR 94-30. 1994.

DESIGN ISSUES 1

Representation of Multi-level Composite Objects in Relational Databases

W. Rahayu,   E. Chang,   T.S. Dillon

La Trobe University, Department of Computer Science and Computer Engineering
Bundoora, Victoria 3083, Australia
{wenny, chang, tharam}@latcs1.cs.latrobe.edu.au

Abstract

Composite objects are objects along a composition or aggregation hierarchy. This hierarchy may span in an arbitrary level. This paper describes multi-level composite object representation in relational database management systems (RDBMS). Composite object representation comprises two main elements: *Composite Object Structuring* and *Composite Object Instantiations*. We formulate a composite index structure for composite object structuring. Using this index structure, composite objects can be presented in any format (e.g. nested relation) when they are instantiated. Our analysis shows that the proposed index structure for composite object representation in RDBMS is more efficient than conventional method through direct querying for retrieving composite objects.

1 Introduction

Aggregated or *composite objects* are built from other component objects. If one gets a composite or aggregated object design that has components objects which themselves composite or aggregated objects, then one gets a two-level aggregation or composition hierarchy. This could be repeated to several levels of composition/aggregation hierarchy. In this paper, the terms composition and aggregation are used interchangeably. The notion of composition is important in the development of many complex database applications, particularly in computer aided design, office applications, and engineering applications. In these applications, object-oriented modeling is often used as a basis in the analysis and design stages. In the implementation, however, relational database management systems (RDBMS) are often employed, due to several obvious reasons, such as the popularity and maturity of RDBMS, etc. Consequently, it is therefore critical to investigate how composite objects are represented in relational databases. The aim of this paper is to present composite object representation, particularly multi-level composition, in relational databases.

In this paper, we propose a method, which stresses the significance of preserving the semantics of each composite object and captures these semantics in the creation of composite object. This will subsequently ensure a direct and smooth transition from a conceptual modeling stage into a design and implementation stage, as well as diminish the gap between the connotations of composite object in the real world and its representation in the DBMS.

We develop a representation for composite objects in relational database systems by creating a structure, which stores indices of composite objects. This structure is formed by running a query on aggregate tables to extract tuple identifiers, which will serve as the indices of the created composite object. Aggregate tables are the tables that store the composition relationships between "whole" objects and "parts" objects. Other details of each object are stored in the base tables. The aggregate tables ensure that every integrity constraint associated with different types of compositions in different levels is preserved. Composite indices are derived from the aggregate tables, and thus the semantics and constraints between each level of the composition are always preserved.

Another benefit attained from the structure of the aggregate tables is the efficiency achieved when querying for the creation of the composite indices. The aggregate tables are designed to support composition hierarchies and the operations to access composite objects. In our earlier paper [12] we show how aggregate tables improve the efficiency of query operations that are designated to access composite objects. In this paper, we will show how aggregate tables can be used to derive composite indices.

Our proposed method does not enforce a particular access method in instantiating the composite objects for user applications. It is rather to improve the efficiency of access and storage of the composite objects. We will also show that the proposed method can be used by most existing methods for representation of objects in conjunction with relational databases to improve the semantics and efficiency in accessing composite objects. The main aims of the proposed method are: (*i*) to allow accesses to the entire level composite object without the necessity for employing path expression techniques, and (*ii*) to facilitate the support of the use of aggregation semantics to improve the adaptability of user queries over aggregation hierarchy of composite objects.

The rest of this paper is organized as follows. Section 2 discusses an overview of composite objects, and existing work on composite object representation. Section 3 presents briefly two layers in composite object representation in relational databases, namely composite object structuring using composite indices and composite object instantiations into a specific format desired by user applications. The details of composite object structuring and instantiations are presented in sections 4 and 5, respectively. Section 6 presents a quantitative analysis of the proposed method. Finally, section 7 draws the conclusions.

2 Background

As a background to our work, we briefly describe composite objects in the next section. The discussion on existing work on composite object representation will follow.

2.1   Composite Objects: A Brief Overview

Composite objects are complex objects with *composition (part-of) semantics*. Most standard textbooks in Object Data Modelling and Object Databases [2], [3], [6] also define another type of complex object that is based on *reference semantics*.

The main difference between the two lies in the links that connect the components of a complex object. In the composition type of complex object (composite object), the links are augmented with semantics that enforce integrity constraints associated with composition of the linked objects. In contrast, there is no special integrity constraint attached to the link in the reference type of complex objects. There could, however, be constraints that arise from the meanings of the relationship within the domain. The components of the reference type complex objects are themselves independent objects, in which at times they may be considered as part of the complex object [3].

In this paper, we focus on the composition type of complex object, since composition truly reflects the important whole-part semantic of complex objects (i.e. aggregation). The reference type itself is actually an association, which is conceptually different from aggregation. In contrast, most existing work on complex object representation in relational DBMS focuses on the reference semantics, not so much on the composite semantics.

2.2   Existing Work

There is a number of existing works on complex object representation in relational database management systems (RDBMS). Eventhough representation of complex object in relational databases is supposed to cover both types of complex objects, most of the existing techniques only cover the reference type of complex object representation. Moreover, those existing techniques mainly address the formation of complex object and the ways to access it, without emphasizing on the maintenance of the semantics of complex object. In this section we discuss existing work on complex objects, particularly the ones by Lee and Wiederhold [8], Pirahesh et al. [10], and Barsolou and Wiederhold [1].

The research by Lee and Wiederhold [8] proposes a *View Object* which is instantiated by delivering a query to a relational database and by converting the result of the query into a nested structure. The main highlight of this research is the formation of complex object (in the form of nested structure) from RDBMS tables using techniques called RF (Relation Fragments) and SNR (Single Nested Relation) which are proven to be more efficient that the ordinary SFR (Single Flat Relation) method. In the SFR method, the query is retrieved into a flat relation format, whereas in both the RF and SNR method the query result is transformed into fragments which are accompanied by an assembly plan for the client to re-assemble into nested structures. However, this research does not consider composition type of complex objects in which there are certain semantics and integrity constraints directly attached to the complex objects. Additionally, if a composition type of complex object is to be formulated using the above methods, the query to be delivered to the base tables become less efficient, since several explicit joins need to be performed for every level of composition. In other words, both composition and reference type of complex objects are treated merely as a reference type.

Pirahesh et al. [10] develops a technique to make relational systems be able to understand (through language extension) and be able to handle (through optimization) complex objects. An extension to SQL to handle complex objects has been proposed. The language is called SQL XNF(SQL Extended Normal Form) and is used to derive complex objects from relational tables. XNF can be seen as an extension to existing RDBMS and, therefore, it avoids the need for building or migrating into an entirely new DBMS. Like other existing work, this approach does not consider the essential semantics of composition type of complex objects. The composition in a complex object is viewed as several interconnected references rather than one whole hierarchy.

Barsolou and Wiederhold [1] develop an implementation of the View Objects model in the PENGUIN system - a system that defines an object-oriented layer on top of an RDBMS. The object layer has three tasks: (*i*) *Object Generator* which maps relations into View Objects where each View Object can be a complex combination of join and projection operations on the base relations, (*ii*) *Object Instantiator* which provides a non-procedural access to the View Object instances, and (*iii*) *Object Decomposer* which maps the View Object instances back to the base relations. Similar to the previous methods, this system mainly addresses the reference type of complex objects. If a complex object of composition type is viewed, join operations must be performed by the Object Generator, which will reduce the efficiency. Another shortcoming, also mentioned in [1], is the limited semantic expressiveness of the structural model. Different kinds of integrity constraints that are attached to the complex objects cannot be captured using this model.

In summary, most existing works on complex objects representation in the RDBMS mainly address the reference type only. The concept of integrity constraints between linked objects has not been considered, and therefore it creates a big gap between the exact notion of the complex object in the real world and its representation in the DBMS. Another consequence of treating composite type of complex objects as ordinary reference type is that composition is not considered collectively as a basic unit of a high level object and thus this makes queries to access the complex object inefficient and tedious [7]. In other words, complex object composition cannot be seen as a whole, encapsulated, object, rather it is depicted as several object interconnections [12]. The main purpose of the proposed method presented in this paper is to address the above issues and to come up with a solution that can be used by other object representation methods as a way to solve the identified problems. Instead of treating the relational base tables merely as data storage, we try to optimize them and to improve their semantics in the relational database level by creating a composite index structure. The final format of the composite objects in the object layer is flexible and can be determined by the user applications.

3 Composite Object Representation

Composite object representation in RDBMS is divided into two layers: namely *Relational layer* consisting of *Composite Object Structuring*, and *Object layer* consisting of *Composite Object Instantiation*. The first layer is called relational layer, since objects are stored in relational tables. It is basically divided into three steps. In the first step, base tables are created. In the second step, aggregate tables are formed. Aggregate tables are employed to maintain the relationship between a "whole" class and all of its direct "part" classes. To create an aggregate table from the given base tables, we apply a composition transformation rule. In the third step, a composite index is created by the composite indices creation rules. Unlike the aggregate tables which maintain one-level composition between a whole class and its direct descendants, the composite index structure preserve the whole composite object structure.

In the object layer, composite objects can be presented in any form requested by user applications. We also provide a nesting algorithm that retrieves and presents composite objects in a form of nested relation.

Figure 1 shows how composite objects are created through composite indices. In the next sections, the steps/rules and algorithms depicted in Figure 1 are explained.

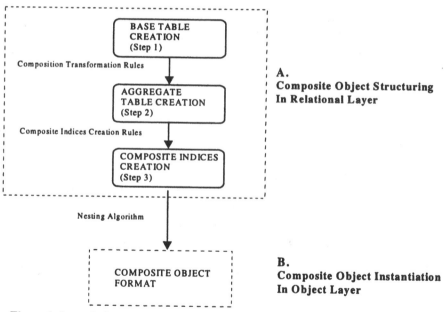

Figure 1. Instantiating composite objects from relational tables through composite indices

As a running example, we use an object schema shown in Figure 2. The PC (Personal Computer) consists of SystemBox and Monitor. Further, SystemBox is composed of CPU and RAM. For simplicity, the attributes are not shown. In this example, PC is the root object. The relationship between the root class and its direct part classes (i.e. SystemBox and Monitor) is known as level 1 of path 1. Further down, the relationships are level 2 of path 1, level 2 of path 2, etc. Later, we call level x of path y to be AGGREGATExy.

The next two sections explain composite object structuring and composite object instantiation.

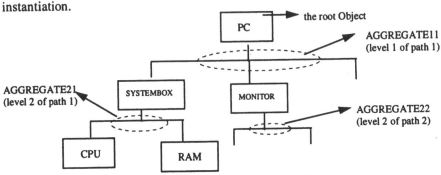

Figure 2. Composite Object PC (Personal Computer)

4   Composite Object Structuring

We recall that composite object structuring is divided into three steps: the creation of the Base tables, the Aggregate tables, and the Composite Indices. These steps show how composite indices are created from base tables for a given composite object schema.

4.1   Step 1: Base Tables Creation

The first step is to create base tables for each of the class in the composite object schema (i.e. the root of the composite objects and each of the part class). Each table is added with an attribute to represent the object identifier (OID) [13], [14], for example PC_oid attribute for OIDs of PCs. It is important to note that each OID that belongs to instances of the objects in the composite object structure has to be unique both in the object domain as well as in the composite object domain. For example, an OID of a SystemBox should not be the same as the OID of a CPU.

The base tables for the PC composite object example in Figure 2 are shown in Figure 3. Each of the class in Figure 2 becomes a table (i.e. PC, SystemBox, CPU, Monitor, and RAM). Each class as an attribute which represents the OID, such as PC_oid, SB_oid, etc. They are also the primary keys of the respective table. Other attributes are additional information about the class, such as MaintenanceDate of PC, Type of SystemBox, Speed of CPU, etc. To give a clear picture of the base table creation process, we inserted a number of records in each of the base table for an illustration.

PC

PC_oid	MaintananceDate
PC1	01/05/97
PC2	01/06/97
PC3	01/07/97

SYSTEMBOX

SB_oid	Type
SB1	Tower
SB2	Server box
SB3	Desktop

CPU

CPU_oid	Speed(MHz)
CPU1	90
CPU2	100
CPU3	120
CPU4	60

MONITOR

M_oid	Size (inch)
M1	14
M2	15
M3	17
M4	21

RAM

RAM_oid	Size (MB)
RAM1	2
RAM2	32
RAM3	8
RAM4	16
RAM5	64

Figure 3. Base Tables

4.2   Step 2: Aggregate Tables Creation

The second step is to create the *aggregate* tables for each composition relationship. A number of aggregate tables are created for a multilevel composite object. Using the running example shown previously in Figure 2, the first aggregate table maintains the relationship between the root class (i.e. PC) and its direct parts (i.e. SystemBox and Monitor), whereas the second aggregate table maintains the relationship between SystemBox and CPU/RAM. Should there be any classes directly below class Monitor, we will need an aggregate table to maintain this relationship.

The rule to create aggregate tables can be explained as follows. Let RW be the relational table of the "whole" object in the composition with Wk as the primary key (PK) of the table, and let $Ra, Rb, ..., Rz$ be the relational tables of the "part" objects in the composition with $ak, bk, ..., zk$ as the PKs of the tables. The general schema of the Aggregate tables which belong to the different types of compositions are defined as follows:

AGGREGATExy (Wk, PartNo, PartType)
Where: PartNo = $(ak | ... | zk)$, and
PartType = the name of the relation $(Ra | ... | Rz)$.

Although the OID of the object, as shown in the attribute Wk, may indicate the part class type, the PartType attribute is still added to simplify the representation. This is also due to that OID may be created and inserted automatically by the system, on which the user applications may not have control. Therefore, by the addition of the PartType attribute, it can be guaranteed that the part class type is still maintained.

Using the example above, the type of composition relationship between PC and its parts: SystemBox and Monitor, is *one-one* existence independent. The deletion of a particular PC may not necessarily cause a deletion of its components (ie. monitor or system box) as another PC can reuse them. Table AGGREGATE11 is created to maintain this relationship. Since it is *one-one* existence independent composition, the primary key is the *PartNo* attribute. This attribute is unique enough to identify each record.

The composition between SystemBox and its parts: CPU and RAM, is *one-to-many* existence independent. This composition is level 2 of path 1 and the aggregate table is called AGGREGATE21 with SB_oid and Part2 is a composite primary key. Figure 4 shows the two aggregate tables. The records are based on the base tables created earlier (see Figure 3).

AGREGATE11

PC_oid	Part1	Part_Type (Pt1)
PC1	SB1	SystemBox
PC1	M1	Monitor
PC2	SB2	SystemBox
PC2	M2	Monitor
PC3	SB3	SystemBox
PC3	M3	Monitor

Primary Key: Part1
Part1 = SB_oid | M_oid

AGREGATE21

SB_oid	Part2	Part_Type (Pt2)
SB1	RAM1	RAM
SB1	RAM2	RAM
SB1	CPU1	CPU
SB2	RAM3	RAM
SB2	RAM4	RAM
SB2	CPU2	CPU
SB2	CPU3	CPU
SB3	RAM5	RAM
SB3	CPU4	CPU

Primary Key: SB_oid, Part2
Part2 = CPU_oid | RAM_oid

Figure 4. Aggregate Tables

4.3 Step 3: Composite Indices Creation

The final step in the composite object structuring is composite indices creation. It is basically a transformation from the aggregate tables created in the previous step into a composite index. The composite index structure is a relational table. The transformation process can be explained as follows.

Let R_{co} be the table that stores the composite object, *oid* be the identifier of the root object, $\{Part_1, Part_2, ..., Part_m\}$ be the identifier of the "part" (component) objects, $\{Pt_1, Pt_2, ..., Pt_m\}$ be the domain (type) of each "part" identifier, $(AGGREGATE11 ... AGGREGATE(m+1)j)$ be the tables that stores the aggregate relationships between each level of the composition, and $(oid_{11} ... oid_{(m+1)i})$ be the identifiers of the aggregate tables. Suppose the level of the composition is m, and the path number in each composition level is i. The composite indices (Rco) is then defined as follows:

$$R_{co} = \Pi \ (oid, Part1, Pt1, ... Partm, Ptm) \ \bigcup_{i=1}^{n(m-1)} R_{(m-1)} \bowtie AGGREGATEmi$$

$$R_{(m-1).}Part_{(m-1)} = AGGREGATE_{mi}.oid_{mi}$$

The full derivation of this transformation rule is given in the Appendix A. Note that we perform a left-outer join in order to prevent from information loss.

Whenever a matching tuple is not found, the tuple will not be discarded, rather a null value will be inserted.

Using the previous AGGREGATE11 and AGGREGATE21 tables, we get the following composite index.

$$R_{co} = \Pi \ (oid, \ Part1, \ Pt1, \ Part2, \ Pt2) \ AGGREGATE11 \ \boxed{\bowtie} \ AGGREGATE21$$

AGGREGATE11.Part$_1$ =AGGREGATE21.oid$_{21}$

Since the OIDs of the root table and the AGGREGATE21 are PC_oid and SB_oid, respectively, the above relational algebra for R_{co} can be translated into the following SQL:

```
SELECT PC_oid, Part1, Pt1, Part2, Pt2
FROM AGGREGATE11 LEFT OUTER JOIN AGGREGATE21
ON AGGREGATE11.Part1 = AGGREGATE21.SB_oid
```

We name the result table *Composite_PC* table. This table is the composite index of the Composite Object PC shown earlier in Figure 2. The tables may not be in 3NF, but anomalies may not occur, since this table is a table derived directly from the aggregate tables.

Composite_PC

PC_oid	Part1	Pt1	Part2	Pt2
PC1	SB1	System Box	RAM1	RAM
PC1	SB1	System Box	RAM2	RAM
PC1	SB1	System Box	CPU1	CPU
PC1	M1	Monitor	null	null
PC2	SB2	System Box	RAM3	RAM
PC2	SB2	System Box	RAM4	RAM
PC2	SB2	System Box	CPU2	CPU
PC2	SB2	System Box	CPU3	CPU
PC2	M2	Monitor	null	null
PC3	SB3	System Box	RAM5	RAM
PC2	SB3	System Box	CPU4	CPU
PC2	M3	Monitor	null	null

Figure 5. Composite Index for PC (Personal Computer)

5   Multi-Level Composite Objects Instantiation

Composite Indices are internal representation (or storage structure) of multi-level composite objects. User applications may generate a more appropriate format for composite object external representation. This can be in the format of nested relation or other formats. General composite object instantiation is explained in Algorithm 1.

In algorithm 1, $t_i = \{t_1, \ t_2, \ ..., \ t_n\}$ denotes the tuples of the composite index table. $Part_j = \{oid, \ Part_1, \ ..., \ Part_m\}$ are the attributes that belong to each tuple of the composite index table, and $Pt_j = \{Pt_1, \ Pt_2, \ ...., \ Pt_m\}$ are the table/domain from where the "part" attributes ($Part_j$) come. $Part_j$ is actually the index that refers to a particular "part" in the Pt_j table. Consequently, the retrieval process is merely a merging process.

```
for each tuple ti from composite index table
    read a tuple from the Root_Object table with oidi as index
        for each Partj
            read a tuple from table Ptj with Partj as index
            form a composite object
        end for
end for
```

Algorithm 1. General Composite Object Instantiation

The next section explains the composite object instantiation to nested relation structures in more details. Following this, it will be shown that the composite index structure can also be used by any existing method in instantiating composite objects.

5.1   Nested Relation Structure

In this section, we present a technique for instantiating composite objects from composite index table and for storing the result into a nested relation structure. As an example, we use the Composite_PC example presented in Figure 5 as a composite index. Figure 6 shows the general technique of instantiating composite objects from a composite index to a nested relation using a nesting algorithm. The algorithm itself is presented in Algorithm2.

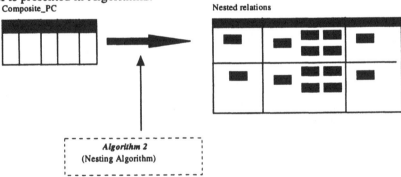

Figure 6. Composite Object Instantiation into a Nested Relation Structure

If we apply algorithm 2 to the example Composite_PC, the input of to the algorithm is the composite index table, which is the Composite_PC table (see Figure 5). The attributes of this composite index table are *(PC_oid, Part$_1$, Pt$_1$, Part$_2$, Pt$_2$)*. Each tuple of the Composite_PC is identified as t_i, where $t_i = \{t_1, t_2, ..., t_n\}$ and n is the total number of tuples in the Composite_PC. Note that each tuple is retrieved only once before it is inserted into the Nested relation structure. The output of the Nesting Algorithm is as follows (The brackets serve as a separator between simple objects):

[PC1, [[SB1, [[RAM1, RAM2] , [CPU1]]] , M1]]
[PC2, [[SB2, [[RAM3, RAM4], [CPU2, CPU3]]], M2]]
[PC3, [[SB3, [[RAM5], [CPU4]]], M3]]

```
for each tuple ti of Composite_PC table
    if ti.oid = t(i-1).oid
        if ti.Part1 = t(i-1).Part1
            if ti.Pt2 = t(i-1).Pt2
                Insert ti.Part2
            else
                Close previous part level2 folder
                Open new part level2 folder and Insert ti.Part2
        else
            if ti.Pt1 = t(i-1).Pt1
                Close previous part level1 folder
                Open new part level1 folder and Insert ti.Part1
                Open new part level2 folder and Insert ti.Part2
            else
                Close previous part level1 folder
                Open new part level1 folder and Insert ti.Part1
    else
        Close previous object folder, except for the 1st tuple
        Create new object folder and Insert ti.oid
        Open part level1 folder and Insert ti.Part1
        Open part level2 folder and Insert ti.Part2
endfor
```

Algorithm 2. Composite Object Instantiation into Nested Relations for the Composite_PC example

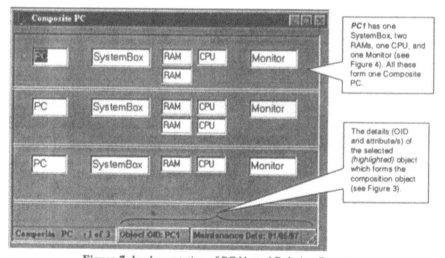

Figure 7. Implementation of PC Nested Relation Structure

We have implemented a nesting algorithm in C++Builder. Through the implementation we show that composite objects presented as nested relations are actually derived from the composite indices. Figure 7 shows an interface of the result of the Nesting Algorithm. Each button represents a simple object, whereas each unit of several simple objects rooted in a PC object represents a Composite_PC object. In the event of a particular object being chosen (by selecting a button), the complete descriptions of the simple object will be displayed.

5.2   Other Methods

Most existing work implements an additional layer (often known as object layer) on top of the relational layer. Because the proposed composite indices structure is created in the relational layer, it can also be employed by other systems that are built on top of the relational layer (ie. the object layer). These composite indices support the necessary functionalities to derive composite objects from relational base tables. Instead of deriving data straight from the relational base tables and employing a RDBMS as mere data storage, the composite index structure will ensure more efficient storage and retrieval.

Figure 8 shows the scope of our proposed structure in the common architecture of composite object creation from relational base tables. In the previous section we have shown that nested relation uses the composite indices to instantiate composite objects. Other methods, such as object views [1], query language [10], and view object [8], can also utilise composite indices to instantiate composite objects.

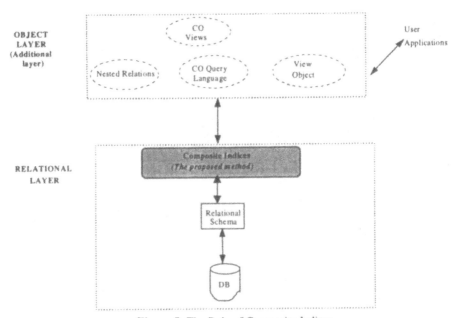

Figure 8. The Role of Composite Indices

Composite objects instantiation through composite indices is more efficient than that through direct querying to the base tables. User application may use the composite objects instantiated in the object layer which are provided in various formats.

The main benefits of using the composite index structure are:

- The composite indices structure builds and stores the composition relationships between every "whole" and "part" objects of the multi-level composite objects, therefore the system on the object layer will only need to retrieve and to store them in a desired object format.
- The semantics and integrity constraints of the composition are maintained by the composite index structure, ensuring no data anomalies are derived from the relational layer.

6 Quantitative Analysis

In this paper, we only analyze the *composite object structuring*. That is the performance of data retrieval from base tables. The main reason is because the composite object structuring step plays a critical role to determine the efficiency and semantics of the retrieved data from the relational storage. No matter what the format or method is used to translate the data into the desired format, the first process of deriving data from relational base tables is always essential. In this section, we will compare the efficiency of using the common method of data retrieval for composite objects as proposed by many publications (called *Direct Query*) versus the ones that utilize our Composite Indices Structure (called *Composite Indices Query*). We call them both query, since both methods use query language to derive composite objects. Existing methods use a query to retrieve data from base tables and present it as a composite object. Our method uses a query consisting multiple left-outer joins to create a composite index.

Because the main purpose of the quantitative analysis is to compare the costs of the queries, not to estimate the full costs, we consider only the factors that will greatly impact the overall cost of the data retrieval. The analysis is mainly based on the number of I/O accesses, as I/O access is considered to be the most expensive processing cost component. Our analysis is based on the cost platform to be described in the next section. The cost comparison will then follow.

6.1 Cost Platform

Most existing work requires a query to the base tables in order to generate relational composite tuples. The query normally involves a number of join operations, in which the number of join operations is proportional to the number of tables (or "part" objects) involved in the query. In contrast, our method generates relational composite tuples through the aggregate tables. Although join operation is still needed between different levels of composition, the number of join operations is not influenced by the number of tables (or "part" objects) within one level of composition. Figure 9 illustrates the difference between our methods and existing work.

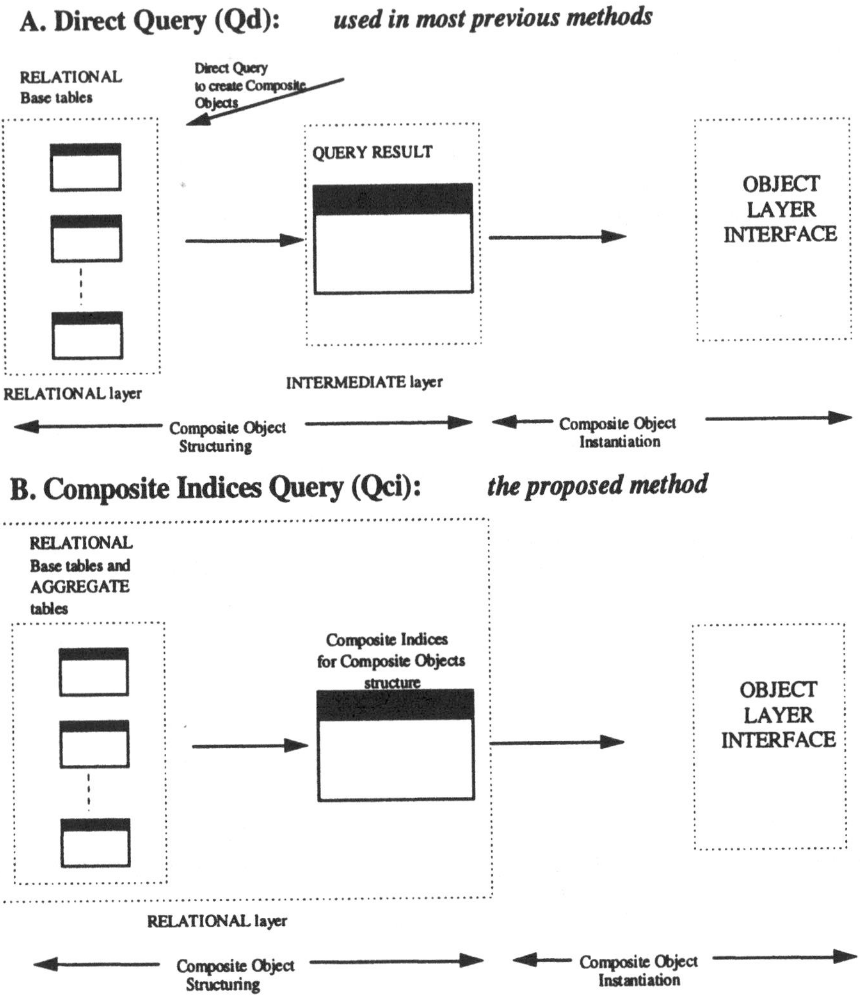

A. Direct Query (Qd):   *used in most previous methods*

B. Composite Indices Query (Qci):   *the proposed method*

Figure 9. Direct Query vs. Composite Indices Query

The key components for these two approaches are as follows. The Direct Query (Qd) method, the process consists of a series of join operation between each of the base table.

- Direct Query (Qd)

Input: Relational base tables $\{R1, R2, ..., Rm\}$

Output: Relational composite tuples : Rd

$$Rd \quad = \quad \{R1 \bowtie R2 \bowtie ... \bowtie Rm\}$$
$$= \quad \bowtie \{R1, R2, ..., Rm\}.$$

Method: M-way pipelined nested loop join [4], [8].

- Composite Indices Query (Qci)
  Input: Relational aggregate tables $\{AGGREGATE11, ..., AGGREGATEmi\}$
  Output: Relational composite tuples: Rm_{ci}

$$Rm_{ci} = \bigcup_{i=1}^{nm} R_{(m-1)ci} \bowtie AGGREGATEmi$$

6.2   Cost Comparison

The cost comparison is divided into two categories: (a) one-level composition, and
(b) multi levels composition. Figure 10 gives an illustration of one-level and multi-
levels compositions.

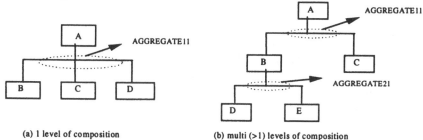

(a) 1 level of composition   (b) multi (>1) levels of composition

Figure 10. One level and Multi level Compositions

We are going to compare the cost of data retrieval for creating composite objects
using both direct query (Qd) and composite indices query (Qci). Note that the cost
equations are expressed in terms of the number of tuples. Thus, A, B, C, D, and E
are the number of tuples in each relational base tables A, B, C, D, and E,
respectively. $AGGREGATE11$ and $AGGREGATE21$ are the number of tuples is each
aggregate table $AGGREGATE11$ and $AGGREGATE21$, respectively.

6.2.1   One-level Composition

The costs for Direct Query (Qd) and Composite Indices Query (Qci) are as follows.
- Direct Query (Qd):
  Cost of $Qd_{(1)}$ = Cost of ($\bowtie \{A, B, C, D\}$)
- Composite Indices Query (Qci):
  Cost of $Qci_{(1)}$ = Cost of (AGGREGATE11)

LEMMA 1. To create composite objects of one-level composition, the cost of using
the proposed composite index method is always less than that of the direct query
method.

PROOF. We shall prove that

$$\text{Cost of } Qd_{(1)} > \text{Cost of } Qci_{(1)} \tag{1}$$

Using the cost formula for *Direct Query* and *Composite Indices*, condition (1)
becomes:

$$\text{Cost of } (\bowtie \{A, B, C, D\}) > \text{Cost of } (AGGREGATE11)$$

As there are 3 join operations (i.e., A join B join C join D) in Qd, and no join operation is needed in Qci, the above condition is true. Therefore, Lemma 1 is shown to be valid.

Notes: The number of join operations in Qd will increase as the number of "part" objects that belong to the root grows. □

6.2.1   Multi-levels Composition

The costs of for Direct Query (Qd) and Composite Indices Query (Qci) for multi-levels compositions are as follows.

- Direct Query (Qd):
  Cost of $Qd_{(2)}$ = Cost of ($\bowtie$ {A, B, D, E, C })
- Composite Indices Query (Qci):
  Cost of $Qci_{(2)}$ = Cost of (AGGREGATE11 $\bowtie$ AGGREGATE21)

LEMMA 2. To create composite objects of more than one-level composition, the cost of using the proposed composite indices method is always less than that of direct query method.

PROOF. We shall show that

$$\text{Cost of } Qd_{(2)} > \text{Cost of } Qci_{(2)}$$

$$(2)$$

Using the cost formula for Direct Query and Composite Indices, condition (2) becomes:

Cost $(\bowtie\{A,B,D,E,C\})$ > Cost (AGGREGATE11 $\bowtie$ AGGREGATE21).

Provided that AGGREGATE11 $\approx$ (B+C) and AGGREGATE21 $\approx$ (D+E), and the unit of the calculated cost is tj (join time), it becomes

$$(A \times B \times D \times E \times C) \text{ tj} \quad > \quad ((B + C) \times (C + D)) \text{ tj}$$
$$\Rightarrow \quad (A \times (B \times C) \times (C \times D)) \text{ tj} > \quad ((B + C) \times (C + D)) \text{ tj.}$$

If it can be proven that:

$$(B \times C) > \quad (B + C) \text{ and} \quad\quad (3)$$
$$(C \times D) > \quad (C + D) \quad\quad\quad\quad (4)$$

to be true, then condition (2) above is trivially satisfied.

Case 1 is where B = C. Condition (3) becomes

$$B^2 > 2 \times B$$
$$\Rightarrow \quad B > 2.$$

Condition (2) is satisfied if B > 2 and C > 2.

Case 2 is where B > C. Based on the first case where C > 2, condition (3) can be derived to

$$(B \times C) > B \times 2$$
$$\Rightarrow \quad (B \times C) > B + B.$$

Since B > C, B x C > B + C is true. Therefore, condition (3) is true if B > C and C > 2. The same proof is applied for C > B and B > 2.

The same method is applicable to satisfy condition (4). Since the conditions (3) and (4) require the number of tuples to be greater than 2 (which is very small), most of the time, condition (2) above is satisfied. Therefore, Lemma 2 is shown to be valid.

□

7 Conclusions

In this paper we have presented techniques for efficient multi-level composite object representations for relational databases. Composite object representation comprises two elements: *composite object structuring* in which composite indices are used to store composite objects in relational tables, and *composite object instantiation* in which composite objects are derived from composite indices into any format specified by user applications (eg. Nested relation).

The main benefits of our proposed method are:

- The improvement of the semantic expressiveness of the created composite objects. This is achieved by having the composite indices structure that maintain integrity constraints associated with different types of composition.
- The improvement of efficiency of the queries for deriving data from relational tables which are then structured to form the composite objects. The composite index structure ensures a straightforward access to the whole composite object without the necessity for path expressions.
- The flexibility due to the proposed composite indices structure being built in the relational layer. It can be used by most RDBMSs, which support composite object representations in their object layer.

References

1. Barsolou, T. and G. Wiederhold (1990) "Composite Objects for relational databases", *Computer Aided Design (Special issue on OO Techniques for CAD)*, 22(8).
2. Dillon, T. S. and P. L. Tan (1993) *Object-Oriented Conceptual Model*, Prentice Hall.
3. Elmasri, R. and S. Navathe (1994) *Fundamentals of Database Systems*, The Benjamin Cummings Company Inc.
4. Helman, P. (1994) *The Science of Database Managament*, Irwin Inc., USA.
5. Kim, W. (1982) "On Optimizing an SQL-like Nested Query", *ACM Transaction on Database Systems*, September.
6. Kim, W. (1990) *Introduction to Object-Oriented Databases*, MIT Press, Cambridge, Mass.
7. Ling, L. (1993) "A Recursive object algebra based on aggregation abstraction for manipulating composite objects", *Data and Knowledge Engineering*, August.
8. Lee, B.S. and G. Wiederhold (1994), "Efficiently Instantiating View-Objects From Remote relational Databases", *VLDB Journal*, 3.
9. ODMG (1994) *The Object Database Standard*, Release 1.1, R.G. Cattel (ed), Morgan Kaufmann Publishers, San Fransisco.
10. Pirahesh, H., B. Mitchang, N. Sudkamp, and B. Lindsay (1994) "Composite Object Views in relational DBMS: An Implementation Perspective", *Fourth International Conference in Advances in DB Technology*, Springer LNCS 779.

11. Rahayu, W, E. Chang, and T.S. Dillon (1998) "Implementation of Object-Oriented Association Relationships in Relational Databases", *Proceedings of International Database Engineering and Applications Symposium IDEAS'98*, IEEE Computer Society Press, UK (to appear).

12. Rahayu, W. ,E. Chang, T.S. Dillon and D. Taniar (1996) "Aggregation versus Association in Object Modelling and Databases", *Proceedings of Australasian Conference on Information Systems*, Tasmania.

13. Rahayu, W. and E. Chang (1993) "A Methodology for transforming an Object-Oriented Data Model to a Relational Database", *Proceedings of the 12th International Conference on Technology of Object-Oriented Languages and Systems*, Melbourne.

14. Rumbaugh, J., et. al. (1991) *Object-Oriented Modeling and Design*, Prentice-Hall.

Appendix A

Relational tables for composite indices are derived from joining (left outer join) the created *AGGREGATE* tables. An *AGGREGATE* table is created for each level of composition for storing the relationships between each "whole" and its "parts" objects. The relations for each level of composition $(R_1, R_2, ..., R_m)$ are as follows.

$R_1 = AGGREGATE_{11}$

$$R_2 = \bigcup_{i=1}^{n1} AGGREGATE_{11} \bowtie AGGREGATE_{2i}$$

$$AGGREGATE11.Part1 = AGGREGATE2i.oid2i$$

$$R_3 = \bigcup_{i=1}^{n2} R_2 \bowtie AGGREGATE_{3i}$$

$$R2.Part2 = AGGREGATE3i.oid3i$$

$$R_4 = \bigcup_{i=1}^{n3} R_3 \bowtie AGGREGATE_{4i}$$

$$R3.Part3 = AGGREGATE4i.oid4i$$

$$R_m = \bigcup_{i=1}^{n(m-1)} R_{(m-1)} \bowtie AGGREGATEmi$$

$$R_{(m-1)}.Part_{(m-1)} = AGGREGATE_{mi}.oid_{mi}$$

where $m >= 2$, and i = path number in each level of composition.

(for $m = 1$ (1 level composition), $R_1 = AGGREGATE_{11}$)

For the Composite_Object table, only oid of the root object and the oids of each part (*Part1 ...Part m*) are selected. Hence, Composite_Object table *Rco* can be generated as follows.

$$R_{co} = \Pi (oid, Part1, Pt1, ... Partm, Ptm) . Rm$$

$$R_{co} = \Pi (oid, Part1, Pt1, ... Partm, Ptm) \bigcup_{i=1}^{n(m-1)} R_{(m-1)} \bowtie AGGREGATEmi$$

$$R_{(m-1)}.Part_{(m-1)} = AGGREGATE_{mi}.oid_{mi}$$

Complex Methods and Class Allocation in Distributed OODBSs

Ladjel Bellatreche   Kamalakar Karlapalem
University of Science and Technology
Clear Water Bay, Kowloon, Hong Kong
E-mail: {ladjel, kamal}@cs.ust.hk

Qing Li
Hong Kong Polytechnic University
Hung Hom, Kowloon, Hong Kong
E-mail: csqli@comp.polyu.edu.hk

Abstract

In a distributed object-oriented database system (DODBS), queries which invoke methods executing at different sites and access different classes need to be executed very efficiently. Therefore, the methods invoked and classes accessed by the queries need to be allocated to sites so as to reduce the data transfer cost in processing a given set of queries. The methods and class allocation(MCA) problem needs to take into consideration complex interdependencies among queries, methods and classes. In this paper, we develop a comprehensive cost model for total data transfer incurred in processing a given set of queries by incorporating the dependencies among the queries, methods and classes. Further, we develop an iterative approach to generate near-optimal solution for the combined MCA problems by using the above cost model. In this approach, we start with an initial class allocation(CA) which is used for method allocation(MA), which in turn is used for CA, and so on. We stop this iterative MCA when there is no further reduction in total data transfer cost incurred in processing the given set of queries. We also present the results of experiments conducted to evaluate the effectiveness of our approach by comparing the results with exhaustive enumeration solution (which guarantees the optimal solution).

1 Introduction

Over the past few years, object-oriented database systems (OODBSs) have been thought of as the next generation database systems for advanced applications such as CAD/CAM, CASE, and multimedia information systems [3]. The distributed databases have also become an important area of information processing. The design of distributed databases enhances the performance of the applications in two ways [10]: by reducing the amount of irrelevant data accessed by the applications and by reducing the amount of data transfered in processing the applications. Two of the main design activities in distributed database system design are: *partitioning* and *allocation*, which refers to partition the data (e.g., relations) and allocating fragments of relations to various

239

site, respectively. The result of an allocation process is an allocation scheme. The research work has demonstrated that the allocation problem in the relational model is *NP-complete* [1, 7], and it has not been satisfactorily solved for distributed relational databases [10]. The data allocation problem for relational model becomes MCA problem in distributed OODBs. The MA problem is tightly coupled to CA problem because of encapsulation. Therefore, allocation of classes will imply allocation of methods to their corresponding home classes. But since applications on OOBDs invoke methods, the allocation of methods affect the performance of applications. Further, there has not been much work done on query/method processing in distributed object processing. Allocation of methods which needs to access multiple classes at different sites is a problem which has been not yet tackled. Another opinion with respect to MCA raised by Karlapalem et al [10] uses the power of partitioning transparency, wherein the end users need not know whether the method invoked is simple, or complex (executed at different sites), and whether the classes accessed are partitioned or not. In this case, the problem of MA and CA can be addressed independently, even though they are interdependent.

In this paper, we address the combined MCA problem in OODBSs. The objective of this study is to allocate methods and classes to various sites so that a minimum total data transfer cost is achieved. As CA problem is also a NP-complete problem [4], an optimal allocation of methods constitutes a complex problem due to the existence of two types of dependencies: 1) method-method dependency which means a method can call other method(s), and 2) method-class dependency which means a method can use objects of some class(es).

1.1   An Iterative Approach for MCA

Since an OODB takes into account the encapsulation of methods and the objects referenced by these methods, the allocation problem in OODB needs to address the allocation of classes and methods together. Indeed, the MCA problems are mutually interdependent. Our objective is to develop a new approach that integrates MCA in DODBSs in an iterative manner, so as to minimize the overall data transfer cost incurred from processing a given set of queries. First, we develop a global cost model which can be viewed as a function with two variables X and Y, where X and Y represent MA scheme and CA scheme, respectively. Our iterative approach consists of fixing one variable and then finding a value for the second to achieve a minimum data transfer cost. Then, based on the value of the second variable, we look for the first variable's value which can further reduce the total data transfer cost. We do this procedure iteratively(see Figure 1), till there is no change in the global cost. Finally, the values of X and Y satisfying the minimal total data transfer cost represent our solution of the MCA problems. The algorithm proposed in [4] provides us with the initial CA scheme to be used for our iterative MCA generation.

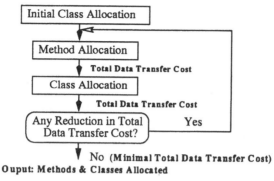

Figure 1: An Iterative approach for MCA

1.2 Related Work

The allocation problem has been first studied in terms of file allocation in a multi computer system, and later on as a data allocation in distributed database systems [1, 11].

The file allocation problem(FAP) was studied by Ramamoorthy et al. [12], and Chen [5]. In [12], the authors analyzed a FAP in the environment of a distributed database and developed a heuristic approximation algorithm for a simple FAP as well as the generalized FAP. They also proposed a model for file migration or reallocation. Chen [5] formulated a queuing model for an open central server network. File request frequencies and execution times are assumed to be exponentially distributed, and standard results for $M|M|1$ queue are applied to obtain file request distributions in order to minimizes average response time.

The problem of data allocation(DA) has been studied in the relational environment [6, 1, 11]. A strategy to integrate the treatment of relation assignment and query strategy is proposed in [6] to optimize performance of distributed database system. Apers [1] considered the allocation of the distributed database to the site as to minimize the total data transfer cost. In [11] the authors developed a site-independent fragment dependency graph representation to model the dependencies among the fragments accessed by a query and used it to formulate and solve DA problem for distributed database systems using *query-site and move-small* query execution strategies. They formulated the DA problem in query-site case as a mapping problem, which can be mapped to a maximum flow minimum cost problem to achieve an optimal solution.

To the best of our knowledge, there is little work done on dealing with the method allocation problem for OODBs, except for some work on distributed design for an OODB [10], and the work of Bhar et al. [4]. Karlapalem et al. [10] have touched the allocation problem under two levels: class fragment allocation and MA, but they did not present an effective algorithm to solve the class or method allocation. In [4] the problem of class fragments allocation in DOODB design has been addressed, and a general taxonomy based on the data model, degree of redundancy and design objectives is developed; and a heuristic algorithm to improve the fragment classes allocation (which is based on the heuristic approach by Kernighan and Lin in their graph partition work) is proposed. However, Bhar et al. ignored the problem of MA completely.

1.3 Contributions & Organization of the Paper

In this paper we formulate the allocation of methods and classes as a mapping problem i.e., to map the methods to sites as well as classes to sites, so as to minimize the overall data transfer cost incurred in processing a given set of queries. The main contributions of this paper include the following:

1) This paper addresses the combined MCA problem in the DODBS environment. This problem had been addressed by others by treating MCA as separate problems.

2) The basic CA or MA problems are NP-complete, and the combined MCA problem is even more difficult and challenging. This is the first piece of work that tackles the combined problem and hence provides a framework for future work.

3) A comprehensive cost model is developed which incorporates the complex dependencies between queries, classes, methods and sites to calculate the total data transfer incurred in processing a set of queries.

4) An iterative MCA approach is advocated to come up with an near optimal solution to this problem. We illustrate our cost model and the solution approach by means of an example.

5) Finally, the MCA problems are solved by using the above-mentioned iterative approach whose solution is further compared with the exhaustive enumeration solution. The complexity of the exhaustive solution is $(M + C)^S$, where M is number of methods, C is number of classes, and S number of sites, and hence takes lot of time for large number of sites, methods and classes. Therefore, for large number of sites, methods and classes, we show the amount of reduction in total data transfer cost achieved by our algorithm, in comparison to the initial solution.

In the rest of the paper, Section 2 presents basis for our object oriented data model, Section 3 formulates the MCA problem, Section 4 presents the algorithms for MCA, Section 5 presents experimental results, and Section 6 presents the conclusions and discusses a few open problems.

2 Distributed OODBS

In this study, we consider an object oriented model with the basic features that are mandatory and/or common to most OODB models and systems [2]. We assume following key features: object identify, encapsulation, class hierarchy(IsA relationship), class composition hierarchy(PartOf relationship, aggregation graph) and method.

The method has a signature including the method's name, a list of parameters, and a list of return values which can be an atomic value (Integer, Real,

String, etc.) or an object identifier (OID). Methods are inherited from the superclass(es). A subclass may alter the method code of an inherited method or additional methods may be added. Two types of methods are identified [10] : simple and complex. A method which does not call/invoke any other method is called a *simple method*, otherwise it is a *complex method*. Method may return atomic values or object identifiers (OIDs). For atomic values, we also include the case where the value returned is empty. A complex method can be represented by method dependency graph (MDG) [9] which represents the structure of a method. A MDG has a set of nodes and a set of directed edges. The classes and methods represent leaf nodes and non-leaf nodes, respectively. Edges represent dependencies between nodes. A MDG can be considered as a directed acyclic graph (note that we don't consider recursive methods).

2.1 A Taxonomy of Method Execution in DODBSs

In this subsection, we describe different approaches for method execution during query processing in a DODBS. Let there be a query invoking a method which accesses a attributes of class(es) allocated at various sites in the DODBS. Four scenarios of method execution are possible:

• *Local method - Local object.* In this case, both the methods and its objects reside in the same site. All the processing of the methods is done locally.

• *Local method - Remote object.* The method m is applied to objects which reside remotely (i.e., these objects are allocated at sites different from the site of m). In this case, we need to transfer all objects needed by the method m to the site of m in order to execute it.

• *Remote method - Local object.* This approach consists of migrating the method m to the site where the objects are located, and then execute the method m.

• *Remote method - Remote object.* This approach consists of migrating the method m and objects to the (query) site which is different from the method site and site where the objects are located.

In all these cases, the results of method execution will be transfered to the query site if it is different from the method(m) site.

Note that the objective of MA is to minimize the total data transfer cost to process all the queries by using one of the above method execution strategies. In this paper, we shall develop an algorithm which allocate all methods at various sites based on the *Local method - Local object* and *Local method - Remote object* strategies. We do not address the method migration strategy in this paper. Method migration is an important issue which requires further work on modeling the data transfer cost incurred in migrating methods, which is beyond the scope of this paper.

3 Formulating MCA Problem

We consider a DODBS with t sites, with each site having its own processing power, memory and a local OODB manager. Let S_j be the name of the site j

where $1 \leq j \leq t$. The t sites of the DODBS are connected by a communication network. A link between two site S_j and $S_{j'}$ (if it exists) has a positive integer $P_{jj'}$ associated with it, giving the cost for a unit data transfered from site S_j to site $S_{j'}$. If two sites are not directly connected by a communication link, then the cost for unit data transferred is given by the sum of the cost of links of a chosen path from S_j to $S_{j'}$. Let a set of N queries $\{q_1, q_2..., q_N\}$ be the most important queries accounting for more than 80% of the processing in the DODBS. We define a query site as the site where the query is initiated. A query can invoke methods or itself is a method. Let $M = \{m_1, m_2, ..., m_n\}$ be the methods to be allocated to various sites. Each query q_h can be invoked from any site with a certain frequency. Let f_{hj} be the frequency with which the query q_h is executed from site S_j. These frequencies of query executions at different sites can be represented by a $N \times t$ matrix, F. We also define the vectors $l = \{l_j \mid 1 \leq j \leq t\}$ and $l' = \{l'_j \mid 1 \leq j \leq t\}$ as the limit on maximum number of methods and classes, respectively, that can be allocated at site S_j; these vectors model the storage constraint for the MCA problem.

3.1 A Cost Model for Total Data Transfer

We now describe in detail the inputs for our MCA problem. These inputs characterize the underlying DODBS and help in formulating the problem. The notations used throughout the paper are summarized in Table 1. We consider a class composition hierarchy having s classes, named, $\{C_1, C_2, ..., C_s\}$. Let m_i be a method used by a query q_h where $1 \leq h \leq N$. Let MDG_i be the method dependency graph corresponding to the method m_i. Let g_{hi} gives the relationship between the query q_h and the MDG of method m_i, implying that the query q_h invokes the method m_i represented by its MDG (i.e., MDG_i). From this relation a matrix $G = \{g_{hi}\}$ can be set up for $1 \leq h \leq N$, $1 \leq i \leq n$, as:

$$g_{hi} = \begin{cases} 1 \text{ if the query } q_h \text{ invokes the method } m_i \text{ represented by } MDG_i \\ 0 \text{ Otherwise} \end{cases}$$

Each class in this hierarchy is defined by attributes and methods. We assume there is a query q_h invoking a method m_i which, as noted above, can be represented by the relation g_{hi}. We note that the MDG of m_i (i.e., MDG_i) can contain n_i number of sub-methods. From g_{hi} and MDG_i, a method-method dependency matrix, $MM = \{mm_{ii'} \mid 1 \leq i, i' \leq n_i\}$, can be defined as:

$$mm_{ii'} = \begin{cases} 1 \text{ if the method } m_i \text{ is dependent on the method } m_{i'} \\ 0 \text{ Otherwise} \end{cases}$$

For each method m_i, we define r_i as the size of returned values of m_i, and let $R = \{r_i \mid 1 \leq i \leq n\}$.
A method-class dependency matrix, $MC = \{mc_{ik} \mid 1 \leq i \leq n, \ 1 \leq k \leq s\}$ is defined as:

$$mc_{ik} = \begin{cases} 1 \text{ if the method } m_i \text{ is accessing the class } C_k \\ 0 \text{ Otherwise} \end{cases}$$

Let o_{ik} be defined as the size of objects of class C_k needed by the method m_i. These sizes of objects can be represented by a $n \times s$ matrix, $O = \{o_{ik} \mid 1 \leq i \leq n, 1 \leq k \leq s\}$. Based on the above inputs we shall develop a cost model for total data transfer incurred to process all the queries and then develop a solution to the (non replicated) MCA problems.

Example

Suppose there are 3 methods, 4 classes, and 2 sites in a DODBS. Let q_1 be a query initiated at site S_1 with access frequency f_{11} equal 50. The graph in Figure 2 is the method dependency graph of q_1. The class nodes at the leaf level are shown by rectangles, with their allocated sites and size of objects needed by methods in curly and small parentheses, respectively. The method nodes are represented by circles along with their size of returned values in parentheses. The corresponding input matrices MM, MC, Y, and O are as shown below, with R denoting the size of returned objects/values for the three methods.

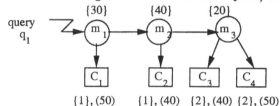

Figure 2: An Example of Method Dependency Graph

$$MM = \begin{bmatrix} 0 & 1 & 0 \\ 0 & 0 & 1 \\ 0 & 0 & 0 \end{bmatrix} \quad MC = \begin{bmatrix} 1 & 0 & 0 & 0 \\ 0 & 1 & 0 & 0 \\ 0 & 0 & 1 & 1 \end{bmatrix} \quad Y = \begin{bmatrix} 1 & 0 \\ 1 & 0 \\ 0 & 1 \\ 0 & 1 \end{bmatrix}$$

$$R = \begin{bmatrix} 30 \\ 40 \\ 20 \end{bmatrix} \quad O = \begin{bmatrix} 50 & 0 & 0 & 0 \\ 0 & 40 & 0 & 0 \\ 0 & 0 & 40 & 50 \end{bmatrix} \quad X = \begin{bmatrix} 1 & 0 \\ 0 & 1 \\ 1 & 0 \end{bmatrix}$$

Assume further the matrix X denotes a possible MA that indicates that methods m_1 and m_3 are assigned at site 1 and m_2 is assigned at site 2.

3.1.1 Total Data Transfer Cost for a Single Query Evaluation

We suppose that all classes of our DODBS are already allocated at various sites. In order to make it easier for the formulation of MA problem, we define the total data transfer cost (TDTC) of evaluating a query q_h accessing a method m_i as $TDTC_i^h$. In the next subsection, we shall generalize this formulation for given set of queries where every query may access more than one method. Intuitively, $TDTC_i^h$ is defined as follows: $TDTC_i^h = Cost_1 + Cost_2 + Cost_3$, where $Cost_1$ is the data transfer cost due to the method-class dependency, (i.e., the cost of processing a method m such that m uses objects of class C), $Cost_2$ is the data transfer cost due to the method-method dependency (i.e., the cost of processing a method m_i which depends on another method $m_{i'}$, with the latter being allocated at a different site from m_i, and $Cost_3$ is the data transfer cost due to possible remote execution of method(s), i.e., the cost of sending results of executing method m at a site different from the query site. We now

Symbol	Type	Meaning
$i,\ i'\ \&\ i''$	Subscripts	For methods
$j\ \&\ j'\ \&\ j''$	Subscripts	For sites
h	Subscript	For a class
M	Variable	The number of methods. The variable m_i is the ith method
q_h	Variable	q_h is the hth query in $\{q_1, q_2, ..., q_N\}$
N	Variable	The Number of queries
S	Vector	The Set of sites in the network: S_j is the jth element of S
V	Matrix	The site of query matrix
v_{hj}	Variable	It is of value 1 if the query q_h is allocated at the site S_j, 0 otherwise
P	Matrix	The unit transportation cost matrix of the network
t	Variable	The Number of sites
C	Vector	The Set of classes: C_h is the hth element of C
s	Variable	The Number of classes in a class composition hierarchy
MDG_i	Graph	The Method dependency graph corresponding to method m_i
n_i	Variable	The number of methods in the MDG_i
G	Matrix	Query-MDG Matrix.
F	Matrix	The Access frequency matrix
f_{hj}	Variable	The access frequency of the query q_h at site S_j
MM	Matrix	The Method-method dependency matrix
Y	Matrix	The class-site allocation input/output matrix
y_{kj}	Variable	It is of value 1 if the class C_h is allocated at the site S_j, 0 otherwise
MC	Matrix	The Method-class dependency matrix
O	Matrix	The Size of objects Matrix
R	Vector	The Size of returned values vector
X	Matrix	The method-site allocation input/output matrix
x_{ij}	Variable	It is of value 1 if the method m_i is allocated at the site S_j, 0 otherwise

Table 1: Symbols and their Meanings

describe the actual calculation of each of the costs.

Data Transfer Cost Due to Method-Class Dependency When a method is executing at site S_j, we distinguish two types of method-class dependency: *direct method-class dependency* and *indirect method-class dependency*.

• Direct method-class dependency means that a method m_i is assigned to site S_j, but this site does not have objects of a certain class required by this method. In this case, the required object of this class has to be transfered to site S_j.

• Indirect method-class dependency means a method m_i is dependent on another method $m_{i'}$ (directly/indirectly), but the site of $m_{i'}$ does not have objects of a certain class required by $m_{i'}$. In this case, the required objects of this class has to be transfered to the site of $m_{i'}$.

Assume we allocate a method m_i to site S_j, and if we use U_{ij}^1 to denote the total amount of objects needed to be transported for executing method m_i, then U_{ij}^1 is defined as:

$$U_{ij}^1 = \sum_{k=1}^s x_{ij} \times mc_{ik} \times (1 - y_{kj}) \times P_{site(C_k),j} \times o_{ik} + \sum_{i'=1,\; i'\neq i}^{n_i} \sum_{j'=1}^t x_{ij} \times x_{i'j'} \times mm_{ii'} \times U_{i'j'}^1$$

The first term of the above equation is due to the direct method-class dependency. The second term, which is a recursive definition, takes care of the cost of possible indirect method-class dependency. This process is guaranteed to terminate because our MDG is an acyclic directed graph.

The total data transfer cost due to the method-class dependency is thus:

$$Cost_1 = \sum_{j=1}^t U_{ij}^1 \times f_{h,site(q_h)}.$$

Example Continued The method-class dependency cost of executing once the method m_1 at site 1 (U_{11}^1) is 130, because the direct method-class dependency cost is 0 since C_1 is at the same site of m_1, and the indirect method-class dependency cost is 130 since (i) m_1 depends of m_2 (which is allocated at site 2), and the size of its returned objects (of class C_2 allocated at site S_1) is 40, and (ii) m_2 depends on m_3 (which is allocated at site S_1) and uses objects allocated at site S_2, which is of size 90. Hence the total cost due to the method-class dependency is $Cost_1 = 130 \times 50 = 6500$.

Data Transfer Cost Due to Method-Method Dependency When a method m_i is allocated to site S_j, we also distinguish two types of method-method dependency: *direct method-method dependency* and *indirect method-method dependency*.

• Direct method-method dependency: When a method m_i is dependent on another method $m_{i'}$ and these two methods are allocated at two different sites, then to execute the method m_i, the result of method m_i' (i.e., returned values of m_i') should be transferred to the site of method m_i.

• Indirect method-method dependency: When the method $m_{i'}$ is further dependent on another method $m_{i''}$ and these methods are allocated at different sites, then the result of method $m_{i''}$ should be transferred to the site of method $m_{i'}$. Assume again the method m_i is allocated to the site S_j, and let U_{ij}^2 be the total amount of data needed to be transported for executing method m_i. This cost can be defined as:

$$U_{ij}^2 = \sum_{i'=1,i'\neq i}^{n_i} \sum_{j'=1,j'\neq j}^t x_{ij} \times x_{i'j'} \times mm_{ii'} \times P_{j'j} \times r_{i'}$$
$$+ \sum_{i'=1,i'\neq i}^{n_i} \sum_{j'=1,j'\neq j}^t x_{ij} \times x_{i'j'} \times mm_{ii'} \times U_{i'j'}^2.$$

The total data transfer cost due to the method-method dependency is then:

$$Cost_2 = \sum_{j=1}^t U_{ij}^2 \times f_{h,site(q_h)}.$$

Data Transfer Cost of Sending Results of Method to Query Site Let $Cost_3$ be the data transfer cost of sending the results of executing method m_i at site S_j to the query site $S_{site(q_h)}$. The cost of sending the results of m_i is defined as:

$$Cost_3 = \sum_{j=1}^t x_{ij} \times (1 - v_{hj}) \times P_{j,site(q_h)} \times r_i \times f_{h,site(q_h)}.$$

Finally, the total data transfer cost for evaluating the query q_h invoking a method m_i (as denoted by $TDTC_i^h$) is given by the following equation:

$$TDTC_i^h = \sum_{j=1}^t U_{ij}^1 \times f_{h,site(q_h)} + \sum_{j=1}^t U_{ij}^2 \times f_{h,site(q_h)} + \sum_{j=1}^t x_{ij} \times (1 - v_{hj}) \times P_{j,site(q_h)} \times r_i \times f_{h,site(q_h)}$$

$$= \sum_{j=1}^t \left(U_{ij}^1 + U_{ij}^2 + x_{ij} \times (1 - v_{hj}) \times P_{j,site(q_h)} \times r_i \right) \times f_{h,site(q_h)}$$

Example(Continued) In our running example, the method-method dependency cost of executing method m_1 at site 1 (U_{11}^2) is 60, because m_1 depends on m_2 and m_2 further depends on m_3. Hence the total cost due to method-method dependency is $Cost_2 = 60 \times 50 = 3000$.

The cost of sending the result of m_1 to the query site (i.e., site 1) is 0, because m_1 and the query have the same site. The overall data transfer cost for a given allocation in this example is thus:

$$TDTC_1^1 = Cost_1 + Cost_2 + Cost_3 = 6500 + 3000 + 0 = 9500.$$

3.1.2 Total Data Transfer Incurred to Execute a set of Queries

Let $TDTC$ be the total data transfer cost for processing all N queries $\{q_1, q_2, ..., q_N\}$. We recall that the $G = \{g_{hi} \mid 1 \leq h \leq N, \ 1 \leq i \leq n\}$ is a matrix representing the relation between queries and MDGs of all methods(see Table 1). $TDTC$ is then given by the following equation:

$$TDTC = \sum_{h=1}^{N} \sum_{i=1}^{n} g_{hi} \times \left[\sum_{j=1}^{t} \left(U_{ij}^1 + U_{ij}^2 + x_{ij} \times (1 - v_{hj}) \times P_{j,site(q_h)} \times r_i \right) \times f_{h,site(q_h)} \right],$$

where: $U_{ij}^1 = \sum_{k=1}^{s} x_{ij} \times mc_{ik} \times (1 - ykj) \times P_{site(C_k),j} \times o_{ik} + \sum_{i'=1, \ i' \neq i}^{n_i} \sum_{j'=1}^{t} x_{ij} \times x_{i'j'} \times mm_{ii'} \times U_{i'j'}^1$, and

$U_{ij}^2 = \sum_{i'=1, i' \neq i}^{n_i} \sum_{j'=1, j' \neq j}^{t} x_{ij} \times x_{i'j'} \times mm_{ii'} \times P_{j'j} \times r_{i'} + \sum_{i'=1, i' \neq i}^{n_i} \sum_{j'=1, j' \neq j}^{t} x_{ij} \times x_{i'j'} \times mm_{ii'} \times U_{i'j'}^2$.

The MA problem is now formulated as assigning zero-one values to x_{ij} under the following two constraints:

1) $\sum_{j=1}^{t} x_{ij} = 1$ for all $1 \leq i \leq n$, and 2) $\sum_{i=1}^{n} x_{ij} \leq l_j$ for all $1 \leq j \leq t$

so as to minimize:

$$TDTC = \sum_{h=1}^{N} \sum_{i=1}^{n} g_{hi} \times \left[\sum_{j=1}^{t} \left(U_{ij}^1 + U_{ij}^2 + x_{ij} \times (1 - v_{hj}) \times P_{j,site(q_h)} \times r_i \right) \times f_{h,site(q_h)} \right].$$

The first constraint ensures that each method is allocated to at least one site, and the second constraint ensures that no site is allocated more methods (or classes) than allowed (set by the upper bound l_j) for that site. Thus the MA problem can be formulated as a quadratic programming problem which is however very difficult to solve efficiently. In next section, we introduce a heuristic algorithm based on the hill-climbing technique so as to provide a near optimal solution.

4 Algorithm for Methods and Class Allocation

We have shown in the previous section that the problem of MA is a quadratic programming problem. Finding the optimal solution by exhaustive search would require $O(n^t)$ in the worst case where n is the number of methods and t is the number of sites. Therefore, we advocate in this section a heuristic algorithm based on hill-climbing technique in order to find a near optimal solution. We note that all hill-climbing techniques need four parameters [8]: 1) the initial state, 2) generation of the next step, 3) determination of the best state, and 4) stop of test. We will describe all these steps in the following subsections.

4.1 Conversion of a MDG to a Weighted Graph

As can be seen from the equations of calculating the total data transfer cost (TDTC), the NP-completeness of the MA stems from the dependency between the methods. To find an initial solution of our hill-climbing algorithm, we therefore first neglect the dependencies between methods (all $mm_{ii'} = 0$, $1 \leq i, i' \leq n$) and, as a consequence, the cost due to the method-method dependency (i.e., $Cost_2$) is equal to 0. To simplify the construction of the weighted graph, we consider only one query q_h accessing m_i represented by it MDG (MDG_i). We recall that n_i represents the number of methods in MDG_i. From this MDG, we construct a weighted graph with sites and methods represented as nodes. An edge between a site S_j and a method m'_i ($1 \leq i' \leq n_i$) implies that the method $m_{i'}$ is located at site S_j. The weight between S_j and $m_{i'}$ represents the amount of objects needed to be transported for executing the method $m_{i'}$ when it is at site S_j. Let $w_i(S_j, m_{i'})$ be the weight between S_j and $m_{i'}$ for MDG_i. The formula of calculating each edge weight $w_i(S_j, m_{i'})$ for all $1 \leq i' \leq n_i$ is then defined as follows: $w_i(S_j, m_{i'}) = \sum_{k=1}^{s} mc_{i'k} \times (1 - y_{kj}) \times o_{i'k} \times P_{site(C_k),j}$

begin
    for j:= 1 to t do % This step initializes weight between every site and method
        for i:= 1 to n do
          $w(S_j, m_i) = 0$; % $w(S_j, m_i)$ is the global weight including all MDGs (1)
    for j:= 1 to t do % j is for sites (2)
        for i:= 1 to n do % i for methods (3)
            for h:= 1 to N do % h for queries (4)
                for i':= 1 to n do % i' for methods (5)
                    if ($g_{hi'} = 1$) then (6)
                        if ($i = i'$) and ($v_{hj} \neq j$) then (7)
                          $w(S_j, m_i) = w(S_j, m_i) + w_{i'}(S_j, m_i) \times f_{hj} + Cost_3$
                        else
                          $w(S_j, m_i) = w(S_j, m_i) + w_{i'}(S_j, m_i) \times f_{h,site(q_h)}$
end

Figure 3: The Weighted Graph Generation for Methods

We can generalize the calculation of the weight between every method and every site to take into consideration all queries and methods in all the MDGs. The algorithm in Figure 3 generates the weight between every method and every site. We note that the step 7 in Figure 3 checks if the method m_i is accessed by the query q_h and whether the query site is different from the method site. If this is the case, we add the cost of sending the result of m_i to the query site (i.e., $Cost_3$).

Example We assume we have two queries q_1 and q_2 employing methods m_1 and m_4, respectively. Let the frequencies of the two queries q_1 and q_2 be 1 to simplify the calculations. The MDGs of m_1 and m_4 are as shown in Figure 2 and 4, respectively.

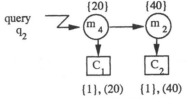

$\{1\}, (20)$ $\{1\}, (40)$

Figure 4: MDG of the Method m_4

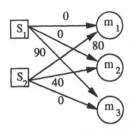 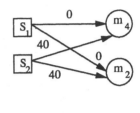

Figure 5a: Weighted Graph for the MDG1　　　Figure 5b: Weighted Graph for the MDG2

Figure 5: Weighted Graphs of Methods m_1 and m_4

First, we calculate all $w_1(S_j, m_{i'})$ as follows:

$w_1(S_1, m_1) = 0$ since m_1 in MDG_1 is at site S_1 and it needs some objects of class C_1 which is also allocated at site S_1.

$w_1(S_2, m_1) = 80$ since m_1 is at site S_2 but C_1 is at site S_1, hence we need to ship all objects of C_1 (i.e., 50) needed by m_1, and after execution of m_1, we should send the result of m_1 (30) to the query site (S_1).

Similarly, we can calculate $w_1(S_1, m_2)$, $w_1(S_2, m_2)$, $w_1(S_1, m_3)$ and $w_1(S_2, m_3)$ which are: 0, 40, 90, and 0, respectively. We perform the same procedure for the MDG of m_4, and get $w_2(S_1, m_2)$, $w_1(S_2, m_2)$, $w_2(S_1, m_4)$ and $w_2(S_2, m_4)$ their respective values: 0, 40, 0, and 40. Figure 5 shows the two resultant weighted graphs for m_1 and m_4.

Based on these, we can calculate the $w(S_j, m_i)$ for each method in the two MDGs. For example, $w(S_2, m_2) = 40 + 40 = 80$.

With the above formalism and the weighted graph generation algorithm, the MA problem can be tackled by a mapping problem. In particular, given the cost of data transfer incurred (i.e., $w(S_j, m_i)$ for $1 \geq j \leq t$ and $1 \geq i \leq n$), the MA problem can be treated as a *maximum-flow minimum-cost* problem for which an optimal mapping can be achieved, as described below.

4.1.1 Maximum Flow Minimum Cost Formulation

The first step in translating the MA problem to a maximum flow minimum cut problem is to calculate the cost of allocating a method m_i to a particular site S_j. This is done by calculating the value of $w(S_j, m_i)$ according to the algorithm in Figure 3. In order to formulate it as a maximum-flow minimum-cut problem, we need to perform the following steps (cf. Figure 6):

1. Two nodes, a source and a sink, are created and named as S and T, respectively.

2. t nodes are created, with each one corresponding to a site from $\{S_1, S_2, \ldots, S_t\}$.

3. n nodes are created, with each one corresponding to a method from $\{m_1, m_2, \ldots, m_n\}$.

4. For each node S_j, an edge from S to it is created and the capacity and cost of the link are assigned as l_j and 0, respectively.

5. For each node m_i, an edge from it to T is created and the capacity and cost of the link are assigned to 1 and 0, respectively.

6. For every pair of nodes S_j and m_i, an edge from S_j to m_i is created and the capacity and cost of the link are assigned to 1 and $w(S_j, m_i)$, respectively.

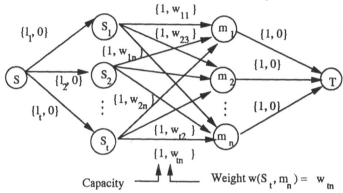

Figure 6: Mapping MA Problem as Max-flow Min-Cut Problem

The key is to find the maximum flow with minimum cost from S to T. It can be observed from Figure 6 that the maximum flow in this case is n (i.e. the number of methods in the MDG of the method m_i), since it is bounded by the sum of capacity of incoming edges to T. The sum of capacity of out coming edges from S must be bigger than n (number of methods) for all the methods to be allocated. This will be true if $\sum_{j=1}^{t} l_j \geq n$. At the point of maximum flow, there must be exactly one incoming edge (say, from method m_i to site S_j) with flow equal to 1 and all other incoming edges (from nodes $S_{j'}$) have flow equal to zero, for $1 \leq j' \leq t$ and $j' \neq j$. This is equivalent to allocating method m_i to site S_j. Since the capacity of flow from S to site S_j is assigned as l_j for $1 \leq j \leq t$, no site will be allocated more than the maximum limit of the number of methods allowed. The problem then is to achieve maximum flow from node S to node T with minimum cost, which is equivalent to assigning each method to a site so as to minimize the total data transfer cost.

When the *method dependencies* are disregarded, the maximum-flow minimum-cut formulation of the MA produces the optimal solution. The proof is given in [11].

4.2 A Near Optimal Solution for MA Problem

Figure 7 shows the the hill-climbing heuristic algorithm we are advocating, which constitutes our solution to the general MA problem. The major steps of this algorithm are as follows:

1. First, neglect the dependencies among methods, and come up with an initial

solution method allocation by using the max-flow min-cut formulation of the problem (as described in subsection 4.1.1).

2. Iteratively improve the initial MA by using the hill climbing heuristic until no further reduction in total data transfer cost can be achieved. This is done by applying the following hill climbing operations:

• ship(m_i, S_j): This operation consists of moving the method m_i allocated at site $S_{j'}(j' \neq j)$ to site S_j, which can potentially reduce the data transfer cost. Note that this operation can be applied to each method, and the method can be moved to any one of $t - 1$ sites it has not been located. Therefore, there can be maximum of $n \times (t - 1)$ ship operations that can be applied during each iteration.

• ship2($m_i, S_j, m_{i'}, S_{j'}$): This operation moves method m_i to site S_j and method $m_{i'}$ to site $S_{j'}$. Note that this operation can be applied to every pair of methods which can be moved to any one of $t - 1$ sites where they are not located. Therefore, there can be a maximum of $(n * (t - 1))^2$ ship2 operations that can be applied during each iteration. As in the case of ship operation, ship2 operations can potentially reduce data transfer costs when a query invokes not one but two methods.

• ship3($m_i, S_j, m_{i'}, S_{j'}, m_{i''}, S_{j''}$) : This operation moves method m_i to site S_j, method $m_{i'}$ to site $S_{j'}$ and method $m_{i''}$ to site $S_{j''}$. This operation can be applied to each triplet of methods, and they can each be moved to any one of $t - 1$ sites where they are not located. Therefore, there can be a maximum of $(n * (t - 1))^3$ ship3 operations that can be applied during each iteration. The ship3 operations can also potentially reduce data transfer costs when a query invokes three methods.

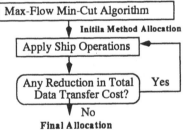

Figure 7: Steps in Hill-Climbing Algorithm for MA Problem

These operations take into consideration the dependency between the methods as modeled by the MDGs. These operations can be iteratively applied till no more reduction can be obtained in the total data transfer cost. Note that we have only incorporated the shipping operations up to three methods (and classes) because, from our experiments, we have found that higher numbers of method/class shippings are not that often used. Also simultaneous method/class shippings may generate allocation schemes which violate the constraints on the number of methods or classes that can be allocated to a site. Finally, the complexity of the hill-climbing algorithm increases significantly with the number of methods (or classes) shipped.

4.3 Class Re-allocation

Based on the near optimal solution to the MA problem described above, we re-examanine the problem of allocating classes to various sites so as to further minimize the data transfer cost, by utilizing the same formulation of the cost as described for MA (cf., subsection 4.1. The only difference here is that the matrix X (MA matrix) is now fixed, and the matrix Y (CA matrix) becomes variable. Still, the CA problem is also NP-complete [4], hence we need to develop a heuristic algorithm in order to find a "near optimal solution" as well. The heuristic algorithm for CA problem is basically the same as that for MA problem. In this case, the nodes in Figure 5 become classes and sites. For each MDG_i accessed by a query q_h, the weight of each edge between the site S_j and a class C_k (i.e., $w_i(S_j, C_k)$) is calculated as follows:

$$w_i(S_j, C_k) = \sum_{i'=1}^{n_i} mc_{i'k} \times (1 - x_{i'j}) \times o_{i'k} \times P_{site(m_{i'}),j}$$

begin

    for j:= 1 to t do % This step initializes weight between every site and class

      for k:= 1 to s do

        $w(S_j, C_k) = 0$; % $w(S_j, C_k)$ is the global weight including all MDGs (1)

    for j:= 1 to t do % j is for sites (2)

      for k:= 1 to s do % k for classes (3)

        for h:= 1 to N do % h for queries (4)

          for i':= 1 to n do % i' for methods (5)

            if $(g_{hi'} = 1)$ then (6)

              $w(S_j, C_k) = w(S_j, C_k) + w_{i'}(S_j, C_k) \times f_{h,site(q_h)}$

end

Figure 8: The Weighted Graph Generation for Classes

The generalization of calculation of the weight between every site and class is given by the algorithm in Figure 8. Further, the ship operations are applied to classes instead of methods.

As illustrated early in Figure 1, we treat the two mutually interdependent problems of the MCA in an iterative manner. Specifically, based on an initial CA we proceed to allocate methods, and based on the resultant MA scheme, we next re-allocate classes, so on and so forth. For each allocation scheme, we calculate the total data transfer cost. This procedure is iteratively applied till no more reduction can be achieved in the total data transfer cost defined. Finally, we pick up the two schemes (corresponding to the MCA) with the minimum cost as our final solution.

5 Experimental Results

Our experiments for validating the hill-climbing approach were conducted as follows: each experiment consisted of 20 allocation problems with number of class, number of method, and number of sites fixed. Each allocation problem has 10 queries. The communication network, size of objects needed by methods, methods dependency graphs, return values of methods are randomly generated.

Classes	Methods	Sites	Number of Problems	Optimal Solutions	Average Deviation
3	3	3	20	14	1.4141
3	4	3	20	12	2.5692
4	3	3	20	13	1.9783
3	4	4	20	11	3.1296
4	4	4	20	8	4.3621
4	5	3	20	10	3.1228
4	5	4	20	13	1.9782
5	3	4	20	12	2.7453
5	4	3	20	9	4.3421
5	5	5	20	12	2.5245

Table 2: Experimental Evaluation of Near Optimality of Hill-Climbing Algorithm

Each allocation problem (method and class) is solved by using the hill-climbing algorithm and its solutions were compared with the optimal solution generated by the exhaustive search.

Table 2 lists the results for each of the experiments conducted, column wise, i) the number of classes, ii) number of methods, iii) number of sites, iv) number of problems solved, v) number of problems for which heuristic algorithm generated the optimal solution, and vi) the average deviation in percentage of near optimal solutions from optimal solution (for those allocation problems for which the hill climbing algorithm did not generate optimal solution). The results in Table 2 shows that hill climbing algorithm does produce optimal solutions for 40% to 70% number of problems. Even when it does not provide the optimal solution the average deviation between hill climbing solution and optimal solution varies from 1.5% to 4.3% which is quite good. The exhaustive solution

# Class	# Method	# Sites	Initial Solution	Final Solution	Percentage (%)
10	10	10	48840	37440	23%
10	10	10	49490	35570	28%
15	15	15	53380	36450	32%
15	15	15	56470	36310	35%
20	20	20	68425	40540	40%
20	20	20	72120	44520	39%
22	22	22	75950	45420	40%
22	22	22	76450	46820	39%
30	30	30	84390	49130	41%
30	30	30	82410	46980	43 %

Table 3: Comparison Between the Initial Solution and Final Solution of Hill-Climbing Algorithm

takes lot of time to get the optimal solution, therefore, we present improvement in the quality of solution achieved for allocation problems with large number of sites, classes and methods. Table 3 shows percentage of improvement in total data transfer cost from the initial solution to the final solution achieved for two examples each when number of sites, methods, and classes range from 10 to 30 each. This percentage of improvement varies from 23% to 43% which is quite substantial. Further this percentage of improvement increases with increase in number of sites, methods and classes. This not only shows the utility of the hill-climbing solution we proposed, but its effectiveness for large data allocation problems. Also, we have shown that the hill climbing algorithm can produce optimal solution. Therefore our solution is a viable solution which can used for large practical data allocation problems.

6 Conclusion and Future Work

In this paper we have studied the general allocation problem in DODBSs, which has so for received little attention from the research community. Although the CA and MA are two different tasks, these problems are nevertheless mutually interdependent. In this paper, we first formulated the combined MCA problem and developed a cost model to calculate total data transfer cost incurred. Therefore, we developed an iterative MCA approach to generate near optimal solution to the problem. We evaluated our approach by comparing our solution with exhaustive enumeration solution approach, for small number of sites, classes and methods. Further, we studied the effectiveness of our approach in reducing the total data transfer cost incurred for large number of methods, classes and sites. Our results show that our approach does provide optimal solution for 40% to 70% of the problems solved with number of methods, classes and sites ranging from 3 to 5. Even when our approach does not provide optimal solution, the average deviation from the optimal solution for the problem sets solved as less than 5 percent. Further, in our experimentation with the number of methods, classes and sites ranging from 10 to 30, we found that there is 23% to 43% reduction in total data transfer incurred. Moreover, our algorithm takes few minutes to get the solution in comparison days and weeks that the exhaustive enumeration solution takes. Thus the solution we have provided is both effective and practical for solving large MCA problems in DODBS. In our on going work, we are in fact addressing the problem of response time reduction by allocation of methods and classes in DODBSs, and also addressing the issue of utilizing combined method migration and CA to process applications efficiently for large-scale multimedia systems.

Acknowledgments We would like to gratefully acknowledge the insightful and helpful comments of Dr. Mukesh Mohania of ACRC, School of Computer and Information Science, University of South Australia, The Levels 5095, Australia.

References

[1] P. M. G. Apers. Data allocation in distributed database systems. *ACM Transactions on database systems*, 13(3):263–304, 1988.

[2] M. Atkinson, F. Bancilhon, F. DeWitt, K. Dettrich, D. Maier, and S. Zdonik. The object database system manifesto. *in Proceeding of the first International Conference on Deductive, Object-Oriented Databases*, pages 40–57, 1989.

[3] E. Bertino, M. Negri, G. Pelagatti, and L. Sbattella. Object-oriented query languages: The notion and the issues. *IEEE Transactions on Knowledge and Data Engineering*, 4(3):223–237, 1992.

[4] S Bhar and K Barker. Static allocation in distributed objectbase systems: A graphical approach. *in Proceedings of the 6th International Conference on Information System and Data Management, CISMOD'95, Lecture Notes in Computer Science 1006*, pages 92–114, November 1995.

[5] P. P.-S. Chen. Optimal file allocation in multilevel storage systems. *in Proceedings of AFIPS National Computer Conference, Volume 42*, pages 277–282, 1973.

[6] D. W. Cornell and P. S. Yu. An optimal site assignment for relations in the distributed database environment. *IEEE Transactions on Computers*, 15(8):1004–1009, August 1989.

[7] K. P. Eswaran. Placement of records in a file and file allocation in a computer network. *Information Processing*, pages 304–307, 1974.

[8] R. Jain. *The Art of Computer Systems Performance Analysis*. Willy Professional Computing, 1991.

[9] K. Karlapalem, Q. Li, and S. Vieweg. Method induced partitioning schemes in object-oriented databases. *in 16th International Conference on Distributed Computing System (ICDCS'96), Hong Kong*, pages 377–384, May 1996.

[10] K. Karlapalem, S.B. Navathe, and M. M. A. Morsi. Issues in distributed design of object-oriented databases. In *Distributed Object Management*, pages 148–165. Morgan Kaufman Publishers Inc., 1994.

[11] K. Karlapalem and N. M Pun. Query driven data allocation algorithms for distributed database systems. *in 8th International Conference on Database and Expert Systems Applications (DEXA'97), Toulouse, Lecture Notes in Computer Science 1308*, pages 347–356, September 1997.

[12] C. V. Ramamoorthy and B. Wah. The placement of relations on a distributed relational database. *in Proceedings of the firsth International Conference on Distributed Computing Systems*, pages 642–649, September Oct 1979.

MODELLING ISSUES 2

Specialization of Object Lifecycles

André Le Grand

Information Systems Department, University of Geneva

24, rue Général-Dufour. CH-1211 Genève 4, Switzerland

e-mail: Andre.LeGrand@cui.unige.ch

Abstract

Object lifecycle is now a standard concept of object-oriented modeling methods. Current works about lifecycle specialization do not regard the structure of the specialized class: This may lead to some inheritance problems highlighted in this paper. A new notion we introduce here, top-down conformity, provides a sound and useful approach to validate the behavior inheritance in relation with the class specialization.

keywords: concepts and methodologies, specialization, behavioral conformity

1 Introduction

The notion of lifecycle is widely used to specify the behavior of objects. Since the object classes are derived from other classes by inheritance and composition, the class derivation mechanism induces some conformity rules to derive the object lifecycles by inheritance and composition and vice versa (Cf fig. 1). These rules are independent of the class or lifecycle models used.

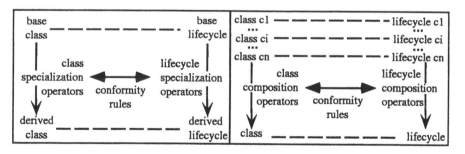

Figure 1: derivation of class and lifecycle

This paper[1] studies the rules and relationships between the lifecycle specialization and the structure of the derived class. We use the UML [1] extension of statecharts [2] to represent the lifecycle diagrams. When considering the derived class structure, the inherited behavior may be not valid, as shown below:

---

[1]This work was partly supported by Swiss CTI grant 2592-1.

example[2]: to gain Member Club status, an Applicant Club must:

1. Acknowledge and abide by the authority of the Executive Board, the Board of Club Representatives, the Constitution and the By-Laws of the NCLA.

2. Pay at least one-half (1/2) of the Annual Dues at the regular meeting during which the Applicant Club wishes to attain Member Club status or by the date prescribed by the Executive Board.

3. Present a verifiable roster of at least twenty five (25) committed players.

4. Receive a simple majority of votes from Voting Members present at the meeting at which a request for Member Club status is made. If the applicant organization does not receive the simple majority of votes necessary for membership, the Applicant Club may re-apply for Member Club status at the next regular meeting. Whenever possible, the Applicant Club shall be advised of the reason(s) for which it was denied membership.

We also consider a special status for some clubs (named PR_Clubs). This new status is decribed by the following rule:

- Survive a minimum of a one (1) year probationary period, as determined by the Executive Board. If some problems occur, a regular member club may come back to the probationary status.

The lifecycle of the classes are illustrated on fig. 2.

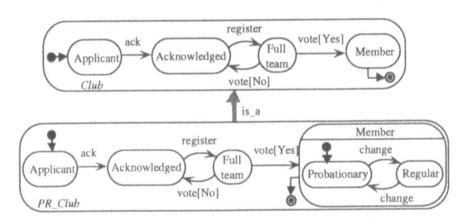

Figure 2: example of a derived lifecycle

In fig. 2 the lifecycle of *PR_Club* class inherits the behavior of the *Club* class, but its behavioral conformity must be carefully studied: the *Member* state is decomposed in the specialized lifecycle into two exclusive substates. When an instance of the *PR_Club* moves into the *Member* state, it should also be in the *Probationary* state (which is the default substate of *Member*). When

---

[2]We illustrate our ideas with examples adapted from the laws of Northern California Lacrosse Association [3], which is dedicated to the promotion of the sport of lacrosse in Northern California.

the transition *vote[Yes]* is fired on any *Club* instance in *Full team* state, the new state of this instance is *Member*. The *PR_ Club* class can inherits this transition (and therefore the corresponding method) if and only if, its firing on any instance of *PR_ Club* in *Full team* state, moves this instance into the right destination state which is *Probationary*. That can or not be the case. If not, the derived class cannot inherit the transition which should be redefined locally.

Since states of instances are defined upon the attributes values, the *Probationary* state is defined according to the structure of *PR_ Club*. Thus the lifecycle specialization is tightly related to class specialization. This paper relates the operators of specialization of these two concepts and describes the inheritance problems which may occur.

To this aim, we introduce a new notion, the top-down conformity:

Definition of top-down conformity 1 (informal) : *a transition of the base lifecycle is conform in the derived lifecycle if and only if, when fired on any instance of the derived class, the instance's new state corresponds to the destination state of this transition in the derived lifecycle.*

Bottom-up approaches (which are described in section 2) define conditions a derived class should conform with respect to a base class. The top-down approach considers the elements of a base class which can be inherited without causing any problem. A more formal definition of top-down conformity is given in section 4.

Outline of this paper.
The main contribution of this paper is to map the top-down conformity problems with the specialization operators of class and of lifecycle. To identify and solve conformity problems, we rely on a formal definition of state interpretation. For each specialization operator, we define the states and the transitions that should undergo a validation from the designers. These validations highlight the methods (included in the transitions) that should be overridden in the derived class.

The remainder of this paper will be organized as follows. Section 2 describes related works which correspond to a bottom-up approach of behavioral conformity. Section 3 defines a formal interpretation of states. Section 4 gives a formal definition of top-down conformity. Section 5 (resp. 6) lists operators to define derived classes (resp. lifecycle). Section 7 (resp 8) presents the validations to ensure the bottom-up (resp. top-down) conformity. Section 9, which ends this paper, presents some conclusions and perspectives.

2 Related work

2.1 Related work on object behavior modeling

The OO modeling methods use various models to specify the object behavior: state transition diagrams [4, 5], logic [6], Petri nets based [7, 8, 9] or statecharts based [10, 1, 11, 12, 13]. Except for OSA [7] and OOA [5], the OO methods ignore the lifecycle specialization. These two exceptions consider the specialization as adding behavior: the derived lifecycle contains as a subpart, the base lifecycle. We believe that this approach is not well suited to specialization since the polymorphic substitution of objects doesn't work: not every state of a derived lifecycle can be substituted to a more general one, in the base lifecycle.

Statecharts-based models include the state decomposition which is very useful for lifecycle specialization. Moreover such models become widely used in OO methods: OOAD [10] uses a simplified model (without orthogonality) of statecharts[2]. OMT [13] and ObjectCharts [11] take the full model. UML [1] extends the Harel's formalism [2] to specify for instance, the object creation and deletion. Harel provides some similar extensions for object modeling [12].

2.2 Related work on specialization of behavior

There are descriptive and constructive approaches. Constructive approaches give a set of operators to specialize lifeycles. Descriptive approaches give a set of rules a derived lifecycle should verify in order to be a specialization of a base one.

2.2.1 Constructive approaches

The work related in [14] presents informally some statechart-based operators of lifecycle specialization. This work takes only the behavior substitutability into account, that is: every object of derived class should also be used wherever an object of the base class could be used.

The approach presented in [15] is both descriptive and constructive. This paper and [16] introduce the idea of long term observable behavior of an object. The long term observable behavior of an object involves a series of transitions whereas the short one involves only one transition (as in [14]). The long term observable behavior prevents the adding of a transitions between two different states in the derived lifecycle.

2.2.2 Descriptive approaches

Another approach [16](an extension of [17]) distinguishes two meanings of lifecycles: observable and invocable behavior. One way is to look at a lifecyle diagram "*as a description of all observable sequences of method calls, i.e of sequences that might occur on objects of this class, though it is not guaranteed that all of these are actually executable or invocable with each instance of the class*". Thus any observable sequence of calls for a subclass should also result (under projection) as an observable sequence according to a superclass. Another way is to look at a lifecycle diagram as "*a description of all invocable services that a client is able to use and where it is guaranteed that they are executable*". This work highlights the difference between locally (as in [14]) and globally observable behavior (as in [15]).

The work described in [18] is based on Object/ Behavior diagrams [8] which rely on Petri Nets, whereas the other works consider different extensions of finite state automata. This paper consider three kinds of behavior consistency: observation (with the same meaning of [16]) weak invocation (which also corresponds to the one of [16]) and strong invocation. The last one "*requires additionally that activities added to a subtype do not interfere with activities inherited from the supertype*". [19] considers only enabling interferences, but this is not sufficient to avoid the inheritance problems.

2.2.3 Limit of existing approaches

All these works focus on the meaning of the lifecycle specialization and do not consider the structure of the derived class which is associated to the specialized lifecycle ([19]. They belong to a bottom-up view of conformity: the derived lifecycle, according to a kind of behavior consistency, should conform to the base lifecycle. [16] and [18] are the most related work to our approach: they have a notion of top-down conformity (invocation) that relies on sequences of transitions: any sequence of transitions that can be performed on an instance of a base class should also be performed on instances of a derived class. These works define the rules the derived lifecycle should conform to in order to be consistent. These rules do not include the structure of the derived class, then some inheritance problems may occur.

The main limit of all these works is that they do not consider at all the structure of the derived class, and thus, there are some hidden inheritance problems, as shown in the above example.

To deal with these problems of lifecycle specialization, we first define formally the interpretation of states.

3 State interpretation

3.1 State structure of a lifecycle

For any class c, in relation with its lifecycle, we define:

- S_c, which is the set of lifecycle states. S_c represents both the basic and composite states which contain other states as substates.

- The total function $children_c : S_c \longrightarrow 2^{S_c}$ which defines, for each state the set of its immediate substates.

A state s is called *basic* if $children_c(s) = \emptyset$, otherwise it is called *composite*. Let's call B_{S_c} (resp. C_{S_c}) the subset of basic (resp. composite) states of S_c. There is a unique root r, i.e. $\exists! r \in S_c \ \forall s \in S_c, r \notin children_c(s)$.

3.2 Types of composite state

For any class c, the function $type_c : C_{S_c} \longrightarrow \{AND, XOR\}$ is a total function that assigns to each composite state its decomposition type:

- if $type_c(s) = XOR$ then $children_c(s)$ is a XOR decomposition of state s: when the object is in state s, it is also in one and only one $s' \in children_c(s)$.

- if $type_c(s) = AND$ then $children_c(s)$ is an AND decomposition of state s: when the object is in state s, it is also in all states $s' \in children_c(s)$.

3.3 Definition of the state interpretation

For an object whose class is linked to a lifecycle, the interpretation of lifecycle states depends on the values of the attributes of this object.

Let's assume that class c with n attributes $A_{c,1}, \cdots A_{c,n}$ (including the inherited ones), where the domain of $A_{c,i}$ is $D_{c,i}$. For simplicity, we consider only simple domains (not object classes). In the general case, if the domain of $A_{c,i}$ is a class, the value of $A_{c,i}$ is an object, we can consider either the state of this value or the OID. Considering complex domains does not change fundamentally the problems of top-down conformity.

The state of an object of c is defined by a value vector $v = (a_1, \cdots, a_n)$ where $a_i \in D_{c,i}$, and a_i is the current value of $A_{c,i}$.

Let us call $\Pi_{c,n}$ the cartesian product $D_{c,1} \times ... \times D_{c,n}$, n being the number of attributes of class c.

The interpretation I_c of a state of S_c is a subset of $\Pi_{c,n}$, and is formally defined as follows:

$$I_c : S_c \longrightarrow \Pi_{c,n}$$

$$I_c(s) = \begin{cases} I \subseteq \Pi_{c,n} & \text{if } s \in B_{S_c} \\ \bigcup_{x \in children_c(s)} I_c(x) & \text{if } s \in C_{S_c} \text{ and } type_c(s) = XOR \\ \bigcap_{x \in children_c(s)} I_c(x) & \text{if } s \in C_{S_c} \text{ and } type_c(s) = AND \end{cases}$$

with (since an object cannot be in several substates of a XOR state)[3]:

$$\forall(x,y) \in children_c(s) \times children_c(s) \quad x \neq y \Rightarrow I_c(x) \cap I_c(y) = \emptyset.$$

Moreover, $r \in S_c$, the lifecycle's root: $I_c(r) = \Pi_{c,n}$

The interpretation of the base lifecycle states and those of the derived lifecycle are related by a property of bottom-up conformity which is introduced in the next section.

3.4 Conservation of state semantics

Let's consider d, a derived class of c. d may contain new attributes and/or the domain of some inherited ones may have been restricted.

When considering the new attributes of the derived class (if any), the value vectors of d instances are: $v \in \Pi_{d,m}$ where:

$$\begin{cases} m \geq n, \\ D_{d,i}(i > n) \text{is the } (i-n)^{th} \text{ added attribute in } d \text{ and,} \\ \forall i \leq n, D_{d,i} \subseteq D_{c,i}. \end{cases}$$

---

[3]Thus the property trivially holds: $\{I_c(x)\}_{x \in children_c(s)}$ is a partition of $I_c(s)$.

The projection $p_{d,c} : \Pi_{d,m} \longrightarrow \Pi_{c,n}$ is a total function that assigns to each state vector, the vector of its first n components. We extend this projection on a set X of state vectors:

$$p_{d,c}(X) = \bigcup_{x \in X} p_{d,c}(x).$$

The following property, named *conservation of state semantics*, should hold between the state interpretations of c and d:

$$\forall s \leq S_c \quad p_{d,c}(I_d(s)) \subseteq I_c(s).$$

The bottom-up conformity (e.g section 2) between d and c requires this property of conservation of state semantics. When the derived class is specialized from a base class without any domain restriction of attributes, the stronger property holds:

$$\forall s \leq S_c \quad p_{d,c}(I_d(s)) = I_c(s).$$

4 Formal definition of top-down conformity

Some other definitions should be introduced before. Let L be the set of labels of transitions. for any class c and its lifecycle , a transition is a tuple (X, l, Y) of $S_c \times L \times S_c$ where X is the source state , l is the label and, Y is the destination state of the transition.

The total function $source_c : S_c \times L \times S_c \longrightarrow S_c$ defines for each transition of the lifecycle of c, its source state: $source_c((X, l, Y)) = X$.

The total function $destination_c : S_c \times L \times S_c \longrightarrow S_c$ defines for each transition of the lifecycle of c, its destination state: $destination_c((X, l, Y)) = Y$.

The total function $default_c$ defines for a state its default states:

$$default_c : S_c \longrightarrow \Pi_{c,n}$$
$$default_c(s) =$$
$$\begin{cases} s \text{ if } s \in B_{S_c}, \\ x \text{ if } s \in C_{S_c} \text{ and } type_c(s) = XOR, \ x \text{ is the default substate of } s, \\ \{default_c(x) | x \in children_c(s)\} \text{ if } s \in C_{S_c} \text{ and } type_c(s) = AND. \end{cases}$$

We also extend the interpretation I_c on a set X of lifecycle states:

$$I_c(X) = \bigcup_{x \in X} I_c(x)$$

Let us call $v_x(obj)$ the current value vector of an instance obj of class x, and $t(v_x(obj))$ its new value after the firing of a transition t, $t(v_x(obj))$ is undefined if t is not firable on $v_x(obj))$.

Definition of top-down conformity 2 (formal) *a transition* t *of the lifecycle of class* c *is top-down-conform in the lifecycle of* d, *a derived class of* c, *if and only if, for any instance* obj *of class* d:

if $v_d(obj) \in I_d(source_c(t))$ and t is fired,
then $t(v_d(obj)) \in I_d(default_d(destination_c(t)))$.

The two next sections define the possible specialization operators for class and for lifecycle. Then the operators appyling to one concept are related with those of the other concept, with regard to top-down conformity.

5 The class derivation operators

A derived class inherits the attributes and methods of its base class. There are many kinds of inheritance [20]. Among them, the following operators are possibly used to define a derived class. We do not claim that the set of all these operators can coexist in one single object model: our aim is to study how these operators relate to those to specialize lifecycles. We consider only single inheritance and mono-valued attributes. These operators are:

- identity

- add a new attribute,

- redefine an attribute with a more restricted domain of values,

- add a new method (possibility of overloading),

- override a method.

The overriding of method may be contravariant (see the functional subtyping rule of Cardelli [21]) or covariant (see Eiffel [22, 23] or O2[24]). We do not enter the debate between these two approaches and refers to [25] for a comparative study.

Next sections present how the specialization of a class by any of these operators affects the specialization of its lifecycle.

6 The lifecycle specialization operators

A derived lifecycle inherits the states and transitions of the base lifecycle. The top-down conformity of these operators is neither a required nor an intrinsic property. The conformity of a derived lifecycle depends on the way the class is specialized. Some lifecycle specializations may require some method overriding (see section 8). These operators are:

6.1 The states specialization operators

These operators decompose a state (by a XOR or AND decomposition) or extend a state decomposition by adding orthogonal components. For each operator the property of state semantics conservation must hold. Figures 2 (a specialization by a XOR decomposition), 3 and 4 illustrate these state specialization operators. The transitions are labelled by an event name instead of a full label, only for clarity.

The specialization by an AND decomposition consists in specializing a basic state into several orthogonal substates.

The NCLA Executive Board shall serve as arbitrator of any disputes between Member Clubs. It also has the power to suspend any Member Club, player, non-playing member of a club, coach, or anyone officially connected with a Member Club or the NCLA, for any period of time deemed necessary for any action contrary to these By-Laws, the NCLA Constitution, sportsmanship, or spirit of the game of Lacrosse.

In fig. 3, the *Member* state is specialized into *Coach*, *Player* and *Team* substates.

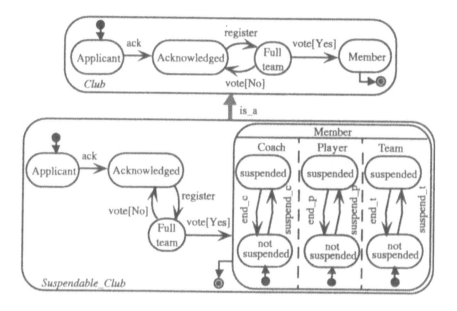

Figure 3: specialization by an *AND* decomposition

The operator illustrated in fig. 4 consists in adding orthogonal substates to an already decomposed state (whatever the decomposition's type is).

> Only players of Member Clubs who have played in at least three regular season games, [...] shall be eligible to participate in the NCLA playoffs or California state finals. A player injured during the season is eligible for the playoffs provided he has played in at least one regular season contest prior to the injury. The NCLA shall sponsor championship playoffs for the top eight (8) teams in the league determined by the following formula for the regular season standings [...].

Thus we define the *PO_ Club* class for teams whose are able to be selected for play-offs. In fig. 4, the *status* substate of the derived lifecycle is orthogonal to the *play_ off* substate of the *Member* state. When considering the class specialization, this new behavior can correspond to the addition of new attributes and of new methods.

The next operator (fig. 5) of state specialization does not decompose a state, but redefines its interpretation is the derived class. *Full team* state of the base lifecycle becomes *New full team* in the derived lifecycle.

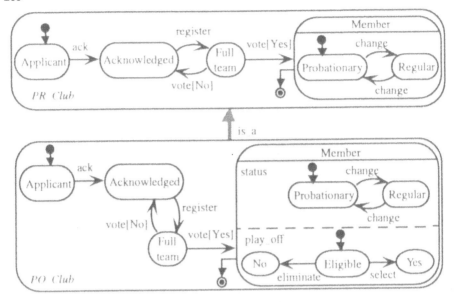

Figure 4: specialization by adding orthogonal substates

Present a verifiable roster of at least twenty five (25) committed players without claiming anymore than thirty-three percent (33%) of the players from an existing Member Club.

The set of value vectors of these states are not equal, since there are also operators that have been applied to derive the class. A new semantics is thus given to the specialized state.

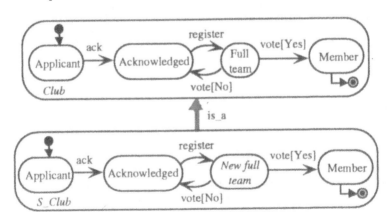

Figure 5: specialization by changing the interpretation of a state

The next two operators must be considered very carefully according to a bottom-up conformity.

6.2 Adding a state

This operator (see fig. 6) may prevent the behavior substitutability and hence the bottom-up conformity. Let us consider some instances of the derived class *PO_ suspendable_ Club*. Moreover consider them in *Eligible_ for_ play_ off* state (these instances are also in *suspended* or *not_ suspended* state according to the other orthogonal substates of *Member*). This means that their value vector belongs to the interpretation of the *Eligible_ for_ play_ off* state. In order to use them wherever an instance of the *Suspendable_ Club* class may be used, the question arises: In which state are these instances? Some of them may be in the *suspended* state (with the interpretation of the base class), other may be in the *not_ suspended* state. This is not very practical. The derived class structure may help if new attributes were added: the interpretation of the states which are added in the derived lifecycle should only depend on these new attributes.

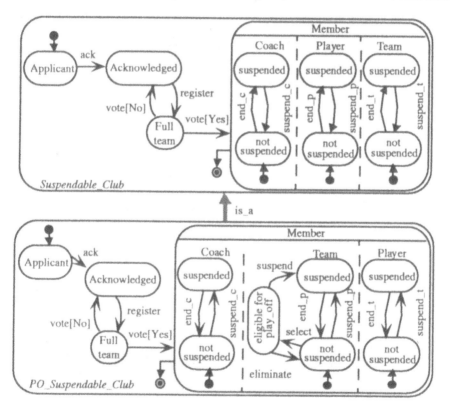

Figure 6: specialization by adding a state

If there is no new attributes in the derived class structure, there are two drawbacks:

- the behavior substitutability is not very clear and practical in this case,

- all the methods of all the transitions should be overridden, since in the above example, the state space (of the *Member* state) is partitioned differently in the derived lifecycle.

Thus, if the bottom-up conformity is wanted, the adding of state requires new attributes in the derived class, and the interpretation of added states relying only on these new attributes.

6.3 State deletion

The state deletion may be explicit or implicit. The explicit state deletion consists in considering, for example, the *Suspendable_ Club* lifecycle of fig. 6 as a specialization of the *PO_ Suspendable_ Club* one (deletion of the *Eligible_for_.play_ off* state). There is no problem about the conservation of semantics for the remaining states. But, if an instance of the derived class is used as an instance of the base class, it will not be used as instance of its original class as long as its vector value belongs to a deleted state.

The implicit state deletion arises when a state becomes unreachable since the restriction of a domain attribute.

All these operators which only involve states may raise problems of behavioral conformity when they are related to the structure of the derived class.

6.4 The transition specialization operators

They are of two types: the adding or deletion of transition between two states and, the specialization of the transitions's label. In UML, the general format of a transition's label is:

event(parameters)[condition]/method(parameters)^target.event(parameters)

Each part of a transition can be specialized. The operators that specialize transition labels[4] cannot cause top-down conformity problems, as this conformity involves only the state interpretation. But they may cause bottom-up conformity problems that are described in the next section.

The adding of transition depends on the requested kind of bottom-up behavior consistency (see section 7). The deletion of transition prevents any bottom-up conformity.

7 Verification of the bottom-up conformity

The lifecycle specialization operators (state-based or transition-based) may lead to some problems of bottom-up conformity when relating them to the structure of the derived class. During the analysis phase, if a kind of bottom-up conformity is wanted, then the lifecycle specialization requires, in some cases,

---

[4]The specialization of event is analogous to those of method; the controversy between covariant and contravariant specialization of event holds. The same approach should be considered for the specialization of event and of method. In case of covariant overriding of methods, the well known problems of type checking are still here. These problems are not related to the lifecycle itself.

the definition of new attributes in the derived class. The table 1 summarizes the verifications to perform.

specialization operator	to be verified
adding a state or orthogonal substates	the interpretation of the new states should only depend on new attributes.
state deletion	caution when using instance substitution.
transition specialization	Some problems may occur if some attributes have been redefined with a more restricted domain. It also depends on the object model (kind of method specialization).
adding a transition	depending on the kind of bottom-up conformity, adding a transition may be forbidden between two different states.
transition deletion	strictly forbidden if bottom-up conformity is wanted.

Table 1: verifying the bottom-up conformity

8 Verification of the top-down conformity

8.1 State-based specialization

The verifications and possible validations are the same for all the lifecycle specialization operators which apply to states. The verifications and possible validations concern the transitions. We assume that specialized transitions are valid since explicitly defined.

This verification applies to all the incoming inherited transitions to all the states that have been decomposed in the derived class. It consists of confirming that the default states are valid when inherited transitions are applied to an instance of a derived class.

example: let us take again the XOR decomposition to describe the state-based verifications (fig. 2). The *Vote* method has to be verified. Its validation depends on the new state of any instance of the derived class for which the transition is fired (and hence the method applied):

- the new state of this instance belongs to the interpretation of the *Probationary* state, which is the destination state of the transition. Thus there is no need to override the method (and hence no validation is required).

- or the new value vector of the instance does not belong to this interpretation. Thus the lifecycle is not valid and the *Vote* method should be overridden to validate the lifecycle. Another way to validate the transition is to add a condition which excludes its firing whenever this case occurs. Since this condition is not always easy to define, we prefer redefining the transition's method.

8.2 Restriction of an attribute domain

Whenever a domain of an attribute is restricted in the derived class, the verification applies to all the inherited transitions. It consists in confirming, for any transition t which is fired on an instance of the derived class, that the new state of the instance belongs to the interpretation of the destination state of t.

> example: let us take the *register* transition in fig. 2: when it is fired on any instance of the derived PR_Club class, the new vector value v of the instance should verify: $v \in I_{PR\_Club}(FullTeam)$.
> If not, the lifecycle is not valid and the transition should be specialized by method overriding.

8.3 Recap

The behavioral conformity of a derived class according to its base class relies on both the bottom-up and top-down conformity. The behavioral top-down conformity of the derived class also depends on its structure. Thus some verifications across the definitions of class and of lifecycle should be carefully studied. The table 2 summarizes these verifications (see the protocol in annexe). The lifecycle's specialization involves usually a series of operators' applications

specialization operator	scope	to be verified
state-based operators	specialized states	methods of the incoming transitions should verify the interpretation of their default substates.
restriction of an attribute domain	all the states	methods of the incoming transitions should verify the interpretation of states

Table 2: verifying the top-down conformity

which imply a series of verifications. When the derived class structure contains at least one restriction of attribute domain, all the transitions methods should be verified. Adding a method does not require any verification. This rule is also valid for adding an attribute, except if combined with the specialization of states in the lifecycle.

Besides the specialization of a transition's method, the transition-based operators induce no verification on class specialization.

9 Conclusion

The OO methods share a common basis of concepts which are grouped into modeling spaces. This paper presents a framework for the integration of two of these spaces, namely the class and lifecycle spaces. Their integration often lead to hidden errors of behavior at the analysis or design levels. With respect to the class specialization, the cornerstone of this integration is the behavioral conformity for which we propose a new approach: we split the behavioral conformity in top-down and bottom-up ways. The bottom-up conformity is usually known as polymorphic substitution whereas the top-down conformity is new. Top-down conformity provides a sound and useful to ensure the full behavioral conformity.

We introduce a set of operators that preserve the bottom-up conformity and circumscribe the top-down conformity to a well defined set of verifications. If they fail, we propose for each case, the validation to establish this conformity, if wanted.

In information systems engineering, the behavioral conformity may not be necessary for all the classes. Moreover, during an analysis phase, some lifecycle may be prescriptive whereas others may be descriptive. However, for the areas in which behavioral conformity is required, we present a validation protocol which relies on specialization only. We further develop on two axes, the formalization of these specialization operators and the composition of lifecycles.

References

[1] Booch G, Rumbaugh J. Unified Modeling Language v1.0. Rational Software Corporation,1996.

[2] Harel D. On Visual Formalisms. Communications of the ACM, Vol 31 (5), may 1988.

[3] Northern California Lacrosse Association. Northern California Lacrosse Web Page. http://www.tol.net/ lacrosse/

[4] Jacobson I, Christerson M, Jonsson P, OEvergaard G. Object-oriented software engineering: a use case driven approach. Wokingham GB ; Reading Mass, Addison-Wesley, 1993 (1993).

[5] Shlaer S, Mellor S J. Object lifecycles: modeling the world in states. Yourdon Press computing series, 1992.

[6] Tari Z. On the design of object-oriented databases. Proceedings of the international conference on Entity-Relationship approach, Lecture Notes in Computer Science, vol 645, pp. 388-405, Springer-Verlag, 1992.

[7] Embley D W, Kurtz B D, Woodfield SN. Object-Oriented Systems Analysis: a model-driven approach. Yourdon Press, 1992.

[8] Kappel G, Schrefl M. Object/behavior diagrams. Proceedings of the 7th international Conference on Data Engineering, pp 530-539, 1991.

[9] Léonard M, Estier T, Falquet G, Guyot J. Six Spaces for Global Information Systems Design. Proceedings of the IFIP working Conference on the Object Oriented Approach in Information Systems, Quebec City, Canada, Oct. 1991.

[10] Booch G. Object-oriented analysis and design with applications. Benjamin Cummings Publishing, 1994.

[11] Coleman D, Hayes F, Bear S. Introducing ObjectCharts or how to use Statecharts in Object- Oriented Design. IEEE Transactions on Software Engineering, vol. 18 (1), january 1992.

[12] Harel D, Gery E. Executable Object Modeling with Statecharts. Proceedings of the 18th International Conference on Software Engineering, pp. 246-257, Springer, 1996.

[13] Rumbaugh J, Blaha M, Premerlany W, Eddy F, Lorensen W. Object-oriented modeling and design. Prentice Hall, 1991.

[14] McGregor J D, Dyer D M. A Note on Inheritance and State Machines. ACM SIGSOFT Software Engineeering Notes, Vol. 18 no 4, Oct. 1993.

[15] Saake G, Hartel P, Junglaus R, Wieringa R, Feenstra R.Inheritance conditions for object lifecycle diagrams. Proceedings of the EMISA Workshop, 1994.

[16] Ebert J, Engels G. Observable or Invocable Behaviour Ð You have to choose. Technical report TR94- 38, University of Leiden, Netherlands, 1994.

[17] Ebert J, Engels G. Structural and behavioral views on OMT-Classes. Proceedings of the int. symposium on Object-Oritented Methodologies and Systems, ISOOMS'94, Lecture Notes in Computer Science, vol 858, pp. 142-157, Springer-Verlag, 1994.

[18] Schrefl M, Stumptner M. Behavior Consistent Extension of Object Life Cycles. Proceedings of the 14th int. Conf. Object-Oriented and Entity-Relationship Modeling, OO-ER'95, Lecture Notes in Computer Science, vol 1021, Springer-Verlag, 1995.

[19] Paech B, Rumpe R. A new Concept of Refinement used for Behavior Modelling with Automata. Proceedings of the 2nd int. symposium on Formal Method in Engineering, FME'94, Lecture Notes in Computer Science, vol 873, pp. 154-174, Springer-Verlag, 1994.

[20] Meyer B. The many faces of inheritance: a taxonomy of taxonomy. Computer, may 1996.

[21] Cardelli L. A semantics of multiple inheritance. Proceedings of the international symposium on the semantics of data types, Lecture Notes in Computer Science, vol 173, pp. 51-67, Springer-Verlag, 1984.

[22] Meyer B. Eiffel: the language. Prentice-Hall 1991.

[23] Meyer B. Object-oriented software construction. 2nd edition, Prentice-Hall, 1996.

[24] Bancilhon F, Delobel C, Kanellakis P. Implementing an object-oriented database system. The story of O2. Morgan Kaufman 1992.

[25] Castagna G. Covariance and contravariance. Conflict without a cause. ACM Transactions on Programming Languages and Systems, 17(3), pp 431-447, 1995.

A   Protocol of top-down verification

The verifications are made according to a search of the inheritance tree. If some verifications fail, then the involved methods should be overridden in the derived class. The search starts with class that is the root of the inheritance tree. The sketch of the search is described below.

procedure search(c: class)
begin
  verify(c);
  for each direct subclass s of c **do** search(s)
end;
procedure verify(d:class)
begin
  if d is the root of the inheritance tree **then return**;
  $S = B_{S_c} \cap C_{S_d}$
  //S is the set of states of lifecycle of c which are refined in the lifecycle of d;
  Let MS be the set of methods of incoming transitions to any state of S;
  for each m in MS **do**
    ask the designer to perform the checks defined in section 8.1;
  if d has attributes that are redefined **then**
    begin
      Let MS be the set of methods of incoming transitions to any state of S_c;
      for each m in MS **do**
        ask the designer to perform the checks defined in section 8.2
    end
end

An Enhanced Definition of Composition and its use for Abstraction

Joël BRUNET

Institut Universitaire de Technologie de Sénart, Fontainebleau
Fontainebleau, France

Abstract

A recent trend in object-oriented modeling is to consider composition as an alternative to aggregation, with enforced constraints. The paper suggests that the aggregation concept is unnecessary by the fact that it can be expressed through the combination of composition and inheritance. It proposes two complementary criteria that enhance the understanding of composition : the first one is based on object life cycles comparisons, while the second one calls for object behavior. Afterwards, an abstraction mechanism is presented. Its aim is to hide some details of an object schema, where links between objects are those of the O* static model : inheritance, composition and reference. A correspondence between these links and the ones of the UML notation is given.

1. Introduction

During the past ten years, hundreds of terms have been proposed in the object-oriented literature to help to specify and develop information systems (for instance 233 distinct notions were counted for UML 1.1. in [1]). Many of them covered similar concepts with different view points, that sometimes leads to confusion but fortunately also to a better understanding of them. This understanding is one of the keys for obtaining suitable object-oriented development methods, that is, methods that assist the analyst during the modeling process and allow to estimate the adequacy of the specification in regards to the user's requirements, before the beginning of the implementation process (even in a process based on prototypes).

So, while the unification of OMT and the Grady Booch's terminologies into UML is a significant step towards the definition of a reduced set of useful concepts, many detailed explanations have to be done about these concepts, in order to enhance the overall modeling process. Indeed, analysts are faced with the diversity of the Universe of Discourse and need guidelines to use concepts in non-trivial concrete situations.

Some modeling problems arise from the difficulty to choose between different concepts when they are insufficiently defined, as for aggregation compared to association. The choice of using one concept rather than another must be done on the basis of a different description of the reality and must have some consequences on the final information system, rather than being a question of fashion.

A profound taxonomy of composition and some of its properties has been proposed in [2] and is still an active research area (e.g. [3]). Winston counts six types of meronymic – or part-whole – relations and five types of relations which are not but can easily be confused with meronymic relations ([2]). The difficulty of perceiving what is and what is not composition seems to be due to the lack of criteria independent of the semantics of the objects in relation.

The work presented in this paper provides an enhanced definition of composition, viewed not as an alternative to aggregation, as in UML (or a special case of aggregation, as in [4]), but as a fundamental concept from which aggregation may be constructed. This definition is based on two complementary criteria on the properties of composite and component objects. These criteria, which represent some underlying properties attached to the semantics of composition, gain to be made clear for two reasons : to provide guidelines during the modeling process and to deduce some important properties of the system, as for instance the way referential constraints will be maintained. Composition allows us to elaborate abstraction mechanisms that cannot be done with aggregation, because in the last case components may become independent of their aggregate during their life span (as for instance engines that may be detached from a vehicule). Some abstraction rules are proposed that abstract the different links of the static O* model [5] : inheritance, composition and reference.

The O* model is used for the illustrations, although a subset of the concepts of the UML object diagram may be used instead (a correspondence between static concepts of O* and UML is provided figure 2).

The paper is organized as follows. Section 2 is devoted to a better understanding of composition. Aggregation and composition are compared in section 2.1. Section 2.2 presents the criterion of life cycle interval equality for defining composition, while section 2.3 describes the criterion of deletion propagation. Finally, Section 3 briefly presents how the composition may be used in an abstraction mechanism of object schemas.

2. Two Criteria for Identifying Composition Links

2.1. Aggregation Versus Composition

In the recent versions of OMT and in the UML notation [4], composition is a particular type of aggregation in which the components are dependent and exclusive – i.e. cannot exist independently and may not belong to more than one composite object –.

The first release of OMT [6] did not mention composition, and just gave some indications on the use of aggregation instead of association : can we use the expression part-of, are the operations and some attribute values of the composite object propagated on the components, and is there a subordination of the components to their composite object ? These indications clearly apply themselves to the current notion of composition, but are problematic when applied to aggregation because there is no constraint on the cardinalities of the classes in relation. This is not a problem on the side of the composite object which may own more than on component, but on the other side, since components may exist independently, any of the indications apply themselves.

B. Henderson-Sellers [3] provides a similar criticism by pointing out that OMT aggregation is bi-directional whereas "it is clear from the wider literature that bi-directional aggregations are exceptions, not the rule".

A point of OMT aggregation that may be viewed as positive is that it takes into consideration the fact that in some cases, composition seems to apply itself but the components (1) may switch between their statute of dependent object and the one of independent object, or in some exceptional cases (2) may belong to more than one composite object. An example of case (1) may be planes which are composed of several engines, each engine occasionally being detached for revision reasons. The paper will try to demonstrate that aggregation is unnecessary : these cases can be modeled by a combination of composition and inheritance (c.f. figure 4, case c). Case (2) seems to happen only when several topological dimensions are concerned in : walls between two adjacent rooms may be viewed as belonging to both ; a two-dimensional game board may be composed of rows and columns themselves composed of squares. Note that, contrarily to the walls case, the shareness exists because squares are subordinated by two composition links, but for each link the composition is exclusive (a square belongs to exactly one row and one column). Thus, only the walls case cannot be represented with composition ; in practice we may specify a wall as an associative object between two adjacent rooms.

UML [4] tackles aggregation in the same way as OMT and presents composition as an aggregation realized by value : components are physically contained by the aggregate object as attribute values. Then, a component object looses its object identity, and it becomes impossible to refer to it, as it is necessary for instance in a room reservation case study : hotels are composed of rooms which are referenced by customer's reservations. This implies that component objects must be considered as real objects, the decision of implementing them as objects or values being postponed until the object schema is reasonably complete. In fact, even in a design model such as the O_2 model [7], the components of a composition link may be implemented either by values or by objects.

2.2. Composition Inferred by Life Cycle Comparisons

In the light of the comments of the previous section, we will consider that, contrary to the usual view of the metamodel that consists in either placing aggregation as a generalization of composition as in [4] (by relaxing the dependence and exclusiveness constraints), or generalizing aggregation and composition in a generic concept as in [3], aggregation is not a relevant concept : if component objects can be independent, we will use a link of composition and a link of inheritance, and if they are shared – in the context of one link –, this is not composition but reference.

Thus, composition means dependence and exclusiveness of the components, and the OMT indications for isolating aggregations links fit well with its semantics. But there are still some imprecisions which may lead to placing compositions links where others may use association instead. Take for instance the case of a customer's order. It is clear for an experienced analyst that an order is an associative object which refers to a customer. But is it absolutely clear that customers are not composed of orders ? After all, orders are dependent and exclusive in regard with their customer, and it is not totally absurd to answer in the affirmative to the OMT indications : orders are part of customers, operations on customers (as canceling the last order) and attribute values (as a "bad payer" value of a reliability attribute) may be propagated on components, and orders are subordinated to customers. Thus, the OMT indications do not allow to avoid the mistake of considering orders as parts of customers.

One way to distinguish between what is composition and what is not is to proceed to object life cycle comparisons. The life cycle $\Gamma(o)$ of an object o has been defined in the O* method [5] as the list of the successive event occurrences which have affected its state. We will focus on the life cycle interval of time, that is, from the first event occurrence which created the object and the last event occurrence, either a deletion event or the event occurrence from which the object does not evolve any more.

Figure 1 shows two examples of comparison between life cycle intervals. In both cases there is an inclusion, which explains itself by the fact that, in the case of composition, the component may not exist without its composite object and, in the case of reference, the associative object cannot exist without the object its refers to.

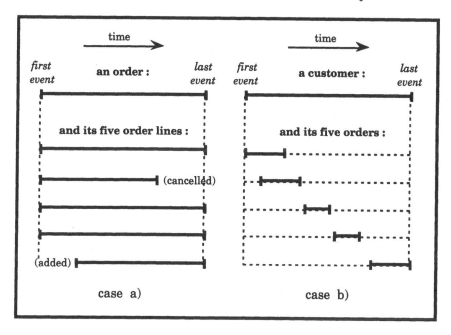

Figure 1 : two examples of life cycle comparisons

A deeper look shows that, in case a), the life cycle intervals are equal (except for a minority) and, in case b), the life cycle intervals are quite different. The following criterion will be adopted : equally means composition while difference means reference, that is, a reference link from an associative object to another object. So an order is composed of order lines, and an order refers to a customer. The wrong answer would be : an order line refers to an order and a customer is composed of orders.

Figure 2 shows the resulting specification of these examples in O*, and the correspondence between the O* and the UML notations. All examples will be represented in O* which is more fitted to our purpose, but UML may be also used.

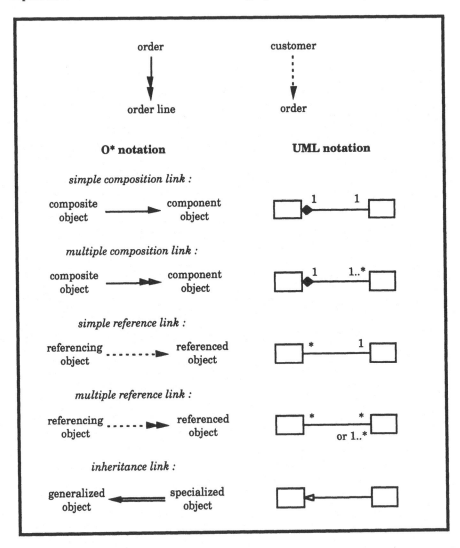

Figure 2 : resulting specification and O* / UML correspondence

Composition and reference links were defined in [5] on the basis of life cycle comparisons, while the definition of the inheritance link was inspired from [8] and [9].

It should be noted that the asymmetry of both composition and reference links is semantic and has no relationship with how they will be realized in the implementation phase, either unidirectionally (a priori in the same direction as the O* arrows) or bi-directionnally, depending on the software environment and on the access needs. In other words, O* links are bi-directionnal.

We have examined associations with a 1..1 multiplicity role. In order to be complete, we must consider other kinds of associations. An association with two multiple roles will become a multiple reference if an inclusion of life cycle intervals is established. This is the case between books and authors for instance (c.f. figure 3). If no inclusion is found, we must reflect upon an object whose life cycle interval is included into the intersection of the ones of the two objects in relation. For instance the study of the association between employees and projects will infer an associative object named assignment. Then the life cycle intervals between assignment and employee, and between assignment and project should be considered.

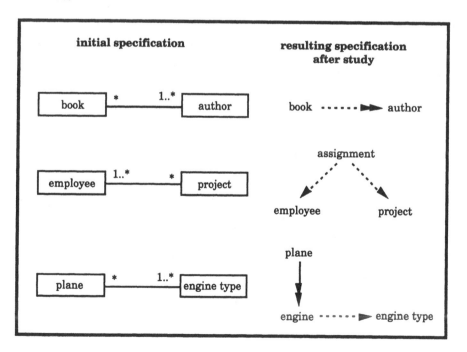

Figure 3 : inferring of new objects by study of life cycle intersections

This process may lead to discover composition links which otherwise would be hidden by the association. For instance, one may consider planes as objects associated with engine types, the two association roles being multiple. The study of the intersection of the life cycle intervals of these objects leads to isolate engine objects. This results in the specification of a composition link between planes and engines and a reference link between engines and engines types.

This mechanism is also relevant for associations whose arity is as greater than two.

2.3. Composition Inferred by Behavioral Dependencies

Another criterion that could be used to discover compositions links concerns behavioral dependencies. By behavioral dependency we mean that sometimes event occurrences may drive or be affected by other ones. Figure 1 shows something inherent to composition that is the synchronization of event creations and deletions between composite objects and almost all their components. On the contrary, reference reflects a clear independence except for marginal cases, as when an order is created at the creation of a customer.

More precisely, the difference of behavior between composition and reference becomes stronger when we ask the question : what happens when a creation or deletion of an object is requested ? For component objects and referencing objects, nothing seems to happen, except when the last component object of a composite object is deleted. This case must be treated because composition implies at least one component object. It is advisable to prevent this deletion rather than to provoke the implicit deletion of its composite object, because this action looks like a user mistake. Some models offer the choice between the two possibilities, as in [10] where deletion propagation may be attached to association roles.

More crucial is the case of composite objects and referenced objects because, in case of deletion, the referential constraint will be invalidated. For composition, the referential constraint is represented by the one-to-one cardinality from components towards their composite, and for reference, it is represented by the one-to-one cardinality from the referencing object towards their referenced object.

The referential constraint is a fundamental contribution of the relational database model, which can be expound as : when a tuple is deleted while one or several other tuples refer to it by their foreign key, we may either prevent the deletion or propagate it to the tuples referencing it. This precision has to be given for each couple (foreign key, primary key), by means of the presence or not of the key words "on delete cascade" attached to each foreign key, when defining SQL tables.

In a surprising manner, this constraint is almost non-existent in the literature on object-oriented modeling, while object models do not resolve the problem by a magic wand tap. [11] briefly mentions it as the existence dependency, but only with the solution of deletion propagation. [12] states that cascading deletion is implied by any role with a 1..1 multiplicity, which appears to be very dangerous.

If its resolution is not specified at the modeling stage, it will necessarily be done at the implementation stage, and then will be a source of misunderstanding for the user. Other problems may arise, depending on the implementation environment. In a relational database environment, there is no problem, except if the programmer decides to opt for prevention for each case, which seems to be the safest solution. At that time, two scenarios may arise when a user has to delete a composite object : either the user has to previously delete all its components, and then possibly be stuck in a vicious circle at the deletion of the last component, or unnecessary code has to be produced in order to propagate the deletion. In an object database environment, the situations are more unpredictable, because of the various ways composition is supported. In the O_2 object-oriented DBMS [7] for instance, objects are never explicitly deleted, but are indirectly erased when no more references point to it. If components are implemented by values, which presupposes no references on them (c.f. section 2.1), then the deletion of a composite object naturally implies the deletion of its components. If components are implemented as objects, they will still exist after deletion of their composite object as long as they stay referenced. For instance in figure 4.a, reserved rooms of a deleted hotel will still exist.

The decision of maintaining the referential constraint by prevention or deletion propagation has an important impact on the behavior of the final information system, so it must be taken at the modeling stage, either implicitly, as it will be proposed here, or explicitly, as in [10]. The advantages of defining them implicitly are that this limits the risks of errors and this will help to distinguish composition links.

Our proposition is to establish an equivalence between composition and the choice of maintaining the referential constraint by deletion propagation. Inversely, the referential constraint implied by the 1..1 multiplicity of a simple reference link will be maintained by prevention. This statement fits well with the semantics of both links : in the examples of figure 1, deletion of an order will cause the deletion of all its order lines, whereas deletion of a customer will be allowed only if no order refers to it. This has a sense, because order lines are subordinated to orders, and orders are more important than customers.

Thus, reflecting on the referential constraint helps to distinguish between composition and reference or, inversely, establishing composition and reference links by comparing life cycles infer automatically a resolution for the referential constraint. Another advantage of this equivalence is that it allows to generate many operation calls at the transition for the modeling to the implementation phase.

The combination of several composition, reference and inheritance links infers some referential links between objects no directly linked. In figure 4, an hotel cannot be deleted if one of its rooms is referenced by a reservation ; a person who is also a customer can be deleted only if there are no orders for him.

Case c) illustrates how the O* model treats some composition cases where components may become independent of the composite object (that is, the OMT aggregation previously discussed), as when the engines of a plane may be detached.

Note that when an engine is mounted on a plane, it is a perfect case of composition : if the plane desappears for some reason, its engine desappears too.

In the O* approach, the engine class has to be split into a general class that contains all engines, regardless if they are mounted on a plane or stocked in the revision shop, and a specialized class that only contains engines mounted into a plane. When a plane is deleted, its components of the mounted engine class are also deleted, which may – or may not – affect them as engines in a general sense. We may want to obtain the first behavior if the plane crashed or became obsolete, and the second one if the engines can be reused. These different behaviors arising when a specialized object is deleted must be taken into account at the modeling phase.

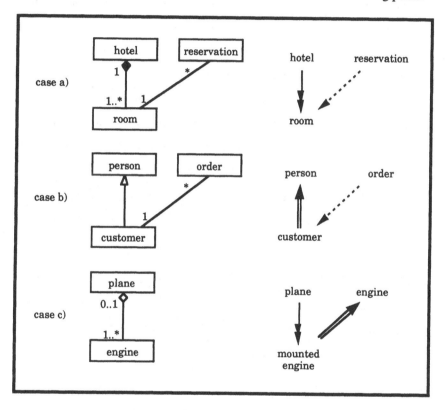

Figure 4 : combination of referential constraints

3. Composition as an Abstraction Mechanism

The main aim of abstraction is to allow things to be represented in a more significant nature by omitting irrelevant details, leading to a better comprehension.

Many approaches have been investigated in the object-oriented paradigm, from entity/relationships-like approaches ([13], [14], [15], [16] amongst others) to software-engineering ones ([17], [18]). These last are amongst the first having presented composition as an abstraction mechanism, by the means of object decomposition. These approaches, however, did not treat referential constraints problems and were designed for improving software development rather than information system specification.

Composition is more flexible than aggregation to elaborate abstractions mechanisms, because component objects are always subordinated to a composite (and only one) object. The evident idea is to hide components into their composite object, but we must pay attention to the different links being involved with the components, because they are still pertinent and must someway be reported onto the composite object. As a matter of facts, abstracting with composition is not always possible : in figure 4 case c, abstracting plane without applying the rules would result in considering planes as inheriting from engines.

Thus, the following rules, based on the work realized in [19], are proposed in order to keep coherent the object schema. Figure 5 illustrates some significant cases.

1. Things resulting from the application of an abstraction mechanism will be called abstract schemes. They may group several classes and so have to be differentiated from the concept of class. They will be represented in dotted rectangles. They may be abstracted like classes under the same conditions.

2. We may abstract a specialized class into its generalized class if and only if the specialized class is not connected with another inheritance link (a).

3. We may abstract a component class into its composite class if and only if the component class is not connected with an inheritance link (b). If the composition link is multiple, all the simple reference links beginning from the component class become multiple (c).

4. We may abstract a referenced class into its referencing class if and only if the referenced class is connected with no other link (d).

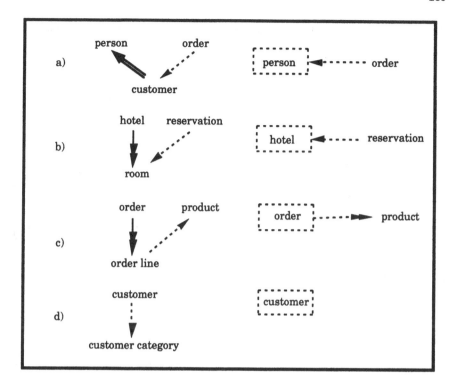

Figure 5 : examples of abstraction

Figure 6 shows an simplified example of two main functions of a business firm, namely, order processing and inventory management. The abstract schemes that may be inferred by a first application of the rules are surrounded.

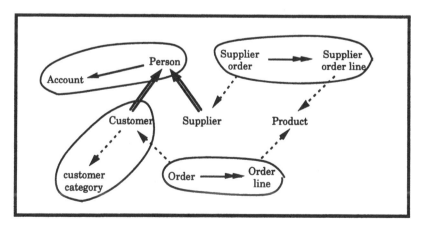

Figure 6 : first application of the rules

The resulting abstracted schema is shown on the left of figure 7, where another abstract scheme derived from a second application of the rules is surrounded. The final schema presented on the right of the figure keeps some essential informations from the initial schema : orders and supplier orders are both placed from a person for a set of products.

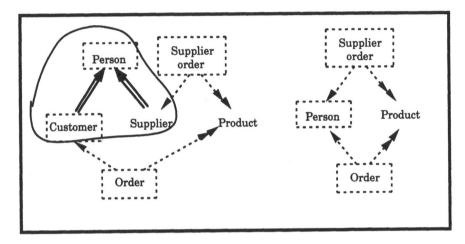

Figure 7 : second application of the rules and final abstract schema

An advantage of integrating such an abstract mechanism into a CASE tool, besides avoiding information overload, is to allow real-time visibility control upon the schema. Classes may be grouped into abstract schemes and inversely abstract schemes may be exploded according to the analysis level needed on the different parts of the schema.

4. Conclusion

In our point of view, aggregation is an unnecessary concept because it can be expressed by the way of more fundamental concepts, such as composition and inheritance. Aggregation is less precise than composition : life cycle interval equality and deletion propagation do no apply oneself. However, aggregation may be useful in describing modeling situations, if it provides precise semantics, as when it is defined as a combination of a composition link and an inheritance link.

The two criteria presented here for finding composition links – life cycle interval equality and deletion propagation – are not only an help for modeling, but also for the elaboration of abstraction mechanisms.

Elsewhere, the decision of maintaining each referential constraint has to be made, by the ways of prevention or deletion propagation, either manually or automatically. Associating deletion propagation with the composition concept fixes this problem in an automatic manner.

References

[1] X. Castellani, "An Overview of the Version 1.1 of the UML Defined with Charts of Concepts", UML'98 Beyond the Notation, International Workshop supported by the OMG, Mulhouse, France, 3-4 June 1998

[2] M. E. Winston, R. Chaffin, D. Herrmann, "A Taxonomy of Part-Whole Relations", Cognitive Science, Vol. 11, pp 417-444, 1987

[3] B. Henderson-Sellers, "OPEN Relationships - Compositions and Containments", Journal of Object-Oriented Programming, Vol. 10, No. 7, Nov/Dec 1997

[4] P.-A. Muller, "Modélisation objet avec UML", Eyrolles, 1997

[5] J. Brunet, "Modeling the World with Semantics Objects", IFIP WG8.1 Conference on the Object-Oriented Approach in Information Systems, Quebec, Oct. 1991

[6] J. Rumbaugh, M. Blaha, W. Premerlani, F. Eddy, W. Lorensen, "Object-Oriented Modeling and Design", Prentice Hall, 1991

[7] M. Adiba, C. Collet, "Objets et bases de données, le SGBD O_2", Hermès, 1993

[8] S. Spaccapietra, C. Parent, "About Entities, Complex Objects and Object-oriented Data Models", Working Conference on Information System Concepts, Namur, Belgium, Oct. 1989

[9] D. Rieu, A. Culet, "Classification et représentations d'objets", Congrès INFORSID, Paris, June 1991

[10] B. K. Ehlmann, G. A. Riccardi, "An integrated and enhanced methodology for modeling and implementing object relationships", Journal of Object-Oriented Programming, Vol. 10, No. 2, May 1997

[11] B. Henderson-Sellers, "OPEN Relationships - Associations, Mappings, Dependencies, and Uses", Journal of Object-Oriented Programming, Vol. 10, No. 9, Feb. 1997

[12] M. Fowler, K. Scott, "UML distilled, Applying the Standard Object-Modeling Language", Eds J. C. Shanklin, Addison-Wesley, 1997

[13] P. A. Bres, J. P. Carrère, "Un Modèle de Comportement d'Objets Naturels", AFCET, Autour et à l'entour de Merise, 1991

[14] P. Desfray, "Object Oriented Structuring : An Alternative to Hierarchical Models", Technology of Object-Oriented Languages and Systems, USA, 1991

[15] W. Kozaczynski, L. Lilien, "An Extended Entity-Relationship (E^2R) Database Specification into the Logical Relational Design", Proceedings of the Sixth International Conference on Entity-Relationship Approach, New York, Nov. 1987

[16] T. J. Teorey, G. Wei, D. L. Bolton, John A. Koenig, "ER Model Clustering as an Aid for User Communication and Documentation in Database Design", Communications of the ACM, Vol. 32, No. 8, Aug. 1989

[17] G. Booch, "Object-Oriented Design with Application", Benjamin/Cummings, 1991

[18] P. Coad, E. Yourdon, "Object-Oriented Analysis", Prentice-Hall, Englewood Cliffs, N. J., 1990

[19] L. S. Peck, J. Brunet, C. Rolland, "Abstraction in the O* object-oriented method", Indo-French Workshop on Object-Oriented Systems, Goa, Nov. 1992

How to Introduce Emergence in Object Evolution

D. Tamzalit, C. Oussalah, M. Magnan.

LGI2P / EMA-EERIE Parc Scientifique Georges BESSE
30 000 Nîmes - France
e-mail: { tamzalit, oussalah }@eerie.fr magnanm@aol.com

Abstract

The model GENOME takes its ideas from artificial evolution and genetic algorithms. It offers analysis and design processes of the evolution in the two components of an object model: classes and instances. It considers that an instance can evolve without being constricted by class specifications. An instance can than provoke the appearance of simple or complex new object: it is the Emergence Process. It outlines therefore its expression through associations, composition or inheritance links.

Key words: analysis and design of evolution - genetic approach - genotype - phenotype - fundamental genotype - evolution filters - development process - emergence process.

1. Introduction

The object-oriented analysis and design has for sometime now permitted the development and reuse of applications which are widely evolutionary. In practice, the result is applications lacking flexibility and subject to problems of adaptation. As a matter of fact, most strategies of evolution take on only the concept of evolution; they do not take on a process of evolutionary analysis and design.

The current paper presents GENOME (Genetic-EvolutioN Object ModEl) in its concepts and evolution processes based on artificial evolution principles. We distinguish two kinds of processes : *development* and *emergence*. These last are constituted of *local* and *global emergence processes*. The former deals with instance evolution causing evolution of their classes. The latter deals with instance evolution requiring creation of new abstractions through new classes.

This paper is organized as follows: section 2 exposes the general problem of the evolution of object representation, and describes succinctly the main strategies of class and instance evolution in many areas (OODB, AI, CAD,...). Section 3 describes our main objectives and goes on to an interpretation of object evolution from artificial life and genetic algorithm viewpoints. Basic genetic concepts and operators are presented for our genetic object model. Section 4 deals with the evolution of such a model by first defining genetic object evolution, then by describing its implementation. Section 4.2.6 concludes this paper.

2. Object Evolution

An object model evolves during the time when one of its components (class/instance) is evolving. In such a case, changes of hierarchy and class definition must be propagated towards instances and sub-classes [20]. Impacts in the model must then be managed. Various object evolutionary strategies have been proposed [15], [24], [26]. They differ in their objectives, axis of interest and adaptation to the needs of use areas.

2.1 Problem

Evolution problems can be encountered as much in design as in operating phases. In the former, the model can often be unstable and partially defined, so needing an incremental specification. In the latter, the model can be revised and re-expressed during its lifetime. An evolutionary object representation must ensure the consistency and pertinence of modeled information and functionality. But most of approaches take on the evolution concept but do not take on the analysis and design process of evolution. In addition, the evolutionary strategies proposed do not always fulfill users' needs. In fact, sometimes a model does not know how to react to evolution stimuli coming from the exterior (environment, users) or the interior (component evolution), particularly if they are not predictable.

2.2 Object evolution: existing strategies

2.2.1 Class Evolution

Experience shows that users' needs are rarely stable and that designers experience difficulties classifying software components into predefined taxonomies. In fact, representing reality by means of classes and instances using links is not always a trivial task. Other problems are linked to the difficulties of building stable and reusable classes. There are five main strategies for managing evolution of classes:

• **Algorithmic approaches: class reorganization$_{(1)}$, class classification$_{(2)}$ and categorization$_{(3)}$**: *class reorganization* [8] presents an algorithm allowing the insertion of a new class by restructuring the class hierarchy; *class classification* in KR and AI [23] turns its attention only to the insertion of a class; *categorization* [19] consists in describing data by distributing amongst a restrained number of homogeneous classes which regroup objects having similarities in features and behavior.

• **Class correction$_{(4)}$**: used in OODB [4], [22]. The principle is to pass the requested update to the implied class or set of classes, changing this latter or even fully reorganizing the hierarchy. All necessary adjustments must be anticipated by defining a taxonomy of update operations.

• **Class adjustments$_{(5)}$**: principally used in AI and Software Engineering. Adaptations are applied to inherited properties when deriving sub-classes, keeping a class hierarchy stable by avoiding modifying it at each evolution [18].

• **Class versioning$_{(6)}$**: widely used in OODB [15], [26], [13], in CAD [25] and in Software Engineering [1]. Any evolution in a class provokes the derivation of a new version of the class. It ensures updates only on copies, by creating new versions of classes in such a way that existing applications continue to use original versions.

• **View points**(7) : the goal of the viewpoints [7] is to make class evolution transparent by translating a class evolution by creation of a view. These mechanisms are adapted to the derivation of new abstractions and the update propagation of virtual instances to real ones [5].

2.2.2 Impacts of class evolution on instances

There are three strategies:

• **Instance conversion**(8): instances are adapted to the new class definition by physical reorganization. There are two principal strategies for this: *immediate conversion* [22] and *deferred conversion* [4], [16]. The first automatically does the instance conversion immediately after the evolution of their class, but the base is inaccessible during the conversion. The second consists in adapting each instance individually the first time it is accessed after its class modification. These two strategies can be combined, as in the system O_2[3].

• **Instance emulation**(9): when the instance is accessed, it is interpreted by means of filter linking the physical representation of the instance and the definition of its class. This technique is often used along with class versioning [24].

• **Versioning**(10): the principle is to associate one version of an instance with every version of its class [9], [25]. This way, after the modification of a class, as soon as an instance is accessed, the system automatically creates a new version conforming to this new version of the class.

2.2.3 Instance Evolution

There are three main strategies to manage the direct evolution of an instance:

• **Integrity constraints**(11): allow the control of instance evolution by defining structural, behavioral and application constraints [18], [6].

• **Versions**(12): these are used to keep a trace of the several states that an instance can take.

• **Classification of instances**(13): widely used in knowledge systems [23]. It connects instances to potential candidate classes in the hierarchy. In this case, the instance is propagated in the class graph, supplying any instance values which are necessary.

Inadequate inheritance structure, absence of abstractions in a hierarchy, too many specialized components, inappropriate behavior... all these are shortcomings that can appear in a classic object modelisation.

The main lack of existing solutions is their inability to face unpredictable situations, to propose evolutionary processes for analysis and design, and to consequently provoke the evolution of their model. In addition, instance evolution is always linked with the evolution of class hierarchies, this constitutes a certain rigidity aspect in object evolution. One aspect is that an instance cannot provoke the creation of a new abstraction in the class model.

We propose an original approach which aims at being more natural, considering an object model as a system moving in an environment. This system evolves and adapts itself on the base of its self-knowledge and any disturbances which an unstable environment provokes.

3. Genetics & Object: what possible connection?

3.1 Objectives

Our main goal is to modelise evolution processes of an object model in a manner to allow it to adapt itself when a change occurs. The model must take into account needs and components not or worse-anticipated and incorporate them. This integrates the generic objectives of object evolution presented in [21].

We consider evolution as an interactive process of adaptation between classes and instances.

Our objectives are to give a model that can:

1. Evolve by itself from its own information but also from the information that it can retrieve and deduce, restricting external interaction with the user to strategic issues only.

2. Derive and abstract conceptual specifications from the evolution of instances for the purpose of achieving adaptation, paralleling the evolution of conceptual specifications and their triggering of evolution of instances: it is the *Emergence Process*.

For that, object concepts can be analyzed from a genetic point of view and adapted in consequence.

3.2 Artificial Life and Genetic Algorithms

We are interested in artificial life [11] in its perception of a system and its evolution, and in genetic algorithms [12] for their representation of a problem and involved mechanisms to find an adequate solution.

3.2.1 Evolution in Artificial Life

An artificial system can evolve by itself thanks to the knowledge it possesses of its own features. These are defined by its *genes*[1], which defines its genetic patrimony, named GTYPE (from *genotype*[2]). Representative individuals of a system are the realization of this GTYPE in a given environment: they constitute its PTYPE (from *phenotype*[3]) [10].

Thanks to its genetic knowledge, the system can cause the evolution of its component individuals and its genetic patrimony. Thus, evolution of artificial life brings the PTYPE and the GTYPE into play through the two processes of *development* and *emergence*[4]:

• The development process describes the development of the GTYPE in order to create new individuals and enrich the PTYPE[5].

---

[1] Genes are encoded in the form of chromosome.

[2] Genotype :"the genetic patrimony of an individual depending on inherited genes from its parents."

[3] Phenotype :" the set of individual features corresponding to a realization of a genotype, determined by the action of the environment during the organism development."

[4] In the literature, the emergence process is often called reproduction. There, we have preferred the term emergence to avoid any confusion with the reproduction mechanism of genetic algorithms.

[5] The development process is often described in the literature as morphogenesis.

• The emergence process describes the emergence of new properties in individuals, so in the PTYPE, which must in turns be inserted in the GTYPE. It is based on the possessed knowledge of the species, the environment and the immediate context.

3.2.2 Genetic Algorithms

Genetic algorithms [12] are adaptive algorithms of combinatory research and modelise artificial systems capable of adapting in response to disturbances in their environment [10].

The *Simple Genetic Algorithm* can be applied to any problem because the fundamental mechanism brought into play is always the same, but is dependent on the way it is specified. The genetic algorithm operates on populations of individuals. Each individual is a potential solution. Its characteristics are encoded by means of a *chromosome* which contains all its genes. The alphabet often used is the binary one {0, 1}. Chromosomes are encoded by strings of bits having the same length. Each bit represents a precise feature: a *gene*. A value of 1 specifies that the corresponding gene is present in the individual, 0 that it is absent.

These solutions evolve thanks to genetic operators. The principle is to take two solutions and to make them reproduce to try to pick up the best genes in child individuals, ensuring thus the survival of solution populations. This is implemented in two phases which complete each other: *exploration* of sub-sets of solutions, and *exploitation* of obtained results. Used mechanisms are the random selection applied to individuals whose chromosomes are best-adapted; the crossover of two *parents* chromosomes generates two child by interchange of genes; the mutation is occasionally used to mutate a gene in order to avoid too early a convergence of solutions. The selection of best adapted chromosomes involves quantitative measurement, *fitness adaptation*, of their adaptation thanks to a *fitness function*.

In addition, genetic algorithms operate on *schemes*. A scheme is an entity having the same genetic structure as the population it represents. This allows the specification of a sub-set of a population's genes and any unspecified genes are considered as indifferent and are represented by an indifference symbol, like #. Thus, the scheme 11### can represent any chromosome of a population having the first two genes present. It is a simple and powerful means to modelise all the members of a sub-population simultaneously.

3.3 Genetic evolution model: basic concepts & operators

We propose adapting artificial life concepts and genetic algorithm mechanisms to object evolution. Basic concepts (section 3.3.1) PTYPE and GTYPE are borrowed from artificial life while basic operators (section 3.3.3) and the scheme concept (section 3.3.4) are taken from genetic algorithms. The advanced concepts of fundamental, inherited and specific genotypes (section 3.3.2) are particular to our model and represent a deeper vision of genotype.

3.3.1 Basic Genetic Concepts: PTYPE and GTYPE

The data of an object model are its classes and instances. They represent the evolving matter. We consider them as the expression of the individuals and the genetic characteristics of the model, more precisely:

•**PTYPE:** from the viewpoint of object modelisation, the representative individuals of a model are its instances, that we qualify by analogy, as PTYPE. To each class is connected its set of instances: its *population*. All instances of the same population have the same genetic code - specified by their parent class. Classes define different genes and consequently, different populations.

•**GTYPE:** the genetic code of instances represents their structural and behavioral characteristics. They are present and specified inside their class - that we qualify as the GTYPE. The classes specify the encoding of instance characteristics through attributes and methods, thus represent the genes through chromosomes.

3.3.2 Advanced Genetic Concepts: Fundamental Genotype, Inherited Genotype and Specific Genotype:

A class defines the genotype of the sub-population it specifies. This genotype is thus constituted of genes. However, each gene doesn't play the same role and hasn't the same predominance either in the semantics it holds nor in the influence it could have on evolution and specifications for possible descendants. From these criteria (semantics and predominance on evolution), we outline the three following types of genotypes:

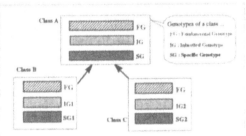

Figure 1: *the three genotypes of a class..*

We consider that every class is entirely specified through three groups of genes, so through three genotypes: the *fundamental genotype*, the *inherited genotype* and the *specific genotype*.

•**Fundamental Genotype FG:** each object presents fundamental features which allow it to exist. For example, an employee may lose his job and become consequently an unemployed worker, but he stays a person (it's obviously supposed that notions of person, employee, and unemployed worker exist in the corresponding model). These features are represented by specific genes held by the class. Without them, an object of this class can no longer concern the population they define or this object can no longer exist. We call this group of genes *fundamental genotype*.

A set of classes having the same FG are classes organized in a specialization tree. Even if the properties they define are different, they all have a common core which expresses their similarity: its their FG. Since an FG changes, the core of another abstraction is expressed : we are talking about something else.

The following genotypes are issued from the specificity of classical object models.

•**Inherited Genotype IG:** a class inherits properties from its super-class through the inheritance link. Except FG, every class inherits the other properties of it super-class that it can redefine or overload. It is the *inherited genotype*. It can differ from one class to another. In Figure 1 for example, $IG1_{class\ B} = IG_{class\ A} + SG_{class\ A}$ and $IG2_{class\ C} = IG_{class\ A} + SG_{class\ A}$.

• **Specific Genotype SG:** it is constituted from properties locally defined within a class.

3.3.3 Object Genetic Operators: Selection, Reproduction, Crossover, and Mutation

It is necessary to define the basic operators that allow PTYPE and GTYPE to be handled. The operators used to handle are those of selection, reproduction, and crossover:

• **Selection:** chooses a class or an instance according to a given criterion: partial or total identity of structure/behavior. The selection of entities according to another entity can be done in sequence or in parallel, and it operates on the adaptation of an entity to a given problem or application.

• **Reproduction:** allows duplication of the genetic code of a class. Instantiation, in the "object" sense, can be seen as the reproduction operator. In the case of single instantiation, it is mono-parental reproduction. In the case of multiple instantiation, reproduction is multi-parental. The instance then has the genetic code of its class, to which it gives value. Values differ from one instance to another, thus giving different PTYPE elements.

• **Crossover:** lets two entities or more exchange their genes in order to define a new chromosome. The chromosome stemming from a crossover is also a potential new entity of the model: a class or an instance. It therefore allows the emergence of new information. It is the evolutionary process par excellence.

• **Mutation:** is used when the selection and crossover operators do not give worthwhile results. It consists of any operation that can modify a genetic code. The consequence is dual: first target another part of the model to carry out research and ensure evolution; second try to restore, if possible, genetic structures lost when modifying the object's structure, or even create a new one.

3.3.4 Notion of Genetic Program and concept of Scheme

• **Notion of *Genetic Program:*** the different basic operators previously presented are defined by programs bound to the class model, called *genetic programs.* They represent all the operators that a model can possess in order to achieve more complex evolutionary processes. This way, each time one of these operators is necessary, its genetic program (GP) is triggered. These programs are independent and thus can operate in sequence or in parallel, if necessary.

• **Concept of Scheme:** the selection process can be applied as well to a class as to an instance. The scheme is the selection unit used in our model in order to achieve evolutionary processes. It is the unit on which the selection works and whose success at a given time governs the population's genetic evolution. The scheme represents the genetic patrimony which is the durable entity because it is transmitted, in opposition to individuals. The scheme is an entity implied in a competition with other similar entities, and whose success, in this competition, and propagation are closely related. The genetic difference will be diffused in the population, and will cause the appearance of new similar units.

This concept presents a double advantage: the expression of the existence or not of genes, and even their indifference at the genetic level of an entity, as well for a class as for an instance. On one hand, it allows to include several entities in the exploration phase, and on the other to apply the concept indifferently to a class or to an instance, thus giving an advantage to the unification of the classes and instances expression, and their manipulation thanks to the aforementioned operators. The scheme is seen as an expression of a *genetic constraint* to which the individuals are submitted, and which is expressed through the specified positions of the scheme. A scheme is also seen as a partial specification of the genetic patrimony. Certain individuals of the population can carry the scheme, others no. This fact will allow to choose the future parents without ambiguity.

We consider two principal kinds of schemes: *permanent* and *temporary*.

• **Permanent scheme:** a scheme is associated to each class. It has a structure identical to a class's because it express the genetic code of its instances. Consequently, a scheme comprises three parts: fundamental genotype, inherited genotype and specific genotype.

• **Temporary scheme:** it is a unit of selection of a set of entities (classes or instances) having the same characteristics. Temporary schemes are especially useful during the evolution of models, for they are used as an initial filter.

The following section deals with evolution of a genetic object model and considers and identifies the general processes of evolution before going into modeling object evolution by means of the concepts and basic operators described above.

4. Towards a Genetic Evolution Object Model

Every entity of the real world is represented in an object model by a couple (class, instance). Every entity is then specified in an object model by a phenotype and a genotype. Reality changes; its model too. It must then evolve to conform to reality. Its evolution must be triggered as well by instance as by class evolution.

Generally in applications, it is instances which evolve more often than class specifications. Changes of class specifications came from the fact that the instances do not respond more to real needs. Thus, for evolution strategies, changes are brought to concerned classes before causing the instances to evolve.

The main reason to consider evolution by class changes is that they hold conceptual specifications and that an instance must always respect them. An instance cannot evolve freely and even less introduce conceptual information.

We propose the GENOME model, which allows instances as well as classes to evolve and to cause the evolution of classes and instances respectively.

4.1 The evolution of a genetic object model from the viewpoint of Artificial Life

We explain the general process of evolution through the following retroactive and iterative loop, from the viewpoint of artificial life, as for genetic algorithms presented in this general process of evolution defined by artificial life [11].

An instance, like any phenotype, is a realization of a genotype for the inherited features; it defines individual features. Its creation and modification issue from classes in the *Development Process*. The genotype is modified by genetic mutations and recombination from new features in the phenotype and/or from disturbances issuing from the environment. In this fashion, existing genes can be combined and modified, and new genes can thus appear. This is the *Emergence Process*.

The strategies and techniques mentioned in section 2 are distributed as follows in Figure 2: the strategies from (1) to (7) are at class level; strategy (3) allows the factoring of common properties of instances into classes. These strategies can trigger the evolution of instances - in the development process, for which strategies (8), (9) and (10) can be used as for strategies (11), (12) and (13), they are at instance level, without any impact at the class level.

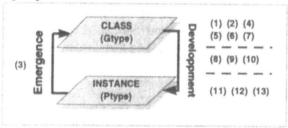

Figure 2: *Object Evolutionary Process from an Artificial Life viewpoint.*

Consequently, we can say that most research work on the evolution of class specifications concerns the development process, because they cause or offer a management of the impact on evolution of instances. However, to our knowledge, only the categorization (3) can concern the process of emergence of new classes from instances.

We consider that object evolution uncovers a shortcoming in the evolutionary process: the processes of emergence and adaptive evolution of new properties from the evolution of instances. We are going to focus on this aspect of evolution - which to our knowledge has not yet been tackled in a dynamic fashion.

4.2 Implementation of evolution

Before turning to the process of evolution, we have to define the way of encoding the genes of handled entities through the scheme concept. Then, we will explain the adaptive function used, and finally we will describe some evolutionary processes. In the outline of evolution and in this first phase of the definition of our genetic evolution model, we consider structural and behavioral genes in the same manner.

4.2.1 Context of modelisation

Our modelisation context is that of complex object modeling. We mean by complex object, an object that defines semantic links towards other objects. These objects are called its *constituents*. The complex object is also defined by a complex structure. Composite objects, for example, are particular complex objects. Its constituents are called its *components*. The semantic links are called *composition links*. A composite object is constituted by its components, and each of them describes a part of the composite object. Note that a complex object model handles also simple objects and that class organization relies on the inheritance link.

We consider that each attribute and method of a class for an instance can be either *compulsory* or *optional*. A compulsory attribute of a class C must be valued by each instance of this class. For an optional attribute, an instance may or may not have a value for it. In the same way, a compulsory method defines a behavior necessarily present for each instance of C, an optional method defines a behavior possibly present for any instance of C. Such a modelisation allows the introduction of flexibility in the modelisation of classes, and consequently of their instances.

A class keeps and possibly restrains its inherited properties. It is the same for the compulsory/optional type of a property or a method. A compulsory property (or method) of a class stays compulsory in its sub-classes. An optional property (or method) can become compulsory in one or more of its sub-classes.

4.2.2 Scheme and coding - Adaptive function

• **The scheme and its coding:** a scheme must be simply and concisely coded in order to allow rapid and accurate expressing and filtering of instances and classes. We describe a scheme with the following minimal alphabet {0, 1, #}. Every time a class is specified, the type of its properties[6] (compulsory or optional) is automatically translated by reference to a scheme. The correspondence between property type and its representing gene in the scheme is as follows: a property compulsorily present is represented by 1; an optional property is represented by #; a property compulsorily absent is represented by 0 (this final point is particularly useful during transitory step in evolutionary processes).

The example in Figure 3, which is a part of a model representing different sorts of members of a research laboratory, outlines notions and concepts used, by distinguishing FG, IG, and SG, and by defining class associated schemes and distinguishing compulsory from optional properties. The adaptive function used is defined here after:

• **Adaptive function:** we use a function which is executed on two schemes having the same length. As entry parameter, it has the scheme of the examined entity, which it compares with the scheme of another entity by a comparison of their genes. Denoting the scheme of the entity as Sch_{obj} and the scheme of the explored entity as Sch_{param}, we define the adaptive function as:

$$Va\ (Schparam) = \sum (i = 1 \rightarrow n)\ \{\ Schobj[i]\ operat\ Schparam[i]\ \}\ /\ n$$

Where:

- operat can be one of the two operators defined subsequently;
- Va is the adaptive value;
- n is the length of the two schemes;
- i is the rate, varying from 1 to n, which defines at each step the gene position of the two compared schemes.

However, the importance of the FG implies that its comparison differs from IG and SG ones. In fact, in order to compare that two entities, it is necessary to have coherency between their respective FG.

---

[6] *By property we mean an attribute as well as a method.*

So, two schemes first have their FG compared thanks to the operator $\oplus$, defined as follow:

$\oplus$	0	1	#
0	1	0	0
1	0	1	0
#	0	0	1

If Va=1, then the comparison can be pursued. It will concern the IG and SG. The operator used is $\otimes$ and defined by:

$\otimes$	0	1	#
0	1	0	0
1	0	1	1
#	0	1	1

A gene absent in one but present in the other is unfavorable and the result is penalized with a 0 value. With different comparisons between 1 and #, and 0 and #, the adaptation value is incremented by one, the reason being that, even if the gene is optional, the corresponding entity contains its genetic code.

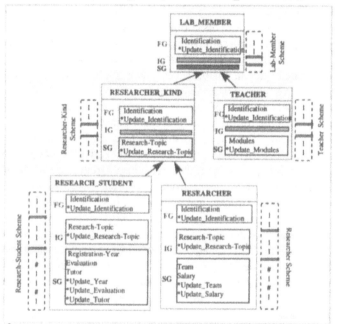

Figure 3: *An example with schemes, different genotypes compulsory and optional properties.*

This manipulation of the instance in two steps has to be done first on a particular group of genes before the other genes. This implies the use of two levels of granularity. The first level is the filtering through the FG. The granularity is a group of genes. The second is one filtering (or several) through the other genes ; granularity is a gene.

Concepts and operators defined in section 1 are the elementary granularity of representation and manipulation for exploration and exploitation.

4.2.3 Evolutionary processes

We are going to treat the case of instance evolution and its various possible impacts on classes.

• **Introduction :** when an instance evolves in its values, while continuing to respect its class specifications, it is an evolution of the phenotype without impacts on the genotype. However, as soon as the instance does not conform to its class, its

304

evolution may require that of its genes: the evolution of the genotype and the emergence of new genetic information are necessary. This evolution is diversify. We classify it like this:

1.**Development processes:** are all processes of phenotypic evolution, i.e. the evolution in the values of instances without requiring modifications at the genotype level (classes).

2.**Emergence processes:** concern any evolution that causes the modification of a class model by emergence of new conceptual information. These modifications can be several:

- Correcting existent specifications of classes without modifying FG.
- Adding/deleting properties in specifications of existent classes without modifying FG.
- Emerging new abstractions, as complex, composite, or simple objects.

• **General principle:** the general principle is to extract from the evolved instance its genetic code into a scheme. This scheme holds references at 1 or 0 whether that the instance valuate or not an attribute, but it does not have an indifferent attribute. So the corresponding scheme has no gene at #.

The evolution processes are divided in an *exploration phase* followed by an *exploitation phase* of the results of the precedent phase (Figure 4). The exploration begins as soon as an instance is modified. This exploration is based on the comparison of the genetic codes of the instance and of every explored class, beginning from its initial class in order to retrieve a parent class candidate.

When an instance evolves, it passes from a coherent state towards another state which must be controlled. In classical approaches of object evolution, the instance is controlled in order to respect specifications of existing classes.

When an evolved instance does no longer corresponds to its class specification and it can no longer remain in this class or be attached to another class, because that FG are different. Before deciding to create a new corresponding class, we propose to exploit eventual links between classes which can bring common information with those carried by the instance. In fact, the instance may express a simple object as well as a complex one.

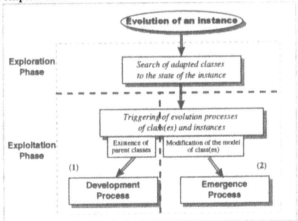

Figure 4: *the evolution through Exploration and Exploitation phases.*

So, the exploration phase can find a candidate class : the evolutionary process yield is the development one. In the other case, the evolutionary processes yield are those of emergence ones. Thus :

• If the exploration phase found a candidate class, their FG are identical, the development process is triggered. It allows to cause the emergence inside the candidate class, new properties. These properties can be simple : it is a simple object. They can be complex : it is a complex object.

• If the exploration phase does not find a candidate class, the instance may involve several other objects. It means that other links than the inheritance one can be involved. The instance expresses than a complex object. The emergence processes may cause the emergence of a new complex object from existent entities. They may also cause the emergence of a new original object.

In order to efficiently recover the conceptual structure yield, we have to organize the analysis of the instance according to very specific criteria. This analysis is based on an *evolutionary filter*.

4.2.4 Evolutionary filter:

A simple object and a complex object are distinguishable in the complexity of their structure. A simple object presents simple attributes, and its only structural link with other objects is the inheritance one which links it strongly to with its super-class(es). A complex object has, in addition, several links with other objects. These links differ in the semantics they hold and thanks to which the objects are more or less strongly coupled.

In order to find which emergence process to trigger, we propose to use a filter which is based on the existence of link expression within an instance.

• **Definition:** links are generally classified according to their cognitive or functional aspect. The functional classification is more rigorous because it is based on the relational theory. It takes into account dependence links between related objects according to the following relational elements: *inclusion, connection,* and *similarity.*

The filter must detect in the instance the eventual expression of association, composition or fusion links. As in the relation theory, we have established an order relation in the filtering of the instance. It is similar to the order relation defined by links. The different links are defined with the relational elements as follows :

- Association (Connection)
- Composition (Connection, Inclusion)
- Inheritance (Connection, Inclusion, Similarity)

By defining the operator $<_{Sem}$, the evolutionary filter follow the following order in the link semantics :

$$\text{Association} <_{Sem} \text{Composition} <_{Sem} \text{Inheritance}$$

In conclusion, the evolutionary filter is used in order to analysis an evolved instance to know which emergence process must be triggered.

These emergence processes must then :

• Retrieve a complex structure from links and components, via an instance.

• Cause new links emerge (association, composition, inheritance) between existent objects via an instance.

• Cause new abstractions emergence in the class model : it is the global emergence process.

It is necessary to note that in the different kinds of evolution handled, we use structures and properties which are known (inheritance, composition, association, ...) by using new concepts and notions. One of these new aspects consists in that we do not first determine the different possible states of an instance. This allows for more openness in its evolution and, in addition, the instance can specify existing information but also to introduce new information. In addition, the user will be able to specify new types of links that he can express with the relational elements of connection, inclusion and similarity. This will enrich the predefined existent links.

4.2.5 Illustrations of evolutionary processes:

• **Development Processes**

Objectives: a development process is any process allowing the modification of instances of a class, either by creation of a new instance or by modification of instance values and/or class membership. Beyond instantiation, we consider the development process and its stages:

1. **Evolution of an instance** Int of a class C taking on a new attribute.

2. **Exploration phase:** search parent classes candidate for the instance:

• **Derivation of the scheme of the instance** in its new state.

• **Search for a candidate parent class:** this process is recursive until it finds a suitable class or not, based on the use of the adaptive function.

• **Verification of the conformity of the instance** Int to the class C being explored. This operation is possible by making their schemes similar in structure. Every one of them is completed by genes of the other scheme: their values are then 0. The verification is first achieved on the FG thanks to the execution of the adaptive function with the operator $\oplus$. If the value is equal to 1, then the adaptive function continuous to progress thanks to the operator $\otimes$ on the IG and SG. If there is conformity, the instance can be attached to C.

• If the Int's IG is more general than that of class C, the system continues its exploration with C's super-class(es) and sister classes having the same FG. The process continues from the precedent step.

• If Int's IG is more restricted than class C's, the system continues its exploration in sub-classes of C. For each sub-class, the process continues from the beginning.

• **Selection of the parent class candidate:** if the exploration phase finds a class of the model whose adaptation value is equal to 1 for the FG, the instance Int must then be attached to this class if the IG and SG of the class's scheme and the instance's scheme are not in contradiction.

3. **Exploitation phase:** instance Int is attached to the selected class. Int's scheme is a temporary one used only during evolution. It is destroyed afterwards. If necessary, the instance must be adjusted to conform to its new class.

• **Emergence Processes**

Objectives: emergence processes enrich existing class specifications in an automatic manner from new information introduced by evolved instances. They allow to refine existing class specifications and to derive new classes in order to represent missing abstractions in the class model.

We present two extreme emergence processes: the *local emergence*, which allows to add or to take off a property from a class, and the *global emergence*, which allows to extract a new class from the instance.

1) - Local emergence process

When an instance introduces new attributes, if no class corresponds to the new instance and the inherited semantics are coherent between the instance and its class, this one must evolve and update its specification: a new attribute will emerge inside it: this is *local emergence*.

When an instance evolves and loses a local attribute, and if this attribute is compulsory, its type changes and becomes optional, which allows the instance to stay attached to its initial class while no danger possessing the attribute in question; this obviates the need to modify previously defined instances.

2) - Global emergence process

When no class can be the parent of the evolved instance, two cases can occur: the instance's genetic code either presents incoherence with its ancestors - thus the user must intervene; or it contains new genes or other genes are present among other classes and must be derived. This situation expresses the need of the specification of a new abstraction inside the class model. The system triggers the crossover operator between the genetic codes of the selected classes and the instance, in order to derive the scheme of the new abstraction. The resulting scheme will permit the definition of a first specification of the new associated class.

Exploitation phase:

• **Application of the evolution filters:** the first filter, the association one, does not find the expression of connection between two objects. The instance will then eventually express a new abstraction.

• **Selection of entities having an adaptation value different then 0:** that means the entities whose FG present coherency.

• **Conformity of schemes of different selected entities and the instance's one:** these entities have possibly a part of conceptual information necessary to the new instance specification. Once respective schemes have similar structures, the crossover operator is invoked through its associated genetic program.

• **Choice of crossing-over points:** this must have a precise semantic. We propose to take a crossing-over point at every gene or group of genes at 0. In fact, a gene at 0 in a scheme is an attribute absent in the corresponding class which cannot transmit it to a new class.

• **Crossover operation:** groups of genes must be crossed-over in order to derive the structural specification of the new class. The instance is then attached to the class.

• **Specification of the new class:** the crossover, when accomplished, allows specifying a new abstraction inside a class, seen as an unrefined class. It is a specification responding minimally to a need expressed by the user, but at the time maximally relative to what the model can offer. The user can then refine it. Subsequently, this class is inserted in the class graph and all consequences must be managed.

4.2.6 Examples:

1) - Development process:

- **Evolution of an instance:** from a research student to a teacher.
- **Exploration phase:** search of candidate parent classes for the instance Int_1 in its new state:
  - **Derivation of the scheme of the instance Int_1:**

Attributes	*Identification*					Modules
Values	"Jean"					C^{++}
Scheme	1	0	0	0	0	1

- **Search of candidate parent class(es):**
- **Verification of the conformity of the instance** Int_1 **to its initial class** Research-Student. Schemes must be adjusted. They become:

1	1	1	1	1	0
1	0	0	0	0	1

- The exploration phase searches in the class model a possible parent class.
- **Selection of candidate parent class(es):** Teacher class is Int_1's parent class.
- **Exploitation phase:** the instance Int_1 is linked to the selected class Teacher. Int_1's scheme is destroyed. The development process has modified the extension of both Research-Student and Teacher classes.

2) - Local emergence process:

- **Evolution of an instance:** an instance Int_2 of Research-Student evolves by acquiring a new attribute:

"Jean"	"Object"	"CNET"	2	"Correct"	"Dupont"

- **Exploration phase:**
  - **Derivation of the instance's scheme:**

1	1	1	1	1	1

  - **Search of a candidate parent class:**

We obtain the following schemes for all handled attributes:

Identif	Topic	**Project**	year	Evaluation	Tutor
1	1	0	1	#	1
1	1	1	1	1	1

Adaptation value	1	1	0	1	1	1	Va= 5/6

- **Exploitation phase = local emergence process:** after the evolution process, The class possesses the following attributes and scheme:

Identif	Topic	Project	Year	Evaluation	Tutor
1	1	#	1	#	1

3) - Global emergence process:

- **Evolution of instance :**

An instance Int_3 of Researcher evolves and become:

Identif	Topic			Team	Salary
"Paul"	"Object"	"C++"	"CNET"	"Object"	10000

- **Exploration phase:** search of candidate parent classes:
  - **Derivation of the instance's scheme:**

Identif	Topic	Modules	Project	Team	Salary
1	1	1	1	1	1

- **Search of a candidate parent class:** at the end of the process, another class than `Researcher` has been selected: the `Teacher` class.
- **Exploitation phase = Global emergence process:**
The most adapted classes: classes whose genetic code is the nearest of the one of instance Int_3 are `Researcher` and Teacher classes. Their adaptation value are respectively 2/3 and 1/3.
- **Choice of crossover points:** information held by Int_3 is present in these two classes and itself introduces a new one. It expresses a different abstraction. As it does not violate existing specification classes, the system can effectively derive from it the specification of a class. To do so, it will achieve a crossover between the three schemes `Researcher`, `Teacher` and Int_3. It must choose one or more crossover points, achieve exchange both genes and obtain an automatic specification of a new class from the three schemes.
- **Crossover:** the crossover done is:

Researcher scheme	1	1	0	0	#	1
Teacher scheme	1	0	1	0	0	0
Scheme of Instance `Int`$_3$	1	1	1	1	1	1
New scheme	1	1	1	1	#	1

5. Conclusion

We have defined the foundations of a genetic object evolution model named GENOME. The evolution of an object model from a genetic viewpoint passes first by the specification in genetic form of the objects (classes or instances).

Our approach of evolution consists in allowing an instance to evolve in a open manner, and then to analyze it in its new state. The first analysis consists in verifying that the instance is not in contradiction with its "species". Subsequently, it is necessary to find to which entity of the model this instance can be attached: a simple, composite or complex object. The interests are multiple: find a complex (composite) object from its constituents (components) by invoking the association (composition) links. The instance can also make it possible to cause the emergence of new links, and even new classes.

Few research works in object world [17], [2] have been interested by the specificity of natural species and genetic algorithms in order to apply them to object modelisation. It seems for us that the object world can benefit from the simple and powerful natural aptitudes surrounding us, which it can further adapt.

References

[1]-M. Ahmed-Nacer « *Un modèle de gestion et d'évolution de schéma pour les bases de données de génie logiciel.* » Thèse doctorat. INPGrenoble, France, Juillet 1994.

[2]-H. Astudillo « *Maximizing Object Reuse with a Biological Metaphor* », pp. 235-251, Theory and Practice of Object Systems, Vol 3, N°4, 1997, A Wiley-Interscience Publication, John Wiley & Sons, Inc.

[3]-F.Bancilhon, G. Barbedette, V. Benzaken, C.Delobel, S. Gamerman, C. Lécluse, P. Pfeffer, P. Richard, F. Velez « *The Design and Implementation of O₂ an OODBS.* » Rapport Technique *Altaïr* 20-88. 13 avril 1988.

[4] -J. Banerjee, W. Kim, H. Kim, H. F. Korth. « *Semantics Implementation of Schema Evolution in OODB.* » ACM 1987.

[5]-B. Benatallah, M-C. FAUVET « *Le point sur l'évolution du schéma d'une BD.* » in L'Objet: Logiciel, BD, Réseaux. Vol 3. N°3- Sept 97. pp 277-297. Ed. Hermes.

[6]-F. Bounaas « *Gestion de l'évolution dans les bases de connaissances* », Thèse doctorat INPGrenoble, France, Octobre 1995

[7]-E. Bratsberg « *Evolution and Integration of Classes in OODB* » PhD thesis, Norwegian Institute Technology, jun. 1993.

[8]-E. Casais « *Managing Evolution in OO Environnements:An Algorithmic Approach* » Thèse - Université de Genève. 1991

[9]-S. M. Clamen « *Schema Evolution and Integration* » Proc. DPD conf., vol. 2, p 101-126. Kluwer Academic Publishers, Boston, 1994

[10]-D. E.Goldberg « *Algorithmes Génétiques* » IA-Edition Addison-Wesley 94

[11]-J-C. Heudin « *La Vie Artificielle* ». Ed. Hermes, 1994.

[12]-J. Holland: « *Adaptation in Natural and Artificial Systems* », University of Michigan Press, Ann Arbor, Mich., 1975.

[13]-R.H. Katz, E. Chang « *Managing change in a computer-aided design database.* »VLDB'87, pp 455-462, Brighton, England, Sept. 1987.

[14]-S.E. Keene « OO Programming in Common Lisp: A Programmer's Guide to CLOS» Addison-Wesley Reading MA, 1989.

[15]-W. Kim, H. T. Chou « *Versions of schema for OODB* » Proc. VLDB88, Los Angeles, Californie, 1988.

[16]-B.S. Lerner, A.N. Habermann « *Beyond Schema Evolution to Database Reorganization* » Proc. ACM Conf. OOPSLA & ECOOP, Ottawa, Canada, Oct. 90, pp. 67-76.

[17]-D. Meslati & S. Ghoul « *Semantic Classification:genetic approach to classification in OO models*» JOOP Jan 97.

[18]-B.Meyer « *OO Software Construction* » International Series in Computer Science. Prenctice Hall, 1988.

[19]-A. Napoli « *Représentation à objets et raisonnement par classification en I.A.* ». Thèse de doctorat, Nancy 1992.

[20]-G. T. Nguyen, D. Rieu « *Schema Evolution in OODB* » DKE, North-Holland, Vol 4, pp 43-67, Juillet 1989.

[21]-C. Oussalah & alii « *Ingénierie Objet: Concepts et techniques* » InterEditions 1997.

[22] -D.J. Penney, J. Stein « *Class modification in the GemStone OODBMS* » SIGPLAN Notices (Proc OOPSLA'87) Vol. 22, No. 12, pp. 111-117.

[23]-F. Rechenman, P. Uvietta « *SHIRKA: an object-centered knowldege bases management system.* » A.Pavé and G. Vansteenkiste ed ALEAS Lyon France pp9-23.

[24]-A.H. Skarra, S.B. Zdonik « *Type Evolution in an OODB.* » Research Directions in OOP, MIT Press Series in Computer Systems, MIT Press, Cambridge, MA, 1987, pp. 393-415.

[25]-G. Talens, C. Oussalah, M.F. Colinas « *Versions of Simple and Composite Objects* »VLDB'93 Aout 93 Dublin-Ireland.

[26]-S. B. Zdonik « *OO Type Evolution* » DPL, F. Bancilhon & P. Buneman eds, ACM Press, NY 1990, pp. 277-288.

EVOLUTION AND
INTEROPERABILITY

Defining Rules for Schema Transformation

Yangjun Chen

Wolfgang Benn

IPSI Institute, GMD GmbH
64293 Darmstadt, Germany
yangjun@darmstadt.gmd.de

Department of Computer Science
TU Chemnitz, 09107 Chemnitz, Germany
benn@informatik.tu-chemnitz.de

Abstract In this paper, we propose a rule-based methodology to do schema transformation as a first step of integrating databases. The methodology consists of three parts: a relational database logic L_{db}, an object-oriented logic L_o and a set of meta-level rules. L_{db} is used to model relational database structures at an abstract level while L_o is used to formalize object-oriented schemas. Then, based on these formalisms, a set of rules is constructed to transform local (relational) schemas into object-oriented ones in such a way that most of tasks can be done semi-automatically. In addition, the transformations w.r.t. view definitions and integrity constraints have been discussed in detail.

1. Introduction

Interoperability is becoming a critical issue for many organizations today, due to the increasing dependence and cooperation between them. Therefore, it is desired for many enterprises to be able to access remote as well as local information sources [LA86, SK92, CW93]. Further, even within a single enterprise several independent information bases may exist as a result of department autonomy [HLM94]. Thus, for many organizations it is important to interconnect existing, possibly heterogeneous, information systems for performing a cooperation. An essential part of this activity is database integration, i.e., the process of constructing a global schema from a collection of existing databases.

The first step of the database integration is the schema transformation, i.e., the transformation of a local schema into an abstract one. For our project, the object-oriented schema is chosen to represent the integrated information. There are several motivations for translating a local relational schema into an object-oriented one: first, to achieve data model homogeneity among the participating database schemas; second, to present clear and logical views of entities present in the local schemas; third, to store all the semantic knowledge gathered about the objects in the local schemas; and fourth, the object-oriented model is specially suitable as a common data model for HIMS (heterogeneous Information Management System) due to its natural framework for integrating heterogenous components and its mechanism of the message protocols which is necessary in a distributed environment.

However, the schema transformation is a time-consuming task and therefore a mechanism is desired to do this work automatically or semi-automatically.

In this paper, we address this problem and propose a method to make the transformation in a semi-automatic manner. As compared to existing procedures [KC93, LA86, LNE89, TS93, PTR96], this procedure lays stress on the rule-based method such that the schema translation can be performed almost automatically. In fact, our method may be viewed as a formalism of some strategies proposed in [KC93, LNE89, SK92, TS93], with the concept of relation classification considered.

The general idea of this method can be depicted as shown in Fig. 1.

Fig. 1. Illustration for a rule-based schema transformation

Here L_{db} represents a relational database logic, and L_o represents an object-oriented logic. L_{db} is used to model a database structure as well as its state, while L_o is utilized to formalize an object-oriented database. Then, based on these formalisms, a set of Horn-clause-like rules [Ll87] is constructed to do a meta-level reasoning for translating a formalism into another. In this way, the schema transformation can be accomplished automatically if the rule set is well defined. Obviously, this method is a flexible strategy, since as the new rules are added to the knowledge base, the system will be stronger and more complete. In addition, the logics proposed in this paper is powerful enough to accommodate most of relational databases and object-oriented databases. Therefore, this method can be used to do the same work in different environments.

The paper is organized as follows. In Section 2, both L_{db} and L_o are discussed. First, in Subsection 2.1, we propose L_{db}, along with the concept of relation classification. Then, in Subsection 2.2, we describe our object-oriented logic L_o, which is a significantly extended version of Kifer's O-logic [KW93]. In Section 3, we show a set of meta-level rules for translating schemas. Section 4 is a sample transformation. Finally, we conclude this paper with a summary in Section 5.

2. Database Logic and Object-Oriented Logic

Our work is based on the (relational) database logic and object-oriented logic developed in the past few years [CRV93, KW93, Ma86]. For our purposes, the database logic is extended to support the concept of relation classification, which is necessary to implement an automatic transformation process. Further, to cope with the aggregation concept in our object-oriented logic, we assume the universe of the semantic structure to be a poset (partially ordered set) instead of a set as done in [KW93]. In this way, the semantic flaws of the logic defined in [KW93] can be removed. In the following, we first discuss the relation classification in Subsection 2.1. Then, we introduce the extended database logic L_{db} and the object-oriented logic L_o in Subsection 2.2 and 2.3, respectively. The goal of these two logics is to provide a basis for formalizing the schema transformation process.

2.1 Relation classification

Here, we consider the problem of classifying relation schemas in a relational schema. For our purpose, we classify the relations in a relational database into four classes: *strong entity relations, weak entity relations, strong relationship relations* and *weak relationship relations,* which can be defined as follows [CBS94, Ch76].

1) A strong entity relation is a relation whose primary key does not properly contains a key of any other relation. For instance, in Fig. 2 (see below), *university, courses, person* and *professors* are typical examples of strong entity relations.

2) A weak entity relation is a relation that satisfies all of the following requirements:
   i) A proper subset of its primary key, denoted K_1, contains the keys of other entity relations. Each key (of some other entity relation) contained in K_1 is called a *supporting key.*
   ii) Each of the remaining attributes of the primary key, denoted $K_i (i > 1)$, is not a key of any other relation. (Then, the primary key is called the composite key, denoted $K_1 \cdot ... \cdot K_i$.)
   iii) This relation represents an entity type whose identifier must properly contain identifier attributes of other entity types (i.e. K_1). This requirement must be confirmed in some

way (e.g., through the interaction with users).

As an example, consider *department* relation in Fig. 2. Its primary key contains the primary key, '*u-name*', of *university* which is a strong relation. Moreover, '*d-name*' is not a key of any other relation, and *department* represents an entity type, then it is a weak entity relation.

3) A strong relationship relation is a relation whose primary key is formed fully by the concatenation of keys of some entity relations. For example, the relation *course_prof* in Fig. 2 is a strong relationship relation, because its primary key, [*course#, ssn#*], is formed fully by the concatenation of the primary keys of *courses* and *professors*.

4) A weak relationship relation is a relation whose primary key is constructed partially by the concatenation of keys of some other entity relations and partially by some attributes of its own. Moreover, it can not be treated as a weak entity relation. Consider the relation *teaching_plan* in Fig. 2. Its key is [*time, classroom, course#*] and '*time*' is not a key of any other relation. Then *teaching_plan* is a weak relationship relation.

university:	[*u-name, city, president*]
department:	[*d-name, u-name, director*]
courses:	[*course#, c-name*]
person:	[*ssn#, name, age, sex*]
professors:	[*p-ssn#, name, address, degree*]
course-prof:	[*course#, ssn#*]
teaching-plan:	[*time, classroom, ssn#*]

(*In the relations, all the keys are underlined.*)

Fig. 2. A sample relational schema

If a relation schema contains an attribute which corresponds to the key of some other relation schema, this attribute is called a foreign key. Any attribute which is not a key, a foreign key, a supporting key or dose not appear in any composite key is called a no-key attribute.

2.2 Database logic L_{db}

In this subsection, we introduce the syntax of our database logic L_{db}, which enriches the logic proposed in [CRV93] with the concept of relation classification. (The definition of semantics of L_{db} can be found in Appendix.)

- syntax of L_{db}

An alphabet of L_{db} consists of:

(1) a countable set of constants $C = \{c_1, c_2, ...\}$;
(2) a countable set of variables $V = \{x_1, x_2, ...\}$;
(3) a set of relation names Σ_1; and a set of attribute names Σ_2;
(4) a set of relation classification labels Ω_1, and a set of attribute classification labels Ω_2;
(5) a set of logic operators: $\wedge, \vee, \neg, \Rightarrow$, and quantifiers $\forall, \exists$;
(6) a set of unary predicates of the form: $\tau_v(x_i)$, where $v \in \Sigma_1$ and $x_i \in V$, and a set of binary predicates of the form: $\delta_{v.z.u}(x_i, x_j)$, where $v, u \in \Sigma_1, z \in \Sigma_2$ and $x_i, x_j \in V$;
(7) a set of (unary) relation classification predicates of the form: $\gamma_v(u)$, where $v \in \Omega_1$ and $u \in \Sigma_1$, and a set of (binary) attribute classification predicates of the form: $\chi_v(u, w)$, where $v \in \Omega_2, u \in \Sigma_1$ and $w \in \Sigma_2$; and
(8) the equality predicate '='.

We assume that the sets $C, V, \Sigma_1, \Sigma_2, \Omega_1$ and Ω_2 are disjoint. Further, for convenience, we regard all the primitive data types: *integer, boolean, character, string* and *real* as (possibly infinite) unary relation names.

The predicates $\tau_v(x_i)$ identify tuples of a particular relation schema. For example, $\tau_{employee}(x_1)$ states that x_1 represents a tuple in relation *employee*. The predicates $\delta_{v.z.u}(x_i, x_j)$ relates tuples of two relation schemas with respect to a particular attribute. For example, $\delta_{employee.name.string}(x_1, 'John')$ states that John is the name of employee object

x_1. The predicates $\gamma_v(u)$ and $\chi_v(u, w)$ are used to classify the relation schemas and attributes, respectively. The following example helps to illustrate the relevant concepts.

Example 1. Consider the relational schema shown in Fig. 2. In this relational schema, there are four kinds of relation schemas: strong-entity, weak-entity, strong-relationship and weak-relationship. Then, $\Omega_1 = \{strong\text{-}entity,\ weak\text{-}entity,\ strong\text{-}relationship,\ weak\text{-}relationship\}$ and a predicate of the form $\gamma_{strong\text{-}entity}(u)$ states that u represents a strong-entity relation schema. Further, in this relational schema, there exist five kinds of attributes: key, supporting-key, foreign-key, no-key and composite-key. Then, $\Omega_2 = \{key,\ supporting\text{-}key,\ foreign\text{-}key,\ no\text{-}key,\ composite\text{-}key\}$, and a predicate of the form $\chi_{key}(university,\ u\text{-}name)$ states that the attribute $u\text{-}name$ of $university$ is its key attribute, while $\chi_{supporting\text{-}key}(department,\ u\text{-}name)$ states that $u\text{-}name$ of $department$ is its supporting-key. $\chi_{composite\text{-}key}(d\text{-}name\cdot u\text{-}name)$ states that $d\text{-}name\cdot u\text{-}name$ of $department$ is its composite key. $\square$

From this alphabet, well-formed formulas may be defined inductively in a usual way. In addition, in the absence of function symbols, a set of terms consists of constants and variables. An atomic formula is an expression of the form $p(x_1, ..., x_n)$, where p is a n-ary predicate symbol (i.e., τ_v, $\delta_{v.z.u}$, γ_v, χ_v and '='') and $x_1, ..., x_n$ are terms. Finally, a set of well-formed formulas is the smallest set of expressions that contains the atomic formulas and for which the following holds:

if F_1 and F_2 are formulas, then so are $F_1\ \&\ F_2$, $F_1 \vee F_2$, $F_1 \Rightarrow F_2$, $\neg F_1$, $(\forall x)F_1$ and $(\exists x)F_1$.

2.3 Object-Oriented Logic L_o

Now we turn to our object-oriented logic L_o and define its syntax as follows, which is an extended version of O-logic proposed in [KW93]. (See Appendix for the semantics of L_o.)

- syntax of L_o

An alphabet of L_o consists of:

(1) a countable set O of constants representing *object identifiers*;

(2) a countable set A_s of *single-valued attribute names*;

(3) a countable set A_m of *set-valued attribute names*;

(4) a countable set Σ of *class names*;

(5) a countable set V_o of *object variables*;

(6) a set of logic operators: $\wedge$, $\vee$, $\neg$, $\Rightarrow$, and quantifiers $\forall$, $\exists$; and

(7) the equality predicate '='.

As in L_{db}, we assume that the sets O, A_s, A_m, Σ and V_o are disjoint. Further, we define the following predicates and structures along the lines of [KW93], including sets, class-hierarchies and aggregation concepts:

(8) an *isa-instanceOf* predicate: *isa-instanceOf*(x, c), where $x \in O$ is an object identifier and c $\in \Sigma$ is a class name;

(9) an *isa-subclassOf* predicate: *isa-subclassOf*(c$_1$, c$_2$), where c$_1$ and c$_2$ are both class names;

(10) an *partOf* predicate: *partOf*(c$_1$, c$_2$), where c$_1$ and c$_2$ are both class names; and

(11) a complex object structure: $(x, X)[A_{s1}: t_1, ..., A_{sk}: t_k, ..., A_{m1}: \{s_{11}, ..., s_{1l_1}\}, ..., A_{mn}: \{s_{n1}, ..., s_{nl_n}\}]$, where x is an object identifier, X is a class name, A_{si} are single-valued attribute names, and A_{mj} are set-valued attribute names; t_i, s_{jl} are complex structures themselves.

Isa-instanceOf predicates classify objects into classes (e.g., *isa-instanceOf*(john, employee)), while *isa-subclassOf* predicates organize classes into subclass hierarchies (e.g., *isa-subclassOf*(employee, person)). *PartOf* predicates specify the aggregation relationships among classes (e.g. *partOf(engine, car)*). Finally, complex object structures are assertions about various properties of objects represented by object identifiers, e.g., *(john, employee)[age*: 30, *salary*: 4000, *parents*: {*mary, david*}].

Either a predicate or a complex object structure is a formula. Formulas are obtained from other (simple) formulas by means of logic operators $\wedge, \vee, \neg, \Rightarrow$, and quantifiers $\forall, \exists$ as described in L_{db}. Finally, we note that the 'object constructor' introduced in [KW93] is not considered in our version, because it is not necessary for our tasks.

3. Rule Set for Schema Transformation

Based on the database logic and the object-oriented logic described above, we can define a set of rules to implement a semi-automatic process of transforming relational schemas into object-oriented ones. In terms of different tasks performed, these rules can be partitioned into six groups. The first four groups are employed to generate classes and the corresponding semantic constraints according to different key structures. Then, the fifth group generates *is-a* links and aggregation (*part-of*) links. Finally, the sixth group deals with inheritance based on some epistemological principles. In the following discussion, a rule of the form: $A_1, A_2, ..., A_n \rightarrow B$ represents a forward reasoning, while $B \leftarrow A_1, A_2, ..., A_n$ represents a backward reasoning.

3.1 OID, Values and Null Values in a Federative Database

Before we present our inference rule set for doing the schema transformation, we first discuss the data-identification problem in a federative environment as well as the null value treatment during a transformation.

- OID and values

The goal of the schema transformation is to remove the model conflicts, so that a component database can be integrated into a cooperation more easily. However, the data residing in a local database should not be translated, but rather be referenced. Therefore, a datum (in some local database) needs to be uniquely identified in a federative environment. In our system, if a relation is translated into a class, each of its tuples (of some relation) will be assigned an OID in order that the transformed schema behaves really like an object-oriented one. The assignment can be done as follows.

First, we show our system architecture, which consists of three-layers: FSM-client, FSM and FSM-agents as shown in Fig. 3. (Here FSM represents "federated system manager".)

The task of the FSM-client layer consists in the application management, providing a suite of application tools which enable users and DBAs to access the system. The FSM layer is responsible for the merging of potentially conflicting local databases and the definition of global schemas. In addition, a centralized management is supported at this layer. The FSM-agent layer corresponds to the local system management, addressing all the issues w.r.t. schema translations as well as local transaction and query processings.

In light of this architecture, each component database is installed in some FSM-agent and must be registered in the FSM. Then, if we number the tuples of a relation in a normal way, the OIDs for tuples will be of the following form:

<FSM-agent name>.<database system name>.<database name>.<relation name>.<integer>,

where "." denotes string concatenation. For example, FSM-agent1.informix.Patient-DB.patient-records.5 is a legal OID for the fifth tuple of relation "patient-records" in a database named "PatientDB". Accordingly, each attribute value will be implicitly prefixed with a string of the form:

<FSM-agent name>.<database system name>.<database name>.<relation name>.<attribute

name>.

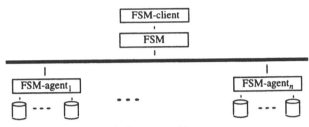

Fig. 3. System architecture

- Null value

In our system, the null value is treated as an applicable null value as defined in [Co86]. This denotes that this value is presently unknown, but can be entered to the database once known. Then, an application null value can be represented using the fuzzy set concept. That is, a null value can be represented (explicitly or implicitly) as a multi-value of the form: $\{(v_1, \frac{1}{n}), ..., (v_n, \frac{1}{n})\}$, where $\{v_1, ..., v_n\}$ is the attribute domain and $\frac{1}{n}$ is the probability of some v_i becoming the corresponding attribute value. As a consequence, if any null value appears, the corresponding attribute will be transformed into a set-valued attribute by the schema transformation to accommodate the relevant values. (Since such a transformation is trivial, we will not list the corresponding rule below for simplicity.)

3.2 Built-in Functions and Semantic Constraints

Another two important concepts are built-in functions and representations of semantic constraints which are frequently used in establishing rules.

- built-in functions:

The following three built-in functions are used to find the classes already created during a process of transformations.

$class(x)$: find the class which has been created in terms of a relation schema named x.

$C(x)$: find the class which has been created in terms of a strong relation whose key attribute is x.

$C_{weak}(x)$: find the class which has been created in terms of a weak relation whose composite key is x.

These functions can be represented using the above logics and implemented using a backward reasoning mechanism.

To this end, we first perform a *function-predicate transformation* which maps a function together with its *functional variable* to a predicate (called *functional predicate*), where the functional variable is the variable which unifies the returned value(s) of the function. That is, each function of arity n is transformed to a predicate of arity $n + 1$, with the last argument representing the functional variable. For example, $V = f(x_1, ..., x_n)$ is transformed to $f(x_1, ..., x_n, V)$. A similar transformation has also been discussed by other researchers [RBS87, Sa91].

Based on the function-predicate transformation, we construct the following backward reasoning rules:

$class(x)$: $\quad class^f(x, y) \leftarrow generate\text{-}class(x), c\text{-}name(x, y)$.

$C(x)$: $\quad C^f(x, y) \leftarrow \chi_{key}(v, x), \gamma_{strong\text{-}entity}(v), class^f(v, y)$.

$C_{weak}(x, y)$: $\quad C^f_{weak}(x, y) \leftarrow \chi_{composite\text{-}key}(v, x), \gamma_{weak\text{-}entity}(v), class^f(v, y)$.

Here '_' means 'do not care' and predicate '$c\text{-}name(x, y)$' in the rule defining $class^f(x,$

y) states that the class generated in terms of x has name y. This rule says that if a class has already been generated in terms of x (*generate-class*(x); see below) and this class has name y, then *class^f*(x, y) holds. Obviously, by executing this rule backwards, the function *class*(x) will be evaluated by instantiating variable y. The second rule says that if x is a key attribute, appearing in some strong relation schema ($\chi_{key}(v, x)$, $\gamma_{strong\text{-}entity}(v)$), and the class for v has been generated (*class^f*(v, y)), then $C^f(x, y)$ holds. The third rule is used to find the classes generated in terms of weak entity relation schemas.

- *semantic constraints*:

The following formalized semantic constraints will be inserted into created classes to specify those semantic relationships (among classes) which can not be expressed by class/subclass or by part-of concepts. In addition, these semantic constraints are always built over the key values and foreign key values of the original relations from which the classes are generated.

$\lambda_1(x, y, z)$: if x is a value of attribute y of some object (represented by the actual value of '*self*' variable) of the current class then $o^{-1}(self)$ should be a value of $o(x).z$, where $o(x)$ represents an object identifier which is determined by x (some key value), $o(x).z$ represents attribute z which appears in object $o(x)$ and o^{-1} represents the inverse function of o. Using the terminology of L_o, $\lambda_1(x, y, z)$ can be illustrated as follows:

$\lambda_1(x, y, z)$:

$self[... y: \{... x ...\} ...] \vee self[... y: x ...] \rightarrow o(x)[... z: \{... o^{-1}(self)...\} ...] \vee o(x)[... z: o^{-1}(self) ...]$.

Note that in the above semantic constraint *self* can be understood as a variable which is always assigned the current object identifier when the corresponding object is referenced by an application. We illustrate the usage of this semantic constraint with the following example.

Example 2. Consider *course-prof*: [*course#, p-ssn#*] of the sample relational schema. If we have created two classes for *professor* and *courses*, respectively, and choose not to generate a class for *course-prof*, we can establish two semantic constraints of the above form to record the relevant information as shown in Fig. 4(b). These two semantic constraints (along with two attributes: *course#* and *p-ssn#*) are inserted into class *professor* and class *courses*, respectively. Then, two objects shown in Fig. 4(c) will both satisfy the constraints. Of course, we can create a class for *course-prof*, but with another form of semantic constraints inserted (see below). ☐

Due to the existence of weak entities, we have to consider more complicated cases that composite keys are involved in a (strong) relationship. In fact, the key of a weak entity consists of a supporting key and several other attributes and can be viewed as a composite key. Foe explanation, see the following relation schema.

    professor-dept: [*p-ssn#, u-name, d-name*]

To deal with such a case, we introduce three variants of $\lambda_1(x, y, z)$ to specify the corresponding constraints. The first variant is of the following form:

$\lambda_1'(<x_1, ..., x_n>, <y_1, ..., y_n>, z)$: $self[... y_1 \cdot ... \cdot y_m: (x_1, ..., x_n) ...] \rightarrow o(x_1, ..., x_n)[... z: o^{-1}(self) ...]$,

where $y_1 \cdot ... \cdot y_n$ represents a attribute name constructed by concatenating y_i ($1 \leq i \leq n$) together and will be inserted into the current class as a new attribute.

The second variant is of the following form:

$\lambda_1''(x, y, <z_1, ..., z_m>)$: $self[... y: x ...] \rightarrow o(x)[... z_1 \cdot ... \cdot z_m: o^{-1}(self) ...]$.

These two variants can be illustrated using the following example.

Example 3. Assume that two classes: *professor* and *dept* have been generated in terms of the corresponding relation schemas. Then, two semantic constraints: $\lambda_1'(<x_1, ..., x_n>, <y_1, ..., y_n>, z)$ and $\lambda_1''(x, y, <z_1, ..., z_m>)$ (as shown in Fig. 5) will be inserted into the corresponding classes, respectively, to establish the relevant semantic relationship. ☐

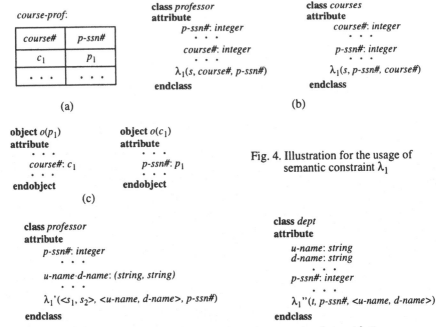

Fig. 4. Illustration for the usage of semantic constraint λ_1

(a) (b) (c)

class *professor*
attribute
    p-ssn#: integer
    . . .
    u-name·d-name: *(string, string)*
    . . .
    $\lambda_1'(<s_1, s_2>, <\text{u-name, d-name}>, \text{p-ssn\#})$
endclass

class *dept*
attribute
    u-name: string
    d-name: string
    . . .
    p-ssn#: integer
    . . .
    $\lambda_1''(t, \text{p-ssn\#}, <\text{u-name, d-name}>)$
endclass

Fig. 5. Illustration for the usage of semantic constraints λ_1' and λ_2''

The third variant is of the following form:

$$\lambda_1'''(<x_1, ..., x_n>, <y_1, ..., y_n>, <z_1, ..., z_m>):$$
$$self[... y_1\cdot...\cdot y_m: (x_1, ..., x_n) ...] \rightarrow o(x_1, ..., x_n)[... z_1\cdot...\cdot z_m: o^{-1}(self) ...].$$

Now we consider another semantic constraint, which can be described as follows. $\lambda_2(x, y, z)$: if x is a value of attribute y of some object (represented by the actual value of '*self*' variable) of the current class then $o(x)$ should be an instance of class z. Its formalized representation is:

$$\lambda_2(x, y, z): self[... y: \{... x ...\} ...] \vee self[... y: x ...] \rightarrow isa\text{-}instanceOf(o(x), z).$$

Example 4. To illustrate the usage of $\lambda_2(x, y, z)$, consider *course-prof*: [*course#, p-ssn#*] once again. If we choose to generate a class for it, two semantic constraints of the form λ_2 should be inserted into the class as shown in Fig. 6. (Assume that classes: *professor* and *courses* have been generated.) ☐

class *course-prof*
attribute
    course#: integer
    p-ssn#: integer
    . . .
    $\lambda_2(s_1, \text{course\#, courses})$
    $\lambda_2(s_2, \text{p-ssn\#, professor})$
endclass

Fig. 6. Illustration for the usage of semantic constraints λ_2

Similar to λ_1, we introduce a variant of λ_2 to deal with composite keys.

$$\lambda_2'(<x_1, ..., x_n>, <y_1, ..., y_n>, z):$$
$$self[... y_1\cdot...\cdot y_m: (x_1, ..., x_n) ...] \rightarrow isa\text{-}instanceOf(o(x_1, ..., x_n), z).$$

3.3 Generating Classes

In this subsection, we consider only the rules for producing classes in terms of strong entity relations, weak entity relations, strong relationship relations and weak relations.

The rules for building links and for handling inheritance will be given in 3.3 and 3.4, respectively. (To understand the following rules well, we suggest referring the definitions w.r.t. the relation classification given in 2.1 once again. In addition, we notice that these rules will be stored as strings and syntactically analyzed using the "*LEX*" unix-utility.)

- *the first group of rules*:

  r_1: $\tau_v(\_), \gamma_{strong-entity}(v) \rightarrow$ *generate-class*(v).
  r_2: $\gamma_{strong-entity}(v), \delta_{v.z.u}(\_ \_) \rightarrow$ *insert-attr*(class(v), z).

These two rules are used to generate classes in terms of strong entity relation schemas. By executing the first rule, a class will be simply created (by executing '*generate-class*(v)'), while by executing the second one, the corresponding attributes will be inserted into the class (by executing '*insert-attr*(class(v), z)'). Trivially, the instances of a class can be identified by performing the following rule.

  r_3: $\gamma_{strong-entity}(v), \delta_{v.z.u}(v_i, \_) \rightarrow$ *isa-instanceOf*($o_t(v_i)$, class(v)),

where $o_t(v_i)$ represents the object identifier corresponding to v_i.

- *the second group of rules*:

  r_4: $\tau_v(\_), \gamma_{weak-entity}(v) \rightarrow$ *generate-class*(v).
  r_5: $\gamma_{weak-entity}(v), \delta_{v.z.u}(\_ \_) \rightarrow$ *insert-attr*(class(v), z).
  r_6: $\gamma_{weak-entity}(v), \chi_{supporting-key}(v, z) \rightarrow$ *insert-constraint*($\lambda_2(x, z, C(z))$, class(v)).

These three rules are used to generate classes in terms of weak entity relation schemas. From r_4 and r_5, we see that for each weak entity relation schema a class will be created in the same way as for strong entity relation schemas. However, a λ_2 semantic constraint will be constructed to specify the semantic relationship between the weak entity and its supporting (strong) entity. We do this by performing '*insert-constraint*($\lambda_2(x, z, C(z))$, class(v))' in r_6. That is, a semantic constraint of the form: *self*[... z: {... x ...} ...] $\vee$ *self*[... z: x ...] $\rightarrow$ *isa-instanceOf*(o(x), C(z)) will be inserted into the class represented by class(v), expressing that the value of a supporting key attribute of an object which belongs to a class created in terms of a weak entity relation schema corresponds to an instance of the class created in terms of the supporting entity (which is represented by C(z) in r_6.) Similar to strong entity relations, we can construct a rule to identify instances of a class created in terms of a weak entity relation. However, here we omit it for simplicity.

- *the third group of rules*:

  (In this group, rules from r_7 to r_{12} are used to determine whether a class will be constructed for a strong relationship relation schema; rules from r_{11} to r_{13} are used to cope with the case that any foreign key of a strong relationship relation schema corresponds to a key of some strong entity; and rules from r_{14} to r_{16} are used to deal with composite keys which appear in a strong relationship as a foreign key.)

  r_7: $\gamma_{strong-relationship}(v), \chi_{no-key}(v, z) \rightarrow$ *no-key*(v, z).

This rule is used to check whether a strong relationship relation schema contains an attribute which is not a foreign key. It is important because for strong relationship relation schemas the method for generating classes can be different in terms of whether a strong relationship relation schema contains any no-key attribute or not. That is, if a strong relationship relation schema contains no no-key attributes, we do not create a class for it (as discussed in Example 2). Instead, we construct a λ_1 semantic constraint for each class which is generated in terms of a relation schema whose key appears in the relationship relation schema as a foreign key (see r_{13}). If a strong relationship relation schema contains a no-key attribute which is not covered (we say that a no-key attribute is covered if it appears in some entity relation schema whose key participates in the relationship relation schema; see r_8), a class will be generated for it. Otherwise, no class will be created at all. As in the case that a strong relationship relation schema contains no no-key attributes, a λ_1 semantic constraint is inserted into the corresponding class (see r_{12} and r_{13}).

r_8: $no\text{-}key(v, y)$, $\chi_{foreign\text{-}key}(v, z)$, $in\text{-}as\text{-}attr(y, C(z)) \rightarrow covered(v, y)$.

This rule is used to define the predicate '$covered(v, y)$', in which '$in\text{-}as\text{-}attr(y, C(z))$' checks whether '$y$' appears as an attribute in '$C(z)$'.

r_9: $\exists z(no\text{-}key(v, z), \neg covered(v, z)) \rightarrow generate\text{-}class(v)$.

r_{10}: $\exists z(no\text{-}key(v, z), \neg covered(v, z))$, $\delta_{v.y.u}(\_\_, \_\_) \rightarrow insert\text{-}attr(class(v), y)$

r_{11}: $\chi_{foreign\text{-}key}(v, y)$, $\exists u(\chi_{key}(u, y))$, $generate\text{-}class(v) \rightarrow insert\text{-}constraint(\lambda_2(x, y, C(y))$, $class(v))$.

These three rules are used to create classes and the corresponding semantic constraints, respectively, in terms of the strong relationship relation schemas which contain some uncovered attributes. Note that by executing r_{11}, corresponding to each foreign key y, a semantic constraint of the form: $self[... y: \{... x ...\} ...] \lor self[... y: x ...] \rightarrow isa\text{-}instanceOf(o(x), C(y))$ will be inserted into the class represented by $class(v)$. In this way, the semantic relationship between $class(v)$ and the class created in terms of an entity relation schema whose key corresponds to y can be established.

r_{12}: $\gamma_{strong\text{-}relationship}(v)$, $(\neg no\text{-}key(v, z) \lor \forall t(no\text{-}key(v, t) \Rightarrow covered(v, t)))$
     $\rightarrow pure\text{-}relationship(v)$.

This rule states that if a strong relationship relation schema contains no no-key attribute or all of its no-key attributes are covered, then it is a pure relationship relation schema, for which no class will be generated. As mentioned above, in this case, several pairs of semantic constraints will be established to specify the relevant semantic relationships (see the following rule).

r_{13}: $pure\text{-}relationship(v)$, $\chi_{foreign\text{-}key}(v, y)$, $\exists u_1(\chi_{key}(u_1, y))$, $\chi_{foreign\text{-}key}(v, x)$, $\exists u_2(\chi_{key}(u_2, x))$
     $\rightarrow insert\text{-}attr(C(x), y)$, $insert\text{-}attr(C(y), x)$, $insert\text{-}constraint(\lambda_1(s, y, x), C(x))$,
       $insert\text{-}constraint(\lambda_1(t, x, y), C(y))$.

For each pair of foreign key attributes, say x and y, appearing in a strong relationship relation schemas, respectively, this rule first creates a new attribute named y in the class represented by $C(x)$ and a new attribute named x in the class represented by $C(y)$. Then, it inserts λ_1 semantic constraints pairwise into the classes generated in terms of those entity relation schemas whose keys appear in the strong relationship relation schema as foreign keys. That is, if x and y are two foreign keys appearing in v, a semantic constraint of the form: $self[... y: \{... s ...\} ...] \lor self[... y: s ...] \rightarrow o(s)[... x: \{... o^{-1}(self) ...\} ...] \lor o(s)[... x: o^{-1}(self) ...]$ will be inserted into the class represented by $C(x)$, while another semantic constraint of the form: $self[... x: \{... t ...\} ...] \lor self[... x: t ...] \rightarrow o(t)[... y: \{... o^{-1}(self) ...\} ...] \lor o(t)[... y: o^{-1}(self) ...]$ will be inserted into the class represented by $C(y)$ (once again, see Example 2 for illustration). Note that before inserting a new attribute into a class, it should be checked whether the attribute already exists in the corresponding class. Therefore, the above rule should take a more complicated form to accomplish this work. Here, however, we omit the detailed discussion for simplicity.

The following three rules will be used to deal with more complex situations that some foreign key(s) of a strong relationship relation schema correspond to a composite key of a weak entity relation.

r_{14}: $pure\text{-}relationship(v)$, $\chi_{foreign\text{-}key}(v, y)$, $\exists u_1(\chi_{composite\text{-}key}(u_1, y))$, $\chi_{foreign\text{-}key}(x)$,
     $\exists u_2(\chi_{key}(u_2, x)) \rightarrow insert\text{-}attr(C_{waek}(y), x)$, $insert\text{-}attr(C(x), y)$,
       $insert\text{-}constraint(\lambda_1'(s, y, x), C(x))$, $insert\text{-}constraint(\lambda_1''(t, x, y), C_{weak}(y))$.

r_{15}: $pure\text{-}relationship(v)$, $\chi_{foreign\text{-}key}(v, y)$, $\exists u_1(\chi_{composite\text{-}key}(u_1, y))$, $\chi_{foreign\text{-}key}(v, x)$,

$\exists u_2(\chi_{key}(u_2, x)) \rightarrow insert\text{-}attr(C_{weak}(x), y), insert\text{-}attr(C_{weak}(y), x),$
$\qquad insert\text{-}constraint(\lambda_1'''(s, y, x), C_{weak}(x)), insert\text{-}constraint(\lambda_1'''(t, x, y), C_{weak}(y)).$

$r_{16}: \gamma_{strong\text{-}relationship}(v), \chi_{foreign\text{-}key}(v, y), \exists u(\chi_{composite\text{-}key}(u, y)), \exists z(no\text{-}key(v, z), \neg covered(v, z))$
$\qquad \rightarrow insert\text{-}constraint(\lambda_2'(s, y, C_{weak}(y)), class(v)).$

Concretely speaking, r_{14} is used to cope with the case that only one of the considered pair of foreign keys corresponds to a weak entity relation schema, while r_{15} is used to handle the case that both the foreign keys come from weak entity relation schemas. In addition, by r_{14} and r_{15}, only pure relationship relation schemas are considered. On the contrary, r_{16} is used to construct semantic constraints for those classes which are created in terms of 'not-pure' relationship relation schemas which contain composite keys as foreign keys. The ideas of these three rules are similar to r_{11} and r_{13} except that composite keys are considered.

Finally, the fourth group of rules is used to generate classes in terms of weak relationship relation schemas.

- the fourth group of rules:

$r_{17}: \tau_v(\_), \gamma_{weak\text{-}relationship}(v) \rightarrow generate\text{-}class(v).$

$r_{18}: \gamma_{weak\text{-}relationship}(v), \chi_{foreign\text{-}key}(v, z) \rightarrow insert\text{-}constraint(\lambda_2(s, z, C(z)), class(v)).$

As for weak entity relation schemas, a class will be created for each weak relationship relation schema, along with a λ_2 semantic constraint constructed to specify the corresponding semantic relationships. (For simplicity, here we do not give the rules for dealing with composite keys which appear in a weak relationship as foreign keys. The corresponding rules can be constructed in the same way as for strong relationship relation schemas.)

3.4 Generating Links

In order to define the rules for establishing *is-a* and *agg* (part-of) links, we need the following two concepts (see [CBS94, MM90, VA95] for original definitions).

Definition 1. (*compatible*) Let $R_i(X_i)$ and $R_j(X_j)$ be two relation-schemata, where X_i and X_j denotes the attribute sets for R_i and R_j, respectively. We say two attributes x ($\in X_i$) and y ($\in X_j$) to be *compatible* if they are associated with the same domain. Two attribute subsets Y ($\subseteq X_i$) and Z ($\subseteq X_j$) are said to be compatible iff there exists a one-to-one correspondence of compatible attributes between Y and Z. $\quad\Box$

Definition 2. (*inclusion dependency*) Let $R_i(X_i)$ and $R_j(X_j)$ be two relation-schemata associated with relations re_i and re_j, respectively. An *inclusion dependency* w.r.t. the current database state (a database state is a set of relations $\{re_1, re_2, ..., re_n\}$, where each re_k is a relation for R_k) is a statement of the form $V(Y) \subseteq V(Z)$, where Y and Z are compatible subsets of X_i and X_j, respectively; $V(Y) \subseteq V(Z)$ is satisfied by re_i and re_j iff $\pi_Y(re_i) \subseteq \pi_Z(re_j)$, where $\pi_X(re_k)$ denotes the projection of re_k on X. $\quad\Box$

In the following group of rules, we denote two compatible attributes x and y by *compatible*(x, y). In addition, the number of tuples of a relation re is denoted *cardinality*(re).

- the fifth group of rules:

$r_{19}: \gamma_{strong\text{-}entity}(v), \chi_{key}(v, z), \gamma_{strong\text{-}entity}(w), \chi_{key}(w, x), compatible(z, x), values(z) \subseteq values(x)$
$\qquad \rightarrow isa\text{-}subclassOf(class(v), class(w)),$

where *values*(z) stands for the actual values of attribute z. This rule is used to establish class/subclass relationships based on the inclusion dependency.

$r_{20}: \gamma_{strong\text{-}entity}(v), \chi_{foreign\text{-}key}(v, z) \rightarrow foreign\text{-}key(v, z).$

This rule is used to collect all the foreign keys appearing in strong entity relation schemas into a temporary relation *'foreign-key(v, z)'*.

r_{21}: $\gamma_{strong\text{-}entity}(v)$, $cardinality(foreign\text{-}key(v, \_)) = 1$, $\chi_{foreign\text{-}key}(v, z)$, $\exists u(\chi_{key}(u, z))$
$\qquad \rightarrow insert\text{-}constraint(\lambda_2(s, z, C(z)), class(v))$.

r_{21}': $\gamma_{strong\text{-}entity}(v)$, $cardinality(foreign\text{-}key(v, \_)) = 1$, $\chi_{foreign\text{-}key}(v, z)$, $\exists u(\chi_{composite\text{-}key}(u, z))$
$\qquad \rightarrow insert\text{-}constraint(\lambda_2'(s, z, C(z)), class(v))$.

If a strong entity relation schema contains only one foreign key, a λ_2 or a λ_2' semantic constraint will be constructed (for the class created in terms of the relation schema) by this rule, depending on the property of the foreign key.

r_{22}: $\gamma_{strong\text{-}entity}(v)$, $\chi_{foreign\text{-}key}(v, z)$, $\chi_{foreign\text{-}key}(v, z)$, $\exists u(\chi_{key}(u, z))$,
$\qquad cardinality(foreign\text{-}key(v, \_)) > 1 \rightarrow partOf(C(z), class(v))$.

r_{22}': $strong\text{-}entity(v)$, $\chi_{composite\text{-}key}(v, z)$, $\exists u(\chi_{composite\text{-}key}(u, z))$, $cardinality(foreign\text{-}key(v, \_)) > 1$
$\qquad \rightarrow partOf(C_{weak}(z), class(v))$.

If a strong entity relation schema contains n ($n > 1$) foreign keys, then n part-of links will be established (with each link corresponding to a foreign key) by these two rules. Trivially, the following rule will be constructed to represent the transitive property of *subclass* relationship.

r_{23}: $isa\text{-}subclassOf(x, y)$, $isa\text{-}subclassOf(y, z) \rightarrow isa\text{-}subclassOf(x, z)$.

3.5 About Inheritance

The next series of rules demonstrates our treatment of inheritance, compared to those in the literature. Principally, these rules are constructed based on the following three epistemological principles:

1) The specification of a concept into some subconcepts is based on the values of at least one attribute of it. All the instances of a subconcept possess the same values of the corresponding attributes. (Therefore, these values of the attributes function as the character of the corresponding subclass, distinguishing it from others.)
2) The set of all instances of the subconcepts of a concept should be equal to or less than the set of instances of the concept.
3) Two concepts with the compatible key attributes are in the same semantic category. That is, both of them should be involved in the same generalization-specification hierarchy.

These principles motivate the following definition.

Definition 3. Let R be a relation schema and *attr* be an attribute of it. If the number of values of *attr* (denoted *cardinality(attr)*) is less than some constant *Const*, then *attr* is called a *division attribute* w.r.t. R. Such a constant *Const* is chosen based upon the ration of the number of distinct values in an attribute over the number of the tuples of the corresponding relation and the largest fan-out of the local generalization/specification hierarchies. □

The observation leading to this definition is that it is possible to partition a class into several subclasses, in terms of some division attribute, with each possessing a value of the division attribute as its characteristic value. For example, attribute *person.sex* in the sample relational schema is a division attribute. Its value set is {man, woman}, in terms of which subclasses *man* and *woman* can be generated. This partition is important in the context of schema integration, since in this way we can eliminate the metadata conflict, i.e., the conflict appearing when the same concepts are represented at the schema level in one database and at the instance level in another.

If uch a partition has be done, each value of the division attribute corresponds to the name of a subclass generated as above. Therefore, the corresponding attribute should be handled as a partially own attribute of the original class. That is, this attribute should not be inherited by the subclasses generated by partitioning the corresponding attribute. For illustration, consider *person.sex* again. If the subclasses *man* and *woman* are generated by partitioning *person.sex*, then *man* and *woman* should not inherit the attribute '*sex*' from *person* for the redundancy reason. However, the other subclasses such as *professor* should inherit it. In addition, if the cardinality of a division attribute is one, this attribute becomes trivially the own attribute of the corresponding class. Based on the above discussion, we construct the following rules to distinguish among division attributes, (partially) own attributes and instance attributes.

- *the sixth group of rules*:

r_{24}: *attr*(x, y), *cardinality*$(y) = 1 \rightarrow$ *own-attr*(x, y).

r_{25}: *attr*(x, y), *cardinality*$(y) \leq Const \rightarrow$ *division-attr*(x, y).

r_{26}: *division-attr*(x, y), *partitioned*(y), $z \in$ *values*$(y) \rightarrow$ *generate-subclass*(x, y, z), *partially-own-attr*(x, y, z).

Rule r_{24} is used to define own attributes, in which predicate *attr*(x, y) holds iff y is an attribute of class y. Rule r_{25} is used to define division attributes in terms of Definition 3. Finally, r_{26} says that if y is a division attribute of x and partitioned, then y is a partially own attribute of x w.r.t. the subclasses created in terms of the values of y. By executing '*generate-subclass*(x, y, z)', a subclass corresponding to z (a value of attribute y) will be generated, possessing all attributes of x except y; and by executing '*partially-own-attr*(x, y, z)', y will be labeled as a partially own attribute of x w.r.t. z. At last, we notice that the execution of the above three rules should be interfered by human beings due to the difficulties of choice of *Consts*. In some cases, the entire schema integration process should be considered to make such a decision.

3.6 About Views and Integrity Constraints

In the previous subsection, a set of rules has been discussed, which can be used to do a transformation almost automatically. Unfortunately, there still are several elements which may exist in a relational database and for which the transformation can be performed only manually. Two examples of such elements are views and integrity constraints.

- *views*

In order to transform a view definition, we have to extend the object-oriented model with deductive abilities. That is, the derivation rules should be allowed in an object-oriented schema. In our system, for the complex object structures in L_o, we define derivation relations in a standard way, as implicitly universally quantified statements of the form: $\gamma_1 \& \gamma_2 \ldots \& \gamma_l \Leftarrow \tau_1 \& \tau_2 \ldots \& \tau_k$, where both γ_i's and τ_k's are complex object structures or normal predicates of the first-order logic. For example, the rule $(o_1, Empl)[e\_name: x, work\_in: o_2 Dept] \Leftarrow (o_2 : Dept)[d\_name: y, manager: o_1 Empl]$ states that department managers work in the department they manage. Here *Empl* and *Dept* are classes, o_1 and o_2 are object variables (over object identifiers) and *work_in* and *manager* are two aggregation functions. Universal quantifiers over o_1 and o_2 are omitted. As another example, consider the so-called '*interesting pair*' problem, which was first addressed in [Ma86] and was further discussed in [KW93]. The problem is to find the pairs *employee-manager* such that the employee's department's manager's name coincides with the employee's name, which can be represented (using our method) as follows:

$pair(o_1, manager(o_2)) \Leftarrow (o_1, Empl)[e\_name: x, work\_in: o_2 Dept], manager(o_2).e\_name = x.$

As we can see, this rule is much simpler than that presented in [KW93] and the semantic ambiguity of [Ma86] is also eliminated. Alternatively, the first rule above may be written in the following form:

$(o_1, Empl)[e\_name: x, work\_in: y] \Leftarrow (o_2, Dept)[d\_name: y, manager: x],$

if *work_in* and *manager* are defined as attribute names. Obviously, any view definition in a relational database can be reformulated in such a way.

- integrity constraints

In terms of L_o's syntax, the integrity constrain w.r.t. an object-oriented schema can be defined to be a formula of the form: $(Q_1x_1) ... (Q_nx_n)e(x_1, ..., x_n)$, where each Q_i is either $\forall$ or $\exists$, $n > 0$, e is a set of complex object structures or normal predicates of the first-order logic, connected with $\land$, $\lor$, $\neg$, or $\Rightarrow$, and $x_1, ..., x_n$ are all variables occurring in e. For example, formula $(\forall o_1)(\forall o_2)\{(o_1, person)[name: \_, age: \_, sibling: o_2] \Rightarrow (o_2, person)[name: \_, age: \_, sibling: o_1]\}$ is a legal integrity constraint, representing that if o_1 is the sibling of o_2, then o_2 must be the sibling of o_1, too. As another example, the following integrity constraint says that if o_1 is a professor, then at least one course must be given by him:

$(\forall o_1)(\exists o_2)\{(o_1, professor)[name: \_, age: \_, degree: \_] \Rightarrow$
$(o_2, course)[course\_name: \_, given\_by: o_1]\}.$

Such integrity constraints will be inserted into the relevant classes and invoked after update operations (on some objects of the corresponding classes) are executed. Intuitively, each integrity constraint represented in a relational schema can be rewritten in this way without loss of any semantics.

Note that such transformations are necessary when we try to integrate a relational database with an object-oriented one. Even if all the participating databases are not object-oriented, the transformation of local schemas into a uniform form is advantageous, since the confusion which may occur during an integration process can be alleviated.

4. A Sample Transformation

To illustrate briefly the usage of the rule set given above, let us trace a sample transformation. The example is so constructed that major ideas can be presented in a simple way.

Example 5. Consider the relational schema given in Fig. 7. In order to translate this relational schema into an object-oriented one, we perform the inference by executing the numbered (forward reasoning) rules in sequence.

First, we note that for the above relational schema we have the following predicates of L_{db}:

$\tau_{university}, \delta_{university.u-name.string}, \delta_{university.u-city.string}, \delta_{university.u-president.string},$
... ...

$\gamma_{strong-entity}, \gamma_{weak-entity}, \gamma_{strong-relationship}, \gamma_{weak-relationship},$
$\chi_{key}, \chi_{supporting-key}, \chi_{foreign-key}, \chi_{no-key}, \chi_{composite-key}$

university:	[*u-name, city, president*]
department:	[*d-name, u-name, director*]
courses:	[*course#, c-name*]
person:	[*ssn#, name, age, sex*]
professor:	[*p-ssn#, name, d-name, u-name*]
course-prof:	[*course#, ssn#*]
teaching-plan:	[*time, classroom, ssn#*]
project:	[*pro#, project-director, foundation*]
foundation:	[*foun#, foun-name, sponsor*]

(In the relational schema, all the keys are underlined.)

Fig. 7. A relational schema

Then, based on the first four groups of rules, we transform the relation schemas into a series of classes, together with some semantic constraints inserted. (See Fig. 8(a) for illustration.) Further, by executing the fifth group of rules (from r_{19} to r_{22}'), a set of links as shown in Fig. 8(b) will be established, leading to a complete object-oriented schema. Finally, by performing the sixth group of rules (from r_{24} to r_{26}), we can partition *person.sex* of *person* and generate two subclasses: *man* and *woman*. In the following, we explain the entire process step-by-step.

By executing r_1 and r_2 repeatedly, the classes: *university, person, professor, courses, project* and *foundation*, together with the corresponding attributes, will be generated, each of which corresponds to a strong entity relation. By executing rules r_4, r_5 and r_6, class *department* will be produced with a semantic constraint of the form λ_2 inserted into it to specify the semantic relationship between it and its supporting entity. Since the relationship relation *course-prof* is a 'pure-relationship', no class is generated for it. (Neither rules from r_7 to r_9 nor rules from r_{10} to r_{11} will be performed because the condition-parts of them are not satisfied by the relational schema.) Instead, two semantic constraints of the form λ_1 will be inserted into *professor* and *courses*, respectively, by executing r_{12} and r_{13}. Further, by executing r_{17} and r_{18}, class *teaching_plan* will be generated with a semantic constraint of the form λ_2 inserted into it. (Note that rules from r_{14} to r_{16} will not be executed because the condition-parts of them are not satisfied.)

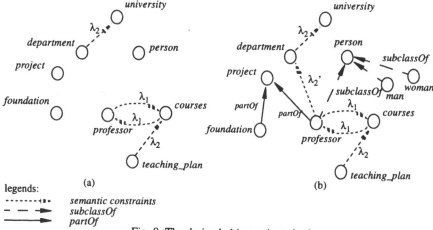

legends:
- - - - - - - ◄■▪   *semantic constraints*
- - - ➤   *subclassOf*
———➤   *partOf*

Fig. 8. The derived object-oriented schema

By performing r_{19}, the *subclassOf* relationship between *professor* and *person* will be built. Then, by executing rules from r_{20} to r_{22}' repeatedly, another semantic constraint of the form λ_2' for *professor* (by r_{21}') and two *partOf* links from *foundation* and *professor* to *project*, respectively, will be generated (see Fig. 8(b)). Finally, by executing r_{25} (r_{24} will not be executed because its condition-part is not satisfied by any class), attribute *person.sex* will be identified as a division attribute if the system constant *Const* is set to be a constant larger than two. Further, if the partition operation has been done, r_{26} will be preformed. In this case, two extra classes *man* and *woman* will be generated and *person.sex* will be labeled as a partially own attribute. □

5. Conclusion

In this paper, a semi-automatic procedure is developed for translating relational schemas into object-oriented schemas for the integration purpose. To implement such a procedure, two logic formalisms: the database logic and the object-oriented logic are proposed as a powerful tool for analyzing schemas. Further, a set of rules are constructed to perform an automatic transformation by generating classes, semantic constraints, class/subclass links and aggregation links in terms of the relational schema at hand. Obviously, this methodology is very flexible due to the extensibility of rule bases. The system becomes stronger and more complete as new rules are added in its knowledge base. For example, a rule of the form:

$Q(x, y)\{\tau_v(\overline{S})\} \Rightarrow \tau_u(\overline{\iota})\}, x \in \overline{S}, y \in \overline{\iota}$, generate-class(v), generate-class(u), $\delta_{v.w.v1}(x, \_)$,
$\delta_{u.z.u1}(y, \_)$ $\rightarrow Q(x, y)\{(o_1, v)[w: x] \Rightarrow (o_2, u)[z: y]\}$

may enable us to translate any relational integrity constraint of the form: $Q(x, y)\{\tau_v(\overline{S})$ $\Rightarrow \tau_u(\overline{\iota})\}$ into an object-oriented one automatically, where $Q(x, y)$ stands for a sequnce of quantifications containing variables x and y. It may be of the form: $\forall x \forall y$, $\forall x \exists y$, $\exists x \exists y$ or $\exists x \forall y$.

Appendix. Semantics of L_{db} and L_o

- semantics of L_{db}

Given a language L of L_{db}, a semantic structure, I_{db}, is a tuple $<U, I_F I_{\Sigma 1}, I_{\Sigma 2}, I_{\Omega 1}, I_{\Omega 2}, I_P>$. Here U is a nonempty (possibly infinite) universe of all elements of an application; the mapping I_F interprets each constant of L as an element in U.

The mapping $I_{\Sigma 1}$ interprets each relation name in Σ_1 as a subset of U^k for some $k \geq 1$ (presumedly, the relation name corresponds to a k-ary relation schema), that is, $I_{\Sigma 1}: \Sigma_1 \rightarrow 2^{\prod U}$, where $\prod U$ denotes the set of all the elements of the form $<e_1, e_2, ..., e_i>$ for all $i \geq 1$ and $2^{\prod U}$ denotes the power set of $\prod U$. The mapping $I_{\Sigma 2}$ interprets each attribute name as a partial function $I_{\Sigma 2}(z)$: $\prod U \rightarrow \prod U$, where $z \in \Sigma_2$. Intuitively, each attribute of a relation associates each tuple of the relation with a value of the attribute. Such a value may be of a primitive data type or may correspond to a tuple of another relation. In the latter case, the corresponding key value will be used in a normal implementation. However, our definition is in a more general form, independent of any concrete implementation, i.e., we use $\prod U$, instead of U, in the above definition to emphasize that the values of an attribute may be a tuple. If the multi-valued attributes are considered, the above function should be rewritten as $\prod U \rightarrow 2^{\prod U}$, with single-valued attributes being handled as a special case. Further, the mapping $I_{\Omega 1}$ interprets each symbol $g \in \Omega_1$ as a subset of $2^{\prod U}$, that is, $I_{\Omega 1}: \Omega_1 \rightarrow 2^{2^{\prod U}}$, where $2^{2^{\prod U}}$ denotes *the power set of the power set* of $\prod U$. Intuitively, the usage of Ω_1 is to classify relation schemas. Let Ω denote the set consisting of all partial functions of the form: $I_{\Sigma 2}(z)$. Then, the mapping $I_{\Omega 2}$ interprets each symbol $h \in \Omega_2$ as the subset of the set Ω, that is, $I_{\Omega 2}: \Omega_2 \rightarrow 2^{\Omega}$. Similar to Ω_1, the usage of Ω_2 is to classify attributes appearing in a relational schema. Finally, the mapping I_P interprets each predicate $p \in \{\tau_v, \delta_{v.z.u}, \gamma_v, \chi_v\}$ as a function $I_P(p): U^i \rightarrow \{true, false\}$.

As in the classic predicate calculus, a semantic structure should be viewed as a possible world that gives an interpretation to the alphabet symbols and formulas of L. For example, the elements of U play the role of 'real' elements in the possible world I_{db}. In contrast, the elements of Σ_1 are the denotation (relation names) given to some structure over these elements (of U), while an element of Ω_1 corresponds to a subset of such structures.

A variable-assignment, va, is a mapping $V \rightarrow U \cup \prod U$. We extend it to predicates in the usual way: $va(p(x_1, ..., x_n)) = I_P(p)(va(x_1), ..., va(x_n))$.

Given a semantic structure I_{db} and a variable assignment va, we can talk about formulas satisfied by I_{db} with respect to va. Formally, formula satisfaction, denoted $I_{db} \vDash_{va} \Gamma$, is defined as follows:

- For $\Gamma = \tau_v(x_i)$, $I_{db} \vDash_{va} \Gamma$ if and only if $va(x_i) \in I_{\Sigma 1}(v)$.
- For $\Gamma = \delta_{v.z.u}(x_i, x_j)$, $I_{db} \vDash_{va} \Gamma$ if and only if $[va(x_i) \in I_{\Sigma 1}(v)] \wedge$
$[va(x_j) \in I_{\Sigma 1}(u)] \wedge$
$[va(x_j) \in I_{\Sigma 2}(z)(va(x_i))]$.
- For $\Gamma = \gamma_v(u)$, $I_{db} \vDash_{va} \Gamma$ if and only if $I_{\Sigma 1}(va(u)) \in I_{\Omega 1}(v)$.

For $\Gamma = \chi_v(u,w)$, $I_{db} \models_{va} \Gamma$ if and only if $va(u) \in \Sigma_1 \wedge I_{\Sigma 2}(va(w)) \in I_{\Omega 2}(v)$.

For any two formulas Γ_1 and Γ_2 of L, the meaning of $\Gamma_1 \wedge \Gamma_2$, $\Gamma_1 \vee \Gamma_2$, $\Gamma_1 \Rightarrow \Gamma_2$, and $\neg \Gamma_1$ is defined according to the standard inductive framework. The meaning of a quantified formula is also standard: $I_{db} \models_{va} \Gamma$, where $\Gamma = (\forall X)F$ (resp., $\Gamma = (\exists X)F$) if for every (resp., some) variable assignment ua that agrees with va everywhere, we have $I_{db} \models_{ua} F$. As usual, the equality predicate '=' gets special treatment:

$$I_P(=) \stackrel{def}{=} \{<u, u> \mid u \in U \cup \prod U\},$$

which is equivalent to saying that for any pair of elements or of data structures, t and s,

$I_{db} \models_{va} (t = s)$ if and only if $va(t) = va(s)$.

Clearly, if Γ is a *closed* formula (no free variables), its meaning is independent of a variable assignment, and we can write $I_{db} \models \Gamma$, omitting va. A semantic structure I_{db} is a model of Γ if $I_{db} \models \Gamma$, in which case we say that I_{db} *satisfies* Γ.

- semantics of L_o

The semantic structure for a given language L' of L_o, I_o, is a tuple $<U'$, I_{OF}, I_{AS}, I_{AM}, I_Σ, I_P, $\leq_\Sigma$, $\prec_\Sigma>$. Here U' is a nonempty poset (partially ordered set, possibly infinite). That is, there exists a relation $\prec$ over U' such that:

    i) $a \prec a$ for all $a \in U'$ (reflexivity).

    ii)   if $a \prec b$ and $b \prec c$, then $a \prec c$ (transitivity).

    iii)   if $a \prec b$ and $b \prec a$, then $a = b$ (antisymmetry).

Note that defining U' to be a poset is the main difference between our version and the logic proposed in [KW93]. According to our observation, all the objects in the 'real' world can be (partially) ordered non-recursively in terms of the part-of relationship. Moreover, the integers with the usual order are a poset and then we can codify the objects of a possible world with the integers in such a way that the part-of relationships of objects are reflected by the partial order of the integers.

Further, we extend this relationship to subsets in the following way. For any two subsets a and b if for each $a \in a$ and all $b \in b$, $a \prec b$ holds, then we have $a \prec b$.

As in the database logic L_{db}, the mapping I_{OF} interprets each constant of L' as an element in U'. The mapping I_{AS} interprets each single-valued attribute $A_{si} \in A_s$ as a partial function $I_{AS}(A_{si})$: $U' \rightarrow U'$. Similarly, I_{AM} maps every set-valued attribute $A_{mj} \in A_m$ into a partial function $I_{AM}(A_{mj})$: $U' \rightarrow 2^{U'}$. The mapping I_Σ interprets each class name in Σ as a subset of U', that is, $I_\Sigma: \Sigma \rightarrow 2^{U'}$. I_P interprets each predicate p as a function $I_P(p)$: $U'^i \rightarrow \{true, false\}$. Further, $\prec_\Sigma$ is a partial order relation such that if $c_1 \prec_\Sigma c_2$ then $I_\Sigma(c_1) \prec I_\Sigma(c_2)$ (i.e., $\prec_\Sigma$ models the part-of relationship.) Finally, if $c_1 \prec_\Sigma c_2$, then $I_\Sigma(c_1) \subseteq I_\Sigma(c_2)$. (i.e., $\leq_\Sigma$ models the subclass-relationship.)

In the following, we view the I_o interpretation of the predicates and the complex object structures as assertions about properties of the objects in U'. Intuitively, a predicate or a complex object structure p is satisfied by a semantic structure, if the properties asserted in p hold for the objects of U'. As in I_{db}, we need to define the formula satisfaction.

A variable-assignment, v, is a mapping $V_o \rightarrow U'$.

Now we can talk about formulas satisfied by a semantic structure I_o w.r.t. a variable-assignment v. The formula satisfaction, denoted $I_o \models_v \Gamma$, is defined as follows:

-    For $\Gamma = isa\text{-}instanceOf(x, c)$, $I_o \models_v \Gamma$ if and only if $v(x) \in I_\Sigma(c)$.

-    For $\Gamma = isa\text{-}subclassOf(c_1, c_2)$, $I_o \models_v \Gamma$ if and only if $c_1 \leq_\Sigma c_2$.

-    For $\Gamma = partOf(c_1, c_2)$, $I_o \models_v \Gamma$ if and only if $c_1 \prec_\Sigma c_2$.

-    For a complex object structure $\Gamma = (x, X)[A_{s1}: t_1, ..., A_{sk}: t_k, ..., A_{m1}: \{s_{11}, ..., s_{1l_1}\},$ ..., $A_{mn}: \{s_{n1}, ..., s_{nl_n}\}]$, $I_o \models_v \Gamma$ if and only if the following conditions hold:

    ·   For each single-valued attribute A_{si}, $I_{AS}(A_{si})(v(x)) = v(t_i)$ and $I_o \models_v t_i$.

    ·   For each set-valued attribute A_{mj}, $\{v(s_{j1}), ..., v(s_{jl_j})\} \subseteq I_{AM}(A_{mj})(v(x))$ and I_o

$\vdash_v s_{jk}$, for $k = 1, ..., l_j$.

Note that in terms of the above definition we derive that $I_o \vdash_v$ *isa-subclassOf*(c_1, c_2) implies $I_\Sigma(c_1) \subseteq I_\Sigma(c_2)$. Similarly, $I_o \vdash_v$ *partOf*(c_1, c_2) implies $I_\Sigma(c_1) \prec I_\Sigma(c_2)$.

As in L_{db}, arbitrary well-formed formulas in L_o are satisfied according to the standard definition. A set of formulas S in L_o is satisfied by I_o if and only if for all $\alpha \in S$, I_o satisfies α. I_o is a *model* of S if and only if I_o satisfies S independent of any variable assignment.

References

CBS94	R.H.L. Chiang, T.M. Barron, and V.C. Storey, "Reverse engineering of relational databases: extraction of an EER model from a relational database," *Data & knowledge Engineering*, vol. 12, 1994, pp. 107 - 142.
Ch76	P.P.S. Chen, "The Entity-Relationship Model: Toward a Unified View of Data", *ACM TODS* 1, No. 1, March 1976.
Co86	E.F. Codd, "Missing Information (Applicable and inapplicable) in Relational Databases", *SIGMOD RECORD*, vol. 15, 1986, pp. 53 -78.
CRV93	J.A. Chudziak, H. Rybinsky and J. Vorbach, "Towards a Unifying Logic Formalism for Semantic Data Models", *Proc. 12th Int. Conf. on the Entity-Relationship Approach*, Arlington, Texas, USA, Dec. 1993, pp. 492 - 507.
CW93	S. Ceri and J. Widom, "Managing Semantic Heterogeneity with Production Rules and Persistent Queues", in *Proc. 19th Int. VLDB Conference*, Dublin, Ireland, 1993, pp. 108 -119.
HLM94	G. Harhalakis, C.P. Lin, L. Mark and P.R. Muro-Medrano, "Implementation of Rule-based Information Systems for Integrated Manufacturing", *IEEE Trans. on Knowledge and Data Engineering*, vol. 6, No. 6, 892 - 908, Dec. 1994.
KC93	J-L. Koh and Arbee L.P. Chen, "Integration of Heterogeneous Object Schemas", in *Proc. 12th Int. Conf. on the Entity-Relationship Approach*, Arlington, Texas, USA, Dec. 1993, pp. 297 - 314.
KRS88	R. Krishnamurthy, R. Ramakrishnan and O. Shmueli, "A Framework for Testing Safety and Effective Computability of Extended Datalog," in: *Proc. 1988 ACM-SIGMOD Int. Conf. on Management of Data*, pp. 154 - 163, Chicago, Ill., June 1988.
KW93	M. Kifer and J. Wu, "A Logic for Programming with Complex Objects," *Int. J. of Computer and System Sciences*, 47, pp. 77 - 20, 1993.
LA86	W. Litwin and A. Abdellatif, "Multidatabase interoperability," *IEEE Comput. mag.*, vol. 19, No. 12, pp. 10 - 18, 1986.
Ll87	J.W. Lloyd, "*Foundation of Logic Programming*", Springer-Verlage, Berlin, 1987.
LNE89	J.A. Larson, S.B. Navathe, and R. Elmasri, "A theory of attribute equivalence in databases with application to schema integration," *IEEE Trans. Software Eng.*, vol. 15, No. 4, pp. 449 - 463, 1989.
LR82	T. Landers and R. Rosenberg, "An overview of multibase," in *Distributed Databases*, H.J. Schneider, Ed. Amsterdam: North-Holland, 1982.
Ma86	D. Maier, "A logic for objects," in: *Proc. Workshop on Foundations of Deductive Databases and Logic Programming*, Washington, Aug. 1986, pp. 424 - 433.
MM90	V.M. Markowitz and J.A. Makowsky, "Identifying extended entity-relationship object structures in relational schemas," *IEEE Trans. Software Eng.*, vol. 16, No. 8, pp. 777 - 790, 1990.
PTR96	M. Papazoglou, Z. Tari and N. Russell, "Object-oriented Technology for Interschema and Language Mappings," in: O. Bukhres and K. Elmagarmid (eds.): *Object Oriented Multidatabase Systems*, Chapter 6, Prentice Hall, Englewood Cliffs, N.J., 1996.
Sa91	Y. Sagiv, "On Testing Effective Computability of Magic Programs," in: *Proc. 2nd Int. Conf. on Deductive and Object-Oriented Databases*, pp. 244 - 262, Munich, Dec. 1991.
SK92	W. Sull and R.L. Kashyap, "A Self-organizing knowledge representation schema for extensible heterogeneous information environment," *IEEE Trans. on Knowledge and Data Engineering*, vol. 4, No. 2, 185 - 191, April 1992.
TS93	C. Thieme and A. Siebes, "Schema Integration in Object-Oriented Databases", in: *Proc. 5th. Int. Conf. on Advanced Information Systems Engineering*, Paris, France, June 1993, pp. 54 - 70.
VA95	M.W. Vermeer and P.M. Apers, "Object-oriented views of relational databases incorporating behavior," in: *Proc. 4th Int. Conf. on Database Systems for Advanced Application (DASFAA' 95)*, Singapore, April 1995, pp. 26 - 35.

Ontology of Object-Oriented Database Evolution

M. L. Hines
University of Missouri-Kansas City
Kansas City, MO   64110 USA
hines@cstp.umkc.edu

Key Words: object-oriented ontologies, knowledge management, object database design, object database development processes

Abstract: The need for expanded data representation and semantic capture resulted in the emergence of object-oriented databases. Representation of relationships beyond inheritance relationships, provision of separate development and working environments, and control of evolution for developing database systems are areas not yet adequately addressed. This work defines a specification hierarchy which provides expanded relationship representation and a development environment for database systems; and an ontological system constraining migration of classes and relationships from the development environment to the working environment.

I.   Introduction

The advent of multimedia, CAD/CAM, and knowledge bases required development of the capability to represent non-traditional data - e.g., 3D images, temporal information, etc. Expanded semantic capture is required to more accurately model real-world entities and their relationships; representation of data has to include not only static, declarative information, but also dynamic, behavioral information including relationship information that is no longer simply syntactic or at the application level. These non-traditional data representation needs require on-going (schema) design in a dynamic working environment. Traditional database models allow little flexibility in the evolution of schema [1,2]. Relationships are statically defined and completely syntactic, resulting in restricted modeling capabilities, and are based on content and content-based operations such as the join [1,2].

Object-oriented databases address some non-traditional data representation needs by expanding possible semantic capture, primarily through encapsulation and representation of inheritance relationships. In object-oriented systems where only inheritance relationships are explicitly captured, ontological constraint is unnecessary, i.e., inheritance is transitive in nature but not restrictive.

Semantic capture in object-oriented database systems can be more fully exploited by expanding representation of inheritance relationships to include representation of other types of relationships. Expanded relationship representation capability helps preserve the integrity of the information in the system, but if it is not constrained the database could become filled with paradoxical and oxymoronic relationships. Representation of relationships other than inheritance relationships requires constraints on how relationships interact with one another to prevent conflicting information. The increase in complexity of represented entities and their interrelationships requires the development of mechanisms within the database data model to regulate and constrain the database such that some state of the database is guaranteed; formalizing an evolutionary mechanism is required.

Constraining evolution in a working database environment also constrains exploratory design, including prototyping. Object-oriented databases must address evolution and flexibility of databases, in particular design databases which characterize CAD, CAM, CASE and CAE technology. Development and working environments, which are separate yet directly related, can facilitate exploratory design while preserving the stability of the working environment.

This work defines a specification hierarchy as a design tool which is explicitly tied to the object-oriented database model, and which provides relationship representation beyond inheritance. The specification hierarchy expands semantic capture through the representation of "prohibited" and "future" relationships in addition to inheritance relationships. This expanded semantic capture sets the ontological framework for modeling other types of relationships.

The specification hierarchy "surrounds" the traditional class hierarchy of an object-oriented database, separating the development environment from the working environment. The development environment allows design to continue without affecting the working environment until the design is complete. The evolution of the working environment is constrained by an ontological system which guarantees the working environment to be closed, consistent, stable, and unambiguous.

Section II briefly overviews the object-oriented database data model used in this research. Section III presents the specification hierarchy and Section IV presents the ontological system. Section V compares this work with other oodb research and summarizes the contributions.

II. Overview of Data Model

The object-oriented database data model used as the foundation for this work is a subset of earlier work which described a complete, formal object-oriented database data model called the COODB data model [3]. The COODB data model formalizes such concepts as object, class, class hierarchy, method, message, and variables. Only those concepts of the COODB data model necessary for understanding of this work are included - i.e., relevant portions of class and class hierarchy. Objects, while a fundamental part of an oodb, are not relevant to the concept of schema (class) evolution as discussed. Only the structure of a class is included; the structure, structural constraints and behavior of the class hierarchy are discussed.

A. Class

A *class* is a template representing a group of objects having certain properties in common. Conceptually, a class represents a collection of user-world entities which are similar within the user's modeling perception. Both procedural and declarative knowledge about the collection of entities are represented by the class definition. The structure of a class, c, is represented by a five tuple such that cls_struct=(CKey, Instance_Var, Class_Var, Method_Set, Superclass_Set). Classes are uniquely identified by their class key, CKey. Methods and class/instance variables may be designed into a class or may be inherited from a superclass. The set of superclasses, c.Superclass_Set, of a class, c, represents the CKeys of the classes of which c is a subclass. Instance_Var and Class_Var of a class represent the set of instance variables and the set of class variables respectively. Class_Var and

Instance_Var are initialized to empty, and are filled either by definition of super-classes or by definition of variables.

The set of methods, Method_Set, of a class contains the methods a class and/or its instances may invoke and execute. Method_Set is initialized to empty, and is filled either through definition of the Superclass_Set or by definition of methods.

B. Class hierarchy

A *class hierarchy* defines the structure of an oodb and contains a set of classes and a set of objects. A graphical representation of the class hierarchy can be obtained where the classes represent the nodes of the graph and the superclass sets of the classes can be used to derive the edges of the graph. All class hierarchies contain at least a root class, which has no superclasses. A root_class is a cls_struct with an empty Superclass_Set. The structure of a class hierarchy, H, is represented by a tuple such that class_hierarchy_struct=(O, C) where the objectbase, O, is a set of object structures initialized to empty, and containing all objects in the class hierarchy.

The *classbase*, C, is a set of class structures, cls_struct, containing the classes participating in the class hierarchy, and is initialized as containing root_class. Classes participating in the class hierarchy are those classes available to users. Classes are related to one another through inheritance relationships exemplified by the presence of the CKey of a class in another class's Superclass_Set. These relationships can be derived by a function *Edges*, which, given a set of classes, returns a set of ordered pairs of CKeys representing inheritance relationships and defining the class hierarchy as a directed graph. In the class hierarchy an ordered pair in the set returned by the function Edges has the following meaning: given an ordered pair, $(class_1, class_2)$, $class_1$ is a subclass of $class_2$, and inheritance occurs from $class_2$ to $class_1$ but not vice versa.

Connectedness and the *no cycles* constraints constrain the structure of the class hierarchy (as formed by the classbase, C, and the set formed by the function

Edges) to a connected graph, and constrains a class from being a superclass of itself. The function *is_path* determines the existence of a path between two classes in a class hierarchy, H.

All members of the Superclass_Set of a class, c, must also be members of the classbase, C, of the class hierarchy, H, to provide closure for the Superclass_Set.

These definitions and constraints provide the foundation for the definition of the specification hierarchy and the evolution system.

III. Specification Hierarchy

The class hierarchy necessarily must be relatively static in nature particularly with respect to evolution of classes, since it is available to users. However, this staticity does not allow an oodb to be as flexible and dynamic as may be needed. Flexibility is primarily needed during design of an oodb, which may be an ongoing process throughout the life of the oodb. With the objective of increased flexibility for designers while also supplying relative stability for users, the *specification hierarchy* is introduced and defined as a design tool for the oodb. The specification hierarchy contains a class hierarchy and also contains other classes and relationships not found in its class hierarchy component. The set *Nodes* in the specification hierarchy includes classes which are still being designed and which are not yet available to the user. The set *Edges* in the specification hierarchy includes inheritance relationships which are still being designed and which are not yet available to the user. Once design of a specification hierarchy Node or Edge is completed, it can be added to the class hierarchy for user availability. The specification hierarchy allows design of an oodb by representing classes, existing and potential, and explicit relationships between those classes.

Each specification hierarchy contains a class hierarchy, H; there is only one class hierarchy in any given specification hierarchy. However, it is perfectly feasible for the class hierarchy to be partitioned into subsets should a need arise, e.g., for security purposes.

A class contained in the specification hierarchy set Nodes may be a class which is available to the user or may be a class still being designed.

Relationships in the set Edges are relationships which can be directly incorporated into the class hierarchy, H, by adding the component classes to H.c (if they are not already there) and adding the superclass component of the Edges relationship to the Superclass_Set of the class component of the Edges relationship. The relationships in Edges may be those affecting the user or may be those still in design.

The set of Prohibited relationships defines those relationships not allowed to exist in the class hierarchy, H. The ability to prohibit certain relationships from existing can increase the semantic capture and integrity of relationships within an oodb, since there are real-world relationships which are, for various reasons, prohibited between real-world entities and enterprises.

The Future set contains relationships recognized to exist between real-world entities and enterprises but not currently part of the oodb. By allowing representation of possible future relationships between classes in the class hierarchy, H, and/or classes in the specification hierarchy, S, planning for incremental growth of the oodb can be facilitated in a more organized manner, since relationships between current classes and potential classes can be recognized at the point when the current class is defined. While not all future relationships in the set Future may be represented, use of the Future set provides a tool for initial definition of relationships. The caveat to using the Future set is to recognize the possibility, and probability, of the incompleteness of the Future set.

Structural constraints, both inter-relational and intra-relational, for the specification hierarchy, including the subcomponent class hierarchy, are presented next. The class hierarchy of an oodb is a subset of the specification hierarchy such that the classbase, c, of the class hierarchy is a subset of the set Nodes of the specification hierarchy, and the set formed by the function Edges of the class hierarchy is a subset of the set Edges of the specification hierarchy.

Since the classbase of a class hierarchy is a subset of the set Nodes of the specification hierarchy and all classes represented by the set Nodes of the specification hierarchy have a unique key, so do classes represented by the classbase of the class hierarchy. Class keys are unchangeable and non-reusable.

The set Edges of a specification hierarchy contains ordered pairs semantically representative of inheritance relationships between classes in the set Nodes of a specification hierarchy. *Faithfulness* constrains the specification hierarchy such that the component class keys of the ordered pairs of Edges are contained in the set Nodes of the specification hierarchy.

The sets Edges, Prohibited, and Future of the specification hierarchy, S, are mutually disjoint, preventing overlap of semantically incompatible sets. The set Future is constrained to be symmetrical, since the relationship represented is semantically unknown.

The oodb data model behavior is defined at a meta-level with respect to a component and the behavior all components of that type exhibit. Behavior, representing procedural knowledge, is defined by providing functions for the components. The behavior of the specification hierarchy consists of functions which allow addition/deletion/update of a class, an Edge set member, a Prohibited set member, an Future set member, addition/deletion/update of a class/edge to the class hierarchy of the specification hierarchy. The class update functions (add-variable, add-method) are not defined for the oodb data model, as their semantics are implementation dependent or dependent on the database management system of the oodb.

The next group of functions allow the creation of classes and relationships including inheritance relationships, prohibited relationships, and future relationships, and the transfer of classes and inheritance relationships from the specification hierarchy to the class hierarchy. These functions impact classes within the specification hierarchy subject to the constraints of the specification hierarchy and its components; they include *create_class* which creates a class within the specification hierarchy, *move_class* which transfers a class from the specification hierarchy to the class hierarchy, *create_edge* which creates an inheritance relationship between two classes in a specification hierarchy, *move_inheritance_relation* which transfers an inheritance relationship from a specification hierarchy to its class hierarchy, *create_prohibited* which defines prohibited relationships for a specification hierarchy and *create_future* which notes future relationships within a specification hierarchy.

The specification hierarchy allows for representation of relationships beyond inheritance relationships, and provides a separation between the development and working environments for an object-oriented database system. The bridging of that separation requires an ontological system for evolution which will constrain the working environment with respect to the relationships represented in the development environment.

IV. Evolution System

The specification hierarchy allows representation of a "mini-world"; the evolution system allows a designer the ability to specify initially, and at any point during system evolution, those relationships possible to represent and those not possible. This *a priori* determination of relationships allows, yet constrains, the evolution of the oodb system within the "open world" left by an incomplete specification hierarchy, i.e., dynamic and flexible evolution is allowed while maintaining a system which is sound; closed; whose inheritance sequences are grounded, stable, consistent, and unambiguous; and whose inheritance relationships adhere to the orthogonality property. Single and multiple inheritance are defined. Single inheritance may require use of virtual classes to represent the breadth of a given "mini-world"; multiple inheritance allows a greater breadth of representation but must be constrained to avoid instability, ambiguity, and inconsistency. Orthogonality, as defined in this work, constrains multiple inheritance in such a way that the desired properties of the oodb system are preserved.

A. Notation

The class hierarchy, H, and the specification hierarchy, S, define sequences of inheritance for an oodb, e.g., class$_1$ inherits from class$_2$ which inherits from

class_n. Symbols used in the evolution system directly represent the class components of the data model by their class keys. Π denotes the set of class keys of all classes in the classbase of the class hierarchy, H.

The relationships between the classes -- inheritance, Future, and Prohibited -- are explicitly represented by "signing" the class keys, i.e., prefixing the class keys in the class hierarchy, H, with a sign - + (positive), − (negative), -- (prohibited), and # (future) - based upon the class's participation in relationships. Θ denotes the set of signed class keys derivable by prefixing the class keys in Π with the four signs +, −, --, #.

Inheritance statements are elements of $\Theta \times \Theta$ -- i.e., they are ordered pairs of signed class keys. Three of the four class signs, (+, --, #), are used to represent relationships explicitly defined in the oodb data model. The fourth sign (−) is used to represent an inferred relationship representing the absence of any explicit relationship between two classes; it cannot be the sign of the first class in any inheritance statement. Its presence as the sign of the first class in an inheritance statement represents usage of a non-class or the complement of a class, and the subsequent non-closure of the system. Non-closure does not assure the desired properties of stability, consistency, and unambiguity necessary for increased semantic capture. A *well-formed ordered pair* is a sequence consisting of two signed class keys where the sign of the first class key is '+'. There are four types of well-formed ordered pairs, each composed of two signed class keys, where p and q represent class keys: (+p, +q) - p is a subclass of q; (+p, −q) - p is not a subclass of q; (+p, --q) - p is prohibited from being a subclass of q (Prohibited relationship); and (+p, #q) - no conclusion whether p is a subclass of q (Future relationship). For example, the assertion "car is a subclass of vehicle" is represented by the signed ordered pair (+car, +vehicle) while the assertion "car is prohibited from being a subclass of animals" is represented by the signed ordered pair (+car, --animals).

Inheritance statements, i.e., facts found in or derivable from the oodb, are represented by the set Γ. Γ denotes a set of well-formed ordered pairs, or inheritance statements, formed from the class hierarchy and the specification hierarchy. For example, the inheritance statement (+car, +vehicle) is true if both car and vehicle exist as class keys within the set Keys(H.c), and if car is a subclass of vehicle represented as a relationship in Edges(H.c). If this statement is true, then it is a member of Γ.

Initially the evolution system is restricted to single inheritance allowing structured growth towards the desired graph representation, and resulting in a finite, labeled, directed tree hierarchy, formed from Γ. Sequences of signed class keys of length greater than two describe sequences through the tree hierarchy. Sequences, formed by ordered pairs within the evolution system, imply subclass inheritance of the properties of the parent class. Sequences may be well-formed or ill-formed. Well-formed sequences are of interest; ill-formed sequences imply the usage of complements of classes which is not allowed. A well-formed sequence has a length of at least 2, and the sign of the first class key in the sequence is positive. the phrase well-formed sequence will subsequently be referred to as sequence. The signs of the remaining class keys in a sequence may be positive, prohibited, non-existent or negative, or future. The set of simple sequences derived from the tree hierarchy formed from Γ denotes the inheritance statements. Σ denotes the set of all sequences of Θ^+ of length at least two, i.e., the set of all possible sequences, both well-formed and ill-formed, of length at least two. Thus Γ is a subset of $\Theta \times \Theta$ which is a subset of Σ. σ denotes a sequence in Σ. Given the class hierarchy H (Figure 1), Γ contains: $\{(+y,+x), (+z,+x),(+w,+y), (+g,+y), (+m,+w), (+h,+z)\}$.

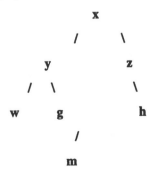

Fig. 1. Class hierarchy example

Z and Φ denote subsets of Σ, with Φ denoting expansions or inheritance theories represented as sequences formed from Γ. Φ contains inheritance theories directly asserted by the sequences derived from the tree hierarchy and inheritance theories inferred or derived from those sequences, including non-existent or negative assertions. Φ is a set of well-formed sequences from Γ formed by concatenating ordered pairs and eliminating duplicates such that given a set of ordered pairs $\{(x_1, x_2), (x_2, x_3), ..., (x_{n-1}, x_n)\}$ where x_i is a signed class key, $1 \le i \le n$, $n \ge 2$, then $(x_1, x_2, ..., x_{n-1}, x_n) \in \Phi$.

Φ for Figure 1 contains: $\{$(+g,+y,+x), (+w,+y,+x), (+m,+w,+y), (+m,+w,+y,+x), (+h,+z,+x), (+m,+w,–g), (+m,+w,–h), (+m,+w,–z), (+m,+w,+y,–g), (+m,+w,+y,–h), (+m,+w,+y,–z), (+g,+y,–w), (+g,+y,–m), (+g,+y,–h), (+g,+y,–z), (+h,+z,–m), (+h,+z,–w), (+h,+z,–y), (+h,+z,–g), (+w,+y,–m), (+w,+y,–g), (+w,+y,–h), (+w,+y,–z), (+y,+x,–m), (+y,+x,–g), (+y,+x,–h), (+y,+x,–z), (+y,+x,–w), (+z,+x,–m), (+z,+x,–w), (+z,+x,–y), (+z,+x,–g), (+z,+x,–h), (+x,–y), (+x,–z), (+x,–w), (+x,–g), (+x,–h), (+x,–m)$\}$ ∪ Γ. Note Φ contains not only the inheritance statements given in Γ, e.g., (+y, +x), but also contains all the inheritance statements and inheritance theories derived from Γ, e.g., (+x,–z) and (+w,+y,–h).

B. Evolution system structure

The evolution system is defined with respect to the symbols representing classes and relationships of the class hierarchy, H, and the specification hierarchy, S. Given an evolution system described as a set of well-formed ordered pairs, Γ, definitions and theorems in this section describe the structure of the expansions of that system. Expansions contain maximal sets of permissible inferences that may be drawn from the system.

Non-structural definitions define a predicate and the conditions for the predicate to hold, e.g., contradiction is defined as a predicate is_contradicted and the conditions for the predicate to hold are given as part of the definition. The variables x and y range over the signed classes and represent signed classes. Signed classes that match except for sign are denoted with a prime notation. If x stands for +p, then x' can signify --p, –p or #p.

The set of simple sequences through the tree hierarchy formed from Γ may be used to derive a set of implied facts called the closure set, $C(\Phi)$. The closure set represents conclusions that may be drawn from the evolution system. $C(\Phi)$ is the set of facts implied by the sequences in Φ. Questions such as "Does the class cars inherit from the class vehicles?" are answerable by examining $C(\Phi)$. For example, if Φ contains the sequence (+dog, +mammal, +animal), then $C(\Phi)$ includes (+dog, +animal). The closure set formed from Figure 1 is :

$C(\Phi) =$
{(+w,+x),(+g,+x),(+h,+x),(+m,+y),(+m,+x),(+w,–g),(+w,–z),
(+w,–h),(+w,–m),(+h,–y),(+h,–w),(+h,–g),(+h,–m),(+m,–z),(+m,–h),(+m,–g),
(+g,–w),(+g,–m),(+g,–h),(+g,–z),(+y,–z),(+y,–h),(+y,–w),(+y,–g),(+y,–m),
(+z,–h),(+z,–y),(+z,–w),(+z,–g),(+z,–m),(+x,–y),(+x,–z),(+x,–w),(+x,–g),
(+x,–h),(+x,–m)} $\cup$ Γ.

Sequences may be contradicted within the closure set by the presence of a negative or prohibited signed class within the intermediary signed classes of a set of sequences being used to derive a fact. Contradiction can be used to prevent any new sequence from appearing in Φ that would conflict with what is already in Φ. For example, (+car, +vehicle) and (+car, --vehicle) are mutually contradictory; if Φ contains one it will contradict the other and preclude its addition to Φ. If the class hierarchy, H, contains, for example, the relation HR = (+car, +vehicle), and the specification hierarchy, S, contains the relation SR = (+car, --vehicle), then SR is precluded from being added to the class hierarchy by the presence of HR in H. In the example given by Figure 1, the sequence (+m,+w,+y,--x) is contradicted.

A sequence does not have to be contained in the evolution system, Φ, to be inheritable. For example, if Φ consists of the two sequences (+beagle, +dog, +mammal) and (+dog, +mammal, +animal), then (+beagle, +dog, +mammal, +animal) is inheritable in Φ. A set of sequences is closed if all of its component sequences are well-formed and are inheritable, i.e., given a sequence, s, and a set of sequences, S, s is inheritable in S if s is longer than 2 elements and all of the sub-sequences of s are elements of S and s is not contradicted in S.

If Φ contains (+beagle, +dog, +mammal) and (+dog, +mammal, +animal) but does not contain (+beagle, +dog, +mammal, +animal), then Φ is not closed under inheritance; (+beagle, +dog, +mammal, +animal) is inheritable in Φ but is not contained in Φ.

If Z ={(+beagle, +dog, +mammal), (+dog, +mammal, +animal)} and Φ={(+beagle, +dog, +mammal, +animal)} ∪ Z, then Φ is an expansion of Z. Given two sets of sequences, Φ and Z, if all sequences contained in Φ-Z are inheritable in Φ, then Φ is grounded in Z. Given two sets of sequences, Φ and Z, Φ is a grounded expansion of Z, if Φ is an expansion of Z and is grounded in Z.

The previous example given of an expansion is also an example of a grounded expansion. Grounded expansions restrict an evolution system to be a connected digraph; for an evolution system to be a grounded expansion of a set Z, all the classes within the evolution system must be reachable by a simple sequence. It can be shown that a) the only well-formed ordered pairs in a grounded expansion are those in the evolution system, i.e., closure; b) all sub-parts of an expansion are also contained in the evolution system; c) multiple expansions are not allowed; and d) only well-formed sequences are allowed.

C. Properties of the evolution system

The properties of the evolution system constrain the structure of an oodb to be unambiguous, stable, and consistent. Ordering relations are used to more directly represent the subclass-class relationships by eliminating the need to use only ordered pairs and sequences to represent relationships in the evolution system. The is_related relation is the "less than" relation under all relationships in Γ; inherits_from is the "less than" relation under subclass relationship alone. It can be shown that the inherits_from relation is a subset of the is_related relation, and the inherits_from and is_related relations are transitive.

An evolution system is said to be consistent if it does not contradict any of its elements, i.e., the ordered pairs within an evolution system do not contradict one another. The set of elements given by the Γ in Figure 1 is consistent. If a prohibited relationship (+w,--y) is added to Figure 1, then Γ is no longer consistent.

Ambiguity is a more global property than consistency; not only must the ordered pairs not contradict one another but the derived sequences must also not contradict one another. An evolution system is said to be ambiguous if it has more than one grounded expansion, i.e., a set of well-formed ordered pairs, Γ, is *ambiguous* iff it has more than one grounded expansion. Γ is unambiguous iff it is not ambiguous.

An evolution system that is ambiguous has more than one grounded expansion such that $\Phi_a \neq \Phi_b$, indicating the presence of a cycle and/or contradicting pairs in the evolution system. Ambiguity is not the same kind of property as consistency. The consistency of a grounded expansion Φ of Γ is a strictly local property of Γ; to show Φ is consistent or inconsistent only the pairs, or sequences, of classes in Γ need be examined. If a pair of the form (x,y), (x,y') or a single sequence of form (x,x') is found, then Φ and Γ are inconsistent. Ambiguity is a more global property; its determination is not by the existence of particular sequences in Γ or in any one expansion, but rather by the existence of multiple expansions.

Stability is more global than consistency; to show an expansion is unstable certain sequences must be shown not to be precluded in it. There is not a minimum number of sequences that must be examined to determine stability; stability depends on the entire expansion. Stability is a more local property than ambiguity; ambiguity can be determined by examining a single expansion for stability. The evolution system given in Figure 2 is unstable.

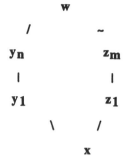

Fig. 2. Unstable evolution system

D. Graph structure of evolution system

Initially, a tree-structured inheritance system has been examined leading to the definition of a tree-structured, object-oriented evolution system with *single inheritance*.

A signed class x, $x \in \Pi$, is a *class node* wrt Γ iff no sequence in Γ begins or ends with $-x$, implying usage of a non-class or the complement of a class (there does not exist a corresponding class in S.H.c) which is not allowed. x may be a *minimal class* in Γ iff there is no class y such that inherits_from(y, x).

Γ is a *tree-structured object-oriented inheritance system* if it is acyclic, all of its signed classes are class_nodes, and only single inheritance occurs. An inheritance system is totally acyclic if none of the classes within the inheritance system participate in a cycle. It can be shown that all classes in an inheritance system are class_nodes [3].

Tree-structured inheritance systems are exception-free if none of the inheritance theories or assertions are contradicted. If it is exception-free, then it is also unambiguous, stable, and consistent since there are only positive signed classes in the system.

The inheritance system can now be expanded to a graph structured inheritance system to allow multiple inheritance; too many situations cannot be adequately modeled with only single inheritance [4]. Tree-structured systems are a subset of graph-structured systems, allowing the previous definitions and theorems to hold for the graph inheritance system; the addition of multiple inheritance and the graph structure necessitates a more thorough discussion of acyclicity. The graph-inheritance evolution system is limited to being acyclic.

The ordering relation for the classes becomes a partial ordering for the graph-inheritance evolution system if the system is totally acyclic [3]. It can be shown that every grounded expansion of a acyclic graph inheritance system is finite.

When two distinct grounded expansions of an acyclic graph inheritance system are unioned, the result is inconsistent [3]. The construction and existence of grounded expansions for acyclic graph-inheritance evolution systems can be shown through the process of successive approximations [3]. Every acyclic graph-inheritance evolution system has a constructible grounded expansion, and if a totally acyclic graph-inheritance evolution system is ambiguous then all of its grounded expansions are unstable [3]. An acyclic graph-inheritance evolution system is unambiguous if and only if it has a single stable grounded expansion.

It is possible, for acyclic graphs, to determine if Γ is ambiguous by constructing one expansion and checking it for stability. An object-oriented graph-inheritance evolution system is defined based on acyclicity. Γ is an *object-oriented graph-inheritance evolution system* if it is acyclic, all of its signed classes are class_nodes and it is stable, consistent, and unambiguous.

The use of multiple inheritance in an oodb system in an unrestricted manner results in a system vulnerable to ambiguity and instability. Multiple inheritance is allowed in a restricted form by introducing an orthogonal object-oriented graph-inheritance evolution system where a class is allowed to inherit from multiple superclasses provided the properties inherited from any two superclasses are disjoint.

Orthogonality of inherited properties in an orthogonal object-oriented graph-inheritance evolution system can overcome name polymorphism of inherited properties by prefixing inherited properties with the CKey of the class from which the property is inherited. Γ is an *orthogonal object-oriented graph-inheritance evo-*

lution system iff it is an object-oriented graph-inheritance evolution system, and allows orthogonal multiple inheritance.

E. Evolution system constraint

By constraining an oodb system to be unambiguous, stable, and consistent, the criteria for establishing an intransitive system have been defined. An intransitive oodb system is unambiguous, stable, and consistent at the beginning of a change (evolutionary action), and at the end of that change (evolutionary action) remains unambiguous, stable, and consistent, whether there have been any changes, additions, or deletions to the structure and/or behavior of the oodb system.

These constraints allow a designer the necessary flexibility and freedom to explore different design possibilities through the specification hierarchy including those designs which might violate the system constraints. The constraints increase the data integrity and knowledge integrity of the oodb by easing demands upon a designer at the design stage while still answering the user's needs with respect to a stable, consistent, and unambiguous system. The design of an oodb system occurs <u>outside</u> the user accessible portion of the oodb decreasing the danger of incurring an anomaly because of an addition, deletion, or change. Before a "new" class or relationship can be made user accessible, -- i.e., moved from the specification hierarchy to the class hierarchy -- it must be checked for stability, consistency, and unambiguity. If it violates any of those three constraints, it cannot be moved to the class hierarchy. The specification hierarchy behaviors to move a class and to move an inheritance relationship from the specification hierarchy to the class hierarchy are modified to reflect these constraints.

IV. Summary

Object-oriented database systems provide expanded semantic capture for emerging data representation needs; this semantic capture can be increased and enhanced by expanding the relationship representations beyond inheritance, and separating the development and working environments. A specification hierarchy has been defined which expands relationship representation and provides a separate development environment that is explicitly tied to the working environment. Migration of design from the specification hierarchy (development environment) to the class hierarchy (working environment) is constrained such that the oodb remains an intransitive system.

The formal definition of an orthogonal object-oriented graph-inheritance evolution system for an object-oriented database provides the foundation for that constraint. The class hierarchy, H, represented as a connected, directed, acyclic graph, and the specification hierarchy, S, are the basis from which the formal mathematical foundation and definition of the orthogonal object-oriented graph-inheritance evolution system is built. The evolution system, allowing multiple inheritance, is defined to be an intransitive system which is unambiguous, stable, and consistent. The evolution of an oodb system, through the change, addition, or deletion of classes or relationships, is constrained by the evolution system.

These two innovations - the specification hierarchy and the evolution system constraint of an oodb - allow object-oriented database evolution while protecting the database user from the database designer. Existing oodb's do not provide a specification hierarchy which allows this style of expanded semantic capture and/or protected working environment. The evolution system work was suggested by [5]; it, or any similar evolutionary constraint mechanism, have not been incorporated as part of an existing oodb.

V. References

[1]   W. Kim, *Introduction to Object-Oriented Databases*, The MIT Press, Cambridge, MA, 1990.

[2]   D. Tsichritzis and O. Nierstrasz, "Fitting Round Objects into Square Databases", *Proceedings 1988 European Conference on Object-Oriented Programming*, Oslo, Norway, August, 1988.

[3]   M. Hines, "COODB: A Formal Data Model", *Information Sciences*, March 1998.

[4]   C. Beeri, "A formal approach to object-oriented databases", *Data and Knowledge Engineering*, Vol. 5, North-Holland, 1990.

[5]   D. Touretzky, *The Mathematics of Inheritance Systems*, Pitman, London, England, 1986.

Capacity-Augmenting Schema Changes on Object-Oriented Databases: Towards Increased Interoperability*

Elke A. Rundensteiner

Department of Computer Science, Worcester Polytechnic Institute
Worcester, MA 01609-2280, USA
rundenst@cs.wpi.edu

Amy J. Lee, and Young-Gook Ra

Department of EECS, University of Michigan
Ann Arbor, MI 48109-2122, USA
amylee@eecs.umich.edu

Abstract

The realization of capacity-augmenting schema changes on a shared database while providing continued interoperability to active applications has been recognized as a hard open problem. A novel three-pronged process, called transparent object schema evolution (TOSE), is presented that successfully addresses this problem. TOSE uses the combination of views and versioning to simulate schema changes requested by one application without affecting other applications interoperating on a shared OODB. The approach is of high practical relevance as it builds upon schema evolution support offered by commercial OODBMSs.

Keywords: Transparent schema evolution, object-oriented views, object-oriented databases, application migration.

1 Introduction

Current schema evolution technology suffers from the problem that schema updates on a database shared by interoperating applications often have catastrophic consequences [BKKK87, KC88, MS93, PS87, TS93, Zic91]. In such a multi-user environment, a schema change demanded by one application could have an undesired impact on other applications, possibly rendering them inoperational. In current OODB systems, schema update capabilities are hence

---

*This work was supported in part by the NSF RIA grant #IRI-9309076, NSF NYI grant #IRI 94-57609, and the University of Michigan Faculty Award Program, IBM Partnership Program, Intel, and AT&T.

more limited by their impact on existing programs rather than by the power of the supported schema change language.

In the context of a 5-year NSF-sponsored effort[1], we are exploring solutions to overcome this schema change problem critical to many industries. Towards this goal, we have proposed a new concept - which we call transparent schema evolution (TSE) – as a promising mechanism for addressing this important problem [RR95]. TSE refers to the notion that a schema change initiated by one user is transparent to (not seen by) other users even though they share a common portion of the schema and the associated data. Our transparency approach is to simulate schema changes as views instead of executing in-place changes on a shared schema, thus shielding other users from these changes [RR97].

However, conventional view mechanisms, being derived functions on the stored database, cannot simulate *capacity-augmenting* [2] schema changes due to their inherent limitation of not augmenting the underlying schema. It has been assumed that one either has to limit oneself to non-capacity-augmenting schema changes or utilize an advanced (capacity-augmenting) view mechanism. In an earlier effort, we [RR95, RR97] as well as Bertino [Ber92] chose the latter approach by extending traditional object-oriented view mechanisms to also support *capacity-augmenting views*. This means that the view mechanism must be capable of the storage of base data directly with view classes. While we have indeed built such an advanced view mechanism, our experiments have shown that this is hard to achieve in an efficient manner [KRR95]. In addition, it imposes restrictions on view classes to be physically materialized so to store these additional attributes with them [KRR95]. More importantly, commercial OODB systems do not support such capacity-augmenting views [3]. For this reason, we now explore an alternative solution to this problem that does *not rely on such powerful (and not available) view support*.

In this paper, we propose a more practical solution to this problem. In contrast to prior work [RR95, RR97], our new approach, which we call TOSE (Transparent Object Schema Evolution), is now neither confined to capacity-reducing or capacity-equivalent schema changes nor requires an advanced view mechanism that supports capacity-augmenting virtual classes. The solution we put forth requires only traditional schema evolution support offered by most commercial OODB systems [BKKK87, PS87] and conventional (derivation-based) view mechanisms [AB91, Run92]. This increases the practical viability of this proposed technology.

The fundamental idea underlying TOSE is a new three-pronged process for

---

[1] We want to express our thanks to the NSF Expert Systems and Database Program, NSF NYI #IRI-94-57609.

[2] The capacity of a schema is defined as the set of possible states of the database under the schema.

[3] As far as we know, the only exception of a fully implemented capacity-augmenting OODB tool is the MultiView research prototype which we have been developing in our on-going NSF-funded research project.

capacity-augmenting transparent evolution. The three steps are: (1) translate the change request specified on the view to the base schema in order to physically restructure the underlying base schema so to hold sufficient capacity as required by the capacity-augmenting schema change operation; (2) derive the desired target view schema from the augmented base schema; and (3) reconstruct the original base schema from the augmented base schema as a view schema in order to preserve all existing input schemas in the system.

Besides the development of this new solution approach for achieving evolution transparency, another contribution of this paper is to provide the first formal treatment of the *transparency* notion for schema evolution. In particular, we establish *sufficiency conditions* under which a schema change operation can be guaranteed to be *transparently achievable*. This represents a characterization of the expressiveness as well as limitations of the TOSE approach. The sufficiency criteria identifies the notion of *update semantic preserving* (usp) as a key requirement of the view derivation underlying TOSE. To ground these formal requirements, we conducted a case study using MultiView [KR96a] that confirms that object-oriented view systems can satisfy the *usp* requirements (needed for TOSE).

Using this formal foundation, we show that the schema change operations achievable in TOSE are comprehensive since they include the standard set of operations commonly supported by OODB systems, i.e., those proposed in [BKKK87] and adopted in most other schema evolution research [Kim88, MS93, SZ86]. The new TOSE framework allows us to achieve transparency not only for capacity-equivalent and -reducing, but also for capacity-augmenting operations. To validate its feasibility, we have implemented a working TOSE prototype [4] using the Gemstone OODB [5].

The remainder of this paper is structured as follows: Section 2 reviews related research, while Section 3 introduces the basic object and view model. In Section 4, we give an overview of the new TOSE approach. Section 5 identifies the *update-semantic-preserving* property as a key requirement of views for TOSE, while Section 6 presents the theoretical background for TOSE. Section 7 explains the transparent schema change process of our TOSE framework using examples, and Section 8 concludes this paper.

2 Related Research

In our previous work, we have built a TSE system using capacity-augmenting views [RR95, RR97]. Our current results go beyond our previous work [RR95, RR97] in several dimensions. New contributions, besides the new TOSE methodology for achieving transparency without requiring capacity-augmenting views,

---

[4] An earlier version of the TOSE system has been formally demonstrated at SIGMOD'96 [RKR+96]

[5] GemStone is a registered trademark of GemStone Inc.

include a formal definition of the transparency notion, analysis of update semantics preservation of views required by our approach, theorems characterizing the properties of the TOSE framework, and an implementation of the TOSE system for a comprehensive set of change operations.

Tresch and Scholl [TS93] also advocate views as a suitable mechanism for simulating schema evolution, but they fail to provide solutions for *capacity-augmenting* schema changes. However, *capacity-augmenting* schema evolution tends to be important for extending an existing database under changing database requirements - this is the problem that we address in this paper.

Bertino [Ber92] presents a view mechanism and indicates that it can be utilized to simulate schema evolution. Similar to our original approach of TSE [RR95], the proposed view mechanism is extended to be *capacity-augmenting* in that new stored attributes are added to views. However, as indicated earlier, dependence on such an advanced view mechanism may restrict the practical usage of the approach. Therefore, we investigate in this paper how such transparent schema evolution can be achieved *without* relying on capacity-augmenting views.

To our best knowledge, there is no working system that performs *transparent* schema evolution with the transparency notion as defined in this paper. Some schema version systems (Encore [SZ86], Orion [KC88], Goose [MNK91], CLOSQL [MS93], and COAST [Lau97]) are however conceptually related to our notion of transparency. A major distinction of these versioning approaches in contrast to TOSE is that (1) duplicates of object instances are typically created, which causes serious limitations; (2) updates through newer schema versions are often not propagated to older (now out-of-date) versions; and (3) data inconsistencies between different versions of an object may arise over time. For these reasons, true interoperability between old and new applications is not achieved. A more detailed discussion of versioning systems can be found in [RR95, RR97].

3   Background Material

Object-Oriented Data Model. Below we describe the fairly standard object model we assume, which is compatible with the ODMG model [ea97]. Let O be an infinite set of object instances. Each object $obj \in O$ consists of state (the attributes), behavior (the methods to which the object can respond), and a unique object identifier (OID). A property refers to either an attribute or a method. Objects that have common properties are grouped into *classes*. We use the term *type* to indicate the set of properties shared by all objects of the class, and the term *extent* for the set of objects that are direct instances of the class.

Let C be the set of all classes in a database. For two classes $C_i, C_j \in C$,

C_i is a *subtype* of C_j, if and only if (iff) $type(C_i) \supseteq type(C_j)$. All properties defined for a supertype are inherited by its subtypes. C_i is a *subset* of C_j, iff $(\forall \, obj \in \mathbf{O}) \, ((obj \in C_i) \Rightarrow (obj \in C_j))$. For two classes C_i, $C_j \in \mathbf{C}$, C_i is a *subclass* of C_j, denoted by C_i is-a C_j, iff C_i is a subtype as well as a subset of C_j. C_i is a *direct subclass* of C_j, if $(C_i$ is-a $C_j)$ and there are no other classes $C_{k_m} \in \mathbf{C}$ with m = 1, ..., n such that the following is-a relationships hold: $(C_i$ is-a $C_{k_1})$ and $(C_{k_1}$ is-a $C_{k_2})$ and $\cdots$ and $(C_{k_n}$ is-a $C_j)$. C_i is called an *indirect subclass* of C_j, denoted as C_i is-a* C_j, if there are one or more classes $C_{k_m} \in \mathbf{C}$ for which the above is-a relationships hold. A set membership *Extent* is defined for a class C_j as $Extent(C_j) = \bigcup extent(C_i)$, $\forall \, C_i$ is-a* C_j. A class C_i has a unique name, a type, and an Extent.

An *object schema* is a rooted directed acyclic graph S = $(\mathbf{V}, \mathbf{E})$, where $\mathbf{V}$, the finite set of vertices, correspond to classes $C_i \in \mathbf{C}$ and $\mathbf{E}$, the finite set of directed edges, correspond to a binary relation on $\mathbf{V} \times \mathbf{V}$ that represents all direct *is-a* relationships. Each directed edge $e \in \mathbf{E}$ from C_i to C_j represents the relationship C_i is-a C_j. We allow multiple inheritance, e.g., C_i is-a C_m and C_i is-a C_n, where n <> m. The *Root* class has an Extent equal to all database objects and an empty type description.

View Model. We distinguish between base and virtual classes. Base classes are usually defined by an initial schema definition. A virtual class is defined by the application of a query operator to one or more source classes, which could be base or virtual classes, that restructures the source's type and/or extent membership. Virtual classes can be added dynamically to the schema throughout the lifetime of the database. The virtual class forming operators include: *hide, refine, select, union, intersect, join, difference,* and *ident,* which defines the type and extent of the virtual class [Run92]. These object operators determine the properties and extents of the virtual classes. The is-a relationship between virtual classes is similarly defined as that between base classes, i.e., a virtual class VC_i *is-a* another virtual class VC_j, iff $Extent(VC_i) \subseteq Extent(VC_j)$ and $type(VC_i) \supseteq type(VC_j)$. We provide three generic update operations, *create, delete,* and *set* for performing updates [SLT91]. We call a database schema that contains all base classes a *base schema* (BS), and one that contains virtual classes a *view schema* (VS). When it is not important to distinguish among these three schemas we use the term *schema* (S).

Schema Capacity. Like in [MIR93], the *capacity* of a schema S = $(\mathbf{V}, \mathbf{E})$ is defined to be the set of all valid database states of the schema S. We use *states*(S) to denote the set of all possible database states of a schema S (at any time) and use $DB_t(S)$ to denote the data in the database at time t. The following relationship holds: *states*(S) $\supseteq \cup_{\forall t} DB_t(S)$. Intuitively, a schema S_j has a larger or equal capacity than a schema S_i if every database state of S_i can be mapped to a database state of S_j without loss of information.

Schema Transformations. A mapping f between two sets A and B, $f: A \rightarrow B$, is *total* if f is defined on every element of A, *functional* if for any $a \in A$ there exists at most one $b \in B$, *injective* if its inverse f^{-1} is functional, and *onto* if its inverse f^{-1} is total. A functional, injective, total, and onto mapping is called a *bijection*.

Capacity-Reducing (CR)	Capacity-Equivalent (CE)	Capacity-Augmenting (CA)
delete-attribute	change-attribute-name	add-attribute
delete-class	change-class-name	add-class
delete-edge		add-edge
change-attribute-domain (new domain: subclass)		change-attribute-domain (new domain: superclass)

Figure 1: Schema Change Operations Supported by TOSE.

A *schema transformation* T is a total mapping, $T : S \to S$ with S a set of schemas. T is *capacity-augmenting* if there exists a total and injective mapping f: states(S) $\to$ states($T(S)$), T is *capacity-equivalent* if f is a bijection, T is *capacity-reducing* if the mapping of the inverse transformation T^{-1} is total and injective, and T is *capacity-incompatible* otherwise [MIR93]. In our work, T corresponds to the standard set of schema change operations proposed in the literature [BKKK87, Zic91] (Figure 1) [6].

4   Transparent Object Schema Evolution (TOSE)

The goal of our proposed TOSE framework is to provide continued support to existing applications cooperating on a shared database, even under a schema change. TOSE achieves this goal by simulating schema changes using views, which shield users/applications from schema changes requested by other users (Figure 2). Users work on their view schemas instead of directly working on the shared schema, while TOSE maintains the shared schema as foundation for all existing view schemas. A user constructs her initial view schema VS by selecting desired base classes from the shared schema and importing them as *ident* virtual classes into VS. Then, the user tailors the view schema according to her special requirements by issuing a sequence of schema change operations upon the view schema (see the user space in Figure 2). Instead of in-place schema changes, TOSE then simulates the schema change requests by a process further explained below [7].

As subschemas (instead of the complete base schema [BKKK87, PS87])

---

[6]Note that we only allow an attribute domain change to take place if the attribute is locally defined. The *change-attribute-domain* operator can be either capacity-augmenting or capacity-reducing depending on whether the new domain is a supertype or a subtype of the old domain.

[7]That is, a user does not create virtual classes directly, instead virtual classes are created by TOSE.

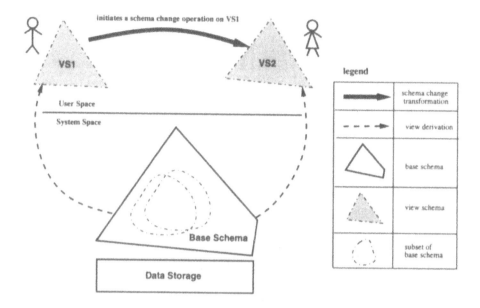

Figure 2: TOSE Simulates Schema Change Using Views.

can be a unit of schema change in TOSE, application developer requesting
the change are more likely to be familiar with the to-be-modified schema -
making the task easier and less error-prone for the users. Unlike previous
research [RR95, RR97, Ber92], TOSE does not rely on the availability of an
advanced (i.e., capacity-augmenting) view mechanism, rather a conventional
view mechanism for OODBs suffices.

4.1 Capacity-Reducing and Capacity-Equivalent Schema Change Operations

The underlying principle of this proposed mechanism is that capacity-reducing
(CR) and capacity-equivalent (CE) schema changes are achieved by constructing a view that reflects the intention of the schema changes (see Figure 3 for
an illustration of the TOSE methodology). For a CR or CE schema change request T_j, TOSE is able to compute the desired schema change by creating a new
view schema VS_j that reflects the intention of the schema change operation.
We have designed a set of virtual class forming queries for all schema change
operations supported in TOSE [RRL97] to simulate the schema change effects
on views. The set of view forming queries that realizes the schema change request T_j is called a *view derivation* operation, denoted as $VS_j = VD^{T_j}(VS_i)$,.
Each of the queries maps virtual classes in the input view VS_i to virtual classes

in the output view VS_j [8].

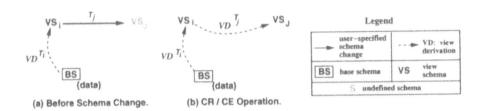

(a) Before Schema Change.   (b) CR / CE Operation.

Figure 3: TOSE Methodology for Capacity-Reducing/Equivalent Schema Change Operations.

The old schema VS_i is kept intact for continued support of existing applications running against it, while the new schema VS_j provides a more appropriate interface for new application programs. Furthermore, VS_j can be viewed as if it were (directly) derived from the base BS, i.e., $VS_j = VD^{T_j} \circ VD^{T_i}(BS)$ – is the sequence of view derivations that derives VS_j from BS. This assures that all interfaces VS_i and VS_j operate on the same base schema (and data).

4.2 Capacity-Augmenting Schema Change Operations

However, capacity-augmenting (CA) schema changes cannot be supported in this fashion due to the inherent limitation of view mechanisms not being able to augment the capacity of the database. For this, we introduce a new solution based on a three-pronged process that does not rely on the availability of advanced (capacity-augmenting) view mechanisms.

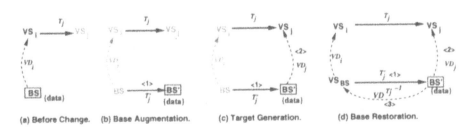

(a) Before Change.   (b) Base Augmentation.   (c) Target Generation.   (d) Base Restoration.

Figure 4: TOSE Methodology for Capacity-Augmenting Schema Change Operations.

First, the base-schema-augmentation step translates the schema change request T_j specified on the view schema VS_i into a corresponding operation T'_j

---

[8] When it is clear from the context, subscripts are omitted for succinctness' sake in remainder of this paper.

to be executed on the base schema BS in order to physically restructure BS, denoted by <1> in Figure 4. This is an essential step as schema evolution semantics have not been defined in the literature when applied to virtual classes but only when applied to base classes. After Step 1 is executed, the original base schema BS does no longer exist in its initial form, rather it now has been modified by either augmenting it with information possibly irrelevant to other applications or even by completely modifying the organization of the schema. For this reason, VS specified upon it may have become undefined (BS and VS_i in Figure 4). Furthermore, the data is associated with the newly modified BS' instead of with the old BS.

Second, the target-view-generation step, denoted by <2> in Figure 4, generates the target view schema VS_j as if the schema change operation T_j had been performed on the view schema VS_i directly (and VS_i were a base schema). Given that the capacity of BS has been appropriately augmented by step 1, we can assure that such a mapping always exists in our context.

Third, since the original BS does not exist any more, for continuing support of all existing view schemas (and thus existing applications) defined on BS, the base-schema-reconstruction step, denoted by <3> in Figure 4, restores the previous base schema BS as a view schema VS_{BS} from the augmented base schema BS'.

5 Update Semantics Preservation (USP) Property of View Schemas

Since the TOSE framework achieves transparency by requiring users to operate on their respective view schemas, we need to assure that the users can work on their view schema as if it were a base schema. For this, we need to make sure that (1) updates on views are unambiguously translated into updates on the base, and (2) the effects of back-propagation from the underlying base schema to the views has the identical effect as if the updates were directly performed on the views. We give the formal definitions of the update semantics of virtual classes, view schemas, and transformations, while proofs can be found in [RRL97, VW94].

Definition 1 *A virtual class VC is* usp, *iff the following generic updates are satisfied at any time t:*

- *create(VC) returns a new object* obj *such that* $Extent_{t+1}(VC) = Extent_t(VC) \cup \{obj\}$ [9].

- *delete(obj), where* obj $\in Extent_t(VC)$, *removes the object* obj *from* $Extent_t(VC)$, *i.e.,* $Extent_{t+1}(VC) = Extent_t(VC) - \{obj\}$.

---

[9]Note that $Extent_t(C)$ is the class extent of the class C at time t.

- *set(*obj, attr, newValue), where* obj $\in$ *Extent(VC), changes the attribute* attr *of the object* obj *to* newValue.

We have conducted a case study on the set of schema change operations supported in TOSE (Figure 1) [RRL97], and found that only the *hide*, *difference*, *ident*, *union*, and *intersection* object algebra operators are needed to simulate this set of schema changes. We then verified that a usp update propagation behavior could be found for all virtual classes generated by these algebra operators for the three generic update operations *create*, *delete*, and *set* (see our technical report [RRL97]). For brevity, the discussion is not repeated here.

Definition 2 *Let VC_i and VC_j be virtual classes. (VC_i, VC_j) is a usp pair iff we have:*

- *If VC_i is a subclass of VC_j, any* create *operation applied to VC_i at time t adds an object to both $Extent_{t+1}(VC_i)$ and $Extent_{t+1}(VC_j)$, and any* create *operation applied to VC_j at time t does not affect $Extent_{t+1}(VC_i)$. If VC_i is not a subclass of VC_j,* create *applied to VC_i does not affect $Extent_{t+1}(VC_j)$.*

- Delete *applied to object* obj *of VC_i at time t removes the object* obj *from $Extent_{t+1}(VC_i)$, i.e., $Extent_{t+1}(VC_i) = Extent_t(VC_i)$ - {obj}. If* obj $\in Extent_t(VC_j)$, *the object* obj *is also removed from $Extent_{t+1}(VC_j)$; otherwise $Extent_{t+1}(VC_j) = Extent_t(VC_j)$.*

- Set *applied to VC_i at time t changes the attribute* attr *of an object* obj *in both $Extent_{t+1}(VC_i)$ and $Extent_{t+1}(VC_j)$, if* attr *is also defined in VC_j and* obj $\in Extent_t(VC_j)$; *otherwise $Extent_{t+1}(VC_j) = Extent_t(VC_j)$.*

Note that an arbitrary combination of two usp virtual classes is not necessarily a usp pair. This is best explained by the example below.

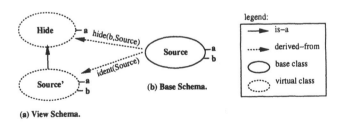

(a) View Schema.

Figure 5: Two Individual Usp Virtual Classes Is not Necessary a Usp Pair.

Example 1 *Let's create two virtual classes, Hide and Source', by applying the hide and ident object algebra operators to the class Source. The Source' virtual class is an identical copy of its source class, Source, and the Hide virtual class hides the property b from its interface. Therefore, the Hide virtual class is a superclass of the Source' virtual class [Run92]. As mentioned earlier (and shown in [RRL97]) individually hide and ident virtual classes are usp, i.e., the Hide and Source' classes are usp. However, Hide and Source' together in one schema do not preserve the update semantics, because an object created for the Hide class (a superclass) is not only visible to the Hide class, but also visible to the Source' class (a subclass)* [10]. *This violates the first condition of Definition 2. Therefore, we have shown that (Hide, Source') is not usp, although both of the virtual classes are usp, individually.*

We call this behavior *downward visibility anomaly*, which is not base-like. This unexpected behavior is caused by the view derivation relating two classes, i.e., Hide derived-from Source and Source' derived-from Source, is not hidden from the user. Theorems for usp pair commutativity, associativity, and so on can be found in [RRL97].

Definition 3 *Let a view schema VS consist of usp classes $\{ VC_1, VC_2, \ldots, VC_n \}$. Then VS is called usp if every pair of the classes in VS is a usp pair.*

Intuitively, a usp view schema has the following characteristics: let VS be a *usp* view schema and $DB_t(VS)$ be the state of the stored database under VS at time t. Then any update on $DB_t(VS)$ results in the next snapshot $DB_{t+1}(VS)$ at time $t+1$ that would have resulted if VS were a base schema. In other words, the derivations defining classes in VS don't cause any unexpected side-effects. A usp view derivation is defined next.

Definition 4 *A view derivation $VD(S_1) = S_2$, which maps the schema S_1 to the schema S_2, is called usp if S_2 is guaranteed to be a usp view schema whenever S_1 is usp.*

Theorem 1 *Let VD^1 and VD^2 be two usp view derivations. Then, the composition $VD^2 \circ VD^1(S) = VD^2(VD^1(S))$, with S any schema and '$\circ$' defined as sequential application, is also usp.*

Again, the proof of the above theorem is omitted due to lack of space [RRL97].

---

[10] The create operation issued on the Hide class is first translated to the create operation on Hide's base class, which is Source. Then the effect is propagated to *all* the virtual classes derived from it, i.e., Hide and Source'.

6 Formal Foundation of Transparency Property of TOSE

All schema transformations supported in TOSE (i.e., they can be specified and correctly executed over view schemas) have the same semantics as the corresponding conventional schema transformations defined over base schemas. Since TOSE aspires to provide users with an environment of a view schema that 'behaves' exactly like a base schema, we now formalize the *transparency* notion of our TOSE framework. We then show that TOSE achieves schema changes *transparently* for capacity-reducing, -equivalent, and -augmenting transformations.

Definition 5 *Let T be a schema transformation as defined in Section 3. The inverse transformation of T, denoted as T^{-1}, is defined as $T^{-1} \circ T(S) = S$, where S is a schema.*

That is to say applying a transformation and then its inverse (or vice versa) to a schema S results in S.

Definition 6 *Two schemas S_i and S_j are said to be "identical" from time t = t_k onward, iff the same sequence of updates $(\mu_t, \mu_{t+1}, \ldots)$ is applied to both schemas, and we have $\mu_t(DB_t(S_i)) = DB_{t+1}(S_i)$, $\mu_t(DB_t(S_j)) = DB_{t+1}(S_j)$, and $DB_t(S_i) = DB_t(S_j)$ for $t \geq t_k$.*

Definition 7 *Let **VS** be a set of view schemas. Let the input view schema VS_i be usp [11], and let T be a schema transformation $T(VS_i) = VS_j$, where VS_i and $VS_j \in$ **VS**. T is said to be transparent iff there exists a usp view derivation VD^T such that either $VD^T(VS_i)$ is identical to VS_j (for capacity-reducing/equivalent transformations), or $VD^{T^{-1}}(VS_j)$ is identical to VS_i (for capacity-augmenting transformations) [12].*

The existence of VD^T or $VD^{T^{-1}}$ in the above definition such that T can be simulated transparently is the *sufficiency condition* for a T to be considered to be *transparent* within our framework. We have shown [RRL97] that for every capacity-reducing and -equivalent schema change operation supported in TOSE (See Figure 1), denoted by T_{re} with $T_{re}(VS_i) = VS_j$, there exists a usp view derivation operation $VD^{T_{re}}$ such that $VD^{T_{re}}(VS_i) = VS_j$. VS_j can be shown to be a usp view schema by Theorem 1, since VS_i and $VD^{T_{re}}$ are both usp. Hence, TOSE is transparent for T_{re} by Definition 7.

---

[11]Assume an initial view schema is constructed by selecting desired base classes from the shared schema – which contains base classes only hence it is usp by definition, then applies one or many usp view derivations to it. The output view schema is guaranteed to be usp by Theorem 1.

[12]$VD^{T^{-1}}$ is a usp view derivation corresponding to the inverse transformation T^{-1}.

Next, we focus on showing that TOSE is transparent also for capacity-augmenting transformations T_a. Four of the transformations we are considering (see Figure 1) are capacity-augmenting, namely add-attribute, change-attribute-domain (when the new attribute domain is a superclass of the original domain), add-class, and add-edge. There are two possible scenarios to consider:

Case 1: The capacity that the transformation asks to be added is already in the base schema though it is not necessarily visible through the current user view.

Case 2: The capacity that the user wishes to add is not available in the base schema.

Next, we argue why TOSE is transparent under both scenarios.

Case 1: Case 1 is relevant for the *add-edge* transformations only, since we assume *add-attribute* and *add-class* transformations add attributes and classes that do not exist in the database before. When the requested information is already in the base schema, TOSE is able to derive the target view schema with a usp view derivation. We have developed a general algorithm to simulate the required schema change by determining a usp view derivation that when applied to the base schema will generate the desired (view) schema interface (see [RRL97] for details). The output view schema is usp by Definition 4. This satisfies the transparency requirement of TOSE. ■

Case 2: When the information that the user requests to be added into VS_i does not exist in the base schema BS, the change request T_a specified on VS_i is translated into an in-place change T_a' on BS such that T_a' augments the capacity of BS to become sufficiently large to include the desired information (Figure 4). For each of the capacity-augmenting schema changes listed in Figure 1, we have proposed an algorithm for translating the schema change into a change on the *primary base* class(es) in the base schema [13].

For each of these CA transformations, the application of a usp view derivation VD_j on the modified base schema BS' generates the target (output) schema VS_j (*target view derivation step*). The target view schema VS_j is usp, since it is specified on an (augmented) base schema and the view derivation is capacity-reducing or -equivalent (shown to be usp for our framework). Again, we have given algorithms for how to compute the view derivation VD_j from BS' to VS_j based on the initial view derivation VD_i that was used to derive the input schema VS_i from the original BS for each of the schema changes [RRL97].

Finally the original base BS is reconstructed from the augmented base BS' (*the original base schema restoration step*) by applying a *view derivation operator* $VD^{T_a'^{-1}}$ that is the inverse of T_a' to the new base BS'. It is proven [MIR93]

---

[13]Basically, a primary class is computed by tracing back the derivation history of a virtual class until a base class in found in the base schema. We have given algorithms for how to search the primary base class for each type of the virtual class used in TOSE in our technical report [RRL97].

that for every capacity-augmenting transformation T there always exists a usp view derivation $VD^{T^{-1}}$ that can be used to get back the original input schema. We thus have:

$$VS_i = VD_i \circ VD^{T_a'^{-1}}(BS') \tag{1}$$

With the theorem from [MIR93], Equation (1) naturally captures the third step of our TOSE framework. Because $VD^{T_a'^{-1}}$ is a usp view derivation [MIR93] and VD_i by assumption of our framework is usp, TOSE is transparent under this second scenario by Theorem 1. ∎

7 Walk-through Examples of TOSE

7.1 A Capacity-Reducing Schema Change Operation: Deleting an Attribute

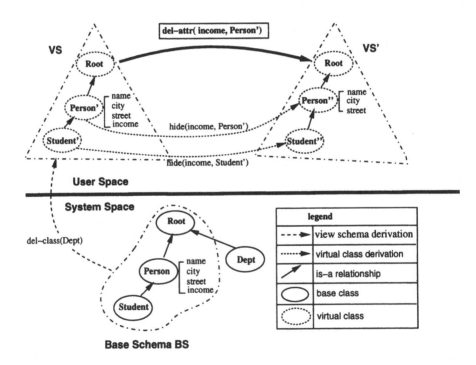

Figure 6: Example: TOSE Simulates a Capacity-Reducing Schema Change Using Views.

A database administer (DBA) may want to remove a sensitive attribute, e.g., *income*, from the database given in the upper left of Figure 6 before allowing access by less privileged users. To do this, the DBA issues the del-attr(*income, Person'*) schema evolution request on VS. Because deleting an attribute from a view schema is capacity-reducing, TOSE simulates this simply by a view derivation. Namely, it creates the new view VS' by hiding the attribute *income* from the *Person'* and *Student'* classes, respectively. The newly derived virtual classes are grouped into the new view schema VS' (upper right of Figure 6). Privileged users can still access the attribute *income* through the original view VS while new users now operate through the modified schema VS'.

7.2   A Capacity-Augmenting Schema Change Operation: Adding an Attribute

Now assume a new application needs to know a person's birthday. To satisfy this newly recognized requirement, the DBA issues the *add-attr(birthday, Person')* transformation on the current view VS (user space in Figure 7) [14]. This is a capacity-augmenting change operation.

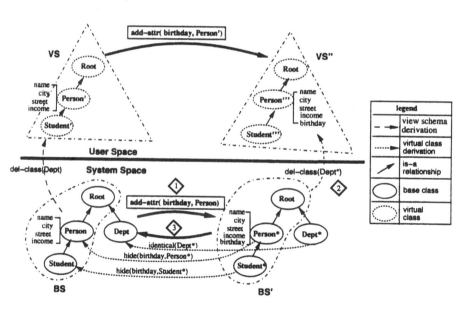

Figure 7: Example: TOSE Realizes a Capacity-Augmenting Schema Change in a Three-Step Process.

First, the *base-schema-augmentation* step translates the *add-attr(birthday, Person')*

---

[14] Add-attr(a,C) means adding a newly defined attribute *a* to the class C. Note that this attribute *a* has to be added to all the subclasses of C, since a virtual class is treated as a first-class citizen in our model [Run92].

originally specified on the view VS into the operation *add-attr(birthday, Person)* on the base schema, where Person is the corresponding primary base class of Person'. TOSE uses a conventional in-place schema change tool to add the attribute *birthday* to Person in BS. The modified class is re-named as Person* for the purpose of easily distinguishing it in our discussion. The *birthday* attribute is inherited into the base class Student as well. After step <1>, the base schema, refined to BS' in Figure 7, has been extended to now hold more capacity. All objects in the database are now associated with the new base BS', instead of the original BS.

Second, the target-view-generation step generates the target view VS$''$ by applying the same view derivation *del-class*, which was used to derived VS from BS, on the new base schema BS'. Thereafter, we can observe that the resulting target view schema VS$''$ is identical to the one we expected if we had directly applied the transformation on the input view schema VS.

Third, since the original base schema and the view schema (and thus applications built on it) become undefined, the *base-schema-reconstruction* step restores the previous base schema BS as a view. The inverse function of *add-attr* is the *del-attr* transformation, which is realized in TOSE by applying the *hide* algebra operators to the base classes Person* and Student*, respectively. Note that every physical object instance is associated with one and the same base schema, even though it appears differently to different users depending on the schema through which it is accessed. In the above example, the unique schema under which all instances are maintained used to be *BS* but after the application of the *add-attr* operation (in Figure 7) it has become BS'.

8 Conclusions

In this paper, we have presented a novel solution to the problem of schema evolution affecting existing programs based on a three-step process called TOSE. This TOSE methodology adds great value to many modern applications, as it addresses the pressing demand for application interoperation in a practical manner by utilizing available technology, i.e., a conventional in-place schema change tool and derivation-based view mechanisms, instead of depending on non-established technology. As proof of concept, a TOSE prototype has been built on top of the usp MultiView subsystem [KR96a, KRR95] and the Gemstone OODB [15]. The TOSE system supports all operations listed in Section 7, including capacity-reducing, -equivalent, and -augmenting transformations.

In the future, we plan to study issues related to the optimization of the TOSE implementation, such as integrating deferred evolution of base classes and incremental materialization of virtual classes used by TOSE.

---

[15] GemStone is a registered trademark of GemStone Inc.

References

[AB91]   S. Abiteboul and A. Bonner. Objects and Views. *SIGMOD*, pages 238–247, 1991.

[Ber92]   E. Bertino. A View Mechanism for Object-Oriented Databases. In *3rd Int. Conference on Extending Database Technology*, pages 136–151, March 1992.

[BKKK87] J. Banerjee, W. Kim, H. J. Kim, and H. F. Korth. Semantics and Implementation of Schema Evolution in Object-Oriented Databases. *SIGMOD*, pages 311–322, 1987.

[ea97]   R. G. G. Cattell et al. In *The Object Database Standard: ODMG 2.0*, chapter 1. Morgan Kaufmann Pub., 1997.

[KC88]   W. Kim and H. Chou. Versions of Schema For OODBs. In *Proc. 14th VLDB*, pages 148–159, 1988.

[Kim88]   H. J. Kim. *Issues in Object-Oriented Database Systems*. PhD thesis, University of Texas at Austin, May 1988.

[KR95]   H. A. Kuno and E. A. Rundensteiner. Materialized object-oriented views in *MultiView*. In *ACM Research Issues in Data Engineering Workshop*, pages 78–85, March 1995.

[KR96a]   H. A. Kuno and E. A. Rundensteiner. The *MultiView* OODB View System: Design and Implementation. In Harold Ossher and William Harrison, editors, *Theory and Practice of Object Systems (TAPOS), Special Issue on Subjectivity in Object-Oriented Systems*. John Wiley New York, 1996.

[KR96b]   H. A. Kuno and E. A. Rundensteiner. Using Object-Oriented Principles to Optimize Update Propagation to Materialized Views. In *IEEE Int. Conf. on Data Engineering*, pages 310–317, 1996.

[KR98]   H. A. Kuno and E. A. Rundensteiner. Incremental Maintenance of Materialized Views in OODBs. *IEEE Transaction on Data and Knowledge Engineering,*, 1998.

[KRR95]   H. A. Kuno, Y. G. Ra, and E. A. Rundensteiner. The Object-Slicing Technique: A Flexible Object Representation and Its Evaluation. Technical Report CSE-TR-241-95, University of Michigan, 1995.

[Kun96]   H. A. Kuno. *View Materialization Issues in Object-Oriented Databases*. PhD thesis, University of Michigan, Ann Arbor, June 1996.

[Lau97]   S.-E. Lautemann. A Propagation Mechanism for Populated Schema Versions. In *IEEE Int. Conf. on Data Engineering*, pages 67–78, 1997.

[MIR93]   R. J. Miller, Y. E. Ioannidis, and R. Ramakrishnan. The Use of Information Capacity in Schema Integration and Translation. In *Int. Conference on Very Large Data Bases*, pages 120–133, 1993.

[MNK91]   M. A. Morsi, S. B. Navathe, and H. J. Kim. A Schema Management and Prototyping Interface for an Object-Oriented Database Environment. In F. Van Assche, B. Moulin, and C. Rolland, editors, *Object-Oriented Approach in Information Systems*, pages 157–180. Elsevier Science Publishers B. V. (North Holland), 1991.

[MS93]   S. Monk and I. Sommerville. Schema Evolution in OODBs Using Class Versioning. In *SIGMOD RECORD, VOL. 22, NO.3*, September 1993.

[PS87]   D. J. Penney and J. Stein. Class modification in the GemStone object-oriented DBMS. In *OOPSLA*, pages 111–117, 1987.

[RKR+96]   E. A. Rundensteiner, H. A. Kuno, Y.-G. Ra, V. Crestana-Taube, M. C. Jones, and P. J. Marron. Demonstration paper: The Multi-View Project: Object-Oriented View Technology and Applications. *SIGMOD*, page 555, 1996.

[RR95]   Y. G. Ra and E. A. Rundensteiner. A Transparent OO Schema Change Approach Using View Schema Evolution. In *IEEE Int. Conf. on Data Engineering*, pages 165–172, March 1995.

[RR97]   Y. G. Ra and E. A. Rundensteiner. A Transparent Schema Evolution System Based on Object-Oriented View Technology. *IEEE Transactions on Knowledge and Data Engineering*, pages 600–624, September 1997.

[RRL97]   Y.G. Ra, E. A. Rundensteiner, and A.J. Lee. A Practical Approach to Transparent Schema Evolution. Technical Report WPI-CS-TR-97-3, Worcester Polytechnic Inst., Dept. of Comp. Scie., 1997.

[Run92]   E. A. Rundensteiner. *MultiView*: Methodology for Supporting Multiple Views in Object-Oriented Databases". In *18th VLDB Conference*, pages 187–198, 1992.

[SLT91]   M. H. Scholl, C. Laasch, and M. Tresch. Updatable Views in Object-oriented Databases. In *Proceedings of the Second DOOD Conference*, pages 189–207, December 1991.

[SZ86]   A. H. Skarra and S. B. Zdonik. The Management of Changing Types in an Object-Oriented Databases. In *Proc. 1st OOPSLA*, pages 483–494, 1986.

[TS93]   M. Tresch and M. H. Scholl. Schema Transformation without Database Reorganization. In *SIGMOD RECORD*, pages 21–27, 1993.

[VW94]   V.M.P. Vidal and M. Winslett. Perserving Update Semantics In Schema Integration. In *Int. Conference on Information and Knowledge Management*, pages 263–271, 1994.

[Zic91]   R. Zicari. A Framework for O_2 Schema Updates. In *7th IEEE Int. Conf. on Data Engineering*, pages 146–182, April 1991.

METHOD ISSUES 2

Model Engineering Using Charts of Concepts: Application to the Model of the UML

Xavier Castellani, Naïma Hamamouche
CEDRIC IIE (CNAM) research laboratory,
Evry, France,
Email: {castellani,hamamouche}@iie.cnam.fr.

Abstract

The models of analysis and design methods are complex and the numbers of their concepts are high. Furthermore, news versions of these methods appear every six months. How to follow the successive versions of the models of these methods? How to create customized versions of these models? To answer to these two questions, we propose to represent models with charts of concepts. These charts allow to select, create, delete, and modify concepts by knowing impacts of these operations. They also allow to verify a model by searching non connected sub-sets of concepts and circuits between definitions of concepts. In this paper we explain how to represent versions, news and customized, of a model defined with charts of concepts. To illustrate our proposition we show charts of concepts of the version 1.1 of the Unified Modeling Language.

1 Introduction

Every year new versions of object-oriented models appear. It is the case for the UML. A new version of a model is defined starting from an existing version of this model by adding new concepts, deleting concepts and sometimes by modifying definitions of some concepts. This process of creation of successive versions of a model is depicted in the upper part of the schema in Figure 1.

Moreover, models have a lot of concepts, for example more than 230 concepts for the UML. Often these models are not adapted to the requirements of the software analysts and designers. That is why it is necessary to create customized versions of models. A customized version is defined starting from a version of a model by selecting concepts, adding new concepts and sometimes by modifying definitions of concepts. This process of creation of a customized version and the creation of successive versions of a customized version is shown in the lower part of the schema in Figure 1.

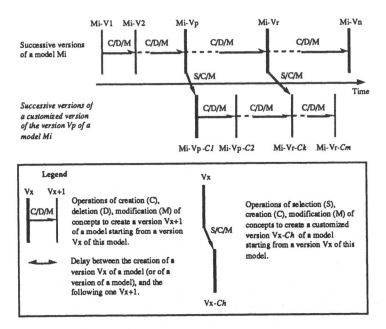

Figure 1. Successive versions of a model Mi and
of a customized version Vp of this model

The upper part of the schema in Figure 1 can be seen as a statechart diagram of a model. The states are the successive versions of this model. The transitions are defined with operations performed to map from a version to the following one. The lower part of this schema can also be seen as a statechart diagram of a customized version of a model for the same reasons.

The two problems that we try to solve are: How to follow the successive versions of a model? How to create customized versions of a model? To solve these two problems it necessary to propose solutions to create, delete, modify and select easily concepts in a model.

1.1 Difficulties to Define Versions, News and Customized, of a Model

Models of methods are generally defined with texts. A lot of works are developed on metamodeling of analysis and design methods. Some of these works allow to compare models of methods to evaluate them or to define core models of methods [1] [2]. The goal of other works is to define meta-case tools as MetaEdit+ [3]. Each case tool, such as GraphTalkMeta, Kogge, MetaEdit+, MetaView, Mviews,... , has its formalism to define meta-models.

Meta-models are defined with the entity-relationship model [4], with an object-oriented model or with the models that these meta-models represent. For example, the meta-model of the model of the UML is represented by its authors with the object-oriented model of the UML itself.

A meta-model of a model can allow to create versions, news and customized, of this model. It represents concepts of a model. But, a meta-model represented with the entity-relationship model or with an object-oriented model does not allow to create, delete, modify and select concepts by seeing concepts that are implied in the selection and those that are not implied. That is why we propose to represent models with charts of concepts to define versions of models.

1.2 Our Contribution to Define Models: Utilization of Charts of Concepts

We propose to represent models with charts of concepts to define versions of a model: its first version, its new and customized versions. A chart represents concepts and dependencies between their definitions. A definition dependency is defined from a concept CPx to a concept CPy if the concept CPx is used in the definition of the concept CPy.

Charts of concepts allow to create, delete, modify and select concepts by seeing concepts that are concerned and those that are not concerned.

1.3. Illustration of the Use of Charts of Concepts to Define Models. Example: Charts of Concepts of the Version 1.1 of the UML

The UML is a language, a notation and so a model to analyze and to design object-oriented information systems. The UML is defined by Booch, Jacobson and Rumbaugh [5]. This model is defined with numerous concepts. It is not useful to use all these concepts in a data processing department of a company.

To illustrate our proposition we have defined charts of concepts of the version 1.1 of the model of the UML. In this paper we propose charts of concepts of this model. We do not recall definitions of the concepts of this model. Justifications of definition dependencies between concepts result from definitions of these concepts. These justifications are not specified in this paper for sake of conciseness. The reader may refer to definitions of concepts in [5].

Before creating, deleting, modifying and selecting concepts, we tried to take into account all the concepts of the model of the UML but we do not guarantee that we have been exhaustive.

We have justified the interest of charts of concepts comparing to meta-models in Section 1.1. We will precise our contribution with regard to conceptual graphs in Section 2.4.

1.4 Outline of this Paper

Charts of concepts of a model are defined in Section 2. Verification of a model defined with charts of concepts is specified in Section 3. The creation, the deletion, the modification, and the selection of concepts in a model defined with charts of concepts are detailed in Section 4. A brief discussion on the use of charts of concepts to define versions, news or customized, of models is presented in the conclusion. In the annex are depicted charts of concepts of the version 1.1 of the model of the UML.

2 Charts of Concepts of a Model

A definition of a concept of a model of an analysis and design method is given in Section 2.1. Definition dependencies defined between concepts in charts of concepts are specified in Section 2.2. Charts of concepts themselves are defined in Section 2.3. Precision on the formalism used to represent charts of concepts comparing to Sowa's conceptual graphs and comparing to dependencies of the relational model is given in Section 2.4.

2.1 What is a Concept of a Model?

For us, a concept of a model is anything of this model that can be used by software analysts and/or designers to represent or to specify phenomena of the real world or technical phenomena.

- What is a Concept of the Model of the UML?

The problem is not simple, even if the charts of concepts presented in this paper prove that it is possible to do that. In documents on the UML is presented the meta-model of the UML. But all the concepts, or supposed to be, are not in this meta-model. We have studied glossaries and indexes of these documents to decide if a notion represents or not a concept. We have also used our culture on the object-oriented approach to take decisions. Other concepts could be chosen; in this case the presented charts of concepts could be modified.

Examples:
    We have taken into account as concepts the notions of "action associated to an entry transition" and "action associated to an exit transition" used in statechart diagrams (that is depicted in the annex in Figure 21), because these two notions are used to define the notion of "point of execution of an operation". This last notion has also be considered as a concept.
    We have not taken into account as concepts notions of "cyclic activity" and "sequential activity" in statechart diagrams considering the little importance granted in the documents to these two notions.

- Difficulties to Find Definitions of Some Concepts in the Model of the UML

Definitions of concepts are informal and hidden in texts. Some concepts are defined several times in documents which present the UML. For these concepts we have considered the union of their different definitions.

2.2 Definition Dependencies Defined between Concepts

The graphic formalism of representation of charts of concepts proposed in this paper settles on the definition dependencies between two concepts.

2.2.1 Definition Dependencies between two Concepts

We say that it exists a definition dependency from a concept CPx to a concept CPy if the concept CPx is used in the definition of the concept CPy.

$$CPx \longrightarrow CPy$$

Figure 2. Representation of a definition dependency between two concepts

If it exists a definition dependency from a concept CPx to a concept CPy and an inverse dependency from CPy to CPx, then we say that a co-definition dependency exists between these two concepts.

$$CPx \longleftrightarrow CPy$$

Figure 3. Representation of a co-definition dependency between two concepts

The existence of a co-definition dependency between two concepts represents the fact that a circuit of dependencies exists between these two concepts.

2.2.2 Non Representation of Definition Dependencies Resulting of Transitivity of Definition Dependencies

If it exists a definition dependency from a concept CPx to a concept CPy and a definition dependency from the concept CPy to a concept CPz, we do not represent link from CPx to CPz to simplify the charts of concepts.

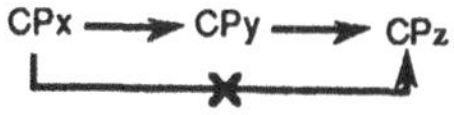

Figure 4. Non representation of definition dependencies resulting of transitivity

2.2.3 And/Or Expressions between Definition Dependencies

If definition dependencies exist respectively from a concept CPx to concepts CPy, CPz, ... , that means that CPx has been defined before CPy and CPz and ... These "and" are not represented in the charts of concepts.

Example taken in the chart of basic concepts relative to objects of the UML (that is depicted in the annex in Figure 16): the graph in Figure 5 represents the fact that the concept of "object" has been defined before the concepts of "key", "object persistence", "object flow" and of "message".

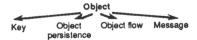

Figure 5. Definition dependencies starting from a concept

If several definition dependencies end to a same concept CPy, an "and/or" logical expression mentioned on the graph specifies how the concept CPy depends on the beginning concepts of these definition dependencies.

Example of logical expression defined with a simple "and" taken in the chart of concepts of the class diagrams of the UML (that is depicted in the annex in Figure 19): the concept of "sub-set constraint" depends on the concept of "constraint" and on the concept of "role".

Figure 6. Definition dependencies ending to a concept with an "and"

Example of logical expression defined with a simple "or" taken in the chart of concepts of the class diagrams of the UML (that is depicted in the annex in Figure 19): the concept of "constraint on an association" depends on the concept of "sub-set constraint" or on the concept of "constraint or".

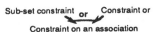

Figure 7. Definition dependencies ending to a concept with an "or"

Example of logical expression defined with "and" and "or" taken in the chart of concepts of the class diagrams of the UML (that is depicted in the annex in Figure 19): the concept of "multiplicity (of a role)" depends on (the concept of "role" and on the concept of "multiplicity") or (on the concept of "role" and on the concept of "composition" and on the concept of "multiplicity").

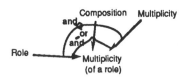

Figure 8. Definition dependencies ending to a concept with an "and/or" expression

2.2.4 Root Concepts and Terminal Concepts

A root concept of a model is a concept which is not defined with other concepts of this model. A root concept is represented under a small black triangle.

▼
Element

Figure 9. Example of root concept

A terminal concept of a model is such that no concept of this model is defined with it. A terminal concept is represented above or near a small black circle.

Key
●

Figure 10. Example of terminal concept

2.3 Charts of Concepts

A chart of concepts is a directed graph such that nodes are concepts and arcs are definition dependencies.

- Representation of Concepts of a Chart of Concepts Used in Another Chart of Concepts

Some models are shared in sub-models. It is the case of the model of the UML which is shared in parts that contain groups of basic concepts and groups of concepts that allow to represent 9 types of diagrams.

If a concept CPx defined in a chart of concepts CCi is used in a chart of concepts CCj, the name of the concept CPx is mentioned surrounded with an ellipse in the chart of concepts CCi. The three cases of surrounding or not a concept with an ellipse in a chart of concepts are illustrated in Figure 11.

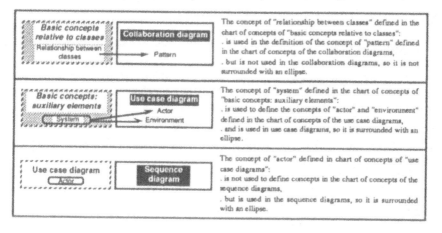

Figure 11. Examples of the three cases of surrounding or not
a concept with an ellipse

For sake of clearness, we have not represented definition dependencies from concepts that begin definition dependencies and that end to concepts that belong to other charts.

If a concept of a chart is beginning of a definition dependency that ends to a concept of another chart, this concept is not therefore terminal. So, it is not represented with the small black circle that would mean that it is terminal.

- Charts of Concepts of the Version 1.1 of the UML

Authors of the UML present concepts of its model in two categories of groups of concepts: basic concepts and concepts used in 9 types of diagrams. We defined charts of concepts for these two categories of groups of concepts.

. Charts of the Basic Concepts of the Model of the UML. Basic concepts of the model of the UML are: basic concepts relative to objects, basic concepts relative to classes, auxiliary elements, extension mechanisms, and data types. Some charts of concepts of these groups of basic concepts are represented in the annex.

. Charts of Concepts of the 9 Types of Diagrams of the Model of the UML. The UML proposes 9 types of diagrams: use case diagrams, class diagrams, object diagrams, collaboration diagrams, sequence diagrams, statechart diagrams, activity diagrams, component diagrams and deployment diagrams. We do not recall definitions of these 9 types of diagrams. The reader may refer to their presentation in [5]. Some charts of concepts of these diagrams are represented in the annex.

Note that the object diagrams and the activity diagrams cannot be represented with the version 4 of the case tool Rose (commercialized by Rational Software) which allows to analyze and design with the UML.

2.4 Precision on the Formalism used to Represent the Charts of Concepts

The formalism used to represent used to represent charts of concepts is an extension of the conceptual graphs of Sowa [6].

The conceptual graphs allow to define a meaning for each conceptual relationship of a graph. All the arcs of charts of concepts have the same meaning which is "the definition of a concept CPy end of an arc, uses a concept CPx beginning of this arc". In this sense, charts of concepts are particular conceptual graphs. But with charts of concepts we can define "and/or" expressions between definition dependencies (cf. Section 2.2.3).

Many operations can be defined on conceptual graphs: copy, restriction, join, projection, specialization, generalization, simplification. On charts of concepts we apply other operations to create, delete, modify and select concepts (operations that we will present in Section 4).

Do not confuse definition dependencies with other types of dependencies, with other types of dependencies, for example with functional dependencies, multivalued dependencies or inclusion dependencies of the relational model [7].

3 Verification of a Model Defined with Charts of Concepts

In this section we explain how to verify a model defined with charts of concepts by searching non connected sub-graphs and circuits.

3.1 Non Connected Sub-graphs in Charts of Concepts

A non connected sub-graph in a chart of concepts relates the fact that the model is fragmented and that we can use the concepts of this sub-graph apart of the other concepts. The existence of a non connect sub-graph in a chart of concepts is very cumbersome because that means that we can use this sub-graph in another chart.

- Non Connected Sub-graphs in Charts of Concepts of the Model of the UML

In the charts of concepts of the version 1.1 of the UML we found four non connected sub-graphs in the chart of concepts of sequence diagrams (that is depicted in the annex in Figure 20). One of these non connected sub-graphs is depicted in Figure 12.

Figure 12. Example of non connected sub-graph

3.2 Circuits Between Definitions of Concepts

The existence of a circuit between concepts relates the fact that the definition of a concept uses a concept of which the definition uses another concept, ... , of which the definition uses the first concept. So, the existence of a circuit between concepts of a model is very cumbersome because that means that the comprehension of a concept of a circuit necessitates the comprehension of all the other concepts of the circuit.

The existence of a circuit means that the deletion of one of its concepts imposes the deletion of all its concepts. Like, the existence of a circuit means that the selection of one of its concepts imposes the selection of all its concepts.

- Circuits Between Definitions of Concepts of the UML

Muller evokes the problem by recalling that the egg and the hen [8]. We found several circuits between definitions of concepts of the model of the UML. We know how it is difficult to delete these circuits. One of them is in the chart of basic concepts relative to objects (that is depicted in the annex in Figure 16), is depicted in Figure 13.

Figure 13. Example of circuit between concepts

Some circuits result from co-definition dependencies between two concepts. The co-definition between the concepts of "interaction" and "collaboration" in the chart of concepts of collaboration diagrams (that is depicted in Figure 15 in Section 4.4), is depicted in Figure 14.

Figure 14. Example of circuit resulting from a co-definition dependency between two concepts

4 Creation, Deletion, Modification and Selection of Concepts in a Model Defined with Charts of Concepts

In this section we present the operations of creation, deletion, modification and selection of concepts in a model defined with charts of concepts.

4.1 Creation of Concepts in a Model Defined with Charts of Concepts

To create a concept in a chart of concepts, concepts used in its definition and concepts that use it in their definitions must be exist in these charts of concepts. The first concepts are the predecessors of the new concept and the second ones are its successors in the considered chart of concepts. If predecessors or successors of a new concept do not exist, they must be created before the creation of the new concept.

- Examples of Concepts that Could be Created in the Model of the UML

In addition to the concepts of "pattern" and "framework", the concept of "generic application" could be created in the UML for reusing applications. Generic applications are also called "application frameworks". Johnson and Wirfs-Brock [9] define a generic application as a skeleton of classes, objects and relationships grouped together for building a specific application. The importance of designing application frameworks is also underlined by Coad [10]. We propose a development process for the creation and reuse of generic applications in [11].

The distinction between different categories of objects, business objects, technical objects,..., facilitates analyses and designs. The model of the UML does not distinguish categories of objects.

The functional OMT model [12], generally appreciated by software analysts and designers, could be created in the model of the UML.

Data flow diagrams (DFD) could be created in the model of the UML. The software analysts and the designers could have the possibility to choose between DFD and use cases, if they consider that the use of DFD's and use cases is redundant.

A new concept can be created with the UML by stereotyping an existing concept if this new concept is a subclass of this existing concept defined with the same form but with a different intent.

4.2 Deletion of Concepts in a Model Defined with Charts of Concepts

The deletion of a concept in charts of concepts of a model is a suppression of this concept for ever. A deletion of a concept necessitates to delete all its successors.

- *Examples of Concepts of the Model of the UML that Could be Deleted*

The concept of "use case" defined in the OOSE method [13] of Jacobson could not be used in the UML.

The concept of "activity", for which we do not see interest in an object-oriented model, could be deleted. Hence, activity diagrams would not be useful.

4.3 Modification of Concepts in a Model Defined with Charts of Concepts

A modification of a concept in a model defined with charts of concepts is either a modification of its textual definition or a modification of its predecessors or its successors.

- *Examples of Concepts of the Model of the UML of which Definitions Could be Modified*

We met difficulties to find definitions of some important concepts in the UML, difficulties specified in Section 2.1. So, it would be better that more precise definitions of concepts would be given in a further version of the model of the UML.

Concepts of "system" and "subsystem" of the version 1.1 of the UML are used to define the physical representation of applications. In a French version of the model of the UML, the notion of "system" could be more general and applicable at all abstraction levels, and not only at the physical level.

In the model of the UML exists the concept of "object flow" of which definition is: an instance of a class Ci is deleted in this class and becomes an instance of another class Cj. This concept is therefore a particular case of transmutation that can be defined between more than two classes. The concept of "object flow" could be modified and becomes the general concept of transmutation allowing to create instances of several classes from instances of several classes, concept proposed in the method MCO [14] [15].

The modification of definitions of concepts of the model of the UML generally necessitates to modify definition dependencies between these concepts and other concepts.

4.4 Selection of Concepts in a Model Defined with Charts of Concepts

A selection of concepts in a model defined with charts of concepts is an extraction of concepts in this model to create a customized version of this model with saving these concepts in the library of the initial model. A goal and criteria must be defined to select concepts in a model.

It is necessary to fix the goals of a customized model so as to select concepts in a starting model. These goals may be about:
. the taking into account of culture on object-oriented approach and on analysis and design of information systems of the persons that will use this version;
. the field of information systems that will be designed with the customized model: management, scientist, real time, etc.;
. the types of applications to design with this customized model: applications managing large volumes of data, of which processing is preponderant, of which communications are essential because data are distributed, etc.;
. the abstraction levels and the stages where this customized model will be used: conceptual level (requirements engineering), logical and physical levels (system engineering);
. the trades of persons that will use it: end-users, software analysts, designers, developers, administrators of libraries, etc.;
. the time that these persons could devote to its apprenticeship, and so the maximal number of concepts that this customized model can have;
. the case tools that will be used to analyze and to design with this customized model and to manage specifications created with this version;
. the financial means that can be spent to the creation of a customized model and to the training of the persons;
. etc.

The mechanism of selection of concepts in a model is the following one. We associate to a node that represents a concept CPy:
. a Boolean function Fy of which arguments represent the selection variables (defined hereafter) of the predecessors of CPy, arguments joined by logical and/or

operators;

. a Boolean choice variable Cy: the value "true" means that the manager of software analysts and designers wants to select the concept CPy;

. and a Boolean selection variable Sy such that: Sy = Cy and Fy; the concept CPy is selected if Sy is true.

The evaluation of a Boolean function Fy associated to a node CPy depends on values of selection variables of its predecessors, which depend on values of selection variables of their predecessors, etc.

To select several concepts we repeat the selection mechanism above-mentioned to select one concept and the selected concepts are marked.

- Selection of Concepts in the Model of the UML

Example of goal and criteria to select concepts in the model of the UML:
. Goal: to initiate to the model of the UML professionals working in computer science not familiarized with the object-oriented approach;
. Selection criteria of concepts in the model of the UML to define a customized version of this model:
  . to only consider object-oriented concepts;
  . to take an interest to classes instead of objects, to the conceptual and the logical levels more than to the physical level, to static representations instead of dynamic representations.

In Figure 15 is presented an example of selected concepts in the chart of concepts of collaboration diagrams. The names of the non selected concepts are hachured. According to our criterion "take an interest to conceptual and logical levels before physical level" we do not select concepts of "passive object", "active object", "argument of a message", "result", "sequence" and "point of synchronization of a message" in chart of concepts of collaboration diagrams.

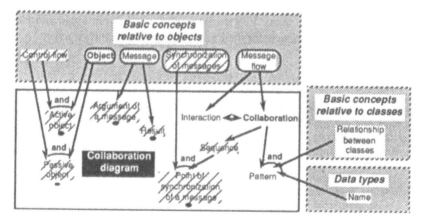

Figure 15. Selection of concepts in the chart of concepts of collaboration diagrams

382

5 Conclusion, Discussion

This paper underlines the use of charts of concepts to define new versions and customized versions of models. The goal of a work in progress is to manage versions of models of which anterior versions must be conserved. Schema evolution models and versioning models will be used. Among the numerous works in this field let us mention for example [16], [17], [18], [19], ...

We explained in Section 1.1 why we think that meta-models do not allow to create, delete, modify and select concepts by seeing concepts which are implied in a selection and those which are not implied. Another work in progress is developed to transform meta-models in charts of concepts and vice versa.

Table 1 summarizes numbers of concepts that we have taken in account in charts of concepts of the model of the UML. The number of concepts of this model (233) is high. This number justifies the necessity to create customized versions of the model of the UML defined with selections of concepts.

The possibility to define selections of concepts in models is exposed in [20] with presentation of the version 1.0 of the UML. This application is developed and extended in [21], paper in which a core of the version 1.1 of the UML is presented. The model of the MCO method and a core of this model are presented in [14] using charts of concepts. As the charts of concepts allow to define selections of concepts in models, they allow to present overviews of models both defined by selections of concepts and macro views of models [22].

As charts of concepts are directed graphs, they allow to evaluate models with metrics usable to measure the size, the complexity, and anomalies of models such as circuits between concepts [23].

So, the charts of concepts are a general proposal in the field of the method engineering [2].

Acknowledgments

The authors would like to thank Vincent Bataille, student in our team, and Hong Jiang, PhD in computer science, for their valuable remarks on this paper.

References

1. Henderson-Sellers B and Firesmith G. COMMA: Proposed core model. Report on Object Analysis and Design, Vol. 4, No. 1, 1997.
2. Welke RJ, Kumar K. Method engineering: a proposal for situation-specific methodology construction, in Systems Analysis and Design: A Research Agenda. Cotterman and Senn(eds), Wiley, 1992.
3. Tolvanen JP, Marttiin P, Lyytinen K, Rossi M, Tahvanainen VP and Smolander K. Modeling Requirements for Future CASE: Modeling Issues and Architectural Consideration. Information Resources Management Journal, Vol. 8, No. 1, 1995.
4. Chen PP. The entity-relationship model. ACM transactions on database systems. Vol. 1, No. 1, March 1976.
5. Booch G, Jacobson I and Rumbaugh J. Unified Modeling Language (UML), Version 1.1. Rational Software Corporation, Santa Clara, 1 September 1997.

Basic concepts

Chart of basic concepts relative to objects	24
Chart of basic concepts relative to classes	8
Chart of basic concepts: auxiliary elements	12
Chart of basic concepts: extension mechanisms	8
Chart of basic concepts: data types	32
Total number of basic concepts	*84*

Diagrams

Chart of concepts of use case diagrams	7
Chart of concepts of class diagrams	42
Chart of concepts of object diagrams	7
Chart of concepts of collaboration diagrams	9
Chart of concepts of sequence diagrams	23
Chart of concepts of statechart diagrams	33
Chart of concepts of activity diagrams	6
Chart of concepts of component diagrams	11
Chart of concepts of deployment diagrams	11
Total number of concepts of charts of diagrams	*149*

Numbers of concepts **233**

Table 1. Numbers of concepts of the model of the version 1.1 of the UML

6. Sowa JF. Conceptual structures: Information processing in Mind and Machine. Addison-Wesley Publishing Company, 1984.
7. Codd EF. Further normalization of the data base relational model. Data base systems, Prentice Hall, Englewood Cliffs, New Jersey, 1972.
8. Muller PA. Instant UML. Wrox Press Inc, Chicago, USA, 1997.
9. Johnson R and Wirfs-Brock R. Object-oriented frameworks. Tutorial notes, in Proceedings of ACM OOPSLA 1991.
10. Coad P. Object-Oriented Patterns. Communications of the ACM, September 1992, Vol. 35, No. 9.
11. Castellani X and Liao S. Development Process for the Creation and Reuse of Object-Oriented Generic Applications and Components. Journal of Object-Oriented Programming (JOOP), June 1998, Vol. 11, No. 3, SIGS Publications, New York.
12. Rumbaugh J, Blaha M, Premerlani W, Eddy F and Lorensen W. Object-Oriented Modeling and Design. Prentice Hall International, 1991.
13. Jacobson I. Object-Oriented Software Engineering, A Use Case Driven Approach. Addison-Wesley Publishing Company, 1992.
14. Castellani X. Méthodologie générale d'analyse et de conception des systèmes d'objets (MCO). L'ingénierie des besoins. Masson Editor, 1993.
15. Castellani X and Jiang H. Specification and Implementation of the Transmutation Concept. International Conference on Object-Oriented Information Systems (OOIS' 94), London, UK, December 19-21, 1994, proceedings published by Springer-Verlag.
16. Fauvet MC. Définition et réalisation d'un modèle de versions d'objets. 5th days on Advanced data bases, Geneva, Switzerland, September 1989.
17. Gançarski S and Jomier G. Managing Entity Versions within their contexts: a Formal Approach. 5th International conference, Database and Expert Systems Applications, Athens, Greece, September 1994.
18. Sciore E. Versioning and configuration management in an object-oriented data model, VLDB Journal, 3:77-106, 1994.

19. Zdonik SB. Version Management in an Object-Oriented Database. Springer Verlag, LNCS, 1986.
20. Castellani X. Cartes de concepts permettant de créer des versions personnalisées d'UML. Journal Ingénierie des Systèmes d'Information (ISI), Volume 5, n° 5/1997, September 1997, Hermès.
21. Castellani X and Hamamouche N. Definition of Customized Models: Application to Define a Core of the UML Model. Tenth International Conference on Software Engineering and Knowledge Engineering (SEKE '98), San Francisco, USA, 18-20 June 1998.
22. Castellani X. An Overview of the Version 1.1 of the UML Defined with Charts of Concepts. «UML»'98 Beyond the Notation, International Workshop supported by the OMG, organized by the ESSAIM, Mulhouse, France, 3-4 June 1998.
23. Castellani X. Evaluation of Models Defined with Charts of Concepts: Application to the UML Model. CAISE'98/IFIP 8.1, Third International Workshop on Evaluation of Modeling Methods in Systems Analysis and Design (EMMSAD'98), Pisa, Italy, 8-9 June 1998.

Annex: Charts of Concepts of the Version 1.1 of the UML

Some charts of the basic concepts and of the concepts of the diagrams of the model of the UML presented are in this annex:

. charts of basic concepts: basic concepts relative to objects, and basic concepts relative to classes (Figures 16, 17); for sake of conciseness we do not present the charts of the auxiliary elements, extension mechanisms, and data types;

. charts of concepts of diagrams: use case diagrams, class diagrams, sequence diagrams, and statechart diagrams (Figures 18 to 21); the chart of collaboration diagrams was presented in Figure 15 in Section 4.4; for sake of conciseness we do not present the charts of the object diagrams, activity diagrams, component diagrams, and deployment diagrams.

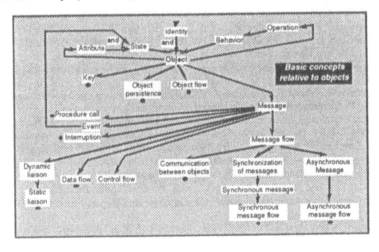

Figure 16. Chart of basic concepts relative to objects

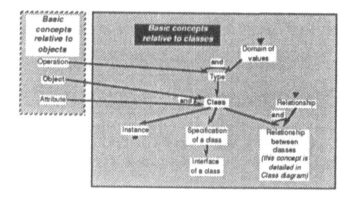

Figure 17. Chart of basic concepts relative to classes

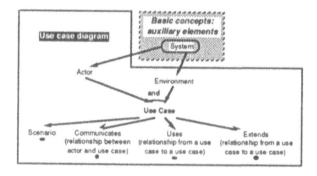

Figure 18. Chart of concepts of use case diagrams

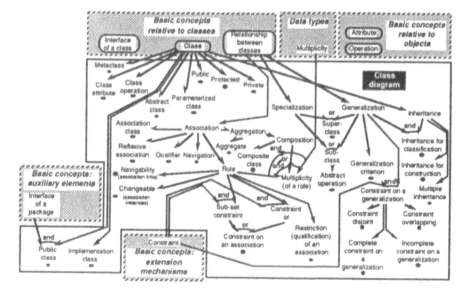

Figure 19. Chart of concepts of class diagrams

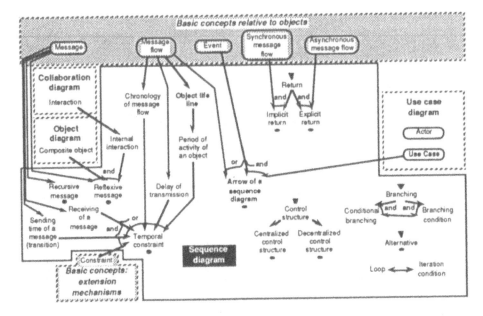

Figure 20. Chart of concepts of sequence diagrams

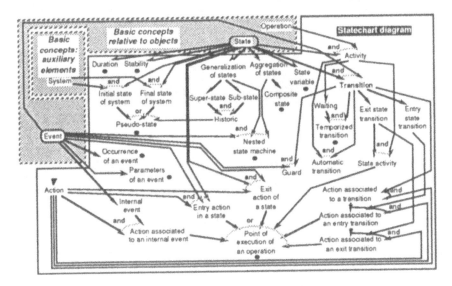

Figure 21. Chart of concepts of statechart diagrams

A CASE Tool for the Modeling of Methods and Information Systems

José Celso Freire Junior

Faculdade de Engenharia-Guaratinguetá - UNESP

Guaratinguetá - Brazil

Monique Chabre-Peccoud - Agnès Front - Jean-Pierre Giraudin

Laboratoire Logiciels Systèmes Réseaux - IMAG

Grenoble - France

Abstract

MODSI is a multi-models tool for information systems modeling. A modeling process in MODSI can be driven according to three different approaches: informal, semi-formal and formal. The MODSI tool is therefore based on the linked usage of these three modeling approaches. It can be employed at two different levels: the meta-modeling of a method and the modeling of an information system.

In this paper we start presenting different types of modeling by making an analysis of their particular features. Then, we introduce the meta-model defined in our tool, as well as the tool functional architecture. Finally, we describe and illustrate the various usage levels of this tool.

1 Introduction

Systems have become increasingly complex with growing needs for safety. Thus there specification must be improved in order to assure better development and it is necessary to use different modeling techniques according to the view of the system that has to be expressed and according to the actors of the various phases in the development process. It is especially necessary to coordinate informal, semi-formal and formal specifications. The clearness needs are satisfied by combining semi-formal modelings and texts, structured or not (informal specifications). The precision needs can be warranted by use of formal methods, linked to the others. In fact, the *multi-modeling* of information systems increases in the CASEs available for modeling, but has still to be improved.

To go from the domain of the problem close to the user, to the domain of the solution close to the implementation machine, we necessarily have to use different models (concepts, notations, languages) to elaborate, verify, enable, coordinate, transform or explain, what implies the definition of these models and the cohesion of their usage. This can induce static rules and their evaluation can be further developed in guiding and controlling the modeling processes. In the presentation, our CASE tool (MODSI) will not approach this guiding process. We will just describe our choices in terms of a meta-modeling tool that allows multi-modeling.

A meta-model supports the definition of a model (its concepts, relationships between concepts, its notations, etc.) but also establishes relationships between models. Different meta-modeling approaches are possible (axiomatic, conceptual graphs, etc.). We choose to develop a meta-model according to several viewpoints: graphs of representation, representation of sub-models and inter-models organization. This approach is the heart of our CASE tool. We present here the prototype of a modeling CASE tool where informal, semi-formal and formal methods are jointly used to produce, as much as possible, a specification that takes into account the advantages of each approach.

Section 2 describes different types of modeling. Section 3 introduces the meta-model supported by our CASE prototype. Section 4 presents the meta CASE environment we use. The architecture and the parts of MODSI are presented in section 5. The different levels of use of MODSI are introduced in section 6. Section 7 presents a specific example using MODSI. Section 8 establishes an assessment of the prototype and draws some future perspectives.

2   Modeling Types

According to the Webster Dictionary, modeling consists in "To plan or form after a pattern; to form in model; to form a model or pattern for". The modeling is therefore the building of a model of something for some purpose. A more complete definition of model is given by M. Minsky [23]: "For an operator O, an object M is a model of an object A if O can use M to reply to questions concerning A".

According to R. S. Pressman [29], modeling used in the *Software Engineering* is composed of three components: the *methods* with there own languages, the *tools* and the *processes*. In relation to the language used in a modeling process, one can class the modeling as being formal, semi-formal or informal.

Table 1, inspired of M. D. Fraser [14], presents categories of language types as well as examples of those languages or of methods that use them. Next section presents, with more details, those three types of modeling.

We concentrate in this paper in the languages approach of the method to integrate them in a tool, but not in the process model.

2.1   Informal Modeling

The process of informal modeling according to an informal language can have a justified use [4]: (1) its ease of understanding allows to build consensus between persons that specify and those that want to use a software; (2) it represents a familiar communication manner between persons.

On the other hand, the use of an informal language makes the modeling process vague and sometimes ambiguous. Also, as the human reasoning is the only process for the analysis and the verification of the specification [13], it can induce errors in understanding, interpretation and verification.

Categories of Languages			
Informal Languages		Semi-Formal Languages	Formal Languages
"Simple"	Standard		
Language that has not a complete set of rules to restrain a model production.	Language with a structure, a format and rules to compose a model production.	Language that has a defined syntax to specify the conditions on the model structuring.	Language that have a syntax and a semantics rigorously defined. A theoretical model can be used to enable a modeling and prove its validity.
Examples of Languages or Approaches			
natural language.	Structured text in natural language.	Entity-Relationship Diagram, Object Diagrams, State Diagrams.	Petri Networks, State Machines, VDM, Z, B.

Table 1: Classification and Use of Languages and Methods

It is possible to use a "Informal Standard Modeling" to restrain these problems, that is, a modeling that uses a natural language while introducing usage rules of the language in the building process of the model.

Such type of modeling keeps advantages of the informal modeling improving the process while making it more precise, less ambiguous and more complete.

2.2 Semi-Formal Modeling

The process of semi-formal modeling is based on graphical or textual languages in order to have precise syntax as well as a semantics; this semantics is not completely defined, but allows, nevertheless, a certain rules and errors checking ability and some computerization of the work [3].

Most semi-formal approaches are strongly based on a graphical language. That can be justified by the power of expression given by a well developed graphical model; the textual language is mostly used as support to graphical models. The semi-formal modeling, using a graphical language, can produce in depth and still readable models : this justifies its large usage. However the lack of a complete semantics hinders strongly this type of modeling; the problem existing for informal languages persists with the lack of precision related to the understanding of the modeling as well as the existing ambiguities of semi-formal languages.

Attempting to solve those problems, some use of constraints on graphical models has been introduced as textual constraints proposed in J. J. Odell's work [24]. Structural constraints are applied there to a modeling based on object-oriented models. Some other proposition was made by S. Cook and J. Daniels [7]. In our work based graphically on the OMT method [32] and D.

Harel state charts [20], we propose to introduce constraints expressed in the Z formal language [34].

2.3 Formal Modeling

A formal approach is a rigorous development process based on formal notations with a precise semantics enabling formal verifications [16]. Expressing a more accurate meaning allows to use the formal model for systematic proof and consistency checking [8].

We resume below the analysis of formal approaches achieved by A. Hall [17] and by J. P. Bowen and M. C. Hinchey [6] concerning some myths inherent on formal languages.

A. Hall [17] explains that formal approaches support the search for errors and decrease their impact through a more complete specification. This specification can be applied to any type of hardware or software system; they do not replace however existent approaches and have to be used jointly with semi-formal approaches. If a solid mathematical knowledge is necessary to make proofs, it is not always imperative to specify a system. The formal approach usage can invoke a lessening of costs and does not produce delays in projects.

J. P. Bowen and M. C. Hinchey [6] show that with an appropriate translation in some other expression mode, formal approaches can support the understanding of a system by its user, including large systems where they are largely applied. Beyond the existent specific formal proofs tools, the numerous studies of wider tools that could cover all specification process, show the interest of the community for these approaches. The formal approach begins even to be imposed by companies in some cases although they are not used everywhere in the modeling process.

3 The Proposed Meta-Model

In this paper, our multi-modeling approach is based on the use of a meta-model. This meta-model integrates informal, semi-formal and formal methods and can be used either for the representation of models proposed by traditional methods in the information system modeling, those method meta-modeling, or for the representation of the models stemming from the use of those methods on the specification process of an information system integrating the various approaches for multi-modeling.

The proposed meta-model (see figure 1) uses the concept of view composed of one or several *schemata*. The number of schemata of a meta-model view is determined by the complexity of the method or model represented. We describe these views hereafter.

- *Formal Model*: this view is employed for the formal declaration of all concepts of the specification. It renders the meta-model compatible with the syntax of the used formal language, by representing the basic types of the model as well as its global declarations.

- *Static Model*: this view contains schemata employed for the representation of basic concepts (i.e. Class, Object, Property, etc.), basic relationships between these concepts (instantiation, static characterization, etc.) and several specific relationship types (inheritance, composition, etc.) used by the modeled approach.

- *Dynamic Model*: this view corresponds to schemata employed to represent the concepts and relationships between these concepts used by an approach for the modeling of the dynamic of a system (state diagram, interactions diagram, data flow diagram, etc.).

- *General Model*: this view presents a synthetic schema representing mostly the relationships existing between different concepts of the static and dynamic models as well as other models part that have not yet been represented.

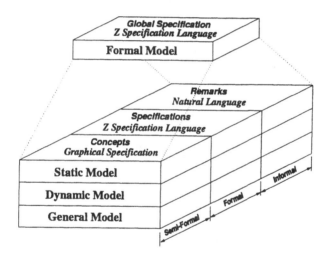

Figure 1: MODSI Meta-Model

The views on the proposed meta-model use the method of schemata with different levels of details: a view is composed of one or several schemata.

The Formal Models view, by its role of global formal specification, is represented by one unique schema, the Global Specification Schema (see figure 1).

Static, Dynamic and General Models views are composed of three different types of schemata : Concepts, Specifications and Remarks (see figure 1).

The integration of informal, semi-formal and formal methods in the meta-model is achieved by these schemata. The four types of schemata are described hereafter.

- *Global Specification*: the *S_Global* schema, is a skeleton, where types, relationships between these types as well as axioms used in a specification of a model are declared formally. The language used is Z [34].

- *Concepts*: the *S_Concepts* schemata represent the integration of the semi-formal approach in the meta-model. They are graphical schemata with a notation that depends on the level in which the tool based on the meta-model is used (meta-modeling or multi-modeling, see section 6).

- *Specifications*: the *S_Specifications* schemata correspond to the usage of the formal approach. They are based on Z [34]. This formal specification allows complete aspects and constraints of a method or a model not clarified with the graphical S_Concepts model. The used language can be Z or Object-Z [9] depending on the level in which the tool is used (see section 6).

- *Remarks*: the *S_Remarks* schemata represent some usage of the informal approach. A S_Remarks schema explains in natural language interesting aspects of a method or a model and clarifies notations employed elsewhere. The S_Remarks schema can be used also to describe literally aspects that can neither be captured with the S_Concepts, nor with the S_Specifications schemata.

This meta-model is the kernel on which our modeling tool is built. This meta-model fills three essentials objective for the modeling of an information system: (1) it eases the integration of informal, semi-formal and formal specifications (to combine OMT and Z for example); (2) it coordinates the joint use of several models according to the same informal, semi-formal or formal paradigm (to combine OMT for static aspects and MERISE for dynamic aspects for example); (3) it might allow the organization of the modeling process using views. The components of the tool described in the next section is built on this meta-model.

4 A Meta Case Environment

We choose to develop the prototype on a meta-case environment, in order to be able to work simultaneously in a graphical modeling environment, and to add and couple the graphical language with formal language, that could be produced or analysed in a parallel process.

A meta-CASE environment is a CASE intended to support CASE description in order to produce CASE generation. Its functionnalities are usually a graphical editor generator, supporting graphical model descriptions, syntactical editors generator or a coupling with a syntactical editor (LEX and YACC for exemple) for the language approach, a repository or a DBMS coupling in order to support the storage of the languages descriptions, the various cohesion rules as well as the models expressed with the CASE, and various external and presentation specifications of the human interface. It often supports the definition of languages coupling in order to produce code generation to.

At the beginning of our work the most common environments of this type were GraphTalk [26], Paradigm Plus [28] and MetaEdit [33]. Some tools were developped in research environment as MetaGen [5] or MetaView [12].

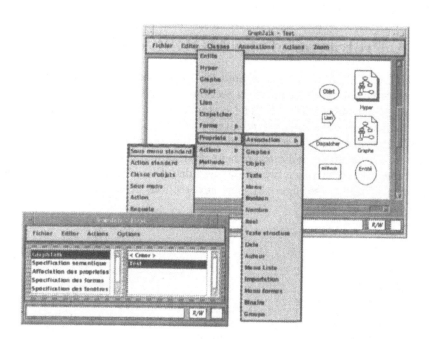

Figure 2: GraphTalk Meta Tool

The contacts we had with Xerox, induced us to concentrate on the Graphtalk-LEdit environment. The product had, like Paradigm Plus, a multiplatform environment, and had developped an object oriented approach, even in the storage model that was appealing for OO-modeling. The strong coupling announced of a graphical editors generator with the syntactical editor LEdit was functionally adapted to the environment we were to build.

A tool generation is obtained combining four views, specifications of the tool with the GraphTalk concepts. The **semantical specification** defines an object oriented metamodel of the model language (objects and relationships or links), a **property specification** attaches text properties, and constraints of type, existence and cardinalities to the concepts and relations and mutual cohesion constraints of the meta-model parts, the **shape specification** introduces the graphical presentation of the model to whom textual properties migth be attached, and finally, the **widget specification** describes the users interface and the documentation process of the tool intended. This incremental process in building the tool gives a good and modular approach of a CASE construction.

Figure 2 presents two windows of the GraphTalk meta-tool. The "Graph-Talk-Essai" window is the main window of the meta-tool and the "GraphTalk-Test" window is an instance of the meta-tool. The "GraphTalk-Test" window presents basic components (entity, graph, link, etc.) offered by the meta-tool for the modeling of a method. One can see also the kind of properties (association, boolean, number, etc.) and actions (menu, query, etc.) that one can attach to the components of a modeling.

5   A Prototype of the MODSI Tool

The MODSI CASE prototype is built on three existent software tools: the meta-tools GraphTalk (presented in section 4) and LEdit [27] as well as with the documents editor Thot [25]. The syntactic editor generator LEdit supports BNF languages definition; it is adapted to take in account formal languages models. It works togheter with GraphTalk. Thot is a syntactic parameterized editor for the definition and management of structured documents. The MODSI prototype is composed on two main modules, the *Models Handler* and the *Documents Handler* (see figure 3). The next sections present the main modules that compose MODSI.

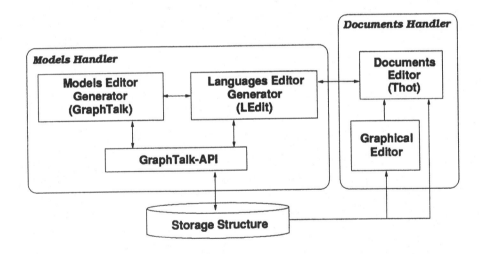

Figure 3: MODSI Tool Architecture

5.1   Models Handler

The Models Handler allows the creation and the maintenance of all schemata used in the meta-modeling, description of a specific multimodel approach of an information system modeling. It might treat the OMT models as well as the meta-description of UML for example.

The Models Handler leans on the meta-tools *GraphTalk* and *LEdit* as well as on facilities provided by GraphTalk, as the *GraphTalk-API* allows the creation and the maintenance of a *Storage Structure* through the joint usage of demons. This structure holds the links between the various parts presented in S_Concepts schemata of a modeling.

At the meta-modeling level, the Models Handler is composed of two bound tools, A2M and A2M'. A2M manages mostly the semantical specification and the property part of a GraphTalk tool while A2M' adds the graphical and presentation specification. These parts A2M- A2M' include all the information through the coupling of formal descriptions generated with LEdit, in order to generate the terminal multi-model tool called AM (see figure 4).

AM is the multi-modeling tool on the target method, it uses the meta-description stored to manage the graphical modeling done by the end-user and generates formal skeleton that the developer can complete using the formal editor generated at meta-level with LEdit.

5.2 Documents Handler

The documents handler allows the creation and the maintenance of a informal standardized specification that validates and maintains the cohesion between the three types of modelings employed (informal, semi-formal and formal). This handler is based on the syntactic editor *Thot* that we use to develop a *"Modeling Canvas"*.

The Modeling Canvas is composed of a *structured descriptive text* that focuses on schemata produced by the Models Handler. In order to create this structured descriptive text in a adaptable manner, it is necessary first to have modeled the system with the Models Handler. This descriptive text is composed by text in natural language with pointers to members stemming from schemata generated by the Models Handler.

The cohesion between this descriptive text and schemata of the Models Handler is ascertained by the use of Views; a view defines a part of a S_Concept. It gives at documentation level the mean to choose the granularity of the model presentation. After the modeling of a model or a system, one has to define views that focus on this modeling to ascertain the coherence between the two handlers. If no view is defined, the whole modeling schema is considered as a unique view.

6 Levels of Usage: Meta-Modeling and Multi-Modeling

The Meta-Modeling Tool

In the *Meta-Modeling Level*, two steps are necessary to create the tool generated from the meta-model of a method and two different parts are used there.

A2M - The first one (*A2M*) implements the four meta views (Formal, Static, Dynamic and General) of the proposed meta-model. Those views are used to produce a first release of the model of a method. At this level, S_Concepts schemata are given by ERA diagrams (Entity-Relationship-Attribute) that represent concepts and relationships between those concepts; S_Specifications schemata and the specification of the Global Specification view are declared formally using Z. The General view is expressed by natural language sentences. Thus A2M parts includes the semantics of the languages modeling. The tool A2M generates for the second part A2M' all necessary components to offer the notion of presentation views in the tool AM that will be generated by A2M' for the proposed method according to the Document Handler needs.

A2M' - The second part (*A2M'*) is generated by A2M. In A2M', the three views (Static, Dynamic and General) are not explicitly used. Objects and relationships present in A2M' are generated from the definitions made in A2M. The model tool designer has to complete the part generated by A2M, declaring the shapes of the concepts and relationships of the method model and adding GraphTalk members and demons in order to be able to generate the AM part of the selected method. One has also to attach a Graphtalk property of type text to each of the nodes that have to exist in the final graph generated in AM, in order to produce the ability to define informal specification parts documenting graphical parts. All those additional information brings no new semantical definition to the specification of the method, so the A2M' tool do not has to manage informal or formal specifications. The only schema of the proposed meta-model that has to be completed is the the S_Concept that uses only GraphTalk notations, syntax and tools.

This uses the property, shape and widget specification of GraphTalk including text and calls to the LEdit syntactic editors through deamon call.

The Multi-Modeling Tool

The *Multi-Modeling* is done with the AM tool and permits to create models of information systems, using the models of the modeled method. This tool is generated by the meta-tool GraphTalk using definitions produced in A2M'. The static, dynamic and general views are meta-model concepts that structure the filed information, but are implicit here. Each approach, through its owns diagrams, defines its views. The notation generated graphically is the one defined in the A2M' part, while the S_Specifications which implicitely manages the generated formal specification, produces Object-Z schematas [9] precising the class definitions. The declaration of classes and inheritance structure conform to A. Hall propositions [18, 19] as well as the representation of aggregation structures. The relations between objects are formal Z relations.

The figure 4 shows a reduced example of our propositions according to the different modeling levels. In this example a part of the OMT method [32] is modeled. The Remarks part, natural language informal specification, has been dropped for readability purpose.

The meta-modeling part of figure 4, related to A2M tool, presents a partial modeling of the Objects Model of OMT. This modeling expresses semi-formally and formally the fact that class and inheritance concepts are defined in the Objects Model. The part relative to A2M' presents necessary GraphTalk descriptions (the shadowed part) for the effective usage of the inheritance concept between classes. In A2M', Class and Inheritance are generated automatically by A2M, because they have been defined at this level. The other concepts (Super_Class and D_Inheritance) are introduced to allow the meta-tool GraphTalk to manage the concept of inheritance and its constraints in the AM tool.

In fact, the concept introduces a new node between superclass and subclass concept as the graphical relation is a (one to n) one. As we said, the formal and informal schemata are not used at this level.

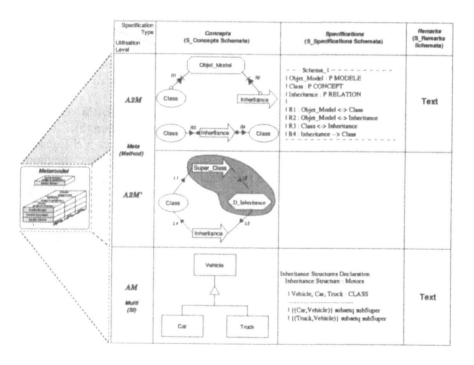

Figure 4: The Proposed Levels of the Prototype

In figure 4, the multi-modeling level describes the usage of the generated modeling tool (AM) through the presentation of the S_Concept schema that shows three classes, Vehicle, Car and Truck linked by an inheritance structure. The S_Specification schema shows a part of the S_Global schema for the S_Concept schema. To simplify, the formal specification of classes is not shown.

7 A Specific Example of MODSI Usage: The STORM Modeling

The example presented in this section is based on the modeling of a part of the STORM model [1]. The STORM model is an object model for the management and modeling of multimedia data including their time evolution. This model offers the means to search, update and compose multimedia data that build *presentations*, playing and coupling video, images and sounds.

Presentations of multimedia objects are stored in a database in the same way as the objects they are constructed on. The running of presentations is enabled by the use of synchronization constraints, especially in the presence of parallelism. The storing of multimedia presentations as objects allows to amend them and to recover them easily and to ascertain the consistency of the method. Each presentation is therefore considered as a STORM multimedia object.

The different objects that compose a presentation are structured by using sequential or parallel operators. Operators can have constraints applied in the synchronization of their components. Sequential operator constraints are of type before and meet and parallel operators of type equal, start, finish, overlap and during [2].

The semi-formal modeling process of a system using the STORM generated tool, produces at the same time its formal specification (see figure 5).

Through the usage of GraphTalk demons, while one defines a S_Concept schema, the tool builds the associated S_Specification schema. Thus, the modeling of a part of the STORM model (the algebraic structure, presented in the right window, "Modèle_Objet-Struc_Algébrique" of the figure 5) produces the formal specification presented in the left window, "gclasseZ-STORM.le" of the same figure. The S_Specification schema presents the formal class declaration, the links, the two inheritance structures and the aggregation structure. We can see the annotation (schema S_Remarks)) that has been provided by the designer of the Storm Model to explain the specialization of the Tree object.

Figure 6 presents the Model document produced with the Documents Handler that instantiates the existing links between the two handlers.

Having modeled a system by using the components of the models handler, and having declared views in the S_Concepts schema (i.e. the two views Str_H1 and Str_H2 defined in the right window, "Modèle_Objet-Struc_Algébrique" of the figure 5), we can begin to build documents using the documents handler. Thus we have declared a view that consists in the structure H1 (classes Tree, TerminalNode and OperatorNode) and another that consists in the structure H2 (classes OperatorNode, ParNode and SeqNode) for the future use of STORM algebraic structure.

The figure 6 example, necessarily limited, includes nevertheless the S_Concept and S_Specification schemata as well as the S_Remark part. Those elements are scheduled according to a modeling canvas. This canvas coordinates formal, semi-formal and informal specifications. Such canvas can schedule a use of semi-formal representations for an eased interpretation of formal description.

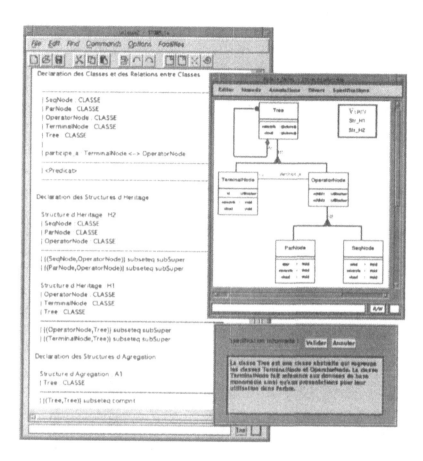

Figure 5: Algebraic Structure - Modeling with the Generated AM-OMT

8 Conclusion

In this paper we present the architecture of a tool intended to ease joint use of three approaches (informal, semi-formal and formal) in the modeling of specifications of information systems. Those approaches can be combined at two different levels: the meta-modeling of models of object oriented methods and the multi-modeling of information systems. This coordinate use of formalisms has been materialized by the development of a prototype, MODSI, a tool generator for building multimodel specification systems documents.

To structure the joint use (informal/semi-formal/formal) of model parts, we have proposed a meta-model. This meta-model enables to model systems according to two axes: one that integrates the three formalisms, and the other, that allows to structure the system according to views integrating its dynamic and static characteristics. This meta-model is at the heart of the generator of modeling tool presented here.

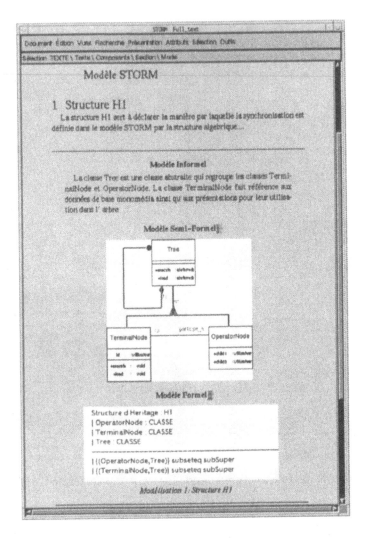

Figure 6: Exemple of Utilisation of the Tool

The main features of the generator are the following: (1) a description of each model according to a same meta-model taking into account the three dimensions, informal, semi-formal and formal; (2) a upgradeability, a portability and an autonomy of the three composers (meta-tools) of the selected architecture; (3) a combination of the object modeling techniques and formal approaches by an organization in schemata; (4) a generalization of the concept of multi-modeling; (5) a help to the documentation of projects; (6) an ability to permit the formal checking of a semi-formal specification.

Our contribution is significant because the architecture and model we propose in this generator prototype allow more strongly than in the usual commercial tools, to combine automatically, coordinate and maintain cohesion for a same information system between parts of documents of different types : formal specifications, semi-formal multi-models and informal ones, even at a fragment level.

The tool includes this management of "fragments" of models as part usable in an hypertext editor dedicated to the documentation of information systems specifications.

The actual developments of meta-CASE migth support a process management specification of the modeling, documentation and validation phases too. A CASE developped on the concepts presented here includes no modeling process description nor process management if those are not included whith special code daemons added to the four specifications parts. We have not treated the process modeling description, necessary to build a more complete modeling tool but we only concentrated in this research on the coupling of multi-languages and multi-view expressions of the information system.

At the beginning of our work, we were promised an internal access to the OMT tool already in development by the developpers of GraphTalk, so we intended to concentrate on the integration of the new functionalities in a real tool environment in order to better prove the feasability and usefulness of our propositions. Various industrial changes proved deceiving but the work was to far away to be modified. Nevertheless, the tool prouved to give a good environment for prototyping modeling tools. So we actually intend to test our proposal on the UML languages using the ROSE tool [30] and the sub-module SODA [31], importing thus whole parts of complete semi-formal models in an hypertext structure and complete specific informal and formal parts. We think that the structure of MODSI would help integrating a precise semantics on UML meta model as proposed by [10] as well as OCL sentences [21] defining more precisely pre and post conditions on operations as well as logical conditions on states and events.

The example we developed in the STORM project [15] allows us to consider the use of those concepts (meta-modeling, generation, etc.) for the development of a prototype running specifications of multimedia presentations. The actual features of the MODSI prototype are well defined for such purpose.

Finally, we would like to explore the MODSI prototype use in the inter-modeling migration (from structured modeling to object model for example). This concerns the difficult domain of models transformation [11, 22, 19], but the multi-modeling approach should help a process that uses heterogeneous approach in building safe "translator".

Further experiment and development has still to be done, a prototype is no tool.

References

[1] M. Adiba. Storm: Structural and Temporal Object-oRiented Multimedia database system. In *IEEE International Workshop on Multimedia DBMS*,

pages 10–15, Minnowbrook Conference Center - Blue Mountain Lake, NY, USA, august 1995.

[2] J. F. Allen. Maintaining knowledge about temporal intervals. *Communications of the ACM*, 26(11), november 1983.

[3] P. André. *Méthodes formelles et à objet pour le développement du logiciel: Études et propositions*. PhD thesis, Université de Rennes I, juillet 1995.

[4] R. Balzer, N. Goldman, and D. Wile. Informality in program specifications. *IEEE Transactions on Software Engineering*, SE-4(2), march 1978.

[5] G. Blain, N. Revault, H. Sahraoui, and J-F. Perrot. A meta-modelization technique. In *OOPSLA '94, Workshop on AI and Software Engineering*, 1994.

[6] J. P. Bowen and M. G. Hinchey. Seven more myths of formal methods. *IEEE Software*, pages 34–41, july 1995.

[7] S. Cook and J. Daniels. *Designing Object Systems - Object-Oriented Modelling with Syntropy*. Prentice-Hall, 1994.

[8] S. Cook and J. Daniels. Let's get formal. *Journal of Object Oriented Programming*, pages 22–24 and 64–66, july-august 1994.

[9] R. Duke, P. King, G. Rose, and G. Smith. The Object-Z specification language: Version 1. Technical Report 91-1, The University of Queensland, Department of Computer Science, 1991.

[10] A. Evans, R. France, K. Lano, and B. Rumpe. Developing the UML as a Formal Modelling Notation. In *UML '98 - Beyond the Notation*, Mulhouse, France, 1998.

[11] P. Facon and R. Laleau. Des spécification informelles aux spécifications formelles : compilation ou interprétation? In INFORSID, editor, *Actes du 13ème Congres INFORSID*, pages 47–62, Grenoble, juin 1995.

[12] P. Findeisen. The Metaview System. http://ewb.cs.ualberta.ca/~softeng/Metaview/doc/system.ps, 1994.

[13] M. D. Fraser, K. Kumar, and V. K. Vaishnavi. Informal and formal requirements specification laguages: Bridging the gap. *IEEE Transactions on Software Engineering*, 17(5):454–465, may 1991.

[14] M. D. Fraser, K. Kumar, and V. K. Vaishnavi. Strategies for incorporating formal specifications in software development. *Communications of the ACM*, 37(10):74–84, october 1994.

[15] J. C. Freire, R. Lozano, and F. Mocellin. Vers un atelier de structuration et construction de présentations multimédias. In INFORSID, editor, *Actes du 15ème Congres INFORSID*, Toulouse, juin 1997.

[16] H. Habrias. Les spécifications formelles pour les systèmes d'information, quoi?, pourquoi?, comment? In *XII INFORSID 17-20 mai 1994*, pages 1–31. INFORSID, may 1994.

[17] A. Hall. Seven myths of formal methods. *IEEE Software*, september 1990.

[18] A. Hall. Using Z as a specification calculus for object-oriented systems. In D. Bjorner, C.A.R Hoare, and H. Langmaack, editors, *VDM and Z - Formal Methods in Software Development*, pages 290–318. Springer-Verlag, april 1990.

[19] A. Hall. Specifying and interpreting class hierarchies in Z. In J.P. Bowen and J.A. Hall, editors, *Proceedings of the Eighth Z User Meeting, Cambridge 29-30 june/1994*, pages 120–138. Z User Group, Springer-Verlag, june 1994.

[20] D. Harel. Statecharts: A visual formalism for complex systems. *Science of Computer Programming*, 8(3):213–274, 1987.

[21] A. Kleppe, J. Warmer, and S. Cook. Informal formality ? the Object Constraint Language and its application in the UML metamodel. In *UML '98 - Beyond the Notation*, Mulhouse, France, 1998.

[22] Y. Ledru. Complementing semi-formal specifications with z. In *Knowledge-Based Software Engineering Conference [KBSE] - 1996*, 1996.

[23] M. L. Minsky. Matter, mind and models. In *Semantic Information Processing*. MIT Press, 1968.

[24] J. J Odell. Specifying structural constraints. *Journal of Object Oriented Programming*, pages 12–16, 1993.

[25] Projet Opéra. Thot - un éditeur de documents structurés. http://opera.inrialpes.fr/OPERA/Thot.fr.html, 1996.

[26] Software Technologies Parallax. Graphtalk 2.5 - méta-modélisation - manuel de référence, 1993.

[27] Software Technologies Parallax. Ledit - interface de programmation, 1994.

[28] PLATINUM Technology Inc. Paradigm plus - information. http://www.platinum.com/clearlake/paradigm30/paradigm30.html, 1996.

[29] R. S. Pressman. *Software Engineering - A Practitioner Approach*. McGraw-Hill Book Company Europe, third edition, 1994.

[30] Software Corporation Rational. Rational Rose 98. http://www.rational.com/products/rose/, 1998.

[31] Software Corporation Rational. What is SoDA. http://www.rational.com/demos/sodademo/soda.htm, 1998.

[32] J. Rumbaugh, M. Blaha, W. Premerlani, F. Eddy, and W. Lorensen. *Object Oriented Modeling and Design.* Prentice Hall, 1991.

[33] K. Smolander, K. Lyytinen, V.P. Tahvanainen, and P. Martin. MetaEdit : a flexible graphical environment for methodology modelling. *LNCS*, (498):168–193, 1991.

[34] J.M. Spivey. *The Z Notation: A reference Manual.* Prentice Hall, 1989.

A Semi-automatic Process of Identifying Overlaps and Inconsistencies between Requirements Specifications

George Spanoudakis
Department of Computer Science, City University
London, UK

Anthony Finkelstein
Department of Computer Science, University College London,
London UK

Abstract

Reconciliation is a method which supports the detection and verification of overlaps and the resolution of certain forms of inconsistencies between requirements specifications expressed in an object-oriented framework. The method identifies a set of candidate overlaps between two specifications by analysing their similarity. These overlaps are assessed by the authors of the specifications. If the authors disagree with the overlaps identified by analysis, the method guides them through an exploration activity aimed at (1) identifying inconsistencies in the modelling of the specifications with respect to the overlaps indicated by them, and (2) resolving these inconsistencies in a way which ensures that the results of further analysis will converge with overlaps indicated by the authors. This paper provides an overview of the method focusing on the process of identifying and resolving inconsistencies between specifications.

Keywords: inconsistency management, requirements engineering, object-oriented methods

1. Introduction

In software engineering settings where different stakeholders may have conflicting requirements for the system to be built, there is no point in worrying about the consistency of the resulting specifications unless you are pretty confident that they refer to the same things within a shared domain of discourse. In other words, unless there is an overlap between these specifications. This paper describes a method, called "reconciliation", which identifies overlaps and particular forms of inconsistencies between specifications expressed in an object-oriented framework, and guides the stakeholders (these may be the authors of the specifications or a third party) in taking steps towards the amelioration of these inconsistencies in a rationalised way. The paper builds upon previous work of the authors on the automated analysis of similarity between heterogeneous specifications [23]. An account of the method at an earlier stage in its development has also been presented in [25].

Overlap may be formally defined as a relation between the interpretations of the components of two specifications [26] and different types of overlap relations may be distinguished. In particular, a pair of specification components have a:

• *total overlap* if the sets of the objects they designate in some domain of discourse are the same (Spanoudakis et al [26] distinguish three types of overlap depending on the exact relation between the interpretations of the specifications)
• *null overlap* if the sets of the objects they designate have no elements in common.

Often, the presence of overlaps dictates the need to check whether specifications satisfy certain consistency rules. A consistency rule is a condition that the two specifications must jointly satisfy. A breach of such a rule manifests itself as a logical inconsistency. The consistency status of specifications needs to be checked and established with reference to specific sets of overlap relations and it might change given different such sets. Formally, two specifications S_i and S_j will be inconsistent with respect to a consistency rule CR when overlapping as indicated by a set of overlap relations O (S_i, S_j) if: $\{S_i ; S_j; O(S_i, S_j)\}$ *entails* ¬ CR. Overlap and inconsistency are two levels of specification interference the first of which is a precondition for the second.

Consider for instance two classes in two object-oriented specifications which have different superclasses and are identified as totally overlapping components. These classes would violate a consistency rule demanding that totally overlapping classes must have exactly the same superclasses. This rule would not be violated if the classes did not overlap. In this case it would not even make sense to check the rule.

Specification interference is not undesirable since it provides scope for innovative thinking, deferment of commitments in teamwork, exploration of alternatives, elicitation of information, and enables the focus of attention to aspects of systems that may deserve further analysis. However, it delivers on these promises only if it is appropriately "managed", that is overlaps and inconsistencies are identified, traced and steps are taken towards the amelioration of inconsistencies [8]. Also, it should be clearly appreciated that specifications might have been constructed independently, by stakeholders with varying concerns, backgrounds and knowledge and expressed in different languages. As a consequence they might be at different levels of abstraction, granularity and formality; and might deploy different terminologies. The complexities arising from these forms of heterogeneity – set alongside the normal software engineering problems of scale – make the identification of overlaps and inconsistencies a very complex activity.

Reconciliation supports this activity. The method identifies a set of candidate overlaps between specifications based on an analysis of their structural and semantic similarities. Then the stakeholders review these candidate overlaps and identify those which in their view are "true" overlaps and those which are "false" overlaps. Based on this assessment the method suggests revisions to the specifications which would ensure that the results of further analysis converge with the assessment of the stakeholders. After a number of overlap identification and specification revision cycles the method delivers a set of agreed correspondences between the specifications and the specifications are revised so as to be consistent with these correspondences. The method is applicable to object-oriented specifications.

The rest of the paper is structured as follows. Section 2 provides an overview of existing work on overlap identification. Section 3 describes the identification of overlaps and their assessment by the stakeholders in Reconciliation. Section 4 describes the process by which Reconciliation guides the stakeholders in elaborating and ameliorating inconsistencies and section 5 overviews the tool support currently available. Section 6 gives an example of ameliorating inconsistencies and section 7 summarises the method and outlines directions for future research. An appendix with a formal definition of the similarity analysis model used by the method is also given.

2.   Related Work

Overlaps between independently constructed specifications have been traditionally identified by:

- *representation conventions* – the simplest and most common representation convention is to assume total overlaps between specification components with identical names and null overlaps between any other pair of elements [5,7,6,9,28,18]
- *shared ontologies* – overlaps are assumed between specification components that have been "tagged" with the same item in a shared ontology used for assigning interpretations to these components [2,14,22]
- *direct human inspection* – the stakeholders explore the specifications and identify overlaps [4]

In essence, the approach, in both the case of representation conventions and shared ontologies, is to identify overlaps between components which satisfy specific consistency rules that should hold between overlapping components.

In the case of the "identical names" convention the rule is:
CR1: *If two components x and y overlap then x and y must have identical names*

In the case of the shared ontologies the rule is:

CR2: *If two components x and y overlap then x and y must be annotated with the same item in the ontology*

Note that the approach is *abductive*: the establishment of the consequent parts of the rules leads to the establishment of their antecedent parts. Clearly this way of identifying overlaps is weak since it assumes that overlapping components are always consistent! In reality – especially in the early stages of requirements acquisition and specification – this assumption turns out to be wrong: there may be components which satisfy the rule but are not overlapping (e.g. homonyms in the case of CR1) and components which overlap but are inconsistent with respect to the rule (e.g. overlapping components tagged with different items in a shared ontology by mistake).

Human inspection, on the other hand, might be safer especially if it is performed by the authors of the specifications. However, it is inefficient when it comes to specifications of substantial complexity. Hence a combination of the two approaches in which overlaps are assumed between components satisfying specific consistency rules but need to be confirmed by inspectors seems to be the right way to go. Human intervention gives confidence in overlap identification which may benefit from automated reasoning, tool and method support, particularly in settings characterized by problems of scale.

3. Reconciliation: identification and assessment of overlaps

The reconciliation method combines automated analysis with inspections by humans to detect and verify overlaps between specifications. The automated analysis available is based on a computational model which detects structural and semantic similarities between specifications classified and represented according to a particular meta-model. This meta-model expresses general, domain-independent, semantic modelling properties, and enables the representation of the specifications in a homogeneous way. Both the meta-model and the specifications are described in Telos, an object-oriented conceptual modelling language [17].

3.1 The Meta-model

The meta-model consists of a kernel and a set of extensions. The kernel includes classes which represent common, domain-independent, semantic modelling constructs [16,27] and the extensions include classes which represent established specification languages in the common representation framework.

The specification components are classified as instances of the kernel classes subject to the properties they possess (some classes of the kernel are shown as light grey boxes in Figure 1). At a high level of abstraction the components are distinguished into those representing entities and those representing relations. Entity representing components are further distinguished into natural, nominal, place, event, activity, state, agent and physical quantity components. Components representing relations are initially distinguished by their arity (e.g. binary or n-ary relations). Binary relations are further specialised according to: cardinality constraints (e.g. 1:1, N:M, total and onto relations); mathematical properties (e.g. symmetric, transitive and set-inclusion relations); existential dependencies between the items they relate; and other general semantic constraints, such as the temporal coexistence, physical separability or homogeneity of the substance of the items they relate [27].

The extensions to the kernel comprise classes which represent modelling constructs of established specification languages. One of the current extensions includes classes which represent the models of the Object-Oriented Software Engineering (OOSE) method [11].

Figure 1 shows a part of the extension which represents the "Problem Domain Object Model" (PDOM) of OOSE. The elements of PDOM have been introduced as subclasses of the classes in the kernel of the meta-model subject to their semantics. Consider for instance the "Inherits" relation in the PDOM. This relation is represented by the class *InheritsRelation* which associates "problem domain object types" and is introduced as a subclass of:

- *BinaryRelation* – Inherits is a binary relation between problem domain object types
- *ManyToManyRelation* – a problem domain object type may inherit from several problem domain object types and may be inherited by more than one problem domain object types
- *OptionalRelation* – there may be problem domain object types which do not inherit from any other problem domain object type
- *NotOntoRelation* – there may be problem domain object types which are not inherited by any other problem domain object type
- *ExistentialIndependencyRelation* – the existence of a problem domain object type does not depend on the existence any of the object types it inherits from

A detailed description of the kernel of the meta-model is given in [23]. The extensions of the meta-model for the various models of the OOSE method are described in [1].

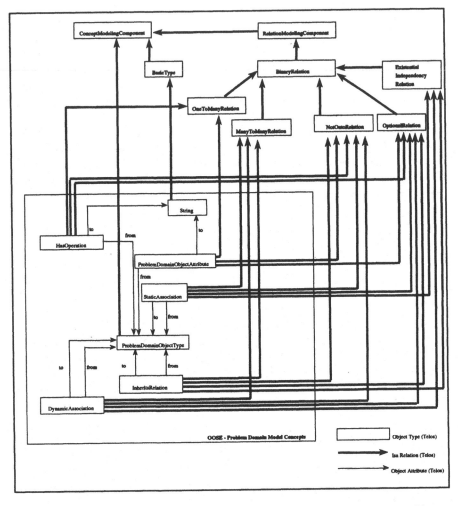

Figure 1: An extension of the kernel meta-model for the "Problem Domain Object Model" of OOSE

3.2 Computational Identification of Overlaps

Specifications are represented by objects which are created as instances of the classes of the meta-model. The attributes of these objects are used to aggregate the components of specifications. This representation makes possible the analysis of the similarity of the specifications according to a computational model which is described in [24]. Similarity analysis is based on three main metric functions. These functions measure the conceptual distances between the specification-objects with respect to the classification and generalisation relations as well as the attributes that constitute their descriptions.

The computation of the distance between two specification-objects with respect to their attributes (called *attribution distance*) determines a morphism I_a between their components, which indicates a set of candidate overlaps between them. By virtue of the definition of the function which computes this distance (see function d_a in the appendix) overlaps are assumed between the components of specifications which satisfy the consequent part of the following consistency rule:

CR3: *If the components x and y overlap then they must be classified as instances of the same kernel classes of the meta-model*

In cases where components which are classified within the same kernel classes of the meta-model can be mapped in many ways, the attribution distance selects a mapping between components violates the consequent part of the following consistency rule to the minimum possible extent:

CR4: *If the components x and y overlap then they must have identical classifications within the classes of the extensions of the meta-model, identical attributes, and identical superclasses.*

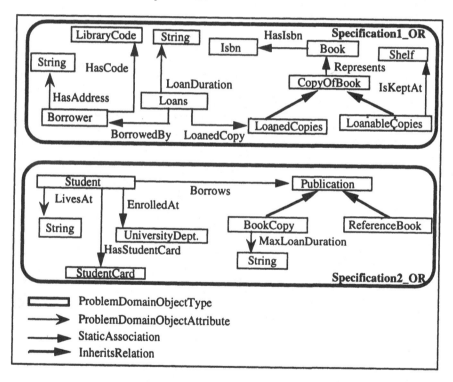

Figure 2: Partial library specifications

The extent to which each pair of components (x,y) in I_a violates the consequent part of CR4 is measured by the overall distance between x and y (see function d in the appendix). Spanoudakis and Constantopoulos [24] have shown that d(x,y)=0 if and only if x and y are identical and therefore satisfy the consequent part of CR4. For non-identical components the more the non-identical classes, attributes and superclasses of them the larger the overall distance between them and therefore the larger the extent to which they violate CR4.

The estimation of the pairwise distances $d(x,y)$ between specification components uses a recursive generation of morphisms between their own substructures and depends on the classification and generalisation distances between these components (see functions d_c and d_g in the appendix). These two distance metrics are computed by identifying the non-common classes and superclasses of the components involved, measuring the importance of these classes, and aggregating these importance measures into distance measures.

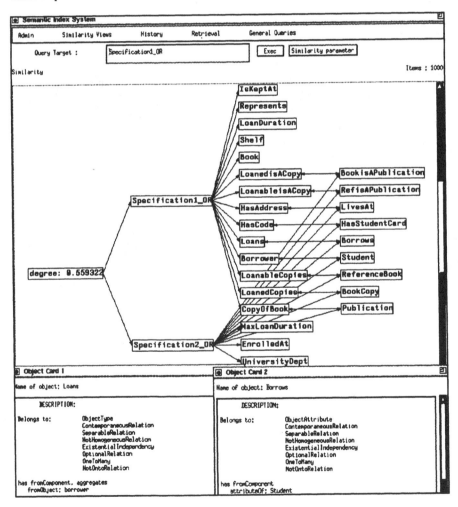

Figure 3: Similarity generated overlaps between two library specifications

Consider for example the two partial specifications of a university library system shown in Figure 2. The analysis of their similarity generates the morphism I_s shown in Figure 3. All the components mapped by this morphism satisfy the consequent part of the consistency rule CR3. For instance as shown in Figure 3, *Loans* and *Borrows* are identically classified as contemporaneous, separable, not homogeneous, optional, 1:M, and not onto binary relations. The fact that *Loans* is classified as a PDOM-ObjectType and *Borrows* as a PDOM-ObjectAttribute does not prevent their mapping because these two classes are not part of the kernel of the meta-model.

The morphism shown in Figure 3 was selected amongst other candidate morphisms. These morphisms mapped the components of Specification1_OR and Specification2_OR in ways which satisfy the consequent part of the rule CR3 but violated the rule CR4 to a larger extent. For instance, one of the other morphisms considered by similarity analysis was identical to I_s except that it mapped the PDOM object attribute *LivesAt* in Specification2_OR onto the attribute *LoanDuration* in Specification1_OR rather than the attribute *HasAddress*. The mapping of *LivesAt* onto *LoanDuration* does not violate the rule CR3 since these attributes are identically classified within the kernel classes of the meta-model. However, it violates the consequent part of the rule CR4 to a higher extent. This is because the object types of *LivesAt* and *LoanDuration* (*Student* and *Loans*) have more modelling discrepancies than the object types of *LivesAt* and *HasAddress* (*Student* and *Borrower*).

3.3 Assessment of Overlaps

Clearly flaws, incompleteness or inability to express the correct semantics in the modelling of specifications might force similarity analysis to generate morphisms indicating overlaps which are not correct. After all the approach of the automated analysis is abductive as discussed in section 3.2. Reconciliation copes with this problem by requiring the stakeholders to review the overlaps detected and identify those which in their view are "true" overlaps and those which are "false" overlaps. The stakeholders may propose a different morphism I_o between specification components which reflects overlaps based on their own interpretation of specifications.

Based on the morphisms I_s and I_o (both assumed to be directed from the specification Spec1 to the specification Spec2 in Figure 4) we distinguish among 7 different types of wrongly mapped components:

• **WU1-components:** WU1 components (wrong unique components of type 1) are components for which no overlap relation was found by similarity analysis. According to the stakeholders these components have overlapping counterparts which in fact are existing components of the specifications that similarity analysis did not map to any other component (Case 1 of Figure 4). Formally, a component x of a specification Spec1 and a component y of a specification Spec2 form a pair of WU1 components if: $I_s(x)=nil$ and $I_s^{-1}(y)=nil$ and $I_o(x)=y$ (*nil* indicates that a component has no counterpart in the morphism).

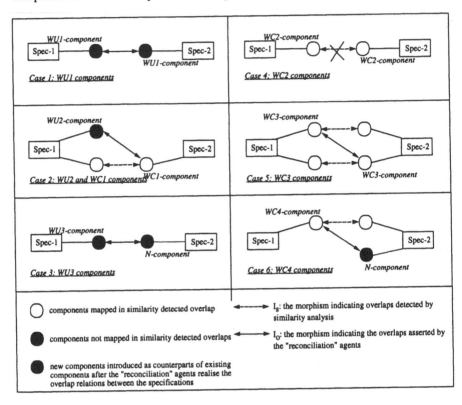

Figure 4: Types of components with "false" overlaps

- **WU2-components and WC1-components:** WU2 components (wrong unique components of type 2) are components for which no overlap relation was found by similarity analysis. According to the stakeholders WU2 components have overlapping counterparts. These counterparts have been mapped on to different components by similarity analysis which will be referred to as WC1 components (wrong corresponding components of type 1) (Case 2 of Figure 4). Formally, a component x of a specification Spec1 and a component y of a specification Spec2 form a pair of WU1 and WC1 components if:
$I_s(x)=nil$ and $I_s^{-1}(y)=z$ and $I_o^{-1}(y)=x$ and $x \bullet z$

- **WU3-components:** WU3 components (wrong unique components of type 3) are components for which no overlapping counterpart was found by similarity analysis. The stakeholders confirm this result but indicate that a new component (*N-component*) must be introduced in the specifications to serve as a counterpart of the WU3 component (Case 3 of Figure 4). Formally, a component $x(y)$ of a specification Spec1(Spec2) is a WU3 component if: $I_s(x)=nil$ and $I_o(x)=N$ ($I_s^{'}(y)=nil$ and $I_o^{'}(y)=N$) (N indicates a new component introduced in a specification as a counterpart of a component of the other specification).

- **WC2-components:** WC2 components (wrong corresponding components of type 2) are components which similarity analysis has mapped onto each other. According to the stakeholders these components do not overlap not only with each other but also with any other component of the specifications (Case 4 of Figure 4). Formally, a component x of a specification Spec1 and a component y of a specification Spec2 form a pair of WC2 components if: $I_s(x)=y$ and $I_o(x)=nil$ and $I_o^{'}(y)=nil$

- **WC3-components:** WC3 components (wrong corresponding components of type 3) are components for which the stakeholders identify overlapping counterparts which are different from those detected by similarity analysis. The counterparts that the stakeholders indicate have been mapped onto different components by similarity analysis (Case 5 of Figure 4). Formally, a component x of a specification Spec1 and a component y of a specification Spec2 form a pair of WU1 components if: $I_s(x)=u$ and $I_s^{'}(y)=w$ and $I_o(x)=y$ and $u{\bullet}y$ and $w{\bullet}x$

- **WC4-components:** A WC4 component (wrong corresponding component of type 4) is a component which the similarity analysis has mapped onto a counterpart but the stakeholders think that should correspond to a new component (N-component) that has to be introduced in the specifications (Case 6 of Figure 4). Formally, a component $x(y)$ of a specification Spec1(Spec2) is a WC4 component if: $I_s(x)=u$ and $I_o(x)=N$ ($I_s^{'}(y)=w$ and $I_o^{'}(y)=N$)

4. The Process of Overlap Elaboration and Inconsistency Amelioration

The components mapped by I_o but not I_s violate the consequent parts of at least one of the rules CR3 and CR4 since similarity analysis failed to map them. Reconciliation guides the stakeholders through an exploration activity aimed at (1) identifying the inconsistencies in the modelling of these components with respect to CR3 and CR4 given the overlaps indicated by I_o, and (2) suggesting resolutions of these inconsistencies.

This activity is described by a process model which articulates a way of identifying elements in the modelling of specification components that caused the inconsistencies and prevented similarity analysis from generating the "true" overlaps indicated by I_o. This process model has been specified as an instance of the NATURE process meta-model [20,21] and represented in Telos.

4.1 Specification of Process Models in NATURE

According to the process meta-model of NATURE a process is described as a graph of *contexts*. A context represents the decision to pursue a specific goal (*intention*) in a given *situation*. A situation is defined as a condition which regards the state of the product being manipulated by the process or has to be confirmed by the person who enacts the process model. Conditions may be atomic or composite (disjunctions or conjunctions of atomic conditions). Contexts are distinguished into:

• *executable contexts* – these are contexts which have intentions that can be directly satisfied by performing an *action* which changes the state of the product
• *plan contexts* – these are contexts which have intentions decomposed into a set of sub-goals and can be achieved only by satisfying these sub-goals in a specific order
• *choice contexts* – these are contexts which have intentions which are refined into one or more alternative goals and can therefore be satisfied by satisfying either of these goals

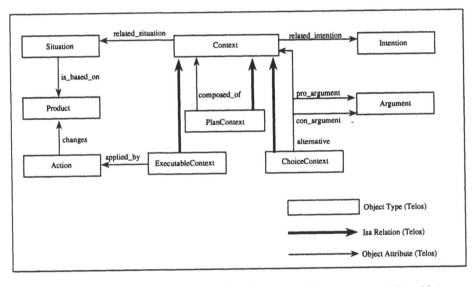

Figure 5: The process meta-model of NATURE (simplified version of Fig. 38 in [20])

Pohl [20] shows how the process meta-model of NATURE can be described in Telos and subsequently how process models can be described as instances of it in the same language. Figure 5 shows a graphical view of the description of the process meta-model in Telos.

4.2   The Process Model of "Reconciliation"

The process model of Reconciliation is shown in Figure 6. Note that the process meta-model of NATURE leaves open the specification of the conditions which define situations. In the case of the Reconciliation process model these conditions are specified as queries over the state of the product of the process and queries that are to be answered by the stakeholders (e.g. atomic conditions *correctIn(x,S)* and *incorrectIn(x,S)* in Figure 6; the stakeholder is assumed to give a "yes" answer if he/she activates the relevant context). The product of the process of Reconciliation comprises four objects that may be modified during it. These include the pair of the specifications involved (Spec1 and Spec2), an object representing the morphism I_s and an object representing the morphism I_o. I_s may change as similarity analysis may be re-performed after a certain number of specification revisions. I_o may also be expanded to reflect overlaps between components overlooked at an earlier stage in the process or modified if the stakeholders change their mind about the interpretations of the specifications and consequently about the overlaps between them. The main paths of the process of Reconciliation are described in the next section.

4.2.1   Starting reconciliation

Reconciliation starts when the stakeholders activate similarity analysis in order to generate the morphism I_s which indicates the candidate overlaps. This is possible by activating the executable context C2. Subsequently they may assess these overlaps by activating the executable context C3. This context invokes an interactive form which is used to define the correct morphism I_o. If I_s and I_o are not identical, the stakeholders may explore the modelling of the components involved in "false" overlaps. This requires the activation of the choice context C4. C4 gives them a number of options, each dedicated to exploring one of the types of the wrongly mapped components discussed in section 3.4.

4.2.2   Exploring inconsistencies between WU1 and WU3 components

The WU1 components are components which similarity analysis failed to map because they were not classified as instances of the same kernel classes of the meta-model and therefore they violate the rule CR3. If these components had been classified as instances of the same kernel classes of the meta-model, similarity analysis would have mapped them (rather than leaving them without counterparts) since this would minimise the overall distance between the specifications (or equivalently it would reduce the extent to which the rule CR4 is violated). Similar classification discrepancies might prevent the mapping of WU3 components onto their newly introduced counterparts (N-components). Thus, the investigation of possible inconsistencies between WU1 or WU3 and N components should focus on their non-common kernel classes of the meta-model (context C9). The activation of C9 leads to the identification of the kernel classes of the meta-model which are classes of only one of the components involved (this is the result of the process enactment mechanism checking the conditions *memberOf(c, x.Km − y.Km)* and *memberOf(c, y.Km − x.Km)* in order to identify which of the options of C9 become available. The classification of one of the components involved as an instance of a kernel class which is not a class of the other might be deemed to be incorrect and consequently removed (executable contexts C19 and C20). Alternatively, if a non common kernel class is confirmed to be correct then the only way to resolve the inconsistency is to add it to the list of the classes of the other component (executable contexts C21 and C22).

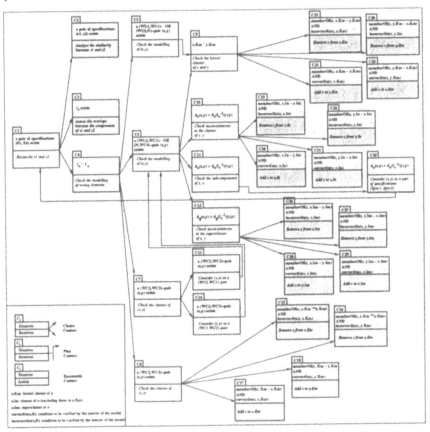

Figure 6: The process model of Reconciliation (details not easily readable, presented for illustrative purposes only)

4.2.3   Exploring inconsistencies between WU2 and WC1 or WC4 components

A pair of a WU2 and a WC1 component or a pair of WC4 components might also have not been mapped on to each other by similarity analysis because of classification inconsistencies with respect to the kernel classes of the meta-model which violate the rule CR3. These inconsistencies can be explored by activating the context C9.

Another reason that may lead to a pair of a WU2 and a WC1 component or a pair of WC4 components is that their mapping in I_o would result in a relatively extended violation of the rule CR4 than their mapping in I_s. In other words the mapping of these components suggested by the stakeholders would result in a relatively higher distance than the mapping suggested by similarity analysis: $d(I_s^{-1}(y),y) < d(x,y)$, $x=I_o^{-1}(y)$. The overall distance between a component y and its counterpart in I_s, $I_s^{-1}(y)$, might be lower than the overall distance between y and its counterpart in I_o, $I_o^{-1}(y)$ if one or more of the following inequalities regarding the classification, generalisation or attribution distances between these pairs of components holds: $d_c(I_s^{-1}(y),y) < d_c(x,y)$, $d_g(I_s^{-1}(y),y) < d_g(x,y)$ or $d_a(I_s^{-1}(y),y) < d_a(x,y)$. Depending on which of these inequalities holds the stakeholders may check for inconsistencies in the classes, superclasses or the subcomponents of the components involved.

If $d_c(I_s^{-1}(y),y) < d_c(x,y)$ is true the stakeholders have the option of activating the context C10 to explore and resolve inconsistencies regarding the classifications of x and y. The process is similar to the process of exploring classification inconsistencies in the case of WU1 and WU3 components, except that the non kernel classes of the components involved are taken into account. This part of the process is described by the contexts C29, C30, C24, and C3.

If $d_g(I_s^{-1}(y),y) < d_g(x,y)$ is true the stakeholders have the option of activating the context C12 to explore and resolve inconsistencies regarding the superclasses of x and y. The classes which are not superclasses of both the components involved are identified (this is the result of checking the conditions memberOf(c, x.Isa − y.Isa) and memberOf(c, y.Isa − x.Isa)) and the stakeholders have the option of declaring them as superclasses of both the components (contexts C28 and C29) or remove the relevant generalisation relationships (contexts C26 and C27).

If $d_a(I_s^{-1}(y),y) < d_a(x,y)$ is true the stakeholders have the option of exploring the discrepancies between the subcomponents of x and y (context C11 and C25). This exploration is similar to the exploration of the modelling of S1 and S2 and therefore may be carried out by considering the components x and y as top level specifications and activating the context C1.

4.2.4 Exploring inconsistencies between WC3 components

A pair of WC3 components might not have been mapped onto each other for the same reasons that do not allow a pair of a WC1 and a WU2 component to map onto each other. Thus WC3 components may be explored by activating the contexts of the process model available for WC1 and WU2 components (contexts C7, C13, and C14).

4.2.5   Exploring inconsistencies between WC2 components

WC2 components may occur due to the assumption made by similarity analysis that overlaps exist between components which satisfy the rule CR4 to a maximum possible extent. Note that due to this assumption even dissimilar components may be mapped onto each other provided that they are classified within the same kernel classes of the meta-model (i.e. they satisfy the rule CR3). This because if these components had been left without counterparts the overall distance between the specifications would be larger. If the stakeholders insist that such components should not overlap, it is worth investigating if their classifications within the kernel classes of the meta-model are identical by incident. If they are the stakeholders have the option to modify them in order to prevent similarity analysis from generating the wrong mappings (executable contexts C15 and C16). Alternatively, they may identify kernel classes of the meta-model which should have been declared as classes of only one of the components involved and add the relevant classification links (executable contexts C17 and C18). This would make the classification of the components involved non identical and therefore it would prevent analysis from generating the wrong mappings.

5.   Tool Support

Currently Reconciliation is supported by a prototype built as a customisation of the Semantic Index System(SIS [3]). SIS is a tool for developing, browsing and querying Telos object bases. The customised SIS tool has been integrated with a module which performs the similarity analysis. The meta-model for specification analysis has been implemented as a kernel SIS object base, which is used as a schema for describing specifications. Specifications are described as SIS objects classified using this schema and are therefore amenable to similarity analysis. This description is supported by a tool of interactive data entry forms used to develop SIS object bases. This tool has been customised to support the task of classifying specification components. Similarly the Reconciliation process model has been implemented as a set of SIS objects classified using a schema which defines the process meta-model. The system enables the browsing of the contexts which are found to be applicable in a current situation as determined by SIS queries which express the conditions of the process model.

6.   Amelioration of inconsistencies

The process outlined in section 4.2 ideally leads to a point where similarity analysis generates a morphism reflecting overlaps which are verified by the stakeholders unless they decide to abandon it before reaching this point. Along the way the specifications are modified in a way that makes them more consistent with the rules CR3 and CR4 given the overlaps indicated by the stakeholders. Note that they may never become entirely consistent with these rules but as we discussed in section 1 targeting full consistency at early stages of requirements specification is not always desirable. Regardless of whether or not full consistency is achieved one of the novel features of Reconciliation is that it provides a way of ameliorating specific forms of inconsistencies and measuring the progress made in this respect.

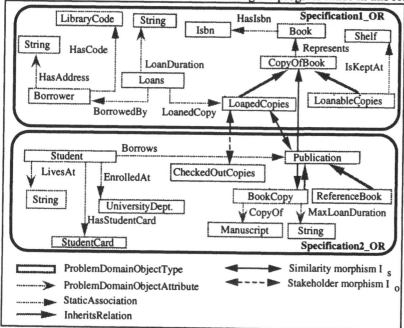

Figure 7 : "False" overlaps

Consider as an example the enactment of the reconciliation process model assuming the specifications and the morphisms I_s and I_o between them shown in Figure 7. *LoanedCopies* and *CheckedOutCopies* constitute a pair of a WC1 and a WU2 component. Thus, the context C6 may be activated to explore the inconsistencies between them. In this particular example, *LoanedCopies* and *CheckedOutCopies* were not mapped onto each other by similarity analysis because as a pair they violate the rule CR4 more than the pair *LoanedCopies* and *Publication*. This is because *LoanedCopies* has three subcomponents (the inherits relation to *CopyOfBook*, the static association *Represents* which is inherited from *CopyOfBook*, and the problem domain object type *Loans*) which have no counterparts in *CheckedOutCopies*. This reflects on the attribution distance between these two components which is d_a(LoanedCopies,CheckedOutCopies)=1. On the other hand, *LoanedCopies* has only two components without counterparts in *Publication* (the inherits relation to *CopyOfBook* and the static association *Represents*) and a subcomponent (*Loans*) with a counterpart in it (the static association *Borrows*). Note also, that although *Loans* and *Borrows* are not identical they are similar (e.g. they both express binary relations of the same cardinalities). The attribution distance between these components is d_a(LoanedCopies,Publication)=0.502. Thus if *LoanedCopies* and *Publication* are taken as overlapping components (as indicated by I_v) they violate the rule CR4 less than *LoanedCopies* and *CheckedOutCopies*.

Since d_a(LoanedCopies,Publication) < d_a(LoanedCopies,CheckedOutCopies) the context C11 becomes applicable and may be activated by the stakeholders to explore the inconsistencies between the subcomponents of *LoanedCopies* and *CheckedOutCopies*. A possible way of exploring and resolving these inconsistencies is to enact the following sequences of contexts of the process model:

- C11, C25, C1,C3: an inherits relation directed to *BookCopy* (N-component) is introduced to *CheckedOutCopies* as the counterpart of the inherits relation of *LoanedCopies* (the N-component is introduced while the stakeholders assess the morphism between the subcomponents of *CheckedOutCopies* and *LoanedCopies*)
- C2, C4, C5, C9, C21: the N-component in *CheckedOutCopies* is classified within the kernel classes of the inherits relation in *LoanedCopies*

After these modifications since *CheckedOutCopies* has only one subcomponent with no counterparts in *LoanedCopies* (the logical attribute *MaxLoanDuration* inherited from *BookCopy*), the extent to which – together with *LoanedCopies* – it violates CR4 is reduced. The formerly unique subcomponents of *LoanedCopies* (i.e. the inherits relation to *CopyOfBook*, the problem domain object type *Loans* and the static association *Represents*) now have got counterparts in *CheckedOutCopies*. These are the inherits relation to *BookCopy*, the static association *Borrows* (inherited from *Publication*) and the static association *CopyOf* (inherited from *BookCopy*). These modifications reduce the attribution distance between *LoanedCopies* and *CheckedOutCopies* and ameliorate their inconsistency with respect to the rule CR4. A quantitative indication of this amelioration is given by the new attribution distance between these components: d_a(LoanedCopies,CheckedOutCopies)=0.34. Note also that as a result of these modifications similarity analysis maps *LoanedCopies* onto *CheckedOutCopies*, too.

7.   Conclusions & Future Work

Reconciliation, the method discussed in this paper supports the management of overlaps and inconsistencies between specifications. It detects overlaps by analysing similarities between specifications and guides stakeholders through a process of assessing and verifying these overlaps and ameliorating the inconsistencies that may arise as their consequence. We believe that the method has promise though there is clearly considerable scope for further work.

Our immediate plan is to apply the method in a large industrial case study involving the integration of independently developed enterprise models of a large British organisation. This case study requires the extension of the meta-model of the method so as to become applicable to specifications expressed in the Unified Modelling Language (UML) [12]. This extension has already started. Two further important issues we hope to investigate thoroughly in this case study regard the effectiveness of the method in reconciling behavioural specifications (for instance sequence and statechart diagrams in UML) and the use of domain specific ontologies to improve the accuracy of the identification of overlaps during the analysis stage of the method. We are also looking at extending the tool support beyond the functionality which is available from the current prototype. One of the extensions that we seek to introduce to the tool is to give the stakeholders the option to reconcile only subparts of the specifications. Our plan is to develop a tool that would support the method in a way providing value-adding services to existing commercial CASE tools supporting the UML.

References

[1]   Apostolopoulos G., (1996), "The Object-Oriented Software Engineering Method in the Viewpoints Framework", MSc Thesis, Department of Business Computing, City University, London, UK

[2]   Boehm B., In H., (1996), "Identifying Quality Requirements Conflicts", IEEE Software, March 1996, pp. 25-35.

[3]   Constantopoulos, P. and M. Doerr (1993), "The Semantic Index System: A Brief Presentation", Institute of Computer Science, Foundation for Research and Technology-Hellas, Heraklion, Crete, Greece. (available by ftp from: http://www.ics.forth.gr/proj/isst/Systems/SIS/index.html).

[4]   Easterbrook, S. (1991), "Handling Conflict between Domain Descriptions with Computer-Supported Negotiation", Knowledge Acquisition 3, pp. 255-289.

[5]   Easterbrook, S., A., Finkelstein, J. Kramer, and B. Nuseibeh (1994), "Co-Ordinating Distributed ViewPoints: The Anatomy of a Consistency Check", International Journal on Concurrent Engineering: Research and Applications 2, 3, CERA Institute, pp. 209-222.

[6]   Easterbrook, S. and B. Nuseibeh (1995), "Managing Inconsistencies in an Evolving Specification", In Proceedings of the IEEE International Conference on Requirements Engineering, York, England, pp. 48-55.

[7]   Finkelstein, A., Gabbay, D., Hunter, A., Kramer, J., and Nuseibeh, B., (1994). "Inconsistency Handling In Multi-Perspective Specifications", IEEE Transactions on Software Engineering, 20, 8, pp. 569-578.

[8]   Finkelstein A., Spanoudakis G., Till D.(1996), "Managing Interference", Joint Proceedings of the Viewpoints 96: An International Workshop on Multiple Perspectives in Software Development, San Francisco, USA, pp.172-174.

[9]   Heitmeyer, C., B. Law, and D. Kiskis (1995), "Consistency Checking of SCR-Style Requirements Specifications", In Proceedings of the IEEE International Conference on Requirements Engineering, York, England, pp. 56-63.

[10]   Hunter, A. and B. Nuseibeh (1995), "Managing Inconsistent Specifications: Reasoning, Analysis and Action", Technical Report TR-95/15, Department of Computing, Imperial College, London, UK.

[11]   Jacobson, I. (1995), "Object Oriented Software Engineering: A Use Case Driven Approach", Addison-Wesley, NY.

[12]   UML, (1997), "Unified Modelling Language", Version 1.0, Rational Software Corporation, CA, USA *(available by ftp from http://www.rational.com)*

[13]   Kotonya, G. and I. Sommerville (1992), "Viewpoints for Requirements Definition", Software Engineering Journal 7, 6, pp. 375-387.

[14]   Leite, J. and P. Freeman (1991), "Requirements Validation Through Viewpoint Resolution", IEEE Transactions on Software Engineering 17, 12, pp. 1253-1269.

[15]   Meyers, S. and S. Reiss (1991), "A System for Multiparadigm Development of Software Systems", In Proceedings of the 6th International Workshop on Software Specification and Design (IWSSD-6), Como, Italy, pp. 202-209.

[16]   Motschnig-Pitrik, P. (1993), "The Semantics of Parts vs. Aggregates in Data Knowledge Modeling", In Proceedings of CAiSE '93, LNCS 685, Paris, France, Springer-Verlang, Berlin, pp. 352-373.

[17]   Mylopoulos, J., A. Borgida, M. Jarke, and M. Koubarakis (1990), "Telos: Representing Knowledge About Information Systems", ACM Transactions on Information Systems 8, 4, pp. 325-362.

[18]   Nissen H., Jeusfeld M., Jarke M., Zemanek G., Huber H., (1996), "Managing Multiple Requirements Perspectives with Metamodels", IEEE Software, pp. 37-47.

[19]   Nuseibeh, B. et al. (1994), "A Framework for Expressing the Relationship between Multiple Views in Requirements Specification", IEEE Transactions on Software Engineering 20, 10, pp. 760-773.

[20]   Pohl K. (1996). Process-Centered Requirements Engineering, Advanced Software Development Series, J. Kramer (ed), Research Studies Press Ltd., ISBN 0-86380-193-5, London

[21]   Rolland C., Souveyet C., Moreno M. (1995). An Approach for Defining Ways-Of-Working, Information Systems, 20, 4, 337-359

[22]   Robinson, W. and S. Fickas (1994), "Supporting Multi-Perspective Requirements Engineering", In Proceedings of the IEEE Conference on Requirements Engineering, IEEE Computer Society Press, Los Alamitos, CA, pp. 206-215.

[23]   Spanoudakis, G. and P. Constantopoulos (1995), "Integrating Specifications: A Similarity Reasoning Approach", Automated Software Engineering Journal 2, 4, pp. 311-342.

[24]   Spanoudakis G., Constantopoulos P. (1996). "Elaborating Analogies from Conceptual Models", International Journal of Intelligent Systems, Vol. 11, No 11, pp. 917-974.

[25]   Spanoudakis G., Finkelstein A. (1997) "Reconciling requirements: a method for managing interference,inconsistency and conflict", Annals of Software Engineering, Special Issue on Software Requirements Engineering, 3, pp. 459-475.

[26]   Spanoudakis G., A. Finkelstein, D. Till. (1997). "Interference in Requirements Engineering: The Level of Ontological Overlap", Technical Report Series, TR-1997/01, ISSN 1364-4009, Department of Computer Science, City University, 1997

[27]   Storey, V. (1993), "Understanding Semantic Relations", Journal of Very Large Data Bases 3, pp. 455-488.

[28]   van Lamsweerde A. (1996), "Divergent Views in Goal-Driven Requirements Engineering", Joint Proceedings of the Sigsoft '96 Workshops – Viewpoints '96, ACM Press, pp. 252-256.

Appendix:

The space restrictions on this paper do not allow us to provide the appendix detailing the similarity model. For those interested in the full details it can be obtained from http://www.cs.ucl.ac.uk/staff/A.Finkelstein.

DESIGN ISSUES 2

Consistency Analysis on
Lifecycle Model and Interaction Model

K.S. Cheung, K.O. Chow & T.Y. Cheung
Department of Computer Science, City University of Hong Kong
Tat Chee Avenue, Kowloon, Hong Kong

Abstract

Two separate models, lifecycle model and interaction model, are generally adopted for specifying object behaviour in object-oriented system development. In this paper, we propose a Petri net-based formal method for analysing consistency between the two models at the logical level. This contributes to improving the consistency in the specification of object behaviour.

1 Introduction

Under the object-oriented (OO) approach for system development, a system is considered as a collection of objects exhibiting features in two essential aspects, namely, object structure and object behaviour [1, 2, 3, 4, 5]. Object structure, involving classes of objects and their structural relationships, is generally specified by a structural model, such as the class diagram (object model) in OMT [6], the class diagram in Booch's method [7] and the static structure diagram in UML [8, 9]. Object behaviour, involving object lifecycle and interaction [10], is generally specified by a lifecycle model and an interaction model, such as the state diagram and event-trace diagram (dynamic model) in OMT [6], the state transition diagram and interaction diagram in Booch's method [7], and the state diagram, activity diagram, collaboration diagram and sequence diagram in UML [8, 9].

In OO system development, lifecycle model and interaction model are separately constructed for specifying object behaviour. The consistency between these models is essentially required in order to deliver an accurate interpretation of the intended behaviour of a system [11]. This is even more vital for large-scale systems which involve hundreds or thousands of objects exhibiting highly complicated and intermingled behaviour. Although many OO methods offer meta-models for ensuring consistency at the syntactic or notation level, the consistency at the logical level that concerns logical implication of models is downplayed. The same issue applies to OO CASE tools where only consistency at the syntactic or notation level is considered. There is an emerging need of ensuring the consistency between lifecycle model and interaction model at both syntactic level and logical level, especially as the multi-modelling trend continues to prevail.

The purpose of this paper is to investigate the consistency between lifecycle model and interaction model at the logical level. A formal analysis on this consistency using Petri Net (PN) [12, 13] is proposed. The analysis starts by constructing a PN with some newly imposed definitions and rules of execution. The PN is then executed and the results would conclude whether the lifecycle model and interaction model are consistent with each other. Similar analysis is rarely reported in the literature where the consistency between lifecycle model and interaction model in particular is not significantly mentioned. Hayes & Coleman addressed the consistency on models and proposed some precise semantics for ensuring consistency [14]. Kirani & Tsai proposed the verification of consistency using method sequence specification with an emphasis on the casual relationship that exists between operations of a class [15]. Harel & Gery proposed an executable specification language using statecharts where object behaviour in the lifecycle aspect is rigorously analysed [16].

The rest of this paper is structured as follows. Section 2 discusses the specification of object behaviour through the lifecycle model and interaction model. Section 3 addresses the consistency between these two models, and elaborates the proposed analysis on consistency and its application in OO system development. A case example is illustrated.

2 Object Behaviour

In this section, the lifecycle aspect and interaction aspect of object behaviour are identified. The specification of them through the lifecycle model and interaction model is discussed.

2.1 Lifecycle and Interaction

Lifecycle and interaction are two aspects of object behaviour [10]. Under the OO approach, a system is considered as a collection of objects. Each object has its lifecycle in which there are changes in behaviour such as the transition of states and execution of operations. This aspect of object behaviour, pertaining to the lifecycle of an object, is referred to the lifecycle aspect of object behaviour. On the other side, objects are interacting with others via messages that exhibit different interaction scenarios. This aspect of object behaviour, pertaining to the interaction between objects, is referred as the interaction aspect of object behaviour. The lifecycle aspect concerns behaviour of single objects while the interaction aspect concerns behaviour of multiple objects. In the existing OO methods, they are generally specified by a lifecycle model and an interaction model.

Table 1 lists the lifecycle models and interaction models of six prevailing OO methods.

OO methods	Lifecycle models	Interaction models
Booch's method [7]	state transition diagram (dynamic view)	interaction diagram (dynamic view)
Coad-Yourdon's OOA [17]	object state diagram (service layer)	message connection (service layer)
Embley's method [18]	state net (object behaviour model)	interaction diagram (object interaction model)
OMT [6]	state transition diagram (dynamic model)	scenario diagram (dynamic model)
OPEN [19]	state transition diagram	collaboration diagram sequence diagram
UML [8, 9]	state diagram activity diagram	collaboration diagram sequence diagram

Table 1. Lifecycle models and interaction models of six OO methods.

2.2 Specification through Lifecycle Model

A lifecycle model specifies object behaviour pertaining to the lifecycle of single objects. Typically, it is composed of nodes and arcs. A state is denoted by a node, with a label showing the event and the operation triggered to execute by the event if any. A transition of states is denoted by an arc connecting the concerned states with a label showing the triggering event, and the operation triggered to execute on the transition if any. Figure 1 shows a lifecycle model consisting four states, s_1, s_2, s_3 and s_4. The transition from state s_1 to state s_2 is triggered by event e_1. The transition from state s_1 to state s_3 is triggered by event e_2. Operation o_1 is triggered to execute on this transition. The transition from state s_2 to state s_4 is trigger by event e_4. In state s_2, event e_3 occurs and operation o_2 is triggered to execute.

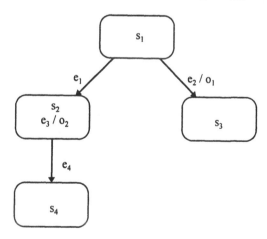

Figure 1. A simple lifecycle model.

A lifecycle model can be formally denoted as a 5-tuple $< S, E, O, T, X >$ where S is a set of states, E is a set of events, O is a set of operations, T is a set of transitions of states and X is a set of executions of operations. A transition from state s_1 to state s_2 is denoted by a 3-tuple $< e, s_1, s_2 >$ where e is the triggering event. The execution of an operation o is denoted by a 2-tuple $< e, o >$ where e is the triggering event. State s_i is considered as the initial state provided that $\forall s \in S \bullet \neg \exists t \in T, e \in E \bullet t = < e, s, s_i >$. State s_f is considered as the final state provided that $\forall s \in S \bullet \neg \exists t \in T, e \in E \bullet t = < e, s_f, s >$. The lifecycle model in Figure 1 can be formally denoted by the 5-tuple $< S, E, O, T, X >$ where $S = \{ s_1, s_2, s_3, s_4 \}$, $E = \{ e_1, e_2, e_3, e_4 \}$, $O = \{ o_1, o_2 \}$, $T = \{ < e_1, s_1, s_2 >, < e_2, s_1, s_3 >, < e_4, s_2, s_4 > \}$ and $X = \{ < e_2, o_1 >, < e_3, o_2 > \}$.

2.3 Specification through Interaction Model

An interaction model specifies object behaviour pertaining to the interaction between multiple objects. In an interaction scenario, the occurrence of an event represents an external stimulus to an object, usually on receipt of a message from another object, that triggers changes in behaviour of the object such as the transition of states and execution of operations. Typically, an interaction model is composed of vertical bars and directed lines. Each interacting object is represented by a vertical bar. Each event, corresponding to the receipt of a message, is represented by a directed line showing the flow of the message. The directed line is labelled with the event, and sometimes the operation triggered to execute by the event. Figure 2 shows an interaction model between two objects x and y involving a sequence of events, e_1, e_2, e_3 and e_4. The occurrence of event e_1 denotes the receipt of a message from object x to object y where operation o_{y1} of object y is triggered to execute. The occurrence of event e_2 applies to object x where operation o_{x2} of object x is triggered to execute. The occurrence of event e_3 denotes the receipt of a message from object y to object x where operation o_{x1} of object x is triggered to execute. The occurrence of event e_4 denotes the receipt of a message from object x to object y where no operation is triggered to execute.

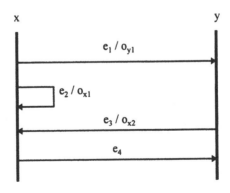

Figure 2. A simple interaction model.

An interaction model can be formally denoted by a 4-tuple $< A, M, EQ, XQ >$ where A is a set of interacting objects, M is a set of flows of messages, EQ is an occurrence sequence of events and XQ is an execution sequence of operations. A flow of message is denoted by a 4-tuple $< e, s, r >$ where e is the event corresponding to the receipt of the message, s is the sending object and r is the receiving object. An execution is represented by a 2-tuple $< r, o_r >$ where r is the receiving object and o_r is the operation of object r that is triggered to execute. The interaction model in Figure 2 can be formally denoted by the 4-tuple $< A, M, EQ, XQ >$ where $A = \{ x, y \}$, $M = \{ < e_1, x, y >, < e_3, y, x >, < e_4, x, y > \}$, $EQ = [e_1, e_2, e_3, e_4]$ and $XQ = [< y, o_{y1} >, < x, o_{x1} >, < x, o_{x2} >]$.

3   Consistency Analysis

In this section, the consistency between lifecycle model and interaction model is addressed. A formal analysis on this consistency using Petri Net (PN) is proposed. Newly imposed definitions and rules of execution of the PN are described. The proposed analysis is elaborated with an illustration of a case example. Its application in OO system development is highlighted.

3.1 Consistency between Lifecycle Model and Interaction Model

In OO system development, lifecycle model and interaction model are separately constructed for specifying object behaviour. Consistency between these models is essentially required in order to deliver an accurate interpretation of intended behaviour of a system [11]. There are two levels of consistency, namely, syntactic level and logical level, which are also regarded by Coleman et al [20] as simple consistency and semantic consistency respectively. Consistency at the syntactic or notation level emphasises the consistency with respect to the notation or syntax of the models. For example, the execution of operations involved in an object lifecycle specified in the lifecycle model should be corresponding to the respective operations defined in a class specified in the structural model. Consistency at the logical level emphasises the consistency with respect to the logic implication of models. For example, the execution sequence of operations involved in an interaction between two objects specified in the interaction model should not contradict the respective transition sequence of states and execution sequence of operations of the object lifecycles specified in the lifecycle model. The focus of this paper is placed on the consistency at the logical level.

The consistency between lifecycle model and interaction model at the logical level can be illustrated using a case example as follows. Figures 3 and 4 respectively show the lifecycle models of two interacting objects x and y. The lifecycle model of object x is formally denoted by the 5-tuple $< S, E, O, T, X >$ where $S = \{ s_{x1}, s_{x2}, s_{x3}, s_{x4} \}$, $E = \{ e_1, e_2, e_3, e_4, e_5, e_6 \}$, $O = \{ o_{x1}, o_{x2} \}$, $T = \{ < e_2, s_{x1}, s_{x2} >, < e_4,$

$s_{x2}, s_{x3} >, < e_5, s_{x2}, s_{x4} >, < e_6, s_{x3}, s_{x4} > \}$ and $X = \{ < e_1, o_{x1} >, < e_3, o_{x2} > \}$. The occurrence of event e_1 refers to the receipt of a message from object y (at state s_{y1}). The occurrence of event e_3 refers to the receipt of a message from object y (at state s_{y2}). The lifecycle model of object y is formally denoted by the 5-tuple $< S, E, O, T, X >$ where $S = \{ s_{y1}, s_{y2}, s_{y3}, s_{y4} \}$, $E = \{ e_7, e_8, e_9, e_{10}, e_{11}, e_{12} \}$, $O = \{ o_{y1}, o_{y2}, o_{y3} \}$, $T = \{ < e_7, s_{y1}, s_{y2} >, < e_9, s_{y2}, s_{y3} >, < e_{10}, s_{y2}, s_{y4} > \}$ and $X = \{ < e_8, o_{y1} >, < e_{11}, o_{y2} >, < e_{12}, o_{y3} > \}$. The occurrence of event e_7 refers to the receipt of a message from object x (at state s_{x2}). The occurrence of event e_9 refers to the receipt of a message from object x (at state s_{x4}). The occurrence of event e_{10} refers to the receipt of a message from object x (at state s_{x4}).

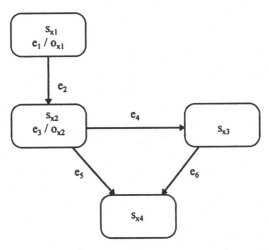

Figure 3. Lifecycle model of object x (case example).

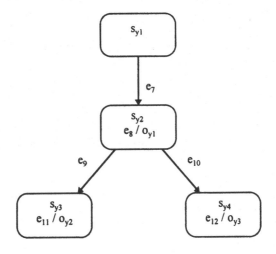

Figure 4. Lifecycle model of object y (case example).

Figures 5 and 6 respectively show the interaction models for two interaction scenarios A and B between objects x and y. The interaction model for scenario A is formally denoted by the 4-tuple $< A, M, EQ, XQ >$ where $A = \{ x, y \}$, $M = \{ < e_1, y, x >, < e_7, x, y >, < e_3, y, x >, < e_9, x, y > \}$, $EQ = [e_1, e_2, e_7, e_8, e_3, e_5, e_9, e_{11}]$ and $XQ = [< x, o_{x1} >, < y, o_{y1} >, < x, o_{x2} >, < y, o_{y2} >]$. The interaction model for scenario B is formally denoted by the 4-tuple $< A, M, EQ, XQ >$ where $A = \{ x, y \}$, $M = [< e_1, y, x >, < e_7, x, y >, < e_3, y, x >, < e_{10}, x, y >]$, $EQ = [e_1, e_2, e_7, e_8, e_3, e_4, e_{10}, e_{12}]$ and $XQ = [< x, o_{x1} >, < y, o_{y1} >, < x, o_{x2} >, < y, o_{y3} >]$.

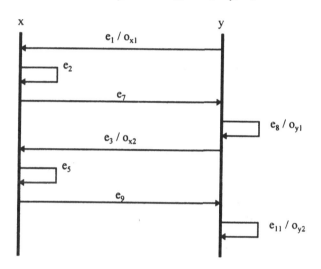

Figure 5. Interaction model of scenario A (case example).

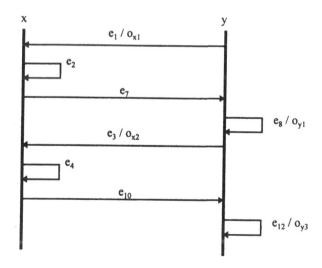

Figure 6. Interaction model of scenario B (case example).

The lifecycle models shown in Figure 3 and 4 are consistent with the interaction model shown in Figure 5 but not consistent with the interaction model shown in Figure 6. More specifically, the execution sequence of operations in the interaction scenario and the transition sequence of states and execution sequence of operations in the object lifecycles are congruent in scenario A but contradictory in scenario B. In scenario B, there is a transition from state s_{x2} to s_{x3} in the lifecycle of object x upon the occurrence of event e_4. The subsequent event e_{10} would never occur as this event refer to the receipt of a message from object x which is at state s_{x4} and not state s_{x3}. Also, the next subsequent event e_{12} would never occur so operation o_{y3} of object y would never be triggered to execute. Object x would be remained at state s_{x3} and object y would remained at state s_{y2}. These states are not final states of the respective objects, implying that the objects do not go through their lifecycle in the interaction scenario.

3.2 Formal Analysis on Consistency using Petri Net

We propose a formal analysis on the consistency between lifecycle model and interaction model using Petri Net (PN) [12, 13]. A PN is an analytical model consisting places and transitions, and can be formally denoted by a 4-tuple < P, T, I, O > where P is a set of places, T is a set of transitions, I and O are input and output functions mapping transitions to places. In the proposed analysis, some new definitions are imposed on a PN as follows.

Definition of a PN place. Each state of an object in its lifecycle is represented by a PN place. The PN place is denoted by a 2-tuple $< x, s_x >$ where x is the object and s_x is the state. Figure 7 shows the PN place $< x, s_{x1} >$ for object x at state s_{x1}.

Figure 7. Representation of a state of an object.

Definition of a PN transition. Each transition of states as well as each execution of operation of an object in its lifecycle is denoted by a PN transition with a label showing the triggering event. A PN transition is denoted by a 3-tuple $< e, x, o_x >$ where e is the triggering event, x is the object and o_x is the operation of object x that triggered to execute. Figure 8 shows a PN transition $< e_1, x, o_{x1} >$ that denotes the transition from state s_{x1} to state s_{x2} of object x upon the occurrence of event e_1 and operation o_{x1} is triggered to execute. Figure 9 shows a PN transition $< e_1, x, o_{x1} >$ that denotes the transition from state s_{x1} to state s_{x2} of object x upon the occurrence of event e_1 where the occurrence of event e_1 refers the receipt of a message from object y (at state s_{y2}) and operation o_{x1} is triggered to execute.

Figure 10 shows a PN transition $< e_3, x, o_{x1} >$ that denotes the execution of operation o_{x1} of object x (at state s_{x3}) upon the occurrence of event e_3. Figure 11 shows a PN transition $< e_3, x, o_{x1} >$ that denotes the execution of operation o_{x1} of object x (at state s_{x3}) upon the occurrence of event e_3 where the occurrence of event e_3 refers to receipt of a message from object y (at state s_{y3}).

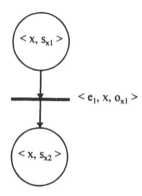

Figure 8. Representation of the transition of states.

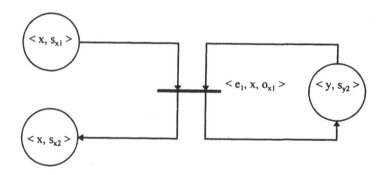

Figure 9. Representation of the transition of states (on receipt of a message).

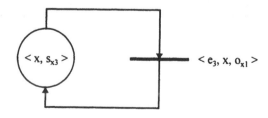

Figure 10. Representation of the execution of an operation.

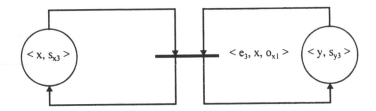

Figure 11. Representation of the execution of an operation (on receipt of a message).

Definition of a token. Tokens are assigned to a PN for execution. Place $< x. s_{x2} >$ holding a token means that object x is at state s_{x2} in its object lifecycle.

Definition of a marking. A PN with a marking μ describes current states of the objects at a particular moments. The marking μ denotes the existence of tokens at the corresponding PN places $< x, s_{x1} >$, $< x, s_{x2} >$, $< x, s_{x3} >$, $< x, s_{x4} >$, $< y, s_{y1} >$, $< y, s_{y2} >$, $< y, s_{y3} >$ and $< y, s_{y4} >$. The marking $\mu = < 0, 1, 0, 0, 1, 0, 0, 0 >$ depicts the holding of tokens at places $< x, s_{x2} >$ and $< y, s_{y1} >$. In other words, object x is at state s_{x2} while object y is at state s_{y1} at that particular moment.

We also proposed to introduce the following procedure for executing the PN.

Initial marking. Initially, one token is given to the PN place which denotes the initial states of an object. For example, the initial state in the object lifecycle of object x is sx1 so a token is given to the PN place $< x, s_{x1} >$. If n objects are involved, then n tokens are given to the PN. The PN has an initial marking $\mu_0 = < 1, 0, 0, 0, 1, 0, 0, 0 >$.

Firing rule. A PN transition $< e, x, o_x >$ can fire upon satisfying two conditions : (i) the occurrence of the triggering event e; and (ii) each input place gets a token. After firing the PN transition, each output place will be given a token. The firing of the transition means that event e occurs and operation o_x of object x is triggered to execute (provided that $o_x \neq \emptyset$).

Execution. The PN is executed by giving the occurrence sequence of events in an interaction scenario. Initially, tokens are given in accordance with the initial marking μ_0. A PN transition may fire upon the occurrence of the first event in the sequence of events. Similarly, PN transitions may fire upon the occurrence of the second, the third and the rest events in the sequence of events. The execution will stop upon the occurrence of the last event in the sequence of events.

There are some implications and properties of the PN. These implications and properties are outlined as follows.

Implication of a marking. A marking of the PN describes the states of objects at a particular moment. An object is always at one state at a particular moment. So, two tokens cannot appear at two places referring to the same object in a marking. The initial marking μ_0 describes the initial states of objects at the start of an interaction scenario. The final marking μ_ω describes the final states of objects at the end of an interaction scenario.

Derived execution sequence of operations. On firing a PN transition $< e, x, o_x >$, the operation o_x of object x is triggered to execute (provided that $o_x \neq \varnothing$). During the execution of a PN, PN transitions fire in accordance with the sequence of events. An execution sequence of event can be derived.

Property of n-safeness. A PN involving n objects should be n-safe. The PN is initially given n tokens. For each PN transition, the number of input places and the number of output places are the same so the number of tokens before firing and the number of tokens after firing should be the same. Throughout an execution, the PN will have n tokens each of which in a PN place referring a specific state of an object. Thus, the PN is n-safe.

The consistency between lifecycle model and interaction model can be analysed through three steps. In the following, these steps are outlined and illustrated with the case example.

Step 1 : Construct the PN. Given lifecycle models of the interacting objects, a PN is to be constructed. Figure 12 shows the PN constructed with the lifecycle models of objects x and y as shown in Figures 3 and 4. The PN consists of places $P = \{ < x, s_{x1} >, < x, s_{x2} >, < x, s_{x3} >, < x, s_{x4} >, < y, s_{y1} >, < y, s_{y2} >, < y, s_{y3} >, < y, s_{y4} > \}$ and transitions $T = \{ < e_1, x, o_{x1} >, < e_2, x, \varnothing >, < e_3, x, o_{x2} >, < e_4, x, \varnothing >, < e_5, x, \varnothing >, < e_6, x, \varnothing >, < e_7, y, \varnothing >, < e_8, y, o_{y1} >, < e_9, y, \varnothing >, < e_{10}, y, \varnothing >, < e_{11}, y, o_{y2} >, < e_{12}, y, o_{y3} > \}$.

Step 2 : Execute the PN. The PN is to be executed with the occurrence sequence of events, which is identified from the interaction scenario as depicted in an interaction model. In the case example, the occurrence sequences of events involved in scenarios A and B are $EQ_A = [e_1, e_2, e_7, e_8, e_3, e_5, e_9, e_{11}]$ and $EQ_B = [e_1, e_2, e_7, e_8, e_3, e_4, e_{10}, e_{12}]$ respectively. Given an initial marking $\mu_0 = < 1, 0, 0, 0, 1, 0, 0, 0 >$, the PN is executed with the sequences of events for scenarios A and B. After execution, the PN will have a final marking μ_ω.

Step 3 : Check consistency. The consistency between lifecycle model and interaction model is achieved upon the satisfaction of two conditions : (i) the final marking μ_ω of the PN depicts the situation that each object is at the final state in its object lifecycle; and (ii) the execution sequence of operations derived from the PN is equivalent to the execution sequence of operations of the interaction scenario depicted in the interaction model.

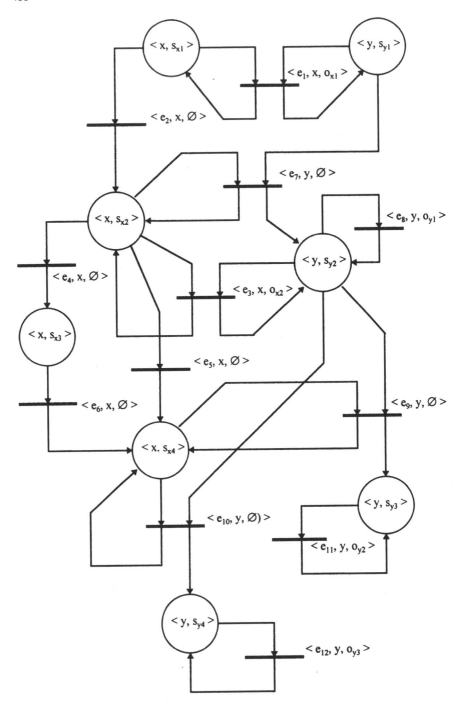

Figure 12. PN model for consistency analysis (case example).

Analysis for scenario A. For scenario A, the sequence of events is $EQ_A = [\, e_1, e_2,$ $e_7, e_8, e_3, e_5, e_9, e_{11}\,]$. The PN has an initial marking $\mu_0 = \,< 1, 0, 0, 0, 1, 0, 0, 0 >$. When the first event e_1 occurs, the PN transition $< e_1, x, o_{x1} >$ fires and operation o_{x1} of object x is triggered to execute. The PN has a new marking $\mu_1 = \,< 1, 0, 0, 0,$ $1, 0, 0, 0 >$. When the second event e_2 occurs, the PN transition $< e_2, x, \varnothing >$ fires and no operation is triggered to execute. The PN has a new marking $\mu_2 = \,< 0, 1, 0,$ $0, 1, 0, 0, 0 >$. After the occurrence of the last event e_{11}, the PN has the final marking $\mu_\omega = \,< 0, 0, 0, 1, 0, 0, 1, 0 >$. The tokens are at places $< x, s_{x4} >$ and $< y,$ $s_{y3} >$ referring the final states of objects x and y. The derived execution sequence of operations $XQ_A = [\, < x, o_{x1} >, < y, o_{y1} >, < x, o_{x2} >, < y, o_{y2} >\,]$ is equivalent to the execution sequence of operations for interaction scenario A depicted in the interaction model. It is concluded that the consistency between the lifecycle models and the interaction model (for scenario A) is achieved.

Analysis for scenario B. For scenario B, the sequence of events is $EQ_B = [\, e_1, e_2,$ $e_7, e_8, e_3, e_4, e_{10}, e_{12}\,]$. The PN has an initial marking $\mu_0 = \,< 1, 0, 0, 0, 1, 0, 0, 0 >$. When the first event e_1 occurs, the PN transition $< e_1, x, o_{x1} >$ fires and operation o_{x1} of object x is triggered to execute. When the second event e_2 occurs, the PN transition $< e_2, x, \varnothing >$ fires and no operation of object x is triggered to execute. The PN has a new marking $\mu_2 = \,< 0, 1, 0, 0, 1, 0, 0, 0 >$. Until the occurrence of event e_4, the PN transition $< e_4, x, \varnothing >$ fires and no operation is triggered to execute. The PN has a new marking $\mu_6 = \,< 0, 0, 1, 0, 0, 1, 0, 0 >$. When the next events e_{10} and e_{12} occur, no transition fire. The PN has the final marking $\mu_\omega = \,< 0,$ $0, 1, 0, 0, 1, 0, 0 >$. The tokens are at the places $< x, s_{x3} >$ and $< y, s_{y2} >$, referring state s_{x3} of object x and state s_{y2} of object y. These states are not final states. The derived execution sequence of operation $XQ_B = [\, < x, o_{x1} >, < y, o_{y1} >, < x, o_{x2} >\,]$ is not equivalent to the execution sequence of operations for interaction scenario B depicted in the interaction model. It is concluded that the consistency between the lifecycle models and the interaction model (for scenario B) is violated.

3.3 Application in OO System Development

There is an emerging need of ensuring the consistency between lifecycle model and interaction model in the specification of object behaviour, not only for the initial system development but also for the subsequent system modification [21, 22]. The analysis on this consistency cannot be trivial, especially on the consistency at the logical level that concerns logical implication of models. In this regard, the proposed analysis offers a formal method to analyse the consistency using Petri Net. With the analysis, individual lifecycle models and interaction models can be analysed against their mutual consistency as soon as they are constructed. This contributes to a more rigorous specification of object behaviour for OO system development, and even more vital for large-scale systems which involve hundred or thousands of objects exhibiting highly complicated and intermingled behaviour. OO CASE tools can also make practical use of this in implementing more sophisticated verification on consistency between models.

4 Conclusion

Lifecycle model and interaction model are generally adopted for specifying object behaviour in OO system development. The consistency between these models is essential required as it directly influences an accurate interpretation of the intended behaviour of a system. Consistency at the syntactic or notation level can be analysed with the meta-models offered by OO methods. The consistency at the logical level, which concerns the logical implication of models that is relatively difficult to analyse, is however downplayed by the existing OO methods as well as the existing OO CASE tools. In this paper, the specification of object behaviour through the lifecycle model and interaction model is first discussed. The two levels of consistency between these models are addressed. With a focus on the consistency at the logical level, the proposed analysis using Petri Net is elaborated with an illustration of a case example. Its application in OO system development is also highlighted. The proposed analysis offers a formal method to analyse the consistency between lifecycle model and interaction model at the logical level, contributing to a more rigorous specification of object behaviour for OO system development.

Reference

[1]   J. Iivari, "Object Orientation as Structural, Functional and Behavioural Modelling : A Comparison of Six Methods for Object-Oriented Analysis", Information & Software Technology, Volume 37, Number 3, Pages 155-163, 1995.

[2]   T. Dillon & P.L. Tan, Object-Oriented Conceptual Modelling, Prentice-Hall, 1993.

[3]   K.O. Chow & S. Yeung, "Behavioural Modelling in Object-Oriented Methodology", Information & Software Technology, Volume 38, Number 10, Pages 657-666, 1996.

[4]   E. Yourdon, Object-Oriented Methods : An Integrated Approach, Prentice Hall, 1994.

[5]   J. Martin & J. Odell, Object-Oriented Methods : A Foundation, Prentice Hall, 1995.

[6]   J. Rumbaugh et al, Object-Oriented Modelling and Design, Prentice Hall, 1991.

[7]   G. Booch, Object-Oriented Analysis and Design with Applications, Benjamin Cummings, 1994.

[8]   G. Booch, J. Rumbaugh & I. Jacobson, The Unified Modelling Language - Document Set, Version 1.0, Rational Software, 1997.

[9]   M. Fowler & K. Scott, UML Distilled : Applying the Standard Object Modelling Language, Addison Wesley, 1997.

[10] A. Wasserman, "Behaviour and Scenarios in Object-Oriented Development", Journal of Object-Oriented Programming, Volume 4, Number 9, Pages 61-64, 1992.

[11] K.S. Cheung, K.O. Chow & T.Y. Cheung, "A Feature-based Approach for Consistent Object-Oriented Requirements Specification", In W. Wojtkowski et al, Systems Development Methods for the Next Century, Pages 31-38, Plenum Press, 1997.

[12] J. Peterson, Petri Net Theory and the Modelling of Systems, Prentice Hall, 1981.

[13] W. Reisig, Petri Nets - An Introduction, Springer Verlag, 1985.

[14] F. Hayes & D. Coleman, "Coherent Models for Object-Oriented Analysis", Proceedings of OOPSLA '91, Pages 171-183, ACM Press, 1991.

[15] S. Kirani & W.T. Tsai, "Method Sequence Specification and Verification of Classes", Journal of Object-Oriented Programming, Volume 7, Number 6, Pages 28-38, 1994.

[16] D. Harel & E. Gery, "Executable Object Modelling with Statecharts", IEEE Software, Volume 30, Number 7, Pages 31-42, 1997.

[17] P. Coad & E. Yourdon, Object-Oriented Analysis, Prentice Hall, 1991.

[18] D. Embley, B. Kurtz & S. Woodfield, Object-Oriented Systems Analysis : A Model-driven Approach, Prentice Hall, 1992.

[19] D. Firesmith et al, OPEN Modelling Language : Reference Manual, Version 1.0, OPEN Consortium, 1996.

[20] D. Coleman et al, Object-Oriented Development : The Fusion Method, Prentice Hall, 1994.

[21] K.S. Cheung, K.O. Chow & T.Y. Cheung, "Verification of Object-Oriented Design Modifications using Feature-based Assertions", Proceedings of SCI '97, Pages 347-354, Venezuela, 1997.

[22] J.D. McGregor & D.A. Sykes, Object-Oriented Software Development : Engineering Software for Reuse, Van Nostrad Reinhold, 1992.

Subjective Method Interpretation in Object-Oriented Modeling[*]

Bent Bruun Kristensen

The Maersk Mc-Kinney Moller Institute for Production Technology

Odense University, DK-5230 Odense M, Denmark

Abstract

In object-oriented modeling an object reacts objectively to an invocation of one of its methods in the sense that it is given which description for the method is interpreted. Subjective behavior of an object means that is not objectively given which description is interpreted — the choice depends on other factors than the invocation such as the invoking object, the context of the objects, and the state of the objects. The notion of subjectivity is defined, and the support of subjectivity by means of object-oriented language mechanisms is investigated.

1 Introduction

In object-oriented modeling the result of a method invocation is always dependent on the actual state of the object involved. The method description interpreted in an invocation is determined only by the type of the object for which the method is invoked. This means that the effect — in the sense of which description is interpreted — of a method invocation clause is dependent on (the type of) the object that is currently referenced. An object could behave subjectively in the sense that other factors will determine its behavior — i.e. which description is interpreted given the same invocation clause. This kind of subjective behavior would support more autonomous and evolutionary objects.

In [18] subjectivity is motivated by real-world object behavior. Various *forces* are described, that affect an object's behavior in the real world: A *sender* force, a *context* force, and a *state* force. The sender of a message can affect how an object responds. For example, the way that you respond to complaints from your boss can be different from the way you respond to your children's. Context also affects the behavior — your response to the complaints from your children in private are different from your response in public. State also affects behavior. Your mood can dramatically affect your response to more or less appropriate complaints. There is some kind of precedence among these forces. The question is how these forces influence each other. The overall problem is to understand the nature of these forces and to support such forces in the modeling.

In terms of one object invoking a method of another object we try to identify subjective behavior at least for the following aspects:

---

[*]This research is supported in part by The A. P. Moller and Chastine Mc-Kinney Mollers Foundation.

- The context of the invoking object and of the object being invoked. The behavior of the objects depends on their context.

- The type (class) of the invoking object. The behavior of the object being invoked depends on the type of the invoking object.

- The state of the invoking object and of the object being invoked. The behavior of the objects depends on their states.

Inspired from the notion of forces, the circumstances under which we in this article support subjective behavior involve at least:

- The roles of the object being invoked. The behavior of the object being invoked depends on one of its roles as seen from the invoking object.

- Multiple implementations of the methods of the invoking object. The behavior of the object being invoked — in terms of the selection among these implementations — depends on the type (class and corresponding class hierarchy) of the invoking object.

- The delegation from the object being invoked. The behavior of the object being invoked can be partially delegated to other objects, either an autonomous object (accessed explicitly by a reference) or an enclosing object (accessed implicitly). In both cases a kind of subjective behavior is obtained by a combination of delegation and a polymorphism variant.

Article Organization. In section 2 we introduce the notion of subjectivity and relate it to the concepts of object-oriented modeling and programming. In section 3 we illustrate a number of mechanisms to support subjectivity. In subsection 3.1 the notion of roles in relation to subjectivity is illustrated. In subsection 3.2 the idea of multiple implementations of a method is discussed. In subsection 3.3 we describe why mechanisms that support polymorphism and locality are not subjective mechanism by themselves. In subsection 3.4 we describe how a combination of mechanisms that support delegation and either polymorphism or locality can be seen as a kind of subjective mechanisms. In section 4 we present related work. In section 5 we summarize the results of the article. In appendix A we quote dictionaries for their definitions of subjectivity and related concepts. In appendix B we illustrate the use of other well-known mechanisms not to be seen as subjective mechanism.

2 Subjectivity in Modeling

Subjectivity & Perspectives. According to the dictionaries *subjectivity* means "belonging to, of, due to, the consciousness or thinking or perceiving subject". Software systems have no consciousness and usually we do not think of executing entities as *subjects*, i.e. as "thinking and feeling entities". In this article we use subjects and subjectivity as metaphors when we explore possible extensions of the object-oriented paradigm. Therefore, we need to specify the meaning of these terms in that context.

In general, in software systems we have descriptions of the execution processes, namely programs. We organize the descriptions according to different perspectives on the execution process. The perspectives include procedural programming, functional programming, logic programming and object-oriented programming. Several definitions of object-oriented perspective exist. It is not the objective of this article to discuss these or to argue which one of these is the correct or better one. We shall rely on a rather weak definition where the perspective is a collection of interacting objects. An object is created according to some description, usually in the form of a class. Classes and objects are related by means of various relations, including generalization and aggregation hierarchies. The objects interact by invoking methods — one object invokes a method of another object. The execution process is a sequence of embedded method invocations among the collection of objects being involved. In general, several threads of such invocation sequences can exist.

Abstractions in Modeling. In programming languages we declare and invoke abstractions. An abstraction has a designation — the designation is given in the declaration of the abstraction and is used in the application of it. The invocation of an abstraction means that the corresponding description is interpreted according to the semantics of the language. In general, when we know the designation we also know which description is interpreted. The interpretation is state dependent. The state of the execution determines how the interpretation evolves and what the result (in very general terms) of the interpretation is.

As an example, in procedural programming we declare a procedural abstraction BinarySearch. We invoke the procedure by its name and we simply execute the body of the BinarySearch procedure. The execution is dependent of the actual values to search among and the key value to search for. The recursive invocations of the procedure behave differently, dependent on these values. But the description to be followed is the same. The situation is similar for a class abstraction. The class has a name and we instantiate objects by the description of the class. A method is also an abstraction. When we invoke a method we instantiate some kind of activation record by means of the method description. The method is interpreted relatively to an object — its interpretation depends on the state of that object.

But in most object-oriented languages method invocation differs form the usual invocation of abstractions. An object is invoking a method of another object. The invoking object does this through a reference to the other object and the designation (the name) of the method. The difference is that the reference dynamically can denote different objects for which the method may be declared differently. In some object-oriented languages the reference is not typed and may denote any type of object. In other languages the reference is typed but may still denote different types of objects (usually any object of a subtype of the type of the reference). The idea is, that even if we give the designation of the method the actual choice of a description of a method is parameterized by the value of the reference (an object). That object solely determines which description is interpreted, namely the method declared for that object. Still, objects of the same type (class) behave the same way — they interpret the same description[1]. In Figure 1, we illustrate the notation for classes, objects, methods and references, that is used in the illustrations.

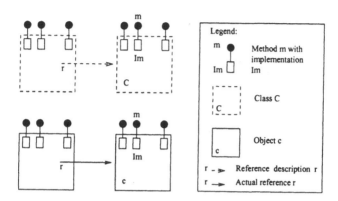

Figure 1: Classes, Objects, Methods and References

Definition of Subjectivity. In object-oriented modeling we can summarize the situation as follows — object a of class A invokes the method m of object b of class B by means of the reference rB (to access an enclosing object the reference rB is implicit):

- The type B of the reference rB to the object b is known. The type determines which types of objects can be referenced by rB.

- The type of the object actually referenced by rB determines which description of m is used.

- The object b interprets the method m in its current state.

- A type (or signature) for the method m may or may not be given. The method m can have different implementations in different classes.

- The type A of the object a that invokes a method is not used, except that a can access the reference rB.

- The state of object a is not used, except that a invokes $rB.m$ in the current state and the values of actual parameters of m reflect the current state.

---

[1]An exception is a singular or one-of-a-kind object, where the class is given only implicitly. A singular object executes its unique, but fixed description upon the invocation of a method.

In Figure 2, we illustrate the objects a and b of types A and B, respectively. By rB.m the implementation of a method in a invokes the method m of b by use of the reference rB.

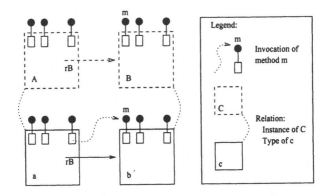

Figure 2: Method Invocation

Given the type of the reference and a named designation of the method, we obtain different interpretations by means of different objects only. That fact, that objects of different types behave differently in terms of the description that is interpreted, is fundamental in object-oriented modeling. In this article we are interested in situations where the objects of the same type in general behave differently (still in terms of the description that is interpreted) dependent of various other circumstances. The objects can legally display positive discrimination in favor of other objects under given circumstances. This includes as a special case that the same object (an object with one given identity) behaves differently under different circumstances. We shall understand this as *subjective behavior* because from the usual objective point of view, we can not determine which kind of behavior to expect. The actual behavior is due to other circumstances, the kind and form of which are the topic of this article.

We shall use the following definitions of subjectivity in the context of object-oriented modeling:

Definition: A denotation of a method invocation for a given object is said to be subjective if different method interpretations can result.

Remarks:

(1) The denotation has two parts: some kind of relation structure between the object invoked and some invoking objects, and the method invocation.

(2) Some precision is appropriate: "a given object" means "an object with a given, same identity" and "different method interpretations" means "interpretation of different implementations of the method".

Definition: A mechanism is subject-oriented if it supports a subjective description. A subject is any entity that offers subjective behavior.

In the JAVA language [2] objects are related by means of references. A reference is explicitly included in the description of an interaction between objects, except if the access is to an enclosing class instance (object). To which extent various forms method invocations in JAVA can be seen as subject-oriented mechanisms is among others the topic of this article. By *method dispatch*, in general, not only in JAVA, it is possible to permit and select among several applicable methods — usually the most specific applicable method among the overloaded methods. By *multiple dispatching*, as in the Cecil language [4] it is possible to test among the classes of all the arguments in the methods. Neither of these mechanisms for method dispatch are subject-oriented mechanisms because by the description of the invocation of the method gives full control over the actual choice among the bodies of the applicable method. The *predicate dispatching* [6] generalizes the method dispatch mechanisms. Arbitrary predicates control the method applicability, and logical implication is used to define the overriding relationship. The method selected to handle the sent message depends not only on the classes of the arguments, but also on the classes of the subcomponents of the arguments, on the state of an argument, and on relationships between arguments and objects. The predicate dispatch mechanism is not a subject-oriented mechanism because the predicates alone control the choice of the method body.

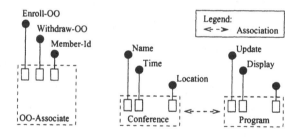

Figure 3: **OO-Associate**, Conference and Program

"Conference Organizing Problem".

We shall use the "Conference Organizing Problem" [16] as an illustrating example. We are not trying to solve what this model originally tried to solve. Instead we use it as a well-known context to illustrate our ideas. A major part of the illustrations are slightly modified examples from [11].

We restrict the model to deal with some "OO" organization only. In Figure 3, we illustrate class **OO-Associate**, that models any person who is related to "OO" and therefore registered in some register of **OO-Associates**. Class **OO-Associate** is not related to any particular conference, but models only the general information and behavior as illustrated. An actual conference is modeled by the class Conference, that is related to an instance of class Program. In the various examples we shall illustrate subjectivity in the interaction between OO-Associate (as a participant in a conference) and the Conference/Program.

3   Subjectivity Mechanisms

In the following subsections we illustrate the notion of subjectivity by means of mechanisms for role classes and multiple implementations of methods. We show that polymorphism and locality are not subject-oriented mechanisms by themselves, but that in combination with delegation, they can be seen as a kind of such.

3.1   Roles

A object can play different roles in relation to different objects. Another object knows the given object from a certain perspective — given by the role. In general, a method of an object with its roles is a combination of a method of the object and a method of the role. The perspective then determine which description of a method is actually interpreted when invoked through a role.

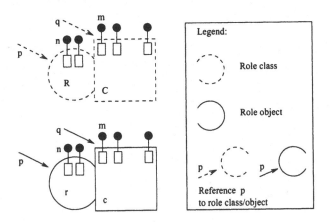

Figure 4: Role Classes and Instances

We introduce a conceptual abstraction mechanism [10], the *role* [11], [12]. The role concept is a natural element in our daily concept formation. The concept has already shown useful in object-oriented methodologies [20] and languages [12]. Role classes support additional perspectives on objects — a role class is a language mechanism that models the dynamic change of the roles of an object. A role can be instantiated and glued onto the *intrinsic* object (the object playing the role) and later removed from the object. Generalization and aggregation hierarchies model the relations of role classes. The properties (instance variables and methods) of a role are additions to the properties of the class of the intrinsic object — in the description of the role class the properties of the intrinsic class/object are directly accessible. An object and its currently available roles are seen as an entity with one identity. However, other objects can access this entity through it roles — by references that are typed by the role classes — to obtain different interfaces and behavior from the entity. In Figure 4, we illustrate the notation for role classes and instances, that we use in the illustrations. The access of role classes is by means of the references q and p. We assume that q is qualified by the class C and that p by R. An object of class C can have (one or several) instances of the role class R as its roles. Through the reference q to the C object only the method m (as an example) is accessible — but not the n method. Through the reference p to the role r the method n (as an example) as well as method m (as an example) are accessible. In the description of the implementation of the method n the method m may be invoked (and the instance variables defined in C may be accessed) directly.

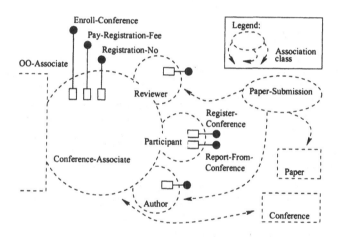

Figure 5: Roles of Conference-Associate

"Conference Organizing Problem". A OO-Associate plays the role Conference-Associate in relation to Conference. An OO-Associate object can have any number of Conference-Associate roles, because it can be involved in a number of conferences — a given conference is related to a specific role of an OO-Associate only and not the entire OO-Associate. During the preparation of the Conference the Conference-Associate can play the roles Participant, Author, Reviewer. These become roles of Conference-Associate as illustrated in Figure 5. The Participant role can have methods such as Register-Conference and Report-From-Conference. We consider Participant, Author, and Reviewer to be roles of Conference-Associate because the various relations to a given conference are related to these specific roles only (and not to Conference-Associate as a whole): A Participant is related to the Conference — an Author, the Paper and its Reviewers are related through a Paper-Submission association.

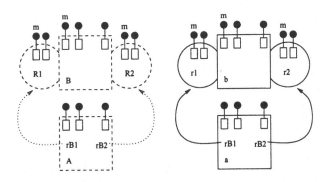

Figure 6: Illustration: Role

Schematic Example. By a schematic example we illustrate why the "Role-of-Object" mechanism is a subject-oriented mechanism. The object b is of class B. The classes R1 and R2 are role classes for B. The objects r1 and r2 are instances of R1 and R2, that are bound to b. The method m is defined for both B, R1 and R2. The implementations of m are ImR, ImR1 and ImR2 in m, R1 and R2, respectively. The object a is of class A. The object a has a reference rB1 of class (type) R1 and a reference rB2 of class (type) R2. The value of rB1 is r1 and the value of rB2 is r2.

In this example we have the *same* designation (m), *different* description (ImB combined with ImR1 and ImR2), *same* object identity (b's identity). In Figure 6,

(1) a invokes rB1.m: ImR1 combined with ImR is executed.

(2) a invokes rB2.m: ImR2 combined with ImR is executed.

"Conference Organizing Problem". When actually attending the conference, the Participant can further play the roles such as Speaker, Panelist, or Session-Chair. We model these as roles of Participant as illustrated in Figure 7. The roles Speaker, Panelist, or Session-Chair all have a method Manuscript to model the paper presentation, the opening presentation for the panel discussion, and the introductions and questions for the session, respectively. These are roles of Participant because the various relations to a given conference are related to these specific roles only (and not to the Participant as a whole): A Speaker is related to the Presentation, a Panelist is related to the Panel-Session, and a Session-Chair is related to a Session (one role for each session to which a participant is related). When the Manuscript method of OO-Associate object is accessed through any of these roles a different behavior is obtained depending on the actual relation used.

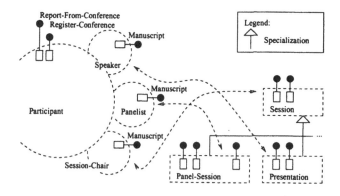

Figure 7: Roles of Participant

3.2 Multiple Implementations

A method can have more than one implementation. The choice among the implementations in an invocation of the method can be determined by various factors, including (the type of) the invoking object. The *timing polymorphism* [22] is an example of a variant of multiple method implementations to support the communication between two distributed real-time objects involving timing constraints. By *performance polymorphism* [21] it is possible to maintain and select among multiple implementations of a method that carry out the same task and differ only in their performance measures.

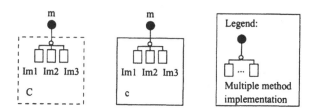

Figure 8: Multiple Method Implementations

In Figure 8, we illustrate the notation for multiple method implementations, that we use in the illustrations. The method m of class C has several implementations Im1, Im2 and Im3. Upon the invocation of the method m of the object c it is entirely up to the object c to decide which of the implementations to be interpreted as response to the invocation. The invoking object has no influence on which implementation is selected. The decision can be made on several kinds of information including the identity of the object invoking the method and the type of this object — in this discussion of the support of subjectivity by means of multiple implementations we shall assume that the type of the

452

invoking object determines the choice.

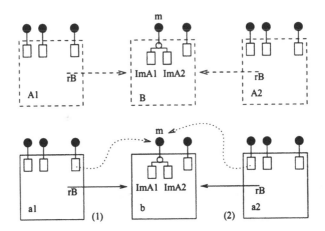

Figure 9: Illustration: Multiple-Implementations

Schematic Example. By a schematic example we illustrate why the "Multiple-Implementations" mechanism is a subject-oriented mechanism. The object b is of class B. The class B has method m. The method m has different implementations ImA1 and ImA2 for invocations initiated by objects of the classes A1 and A2, respectively. The reference rB is of class (type) B. The value of rB is b. The objects a1 and a2 are of classes A1 and A2, respectively.

In this example we have the *same* designation (m), *different* description (ImA1 and ImA2), *same* object identity (b's identity). In Figure 9,

(1) a1 invokes rB.m: ImA1 is executed.

(2) a2 invokes rB.m: ImA2 is executed.

"Conference Organizing Problem". The Participant has the roles Speaker, Panelist, or Session-Chair. The classes Speaker, Panelist, and Session-Chair are all related to the Conference class, because of the relations between Participant (or actually Conference-Associate) and Conference. The class Conference can have a method Registration-Information to model request from the Participants concerning for example the various kinds of fees for attending the conference. These fees vary according to the kind of Participant. In Figure 10, we illustrate the multiple method implementations for Registration-Information and the relation between Conference class and the classes Speaker, Panelist, and Session-Chair (implicitly through Conference-Associate). When the Registration-Information method of Conference object is invoked through any of these objects a different behavior is obtained depending on the actual type of the invoking object (in this example a role object).

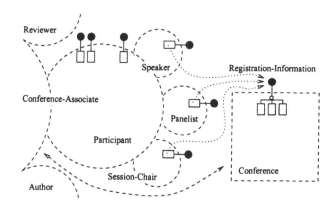

Figure 10: Method `Registration-Information`

3.3 Non-Subjectivity

By the use of polymorphism[2] (and by "local/enclosing class" to be discussed later) it is not possible from the invocation of an abstraction (a method) to determine the actual description of the abstraction (the method) to be interpreted (the determination of the actual description is dependent on the execution state, in this case the value of the reference).

Schematic Example: Polymorphism. By a schematic example we illustrate why polymorphism cannot be seen as a subject-oriented mechanism. The object b is of class B. The classes B1 and B2 are subclasses for B. The objects b1 and b2 are instances of B1 and B2. m is a method of B. The method m is redefined in B1 and B2. The implementations of m are ImB, ImB1 and ImB2 in B, B1 and B2, respectively. The object a is of class A. The object a has a reference rB of class (type) B. The value of rB can be b, b1 or b2.

In this example we have the *same* designation (m), *different* descriptions (ImB, ImB1 and ImB2), and **different** objects (b, b1 and b2). In Figure 11,

(1) a invokes rB.m and rB's value is b: ImB is executed.

(2) a invokes rB.m and rB's value is b1: ImB1 is executed.

(3) a invokes rB.m and rB's value is b2: ImB2 is executed.

The "Locality" Mechanism. Classes can be defined locally to enclosing classes, and the existence of objects of local classes is dependent on — and exist in relation to — an object of the enclosing class. Examples of object-oriented programming languages that include the locality mechanisms are BETA [15] and JAVA language [2] — but both excluding multiple enclosing classes.

---

[2]The term polymorphism is used with the meaning that different objects interpret the invocation of a given method differently, namely according to the definition of this method

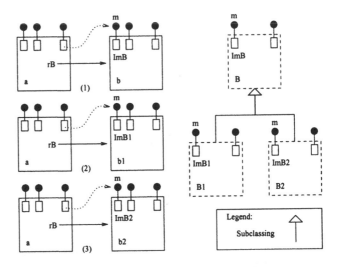

Figure 11: Illustration: Polymorphism

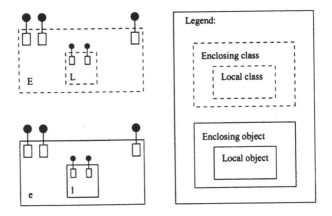

Figure 12: Enclosing/Local Classes/Objects

In Figure 12, we illustrate the notation for enclosing/local classes/objects, that is used in the illustrations. The class L is defined local to the enclosing class E. The properties (instance variables and methods) of E are available to L, and can be accessed directly in the description of the properties of L. The same class L can be defined to be local to several classes — as a part of the definition of the local/enclosing relation the class L must specify its requirements to the properties of the multiple enclosing classes. An object 1 exists always in exactly one instance of one of the enclosing classes of its class L. The object 1 is shown in object e of class E, but 1 can change its enclosing object during its lifetime. The accessibility of 1 from outside e can be specified in a similar way as for accessibility of methods.

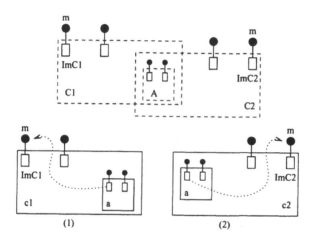

Figure 13: Illustration: Locality

Schematic Example: Locality. By a schematic example we illustrate why the "Local/Enclosing Class" mechanism is not a subject-oriented mechanism. The object a is of class A. The class A is declared local to both the classes C1 and C2. c1 and c2 are objects of C1 and C2, respectively. The method m is defined in both C1 and C2 (the implementations of m are ImC1 and ImC2, respectively).

In this example we have the *same* designation (m), *different* descriptions (m invokes ImC1 or ImC2), and **different** objects (c1 and c2). In Figure 13,

(1) a invokes m and a is local to c1: ImC1 is executed.

(2) a invokes m and a is local to c2: ImC2 is executed.

---

for the object's class.

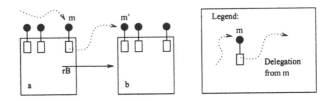

Figure 14: Delegation

3.4 Delegation

Delegation combined with polymorphism or the locality mechanism can be seen as a *not quite* subject-oriented mechanism. The combination at least support a kind of subject-oriented behavior. In this combination the distinct behavior is obtained by that the given object delegates the behavior to either different objects by use of polymorphism (to which the given object has a reference) or to different enclosing objects (to which the given object is local).

In Figure 14, we illustrate delegation: The method m of the object a is invoked. The object a delegates the invocation to the method m' of the object b. The implementation of the method m of a includes the invocation rB.m'.

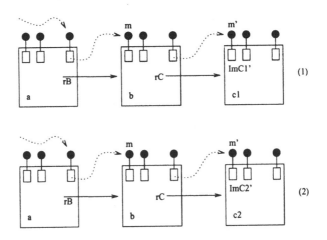

Figure 15: Illustration: Delegation and Polymorphism

3.4.1 Delegation and Polymorphism

Schematic Example. The object b is of class B, and m is a method of B. The reference rC is of class (type) C. The classes C1 and C2 are subclasses for C. The objects c1 and c2 are instances of C1 and C2 and m' is a method of C. The method m' is redefined in C1 and C2. The implementations of m are ImC1' and ImC2' in C1 and C2, respectively. The object a is of class A. The object a has a reference rB of class (type) B. The object b has references rC, rC1 and rC2 of class (type) C, C1 and C2, respectively. The value of rC1 is c1 and the value of rC2 is c2. The method m invokes rC.m'.

In this example we have the *same* designation (m), *different* description (m delegates to ImC1' or ImC2'), *same* object identity (b's identity). In Figure 15,

(1) a invokes rB.m and rC's value is c1: ImC1' is executed as part of the execution of the implementation of m.

(2) a invokes rB.m and rC's value is c2: ImC2' is executed as part of the execution of the implementation of m.

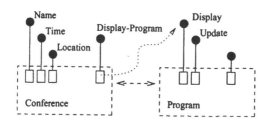

Figure 16: Display-Program and Display Methods

"Conference Organizing Problem". An actual conference is modeled by the class Conference. Related to a conference is an instance of class Program. Conference has methods such as Location, Time, Name, etc. and Program has methods such as Update, Display, etc. We imagine that several types of programs are declared in a classification hierarchy. In Figure 16, we illustrate how the method Display-Program of Conference delegates the behavior (probably only partially) to the method Display of Program. The actual Program object related to the Conference object will then determine which program is actually displayed.

3.4.2 Delegation and Locality

Schematic Example. The object b is of class B. The class B is declared local to both the classes C1 and C2, and c1 and c2 are objects of C1 and C2, respectively. The class B has a method m. The method m invokes a method m', that is a method of both C1 and C2 (the implementations of m' are ImC1' and ImC2', respectively). The object a is of class A. The reference rB is of class (type) B. The value of rB is b.

In this example we have the *same* designation (m), *different* description (m delegates to ImC1' or ImC2'), *same* object identity (b's identity). In Figure 17,

(1) a invokes rB.m and b is local to c1: ImC1' is executed as part of the execution of the implementation of m.

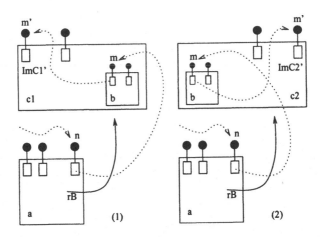

Figure 17: Illustration: Delegation and Locality

(2) a invokes rB.m and b is local to c2: ImC2' is executed as part of the execution of the implementation of m.

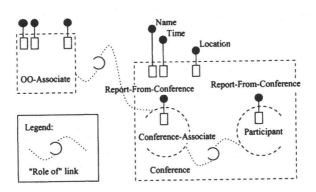

Figure 18: Delegating Method: Report-From-Conference

"Conference Organizing Problem". The class Conference-Associate is meaningful only in the context of a Conference. We apply the locality concept to support this relation and define Conference-Associate local to the enclosing Conference. The methods of the enclosing class Conference are directly available to the methods of the local class Conference-Associate. The method Report-From-Conference can use the methods Name and Time directly. Concerning the dependability, an instance of Conference-Associate is dependent on — and can always assume the existence of — an instance of Conference (or of some other class to which it is also declared local). In Figure 18, we illustrate how the method Report-From-Conference of the local (role) class Conference-Participant — and its role class Participant (also local to Conference) delegate their behavior (probably only partially) to the methods Location, Time, Name, etc. of the enclosing Conference class. The actual Conference object enclosing to the Conference-Associate and Participant objects will then determine which conference that is actually used.

4   Related Work

The subjects [8] model that different agents might view the same object from different perspectives. The agents do not only have a filtered view of an object, but some of the methods of the object may be there only because of the given perspectives of an agent. Usually, the criteria for deciding which properties of real-world phenomena to include in a model are based on a single perspective only.

In [17] subjectivity is discussed in the context of the mutual dependent development processes of language mechanisms and design patterns. The thesis gives an outline of two kinds of subjectivity. *Perspective based subjectivity* is supported by means of roles. *Message based subjectivity* is defined in terms of either the identity or the type of the sender of a message. The thesis also distinguishes between the identity of objects and individuality of subjects (subject here restricted to object with roles). Each object (as well as any kind of instance of classes and other kinds of concepts) has its own unique identity. A subject can be a combination of a number of such instances and may therefore have no unique identity. But subjects are still individual entities. Two subjects are defined to be the same individual if the intrinsic objects of the two subjects have the same identity [3].

[1] describes an experiment on programming language support including enclosing classes. The background for the experiment is [9] and [19]. The objective is to gain more experience with the design of abstraction mechanisms of this kind and to consider efficient implementation techniques. Based on a general model, language mechanisms (as additions to an existing object-oriented programming language, the Beta language [14]) were constructed as well as an experimental implementation for these. The general model allows an object to move from one enclosing class to another; the model is based on static binding of names and the movability of local objects introduces *multiple binding* of names. For the class an optional clause is introduced where the potential enclosing classes, in which an object of the class can be a local object, can be listed. The experiment is based on the implementation of the Beta language [14]. A preprocessor transforms the additional clauses into Beta code. The experience is that movable local objects introduce a complex[3] look-up

---

[3]In static languages the binding of a method is usually done at run-time, dependent on which object is currently denoted. In dynamic languages (methods may be added and deleted at run-time) there is a need for dynamic look-up of the method in one and the same superclass hierarchy only. The look-up required in the case of multiple binding varies between different, but fixed superclass hierarchies because the object (or some of its enclosing

mechanism for method activations, but the implementation shows that efficient, though complex run–time structures for multiple binding of names are available.

5 Summary

We have defined subjectivity in terms of object-oriented mechanisms as class, object, method etc., although the objective is to investigate subjectivity as a further development of object-oriented modeling. Objects behave objectively in the sense that the behavior of an object is known no matter the circumstances of the invocation. With subjectivity the objects can display different behavior dependent on the circumstances — although still deterministic behavior.

We have investigated a number of language mechanisms and clarified to which extent these support subjectivity — and thus can be classified as subject-oriented mechanisms. The discussion is guided by illustrative examples to help the intuitive understanding. Specifically for the JAVA language we find that method invocation and object instantiation can appear as a kind of subjective descriptions only by a combination of delegation and polymorphism. By mechanisms in general, we obtain explicit support of subjectivity. The alternative, simulation of support of subjectivity by means of patterns is not discussed in this article.

The intention of this article is to present an understanding of subjectivity objectively — whether or not we succeeded is probably subjective. However, it seems to be an objective fact that subjectivity is more powerful than objectivity.

Acknowledgments. We thank Pablo Victory for his inspiring contribution at the Workshop on Subjectivity in Object-Oriented Systems at OOPSLA'95 as well as the succeeding private communication. We also thank Johnny Olsson for fruitful discussions about subjectivity in relation to his Masters Thesis [17]. Finally, we thank Lars Kirkegaard Bækdal and Bo Nørregaard Jørgensen for comments and suggestions.

References

[1] E. F. Andersen, P. Gilling, P. Holdt–Simonsen, L. Milland: OOP –med Sammenhæng og Overblik. Thesis (in Danish), Aalborg University, 1993.

[2] K. Arnold, J. Gosling: The JAVA Programming Language. Addison-Wesley, 1996.

[3] M. Bunge: Treatise on Basic Philosophy, Ontology I: The Furniture of the World. Volume 3. D.Reidel Publishing Company, 1977.

[4] C. Chambers: Object-Oriented Multi-Methods in Cecil. Proceedings of the European Conference on Object-Oriented Programming, 1992.

[5] J. Coplien: Advanced C++ Programming Styles and Idioms. Addison-Wesley, 1992.

[6] M. Ernst, C. Kaplan, C. Chambers: Predicate Dispatching: A Unified Theory of Dispatch. Proceedings of the European Conference on Object-Oriented Programming, 1998.

---

objects) may have moved.

[7] E. Gamma, R. Helm, R. Johnson, J. Vlissides: Design Patterns: Elements of Reusable Object-Oriented Software. Addison Wesley, 1994.

[8] W. Harrison, H. Ossher: Subject-Oriented Programming (A Critique of Pure Objects). Proceedings of the Conference on Object-Oriented Programming Systems, Languages and Applications, 1993.

[9] B. B. Kristensen: Complex Associations: Abstractions in Object-Oriented Modeling. Proceedings of the Object-Oriented Programming Systems, Languages and Applications Conference, 1994.

[10] B. B. Kristensen, K. Østerbye: Conceptual Modeling and Programming Languages. Sigplan Notices, 29 (9), 1994.

[11] B. B. Kristensen. Object-Oriented Modeling with Roles. Proceedings of the 2nd International Conference on Object-Oriented Information Systems, Dublin, Ireland, 1995

[12] B. B. Kristensen, K. Østerbye. Roles: Conceptual Abstraction Theory & Practical Language Issues. Theory and Practice of Object Systems, 1996.

[13] B. B. Kristensen: Architectural Abstractions and Language Mechanisms. Proceedings of the Asia Pacific Software Engineering Conference '96, 1996.

[14] O. L. Madsen, B. Møller-Pedersen, K. Nygaard: Object Oriented Programming in the Beta Programming Language. Addison-Wesley 1993.

[15] O. L. Madsen, B. Møller-Pedersen: Part Objects and Their Location. Proceedings of International Conference on Technology of Object-Oriented Languages and Systems, 1992.

[16] T. W. Olle, A. A. Verrijn-Stuart, H. G. Sol, Eds.: Information System Design Methodologies: A Comparative Review. North-Holland, 1982.

[17] J. Olsson: Language Mechanisms and Design Patterns. Masters Thesis. Aalborg University, 1996.

[18] M. Prieto, P. Victory: Real World Object Behavior. Workshop on Subjectivity in Object-Oriented Systems, The Object-Oriented Programming Systems, Languages and Applications Conference, 1995.

[19] J. Rumbaugh: Relations as Semantic Constructs in an Object–Oriented Language. Proceedings of the Object–Oriented Systems, Languages and Applications Conference, 1987.

[20] J. Rumbaugh, M. Blaha, W. Premerlani, F. Eddy, W. Lorensen: Object-Oriented Modeling and Design. Prentice Hall 1991.

[21] L. Zhou, E. A. Rundensteiner, K. G. Shin: OODB Support for Real-Time Open-Architecture Controllers. Proceedings of the Fourth International Conference on Database Systems for Advanced Applications, 1995.

[22] K. Takashio, M. Tokoro: Time Polymorphic Invocation: A Real-Time Communication Model for Distributed Systems. Proceedings of 1st IEEE Workshop on Parallel and Distributed Real-Time Systems, 1993.

A   Dictionary

Oxford Dictionary:[4]

---

[4]The Concise Oxford Dictionary of Current English. Oxford University Press, 1964.

- **subject**:
  ... *3. (philos.). Thinking & feeling entity, the mind, the ego, the conscious self, as opp. all that is external to the mind (& object, the ego & the non-ego, self & not-self, the consciousness & what it is or may be conscious of); the substance or substratum of anything as opp. its attributes. ...*

- **subjective**:
  ... *1. (Philos.) belonging to, of, due to, the consciousness or thinking or perceiving subject or ego as opp. real or external things; ...*

- **Object**:
  ... *5. (philos.). Thing thought of or apprehended as correlative to the thinking mind or subject, external thing, the non-ego. ...*

- **Objective**:
  ... *1. (philos.). Belonging not to the consciousness or the perceiving or thinking SUBJECT, but to what is presented to this, external to the mind, real. ...*

B   Other Mechanisms

Ordinary Execution.   The execution of a given description will usually both execute different parts of the description, and give different results (in a broad sense). The execution depends on the state of the executing object, the possible input parameters, etc. This is an ordinary execution, because different parts or different results does not imply that the invocation is subjective. The invocation of the method n of a Q object implies that different descriptions, namely m1 and m2 of P, are executed dependent on the state of the Q object — the value of the parameter b.

```
class P {
   public void m1 () {
     //
   };
   public void m2 () {
     //
   };
};
class Q {
   P rP = new P();
   public void n (boolean b) {
      if (b)
         rP.m1();
      else
         rP.m2();
   };
};
```

Additional Descriptions.   Different additional descriptions can be executed as part of the execution of the given description. Again, if this is obtained only by executing different parts of the given description this is ordinary execution — not subjectivity. However, if the execution of different additional descriptions can be obtained by the same element of the given description then we shall understand this as some kind of subjectivity — namely *not quite* subjectivity. The invocation of the method n of a Q object implies that two different descriptions, namely m of P1 and m of P2, can be executed from the same element in n, namely rP.m().

```
class P  {
   public void m () {
      //
   };
};
class P1 extends P  {
   public void m () {
      //
   };
};
class P2 extends P  {
   public void m () {
      //
   };
};
class Q  {
   P rP;
   P1 rP1 = new P1();
   P2 rP2 = new P2();
   public void n (boolean b)  {
      if (b)
         rP = rP1;
      else
         rP = rP2;
      rP.m();
   };
};
```

Method Overloading.   For example in JAVA each method has a signature, which is its name together with the number and types of its parameters. In JAVA method overloading means to allow two methods to have the same name if their signatures have different numbers or types of parameters.

The method overloading mechanism is not subject-oriented because the signature as such is seen as the designation — the designation is the combination of the name and the number and types of the parameters. In the following the methods with name m of P have different types of their parameter. Therefore, their signatures are different, and they are different designations.

```
class P  {
   public void m (int i)  {
      //
   };
   public void m (boolean b)  {
      //
   };
};
```

Composition of UML Design Models: A Tool to Support the Resolution of Conflicts

Siobhán Clarke, John Murphy, Mark Roantree

School of Computer Applications,
Dublin City University,
Dublin 9,
Ireland.

Contact: sclarke@compapp.dcu.ie

Abstract: Design models are valuable deliverables of the software development process but have the potential to be large and unwieldy. Sound software engineering practice guides us towards the break-up of design models into manageable components. These smaller design models, however, need to be considered together in order to get the "big picture" of the full design. In order to integrate a design model, it must be possible to merge that model with the remainder of the design. There is considerable potential for conflict between the design models being composed. We introduce a tool that supports the resolution of conflicts when composing UML class models, and the definition of composition rules to make the process as automated as possible.
Keywords: Software Composition, UML Design Models, CASE Tools

1. Introduction

Object-oriented design models represent a considerable amount of the decision-making for the final product of a software development effort. Therefore, in any large-scale system, the design models might be large and difficult to maintain. As with similar problems in object-oriented programs, splitting the design into smaller models and/or re-using existing designs is a useful tool for managing size and complexity. There is considerable research and technical support for the composition of programs. We believe that there is also much to be gained from the composition of design models as it provides a software engineering mechanism which is valuable for many different kinds of purposes, only some of which are:

- Support for different portions of the design being developed separately by different groups and subsequently merged for the final design model.
- Support for extensions to the design for later versions of the product being developed separately from the previous version and subsequently merged for the new version.
- Support for the design of multiple, different models to cater for different requirements of the final product and the subsequent composition into the final design model.

- Support for the integration of a design model which may have been developed separately and which caters for a problem which might be reused in the design model under development.

While there are many benefits to composing design models, there are many conflicts which might occur during the composition process. In this paper, we describe the functionality of a research tool we are developing to support the automation of the composition process as far as possible. Using a small example of composing UML class models, we first show how the tool might notify the designer to resolve those conflicts during the composition process. We then consider how the tool might support the definition of composition rules to automate the resolution of conflicts by allowing the tool make decisions based on those rules to resolve related conflicts. The paper is organised as follows:

- In Section 2 *"Related Work"* we look at just three of the many different composition mechanisms supporting both program composition and design composition.
- In Section 3 *"Composing UML Design Models – An Example"* we present a small example of a composition problem which is used throughout the paper.
- In Section 4 *"Requirements for Tool Support"* we consider what support and options a tool should provide a designer in the task of composing design models.
- In Section 5 *"Resolving Conflicts"* , we work through the example of composing two UML class models and illustrate how the tool notifies the designer to resolve conflicts which are encountered.
- In Section 6 *"Customising Composition Rules to Maximise Automation"* , we look at how the tool would support the designer in specifying composition rules which could be re-used in the software composition process.
- In Sections 7 and 8, *"Other Work"* and *"Future Work"* we put the research described in this paper inside the perspective of the overall picture of the research being undertaken.

2. Related Work

There is considerable research on-going into object-oriented software composition. Indeed, one of the main problems facing the achievement of true composability as discussed in [1] is the "lack of consistent terminology and insight in the relations between different composition techniques". Different techniques include frameworks, adaptive components, open implementation, computational reflection and meta-level architectures, role modelling, subject-oriented programming, contract specification, and much more. In this look at related work, we consider just three composition techniques, one from the programming domain called subject-oriented programming, and two from the analysis and design domain (model templates and role modelling).

2.1. Composing Object-Oriented Programs

One mechanism to support the composition of object-oriented programs, called subject-oriented programming, is based on the packaging of object oriented systems into "subjects"[1], with a compositor program used to compose subjects into larger subjects, and eventually entire systems [2]. A *subject compiler* produces a subject label, which describes the aspects of the subject which are required for composition purposes. Information in the subject label includes: 1) the classes defined and/or used by the subject, 2) the operations defined and/or used by the subject, with their signatures, 3) the method mapping that maps (operation, class) pairs to sets of method bodies to be executed and 4) a set of aliases which specify the relationship between the symbols which refer to classes and operations in the subject with the names used in the label.

When composing subjects, composition designers consider issues of both correspondence and combination. Correspondences between different elements of the subjects, like operation correspondence, class correspondence, instance variable correspondence and method combination are chosen. One example of a correspondence rule available to the composition designer is *MatchByName* which sets name-matching (i.e., string matching on the element name) as the rule for correspondence. Once element correspondence has been established in subject-oriented programming, and documented as a set of correspondence rules, rules to specify the combination strategy of the compositor program are defined (or re-used). Combination can be performed in a variety of different ways. For example, one subject's elements may *replace* those of another. Alternatively, use of *join* combination aggregates, rather than replaces, functionality. The full composition process composes subjects into larger subjects, which themselves can be further composed into larger subjects, and eventually the entire system.

2.2. Composition in Object-Oriented Design Models

Composition at the design level is also a very useful mechanism as all the benefits associated with component-based programming like reducing complexity and increasing flexibility (and more) are equally applicable at the design stage. We look here at mechanisms for building specifications from the composition of generic reusable parts as described in [3] and the process of synthesis of role models in [4].

2.2.1. Model Templates

The notion of model templates is discussed in [3]. A template is a model of a design pattern – i.e., a generic piece of model. Designs may be built by application of the templates. Applying a template to the design model effectively merges the specification of the template with the model, ensuring that the model is refined

---

[1] A subject is defined as an object-oriented program or program fragment that models its domain in its own, subjective way.

with the generic template. Specification of the model template is similar to the specification of the design model. On application of the template to the model, the names of the template are replaced by the names in the model. If we take the liberty of applying subject-oriented programming terminology to this example, we could see the application of a correspondence rule like *Correspond²* to cover this case.

2.2.2. Roles

A mechanism for role-modelling described in [4] allows the designer construct a role model for each activity or task carried out in the overall system, or construct several role models for the same activity at different levels of detail. The key to this mechanism is the facility for *synthesis* – the process of composing the different role models. In general, the domain of the roles resulting from the synthesis is the union of the domains of the synthesised roles. Synthesis may lead to intended or casual name collisions, which are resolved by re-naming. Again, applying subject-oriented programming terminology, we might see the application of the *MatchByName* correspondence rule for the general case, with the *Correspond* correspondence rule used for exceptions.

3. Composing UML Design Models – An Example

Let us consider a small, contrived example of composing two static class models. In two different departments of a company, Personnel and Payroll, a class for Employee has been specified. Personnel are interested in the personal details and work experience of the employee. Payroll are interested in the salary scale of the employee and whether the employee is on an incentive plan. Such a plan will have an impact on the percentage of the base salary which the employee will be paid each month.

In Figure 1, the Employee class shows details of attributes of interest to personnel like name, personnel id, address, marital status, date of birth and level. Personnel also maintains an indication of the total amount earned by the employee in the previous tax year in an attribute name "salary". Employees may be promoted which sets the value of the level attribute. Associated with the Employee class in the Personnel model is a class called ProfessionalExperience, which holds a history of previous positions held by the employee. It was the designer of this model's view that the class Employee should not have any subclasses and therefore, the isLeaf property of the class was set to true.[3]

---

[2] In subject-oriented programming, an explicit correspondence rule *Correspond* establishes correspondence between the label elements explicitly listed in the rule's parameters. Typically, the elements will not have the same name.

[3] The isLeaf property (inherited from the UML GeneralizableElement meta-class [5]) is not explicitly illustrated on the UML class model.

468

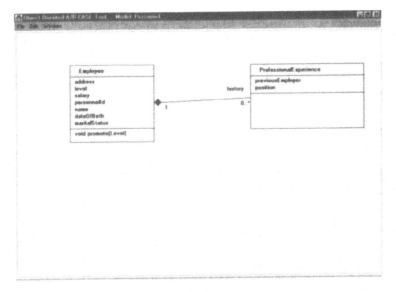

Figure 1: Personnel Model

Meanwhile, in the Payroll model illustrated in Figure 2, an Employee class also provides a definition for a "salary" attribute, but this attribute indicates the salary payment type of the employee with valid values such as "monthly" or "weekly". The employee class also defines the personnel id, name and base salary of the employee. Unlike the Personnel model, however, a need was seen for a subclass called SalesIncentiveEmployee which uses different algorithms to calculate the annual and monthly salary of the employee based on the allowances and restrictions specified in the attributes defined for it.

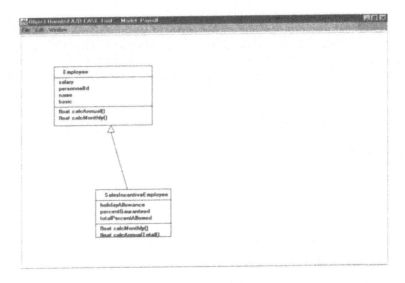

Figure 2: Payroll Model

Notwithstanding some of the "interesting" design and naming decisions made in the examples, a consolidation of the two models could be useful for maintenance purposes. In the next section we discuss what is currently supported by the tool and briefly look at what is under development. In section 5 we work through the example and illustrate how the tool supports the designer in handling the conflicts.

4. Requirements for Tool Support

It is important that tool support for the managing of conflicts in the composition of design models be as flexible as possible by including support for different kinds of correspondence and combination strategies (inspired by [2]). We have already implemented support for correspondence based on a name-match (described here). The supported combination strategy is similar to "Replace" (only one of a name-matching set of elements survives the composition), but giving the option for a "Join" when there is an attribute conflict. However, a correspondence rule such is MatchByName may not be applicable in a situation where two designers may have used the same name for two different concepts. The tool must allow the designer either specify exceptions to a MatchByName rule, or define a different rule entirely. In order to assess the level of flexibility which might be required, we looked at the possibilities as follows in Table 1.

Same name, Equal properties	MatchByName would not see a conflict. But, the elements might still be different. A DontMatch rule might be applied, where the designer states that elements with the same name are different, so some kind of automatic rename is required. However, we can see a situation where a combination of both might be required.
Same name, Conflicting properties	MatchByName throws a conflict. Designer chooses either to resolve the conflicts for a single element in the composed model, or to have two elements in the composed model. Renaming of at least one of the elements is required in the later case.
Different name, Equal properties	MatchByName assumes these elements to be different and will include both in the composed model. However, the elements might support the same design concept. Therefore, a tool must support a designer indicating this during the composition process. This would go a long way towards supporting the Catalysis notion of templates.
Different name, Conflicting properties	MatchByName assumes these elements to be different and will include both in the composed model. However, the elements might support the same design concept. Therefore, a tool must support a designer indicating this during the composition process.

Table 1: Composition Possibilities

In Table 1, we consider the simplest cases of element composition decision-making to illustrate that restricting the designer to one rule or another is not feasible. These cases are "simple" in the sense that elements which are instances of UML meta-classes, such as Attribute, Operation, Class etc., are examined without consideration of their relationships to other elements. When composing elements from UML design models, properties of the element may conflict even when their names are the same.

For example, the *Class* meta-class from [5] inherits properties from *GeneralizableElement* through *Classifier*. These properties specify, for example, whether the class is a root class *(isRoot)*, and therefore may have no superclasses, or whether the class is a leaf class *(isLeaf)*, and therefore may have no subclasses. If we are composing two classes with a *MatchByName* correspondence rule, from two separately defined models, properties such as isRoot and isLeaf must be resolved if there is a mismatch. While we do not mean to attach undue importance to the specification of isRoot and isLeaf particularly, the point we are illustrating is that design elements in a UML model are constrained by the rules and properties of the UML meta-model. As a result, conflicts may arise in the composition of the design elements relating to those UML properties and rules and those conflicts must be resolved.[4] We can see from this table that an automatic composition tool, while allowing for a different kinds of general rules for correspondence and combination, must also allow for exceptions to that general rule.

In this paper, we describe the resolution of conflicts arising from name-matching correspondence. We are also working tool support for the specification of synonym matching correspondence which will be documented in future papers.

5. Resolving Conflicts

In this section, we look at how the tool handles conflicts which are detected on selection of the option to merge our Personnel and Payroll models based on MatchByName correspondence and a "Replace" combination strategy. To recap on the model conflicts, we have:

1. The Employee class defined as being a leaf class in the Personnel model, but having a subclass in the Payroll model.
2. The salary attribute of the Employee class in the Personnel model is intended to hold the total salary earned by the employee in the previous year and therefore, is defined with type "float" (not illustrated in the class model). An attribute of the same name appears in the Employee class of the Payroll model, but with a type "string" as it is intended to hold a salary payment type.
3. One final conflict was not obvious from the example description, but the tool detects on checking whether the properties of an attribute are the same. The personnelId attribute in the Employee class of the Personnel model was

---

[4] In section 5.*Resolving Conflicts* we illustrate the impact of changing a class's properties when this change breaks a UML rule associated with the "Generalization" relationship.

defined as having a type "string", but in the Payroll model, the attribute of the same name was defined as having a type "int".

5.1. Class Conflicts

Once the request has been made to compose the Personnel and Payroll models with a MatchByName correspondence rule, the tool takes each of the models in turn (there could, of course, be more than two models selected for composition) and builds the new composed model. The tool iteratively adds any class which was not previously added (check is on name-match). On the pass through the second model (regardless of whether the first pass was over the Personnel or the Payroll model), the first class that is determined to be a duplicate is the Employee class (indeed, this is the only duplicate class). The tool then compares the class properties of each Employee class to determine if there is a conflict. If there was no conflict on class properties, the tool would then check the attributes and operations of the two classes in order to similarly compose them. However, with the Employee class, a conflict is encountered. The Employee class in the Personnel model has been defined as being a leaf class (and therefore does not allow subclasses), but the Employee class of the Payroll model has been defined as allowing subclasses. Other class properties which might have had a conflict are whether the class is a root class (may not have superclasses), whether the class an abstract class and whether the class is an active class.

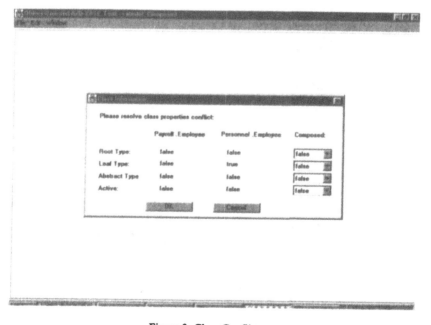

Figure 3: Class Conflict

Because of the range of conflicts which are possible, the tool simply presents a dialog to the designer, indicating that a conflict has occurred and illustrating the class details of the two classes where the conflict occurred (see figure 3). The designer may then choose the required properties for the class in the composed model. It is important to note that the composed model is subject to the same UML rules as the component models. Therefore, if the designer chooses to reiterate that Employee is a leaf type, then the composition mechanism will determine that this will leave the composed model in an invalid state once the generalization relationship between Employee and SalesIncentiveEmployee is added to the model. The designer is notified immediately and must set the leaf type property back to false (see figure 4).

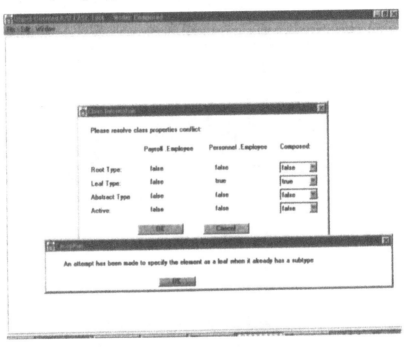

Figure 4: Generalization Exception

Of course, another approach for the tool could have been to deduce that since the only difference between the two classes was whether subclasses was allowed, and that one of the two had a subclass defined, then the correct course of action was to automatically make the required changes without reference to the designer. On the other hand, it sounds more like this could be a standard correspondence rule that might be applied selectively. It is the later approach we have taken and are currently working on (see section 6).

5.2. Attribute Conflicts – Join or Replace

Once class conflicts are resolved, the attributes of Employee are composed. The same correspondence rule of MatchByName applies to all design model elements that are instances of the same UML meta-class, and therefore, applies to attributes. The tool iteratively passes through the attributes of the Employee class, and adds any attribute that has not already been added. If two attributes of the same name are encountered, the properties of the attribute are compared. If any conflict occurs, a dialog is presented to the designer illustrating where the conflict exists. The designer may choose to specify the properties for a single attribute of this name to included in the composed model using a replace option, or may choose that both attributes be included in the composed model using a join option. In the later case, the tool will automatically rename the attributes by including the model and class name information.

In our example, two attribute conflicts are encountered which cover both cases. Figure 5 illustrates the dialog which is presented to the designer when it is determined that the types of the two salary attributes are different. We can see from the dialog that the potential for conflict between properties of attributes is wider than a difference in the attributes' types. Properties such the initial value, the multiplicity, the scope, the changeability and the visibility might also have conflicting values. In this case, the intention of the two salary attributes was entirely different, so the designer chooses the "Join" option to ensure that both appear in the composed model. The tool includes two attributes in the composed model, one with the name Personnel.Employee.salary and another with the name Payroll.Employee.salary.

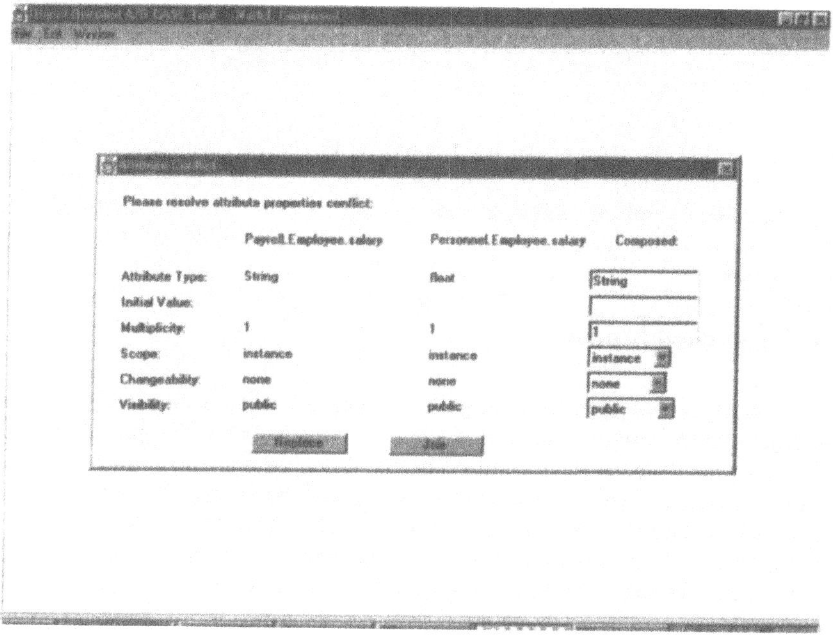

Figure 5: Attribute conflict: Join required

Figure 6 illustrates a similar dialog with the appropriate information to indicate the difference in the types specified for the personnelId attribute. In this case, the concept to be represented by the attribute personnelId is the same in both cases, so the designer decides what the required properties for the attribute in the composed model are, and chooses the "replace" option.

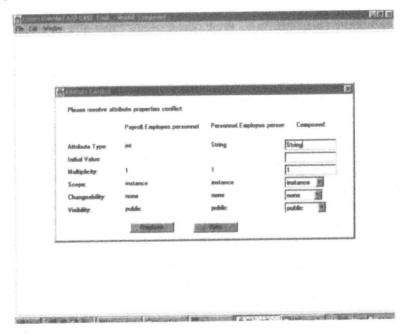

Figure 6: Attribute conflict: Replace required

We can see that the mechanism used compose the classes within a model is the same as the mechanism used to compose attributes within a class. The processes for composing operations within a class and associations within a model are also the same, with the designer guided through the resolution of any conflicts encountered.

5.3. Composed Model

The composition tool iterates through the models for composition and builds the composed model based on the design elements it encounters. We have previously illustrated what happens when conflicts occur. When there are no conflicts, the tool assumes that the design elements are the same and does not notify the designer but simply does not add the element a second time. This is based on a MatchByName correspondence rule, which assumes that elements with the same name and properties are the same. In figure 7 we show the resulting composed model from our example.

The ProfessionalExperience and SalesIncentiveEmployee classes have been added without reference to the designer as, since they occurred only once in the models, there could have been no conflicts. The same applies with the association between the ProfessionalExperience class and the Employee class.

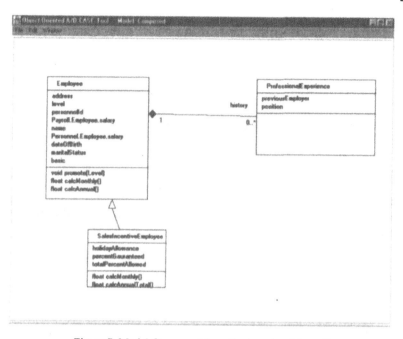

Figure 7: Model Composed from Personnel and Payroll

6. Customising Composition Rules to Maximise Automation

Throughout the development of the first version of this tool to support the basic resolution of conflicts in the composition of design models, it became evident how much more flexible the support could be. We have already discussed the need for different high-level correspondence rules such as one that allows the designer specify that design elements with different names are the same. In this section, we look at two more areas where flexibility might be applied:

In our example, a situation exists where if the value of a property in a class in one model is propagated to the composed model, this would result in an invalid model according to the UML rules. The approach of the tool was to notify the designer to make the appropriate change. In section *6.1. Generic Rules* we look at a mechanism to allow the designer define the automatic approach the composition tool should take in similar circumstances, without reference to the designer.
In addition, we notice from our small example that the designer may make some decisions based on knowledge of the problem domain. In section *6.2. Rules specific to the problem domain* we discuss building rules around such decisions for future use by a compositor tool.

We envisage a library of such rules which would allow the designer selectively refine higher level rules like "MatchByName" to increase the automation of the composition process. Only conflicts which are not covered by the rules applied to the composition process will result in the notification of the designer for resolution.

6.1. Generic Rules

Design elements in a UML design model are constrained by the rules of the UML meta-model. As an instance of a meta-class, a design element has properties and rules associated with it. During the design of a class model (or any UML model), the tool ensures the "correctness" of the model at all times. In the same way, a tool composing models into a new model must ensure that the composed model also conforms to the "correctness" rules of UML. If we first look at our individual models Personnel and Payroll, we might see the application of the UML rule which states that:

*"No **GeneralizableElement** can have a supertype **Generalization** to an element which is a leaf"* [5].

This results in a two-way check in our tool. In the Personnel model, the Employee class is defined as a leaf. Therefore, if there is an attempt to add a subclass to Employee, the tool will notify the designer that this is not possible as Employee is a leaf. On the other hand, in the Payroll model, Employee has not been defined as a leaf, and has a subclass. If the designer attempts to change Employee by making it a leaf, the tool will notify the designer that this is not possible as Employee has a subclass.

In general, where we have a design element property with a rule attached, these must be considered as a pair with a two-way impact. The design element's properties in a particular stage of the design will impact, based on a UML rule, the creation or change of the other properties of the same design element and/or the creation or change of other design elements. Conversely, an attempt to change the properties of a design element may be restricted, based on a UML rule, by the values of other properties in the same design element and/or the values of the properties of other design elements.

This generalisation has prompted our design of the support for the creation of generic rules which could be applied to the composition process. Figure 8 illustrates a dialog which allows the selection of a meta-class property and rule pair. A list of the (supported) UML meta-constructs is presented to the designer, with corresponding properties and, in turn, corresponding rules being displayed on selection of a construct or property, respectively.

Given that we support a two-way impact associated with a (property,rule) pair, we allow the designer choose the action of the compositor tool based on either overriding the property value to a valid value, or removing the related design element. To support our example, the designer creates a generic rule called "OverrideIsLeafAttribute". The designer chooses the class meta-construct and is presented with a list of properties associated with that construct.[5] On selection of the (Boolean: isLeaf, "Element already has subtype") (property,rule) pair, the designer chooses to the option to override the value of the isLeaf property when the composition tool encounters a conflict in this (property,rule) pair. If the designer had applied this rule to the composition of the Personnel and Payroll models, then the compositor tool would have automatically changed the isLeaf property of Employee to a "correct" value without notifying the designer. The "correct" value is obtained from the component in the tool handling rules. If the request for a correct value from the compositor tool results in more than one value, a default value is returned.

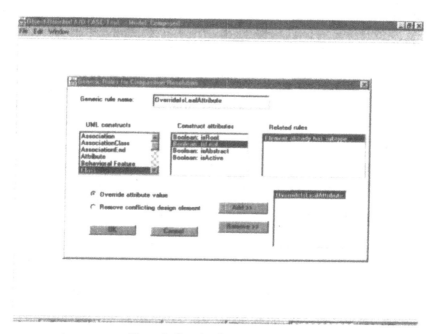

Figure 8: Creating Generic Rules

Similarly, composition rules for every (property,rule) pair may be created and applied to the composition of design models.

6.2. Rules specific to the problem domain

We also notice that during the composition of design models, designers may be asked to resolve conflicts between design elements. These conflicts might result from differences between different designers' knowledge of the problem domain. From our example, both the salary attribute and the personnelId attribute had been defined with different types, which results in a conflict. The designer attempting the composition of design models may intercede in these conflicts by defining the

---

[5] The tool presents the union of the properties of the selected meta-class and all its superclasses.

properties for the design elements in the composed model. We consider that there is potential to build a specific rule for each decision made by maintaining the design element values selected for the composed model. In every future encounter with that design element, even if not in this composition effort, the chosen properties would be applied.

7. Other Work

The overall direction of our research is to develop a tool which supports the composition of all types of components, from design or code components that support some business functionality to more technical kinds of components which may cross-cut the entire application [6]. We have described here the composition of functional design components. When considering more technical concerns, we have based our composition technique on the notion of aspects from Xerox Parc Research and described in [7]. Here, technical aspects of a system, like concurrency support, are separated from the functional component completely. The aspects are written in some aspect language, with an AspectWeaver™ to compose the aspect program and the functional component into the final application. The programmer need only ever work with the functional component or the aspect program, making the programming task simpler. We have developed support in the tool for creating an aspect language and generating an aspect program related to a UML functional design component [8].

8. Future Work

This paper just illustrates the composition of UML class diagrams. It is in our plan to extend the UML constructs supported by the tool to include some models supporting the dynamic design. In this paper we discussed the requirement for other kinds of composition rules. Next, we will implement support allowing the designer relate corresponding design elements which might have different names. One test of the value of this support will be whether this tool supports the "Templates" concept from [3]. In keeping with the ultimate objective of our design tool to include a compositor which can compose many different kinds of components, we plan to include support for the definition of design patterns with associated merge into the class model. The approach to the visualisation of design patterns under consideration is from [9].

References:

[1]   Lucas C, Steyaert P. Research Topics in Composability In: Workshop on Composability Issues in Object-Orientation, ECOOP, 1996

[2]   Ossher H, Kaplan M, Katz A et al. Specifying Subject-Oriented Composition. In: Theory and Practice of Object Systems, Volume 2, Number 3, 1996

[3]   D'Souza D, Wills A. Objects, Components and Frameworks with UML: The Catalysis Approach. Addison-Wesley, 1998.

[4]   Reenskaug T. Working with Objects. The OOram Software Engineering Method. Manning Publications Co., 1996

[5]   UML Consortium. Unified Modeling Language Semantics Version 1.1. available from http://www.rational.com

[6]   Clarke S, Murphy J. Developing a Tool to support the Composition of the Components in a Large-Scale Development. In: Workshop on Object-oriented Behavioural Semantics, OOPSLA, 1997

[7]   Kiczales G, Lamping J, Mendhekar A et al. Aspect-Oriented Programming. In: ECOOP, 1997

[8]   Clarke S, Murphy J. Developing a Tool to support the Application of Aspect-Oriented Programming Principles to the Design Phase. In: Workshop on Aspect-Oriented Programming, ICSE, 1998

[9]   Lauder A, Kent S. Precise Visual Specification of Design Patterns. to appear, ECOOP, 1998

PANEL: 00 TRENDS AND PERSPECTIVES

An Object Oriented Architecture Model For International Information Systems? An Exploratory Study

Hans Lehmann

Department of Management Science and Information Systems, University of Auckland, New Zealand

Private Bag 92019, Auckland, New Zealand, Email: *h.lehmann@auckland.ac.nz*

Abstract. This exploratory paper investigates the architecture and design principles of international information systems. Case study research has evolved a two-dimensional topology as a 'seed concept' for an architecture paradigm. The nature of the architecture in turn suggested that Object Orientation be investigated as the fundamental design principle. For enabling implementation differentiation and future changeability, it is conjectured that object technology is the optimal development strategy for international information systems. Directions for further research are outlined.

1   Introduction

Information systems technology is often critical to the international operations of the globally oriented firm, either as the key to its expansion, or even as the main profit driver. Despite their obvious importance transnational information systems technology is still "largely unreported [and] unstudied" [1] and "...generally ignored "[2]. While scholarly research into this field is sparse, there is an increasing amount of anecdotal evidence and technical reports indicating a strengthening interest by practitioners in this field. This exploratory paper investigates whether there is a generic architecture common to international systems *sui generis* which would allow a more successful development approach.

The literature does not clearly identify a generally accepted term for information systems technology applied across borders. In this paper the term "international information system" (IIS) is used. Furthermore, to distinguish international information systems from other distributed systems (as elaborated in [3]), they are defined as *distributed information systems which support similar business activities in highly diverse environments commonly found across country boundaries.*

The paper is structured as follows:

First, the notion of a specific architecture as the basis for the development methodology for international systems is evolved;

Next, three case studies, which assessed the usefulness of the suggested architecture model, are summarised;

Finally, the object nature of the architecture model and the need for object-orientation as the basis for the design of international information systems is set out and directions for further research are proposed.

2 An architecture for international systems?

Many researchers of IIS architectures use a framework developed by Bartlett and Ghoshal [4] for the classification of enterprises operating in more than one country. Butler Cox [5] developed a model of IIS where there is a direct, one-to-one relationship between Bartlett and Ghoshal's global business strategies and these systems architectures. Other researchers ([6]; [7]; [8]; [9]; [10];[11]) propose similar relationships between information systems structure and global business. Table 1 contains a comparison of the four frameworks discussed:

Bartlett & Ghoshal	Butler Cox	Kosynski & Karimi	Sankar et al	Ives & Jarvenpaa
Global	Centralised	Centralisation	Centralised	HQ-driven
Multinational	Autonomous	Decentralisation	Decentralised	Independent
International	Replicated	Inter-organisational	(undefined)	Intellectual Synergy
Transnational	Integrated	Integrated	Integrated	Integrated

Table 1: Comparison of architecture styles/configurations identified in the literature

It seems that just as the 'international' business strategy is an intermediary stage, so are the corresponding global information technology configurations. If these replicated/inter-organisational/intellectually-synergised structures are regarded as embryonic 'integrated' architectures, then just three generic architectures could be defined, namely

- Centralised;
- Decentralised (including autonomous and independent); and
- Integrated.

The basic underlying need for differing structures comes from the requirement to accommodate differing local needs in the IIS. This had been established early on by Buss[12], when he found that using 'common' systems across different countries can be fraught with difficulty. In the same year Keen, et al. [13] first articulated a paradigm of a 'common core' of information systems applications with 'local' alterations. There has been little further development of this model as far as the functionality of application systems is concerned, and Ives & Jarvenpaa, [9] conclude that "the literature offers little guidance for...local versus common applications".

The notion of a common structure, linking together divergent (local) elements of a global system, however, has been further developed by Keen [14] who states that a 'transnational platform' is required to carry the 'transnational information technology capability' required for global operations.

Based on these fundamental notions, an architecture for international systems can be postulated in the form of a two dimensional topology with a common 'core' and 'local' parts. (see Figure 1.) Conceptually, the 'Core' is similar to Weill's [15] notion of an information technology infrastructure. The Core's main purpose too is "to provide a stable base of reliable services" and furthermore to ensure that local applications can be implemented in the right balance of functionality to adapt optimally to local culture and provide at the same time the required level of global control.

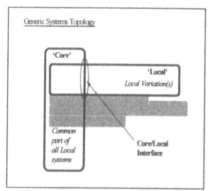

Figure 1. The generic 'Core/Local' topology. The local implementations of the 'Core' and the extent of their local systems varies from site to individual site (indicated bt the grey area)

The degree to which applications are included in the core corresponds to Keen's [14] notion of 'infrastructure range', whereas the extent of integration and the number of local sites correlate with his concept of 'reach'. The 'Local' parts of the IIS are the ones unique to the local site. In both Weill's [15] and Earl's [16] models, this would encompass the parts of the business-unit infrastructure together with business process technologies unique to the respective local business environment. In practical terms, moreover, there will be a third part to the architecture, namely a 'Core/Local Interface' which links the 'Core' and the 'Local' systems structures together.

3 Comparison with some Empirical Observations

Three case vignettes from the author's own experience were used to explore whether the architecture model is useful, initially from two viewpoints:

(a)   As a *framework* for describing the structure of a wide variety of international information systems supporting an equally wide variety of multinational businesses; and secondly

(b)   As a *blueprint* and/or *template* for the design of international information systems.

The analysis of the three case vignettes and their international information systems is contained in more detail in Lehmann [3]. Table 2 (overleaf) summarises the topology and systems element characteristics of the three cases.

According to the criteria explained above, the usefulness of the architecture model can now be assessed in terms of its use as a *framework* and, secondly, in terms of the potential *economies* of design and development of international information systems.

3.1.   A Descriptive Framework

The two dimensional topology is flexible, as a variety of systems architectures can be accommodated. Variety can occur not only in terms of 'core' versus 'local' across the board, but each 'core'/'local' mix and interface can be defined, maintained and changed in precise response to individual local site requirements. The two dimensional topology can therefore implement all the architectures cited above:

Architecture Elements	LEASING FIRM	MERCHANT BANK	COMMODITY BOARD
'Core'	'Medium' core; Data Base of International Customers; Central, Compulsory 'Deal-Set-up' application	'Thin' core; Data & Information standards and communication standards for risk management (stringently enforced);	'Fat' core; Large central Sales and Inventory Management system at the production sites and head office,
'Locals'	Local Variations: Leasing Payments and Receivables systems; Marketing applications;	Locally selected packaged technology for all business operations (e.g. stock broking, capital markets);	Message formats and protocols for communication to smaller, independent local systems;

Table 2: Summary of three case vignettes

- *Centralised* architectures have a 'local' content of (near) zero;
- *Decentralised* architectures have a 'core' of (near) zero;
- *Integrated* architectures have a varying 'core' to 'local' ratio for each element and/or for each location.

3.2. Design Economies from the Model

The 'Core' of common systems, the 'Local' systems and the 'Core'/'Local' Interfaces' could all be developed in three distinct steps and by independent teams within overlapping, or, in the case of 'local' systems acquisition projects, parallel time frames. This would

- Break down and simplify the IIS design task and defuse its complexity;
- Increase the predictability of project outcomes;
- Spread, and thereby reduce, the development risk;

The definition of the 'Core' technology (infrastructure as well as application systems) is, however, crucial for the success of the whole process. Despite guidance from the global business strategy, designing and specifying the common parts of an IIS in the operational detail required for building and installing it is very difficult to do in practice. The following paragraphs discuss this process and suggest a direction for simplifying and error-proofing this process.

4   Object Orientation of the IIS architecture?

CSC [17] carried out a broadly based study of the way in which a number of multinational firms deals with the issues of global information systems versus local business requirements. They found that the firms who had difficulties building IIS design their 'common' requirements in one of two ways:

- The 'core' system is formed around the *'lowest common denominator'* of all the requirements (i.e. the sum of all local business system needs) in system building terms; however, this can be a disappointingly small proportion of the overall information system;

- The opposite stratagem, in CSC terms *'the grand design'*, attempts to specify a system which contains all local and global requirements and agglomerates them into one information system; in mathematical terms this may be called the *'lowest common multiple'* - and just as such a number can be alarmingly large, so can information systems built along this principle; some of the more spectacular information systems failures fall into this category: during the systems development time the business changed so much that there could never be a 'final version' of the software.

In mathematics, however, there is a third possible stratagem for finding common elements among divergent number sets - multiples of *common prime factors*. In systems terms, these would be 'components' in the form of building blocks that would be used to assemble systems. The 'components' would carry the *global* standards, but their assembly could then follow individual *local* requirements. Information systems built in this way would satisfy both 'common' and 'local' needs and would avoid the conflicting trade-off stance altogether.

Such 'prime factors' for the establishment of global commonality can be implemented in three forms:

1. as infrastructure to enable common basic applications (such as email in the case vignette of the *Merchant Bank*); in this way, global standards are implemented in a form which would be immediately useful for the local business unit;

2. as a 'design template', i.e. a set of design outlines and specifications for the global standard part of an application, from which the individual local systems can be built; the case vignette of the *Leasing Subsidiary* is a variation on this theme, with the template fairly firmly embedded in actual software templates;

3. as software components;

Both design templates and actual software components will consist of data and processes - defining them unambiguously as *objects*.

5 'Object' qualities for 'Core' systems elements

Three key qualities of object orientation with respect to the common/local issue in international information systems are discussed below.

Objects are defined as *encapsulating* both data and processes/functions in one unit. This combination makes them very useful for vehicles of 'global;' standards, incorporating both data/information standards as well as 'prescribing' standard ways of operating.

Objects communicate with other objects using 'messages'. *Polymorphism*, defined as the capability of objects to deal differently with identical messages, is an essential quality for implementing 'local' requirements onto standard processes. Examples are

- The application of direct/sales taxes where the local applicability rules, rates, etc. are kept with the local accounting object, reflecting the different local statutory and tax regimes.

488

If the 'Lease-Set-up' part of global standard information system in the case vignette *Leasing Subsidiary* were an object oriented system, one such a globally enforced message would have been the compulsory calculation and reporting of the profitability of each lease deal. Again, the processing modules in the 'message' would act on 'local' and individually different data (e.g. local cost-of-money rates, tax-rebate rules, etc.). Figure 2 depicts this.

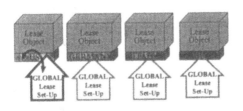

Figure 2. The standard LEASE-SETUP 'message' acts on all objects, taking country variations into account.

Inheritance is the quality of objects to structure themselves hierarchically into 'super-classes and sub-classes pass 'down' characteristics (data and/or processes). This has two main uses in the global/local dichotomy.

First, consider 'Payments' transactions in the *Leasing Subsidiary* case vignette: whilst the gist of payment processing (application into a ledger, cash-book/bank reconciliations, etc.) is common, the operational detail of the payment process is not; each 'local' object would inherit the common processes from a standard Accounts Receivable module, but implement typical local payment types (e.g. 'Fedwire' transfers in the US, Direct Debits in the UK, Bank-Account-Transfers in Germany, negotiable promissory notes in Italy, etc.). Figure 3 shows that.

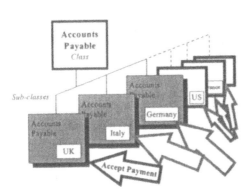

Figure 3. The PAYMENT transaction is applied differently in each country, although the accounting module/object is a global standard.

The second use would be the introduction of new functionality across the organisation - be they new and/or updated global standard/common data and process prescriptions or new operational software developed for local needs in one site but - perhaps - useful elsewhere. In the case vignette of the *New Zealand Commodity Board* (Figure 4) the UK subsidiary developed a system of vendor-managed-inventory with a large supermarket chain whereby the supermarket would pay for goods sold on the basis of their own point-of-sale records, without orders or invoices involved: the Board would replenish their wares in their allocated space as they saw fit. Implemented in object-oriented form, this functionality would have been instantly available to all other local sites through *inheritance* from the Sales & Inventory object.

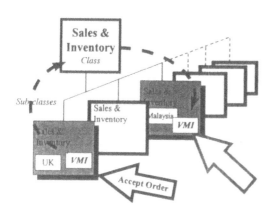

Figure 4. The Vendor-Managed-Inventory system enhancement (developed locally in the UK) becomes part of the SALES & INVENTORY object class - and thus instantly available to Malaysia (and others, if they choose to adopt it).

The advantages of using an object oriented approach to the design/definition of the common and local parts of an international information system are, however, not restricted to the building of the system. As Butler Cox [5] postulate, the business style of multinational enterprises is fluid and changes with their development. Moreover, King and Sethi [2] demonstrated that multinational enterprises are hardly ever homogenous - they work at the same time in different modes and at differing degrees of 'penetration' into the 'Local' systems of different countries (e.g. applying a 'global' style in small subsidiaries and a 'transnational' style in larger, more sophisticated local environments). The ease and flexibility with which an object oriented information systems architecture can be maintained and changed would certainly seem to make such an object oriented approach an essential design consideration.

Conclusion:

The - sparse - literature on international information systems has lead to the definition of a proposed architecture model consisting of a two-dimensional topology, which describes any international information system as consisting of a common 'Core' and 'Local' variations in each individual, subsidiary, site. This generic structure model has been shown to be a practical and flexible tool to describe and understand international firms' information systems. It also seems to fulfil some main criteria important for a candidate for valid information systems theory.

Because the architecture model prescribes a way of structuring international information systems it could also have significant implications for designing and building them. The 'goodness' of the design for an international information system seems to hinge on how well the 'Core' systems (technology and applications) is designed, as this determines to a large extent how easy it will be to apply, maintain and change the global standards of the enterprise. 'Local' systems - and their interfaces - are contingent on the 'Core's ' technology. Object Orientation as a base paradigm for the design of 'Core' elements, in particular the principles of *encapsulation*, *polymorphism* and *inheritance,* are found to be of great usefulness. They would ensure that the 'Core' systems are flexible for being implemented in differing degrees of 'penetration' and are furthermore easy to maintain, enhance and/or change as future business needs and the evolution of the international firm itself dictate. Although so far neither the literature nor the author's own experience and research have witnessed Object Orientation used as the main design principle in international information systems projects, it is conjectured that Object Orientation should be the preferred modus of analysis, design and development for international information systems.

References

1. Cash, J.I. Jr., McFarlan, W.F. and McKenney, J.L. (1992). *Corporate Information Systems - The Issues Facing Senior Executives.* Homewood. Irwin.

2. King, W. R. and Sethi, V. (1993). Developing Transnational Information Systems: A Case Study. *OMEGA International Journal of Management Science,* 21, 1, 53-59.

3. Lehmann, H., P. (1996) 'Towards a common architecture paradigm for the global application of information systems' *in* Glasson, B.C., Vogel, D.R., Bots, P.W. and Nunamaker, J.F. (Ed's) *'Information Systems and Technology in the International Office Of The Future'*, Chapman and Hall, London, 1996, p199-218.

4. Bartlett, C.A., Ghoshal, S. (1989). *Managing Across Borders: The Transnational Solution.* Boston. Harvard Business School Press.

5. Butler Cox plc. (1991). Globalisation: The Information Technology Challenge. *Amdahl Executive Institute Research Report.* London.

6. Karimi, J. and Konsynski, B. R. (1991). Globalisation and information management systems. *Journal of Management Information Systems.* Vol. 7, (No 4), 7-26.

7. Sankar, C., Apte, U. & Palvia, P.(1993). Global Information Architectures: Alternatives and Trade-offs. *International Journal of Information Management,* (1993), 13, 84-93.

8. Ives, B., Jarvenpaa, S.L. 1991. Applications of Global Information Technology : Key Issues for Management. *MIS Quarterly, 15,* 1 (March) p33-50.

9. Ives, B., Jarvenpaa, S.L. 1992. Air Products and Chemicals, Inc. *International Information Systems,* (April) p77-99.

10. Ives, B., Jarvenpaa, S.L. 1994. MSAS Cargo International: Global Freight Management . In T. Jelass, C. Ciborra (Eds.) *Strategic Information Systems: A European Perspective.* John Wiley and Sons, New York.

11. Jarvenpaa, S.L., Ives, B. 1994. Organisational Fit and Flexibility: IT Design Principles for a Globally Competing Firm. *Research in Strategic Management and Information Technology,* Vol. 1, pp.-39

12. Buss, M. D. J. (1982). Managing International Information Systems. *Harvard Business Review,* 153-162.

13. Keen, P. G. W., Bronsema, G. S. and Auboff, S. (1982). Implementing Common Systems: One Organisation's Experience. *Systems, Objectives and Solutions.* 2.

14. Keen, P. G. W. (1991). Shaping the Future: Business Design Through Information Technology. *Harvard Business School Press.* Boston, 1991

15. Weill, P. (1992). The Role and Value of information Technology Infrastructure: Some Empirical Observations. *Working Paper No. 8, University of Melbourne.* Melbourne, July 1992.

16. Earl, M. J. (1989*). Management Strategies for Information Technology.* Prentice-Hall, London.

17. CSC Research and Advisory Services, 1995, *Globalisation and Localisation: Implications for IS.* CSC Foundation Final Report 101, London.

A Perspective on Foundations of Object-Oriented Information Systems

Yingxu Wang [1] Islam Choudhury [2] Dilip Patel [2] Shushma Patel [2]

Alec Dorling [1] Hakan Wickberg [1]

[1] Centre for Software Engineering, IVF
Argongatan 30, S-431 53, Molndal, Sweden
Tel: +46 317066174, Fax: +46 31276130
yingxu.wang@ivf.se, alec.dorling@ivf.se
hw@ivf.se

[2] School of Computing, IS, and Mathematics
South Bank University
103 Borough Road, London SE1 0AA,UK
choudhia@sbu.ac.uk, dilip@sbu.ac.uk
shushma@sbu.ac.uk

Abstract

In this paper object-oriented information system (OOIS) is defined as an information system which employs object-oriented technologies in system design and implementation. This paper attempts to clarify the concept of OOIS and its implication, and to summarise research and practices in the OOIS area. At the top level, perspectives on foundations of object-orientation, information, information systems and OOISs are presented systematically. Then the domain of OOIS is analysed and a generic structure of OOIS as a branch of computer science is derived. Finally trends in OOIS technologies are analysed based on the review of the past OOIS proceedings.

Keywords: Information systems, object orientation, foundations, problem domain, generic structure, trends

1. Introduction

In tracing the history of programming and system design methodologies, it can be seen that functional decomposition had been adopted in programming since the 1950s [1]. In the 1970s the most significant progress in programming methodologies were structured programming [2] and abstract data types (ADTs) [3]. Since the 1980s object-oriented programming have been adopted in almost every software engineering branch.

Because object-orientation methodologies have taken the best ideas in structured programming and ADTs, and combined them with several new mechanisms such as encapsulation, inheritance, reusability and polymorphism, their applications have been naturally extended to information systems design and implementation in the 1990s. This progress has formed a new area of research named object-oriented information systems (OOISs).

This paper attempts to clarify the implication of OOIS, and to summarise research and practices in the OOIS area. At the top level, perspectives on foundations of object-orientation, information, information systems and OOISs are discussed systematically. Then the domain of OOISs is analysed and a generic structure of OOIS is derived. Finally trends in OOIS technologies are analysed based on the review of the past OOIS proceedings.

2. Fundamentals of object-orientation

Although OO is one of the broadly used concepts in software engineering and information systems, the literature presents few clear and unified definitions of OO. This section tries to trace the history of object-orientation, describe the implication of object and OO, analyse the extension of the concept and categorise the technologies for OO.

2.1 What is object-orientation?

To enable the question of what is object and object-orientation to be answered, one needs to address the following issues: what is the implication of OO? what is the intention and extension of OO? Tracing back the history of programming methodologies, it can be concluded that object-orientation is a natural extension and combination of two main stream programming methodologies: the functional-oriented programming and the data-oriented programming. Therefore, the definition of object-orientation would be based on the concept of object in programming and system design. A definition of object is given below:

Definition 1. Object is an abstract model of a real world entity and/or a computational module which is packaged by an integrated structure of interface and implementation, and is described by methods for its functions and by data structures for its attributes.

For a well packaged object, the only access means to it is via the interface of the object. Its implementation of methods and related data structures is hidden inside the object, which enables the implementation to be changed independently without affecting the interface of the object.

Object-oriented technologies were originally designed for programming. Therefore OO was initially an implementation tool rather than a design tool. However, as OO programming became broadly accepted, it was found that OO technologies could be used not only in programming, but also in system design and analysis. OO technologies are fairly generic and are applicable in almost every phase of the software development lifecycle. Based on this view, object-orientation is defined as below:

Definition 2. Object orientation is a type of system design, analysis and/or implementation methodology which supports integrated functional-and-data-oriented programming and system development.

2.2 Basic attributes and classification of OO technologies

The fundamental attributes which can be commonly identified in OO technologies are encapsulation, inheritance, reusability and polymorphism. Within this set of basic attributes, encapsulation is a direct representation of the fundamental methodologies of abstraction, information hiding and modularization in objects; inheritance and reusability are powerful features for improving productivity and quality in software and system development; and polymorphism is a supplement of flexibility to the other attributes of OO.

In viewing OO technologies as generic system analysis, design, implementation and reengineering methodologies, a classification of existing OO methodologies can be presented as in Table 1.

Table 1. Classification of object-oriented methodologies

OO category	OO methodology
OO design	
	OO requirement analysis
	OO specification languages
	OO system design
	OO class hierarchy design
	OO framework design
OO implementation	
	OO programming
	OO testing
	OO system integration
OO reengineering	
	OO application systems
	OO operating systems
	OO database systems
	OO information systems

According to the classification in Table 1, when an OO system is referred to, it implies that the system is designed, implemented and / or reengineered by OO technologies. This will be useful in defining what is an OO information system in the following section.

3. Foundations of object-oriented information systems

To formally define the terminology of OOIS, implications of information and information systems and their philosophical foundations are investigated in this section.

3.1 What is an information system?

The classical information theory is commonly regarded to be founded by Shannon during 1948-1949 [4,5], while the term information was first adopted in Bell and Goldman's work in 1953 [6,7]. According to Shannon's information theory, information was defined as a probabilistic measure of the quantity of message which can be obtained from a message source. It is noteworthy that the classical information theory has been flavoured by communications, signals analysis and coding theories.

In the domain of modern applied computer science and in the software and information technology industries, the term information has a much more practical and concrete meaning that focuses on data and message presentation, storage and processing. With this orientation, information is regarded as an entity of messages, rather than a measurement or metric of messages in the classical information theory. From this perspective, a definition for information and information systems can be derived, as shown below:

Definition 3. Information is a set of organised data that represents messages, knowledge and/or abstract real-world entities.

With above definition of information, an information system can be described as a system which manipulates information as shown below:

Definition 4. An information system is a computer-based system for collecting, storing, processing (adding, deleting, updating), producing, presenting, searching and/or retrieving information.

Definition 4 is a broad implication of the concept of an information system, rather than the conventional implication on database systems only. For instance, with this definition, an advanced word processing system in a PC can be regarded as a typical personal information system.

3.2 Philosophical foundations of information systems

Information system engineering is a unique discipline that relies on special philosophical foundations at the top level. By contrasting the nature of information system with other science and engineering branches, the authors have found a number of interesting fundamental differences as described below.

Information vs. matter: The knowledge of human beings about the world can be categorised into two systems: concrete and abstract worlds. The first is formed by matter or natural entities; and the latter is represented by information – the human abstraction of the real world.

Based on this view, it can be considered that our world exists in two basic forms: information and matter. Therefore information science and technology are fundamental branches of science in the human knowledge structure which study theories and methodologies of information processing.

Accumulation of information vs. conservation of matter: According to the natural law of conservation, matter can neither be reproduced nor destroyed. However, contrasting to the properties of matter, important attributes of information are that it can be reproduced, destroyed and accumulated. The accumulation of information is the most significant attribute of information which human beings rely on for evolution.

Virtuallization vs. realization: In conventional manufacturing engineering, the common approach moves from abstract to concrete and the final product is the physical realization of an abstract design. However, in information system engineering, the approach is reversed. It moves from concrete to abstract. The final software, database and knowledge-base are the virtuallization (coding) and invisibility of an original design which describes the real world problems. The only tangible part of an information system is the storage media or its run-time behaviours. This is a unique feature of information system engineering.

3.3 Object-oriented information systems

Based on the discussion of the implications of information systems in Section 3.1, the analysis of the nature of information in Section 3.2, and the formal description of object and object-orientation in Section 2, an OOIS can now be defined as follows:

Definition 5. An OOIS is an information system which employs object-oriented technologies in system design, analysis and/or implementation.

This definition indicates that an information system can be classified as an OOIS if its analysis, design, implementation and testing adopt object-oriented technologies. Definition 5 also shows that reengineering of legacy information systems into object-orientation can be achieved by means of both OO design and implementation technologies.

4. An overview of OOIS research and trends

In this section, by reviewing the research reported in OOIS'94-97, the entities and problem domain of OOISs is identified. Based on this, a generic structure of OOISs is derived systematically, and trends in OOIS technologies are analysed.

4.1 Domain of OOIS

A review of the subject areas in the past events of OOIS'94-97 [8-11] has identified that the domain of OOIS has covered a wide range of areas, such as hardware, software, people, organisational infrastructure, networking, communications, processes, incoming data, outgoing data, and other resources.

Analysing the distribution of the OOIS subject areas, it can be found that the areas of increasing interest in OOIS include OO methodologies, OO reusability, applications of OO methods, OO software engineering, and OO Web and hypermedia. The areas of declining interest include OO modelling, OO environment/tools, OO programming languages, OO formal methods, OO metrics, and OO knowledge-bases. But the decline of research in certain areas is by no means to show that those areas were no longer important in OOISs.

4.2 Generic structure of OOISs

With the fundamental studies on OOISs and the analysis of their domain coverage, a generic structure of the OOIS knowledge hierarchy can be derived in Figure 1.

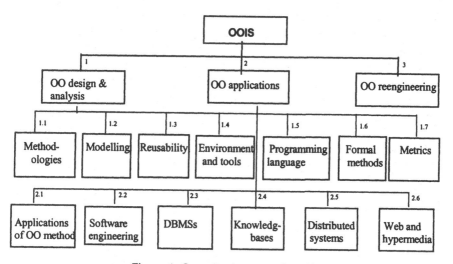

Figure 1. Generic structure of OOIS

Generally, with respect to design and analysis of OOISs, research has concentrated on OO modelling. With regard to applications of OOISs, practices have been dominantly focused on OO database systems. That is why some authors had perceived that OOIS, in its narrow meaning, is equivalent to OO databases. However, in this paper, the authors intend to explore the generic implication of the OOIS concept as a branch of computer science. This has been formally addressed in Sections 2 and 3 especially by Definitions 4 and 5, and is summarised practically in this subsection.

Based on Figure 1 and the fundamental studies in Sections 2 and 3, it can be asserted that OOIS has formed an important branch in computer science with sound theoretical foundations and a wide range of applications.

4.3 Progress and trends in OOIS technologies

Reviewing the work on OOISs with regard to the generic structure of OOISs described in Figure 1, it has been found that research interests in OOIS have mainly focused on how to develop new systems. An increasingly important aspect on OO reengineering of legacy information systems have been left relatively uncovered. Thus the authors suggest that research on methodologies, processes and case studies of OO reengineering of a large number of legacy information systems would be a worthy area to explore. Some other trends identified are for example, integration of existing OO methodologies, development of formal OO methodologies, temporal OOIS technologies, development of OOIS tools, and built-in tests in OOISs [12].

5. Conclusions

This paper has reported on basic research in seeking the foundations of OOIS. Fundamental concepts of object, information, information system, object-orientation, OOIS and their relationship have been formally described. A generic structure of OOIS domain has been derived. Based on a review of the past OOIS proceedings, trends in OOIS research and development have been analysed.

It has been shown that the area of information systems is an important branch of computer science, and that OO technologies are a universal and powerful means not only for improving the design and implementation of new OOISs, but also for reengineering a huge number of legacy information systems.

Trends of OOIS technologies in reengineering, integration of existing OO methodologies, development of formal OO methods, temporal OOIS design, development of OOIS tools, and built-in tests in OOISs have been identified for future research.

References

[1] McDermid, J.A.(ed.)[1991], Software Engineer's Reference Book, Butterworth-Heinemann, Oxford.

[2] Hoare, C.A.R., E-W. Dijkstra & O-J. Dahl [1972], Structured Programming, *Academic Press*, NY.

[3] Liskov, B. & Zilles, S.[1974], Programming with Abstract Data Types, *ACM SEN ,Vol.9*, pp.50-59.

[4] Shannon, C.E. [1948], A Mathematical Theory of Communication,*Bell System Technical Journal*, Vol.27, pp.379-423 and 623-656.

[5] Shannon, C.E. and Weaver, W. [1949], The Mathematical Theory of Communication, *Illinois University Press*, Urbana, IL, USA.

[6] Bell, D.A. [1953], Information Theory, *Pitman*, London.

[7] Goldman, S. [1953], Information Theory, *Pretive-Hall*, Englewood Cliffs, NJ, USA.

[8] Patel, D., Sun, Y. and Patel, S. (eds.) [1995], Proceedings of 1994 International Conference on Object-Oriented Information Systems (OOIS'94), London, December, *Springer-Verlag*.

[9] Murphy, J. and Stone, B. (eds.) [1996], Proceedings of 1995 International Conference on Object-Oriented Information Systems (OOIS'95), Dublin, December, *Springer-Verlag*.

[10] Patel, D., Sun, Y. and Patel, S. (eds.) [1997], Proceedings of 1996 International Conference on Object-Oriented Information Systems (OOIS'96), London, December, *Springer-Verlag*.

[11] Orlowska, M. E. and Zicari, R.(eds.) [1998], Proceedings of 1997 International Conference on Object-Oriented Information Systems (OOIS'97), Brisbane, December, *Springer-Verlag*.

[12] Wang Y., Patel, D., King, G. and Patel, S. [1998], BIT: a Method for Built-in Tests in Object-Oriented Programming, Chapter 47 in Zamir, S. (ed.), *Handbook of Object Technology*, CRC Press.

AUTHOR INDEX